ARUN JOSHI'S NOVELS

A CRITICAL STUDY

ARUN JOSHI'S NOVELS

A CRITICAL STUDY

SIDDHARTHA SHARMA

Published by
ATLANTIC PUBLISHERS AND DISTRIBUTORS
B-2, Vishal Enclave, Opp. Rajouri Garden, New Delhi-110027
Phones : 25413460, 25429987, 25466842

Sales Office
7/22, Ansari Road, Darya Ganj, New Delhi-110002
Phones : 23273880, 23275880, 23280451
Fax : 91-11-23285873
web : www.atlanticbooks.com
e-mail : info@atlanticbooks.com

ISBN 81-269-0318-X

Printed in India at
Mehra Offset Press, Delhi

PREFACE

Arun Joshi, educated in India and the United States of America, stands out as a highly significant novelist on the contemporary scene of the Indian-English novel. He is a remarkable thought-provoking novelist with uncompromising propensity towards the moral and the numinous. Thus, he has kept the novel form serious. He has received the prestigious 1983 Sahitya Akademi Award, India's highest literary honour, for his novel *The Last Labyrinth* (1981). Besides, his five novels and a collection of short stories earned him highest recognition and critical acclaim as an author of rare sensitivity. His novels concern the post-Independence Indians with Western education. They are set against the post-Independence socio-cultural milieu with moral and spiritual problems of the contemporary Indians. Trapped between the Indian ethos and Western influence, his protagonists suffer from uprootedness, cynicism, evils of materialism, loss of faith and identity crisis. Joshi takes up the challenges and problems resulting from the bi-cultural milieu of the country and suggests ways out of the beleaguered existence of the contemporary Indians.

His fiction demonstrates the universal lessons of our spiritual heritage that might have been temporarily relegated to the background but are still relevant despite the materialism and rapid westernization of our country. For

Joshi they still hold the key to the tormenting problems of our times.

Arun Joshi belongs to the tradition of existentialist writers like Camus, Sartre, Kierkegaard, Kafka, Marcel, Jaspers, Buber, Paul Tillich, Beckett, Saul Bellow and others. Invariably his protagonists are questers and seekers. Influences of other Western novelists and poets have also gone into the making of the novelist. They provide Arun Joshi with a body of suggestions in terms of themes and techniques, but he has taken these influences on his own terms, and fused them with the indigenous, transmuting them into organic, well-orchestrated novels with the indelible imprint of his own individuality.

SIDDHARTHA SHARMA

Contents

1

The Modern Indian-English Novel and Arun Joshi

Lord Macaulay wanted the westernization of Indians through the introduction of the English language. Then, he had no inkling that the Indians would ever try their hand at creative writing in English, especially the novel writing. The various Commonwealth countries easily adapted this genre with its comparative flexibility and amorphousness. It became a vehicle for the expression of their indigenous ethos. With this started a unique literary phenomenon: a novel having the graces of English language and technique with the indigenous content.

The Indian-English novel was no exception to it. The historical romances of the 19th and early 20th century are an ample proof of it, for example, S.K. Nikambe's *Ratnabai* (1895), R.C. Dutt's *The Slave Girl of Agra* (1909), S.K. Ghosh's *The Prince of Destiny* and S.K. Mitra's *Hindupur* (1909).

Then in the 1930s and 1940s there emerged a new trend in the Indian-English novel exhibiting social and political realism. The authors took up contemporary social and political problems. The freedom movement of Mahatma Gandhi inspired several Indian English novels, for example, K.S. Venkatramani's *Murugan the Tiller* (1927) and *Kandan, the Patriot* (1932). Even after Independence, the freedom movement of Mahatma Gandhi continued to inspire quite a few Indian-English novelists such as R.K. Narayan, K.A. Abbas, N. Nagarajan, Raja Rao, Manohar Malgaonkar, Nayantara Sahgal and Chaman Nahal. But the greatest fillip to the Indian-English novel was given by the "Big three"—M.R. Anand, R.K Narayan and Raja Rao. William Walsh aptly writes: "It was these three who defined the area in which the Indian novel was to operate. They established the suppositions, the manner, the idiom, the concept of character and the nature of the themes, which were to give the Indian novel its particular distinctiveness."[1]

Mulk Raj Anand is the first writer to give the Indian-English novel a definite tone and texture. In his *Untouchable* (1935), *Coolie* (1936) and *Two Leaves and a Bud* (1937), he takes a broadly humanitarian stance for the oppressed and the have-nots. He is, as Iyengar says, "the advocate of the downtrodden and the underprivileged."[2] He was deeply influenced by Sarat Chandra Chatterjee, Prem Chand, Tolstoy, Ruskin, Gandhi, Balzac and Dickens. With his leftist leaning, he is a "committed" writer standing for the India pariahs—the untouchables, the serfs, the coolies and other suppressed members of the Indian society.

R.K. Narayan, a product of the South Indian Hindu middle class family remained aloof from the contemporary social-political issues and explored the South Indian middle class milieu in his Malgudi fiction: *Swami and Friends* (1935), *The Bachelor of Arts* (1937), *The Dark Room* (1938), and *The English Teacher* (1946). His *Vendor of Sweets* (1967) and *The Man-Eater of Malgudi* (1962) present the clashing and coalescing together of the traditional and the transitional values. Narasimhaiah remarks that Narayan explores 'the staying power of the society...whose hundred ills have not destroyed the moral and spiritual base of the individual."[3] Narayan shares their hopes, fears, aspirations, superstitions of the Indian middle class engaged in a struggle "to extricate themselves from the automatism of the past."[4] In his novels we meet college boys, teachers, guides, tourists, municipal members, taxi-drivers of Malgudi, but through the provincial theme he forges universal vision. Using Western technique but Indian material Narayan has been commendably successful, to use William Walsh's words, "in making an Indian sensibility at home in English art."[5]

The tradition of social realism by Mulk Raj Anand has been followed by Bhabani Bhattacharya, Kamala Markandaya, Khushwant Singh and Chaman Nahal. The poverty, hunger and deprivation consequent upon World War II and the Bengal famine have been rendered realistically by Bhabani Bhattacharya in *So Many Hungers* (1947) and *He Who Rides a Tiger* (1954). The hungers, fear and misery faced by the people after Independence find poignant expression in Kamala Markandaya's *Nectar in a Sieve* (1954) and *A Handful of Rice* (1966). While the clash between tradition and modernity, Gandhi's vision of rural reconstruction and Nehru's plan of rapid industrialization constitute the theme of Bhabani Bhattacharya's *Music for Mohini* (1952) and *Shadow from Laddakh* (1966). The horrors and inhuman atrocities of partition in the name of religions find powerful expression in Khushwant Singh's *Train to Pakistan* (1956), Chaman Nahal's *Azadi* (1975), and Manohar Malgaonkar's *Distant Drum* (1960) and *A Bend in the Ganges* (1964). The theme of social change from traditional values to modern ones and the transformation of the socio-cultural milieu have been dealt with in Menon Marath's *The Wound of Spring* (1961), Venu Chitale's *In Transit* (1950) and Attia Hussain's *Sunlight on a Broken Column.* In Sudhin Ghose's tetralogy—*And Gazellas Leaping* (1949), *Cradle of the Clouds* (1951), *The Vermilion Boat* (1953) and *The Flame of the Forest* (1955)—we find the protagonist endeavouring to adjust himself to the changing times. An altogether different kind of novel appeared entitled *All About H. Hatterr* by G.V. Desani. It is an experimental kind of outstanding novel full of practical wisdom.

Many post-Independence novelists endeavour to explore the theme of encounter between the East and the West. The theme has been explored in Kamala Markandaya's *Possession* (1963), Balchandra Rajan's *The Dark Dancer* (1959), Ruth Prawer Jhabavala's *Esmond in India* (1958), and *Heat and Dust* (1975), Santa Rama Rao's *Remember the House* (1956), Nayantara Sahgal's *Bye Bye Blackbird* (1978). We find the finest example of the East and West encounter in Raja Rao's *The Serpent and the Rope* (1960) wherein Ramaswami, an Indian scholar and Madeliene, his French wife, part ways because of the basic incompatibility of these two cultures.

Social realism notwithstanding, the authors now shifted their focus from the public sphere to the private sphere of individuals by probing deeper into individual psyche. Kamala Markandaya's *The Nowhere Man* (1972) is about the psychological crisis of an Indian immigrant in London. Similarly B. Rajan's *The Dark Dancer* (1959) depicts the thought processes of an embittered woman persecuted and alienated from her family. In *A Time to be Happy* (1958) and *This Time of Morning* (1968), Nayantara Sahgal has interwoven the political turmoil of the world outside and the private torment of the inner world of individuals. In these we find the theme of loneliness, self-realization and sexual liberation. The novels of Anita Desai and Arun Joshi are the result of the complex socio-political situation in the post-Independence days, which only got a fillip by the West.

Anita Desai tried to explore the sensibility of modern Indian generation ill at ease in the modern, rudder-less, chaotic set-up. With this emerged the anti-hero in the Indian English novel. Anita Desai writes in *Voices in the City* (1956) that an unheroic hero is "a man for whom aloneness alone was the sole natural condition, aloneness alone was the treasure worth treasuring."[6] Her novels explore the loneliness of individuals. The crisis in her novels such as *Cry, the Peacock* (1977) and *Clear Light of Day* (1980), *In Custody, Baumgartner's Bombay* (1988) and *Journey to Ithaca* emerge from the pain born of broken marriages, emotional trauma and the failure of communication between individuals. She proved to be a crucial pioneer in the psychological exploration of feminist concerns and proved to be a major post-colonial Indian novelist.

Arun Joshi is an original talent exploring deeper into the moral and spiritual crisis of the contemporary Indians. Joshi has to his credit five novels—*The Foreigner* (1968), *The Strange Case of Billy Biswas* (1971), *The Apprentice* (1974), *The Last Labyrinth* (1981) and *The City and the River* (1990). His protagonists' dilemma issues from the lack of any moral norm in the society. His novels deal with their social-alienation and self-alienation and the concomitant restlessness and their search for a way out of the intricate labyrinth of contemporary life. They simultaneously explore in the Indian context some universal questions of human existence and delineate, to use Verghese's words, "the search for the essence of human living."[7] Joshi gives a proper shape and form in fiction to the chaos and confusion in the mind of contemporary man. His coalescing of self-introspection with self-mockery adds a new dimension to the art of Indian English fiction, as Tapan Kumar Ghosh says:

> Joshi may be regarded as *avante garde* novelist in the sense that for the first time in the history of Indian novel in English he has powerfully exploited and given sustained treatment to a very potent theme of his times, namely a maladjusted individual pitted against an insane, lopsided society which is unhinged from its cultural as well as spiritual moorings, and his uncompromising search for identity.[8]

Unlike the other authors Joshi's novels are not a mere "pathological study of his characters."[9] Like a realist he does suggest a pragmatic way out of the labyrinth of the contemporary beleaguered existence. He avoids mere didacticism, to use Bandopadhyaya's words, "realism in his hand becomes the consequences of psychological elaboration."[10] His fiction demonstrates the universal lessons of our spiritual heritage that might have been temporarily relegated to the background but are relevant despite the materialism and the rapid westernization of our country. For Joshi they still hold the key to the tormenting problems of our times.

In the Eighties yet another breed of novelists emerged. It includes Salman Rushdie, Vikram Seth, Upamanyu Chatterjee, Allan Sealy, Shashi Deshpande, Shashi Tharoor, Farukh Dhondi, Amitav Ghosh, Bapsi Sidhwa, Ipsita Roy Chakraverti, Sudhir Kakkar, Dina Mehta, Dolly Ramanujan and others. Apart from these some lesser novelists have also emerged on the contemporary scene such as Shiv K. Kumar, Saros Cowasjee, Raji Narasimhan, Vasant A. Shahane, K.V. Subbaram, Ranga Rao, Raj Gill, Balraj Khanna and others. Salman Rushdie's *Midnight's Children* and *Shame* changed the substance and tenor of the Indian-English novel. From the corridors of St. Stephen's College alone emerged Vikram Seth, Amitav Ghosh, Upmanyu Chatterjee, Allan Sealy and Shashi Tharoor. They have produced works that exhibit their remarkable ease with language. New novelists with new visions, new themes and new technical and linguistic devices are gaining recognition abroad, which insures a bright future for the Indian-English novel.

Salman Rushdie has published *Grimus* (1975), *Midnight's Children* (1981), *Shame* (1988), *The Jaguar Smile* and *The Satanic Verses* (1988), *Moor's Last Sigh, East West* and *Ground under Her Feet* (1999). Another writer of great worth is Vikram Seth, the youngest among Indian English novelists, he has published *The Golden Gate* (1986), *A Suitable Boy* and *An Equal Music* (1999). Amitav Ghosh has written *The Circle of Reason, Shadow Lines, In an Antique Land, The Calcutta Chromosome, Dancing in Combodia, At large in Burma, Countdown,* and *The Glass Palace.* Upamanyu Chatterjee has written *English, August: an Indian Story* (1988) and *The Mammaries of the Welfare State* (2000). Rohinton Mistry, a distinguished Indian expatriate settled in Canada, has produced two significant novels entitled *Such a Long Journey* and *Bombay Duck.* Bharati Mukherjee, an Indian expatriate in Canada has written *Wife, The Tiger's Daughter* and *Jasmine.* Allan Sealy has published *The Totternama* and *The Hero.* Vasant A. Shahane has published *Prajapati: God of the People* and *Faust.* Shiv K. Kumar has written *The Bone's Prayer* (1997) and *Nude before God* (1987). K.V. Subbaram has written *From Me to You* (1984). Saros Cowasjee has published *Goodbye to Elsa* and *Suffer Little Children.* Ranga Rao has to his credit *Fowl Filcher* (1987). Raj Gill has written *The Rape, The Golden Dawn, The Infidel* and *Ripples* (1991). Raji Narasimhan has published *The Heart of Standing is That You Cannot Fly* and *Forever Free.* Balraj Khanna has published *Nation of Fools* (1984) and *Sweet Chillies* (1991). Ipsita Roy Chakraverti has written *Beloved Witch* (2000). Sudhir Kakkar has written *Ecstacy* (2000). Bapsi Sidhwa has published *The Pakistani Bride* and Shashi Tharoor has published *The Great Indian Novel.*

Another Indian-English novelist of great worth is Shashi Deshpande. She is perhaps the only Indian author to have made bold attempts at giving a voice to the disappointments and frustrations of women despite her vehement denial of being a feminist. *Roots and Shadows*, her first novel, depicts the agony and suffocation experienced by the protagonist Indu in a male-dominated and tradition-bound society. *The Dark Holds No Terrors*, her second novel is all about male ego wherein the male refuses to play a second fiddle role in marriage. *That Long Silence*, her third novel, is about self-doubts and fears Jaya undergoes till she affirms herself. *The Binding Vine*, her fourth novel deals with the personal tragedy of the protagonist Urmi to focus attention on victims like Kalpana and Mira. In her novel, *A Matter of Time*, Deshpande for the first time enters into the metaphysical world of philosophy. It is about three women from three generations from the same family and the way they cope with the tragedy that overwhelms them. *Small Remedies*, her latest novel, is about Savitribai Indorekar, the aging doyenne of Hindustani music, who avoids marriage and a home to pursue her genius.

Another writer of immense worth is Arundhati Roy. She won the Booker Prize for her maiden novel, *The God of Small Things* (1997). It is a tale of shock and horror. Death and decay is the theme of the novel. It is a story of horror about a quiet and sensible worker who, accepting the label of a Paravan with a stoic resignation, is brutally beaten and done to death. Arundhati Roy has not conformed to any of the existing conventions of fiction writing, and her work strikes us as new. She does not follow any existing genre or category known so far.

Indisputably, the Indian-English novel has come of age and gained a unique viability, vibrancy and vitality, attracting remarkably wide readership and universal acclaim, to which Joshi has made a positive contribution. Thus, the contemporary Indian-English novel enjoys a bright future.

NOTES AND REFERENCES

1. Meenakshi Mukherjee, *The Twice-Born Fiction: Themes and Techniques of the Indian Novel in English.* New Delhi: Arnold Heinemann, 1971, 26.
2. William Walsh, "India and the Novel," *The New Pelican Guide to English Literature,* edited by Boris Ford. Penguin, 1983, Vol. 8, 247.
3. K.R. Srinivas Iyengar, *Indian Writing in English.* Bombay: Asia Publishing House, 1973, 335.
4. C.D. Narasimhaiah, *Awakened Conscience: Studies in Commonwealth Literature.* New Delhi: Sterling, 1978, xxiv.
5. Mukteshwar Pandey, *Arun Joshi: The Existential Element in His Novels.* New Delhi: B. R. Publishing Corporation, 1998, 24.
6. William Walsh, *op. cit.*, 250.
7. Anita Desai, *Voices in the City.* New Delhi: Orient Paperbacks, 1982, 26.
8. C. Paul Verghese, *Problems of the Indian Creative Writer in English.* Bombay: Sumaiya, 1971, 125.
9. Tapan Kumar Ghosh, *Arun Joshi's Fiction: The Labyrinth of Life.* New Delhi: Prestige, 1996, 30.
10. Manohar Bandopadhyaya, "The Strange Case of Billy Biswas," *The Patriot,* 1 August 1982.

2

The Foreigner

Arun Joshi is indisputably one of the few front-ranking fictionists of today. He made his debut in Indian-English literature with his maiden novel *The Foreigner* (1968). It has been hailed as "one of the most compelling existential works of Indian English Fiction."[1] With it began Arun Joshi's "odyssey into the dark, mysterious and uncharted hinterland of the soul to plumb some perennial problems of human existence."[2]

The novel is thorough existentialist as it is about an individual's loneliness and feelings of anguish emanating from his estrangement from the environment, tradition and his true self. As Madhusudan Prasad aptly remarks: "They are singularised by certain existentialist problems and the resultant anger, agony, psychic quest and the like."[3] In his novels Joshi has very dexterously handled some serious thought-provoking themes in an unpretentious manner such as rootlessness, detachment, quest for better alternatives in this ostentatious world and self-realization, highlighting our glorious cultural heritage and imperishable moral values. O.P. Bhatnagar also remarks: "A strange feeling of aloneness and aloofness... permeates the entire narrative and provides the necessary texture and structure to the novel."[4]

It deals with the problem of involvement in and detachment from the world, and the lack of courage to face the bitter realities of life and eventual resolution of the problem as an illustration of the *Karmik* principle propounded by Lord Krishna in the *Bhagavadgita*. The formative part of the novel develops against the backdrop of the West, and the later part set in India brings in "acculturation" at the end. In response to

Purabi Banerji's enquiries, Joshi acknowledges that the novel is "a study in alienation,"[5] and is based on observation and personal experience. He admits: "It is largely autobiographical. I am a somewhat alienated man myself."[6] Joshi himself says, "Some parts of *The Foreigner*, my first Book, were written when I was a student in America. I gave it up then and completed it later in 1966."[7]

The Foreigner relates how Sindi Oberoi, an immigrant Indian, suffers in the course of his search for meaning and purpose of his life. Sindi's alienation from the world is similar to the one that many existentialist heroes in the West suffer from. The novel is an enactment of the crisis of the present in the story of Sindi Oberoi. He is an existentialist character—"rootless, restless and luckless in a mad, bad and absurd world."[8] He is a "perennial outsider,"[9] "an uprooted young man living in the latter half of the twentieth century" (207) who belongs to no country, no people and finds himself an outsider in Kenya, Uganda, England, America and India. His rootlessness is rooted within his soul like an ancient curse and drives him from crisis to crisis. He has no roots as he himself admits, "I have no roots" (143). Sindi is trapped in his loneliness, which is "accelerated by his withdrawal from the society around him."[10] He mulls over his foreignness which is almost Kierkegaardian:

> I wondered in what way, if any, did I belong to the world that roared beneath my apartment window. Somebody had begotten me without a purpose and so far I had lived without a purpose, unless you would call the search for peace a purpose. Perhaps I felt like that because I was a foreigner in America. But then, what difference would it have made if I had lived in Kenya or India or any other place for that matter. It seemed to me that I would still be a foreigner. My foreignness lay within me and I wouldn't leave myself behind wherever I went (65).

As R.S. Pathak observes: "His alienation is of his soul and not of geography."[11] He leaves the impression of being an alien on all those whom he meets. June in one of her meetings with Sindi tells him that "I have a feeling you'd be a foreigner anywhere" (35). Even Shiela once tells him that "you are still a foreigner, you don't belong here" (149).

Sindi Oberoi, born of a Kenyan-Indian father and English mother, is orphaned at the age of four when his parents met their end in an air crash near Cairo. He is brought up by his uncle who works as an emotional anchor, and "the thought that he [Sindi's uncle] moved about in that small house on the outskirts of Nairobi gave me a feeling of having an anchor. After his death the security was destroyed" (65).

Deprived of parental love and affection in his very childhood, he becomes broken and anchorless. On being asked by Mr. Khemka as to how his parents died, he betrays Camus' Meursault-like indifference, "For a hundredth time I related the story of these strangers whose only reality was a couple of wrinkled and cracked photographs" (12). Actually, he is incapable of any emotional involvement with his social milieu. He is a born "foreigner" and "is an alien everywhere physically as well as metaphorically."[12] He is a foreigner everywhere, in Nairobi, in India and even in America, as he himself puts it, that "And yet all shores are alien when you do not belong anywhere" (92). Whosoever comes in contact with him notices this foreignness in him. Babu Rao Khemka's sister, Shiela, says: "You are still a foreigner. You don't belong here" (141). Mr. Khemka asks him: "Why are you so strange?" (134). June, in their very first encounter says, "There is something strange about you, you know. Something distant, I'd guess that when people are with you they don't feel like they are with a human being. May be it's an Indian characteristic, but I have a feeling you'd be a foreigner anywhere" (33).

H.M. Prasad writes: "Denied of love, familial nourishment and cultural roots, he grows with a built-in fissure in his personality and becomes a wandering alien, rootless like Naipaul's unanchored souls or Camus' outsider."[13] He turns out to be an anomic man, responsible to no one, having no morality, no ambitions, no purpose in life and becomes a "case of sociological anomic resulting in ontological insecurity or the psychosis of engulfment."[14]

Totally isolated from the society, he spells out his predicament in his dialogue with Mr. Khemka:

> But you at least knew what made an ass of a man; we don't even know that. You had a clearcut system of morality, a caste system that laid down all you had to do. You had a God: you had roots in the soil you lived upon. Look at me, I have no roots, I have no system of morality. What does it mean to me if you call me an immoral man. I have no reason to be one thing rather than another, you ask me why I am not ambitious: well, I have no reason to be. Come to think of it I don't even have a reason to live! (143-44).

Like Camus's outsider, Sindi is spiritually sterile as he is devoid of any religion and faith. He believes that "there is no end to suffering, no end to the struggle between good and evil" (43).

On being asked by June whether he believed in God, he shows his leanings towards the negative side: "Anyway, I can't really be called a Hindu. My mother was English and my father, I am told a sceptic. That doesn't seem like a good beginning for a Hindu, does it?" (95). On another occasion, while wondering aimlessly for something, he replies, "Yes—Have you seen God?" (221). His reply also shows that he has become indifferent to the impression he would make on people around him.

Even morality and immorality mean nothing to him. When Shiela says that June was not virtuous as she was not a virgin, he feels hurt (for he is in some way attached to her despite his expression of detachment through thought and word) and asks, "Is that all?" and further adds: "So you think one of these Marwari girls is really superior merely because of a silly membrane between her legs?" (60). Thus, Sindi is against the sex-centred attitude of morality.

Sindi's total alienation and isolation makes him what he is—cynical and frustrated. Many of the characters in the novel point their fingers at this aspect of Sindi's. Babu Rao Khemka, his friend and a student at Boston, writes to his sister Shiela that Sindi is "so terribly cynical" (55). His flat-mate Karl says to him, "I didn't know you could laugh, too," to which Sindi replies: "I can if I am drunk enough" (77). June's mother tells Sindi: "You are just a cynic, my boy" (108). Shiela even goes to the extent of telling him: "You are the saddest man I have ever known" (148). Sindi, aware of his real plight, confesses: "I was cynical and exhausted, grown old before my time, weary with my own loneliness" (161). Nothing could be truer than what Mr. Khemka tells him that he (Sindi) is "Living, but as bad as dead" (145). Like Camus's outsider Sindi was "tired of living" as a boy and was contemplating suicide" (174-175). Despite being a brilliant student, he was indifferent to studies. At London University and even at Boston, he "cared two pins for all the mechanical engineers in the world" (15). Like Camus's outsider, Meursault, he too rejects his professor's offer of a placement in the college faculty "Instead he takes up a job in New York from where he comes to New Delhi." His rootlessness takes him from Kenya to London and thereafter to Boston and finally to New Delhi. His quest carries him to London, but his tiresomeness and exhaustion don't spare him there also. He remarks:

> I joined London University, but soon I got tired of the classroom lectures. I didn't have any trouble with my courses and I passed the exams creditably enough when they came, but the question that bothered me was very different. I wanted to know the meaning of my life. And my classrooms didn't tell me a thing about it (175).

As R.S. Pathak opines that "His existential drifting over the surface of the earth and his experimentation with self only intensify his dismal loneliness and acute sense of meaninglessness of life."[15]

Consequently, he accepts an evening job as a dishwasher in a nightclub in Soho. He works there for three months and thereafter he is transferred to the bar where he happens to meet Anna, "a minor artist who has separated from her husband" (176). He has a love affair with her and comes to realize that "Anna was not yearning for me or anybody, but for her lost youth" (177).

At one of her own parties he chances to meet Kathy, an English housewife who hungers for adulterous love. He gets deeply involved with her physically, but she leaves him and goes back to her husband for the sacredness of marriage which "had to be maintained at all costs" (178). These experiences at London enrich his mind: "The essence of my life in London lay in what I had learnt from Anna and Kathy" (178).

His quest for the meaning of life makes him befriend a Catholic priest in Scotland. He spends much of his time "discussing religion and God and mysticism" (179) and gradually things begin to clear. Once it so happens that he climbs a hill top one morning and as the sun rises it comes to him in a flash: "All love—whether of things, or persons, or oneself—was illusion and all pain sprang from this illusion. Love begot greed and attachment, and it led to possession" (180). He feels that this philosophy of the so-called detachment (a euphemism for non-involvement arising out of his cowardice to take on the challenges of life headlong) would enable him to meet the challenges of life, though he is grossly mistaken.

Sindi meets June at a foreign student's party. She is an American girl, beautiful, benign, sensual, affectionate, free, frank, uninhibited and generous. Arun Joshi has modelled her after the *Panchamahakanyas.* Hindu tradition looks upon Ahalya, Sita, Mandodari, Draupadi and Tara as models of chastity, *mahapativrata.* Thomas Hardy long back asked the readers to look upon Tess as a pure woman for chastity is a condition of mind.

Sindi and June have a passionate love affair and have sex abundantly. She wants to marry him and requests him time and again that "Let's get married, Sindi. For God's sake, let's get married" (133). But being emotionally sterile, he replies that "Marriage wouldn't help, June. We are alone both you and I. That is the problem. And our aloneness must be resolved from within" (133). He further tells her plainly that "I can't marry you because I am incapable of doing so. It would be like going deliberately mad" (133).

This is reminiscent of the relation between D.H. Lawrence's Paul Morel and Miriam. When Mirian becomes possessive, Paul feels that his self is threatened, and he therefore tells her that "I can only give you friendship—it's all I am capable of—it's a flaw in my make-up."[16]

Sindi has misconstrued the term "detachment." His utter selfish notion of detachment is just a euphemism for non-involvement and thus shirks the most needed responsibility towards June. As S. Rangachari aptly observes: "Detachment which he clings to with perverse obstinacy, misconstruing the lofty concept in a manner suiting his awareness, is a euphemism for self isolation, callous indifference, gross selfishness and inhuman passivity."[17] Actually Sindi wants to love and be loved but fears commitment owing to his inherent cowardice: "The real Sindi is not of the cynical image he wishes to project—the real Sindi is a lonely individual wanting to love and be loved but afraid of committing himself."[18] His estrangement compels June to love Babu Rao Khemka who is gullible and has his root embedded in the Indian soil. America for him is a dreamland of free sex, and he argues with Sindi: "What is the good of coming to America if one is not to play around with girls?" (23). But Babu and June come close to each other, but June being accustomed to free sex life of America asks for sex which he flatly refuses, though later agrees. June commits a blunder by telling him that she had been earlier sleeping with Sindi. This was too much for Babu; he goes mad, slaps her on her face and drives away in his car recklessly and meets with his end in the car crash. Babu is like Henry James's Roderick Hudson in *Roderick Hudson*, who is transferred from a lawyer's office in a Massachusetts town to a sculptor's studio in Rome, is unable to adapt himself to the new environment, fails in art and love, and finally comes to a tragic end. As K. Radha aptly observes: "Sindi and June know that Babu had really committed suicide. He has been sent out of his college as he had failed in all his examinations. He has been disowned by his father for intending to marry June. And on the top of it all comes June's tragic death."[19]

Later June comes to know that she is pregnant by Babu and asks Sindi to marry her, but under the garb of detachment he shirks his duty of extricating her from the situation. Finally, she has to undergo an operation for abortion and, during the course of operation she dies. Thus, Sindi's false and cold "detachment" leads to the tragic death of both—Babu and June. He himself confesses: "All along I had acted out of lust and greed and selfishness and they had applauded my wisdom. When I had sought only detachment I had driven a man to his death" (6).

Not that he does not love her, actually he does not accede to her proposal of marriage owing to certain notions and experiences he has had in the past.

He realizes the folly of his perception. He looks upon himself as the victim of "a tremendous illusion" (208). The so-called "detachment" immediately vanishes and he feels extremely miserable. June could have proved to him one last emotional anchor, but his pompous philosophy of "detachment" alienates June from him and sends her to his friend Babu and in the process she meets her tragic death, thereby intensifying his feeling of "the abominable absurdity of the world" (202). Vyvyan Richards in his *Person Fulfilled* rightly remarks: "Isolation and neglect are man's hell: fellowship is heaven."[20] Now he comes to realize true detachment—it consisted of right action and not escape from it.

After coming to India, he gets a god-sent opportunity to redeem himself. When Mr. Khemka is sentenced to jail for committing fraud with income-tax accounts. Mr. Khemka's business begins to collapse and the workers begin to starve. The workers persuade him to take over the charge of Mr. Khemka's business. Sindi is still not sure but his visit to Muthu's place changes his whole attitude towards life and others. When Sindi says that he does not want to get involved, Muthu replies: "But it is not involvement, sir. Sometimes detachment is in actually getting involved" (239). Sindi now sticks to Muthu's words and confesses to having realized "detachment" though belatedly: "Detachment consisted of right action and not escape from it" (204). Usha Pathania writes, "The Buddha teaches that in order to arrive at the highest stage of human development, we must not crave possessions and selfish individualism."[21] According to this principle "no one being will exist by itself and for itself but the world will move and act in unison as if the whole were under general organisations."[22] Sindi is now on the right path of becoming. As Vyvyan Richards remarks: "Every touch of kindness that opens one's isolated self to others and theirs to us, begins to enrich and perfect our being."[23]

Thus, we find that Sindi's quest for identity as well as meaning and purpose of life does not end in despair. He is lucky enough not to find absurdity and estrangement as the ultimate condition of life, and shows a tremendous capacity for transcendence. Sindi comes out of the impasse after intense suffering, as he himself confesses after June's death: "The Gods had set a heavy price to teach me just that" (204). Like Lord Jim in Joseph Conrad's *Lord Jim,* who was sent to a remote trading station in Patusan, where he created order and well-being in a previously chaotic community and wins the respect and affection of the people, Sindi takes up the charge and thus earning the workers' respect. Erich Fromm writes:

> He [man] is the only creature who is able to say not only 'no' to life but 'yes' and to make for himself a life that is human. In this decision lie his burden and his greatness.[24]

Besides a kind of understanding develops between Sindi and Shiela amidst suffering and chaos. Arun Joshi gives us an inkling of their relationship culminating in marriage. It is a kind of surrender to Shaw's Life Force. This is reminiscent of Don Juan Tenorio's marriage to Ann Whitefield in *Man and Superman.* Unlike Camus' *The Outsider,* the novel ends on an affirmative note. As Tapan Kumar Ghosh rightly puts it: "The novel records his [Sindi's] movement from illusion to reality, from darkness to light and from death's twilight kingdom to the new shores of life."[25]

In *The Foreigner* there is a deep influence of the *Bhagavadgita* as we see that Sindi Oberoi quotes certain verses from it and tries to practise the principle of detachment preached therein. Actually the novel turns out to be Sindi's spiritual odyssey for the central message of the novel comes from the *Bhagavadgita*.

Sindi is demoniacal in nature. He is full of desire, does not believe in God or religion, lacks purity and good conduct and cannot make out the difference between the way of action or the way of renunciation. Deprived of parental love and affection in his very childhood, Sindi becomes broken and anchorless. He is full of passion and has sexual relations with Anna, Kathy, and Christine and later with June. He wants to love June without possession. He dreads involvement and hides it in the garb of detachment. He does not believe in God. On being asked by June whether he believes in God, he shows his leanings towards the negative side. Even morality or immorality means nothing to him. When Shiela says that June was not virtuous, as she was not a virgin; he feels hurt and says, "Is that all?" and further adds: "So you think one of these Marwari girls is really superior merely because of a silly membrane between her legs?" (60). He does not follow the norm of social conduct while talking to Shiela, an Indian girl leading a sheltered life. Lord Krishna tells Arjuna in the *Bhagavadgita*:

pravrttim ca nivrttim ca
jana na vidur asurah
na saucam na'pi ca caro
na satyam tesu vidyate (Chapter XVI, Verse 7)

That is: "The demonic do not know about the way of action or the way of renunciation. Neither purity, nor good conduct, nor truth is found in them."[26] Further, the next verse says:

asatyam apratistham te
jagad ahur aniswaram
aparasparasanibhutam
kim anyat kamahaitukam (Chapter XVI, Verse 8)

That is: "They say that the world is unreal, without a basis, without a Lord, not brought about in regular causal sequence, caused by desire, in short."[27]

Sindi believes that "there is no end to suffering, no end to the struggle between good and evil" (43). This is reminiscent of what Lord Krishna tells Arjuna:

yada-yada hi dharmasya
glanir bhavati bharata
abhyutthanam adharmasya
tada' tmanam srjamy aham. (Chapter IV, Verse 7)

That is: "Whenever there is a decline of righteousness and rise of unrighteousness, O Bharata (Arjuna), then I send forth (create incarnate) Myself."[28] And again in the next verse he says:

paritranaya sadhunam
vinasaya ca duskrtam
dharmasamsthapanarthaya
sambhavami yuge-yuge. (Chapter IV, Verse 8)

That is: "For the protection of the good, for the destruction of the wicked and for the establishment of righteousness, I come into being from age to age."[29]

The problems and bitter realities of life make Sindi seek refuge in non-involvement and inaction; but in the process he becomes the more pained. After Babu's death, June finds that she is pregnant by Babu, and asks Sindi to marry. The hypocrite and selfish Sindi, in the garb of detachment, refuses to marry her. She undergoes an abortion and dies. Sindi comes to a more sorrowful and repentant state. As Lord Krishna tells Arjuna:

duhkham ity eva yat karma
kayaklesabhayat tyajet
sa krtva rajasam tyagam
nai krtva tyagaphklam labhet
(Chapter XVII, Versc 8)

That is: "He who gives up a duty because it is painful or from fear of physical suffering, performs only the relinquishment of the 'passionate' kind and does not gain the reward of the relinquishment."[30]

He misconstrues the meaning of "detachment" which refers to the absence of desire, which means detachment not only towards the world but towards oneself as well. As Lord Krishna teaches Arjuna:

na karmanam anarambhan
naiskarnyam puruso' snute
na ca samnyasanad eva
siddhim samadhigacchati (Chapter III, Verse 4)

That is: "Not by abstention from work does a man attain freedom from action, nor by mere renunciation does he attain to his perfection."[31]

In reality he is a hypocrite. He indulges his passions but dreads involvement. He talks of "illusion" and "detachment," but behaves like a selfish man all along. As the *Bhagavadgita* says:

karmendriyani samyamya
ya aste manasa smaran
indriyartham mimudhatma
mithyacarah sa ucyate. (Chapter III, Verse 6)

That is: "He who restrains his organs of action but continues in his mind to brood over the objects of sense, whose nature is deluded is said to be a hypocrite (a man of false conduct)."[32] Hence, like Arjuna, Sindi behaves in terms of "enlightened selfishness."[33] He is still ignorant and selfish and has learnt "only half the lesson" (192). The more pain smites him, the more he tries to detach himself, and the more he fails to relate himself meaningfully to the world.

His detachment receives a terrible jolt in his encounter with June Blyth, wherein he helplessly watches the crumbling edifice of his detachment and tries to resist it. He appears to believe in *"Brahma satyam jaganmithya"*—(God alone is truth the entire world is illusion). Once he told June that nothing ever seemed real to him, let alone permanent.

Sindi's attitude to life and love is in total disregard of the values of human relations, which leads to his obsession with non-involvement. When the moment of real involvement and commitment with June comes, it becomes "almost a countdown of my courage" (58). He knows "Love was like a debt that you had to return sooner or later. And if you didn't you felt very uncomfortable" (60). Herein lies the rub. As Asnani aptly puts it: "Pleasure without involvement and love without possession are the values that condition the attitude and overall vision of Sindi."[34]

The small fortifications of detachment that Sindi had built around himself all his life are shattered to pieces when the redeeming episode of the crumbling of Khemka's business and the appalled spectacle of the "bundles of soggy humanity" (43). He identifies himself with them: "These are my people, I thought" (198). Khemka's arrest following Income Tax raid for swindling the Government gave him a god-sent opportunity to redeem himself. But Sindi, dreading involvement, refuses "to be dragged into the mess" (199). He believes that one must accept the responsibility of one's actions: "Mr. Khemka had to suffer for his own actions. In the past I had tried to put the consequences of my action on others, or presumed to take over their actions as my own. Both had boomeranged. In the end both had done more harm than good" (209). He tells Shiela: "Who are you and I to stand in the way? He must suffer if he wants to stop being a jackal and become humane" (217-18). These highlight the significance of the *Karmic* principle of the *Bhagavadgita* (no action of ours goes unrewarded or unpunished); "we reap what we sow."[35]

Sindi, not being totally devoid of emotions, could not maintain his non-chalance for long. Sindi happens to visit Muthu's one-roomed house in the slum where he lived with his tubercular wife and realises the "accumulated despair of their weary lives." (226)

Muthu, an illiterate labourer comparable to Sindi Oberoi, a Ph.D. in mechanical engineering from the prestigious university of America, teaches him the distinction between detachment and involvement: "Sometimes detachment lies in actually getting involved. He spoke quietly, but his voice was firm with conviction" (225). Muthu becomes for him the most appropriate example of the ideal man—the man of steady wisdom. In the *Bhagavadgita*, Lord Krishna tells Arjuna:

dukhesu anudvigamanah
sukhesu vigatasprhah
vitaragabhaya krodhah
sttitadhir munir ucyate (Chapter II, Verse 56)

That is: "He whose mind is untroubled in the midst of sorrows and is free from eager desire amid pleasures, he from whom passion, fear, and rage have passed away, he is called a sage of settled intelligence."[36]

He has learnt from experience that it is not action or escape but right action or involvement that turns out to be genuine detachment, the state of '*sthitaprajna*' of the *Bhagavadgita*, having the stability of mind and that 'yoga' and selfless action alone can redeem man.

He becomes more or less a "*sthitaprajna*" abandoning attachment whatsoever as per Lord Krishna's preachings in the *Bhagavadgita*:

yagasthah kuru karmani
sangam tyaktva dhanamjaya
siddhyasiddhyoh samo bhutva
Samatvam yoga ucyate (Chapter II, Verse 48)

That is: "Fixed in yoga, do thy work, O winner of wealth (Arjuna), abandoning attachment, with an even mind in success and failure for evenness of mind is called Yoga."[37]

Sindi realizes that for him, "detachment consisted in getting involved with the world" (225). He decides to act in right earnest without any desire for "*lokasamgraham*" (preservation or maintenance of the world), as Lord Krishna tells Arjuna:

lokasamgraham eva' pi
sampasyan kartum arhasi
(Chapter III, Verse 20, Lines 3-4)

That is: "Thou shouldst do works with a view to the maintenance of the world."[38]

Krishna's injunction to Arjuna is:

Karmany eva' dhikaras te
ma phalesu kadacana
ma karmaphalahetur bhrs
ma te saigo' stv akarmani (Chapter II, Verse 47)

That is: "To action alone hast thou a right and never at all to the fruits; let not the fruits of action be thy motive; neither let there be in thee any attachment to inaction."[39] Dr. Susheel Kumar Sharma aptly remarks: "Sindi's fatal flaw is that he forgets duty but remembers detachment which for Lord Krishna is a vital necessity to do one's duty."[40]

Dr. S. Radhakrishnan explains the meaning of the term thus: "We have to act in the world as it is while doing our best to improve it. We should not be defiled by disgust even when we look at the worst that life can do to us, even when we are plunged in every wind of loss, bereavement and humiliation."[41] Towards the end Sindi becomes oriented towards duty without selfish desires; and says, "The fruit of it was really not my concern" (228).

Sindi becomes a man of action. He takes upon himself the crumbling Khemka's business empire for "there would perhaps be useful tasks to be done" (234) in future and thus he would have "a chance to redeem the past" (234).

Lord Krishna enjoins Arjuna:

Yad ahamkaram asritya
na yotsya iti manyase
mithyai' sa vyavasayas te
prapritis tvani niyoksyati (Chapter XVIII, Verse 59)

That is: "If indulging in self conceit, thou thinkest 'I will not fight,' vain is this, thy resolve. Nature will compel thee."[42]

Thus, impelled by his intrinsic nature, Sindi's higher and enlightened self accepts involvement as the only sane option. He takes up the responsibility of steering Mr. Khemka's bankrupt business ashore. Thus, in *The Foreigner* we find a deep influence of the *Bhagavadgita* in the formulation and the resolution of the problem according to the *Karmic* principle propounded by Lord Krishna. As H.M. Prasad aptly observes: "The central message of the novel comes from the *Geeta*."[43]

Right from the beginning to the very end of *The Foreigner* we find T.S. Eliot's influence. The themes associated with Eliot's poetry are prominent in *The Foreigner*. We find the elements of alienation, rootlessness and purposelessness and moral and spiritual bankruptcy in the novel. As S. Rangachari aptly remarks: "The themes of alienation, of rootlessness of individuals, of inanity and purposelessness of human existence, of moral vacuity, spiritual bankruptcy and apathy—the themes which are associated with Eliot's early poetry figure prominent in *The Foreigner.*"[44]

Sindi appears to be a typical Eliotean character. Like Prufrock, he is a coward and for him "detachment" becomes a euphemism for non-involvement that sparks off many tragedies—especially in the lives of Babu and June. Towards the end of the novel he becomes involved (*karmayogi*) which is again a page from Eliot's *The Four Quartets.*

Arun Joshi's Boston is Eliot's Boston of *The Waste Land*—insipid, sterile, degenerate, with no hope of resurrection. Arun Joshi fails for words to highlight the hypocrisy of the modern, degenerate, spiritually dead American society and straightaway borrows the idea from Eliot's "Love Song": "...there will be time/To prepare a face to meet the faces that you meet." Even the ball and parties in America are, for him, quite a fraud. The show of being courteous was a sham, and the promise to meet again after the party was over, was merely a lip-service. The unreality and artificiality of the Boston community makes him feel out of place, an alien, and an outsider: For him all the roads lead to alienation. Like Eliot's Harry in *The Family Reunion,* he undergoes experiences of a "solitude in a crowded desert." Sindi observes: "I drank and watched the crowd bob up and down in the huge mirror behind the bar. All those faces distorted in the cheap mirror made me feel even more like an alien. Except for the bartender and me there wasn't a soul in the room who wasn't dancing or talking or beating his feet to the music. It is remarkable how you can be in a crowded room like that and still feel lonely like you were sitting in your own tomb" (24). The reference to the bundles of soggy humanity whether he is in Boston or London or India, for Sindi the show remains unchanged. For Eliot all cities are one, all men are one. It appears to be an echo of Eliot's description of people in *The Waste Land*:

A crowd flowed over London Bridge so many,
I had not thought death had undone so many.

Kenya, London, America and India—all shores—are alien to him. He tells Khemka, "I have no roots; I have no system of morality" (143). He has no roots, as he himself confesses, so the question of his culture or morality simply doesn't arise. T.S. Eliot subscribes to this very view—a man acquires culture only when he has roots—in his famous social criticism "Notes Towards the Definition of Culture." He is like the self-isolated Eliotean characters as Prufrock, Gerontion, the Chamberlaynes, Celia, Lord Claberton, etc. He has gained a different set of experiences, and is convinced of the impermanence of things. He says to June, "Nothing ever seems real to me, leave alone permanent. Nothing seems to be very important" (107). His entire life is geared around his quest for permanence in life. When June suggests that they get married, he tells June, "we are alone both you and I. That is the problem. And our aloneness must be resolved from within (126). It is reminiscent of Prufrock's interior monologue, "Let us go then, you and I," as the two live in their own private hells.

Sindi regards life as absurd, which is akin to Eliot's view that life is a "panorama of futility."[45] It is this feeling of the meaninglessness of life that makes him withdraw from the world into the nightside of life. Earlier also he had attempted suicide when he was a college student in Nairobi as he was tired of living. Sindi had been indifferent to June and Babu which leads to their death. For Babu's death his own innocence born of his sheltered life is responsible, as T.S. Eliot writes in a different context, of "the absolute parental care/ that will not leave [him], but prevents [him] everywhere."[46] Eliot's shadow can also be seen in the recurrent death images in the novel, especially in the first part. He leads a death-in-life like the wastelanders. His asthmatic illness, he says, leaves a taste of death in his mouth. After his uncle's death, he says, he existed only for dying. Early in the narrative while watching a lone beauty in one of Khemka's giant parties, Sindi becomes aware of his own loneliness and feels: "Between her and me the chasm of a living world prevailed. I had a feeling that I was watching her from the edge of the world just where Death's kingdom began" (16). It is reminiscent of "death's twilight kingdom" in T.S. Eliot's "The Hollow Men." Like Eliot's strawmen, he ekes out an existence which is a veritable death-in-life.

All his weaknesses he covers with the blanket term "detachment" which is nothing but a euphemism for his non-involvement, which does not accord with the sublime concept of detachment as enunciated in the *Bhagavadgita*. This emotional aridity and cowardice are obvious as he suffers from a Prufrockean aboulia: "And indeed there will be Time/ To wonder, 'Do I dare?' 'Do I dare?'

Sindi's vision is a morbid one, littered with the images of death, and thereby serving as the 'objective correlative,' Khemka finds him "living but as bad as dead" (137). His feeling of the utter futility of his life can be seen in the following lines, where Prufrock-like he has "measured out with coffee spoons."[47] "Twenty-five Christmas on this planet, twenty-five years largely wasted in search of wrong things in wrong places. Twenty-five years gone in search of peace, and what did I have to show for achievement; a ten-stone body that had to be fed four times a day, twenty-eight times a week. This was the sum of a life-time striving" (92).

Like a Wastelander, he remains neutral or indifferent to almost everything. On being asked by June as to what he was thinking; he non-chalantly replies "nothing," which is reminiscent of the answer the lover gives to the lady in "The Game of Chess." Even the mechanical nature of sex between Sindi and June is suggestive of the sexual act between the lady-typist and the young man in *The Waste Land*.

Sindi's affair with Anna reminds us of the love depicted in Eliot's "Portrait of a Lady." Like Eliot's lady, Anna too, as Sindi later comes to realise did not yearn for his company but for her lost youth.

But Sindi shows exemplary courage in his capacity for regeneration when he is thrown into managing Khemka's chaotic business. At dawn it starts raining: "It was the first of the monsoons, carrying a freshness and coolness that was a welcome change from the humid heat of the previous day" (234). The shower, like in T.S. Eliot's *The Waste Land,* is a fertility symbol. It symbolizes reawakening, his rebirth, his regeneration. That afternoon the sky is clear and he goes to Muthu's wretched dwelling place. The clear sky, as Mukteshwar Pandey opines, "symbolises the light of knowledge that will dawn upon Sindi."[48] He condescends to visit Muthu's dwelling place, where Muthu asks him to take charge of the management, and further telling him that sometimes detachment lay in getting involved. Sindi is wise enough to comply with Muth's request, as Eliot says in "East Coker": "The only wisdom we can hope to acquire/Is the wisdom of humility: humility is endless."[49] It is a humble admonition from Muthu to the escapist Sindi in the manner Eliot says in "The Dry Salvages": "So Krishna, as when he admonishes Arjuna on the field of battle. Not fare well,/But fare forward, voyagers."[50] His past has been a colossal waste which he thinks of redeeming through right action, irrespective of the consequences or failures. As Eliot says in "The Dry Salvages": "And right action is freedom/ From past and future also."[51] and in "East Coker," "For us, there is only the trying, rest is not our business."[52] Like Arjuna, he decides to perform "*nishkama karma*" as Eliot writes in "The Dry Salvages" "And do not think of the fruit of action/ Fare forward."[53]

Although we perceive the influence of many Western thinkers and writers that go into the shaping of Joshi's thematic and technical structure and narrative skill, the same have been made use of in a very cautious manner that renders the novel an organic whole. The novel ends on an affirmative note transmuting it into a positive vision. It is this Indian spiritual sensibility that irradiates the novel and thereby according it a distinctive place.

NOTES AND REFERENCES

1. Madhusudan Prasad (ed.), "Arun Joshi," *Indian English Novelists.* New Delhi: Sterling Publishers Private Limited, 1982, 51-52.
2. Tapan Kumar Ghosh, *Arun Joshi's Fiction: The Labyrinth of Life.* New Delhi: Prestige Books, 1996, 38.

3. Madhusudan Prasad, "Arun Joshi," *op. cit.*, 51.
4. O.P. Bhatnagar, "Arun Joshi's *The Foreigner: A* Critique of East and West," *The Journal of Indian Writing in English.* 1/2 July 1973, 13-14.
5. "A Winner's Secrets: An Interview with Purabi Banerji," *The Sunday Statesman*, 27 February 1983.
6. *Loc. cit.*
7. *Loc. cit.*
8. Thakur Guruprasad, "The Lost Lonely Questers of Arun Joshi's Fiction," *The Fictional World of Arun Joshi,* edited by R.K. Dhawan. New Delhi: Classical Publishing Company, 1986, 152.
9. Meenakshi Mukherjee, *The Twice-Born Fiction: Themes and Techniques of the Indian Novel in English.* New Delhi: Arnold Heinemann, 1947, 22.
10. R.S. Pathak, "Quest for Meaning in Arun Joshi's Novels," *The Novels of Arun Joshi,* edited by R.K. Dhawan. New Delhi: Prestige, 1992, 47.
11. *Loc. cit.*
12. Meenakshi Mukherjee, *op. cit.*, 202-3.
13. H.M. Prasad, *Arun Joshi.* New Delhi: Arnold Heinemann, 1985, 29.
14. *Ibid.*, 28.
15. R.S. Pathak, "Quest for Meaning in Arun Joshi's Novels," *The Novels of Arun Joshi,* edited by R.K. Dhawan, 51.
16. D.H. Lawrence, *Sons and Lovers*. Penguin, 1948, 271.
17. S. Rangachari, "T.S. Eliot's Shadow on *The Foreigner*," *Scholar Critic* edited by N. Radhakrishnan, January 1994, 2.
18. Jasbir Jain, "Foreigners and Strangers: Arun Joshi's Heroes," *The Journal of Indian Writing in English*. Vol. 5, No. 1, January 1977, 53.
19. K. Radha, "From Detachment to Involvement: The Case of Sindi Oberoi," *The Novels of Arun Joshi,* edited by R.K. Dhawan. New Delhi: Prestige, 1992, 111.
20. Vyvyan Richards, *Person Fulfilled*. Cambridge: W. Heffer, 37.
21. Usha Pathania, "Having and Being: *The Foreigner*," *The Novels of Arun Joshi, op. cit.*, 135.
22. Wing-Tsit Chan and Charles A. Moore. *The Essentials of Buddhist Philosophy.* Honolulu: T.H., 1956, 43-44.
23. Vyvyan Richards, *op. cit.*, 11.
24. Erich Fromm, *et. al.*, *Zen Buddhism and Psychoanalysis.* New York: Harper and Row, 1970, XVI.
25. Tapan Kumar Ghosh, *Arun Joshi's Fiction: The Labyrinth of Life.* New Delhi: Prestige, 1996, 45.
26. S. Radhakrishnan, *The Bhagavadgita.* New Delhi: Harper Collins, 1996, 336.

27. *Ibid.*, 336.
28. *Ibid.*, 154.
29. *Ibid.*, 155.
30. *Ibid.*, 354.
31. *Ibid.*, 133.
32. *Ibid.*, 134.
33. *Ibid.*, 91.
34. Shyam M. Asnani, " Exploration of the Inner World: A Study of Arun Joshi's Fiction," *The Literary Half-Yearly*. Vol. XXX, No. 2, July 1978, 99.
35. S. Radhakrishnan, *Indian Philosophy*. London: George Allen and Unwin, 1923, 244-45.
36. S. Radhakrishnan, *The Bhagavadgita, op. cit.*, 123.
37. *Ibid.*, 120.
38. *Ibid.*, 139.
39. *Ibid.*, 119.
40. Susheel Kumar Sharma, "Philosophical Reverberations in *The Foreigner,*" *The Novels of Arun Joshi,* edited by R.K. Dhawan, 132.
41. S. Radhakrishnan, *The Bhagavadgita, op. cit.*, 69.
42. *Ibid.*, 373.
43. H.M. Prasad, *Arun Joshi, op. cit.*, 49.
44. S. Rangachari, "T.S. Eliot's Shadow on *The Foreigner,*" *op. cit.*, 1.
45. T.S. Eliot, "Ulysses, Order and Myth," *Selected Prose of T.S. Eliot,* edited by Fronk Kennode. Harcourt Brace, 1975, 177.
46. T.S. Eliot, *Four Quartets.* Delhi: Oxford University Press, 1974, 30.
47. T.S. Eliot, *Selected Poems.* London: Faber and Faber, 1954, 13.
48. Mukteshwar Pandey, *Arun Joshi: The Existential Element in His Novels.* New Delhi: B.R. Publishing Corporation, 1998, 53.
49. T.S. Eliot, *Four Quartets.* London: Faber and Faber, 1970, 27.
50. *Ibid.*, 42.
51. *Ibid.*, 45.
52. *Ibid.*, 31.
53. *Ibid.*, 42.

3

The Strange Case of Billy Biswas

Arun Joshi's second novel, *The Strange Case of Billy Biswas* (1971), though different from the first novel, is existentialist in essence. There is recurrence of the themes of the first novel—the crisis of self, the problems of identity and the quest for fulfilment. Joshi, in one of his interviews admits to having been led to explore "that mysterious underworld which is the human soul."[1] In his reply to Mr. M.R. Dua in an interview, he says: "My novels are essentially attempts towards a better understanding of the world and of myself."[2] In yet another interview with Purabi Banerji, he admits that he has been influenced by the existentialists like Camus, Sartre and Kierkegaard. The themes of angst and alienation are more prominent in *The Strange Case of Billy Biswas* than, in the first one, *The Foreigner*. As K.R.S. Iyengar observes: "In *The Strange Case of Billy Biswas* (1971), Arun Joshi has carried his exploration of consciousness of hapless rootless people a stage further, and has revealed to our gaze new gas-chambers of self-forged misery."[3]

Billy's quest is deeper than Sindi's. It is a change from the Prufrockean aboulia and Hamlet-like introspection of Sindi Oberoi to the catastrophic but decisive action. Combining the Lawrentian quest for the essence of life with Upanishadic search for soul's spiritual reality, Arun Joshi carries the exploration deeper. The novel is a severe condemnation of the spiritual uprootedness of the post-Independence Westernised Indian society and is also a representation of the union of the male and the female as expounded in the *Sankhya* system of the *Bhagavadgita*.

In his lecture at Dhranyaloka, Joshi remarks:

> The first three novels to me, concern generally about questions of identity and, probably ethics. The protagonists feel truncated, unfulfilled in some way. There is a withdrawal from the world, then a return to it, the process making them somewhat more whole. In Billy Biswas this withdrawal and return—something Toynbeen calls transfiguration—is more clear. ...As I see it, Billy Biswas "is not about 'return to nature' as some people have made out. If Billy had not decided, with a deliberate act of decision to establish contact with the collector it might have been said to be that."[4]

It is this mystical urge that makes Billy Biswas leave family and relation for the primordial forest in Central India for spiritual healing to achieve self-realization the way ancient sages and seers in the Indian legends and religious texts did for spiritual sublimation. Actually Billy is haunted by the vision which the seers, the mystics and the visionaries in all ages and in all countries were haunted with. Like Matthew Arnold's Scholar Gipsy, nauseated by the superficial, civilized society with its innumerable ills, Billy makes the decisive and hard choice of living with the company of the primitive community. Like Siddharth, the prince, he renounces the comforts of a well-established sheltered life.

The Strange Case of Billy Biswas is a record of a romantic nostalgia for the simple mode of life—the kind Rousseau, Thoreau, Gandhi and Wordsworth talk about. Billy is totally fed up with the superficialities of a grossly materialistic and sterile Indian society in defiance of its traditional values and beliefs, and impelled by his "urkraft" leaves the family and relations for the primitive life in the Maikala hills. There is also a simultaneous endorsement of an essentially anti-materialistic, Hindu way of living. Billy Biswas finds himself trapped like Willy Loman in Arthur Miller's *Death of a Salesman,* a travelling salesman brought to disaster by accepting the false values of the contemporary society. To escape this disaster Billy decides to flee from the phony society. Tuula Lindgren, Billy's Swedish girl friend, and Bilasia, his tribal wife, represent the traditional Hindu ideal of life without ambition and few needs, and "total disregard of money" (176). The tribal life of Maikala hills in Central India is the ideal world-view for which he rejects the post-Independence, pseudo-Western values of the Delhi society, New Delhi and Maikala hills with their distinctly identifiable cultures reveal in contrast the utter falsehood, superficial sophistication and spiritual uprootedness of the Indian upper society. The novel focuses the spiritual decay of the westernized Indian society and presents spiritual rejuvenation of Billy Biswas, the dramatic conflict between an individual and society turns out to be a conflict between two anti-thetical cultures and attitudes to life.

As a matter of fact, Billy is an outsider like the Savage in Aldous Huxley's *Brave New World*, who is fascinated by the new world in the beginning but finally revolts telling Mustafamond, World Controller, that individual freedom is incompatible with a scientifically trouble-free society. As Joshi puts it, Billy rejects "The post-Independence pseudo-Western values,"[5] the conflict being more of a psychological nature is presented. Billy's own inner struggle, his determination to make his choice to stand up against the society results in his tragic death for the society has no place for its seers and rebels.

The very epigraph of the novel is from Arnold's "Thyrsis": "It irked him to be here, he could not rest" makes the thematic direction of the novel clear. Like Arnold's Scholar Gipsy, Billy Biswas too flees from the so-called civilized society and seeks shelter in the idyllic Maikala Hills. The Scholar Gipsy, nauseated by the "strange disease of modern life,/With its sick hurry, its divided aims," sought the company of the "wild brotherhood" to learn their secret art and waited to receive "the spark from heaven." He was in search of something that reminds us of the following four lines from Matthew Arnold's "Thyrsis":

> This does not come with houses or with gold,
> With place, with honour, and a flattering crew;
> 'Tis not in the world's market bought and sold.

Similarly, Arun Joshi's novel is a scathing attack on the materialistic civilized society and an exaltation of the primitive culture wherein lies the panacea for the ills of the modern society.

Primitivism, especially literary primitivism finds most distinctive expression in *The Strange Case of Billy Biswas.* It is a critique of the upper class Indian society and exalts primitivism born of an anguished awareness of the dehumanising effect of the urban society—a theme exploited by many writers as a critique of the rotten shallow civilized society to justify the rebellion against it. The startling discoveries in psychology and anthropology in the 20th century have only accentuated this sensibility among the writers. Primitivism is actually a revelation of modern man's alienation from his deepest self and from nature. The theme of primitivism makes *The Strange Case of Billy Biswas* very much akin to the story line adopted in D.H. Lawrence's *The Woman Who Rode Away* and *The Plumed Serpent.* Billy Biswas also has a strong urge for reintegration and struggles sincerely to recover the lost vitality and wholeness of being. As Mathur and Rai observe that *The Strange Case of Billy Biswas* is a fictional representation of the "universal myth of the primitive in the heart of man ever alienating him from the superficial and polished banalities of modern civilization."[6]

Like Marlow in Conrad's *Heart of Darkness,* Romi (Romesh Sahai) becomes the narrative voice for Billy Biswas in the novel. He maintains an air of objectivity by keeping some distance from the real events, and thereby functioning as a disguise for the subjective, spiritual and autobiographical journey of the protagonist. Romi presents the events in such a matter-of-fact and down-to-earth manner that "the strange case" as the title suggests becomes convincing and credible. The first-person narrative of Romi is interspersed with introspection, retrospection, monologue and flashback.

Like Marlow in Conrad's *Lord Jim,* Romi performs the task as an involved friend and a detached narrator. As the novel progresses, the narrator becomes more and more involved towards the end. Like Romi, Marlow expresses his failure to comprehend Jim fully: "He [Jim] was not—if I may say so—clear to me. He was not clear."[7] The entire mood of the narrator in the novel is that of reminiscence. The narrator tries to understand the strange case of Billy Biswas, "a man of...extraordinary obsessions" (7). He says," I had neither the imagination nor the obsessive predilections of Billy Biswas" (152). The statement again reminds one of the narrator in Conrad's *Under Western Eyes* who at the very outset disclaims "the possession of those high gifts of imagination and expression which would have enabled my pen to create for the reader the personality of the man who called himself...Razumov."[8]

At the very outset and throughout the novel as well, Romi expresses his inability to comprehend the mysterious urge that impelled Billy to shun the so-called civilized society. Unlike Sindi in the preceding novel *The Foreigner* and in the succeeding novel *The Apprentice*, Billy is a rebel against the modern ostentatious society. He doesn't make compromises, never falters and avoids self-pity like Hamlet and Prufrock. Being a man of courage, he is capable of facing the crisis of life. With absolute self-confidence, he translates his vision into reality. As Billy had once told Romi: "...before the eyes of each one of us sooner or later, at one time of life or another a phantom appears. Some, awed, pray for it to withdraw. Others, ostrich-like, bury their heads in sand. There are those, however, who can do naught but grapple with such faceless tempters and chase them to the very ends of the earth. These last...run the most terrible of perils that man is capable of' (7-8). Billy obviously belongs to this third category of rebels and visionaries, and it is this deep concern for his soul that prompted Billy to abandon himself so recklessly to its call and desperately pursue "the tenuous thread of existence to its bitter end" (8), "no matter what trails of glory or shattered hearts he left behind in his turbulent wake" (8). Billy's strange case is reminiscent of Aaron's case in Lawrence's *Aaron's Rod*. In the novel, Aaron Sisson amateur flautist forsakes his wife and job for a life of flute playing, quest and adventure. His flute is accidentally broken towards the end of the novel, which symbolises the failure of his quest. Billy too after leading a life of his own inherent nature finally meets his tragic end accidentally which symbolizes the end of his quest.

To make this strange case convincing the extraordinary circumstances of Billy are suggested in the first 98 pages of the novel, the background which gives insight into the strong primitive urge in him that impelled him to exile himself from the society. The second part consists of 146 pages which depicts his new life in the primitive world of Maikala Hills, his renewal of contact with Romi, and the consequent disaster. The most striking aspect of the structure of the novel is, the polarity of these two opposite worlds and the modes of living they represent. The deliberate choice of two diametrically opposite geographical locales—New Delhi and the Maikala Hills—has been made "not so much to dramatize the yawning gap but...to reveal what has been lost and to reinforce the utter falsity of the so-called refinement of the Indian upper-crust."[9] This inevitability reminds us of Lawrence's *The Woman Who Rode Away.* The author, first of all, establishes the character of the white lady and the void within and the degradation without. As Hough writes: "Her surroundings are already so squalidly dead that we can well believe that she would choose another kind of death."[10] The riding away of Lawrence's woman to escape from the deluge of civilization appears convincing when the true nature of the woman and the degraded surrounding she is entrapped in are laid bare before us. Her riding away in search of the Childmi tribe and their god symbolizes, to use Hough words, "the sacrifice of her old way of life—a kind of psychic death."[11] This narrative technique of juxtaposing two distinctly opposite geographical locales and their respective cultural ethos has been brought into use by Arun Joshi in *The Strange Case of Billy Biswas,* which again is to be found in his mode of characterization.

The first section establishes the character of Billy and his degraded and sterile surroundings, thereby making his escape convincing. Therefore, Billy's decision to leave the civilized world is not made on the spur of the moment, as some critics make it out to be, but is naturally consequent upon what preceded it.

Billy's case is actually much different from Sindi's. Unlike Sindi, he hails "from the upper-crust of Indian society" (9), and has "claims of aristocracy" (12). Originally from Bengal, his grandfather had been the Prime Minister of a famous princely state in Orissa. His father practiced law at Allahabad and Delhi, and had been the Indian ambassador to a European country. While he is in America, his father is a judge in the Supreme Court. After gaining a Ph.D. in anthropology, he is a lecturer at Delhi University. Despite having such a background, he is ill at ease in the so-called civilized set-up of society, and is much interested in exploring his inner being. As Romi remarks:

> If life's meaning lies not in the glossy surfaces of our pretensions but in those dark mossy labyrinths of the soul that languish forever,...then I do not know of any man who sought it more doggedly and, ...abandoned himself so recklessly to its call (8).

Even in his family, he feels alone and alienated like Camus's outsider. He wrote to Tuula Lindgren:

> It seems, my dear Tuula that we are swiftly losing what is known as one's grip on life. Why else this constant blurring of reality? Who am I? Who are my parents? My wife? My child? At times I look at them sitting at the dinner table and for a passing moment I cannot decide who they are or what accident of creation has brought us together (97).

His exploration of his real inner being makes him an existentialist being, estranged and alienated; and never feels at home in the bourgeois society for he knows his innermost voice will go unheeded. Romi also conveys this at the very beginning of the novel:

As I grow old, I realize that the most futile cry of man is his impossible wish to be understood. The attempt to understand is probably even more futile.... I propose to relate Billy's story...on account of a deep and unrelieved sense of wonder that in the middle of the 20th century, in the heart of Delhi's smart society, there should have lived a man of such extraordinary obsessions (7).

Romi describes Billy as a man "of extraordinary obsessions" (7). He is an unusual person of brilliant intellect, profound sensibility and extraordinary obsessions. The listener is bound to notice "the strong, rather British accent of his speech," "that soft cultivated voice," and "the words having a cadence, a compulsive quality that engaged you in spite of yourself" (11). Romi discovers Billy's "almost inhumanly sharp eyes" (43). He always carries a "singular air" and has a "peculiar intensity of concentration" (44). Later, Romi says, "I had neither the imagination nor the obsessive predilections of Billy Biswas" (153).

A very human association between two Indian students in New York is depicted where Romi meets Billy while desperately searching for a room. Billy offers to share his apartment with Romi, which is situated in one of the worst slums of New York City. It is very surprising for Romi to find the upper class Billy living in Harlem, a black ghetto in white America, which is "much too civilized for him" (9). Romi praises his elegant demeanour: "He was one of those rare men who have poise without pose" (11), but his eyes remain serious even when he laughs or banters: "Most people who meet him considered him a light-hearted good sport without quite noticing the incongruity of his eyes or suspecting what went on in their dark depths" (12). Tuula Lindgren, Billy's Swedish girl friend, and Romi are the only persons "who had any clue to what went on in the dark, inscrutable, unsmiling eyes of Vimal Biswas" (19).

Though he was born into an aristocratic family, he dislikes organized life, and this aggravates his problem of identity instead of resolving it. He gains "a sudden interest in my own identity, who was I? Where had I come from? Where was I going?" (122). His active preparations for his Ph.D. in Anthropology while his father has no inkling about it, is proof enough of his quest for his identity. Billy once says, "All I want to do in life is to visit the places, meet the people who live there, find out...the aboriginalness of the world" (14). A cursory glance at his library evinces not only the "staggering range of his knowledge" but also his "passionate involvement with his subject" (14). Romi sums up his impression of Billy: "It was around his interest in the primitive man that his entire life had been organized" (14).

In the first section, Billy's awareness of a reality other than the tangible one is laid bare before this experience in the mental hospital in America where he works for some time and the arguments he puts forth about the Krishna murder case (a petty government clerk, having received a message from a goddess in a dream, sacrificed a child to cure his dying son) before his father unmistakably prove his perception of the other world. He tells his father, "there are worlds at the periphery of this one, above it and below it, and around it, of which we know nothing until we are in them...something happens, something strong and sudden like the clerk's dream or something very gradual, and you are catapulted into them" (54-55).

A glimpse of Billy's inner life can also be had from the discussion of the play *Avocambo* with Romi. It is a play running off-Broadway at the time Billy meets Romi. It is a play about a quite educated New York man who goes down to the Congo and is so incensed by the heat and the light and the primitive music that he just goes out with his shotgun and starts killing everybody. What is fascinating, of course, are the workings of his deranged mind, what he says between each shot. Billy thinks, "one can quite imagine something like that happening to oneself" (10-11). The Bongo-session in George's apartment is also very revealing. The sound of the drum that Billy played on while sitting perfectly immobile had "a mesmeric pull that held [the audience] by its sheer vitality" and "carried a more fundamental message" (21).

Billy's case is a strange case as his personality is split between the "primitive" and the "civilized." His strange case becomes a universal myth of the primitive in the heart of man ever alienating him from the superficial and polished banalities of modern civilization. For Billy the modern civilization is degenerate, shallow and self-centred:

> What got me was the superficiality, the sense of values. I don't think I have ever met a more pompous, a more

mixed-up lot of people. Artistically, they were dry as dust. Intellectually, they could no better than mechanically mouth ideas that the West abandoned a generation ago (178-79).

He finds himself a misfit in this world, and is in search of a place where he could fit in and feel at home. He could easily afford to stay at any place in Manhattan, but his primitivism carries him to a black ghetto in Harlem, which is "the most human place he could find" (9).

Right from his early childhood, this powerful mysterious force urged Billy. One may say about Billy with Matthew Arnold, "Thou hadst one aim, one business, one desire" "Because thou hadst—what we alas! have not."

When he is fourteen, he goes to Bhubaneshwar "The first thing that hit me about Bhubaneshwar was the landscape" (123). He visits Konark, and the sculptures threat, he felt, had the solutions to the problem of his identity. He says, "I know now, that the spirit was a much, much older force, older than the time when man first learned to build the temples. If anyone had a clue to it, it were only the *adivasis* who carried about their knowledge in silence locked behind their dark inscrutable faces" (124). His visit to the tribal people with his uncle's Chauffeur proves to be a turning point in his life. He watches them dancing, drinking, singing and making love and feels a surge of strange sensation. He says, "First a great shock of erotic energy passed through me, although, mind you, ...this is what I have always dreamt of" (125). Every time he listened to folk music, he couldn't help getting transported to the world of the primitive.

Only Tuula Lindgren, his Swedish girl friend well versed in Western philosophy and psychology "had any clue to what went on in the dark, inscrutable, unsmiling eyes of Billy Biswas" (19). Tuula keeps herself cut off from the commercial civilization and has mastered hypnotism, intuition and auto-suggestion. She is "strongly interested in India, especially in her tribal people, a subject about which Billy knew enough to keep her engaged not one but a hundred nights" (17-18).

As she tells him about the theories of Freud, Carl Jung, Adler and Karl Menninger it is in her company that he comes to have a glimpse of "the other side" (18-19). As she tells Romi: "Billy feels something inside him, but he is not yet sure. Sometimes he is afraid of it and tries to suppress it" (23). She calls it "a great force, *urkraft*...a primitive force" (23) and it can explode any time. Even his drum beating has a "mesmeric pull" (21) for Romi and the audience as their dormant primitive impulse gets aroused. As a result, a little Negro girl gets him and sat so close to him that their knees nearly touched and the two stayed that way the rest of the night. Billy always had hallucination and was continuously nagged by "the old depressing feeling that something had gone wrong with my life. I wasn't where I belonged" (181). Billy occasionally discussed his problems with Tuula and she would Freud-like tell him: "...in a very mild form such hallucinations occurred in everyone—all art in a way flowed out of them," and gave her friendly advice that "I should not encourage them too much" (181).

Billy, a thorough misfit in white America, finds himself "itching to be back" (27) in India. Billy returns to India and experiences only a change of scene and, Eliot-like finds the society in Delhi as spiritually dead and emotionally empty as materialistic America. The people everywhere are the same—artistically dry and intellectually barren. He returns to India and joins Delhi University as Professor in anthropology. But here too his hallucinations keep haunting him and "I had grown terribly afraid of myself, some part of me" (182). Terribly frightened "the only thing I could think of was to get married. It was like taking out an insurance on my normalcy" (182). He marries Meena Chatterjee who is "quite unusually pretty in a Western sort of way" (37), loquacious and shallow. But this hurried marriage, as he later realizes, is a blunder. Meena's money-centric outlook, lack of empathy and of a "sufficient idea of suffering" (185) lead to the marital fiasco. With every passing day, the estrangement between the two mounts and their conjugal life turns into the "most precarious of battle-fields" (81). Billy could have been saved had Meena attempted to understand him and tried to extricate him from his trouble, as she acknowledges to Romi, "Perhaps I just don't understand him as a wife should" (76). And this leads to his total sense of alienation and isolation from his wife, family and his own self. This tells upon his health and outward appearance and his "inhumanly sharp eyes" (43) were a haggard expression which betray "emotions that one tends to associate with a great predicament" (44), Romi's expression of Billy's poignant plight after a year of his marriage is revealing: "Gone was the staggering intelligence, the spectroscopic interests, the sense of humour...the Billy Biswas I had known was finished, snuffed out like a candle left in the rain" (70). His sense of disgust at the civilized society can be seen in his Hamlet-like outburst, "Oh, how dreary, how dreary, how dreary!" (47). As R.K. Dhawan opines: "All of a sudden, Billy is seized by a phantom which makes him anxious to have the so-called civilized world of greed, avarice, riches and hypocrisy."[12] He even once becomes violent in a picnic party arranged by Meena, when one of the boys passes remark that "all *banjaras* were thieves and their women no better than whores" (60), he almost goes mad and picks fight with them.

In reality, Billy—a misfit in white America and the Delhi society—fits into the world of tribals. He even defends before his father the child-sacrifice by a clerk "to propitiate Goddess *Kali* in order that the clerk's young son suffering from leukamia, should get well" (52). He vehemently defends: "Similar cases have been reported from Africa, Indonesia, Japan, from even a country like Sweden. As far as India is concerned, there are enough such cases to fill a thousand-page volume. Look up the court records of any of the tribal agencies, and you will know what I mean" (54). He tells his father earnestly: "It is only after it happens to oneself that one comes to believe" (54).

A look at Billy's psychograph can be had from the letters that he wrote to Tuula Lindgren, his Swedish girlfriend. Certain excerpts from the letters are worth citing. The first excerpt is expressive of his feeling as an outsider in the civilized world:

"When I return from an expedition, it is days before I can shake off the sounds and smell of the forest. The curious feeling trails me everywhere that I am a visitor from the wilderness to the marts of the Big city and not the other way round" (96).

The next two excerpts are scathing attacks on Westernized Indian upper-crust society and its materialistic value system. The animal-imagery used to describe the so-called civilized people is an objective correlative of Bill's deep-seated hatred for the society. He writes: "I see a roomful of finely dressed men and women seated on downy sofas and while I am looking at them under my very nose, they turn into a kennel of dogs yawning (their large teeth showing) or snuggling against each other or holding whisky glasses in their furred paws" (96). The height of his hatred for the Elite class can be seen in his use of the imagery of dogs with large teeth and furred paws. The modern civilization to him is monster-like, devouring all the human qualities of head and heart. Billy reflects: "I sometimes wonder whether civilization is anything more than the making and spending of money. What else does the civilized man do? And if there are those who are not busy earning and spending—the so-called thinkers and philosophers and men like them—they are merely hired to find solution, throw light, as they say, on complications caused by this making and spending of money" (96-97). This is reminiscent of Wordsworth:

> The world is too much with us; late and soon,
> Getting and spending, we lay waste our powers;
> Little we see in Nature that is ours;
> We have given our hearts away, a sordid boon.

In yet another letter, he writes about a "strange woman" who keeps haunting him "causing in him a fearful disturbance, the full meaning of which he has yet to understand" (97). The fifth letter is manifestation of Billy's soul-searching and his agonising quest for identity: "Who am I? Who are my parents? My wife? My child? At times I look at them, sitting at the dinner table, and for a passing moment I cannot decide who they are or what accident of creation has brought us together" (97). Thus, he fails to have any communion not only with the society but with family as well: "To speak, I am afraid, is to address the deaf" (98). The letters not only show what's going on in Billy's mind but also support his disappearance into the primitive world "without his having to verbalize such vulnerable thoughts even in private conversation."[13] As R.K. Dhawan aptly observes: "In a bid to seek communion with the primitive world, Billy opts out of the modern world."[14]

On the contrary, he is all praise for Tuula Lindgren who is educated and human and has great influence on Billy. She is very friendly towards him and yet remains detached from others. She is devoid of any self-consciousness and exhibitionism. Unlike Meena and her ilk, she has a "total disregard of money" (177) who treats money for "a whole lot of paper" (176) and hates the world that hangs "on this peg of money" (97). Her philosophy borders on "Hindu beliefs" (176). According to Tuula, a man's needs are very few *i.e.* to use Rousseau's concept, one should see how many things one can do without. Once his livelihood is assured, he should exploit his inborn gifts to the full—this is what Thoreau and Gandhi said: "Simple living and high thinking"—and "contribute as much to the society as one can" (176). Billy is greatly influenced by Tuula's belief that the search for truth is a lonely business: "...you had to be prepared to go it alone if you really wanted to be honest to yourself" (177). It was she who had insight into Billy's mind. But Meena, as she lacked these very qualities of the head and heart, fails ignominiously to understand her husband. As Billy confides to Romi: "Her upbringing, her ambitions, twenty years of contact with a phony society—all had ensured that she should not have it. So the more I tried to tell her what was corroding me, bringing me to the edge of despair so to speak, the more resentful she became" (186).

Thus, he begins to lose his grip on life and becomes an introvert. As Tapan Kumar Ghosh observes: "Thus, even before his physical disappearance, Billy ceases to belong to the civilized world."[15] His seduction of Rima Kaul is evident of his alienation from the society, his family and his own true self. The shameful affair with Rima shows his fraudulent nature and his abysmal degradation. One afternoon, "like any common rogue" (188), he takes her to a cheap hotel and seduces her. And soon he realizes: "After it was over I looked into her clear trusting eyes, and I had a first glimpse of my degradation" (188). He delves deep into his corrupt, fraudulent ways and affirms: "It gradually dawned on me that a tremendous corrupting force was working on me. It was as though my soul was taking revenge on me for having denied for so long that other thing that it had been clamouring for" (189). And this shocking realization expedites his flight from civilization. In order to escape from the agonies of life, he takes to anthropological expeditions to the various parts of India with the students. Once he takes his students on an anthropological expedition to the tribal areas of the Satpura Hills in Madhya Pradesh and becomes enamoured of the idyllic surroundings and its inhabitants.

A great change overtakes him when he reaches Dhunia's hut and sees Bilasia, to use the very first sentence from Joseph Heller's *Catch-22*: "It was love at first sight."[16] The oil lamp in Dhunia's hut is "lending a voluptuousness to her full figure until the whole hut seemed to be full of her and only of her" (116). His inner self manifests itself: "It was I who had changed. Or, rather, quite suddenly and unaccountably, I had ceased to resist what was the real in me" (116). Billy undergoes "His final metamorphosis" (141) for he had realized that he has been "squandering the priceless treasure of his life on that heap of tinsel that passed for civilization" (141). Billy gets totally enamoured of Bilasia's sensuality: "Her hair was loose. Just behind her left ear there was a red flower. The necklace of beads glowed a little in the darkness. Her enormous eyes, only a little foggier with drink, poured out a sexuality that was nearly as primeval as the forest that surrounded them. Come, come, come, she called, and Billy Biswas, son of a Supreme Court Justice went. The top of her "lugra" came down. Her breasts, when he touched them, were full" (141-42). It is not only a union of two separate bodies but a union of a split self to realize the whole. He discovers in her "that bit of himself that he had searched all his life and without which his life was nothing more than the poor reflection of a million others" (142). Bilasia was his missing self and the union with her make him whole; something analogous to the Lawrentian concept of achieving the wholeness of the personality through the physical union of man and woman on the Jungian idea of the integration of split or missing selves through the idealized union of 'anima' and 'animus.'

Here Joshi is suggesting the union of the male and female in the ultimate embodiment of the human spirit as laid down in the *Sankhya* system of Indian philosophy. According to the *Sankhya* system of Indian philosophy, evolution takes place when *"Purush"* and *"Prakriti"* come into contact. Bilasia is *"Prakriti"* and Billy is *"Purush."* *"Prakriti"* is called *"Shakti."* Bilasia is Billy's *"Shakti."* It is only after Billy's unification with Bilasia that he realizes his self and becomes whole. Bilasia symbolises the life spirit in woman, representing the feminine principle of the *Sankhya* system. She plays a momentous role in Billy's life by letting him realize for himself as to who he is. As H.M. Prasad aptly remarks:

> In the retreat of Mr. Billy Biswas from the modern wasteland of Delhi to the ancient Garden of Eden in Maikala Jungle, from the smothering clutch of Meena to the primeval possessiveness of Bilasia. *"Purush"* meets *"Prakriti"* serving the two ends of evolution, outlined by *Sankhya,* enjoyment (*bhoga*) and liberation or *Sansar* as well as *"Kaivalvya."*[17]

According to *Sankhya* system of philosophy, evolution results when *"Purush"* meets *"Prakriti."* *"Prakriti"* needs *"Purush"* in order to enjoy and also in order to obtain liberation (*upavarga*). In this system *"Prakriti"* is called *"Shakti."* Bilasia here becomes Billy's *"Shakti."* When a man acquires perfect knowledge of reality, it achieves total freedom and the vicissitudes of the body and the mind don't affect him; this state of consciousness is called *"kaivalvya."*

Bilasia is like Tuula Lindgren. She is a remarkable woman character in Joshi's fiction. She exerts great influence on Billy. She has "total disregard of money" (176) and treats money for "a whole lot of paper" (177). Her philosophy borders on "Hindu beliefs" (176). According to Tuula, a man needs a minimum of goods in order to survive. Once this is ensured, a man should devote himself to the fullest exploitation of his inborn gifts and "in the process contribute as much to the society as one can" (176).

Bilasia thus symbolises the primitive ethos. She enlivens Billy's soul that has been deadened by Meena Biswas and Rima Kaul, and this is made possible only by a perfect union of the two. Unlike Meena and Rima, Bilasia is not sophisticated and shallow. She is an integral part of the rhythmic life of nature: "She had that untamed beauty that comes to flower only in our primitive people. It was as though nature were mocking a snook at the Meena Biswases of the world, informing them once again how little it cared for their self proclaimed superiority" (143). Her graceful eyes exude "a grief so tragic that it might well have brought tears to the eyes of a stone God" (143). It is these qualities of hers that heal the lacerated soul of Billy. Bilasia is the right woman to satisfy his soul, as H.M. Prasad observes:

> Meena deadens his senses, Rima corrupts him and the material civilization kills his innate natural instinct. It is Bilasia who causes explosion of senses—the proper medium to reach soul. Billy renounces the civilized world and its symbols in Meena and Rima. From Meena to Rima and from Rima to Bilasia is not a mere trifling in Billy's life, it is a development from sex to sympathy and from sympathy to sublimation. In Bilasia the physical and the elemental meet. She is both Lawrentian and Blakean.[18]

Bilasia, to use Jungian concept, is his missing self. Arun Joshi's protagonists are Pirandello's clusters of identities in search of wholeness. In terms of psychoanalysis, "Billy and Bilasia are two selves of the same personality."[19]

To Meenakshi Mukherjee, *The Strange Case of Billy Biswas* is "a compelling novel about a strange quest drawing upon myth and folklore to reiterate its elemental concerns."[20] The oral tradition of story telling is very successful as the narrator and the audience share a common mythology. The union of the two is taken as the union of *"Jeevatma"* and *"Parmatma,"* the union of *"Purush"* and *"Prakriti."* As Joy Abraham opines: "It is interesting to note, that the union of Billy and Bilasia can be taken as the human soul's longing for reunion with the divine as symbolised by Krishna, the union of 'Jeevatma' and 'Parmatma.'"[21] It is to use Jungian concept, the collective unconsciousness of the whole nation, which makes for the success of this novel. As P. Lal remarks: "Without an absorption in the myths of the lands of one's forefathers, it isn't even possible to live a meaningful life."[22] Indian myths have been used to bring into sharp focus Billy's pursuance of reality in the manner of the *rishis* and *mahatmas,* of our rich Indian heritage. The influence of our religious thinkers is, of course, there in the novel that is primarily concerned with religious issues—the problems of an essentially Hindu mind.

Billy renounces the sophisticated Delhi urban society in favour of the primitive life in the Maikala forest. Meenakshi Mukherjee writes: "Renunciation has always been an Indian ideal of life.[23] Like Prince Siddhartha, later Gautam the Buddha, though brought up in a royal family but from his very childhood he is of a different frame of mind. Billy had "run away from home" (51), at the age of fourteen and gets stranger and stranger with "every passing day" (75). Billy too renounces his wife and son in pursuit of his identity and spiritual perfection to become like the Buddha, the Enlightened one.

Although some critics have raised eyebrows regarding his decisive action and have branded him an escapist. But it is not so. To Romi's question, "But don't you think you had responsibilities towards her, towards your son?" Billy's answer is, "I had greater responsibilities towards my soul" (186). It was a moral conviction that had led Billy to ignore the commonly accepted standards of right and wrong in response to a more deeply founded moral imperative. What was at stake was Billy's self, his struggle to exist as the individual he knew he ought to be. As Mukteshwar Pandey says: "His is not a escape from reality but an escape into reality on the lines of Prince Siddhartha."[24]

After he settles with Bilasia in the Maikala forest his regenerative process takes place and he comes out in a new role. Billy becomes as he himself thinks, is some sort of "a priest" (191). He is regarded as a mangod, an "*avatara*" to the tribals, something that is in tune with the Indian tradition: "The East is trying to see God in man (hence the *avataras* or incarnations) while in the West the difference and distance between God and man is unbridgeable."[25] He performs miracles warding off a tiger, curing children and helps the tribals out of their worldly and spiritual troubles. To the primitive folk he is "like rain on parched land, like balm on a wound" (159-60).

To Romi, Dhunia narrates the legend of the mythical king who was an excellent sculptor, an ideal lover, a magician and a sage. To build a temple unparalleled in the world, he employed the best sculptors of his country but decided to sculpt the chief idol himself. He neglected everything to work upon the hard granite, finally a beautiful idol came into shape and God decided to enter it. God asked the king for a boon and gave a day to think over it. When the brother came to know about it, they poisoned him out of jealousy. In utter grief the queen immolated herself on her husband's pyre, promising that she would be back when her husband is reborn and then the white-cliff of Chandtola would again glow. With Billy's arrival the white-cliff begins to glow and the tribals begin to consider Billy as their legendary king and Bilasia, the Devi Mata.

It is not civilization that Billy rejects, but the westernized upper class Indian society that is spiritually sterile and depraved. Arun Joshi on being asked by Banerji in an interview, if Billy's escape implies a total rejection of modernity, remarks: "Tribals are very civilized according to mine and Billy Biswas's understanding. It is the post-Independence pseudo-Western values that he rejects."[26] Thus, Tapan Kumar Ghosh opines: "It is for him a movement from his feeling of alienation from civilized society to a sense of communion with primitive life."[27] Or, as R.K. Dhawan says, "Billy renounces a life of hypocrisy and deceit to take to a life of noble savageness."[28]

Like Kurtz in Conrad's *Heart of Darkness,* Billy forsakes civilized human society, "adapts himself to the primitive, and even has a native mistress,"[29] and like the Scholar Gipsy "returned no more." Thus, Arun Joshi may have been influenced by Conrad's *Heart of Darkness,* but he goes beyond it as Billy's quest for identity and his search of the meaning of life make him revolt against civilized society, and his mistress Bilasia unlike Kurtz's mistress plays a very significant role in his self-realization.

The second part of the novel begins ten years after the disappearance of Billy. Romi is now posted as a district collector in Central India. The plains of Central India are drought hit and he undertakes to visit the area. In his visit he runs into Billy in loincloth. Ignorant of what Matthew Arnold had to tell the Scholar Gipsy: "Fly hence, our contact fear! Still fly, plunge deeper in the bowering wood" or, "Then fly our greetings, fly our speech and smiles!," he does not flee from Romi's contact. Although shocked, Romi brings him to his bungalow and breaks him the news of his mother's death which, like Camus's Meursault, he receives with astonishing stoicism. And then he narrates to Romi all that happened during his disappearance. The long account of it is given in the first person by Billy through his memory monologue, partly gathered from Dhunia, the tribal headman, and partly summarised by Romi. This use of multiple points of view is reminiscent of Conrad's *Lord Jim,* thereby helping to reveal the various facets of the truth about Billy. The narrative is mostly in the first person and Romi's function is to reproduce the account with absolute objectivity. The novel could have ended up being a melodrama but Joshi handles his plot with remarkable detachment. Firstly he depicts the circumstances in New York, Delhi and Maikala hills where Bill's character and problems, are revealed of its own accord. Despite Romi's deep concern for his friend, he remains a detached narrator, as Tapan Kumar Ghosh opines: "This balanced presentation of the narrative in a superbly controlled style saves the book from ending as a factual case history and turns it, instead, into an imaginative restatement of the human quest for integration and spiritual regeneration."[30] In the second part language is more direct and urgent, hence, artistically satisfying.

It is here that Billy meets Bilasia, the niece of the tribal chieftain Dhunia. During that half hour meeting with Bilasia in Dhunia's cottage, he feels as if "it was not Bilasia I had been waiting for but my future, my past, indeed the very purpose of my life" (113), the thing he had been running after all through his life "had been crystallized, brought into focus" (116). The change that began to sweep his entire being frightened him so much that he began to weep like a child. This mystical communion with the primitive world brings about his regeneration, which has been rendered in a language, at once, poetic, hallucinating and evocative. For the first time Billy feels the call from within becoming articulate and strident. The entire forest, the moonlit night and the multitudinous objects of nature call him to merge with the primitive world: "Come, come, come, come. Why do you want to go back? ...You thought New York was real, you thought New Delhi was your destination. How mistaken you have been! Mistaken and misled. Come now, come take us. Take us until you have had your fill. It is we who are the inheritors of the cosmic night" (121). The call has such a deep impact on him that "he had the first terrible premonition that he might not go back" (137).

But the choice of escaping into the Maikala hills is not drastic. Even as a child, at Bhubaneshwar, while watching a tribal dance at night, a slumbering part of Billy had suddenly awakened and the questions that scathed his mind were: "Who was I? Where had I come from? Where was I going?" (122). Even at Konark, it was not the eroticism of the sculptures, but something beyond it that had appealed to him, his spiritual journey had begun at Bhubaneswar and the destination was the Maikala forest. The final leap was the result of a prolonged mentally traumatic strife. His acceptance of the new way of life after rejecting the old ways of life entails a kind of psychic death that gives rise to an experience of spiritual rebirth. This reminds us of the white lady in *The Woman Who Rode Away*. But Arun Joshi's narrative style differs from Lawrence's. As Tapan Kumar Ghosh aptly remarks:

> But while Lawrence resorts to a highly symbolic description to recreate, "the flight of a human soul into the unknown"[31] ...and revivify the process of psychic renewal, Joshi depends almost entirely on the resources of his narrative and his evocative language.[32]

Billy's process of psychic integration and his disjointed, jerky monologues have been abridged and presented in a superbly controlled style.

The novel's story-line is very much akin to the story-line in Lawrence's *The Plumed Serpent* which runs thus: Kate Leslie, an Irish widow of forty, weary of Europe, arrives in Mexico at a turning point in her life. The theme of the novel is Kate's struggle for deliverance, for a mystical rebirth. She is drawn to General Don Capriano Viedma, who introduces her to Don Ramon Carrasco, a mystic and revolutionary leader, reviver of the cult of the ancient god Quetzalcoatl, the plumed serpent. Kate is fascinated by the darkness and elemental power of Mexico and its people, and enters the cult as the fertility goddess Malintzi and the bride of Capriano.

Like Kate, Billy is also fascinated by the Maikala forest. But prior to this step, he tries to control his "runaway imagination, bordering on hallucination" (128), to control himself about the undesirability of the primitive world. Back in tent, he hugs the magazines and the newspapers "as though they were talismans, certificates of his normalness" (131). But all his attempts are in vain and the only way out to normalise himself was to totally integrate himself with the cosmic world.

Once he settles with Bilasia and performs many miracles in the eyes of the tribals, he wishes to go beyond leading the life of simple primitivism. He is "the primitive pilgrim"[33] and it is primitivism that will lead him to his destination. In a conversation with Romi Sahai, Billy says, "Becoming a primitive was only a first step, a means to an end, of course, I realized it only after I ran away, I realized then that I was seeking something else. I am still seeking something else" (189). Like Indian sages, he was seeking divinity in man, a god-head.

Like the Indian sages, he too, goes into the forest to heal himself and also to attain the highest state of self-realization or sainthood. This is what Joshi probably had in his mind when he wrote that *The Strange Case* and *The Foreigner* "are primarily concerned with religious issues—the problems of an essentially Hindu mind."[34]

Billy's "unbearably tragic" (241) death is the result of his renewable of contact with Romi. Actually during one of the tours to the drought-hit area in the Maikala hills that he runs into Billy. This contact results in Billy's curing Romi's wife Situ of a chronic migraine—he gives her some herb to eat and places a metallic rod on her head. But Situ, yet another Meena-like shallow lady of the urban civilization keeps nagging Romi to divulge the secret. He discloses—despite Billy's warning against doing such a thing—and the same is conveyed to Mr. Biswas and Billy's wife Meena. Mr. Biswas sets the entire state machinery "to drag him up to Delhi by force" (207). In one of the raids on tribals, a constable is speared to death by Billy, which was not intentional but circumstantial, and in defense. Mr. Rele is greatly irritated and is bent upon getting the culprit dead or alive. Despite Romi's best efforts, Billy is shot dead by a Havilder. And then Romi reflects:

> Gradually it dawned upon us that what we had killed was not a man, not even the son of a 'Governor,' but someone for whom our civilized world had no equivalent. It was as though we had killed one of the numerous man-gods of the primitive pantheon (236).

Mr. Biswas, Meena, Situ, Mr. Rele and others failed to understand Billy and his unconventional act for they were "only the representatives of a society which in its middle class mediocrity, bracketed men like Billy with irresponsible fools and common criminals and considered it their duty to prevent them from seeking such meagre fulfilment of their destiny as their tortured lives allowed" (131-32).

His tragic death becomes the more tragic when we concentrate on what he said prior to his death. He opened his fast-glazing eyes for a moment, looking at Romi, and said, "You bastards" (233), and died. This is his final verdict on the so-called civilized society, which is 'bastardly.' What reaches the civilized world is not his message for which he had even sacrificed himself but a handful of ash in a pot. Thus, Billy's 'strange case' is "disposed of in the only manner that a humdrum society knows of disposing its rebels, its seers, its true lovers" (240).

Billy knew full well that nothing but blind blundering vengeance howsoever camouflaged awaits all those who dare to step out of its stifling confines. It is a confrontation whose outcome is as certain as the end of "solitary boats beating against a maelstrom" (240). He knew that the price of making a choice is great, but of not making is even greater. This is what exalts him to the height of a tragic hero in our eyes and wins our sympathy.

Billy Biswas may be termed as "New Tragic Hero." As Richards B. Sewall defines the term thus: "He struggles not so much with a crisis as with a condition, and the condition is the contemporary confusion of values and the dilemma in his own soul. He does not shape events in bold strokes, rather, events to a great extent shape him."[35] Billy also confronts a condition, a system and in trying to escape this situation, he meets an "unbearably tragic death" (241). *The Strange Case of Billy Biswas* too reveals some Western influences on Arun Joshi. But this novel remains tremendously original and remarkable as the Western influences get submerged under Joshi's outstanding originality, ingenuity and sensibility as they are derived from the rich Indian heritage. Joshi's originality and genius consist in the projection of an essentially Hindu view of life, which informs the novels.

NOTES AND REFERENCES

1. Sujatha Mathai, "I'm a Stranger to My Books," *The Times of India,* July 9, 1983.
2. M.R. Dua, "An Interview with Mr. Arun Joshi," September 3, 1971.
3. K.R.S. Iyengar, *Indian Writing in English.* New Delhi: Sterling, 1985, 514.
4. Arun Joshi, "Excerpts from a Talk by Arun Joshi at Dhvanyaloka," Mysore, Sept. 1981, *IACLALS Newsletter,* No. 10, January 1982, 5-6.
5. R.K. Dhawan, "The Fictional World of Arun Joshi," *The Novels of Arun Joshi,* edited by R.K. Dhawan. New Delhi: Prestige, 1992, 21.

6. O.P. Mathur and G. Rai, "The Existential Note in Arun Joshi's *The Strange Case of Billy Biswas* and *The Apprentice," Commonwealth Quarterly,* December 1980, 35.
7. Joseph Conrad, *Under Western Eyes.* New York: Doubleday, 1925, 177.
8. Joseph Conrad, *Under Western Eyes.* New York: Doubleday, 1952, 3.
9. D. Prempati, *"The Strange Case of Billy Biswas*: A Serious Response to a Big Challenge," *The Fictional World of Arun Joshi,* edited by R.K. Dhawan. New Delhi: Classical Publishing Company, 1986, 187.
10. Graham Hough, *The Dark Sun: A Study of D.H. Lawrence.* London: Gerald Duckworth, 1956, 141.
11. *Ibid.*, 142.
12. R.K. Dhawan, "The Fictional World of Arun Joshi," in *The Novels of Arun Joshi, op. cit.*, 20.
13. C.N. Srinath, "Crisis of Identity: Assertion and Withdrawal in Naipaul and Arun Joshi." *The Literary Criterion.* Vol. 14. No. 1, 39.
14. R.K. Dhawan, "The Fictional World of Arun Joshi," in *The Novels of Arun Joshi, op. cit.* 21.
15. Tapan Kumar Ghosh, *Arun Joshi's Fiction: The Labyrinth of Life.* New Delhi: Prestige Books, 1996, 75.
16. Joseph Heller, *Catch 22.* London: Corgi Books, 1955, 13.
17. H.M. Prasad, *Arun Joshi.* New Delhi: Arnold Heinemann, 1985, 46.
18. *Ibid.*, 58.
19. *Loc. cit.*
20. Meenakshi Mukherjee, *The Twice-Born Fiction: Themes and Techniques of the Indian Novel in English.* New Delhi: Arnold Heinemann, 1974, 203.
21. Joy Abraham, "The Narrative Strategy in *The Strange Case of Billy Biswas," The Novels of Arun Joshi, op. cit.*, 191.
22. P. Lal, "Myth and the Indian Writer in English, A Note," *Aspects of Indian Writing in English,* edited by M.K. Naik. Madras: Macmillan, 1979, 17.
23. Meenakshi Mukherjee, *op. cit.*, 97.
24. Mukteshwar Pandey, *Arun Joshi: The Existential Element in his Novels.* New Delhi: B.R. Publishing Corporation, 1998, 84.
25. Prabhakar Machwe, *Modernity and Contemporary Indian Literature.* Delhi: Chetna, 1978, 105.
26. "A Winner's Secrets, An Interview with Purabi Banerji," *The Sunday Statesman,* Feb. 27, 1983.
27. Tapan Kumar Ghosh, *op. cit.*, 77.
28. R.K. Dhawan (ed.), *The Fictional World of Arun Joshi,* New Delhi: Classical Publishing Company, 1986, 35.

29. *Loc. cit.*
30. Tapan Kumar Ghosh, *op. cit.*, 78.
31. *Ibid.*, 80.
32. Graham Hough, *op. cit.*, 142.
33. H.M. Prasad, *op. cit.*, 46.
34. M.R. Dua, "An Interview with Mr. Arun Joshi," September 9, 1971.
35. Richard B. Sewall, *The Vision of Tragedy.* New Haven: Yale University Press, 1959, 110.

4

The Apprentice

Arun Joshi's third novel *The Apprentice* (Orient Paperbacks, 1974), like his first two novels explores, to use Arun Joshi's words, "that mysterious underworld which is the human soul."[1] In this novel, Joshi delineates the agonising predicament of his protagonist, Ratan Rathor, who feels confused and lost in a world full of chaos, corruption, hypocrisy and absurdity. Its theme is akin to Graham Greene's *The Heart of the Matter* where the protagonist undergoes a painful struggle to maintain faith in a hostile environment of corruption, with concept of justice and religion.

Feeling powerless and alienated from his own self as well as his surroundings, he becomes an existentialist character. As Tapan Kumar Ghosh observes:

> Crisis in the soul of an individual, who is entangled in the mess of contemporary life with its confusion of values and moral anarchy and his untiring quest for a remedy lie at the core of Arun Joshi's exploration of human reality in *The Apprentice*.[2]

It is the story of an individual with a guilty conscience, "a man without honour...without shame...a man of our times" (147) trying painstakingly to retrieve his lost innocence and honour. At the same time it is a severe indictment of a rotten, rudder-less, materialistic society with its unscrupulous amassing of wealth in defiance of the sanctity of means and its absurd pursuit of success in career. Thus, the novel is about, unlike Sindi's escapism or Billy's rebellion, the protagonist's conformity to, and victimization by a crooked and corrupt society, thereby lending it a wider social relevance.

The other important theme is about the inevitability of evil boomeranging on the evil-doer. Despite the chaotic circumstances the choice always lies with the individual, and when one deliberately chooses evil, it boomerangs. Although technically the novel bears a close resemblance to Albert Camus's *The Fall,* thematically the most prominent influences noticeable in the novel are those of the *Karmic* principle of the *Gita* and the teachings of Mahatma Gandhi.

The Apprentice seems to be largely influenced by Albert Camus's *The Fall* as the protagonists of the two novels use the confessional mode to express existentialist dilemma amid the social reality. The narrative consists of a long confessional monologue addressed to a young college student from the Punjab by Ratan Rathor, a Government official who also hails from the Punjab. He relates to the student the story of his fall over a period of three months during the time he was rehearsing for the NCC Parade on the Republic Day. The novel concerns the miserable plight of the contemporary man "sailing about in a confused society without norms, without direction, without even, perhaps, a purpose" (74). Ratan Rathor, who is both the hero and the anti-hero of the novel, probes into his inner life and exposes the treachery, pettiness, chicken-heartedness and the degeneration of his own character. He fully conforms to the doctrine that man forms his essence in the life he chooses to lead, and, as Sartre would put it, in his choice lies his freedom. He is a man of the world, pragmatic to the core and rises in the hierarchy by making deals and sucking up to the bosses. It reminds us of Charles Dickens's *Hard Times* by its painful presentation of the corrupt social and political scene. As Ratan Rathor, coming face-to-face with the social reality, conforms to the phony social norms and subsequently suffers like the typical existentialist characters. He is like Willy Loman in Arthur Miller's *Death of a Salesman,* brought to disaster by the false values of contemporary society.

Ratan Rathor, like Coleridge's *Ancient Mariner,* and Jean-Baptiste Clamence in Albert Camus's *The Fall,* detains a young national cadet to narrate to him the gruesome details of his own hypocrisy, cowardice, corruption, degeneration, debauchery and, finally, his great betrayal. He holds his own portrait as a mirror to his contemporaries, "the image of all and of no one" (102), as Clamence calls it, and the narrative turns out to be "the aggregate of the vices of our whole generation in their fullest expression."[3] Ratan is not boastful when he calls himself "a man of our times" and Arun Joshi, calls him, as Banerji says, "everyman."[4]

Though the confessional note is present in Joshi's first four novels, but the mode becomes persistent in *The Apprentice.* As Thakur Guruprasad remarks: "The narrator in this novel is an insistent confessionalist; confession is a factor in his redemption."[5] The protagonist reflects upon his wasteful past after Brigadier's death and gives us an insight into his degenerate soul to gain some perception of truth in life. As Peter M. Axthelm defines the confessional novel as one which "presents a hero, at some point in his life, examining his past as well as his innermost thoughts, in an attempt to achieve some form of perception."[6] A clean confession is not possible without a thorough cleansing of the soul.

His seems to be the cleanest of confessions in the entire range of Indian English literature. As Gandhi writes: "A clean confession, combined with a promise never to commit the sin again, when offered before one who has the right to receive it, is the purest type of repentance."[7]

Like Raskolnikov in Dostoevsky's *Crime and Punishment,* he too makes a clean confession to rid his breast of the guilt, for the unbearable oppression of, to use Shakespeare's phrase, "the worm of conscience" was terrible. As Raskolnikov says, "Any man who has a conscience must pay the price if he is aware of his error. That is his punishment."[8]

A very important aspect of the novel is that Ratan Rathor fails to confess his guilt or crime before anybody except the young student for the latter reminds him of his father: "You look a little like him (Ratan's father), if I may take the liberty of mentioning. Fifty years younger, of course, but grave and clear-eyed. Not a wash-out like me" (8). His father's selfless sacrifice had made such an indelible impression on his psyche that the memory kept haunting Ratan all his life. It is to the image of his father that he is making this honest confession of his fall and degeneration.

The Apprentice can be divided into three phases. H.M. Prasad remarks:

> The novel enacts three stages in the human divine comedy of Ratan. The pre-Independence period is the dawn, the period of idealism, the phase of innocence, the post-Independence India is the broad daylight of experience, the inferno of corruption, the last part the area of expiation, is the door to the purgatory.[9]

Ratan, a child of double inheritance, was brought up in an atmosphere of antithetical philosophies of life. On the one hand is the patriotic and ideal world of his father and on the other is the wordly wisdom of his mother. It was the age of Mahatma Gandhi, and under the magic spell of the Gandhian values like simplicity, honesty, selfless service and non-violence he gave up his career as a successful lawyer, gave away his property to join the freedom movement and is ultimately shot dead while leading a procession. The advice of his father keeps ringing in his ears: "To be good! Respected! To be of use!" (19) Ratan's mother, a tubercular woman, with a pragmatic attitude towards life tells him to earn money: "Don't fool yourself, son.... Man without money was a man without worth. Many things were great in life, but the greatest of them all was money" (20). She further tells him: "It was not patriotism but money—that bought respect and brought security. Money made friends. Money succeeded where all else failed. There were many laws—but money was law unto itself" (20). Ratan is torn between these two conflicting choices—one shown by his idealist and patriotic father, the other by his down-to-earth mother.

Another person whose memory keeps haunting him all his life is that of the Brigadier. His memory is associated with the boyhood escapades amid idyllic setting, the cross-country they undertook together. He remembers how the Brigadier fought for Ratan when half a dozen miscreants accost him while the two were returning after one of their boyhood escapades. Ratan feels the Brigadier's selfless love for "...me who no one had ever fought for" (16). He felt "I was not alone amidst the sugarcane, abandoned on the planet" (17). This incident proves another contrast to his life after the "fall" which has resulted in the loss of paradisaical innocence.

The greatest flaw in Ratan Rathor's character is his cowardice. As his higher self goads him to emulate his father's example, his lower self dictates him to pursue, as his father calls, "careers and bourgeois filth" (33), and torn between the two he is reduced to a split personality. An extremely ironic situation is created when he decides to join Subhash Chandra Bose's army: "I am very excited. I am on my way to greatness... about to lay the foundations of the glorious future" (21). As he set out on his promising journey, with every mile that he traverses, his courage gives in, and "sweating and exhausted, in sight of his destination, he sat in a mangrove and wept" (22). This was the first time he falls prey to his lower self, indicative of the future that awaits him.

His tubercular mother advises him to seek a job in Delhi with the help of his father's friends who now were well established and wielded some clout in the political corridors. "Tight in the stomach, no doubt, but quite full of hopes," he goes to Delhi where to fail would have been "the sign of the greatest incompetence" (31). He makes a futile search for a job and his "back has nearly been broken by the world's unjust thrashing" (44). Wherever he went, he was "examined, interviewed, interrogated," only to be "rejected" (30).

Now Ratan realizes that martyrs like his father and the Gandhian values they had fought for have been replaced, as Victor Anant says, "by opportunism, treachery, cowardice, hypocrisy and wit."[10] The nation his father had laid his life for, was a nation "of frustrated men sailing about in a confused society, a society without norms, without direction, without even, perhaps, a purpose" (74). As M.K. Naik writes:

> The most disturbing phenomenon on the sociopolitical scene has been the steady erosion of the idealism of the days of the freedom struggle, the new gods of self-aggrandizement and affluence having rather too easily

dethroned those of selfless service and dedication to a cause.[11]

In one of his anguished outbursts, Ratan tells the student: "There is nothing in the world as sad as the end of hope. Not even death" (26). His sojourn for a few weeks at Delhi changed him altogether, as he confesses: "I had added a new dimension to my life. I had become, at the age of twenty-one a hypocrite and a liar; in short, a sham" (28). He now loses his identity and is not his own self, and with this "all started to crumble" (26).

The most important aspect of Ratan's character is that the confession is sincere. He never blames others for his debasement and failure, though they might actually be at fault. He never shrinks from personal responsibility. Dr. Faustus also does not put the blame for his fall on his parents. He too, like Faustus doesn't blame others. Shrinath aptly opines: "*The apprentice* shows a remarkable self-awareness in ruthlessly exposing his over-subtle ties, fads, self deceptions, preoccupations, ego and boredom of the dark phase of his life."[12]

Although he remains estranged from the society devoid of any hope or promise, he acclimatized himself to it. He is able to procure a job of a temporary clerk in the department of war purchases, with assistance from a fellow inn-dweller. Thereafter, like a careerist, he devotes himself wholeheartedly to the secret cult of career in utter defiance of the purity of means. He soon forgets his friends as he considered himself superior to them "in education, in polish, in even intelligence" (27). It is not through diligence and efficiency, but through obedience, docility, servility, flattery, cunningness and "shameless sucking up to bosses," that helps him reach higher than the others. Ratan frankly confesses which verges on Bacon-like aphorism: "Some survive through defiance, others through ability. Still others through obedience, by becoming servants to the powers of the world" (35). He is branded "a whore," "an upstart," by his colleagues, but this doesn't affect him as he has turned shameless. He tells the young student:

> I am a thick-skin now, a thick skin and a wash out but, believe me, my friend. I too have had thoughts such as these. But what was to be done? One had to live. And, to live one had to make a living. And, how was a living to be made except through careers (41).

Here the tone is almost Pascallian, wherein he exposes the atrocities of the world through self-mockery and self-ridicule.

Ratan had become so ambitious that he does not hesitate to betray his colleagues for a promise of confirmation from his bosses. The insults hurled on him by his friends had the least effect on him: "One day they refused my tea. It was a considerable snub as such things go, but, to my surprise, I discovered that it made no difference to me" (42). A definite degeneration had set in, and the higher he rose in the echelons of power, the lower his character fell and *vice-versa.*

The Gandhian purity of 'means,' which his selfless and patriotic father believed in, was replaced by the Machiavellian dedication to the 'end.' His fall can be gauged from two incidents concerning contractors when he was new to the job. Ratan was offered a bribe of ten thousand rupees to change his note on the file of the contractor in question. He turned down the offer although he needed money most, and felt proud and self-righteous. In another incident he takes a big sum for changing his note on another contractor's file, although he had no need for money. In the first incident the contractor went bankrupt, and Ratan came face to face with the anarchy of the world. Ratan is like the protagonist in Graham Greene's *The Heart of the Matter* who undergoes painful struggle to maintain faith in a hostile environment of corruption, with concepts of justice and religion.

The utter servility people showed to him also amazed Ratan. He was confused by the ways of the world and confided his doubts and fears to the Superintendent, his mentor. But the latter's reply leads to Ratan's confusion worse confounded: "You know, Rathor, he said, nothing but God exists. You can be certain only of Him" (45). He further says, "there was no point in looking for truths aside from the truth of God. Money in the world always changed hands. God was only concerned with what one did with the money" (45). But Ratan couldn't take an explanation that took no cognizance of the purity of means and the consequences of one's actions. His perplexity knew no bounds:

> Was graft, in His eyes, the same as any other money? And what about the consequences, consequence for what was termed as the "character," of the giver and the taker? Or, was 'character' just a myth that I had somehow picked up? (45).

Here, we find an indelible impression of the Gandhian values on Arun Joshi. For Arun Joshi it is the means that justify the end and its sanctity is all important. But the superintendent neither believed in the validity of the means nor did he take cognizance of the consequences of one's actions. But Arun Joshi, under the influence of the Gandhian values and *The Bhagavadgita* is of the conviction, as he tells Banerji in an interview that "individual actions have effects on others and oneself. So one cannot afford to continue with an irresponsible existence but has to commit oneself at some point."[13] Ratan's father used to tell him: "Whatever you do touches someone somewhere" (149). And at the end of his poignant spiritual odyssey he does follow in the footsteps of his father "to be good! Respected! To be of use" (19).

Ratan Rathor understands that a successful career cannot be realized through diligence and sincerity but through "flattery and cunning" (69). His apprenticeship with the world gives him the realization that it "is not the atom or the sun or God or sex that is at the heart of the universe; it is deals DEALS" (51). In one such deal he marries the Superintendent's niece, gets his job confirmed, and is upgraded as an assistant with a dozen clerks under him. Later, he is made an officer in the department.

Though he marries and gets promoted, he suffers from humiliation. After many "nights of humiliation, nights when you are ashamed of something, ashamed of yourself, when the darkness is full of insults, pointing fingers and mocking laughters" (49) an intense inner conflict, almost Hamletian, rages within him.

Ratan Rathor exercises his 'choice' to pursue his material ends. Now he readily accepts bribes, owns a car, a flat of his own, a refrigerator, and also twenty thousand rupees in the bank. But the irony is, the more he gets, the more he wants: "The more money I accumulated, the more I was dissatisfied and the more I was determined to 'enjoy life'" (89).

He is all praise for the Superintendent who has taught him the secrets of the trade: "More than a teacher, he was sort of sage, priest of that obscure cult that rules this country. The officers might have been its princes, but he was without doubt the priest" (43).

But his discontent was troublesome to him. Now he realizes that "Nothing is more deceptive than men's ideas about getting ahead" (50). Life now appears to him as a complex sum in algebra where the elusive X remains elusive. He tells his young listener that the sum "demands that you set up the equations first, one after the other, one on top of the other" (52). It is a difficult task, which sometimes consumes an entire lifetime. He now begins to behave like a patriot and a true Samaritan. He talks about the miserable condition of the country, collects donations for the soldiers at the war-front. He even writes an article entitled "Crisis of Character." The document begins with quotations from Mahatma Gandhi and *The Bhagavadgita* and consists of a general review of the glorious past of the country, which Ratan had copied from third-rate history books and tourist's pamphlets. He describes the Indian people as "a glorious monument in ruin, a monument of which even the foundations had caught canker" (59). His hypocrisy knows no bounds. The tragedy is that he has been gradually sinking into the abyss of darkness, of corruption, exploitation and bourgeois filth, and yet he thinks he is swimming. As he himself confesses: "We sink and we think we are swimming" (53). Soon after this he confides to the young man an anti-climactic personal revelation: "You see, to cut a long story short, just before the war started I took a bribe. An enormous bribe. Yes, Mr. Crisis of

Character took an enormous bribe. No more, no less" (60). This anti-climactic revelation is reminiscent of Clamence's confession soon after his incisive criticism of society's hypocrisy about slavery: "But on the bridges of Paris I too learned that I was afraid of freedom."[14]

A month before the Chinese invasion Ratan cleared a huge pile of useless war materials lying in Bombay. This results in the Brigadier's abandoning the post for which he is later court-martialled, and in great depression commits suicide. This incident kept haunting Ratan all his life like a dead albatross. He is unable to pin-down the motive behind his act, like the Ancient Mariner's killing of the innocent albatross or of Raskolnikov's murder of the pawn-broker's widow and her sister in *Crime and Punishment.*

He was in real need of some kind of consolation, and he seeks "solace from the annals of corruption" (112). He justified his misdeed thus:

> If I had taken a bribe I belong rather to the rule than the exception. Peons were frequently taking bribes. So were government officials and traffic policemen and railway conductors. A bribe could get you a bed in a hospital, a place to bury your dead. Doctors had a fee to give false certificates, magistrates for a false judgement. For a sum of money politicians changed sides. For a larger sum they declared wars. Bribery was accepted by factory inspectors, bank agents and college professors; by nurses, priests and chartered accountants; by all those who acted in the public interest. Men took the bribes to facilitate the seduction of their wives; women for seduction of other women. All this I knew and had known for twenty years (112).

He takes a bribe for clearing a consignment of sub-standard war material meant for the war-front. He finds every official making money out of the heaven-sent opportunities provided by a war. The words of a Member of Parliament shock him: "Nobody lost a war these days, the M.P. said. There were always compromises. To be candid he whispered who cared for the wilderness that we are quarrelling over" (86). What surprises him most is that Himmat Singh, the Sheikh "conducts his operation for neither money nor power but in order only to destroy" (81). Like Camus's Caligula, he is out to destroy the world that made a whore of his mother. Like Caligula, he derives sadistic pleasure in destroying "everything from top to bottom from one end of the continent to the other" (81).

The Sheikh tells Ratan: "This country had two kinds of people—the rulers and the ruled." (84) While the rulers were a phoney people, the ruled were "brainless." (84) But Ratan is afraid of accepting bribe for fear of losing respect in the eyes of the people, he sets his fear at rest: "There was no such book Rathor—what existed—was not written by God but by a silly society that would do anything for money." (76) He accepts the offer with a feeling that something had gone wrong with his life. He wasn't where he belonged. He is unable to understand as to "why did I take that bribe?" (61). His mental state is like that of the protagonist in Camus's *The Fall* when the latter says, "yet I was unhappy about this as if I had violated the code of hour."[15] Though he consoles himself by what he sees—ministers, secretaries and officials sunk neck deep in corruption—he is worried about the sharp slump in people's morality. As Ratan says, "I felt choked, oppressed, rebellious but tied up totally in knots" (66). It is this conflict and existentialist compulsion that provides existentialist dimension to the novel. What elevates the novel from merely being socio-political treatise on post-Independence India is "the author's sense of the concrete and his eye on situation and character."[16]

He looks into the causes of his indulgence in this nefarious act, and recounts how "the gears began to slip" (67) after his country's "tryst with destiny" (62). After India's freedom, the people's dream of a prosperous and strong nation remained unfulfilled leading to disappointment. The corridors of power became a hot bed of politics and the fourth estate published incredible stories. Flouting the self-laid sanctified norms, the ministers began to give misleading statements in the Parliament. A new set of politicians and statesmen surfaced occupying the centre-stage: "So, they had appeared again. That is if they had ever left the scene in the first place. There was the public and there were They" (63).

What really had happened was that the people were shell-shocked like the animals in George Orwell's *Animal Farm* where the last sentence says "the creatures looked from pig to man and from man to pig; but already it was impossible to say which was which." The English *sahibs* were only replaced by brown *sahibs*: "We thought we were free. What we had, in fact, was a new slavery" (63). In the new set-up money and power was the ruling motive with merit and decency thrown to the winds. In a nutshell, it was "a free-for-all. A great darkness. Blinding us. And blind following the blind. And everybody lying" (70). The mercenary motives with which the various characters in the novel indulge in is reminiscent of Joseph Heller's *Catch 22* wherein the defense and administrative set-up rob the U.S. Federal government of billions of dollars through lying, corruption and hypocrisy.

On the one hand we find Ratan a coward, "a weather vane turning its head where the wind blows" (66) and on the other a slave to his circumstances: "The wide world took me in its wake, overwhelmed me, smothered me" (65). Despite this Ratan is finally responsible for his deeds as he betrays his conscience. We find that Ratan's lot is thoroughly existentialist. As R.G. Das remarks:

> Arun Joshi appears very close to Joseph Conrad, Graham Greene and William Golding in the sense that the act of treachery inflicts an irreparable injury upon the moral nature of man, and that a guilty Ratan lives inescapably in the presence of his conscience. He too realizes as Razumov does in Conrad's *Under Western Eyes,* that all a man can betray is his conscience.[17]

His self-betrayal leads him to a feeling of being a non-entity. His loss of identity is total as he says, "I was a nobody. A NOBODY—Deep down I was convinced that I had lost my significance: As an official, as a citizen, as a man" (73). Joshi delineates Ratan as a modern man "at once everyman and nobody."[18] He wants to know what he really is, if not a 'master-faker.'

Although he enjoys his life in Bombay, all the time he is conscious of the evils of the so-called elite suffers from, which is laid bare by the accounts of a party in Bombay:

> A retired major-general was roundly abusing, in the filthiest of language, those who were fighting; some already dead. It seems to me that nearly everything I heard or said or did that evening was in one way or another obscene. I was, in fact, at the peak of the dung heap that I had been climbing all my life (85).

His fall is complete when once he "had merely walked into a brothel hounded by a strange disturbance" (89). His utter vacuity and dissatisfaction is complete.

Ratan's sense of insignificance and the resultant anguish at the destruction of his authentic self was not his own self and had to lick the boots of his bosses and put on smiles for their pleasure. As Tapan Kumar Ghosh aptly remarks: "He was not himself but simply a cipher in the mass existence of the crowd, a cog in the social mechanism."[19] His soul had been rendered sterile by the perverted modern civilization and by his own inherent cowardice, and he saw his "soul turn to ashes" (75).

T.S. Eliot's influence on Joshi is very marked as the latter uses imagery and symbols, as Axthelm says, "portray a mind gone beyond conventional limits, a mind which cannot be comprehended in the context of objective reality, but is so unique that only its own strange creations can properly reflect it."[20] The purpose of these images is, as R.K. Srivastava says, "by their cumulative effect reflect their being."[21]

The influence of Fyodor Dostoevsky is also not missing. Like a Dostoevskian 'mirror,' Himmat Singh, the Sheikh lays bare in his face the putrefied self of Ratan. As Ratan confesses: "It was perhaps something of me that I saw in him. And *vice versa*" (81). To Ratan, he was: "Mon semblable,—Mon frere!"[22] When Ratan expresses his apprehension regarding the disclosure of the deal, Sheikh taunts him:

> You are a fool, he said...people thought there was a law book laid down by God which they must follow.... There

> was no such law-book, Rathor, he said, what existed, he said, was not written by God but by a silly society that would do anything for money (76).

His faithful wife, Geeta also turns out to be another Dostoevskian mirror. She reminds one of the ladies in Henry James's *The Portrait of a Lady.* Isabel Archer, the 'Lady,' an attractive American girl is married to a worthless and spiteful dilettante, Gilbert Osmand, who marries her for her fortune and ruins her life; but to whom she remains loyal in spite of her realization of his vileness.

The result of what Ratan and his likes did was that the Indo-China war is lost. The Brigadier had to desert his post ignominiously for which he is to be court-martialled, who in utter shame commits suicide. It reminds us of Arthur Miller's *All My Sons* where the father passes a consignment of faulty cylinders for a bribe, and becomes responsible for killing his own pilot-son.

The theme of evil boomeranging on the evil-doer in *The Apprentice* is reminiscent of Joseph Conrad's *Nostromo* and *The Secret Agent.* Nostromo, an Italian sailor, now Capatez de Cargadores is a hero to all, but betrays his own self when entrusted with the task of safeguarding Charles Gould's silver. The temptation is too much for him to remain honest and grows rich by pilfering. But his evil boomerangs on him when he is shot dead when mistaken for an intruder by his old friend Viola who had been appointed lighthouse keeper on the silver treasure island and with whose daughter he trifles with. Similarly in *The Secret Agent,* Verloc, a secret agent, is a spy for a foreign embassy. His wife Winnie has married him chiefly to provide security for her gullible younger brother Stevie, but is ignorant of Verloc's spying activities. The evil boomerangs when he uses the poor and innocent Stevie as an accomplice in a bomb-explosion, and the boy is blown to pieces while carrying the bomb and an enraged Winnie kills Verloc with a knife.

Although the Superintendent of Police detects his involvement and he is put behind bars, but is subsequently released on the interference of the Secretary and the Minister who were accomplices in the crime. Though he is released his guilty conscience haunted him as to his own identity—"Was I the murderer they said I was"? (109). The absurdity of his existence consequent upon his being alone in this wide world makes him "descend into madness," "immobilized, fuddled, tongueless, ununderstood, laughed at" (129).

Totally despaired, he consoles himself with incidents in the annals of corruption where the guilty have gone scot-free: "I thought with satisfaction of a recent fraud executed by the scion of one of the country's first families; the arrest of an Inspector-General of Police for accepting the bribe from a racketeer, recall of an ambassador who had exchanged his country's secrets for a mistress" (112). But his attempt at consoling himself proves fruitless. For the Brigadier's death, Ratan makes himself fully responsible; but for his own fall and degeneration, Himmat Singh.

Himmat Singh, the Sheikh is Camus's Caligula-like character —out to destroy the world. He hated the world for, as he thought, the world hated him. It was in Bombay that Ratan came to know a bit about this underground man. Immaculately dressed, with his extra-large cigarette, his perpetual goggles and twisted lips, he would always mock the world with his rough and sarcastic voice. Though he had extraordinary intelligence, it was made perverse by unknown suffering. The Sheikh would carry out his operations stealthily not to make money but to destroy "everything from top to bottom, from one end of the continent to the other" (81). Once while Ratan was recounting his childhood and his father's martyrdom, the Sheikh asks him, "Was it not intriguing that the son of a revolutionary should be doing what he was doing?" And when Ratan says that his father's death had a deep impression on him and had made him "a man of courage," the Sheikh cut in: "You are a fool, Ratan Rathor, he said, a fool or a great hypocrite. Why did I not admit, he said, that my father's death had meant nothing to me. It might have shaken me up.... It certainly had not meant to me what I said" (83). Ratan was stunned to realize that his father's death had meant only one thing to him: it was "stupid and meaningless" (83) to get killed like that.

The Sheikh, a perpetual outsider could never careless if a war broke out taking a heavy toll of life and property in its wake: "...he could not be bothered with the quarrels of a society whose circle he was outside of and...which he despised" (84). It was this enigmatic Sheikh who made Ratan to realise "some parts of his life, leaving behind a heap of slush to be pondered over" (84).

The darkest part of Ratan's confession comes on the night before the Republic Day, as he says, "a secret darker than the darkness of the night," (100) and the young man lends his keen ear to him.

He visits the hospital to see the Brigadier but is denied admittance: "Great friends, they told him, were usually the most harmful" (95). When he encounters the anonymous multitude of maimed soldiers whose very respectable existence was at stake, he is shocked at the devastation he and his likes had wrought upon the soldiers. It is this encounter which impels him to be good: "I shall be good. I shall not be greedy. I shall not be afraid. I shall be decent" (103). To make good the loss he decides to confess, but when the moment comes to make amends, he retraces his steps.

Next morning he is summoned to the Police Station to confess his guilt, as the S.P. requested Ratan, unless he confessed, "there was no hope for the Brigadier" (116).

A furious debate raged within him: "What good would the confession do? The men who have died have died. And even if it were to do good, why should I go and confess" (110-11). The debate between his conscience and his cocky self express, as Abraham says, "the archetypal pattern of conflict between good and evil which is typically Indian."[23] He spends many sleepless nights on account of this.

He goes to the temple to seek some solace and moral courage, but to his great consternation the malignant tentacles of corruption had the temple as well in its grip. The priest, the agent of God, offered him bribe to save his son, a dishonest contractor, from punishment for having mixed too much of sand in the mortar. He now knew religion was not a remedy for his malaise.

Finally, he decides to write down his confession but it is not a neat confession for he tones down every insinuation of his personal guilt and having "escape routes...to wriggle out of the net" (125). He wants to save the Brigadier but not at his own cost as he does not want to own moral responsibility for his crime. But at the appointed hour, he does not send it to the concerned authorities. But things wouldn't stand for want of Ratan's confession and resulted in the ultimate tragedy. As Tapan Kumar Ghosh sarcastically remarks: "The Brigadier could not wait for Ratan's martyrdom: he committed suicide."[24] This incident reminds us of George Lillo's *The Fatal Curiosity* in which old Wilmof urged by his wife murders a stranger who has deposited a casket with them, only to find the victim is his own son, supposed to have been lost in a shipwreck. Thus evil boomerangs on the evil-doer.

For the first time Ratan is confronted with death that leads to an honest appraisal of life. The sight of the shattered skull of the Brigadier shocked Ratan out of his self-complacency and illusions. He had played havoc with many lives, but when the pain of his dearest one was thrust in his face, he learns: "God is not mocked.... He has got a stick all right and he is not mocked and sooner or later, some place or another, he still raps your knuckles" (129).

Despite this painful experience he kept up appearances but had to undergo terrible loneliness through many days and nights: "No conversation, no visit of either friend or foe, no sleep, in spite of the sleeping pills that our good doctor gave me, no relief, no respite from the hands that pulled me steadily down towards those caverns where I felt certain, the Brigadier had gone" (130). Like it did in the case of Raskolnikov and the Ancient Mariner the worm of guilt kept nibbling away at his conscience and his grief stricken soul suffered inconsolably.

Ratan holds Himmat Singh responsible for his degeneration that led to the Brigadier's death. He takes a gun and decides to kill the Sheikh, but in the dramatic encounter the Sheikh tells him that he was dying and that he had come to the wrong place for the villain. He further discloses the fact that the whole idea of clearing the substandard consignment had originated not with Himmat Singh but with the Minister and the Secretary, and they picked Ratan as a pawn because he was a "spineless flunkey" (136). Actually Ratan had become as Sheikh tells him, "the victim of the most ancient of jokes that man had ever played upon other men," and that he had been "sold over, double-crossed" (135) by the secretary himself. Himmat Singh pronounces his final verdict on Ratan's character: "You are bogus, Ratan Rathor. ...from top to bottom. Your work, your religion, your friendships, your honour, nothing but a pile of dung. Nothing but poses, a bundle of shams" (137).

The Sheikh also reveals to him that it was this very society that had made his mother a whore and his sister a vagrant and so vindictively he sold his soul to the devil. Ratan now realizes that the villain lay within him. As he says: "...to know good, and to know evil and to choose evil: what greater betrayal of the spirit is there? And who does this choosing. I ask you? Who does this choosing but ourselves. And yet we roam the world, beating our breasts, looking for scapegoats" (142). It is in the line of what Gandhi says that everybody knows the truth but few dare to follow it. Ratan takes stock of his life and realizes that the twenty years he spent in the city were a waste: "Twenty years earlier, I had come to this city...to learn, to work, and in the process to make my mark. I had come full of hope, ambition, a good will; and all that was left was a pile of dung" (138). For the first time the memory of his father becomes well pronounced: "Father, Father, what have I done?" (139). At the Sheikh's suggestion he decides to kill the Secretary, but realizing that had his father been in his stead he wouldn't have thought of killing the Secretary, avoids it: "He would not have killed this man...because it would have been too much of a simplification, too primitive a solution" (141). But at last takes, unlike Clamence the blame upon himself. His sense of shame helps him in his moral awakening. Like the Ancient Mariner who later begins to love all creatures of Nature and Raskolnikov who later begins to love the saintly prostitute, Sonia, in him a definite transformation takes place. Like Mahatma Gandhi, Joshi believes that man's transformation lies in man himself.

That very night the Sheikh takes Ratan to a shack in the shanty town where his mother lived and died as a whore. He tells Ratan that his father too was a revolutionary. He wanted to avenge himself of his mother's tragic death. Unlike Ratan, he does not sell himself, but only becomes an instrument of the Devil: "He was born in filth and in filth he had grown. But he had dealt with them, the bosses, men like my Secretary...on their own terms and he had troubled some of them. He was not proud of it, not anymore, but he had at least not sold himself, like I had, nor, for that matter, had he betrayed a friend. You are a man without shame, Ratan Rathor, he said suddenly raising his voice" (144). The Sheikh's mother was shocked at his antisocial ways and cursed him: "God's darkness has come over you" (145). And Himmat Singh would give a poignant cry: "But if it was God's darkness. What was the cure? What was the cure of a crooked world. None, perhaps. Revolution, perhaps...perhaps God himself. God alone perhaps could remove His darkness. But where was God? ...What was God? And where?" (145-46).

Ratan awakens to the fact that there was no cure to the crooked ways of the world; one could only reform oneself. Ratan hasn't lost hope. The Sheikh tells Ratan: "My soul was killed, you put yours to pawn. But souls that were pawned could perhaps be retrieved," (146) that he should try to "put yourself to use, Ratan Rathor.... It might be too late. You have been too long the slave. But give it a try. One lost nothing" (147). In his monologue with the student regarding the *Bhagavadgita* he realizes: "There might be births without number awaiting us and a ceaseless accumulation of Karmas but does one not get paid as one goes along, right here, in this birth, in this world?" (91).

Earlier he had considered life in terms of an Algebra sum where the value of the missing X could never be attained and in the process of solving even X was lost. For him life was "a zero" (148) out of which nothing could be deducted. But now he realizes the fallacy of it for life could very well be made negative if one lost one's sense of shame" (148). As Tapan Kumar Ghosh say:

> This change is effected by a deep-seated belief in the metaphysical *Weltanschauung* of a tradition that regards "*shunya*" or "*zero*" not as something negative but as something meaningful and positive. Ratan's despair and extreme sense of nothingness were, thus, metamorphosed into a wholesome and constructive attitude.[24]

Now he firmly decides upon putting himself to social use and thereby expiates his sin. But the question was as to how to put oneself to social use and to have faith in what kind of God:

> The Superintendent's God is no use. Of that I am sure. Whose God then? The God of Kurukshetra? The God of Gandhi? My father's God, in case he had any? And whose revolution? The Russian? The Chinese? The American? My father's? Whose? Could they possibly be the same—Revolution and God? ...Coinciding at some point on the horizon (148).

According to Gandhi, the greatest religion of man was to put oneself to selfless service which only suffering and sacrifice can make possible. Once he wrote: "If I found myself entirely absorbed in the service of the community, the reason behind it was my desire for self realization. I had made the religion of service my own, as I felt that God could be realized only through service" (155). He chooses to have complete faith in God and in selfless social service. Thus, he opts for the ethical choice by which, in Kierkegaardian sense, he surrenders his self to God.

Leaving the world to its incorrigible crooked ways, every morning he goes to the temple to wipe the shoes of the congregation and begs forgiveness of all those whom he had harmed deliberately or unwittingly:

> I never enter the temple. I am not concerned with what goes on in there. I stand at the doorstep and I say things. Be good, I tell myself. Be good. Be decent. Be of use. Then I beg forgiveness of a large host: my father, my mother, the Brigadier, the unknown dead of the war,

> of those whom I harmed. With deliberation and with cunning, of all those who have been the victims of my cleverness, those whom I could have helped and did not (148-49).

Here we find Ratan Rathor's metamorphosis from Marlowe's Dr. Faustus to Goethe's Faust towards the end. Like Faust and unlike Dr. Faustus, he retrieves his lost soul by putting himself to social use.

He remembers his father's words: "Whatever you do touches someone somewhere" (149). So much importance his father laid on "karma." He now begins to lead his life on the lines of Mahatma Gandhi and the *Bhagavadgita.* Thus, by polishing the shoes of the congregation, he seeks to rid his heart of the 'bourgeois filth" that had settled all through his pursuit of career.

Ratan starts anew with a firm faith in life and himself. As Ratan says, "I know it is too late in the day. But one must try and not lose heart, not yield, at any cost, to despair" (149). This is reminiscent of the lines in Tennyson's "Ulysses:" "To strive, to seek, to find, and not to yield." Arun Joshi's vision has a deep impact of the *Karmic* principle of the *Gita*: "There is no intervening agent between you and God. What you sow you reap."[25] This is reminiscent of what Dostoevsky's character, Father Zossina says, "everyone of us is undoubtedly responsible for all men and everything on earth."[26]

Thus, Arun Joshi's greatness resides in his having added a social dimension to *The Apprentice* through his moralistic vision of responsible existence.

Ratan expresses, the hope that the young generation of the unpolluted listener like him "might yet hold back the tide" (150) if they are "willing to learn from the follies of their elders. Willing to learn and ready to sacrifice. Willing to pay the price" (150). The novel ends at dawn, symbolic of Ratan's transformation and regeneration: "It is a cold dawn. But no matter. A dawn, after all, is a dawn" (150). He does not give way to despair like Clamence does: "It's too late now. It'll always be too late."[27] It is this difference towards the end of *The Apprentice* that reserves for Joshi a high place in the hierarchy of Indian English writers. As Tapan Kumar Ghosh says:

> It is this balanced combination of contemporary experience and aspiration for transcendence that gives Joshi's novel a place of distinction in post-Independence Indian fiction in English and accounts for its difference from Camus's novel that ends in an abyss of nihilism.[28]

NOTES AND REFERENCES

1. Sujatha Mathai, "I'm a Stranger to My Books," *The Times of India,* July 1, 1983.
2. Tapan Kumar Ghosh, *Arun Joshi's Fiction: The Labyrinth of Life.* New Delhi: Prestige Books, 1996, 90.
3. Preface to *A Hero of Our Time* by Mikhail Lermontov, quoted by Albert Camus as the epigraph to *The Fall.*
4. "A Winner's Secrets: An Interview with Purabi Banerji," *The Sunday Statesman,* 27 February 1983.
5. Thakur Guruprasad, "The Lost Lonely Questers of Arun Joshi's Fiction," *The Fictional World of Arun Joshi,* edited by R.K. Dhawan. New Delhi: Classical Publishing Company, 1986, 162.
6. Peter M. Axthelm, *The Modern Confessional Novel.* New Haven and London: Yale University Press, 1967, 8.
7. M.K. Gandhi, *An Autobiography* or *The Story of My Experiments With Truth,* translated by Mahadev Desai. England: Penguin, 1982, 41.
8. Quoted by Tapan Kumar Ghosh, *op. cit.,* 90.
9. H.M. Prasad, *Arun Joshi.* New Delhi: Arnold Heinemann, 1985, 65.
10. Victor Anant, "The Hypnotised People," in *Partisan Review,* 27/2, 1960, 311-12.
11. M.K. Naik, *A History of Indian English Literature.* New Delhi: Sahitya Akademi, 1982, 189.
12. C.N. Srinath, "The Fiction of Arun Joshi: The Novel of Interior Landscape," *The Literary Criterion,* Vol. 12, Nos. 2-3, 1976, 129.
13. "A Winner's Secret: An Interview with Purabi Banerji," *The Sunday Statesman,* February 27, 1983.
14. Albert Camus, *The Fall,* translated by Justin O'Brien. Penguin, 1963, 99-100.
15. Albert Camus, *The Fall, op. cit.,* 41.
16. C.N. Srinath, "The Fiction of Arun Joshi: The Novel of Interior Landscape," *op. cit.,* 129.
17. R.J. Das, "Moral Dilemma in Arun Joshi's *The Apprentice,*" *Journal of Literature and Aesthetics,* Vol. 1, No. 2, March 1981, 43.

18. William Barret, *Irrational Man: A Study in Existential Philosophy*, Garden City, 1958, 5.
19. Tapan Kumar Ghosh, *op. cit.*, 106.
20. Peter M. Axthelm, *op. cit.*, 85.
21. R.K. Srivastava, *Six Indian Novelists in English*. Amritsar: G.N.D. University, 1987, 322.
22. Charles Baudelaire, *Selected Poems*, translated Joanna Richardson. England: Penguin, 1975, 28.
23. Joy Abraham, "Vision and Technique in *The Apprentice*," *The Fictional World of Arun Joshi*, *op. cit.*, 219.
24. Tapan Kumar Ghosh, *op. cit.*, 115.
25. Sujatha Mathai, "I'm a Stranger to My Books," *op. cit.*
26. F. Dostoevsky, *The Brothers Karamazov*, translated by Constance Garnett. New York: Signet, 1960, 155.
27. Albert Camus, *The Fall*, *op. cit.*, 108.
28. Tapan Kumar Ghosh, *op. cit.*, 117.

5

The Last Labyrinth

Arun Joshi's fourth novel, *The Last Labyrinth* (1981), won him the prestigious 1983 Sahitya Akademi Award. This time he lends a wider perspective on the major thematic concerns of his earlier novels. H.M. Prasad observes: "*The Last Labyrinth* assimilates the existential anxiety, the *Karmik* principles, the longings for the vitals of life in the mystical urge of Som Bhaskar."[1] Mukteshwar Pandey observes:

> It exhibits the confluence of the existentialist anxiety as exemplified in *The Foreigner*, the "*Karmik*" principles of 'detachment' and 'action' on the pattern of the *Bhagavadgita* as shown in *The Apprentice*, and the ceaseless longing for the essence of life being observed with a latent quest for "a great force, *urkraft*" as observed in *The Strange Case of Billy Biswas*. Thus, the confluence of the '*Triveni*' in the form of the mystical urge of Som Bhaskar is presented in his incessant longing for the vitals of life and existence.[2]

At one level, *The Last Labyrinth* is the story of Som Bhaskar, a shrewd Bombay businessman trying to grab a plastic manufacturing company of one Aftab Rai who lives with his pretended wife Anuradha in his ancestors' feudal-like Lal Haveli at Banares. At another level, as Tapan Kumar Ghosh says, "it is a story of deeper seeking through love, the spiritual autobiography of a lost soul groping for the meaning of life and death."[3]

Som Bhaskar, the narrator-hero, relates in flashback his infatuation with Anuradha, whom he wants to possess by all means, thus endangering his life and business. It is reminiscent of Jay Gatsby, a shady mysterious financier in F.S. Fitzgerald's *The Great Gatsby,* whose infatuation for Daisy Buchanan proves destructive for him. Som's mad pursuit of Anuradha to possess her physically and spiritually results in his quest for the meaning of life, love, God and death.

Som Bhaskar, 35, is a millionaire industrialist who inherits a gigantic Plastic manufacturing industry. He had been educated in the world's finest universities at a quarter million expense. This led to his western outlook on life, penchant for materialism and a faith in reason. He is married to Geeta, "an extraordinary woman" (11), who has borne him two children and is "all that a wife could be" (40). Yet he suffers from an insatiable hunger: "Hunger of the body. Hunger of the spirit" (11). He is a millionaire; yet he knew that "money was dirt, a whore. So were houses, cars, carpets" (11). A strange sense of discontent keeps gnawing at his soul resulting in the disruption of his life. Since he was 25, he has been singing the song of discontent: "I want, I want, I want" (11). The discontent leads him to run after the carnal pleasures. Despite having a faithful, intelligent and educated wife and a near impossibility of his life without her, he runs after several women—*ayahs,* librarians, nurses, aunts, friends' wives and others and develops sexual relations with them, but his hunger remains insatiable as ever. These new experiences ironically lead him to a terrible sense of emptiness—voids within and voids without: "It is the voids of the world, more than its objects that bother me. The voids and the empty spaces, within and without" (47). He is perpetually haunted by "a great roaring hollowness" (25) and "the boredom and the fed-up-ness" (21). The first time he had this feeling of "void" was when he visited the caves of Ajanta at eighteen. Events like death and its sight make Som's consciousness of void the more intensive. Like Camus's Meursault he betrays no emotions at the news of his mother's death, but feels the same strange hollowness behind his eyes in the cavities of his skull. Even on the Manikarnika Ghat at Banares, the sight of funeral pyres, the smell of burning flesh and the sound of bursting bones gave him the same sense of void. As Som says, "You have to have a little incident or get a telephone at midnight about so and so popping off or catch your wife with another man or be told you have cancer to see the voids within" (48). But he doesn't know the cause of this void and would spend nights without having a wink of sleep: "If I stayed up all night choffing tranquilizers, not knowing why I was awake, and come close to tears because I did not know, it came pretty close to sorrow" (103).

He tries to fill this void with sex, wealth and fame but, ends up confronting, to use Keats's phrase, "sad satiety" for he has no clue to what he wants: "If only one knew what one wanted, or, may be, to know was what I wanted. To know just that. No more. No less. This, then, was a labyrinth, too, this going forward and backward and sideways of the mind" (55). Life seems absurd to him and he develops a kind of loathing for the squalid world that carried on beneath my hospital window. All those buses and cars and taxis and men scurrying back and forth like cockroaches (46). He is in a haze and is unable to think clearly. As he tells Anuradha: "I am dislocated. My mind is out of focus. Why am I here? Why do I come here? (107). These afflictions plunge him into an abyss of despair, like a ship-wrecked sailor sinking into the ocean" (144).

Som is unable to come to terms with the world because he hasn't been able to come to terms with himself. He wants everything in life—whether it be business shares, or faith in God, or the unfathomable mystery of a women or "the secret of the universe" (129). He wants to know if there is a mystery in life where everything fits properly. But his rational analytical mind fed on western thought and outlook makes his quest impossible. His logical analysis gives him no clue to his afflictions. He is aware that he is " wondering, curious, analyzing, correlating, but getting nowhere" (80). This failure leads him to bitterness and makes him vindictive towards those who had put him on this planet; and like Hamlet he is led to question the very purpose of life. If death is to terminate all, there is no point in seeking "little pleasures or little vendettas" (65). For him, if life is incomprehensible, death "the last labyrinth" was the most incomprehensible: "And always in various shades of coherence, the spoken or unspoken question, like a vulture, circled the corpse of my life: what lay in the last labyrinth?" (122). Ever since his mother's death he has been in the grip of this fear-psychosis. Once at a *dargah* in Delhi, he feels: "There was nothing I loathed more than I loathed the sight of death and here, amidst the cenotaphs and the gravestones, there was death with a vengeance. I felt tricked" (15). When Som confides his fear of death to his doctor-friend K, he tells him, "it is not death but life you are bothered about" (203).

Like Hamlet, Som also shrinks from death but has to undergo the absurd exercise of living in the wilderness of this planet. To come to terms with either he tries to comprehend the mystery of life and death through logistics and reasoning, but these mental exercises are rendered infructuous.

But we cannot make Som Bhaskar solely responsible for his peculiar situation. He has inherited, as much from his ancestors as from his age; heredity and environment both are responsible for his mental make-up. He inherits contrary influences from his parents, with the grand father's genetic influence remaining uppermost. His Epicurean and hedonistic grand father is "a man-about-town, a gourmet, fond of women and drink. He had mistresses among the young starlets. He was a good friend but a terrible enemy, not above taking recourse to the gun. He lent and borrowed millions. Twice he lost fortunes without losing a night's sleep" (156). He was a thorough atheist: "Anything to do with God embarrassed him. He disappeared whenever my grand mother held *kirtans*" (156). On the other hand his father is a scientist absorbed in philosophical speculations who wanted to explore "the First Cause." As Som says, "He was given to bigger interrogations which he probably carried on during those nights of insomnia" (154) which followed the death of Som's mother. Thus Som, a child of double inheritance finds himself a misfit everywhere. His painful utterance is a reflection of this:

> And where did I fit in? I was a womanizer all right, and a boozer, but my womanizing and boozing had not settled anything. I had inherited the afflictions of both of them—for what were they if not afflictions, affliction that had led me into unbearable entanglement while I lived I made a fool of myself. For K, for Geeta, for many others I have become a pain in the ass. So where was I at? And why? Why else if not for the afflictions bestowed upon me by my genes: I was in deep trouble. And I knew it (156-57).

Som's mother is, contrary to Som's father and grandfather, a religious lady—a woman of profound faith and endurance. She develops cancer, but does not take the pills. She believes that only Lord Krishna would cure her, and finally she dies of cancer. Som says, "She died of cancer and Krishna." Despite Som's importune requests to get hospitalized, she doesn't agree. Nobody could shake her trust in Lord Krishna, who "sat on top of her bureau and smiled and smiled, and smiled until she was dead" (57). After her death he gave himself over to the mystery of life and death and "the First Cause," "that would explain everything, whose nature might lie behind the nature of all the rest?" (27). He realized science could not give any clue to the riddle of causes, and wondered "If only the mystics could offer their evidence of God like the scientists do" (27). He even watched through his telescope the never-ending space, but to no avail. Then he turned to philosophy and metaphysics that in turn led him nowhere:

> Who knows the truth? Who can tell where and how arose the universe? The gods are later than its beginning: Who knows, therefore, whence came this creation? Only that God who sees in highest heaven; He only knows whence came this universe. He only knows. Or, perhaps, He knows not (155).

The realization that there were no such verities resulted in melancholia and he died: "Wasn't his knowledge, then, a knowledge of verities sparsely known among ordinary men, that had pushed him over the brink, had convinced him that there were no verities at all" (156). In the very opening sentence of the novel, Som Bhaskar says, "Above all, I have a score to settle. I forget nothing, forgive no one," (9) which reminds us of what Dostoevsky's Underground Man says, "I am a sick man.... I am a spiteful man. I am an unattractive man. I believe my liver is diseased,"[4] or, for that matter, the words of Roquentin in Sartre's *Nausea*, "Something has happened to me. I cannot doubt that any more. It came as an illness does."[5] H.M. Prasad aptly remarks: "From his father he derives a Pascalian inclination to know, and if possible to believe, and the mother impulse goads him to trust, to surrender. Thus, emotionally, Som has become a labyrinth."[6] Thus, Som is aware of the inherent contradictions in his genetic constitution.

Som then consults many psychiatrists who "said a lot of things that either made two obvious a sense or no sense at all" (73). At last he gets the explanation to his malaise by an old psychiatrist:

> It is possible...to conceive of this world as being populated not with people of flesh and blood, with certain sexual orientations, but with souls. You can imagine this planet humming with souls, each wanting something. Of course, many might want the same thing. A soul might also imagine that his wants, desires are best met through another soul, if that soul is the right one. That, no doubt, is a big if. Until he meets this right soul there is no peace. When you meet the right soul then, of course, things might be peaceful, may even move on towards, a higher goal (74).

This explanation is akin to Jung's theory of the union of 'animus' and 'anima,' or the *Sankhya* philosophy which talks of the union of "*Purush*" with "*Prakriti*." Until this encounter takes place, discontent corrodes away the 'animus.' Som demands a proof of the existence of souls, it is denied him by the psychiatrist: "We assume certain things 'a priori' in all exercises of logic" (75). But the incorrigible rationalist as he is, he constantly suffers from a facelessness, a blurring of reality. His is a psychological case: "Like Jungian or Pirandellian man, he is full of inner disharmony and is a loose cluster of masks or fragments of identity."[7]

Leela Sabnis, Som's friend and lover, is "professor, descendent of a long line of professors, M.A. and Ph.D from Michigan, something else from London" (75). She has linguistic talents and is well versed in the thoughts and ideologies of philosophers like Descartes, Freud, Jung, Spinoza and others, but she admires Descartes and Freud most. She has an obsession for explanations. According to her, nothing existed that could not be reasoned through. Som asks her to reason through his malaise, she tells him: "You are much too high strung. Without reason. You are neurotic. A compulsive fornicator" (80).

To his problem of discontent and the feeling of void, she attributes to his problem of identity. She says, "Maybe what you want is a mystical identification, identification with a godhead, as most Hindus want, sooner or later" (113). She prescribes Descartes for his malaise ('I think, therefore, I am') asserting that intuition, faith or soul could also be reasoned through. When she affirms that the world of matter and the world of spirit "did not meet, could not meet," (82) he realizes that Leela wasn't the person he wanted, and the six-month love affair between the two terminated for good. As he says, "What I needed, perhaps was something, somebody, somewhere in which the two worlds combined." But real life rarely offers such vain wishes, and he remains frustrated and disillusioned.

Som is a split personality. He has inherited the sensuality of his grandfather and the spirituality of his father. He craves for somebody in whom the physical and the spiritual worlds meet. It is this craving that made a mess of his married life with Geeta. Although she is sensible and sensitive and all that a wife could be, he remains discontented. During these ten years of her married life she has developed her "own guide book of grief" (62). She has no complaint, no reproach for Som's adulteries: "Where she has every right to the adulteries of the body she had only taken to the cleansing of the soul" (63). Geeta is, like Som's mother a child of another world, traversing, like a plane at a higher altitude, "a corridor separate from the dark vestibule" (69) that Som has crossed. Though he cannot imagine life without Geeta, like G.V. Desani's

H. Hatterr, he remains strangely obsessed with women. Things take a dramatic turn with his encounter with Anuradha.

Apparently, the novel seems to be Som's mad pursuit to possess her, but this mad pursuit lends metaphysical dimensions to it as he encounters the mysteries of life, death, love and God. As Tapan Kumar Ghosh says:

> Som's obsession with Anuradha is one of love, a love that does not liberate him and sublimate his desires, as the love of Bilasia and Billy in *The Strange Case*. It freezes him as he is ego-centric and possessive. Som's hysterical and relentless pursuit of Anuradha is a tortuous affair that brings him face to face with the mysteries of life, death and God, and constitutes what may be called the nucleus of the story. This complex affair in which the sensuous and the spiritual dimensions are interwoven inextricably, unfolds in an intriguing juxtaposition of locales.[8]

Som's first encounter with Anuradha takes place at a meeting of the Plastic Manufacturers' Association at Intercontinental Hotel in Delhi. She appears to him "a monument: tall, handsome, ruined" (12). He is bewitched by her dark, sexy eyes and "the body of whose grace and sensuousness she seemed unaware" (41). At Aftab's invitation, Som visits him and Anuradha at the Lal Haveli which "had been built as a maze" (34-35). It is here that he comes to know that Anuradha is not married to Aftab and lives with him. She tells him: "I have not married—It is better not to be anybody's wife. You can't marry everyone you love. So why marry anyone at all?" (43). On being asked whether or not she would like to get married to someone, she says, "I can imagine I am married to Aftab. I can imagine I am married to you. My mother used to imagine she was married to Lord Krishna" (128). The closer he came to her, the more mysterious she appeared to him.

Anuradha is a woman of obscure origin. Her past is a saga of intense suffering and harrowing experiences that have left an indelible mark not only on her body but also on her soul. She was an illegitimate child of an insane mother. She had been molested as a child and had to witness "murders, suicides, every conceivable evil of the world" (190). She was born in Bihar Sharif in a one-roomed house where her mother sang for strangers in the evening and, perhaps sold her body. Her mother had not married, as she believed she was married to Lord Krishna. After she died (she was murdered by one of her many lovers) Anuradha was brought to Bombay by her aunt. She was sent to a convent but there she undergoes great humiliation. In her utter loneliness "All those years she does not make a single friend. She thinks only of her dead insane mother" (190). After schooling her aunt put her on the screen. Anuradha laboured, and her aunt made money. After some success for a year or two, she left the film world and began to live with Aftab in Lal Haveli. It was Gargi, a deaf-mute mystic with profound compassion and insight that brought Anuradha and Aftab together. After a year he almost lost his eyesight and became mentally run down. Anuradha too lost her looks in smallpox and attempted suicide but was miraculously saved by K. Her past is enough to suggest the ineffable suffering and humiliation that she underwent. As K tells Som: "You know, Som, my life has been spent amidst misery and suffering but I know of no other human being who suffered as much as Anuradha" (189-90).

Anuradha has inherited an unflagging faith in Lord Krishna, and her miserable past has made her stay detached and composed whatever the circumstances be. Surprisingly enough she does not believe that by loving Som she is being "particularly unfaithful" (134) to him.

Aftab and Anuradha go to a cottage on the bank of Ganga where they meet Gargi, "a fair, rosy woman of about forty" (150). When the three are back from the visit, Aftab goes to sleep. When Anuradha is left alone with Som, she tells him the mystery shrouding Gargi. Gargi's father was a prince who later turned a Sufi *pir*. He lived with Aftab's father and cured Aftab of his losing eyesight. When Anuradha finds him unbelieving, she tells Som: "You are not as clever as you think. You are wrong about many things. You are wrong about yourself. You think you know a lot, when, in fact, you don't" (61). He tries to make love to her, which annoys her, and she tells him: "It is not me you want—I know. You want something. You badly want something. I could see that the first time we met. But it is not me. That too, I can see. I told you so in the *dargah*" (58-59). She is unable to stand Som for he does not have faith even in her and she pushes him away.

Som is not able to bear her cold rather insulting response and decides to meet her in Banares after many months. In Aftab's Haveli, he is unable to have a sound sleep and is restless. When he wakes up he finds Anuradha standing at his bedside. He lusts madly for her, and is able to have "physical contact." (107) But like Cleopetra in *Antony and Cleopatra* she only fuels his passions.

With a view to forgetting her, he goes on a tour with Geeta to Europe, America and Japan, but to no avail. He goes to Gargi for help. She passes him a note: "God will send someone to help you.... Someone who has known suffering" (118). When she further says, "Go with her. Don't quarrel. She is your *shakti*," (121) he realizes for himself that she is indispensable to him. What Bilasia is to Biswas, Anuradha is to Som, like the "anima" of Jung. She is the life-spirit in women, the Feminine principle of the *Sankhya* system of Indian philosophy. It is she who plays a vital role in his realization of self.

Anuradha becomes a riddle, a puzzle, a mystery to Som and he thinks that she may have the key to his malaise. He says, "She was like the ocean; one could never reach the bottom of her" (132). He even confides to K: "There was more to her than met the eye. A world spinning all by itself. I was infatuated with this mysterious world" (189). It is only towards the end of the novel that he comes to realize his own inadequacy in dealing with her. Suffering and humiliation have endowed her with a special vision to see into the heart of things. Som feels her eyes have been forged for carrying out transactions of the soul.

Som had become completely infatuated with her; he was now bent upon possessing her completely. Every time he goes to Bombay on his business tour, memories of the enigmatic Anuradha keep haunting him. He keeps shuttling between Bombay and Banares to possess her: "All I wanted was her, I wanted her body and soul, every bit of her. I wasn't willing to share a hair of her body with anyone" (133). Anuradha could have ditched Aftab, for very soon Som was to own everything Aftab owned. But like Verne in Henry James's *The Bostonians* who leaves the possessive Olive Chancellor, and goes away with Ransom, a docile man after her heart. Again Anuradha is reminiscent of Eliza Doolittle in Shaw's *Pygmalion* who revolts against his mentor Henry Higgin's possessive and dictatorial behaviour and "bolts" from his tyranny. She achieves freedom and independence and accepts docile and devoted Freddy Eynsford Hill. It is this possessive love of Som that proves fatal for both Anuradha and Som.

Where Som is possessive, Aftab is not; where Som is Western, Aftab is oriental. He hails from a zamindar family. His great grand father had been a courtier of Wajid Ali Shah. His family fled to Banares after the Sepoy Mutiny in 1857. He respects Anuradha's personality and his love is sincere but not possessive. He, too, like Anuradha, has had his share of grief and suffering and has some of the understanding that Anuradha has and which Som is totally devoid of. And so, like Som, he does not know what he wants, he does not know what to believe in. He being a man-of-the-world fails to understand the mysterious and labyrinthine world of Anuradha, Aftab and Gargi where, as Tapan Kumar Ghosh says, "Beauty and horror, life and death, sensuality and spiritual ambience, the dancing girls and the god-woman strangely co-exist."[9] Lal Haveli is, for Som "the mysterious labyrinth of life and reality."[10] He remains an alien to himself: "But I was just not myself. That was where the rub lay. I spent hours—in the office, at home, amidst the din of parties—struggling with her memory trying to untie the riddle" (109). He is so obsessed with the idea of unravelling the mystery shrouding Anuradha and the labyrinthine Lal Haveli that in dreams and memory it becomes difficult for him to extricate one from the other. His business dwindles, his health declines and his mind becomes dazed. His rational and analytical approach fails to bridge the gap between his own world and the world of Anuradha and

Aftab. As Aftab tells Som: "I don't want to discuss, I find it difficult to argue with you...you have such strong ideas. And you hold them so...feverishly" (36).

Anuradha is Som's "Shakti" but the incorrigible sceptic as he is, he is not satisfied with what Gargi says, and he asks her: "But what if there is no God?" (118). To this she only gives him an enigmatic smile. He does not want to take recourse to faith in God or Krishna as did her mother, Anuradha and others, as it will be tantamount to a moral and spiritual death. Wherever he goes he finds the presence of God or Krishna—Mother's room, or Banares. He fails to comprehend Anuradha's unswerving devotion to Lord Krishna which appears nothing to him but ridiculous. Equally incomprehensible is the enthusiasm with which hordes of pilgrims swarmed the Krishna temple on the "*Janmashtami,*" when Anuradha is dressed "as if for a wedding" (129). To Som the entire panorama seems absurd and the enthusiasm misplaced:

> Indifferent to the shit under their feet, indifferent to the smell of a thousand bodies, the pilgrims jostled from step to step, ecstasy on their faces, when I would expect disgust. Anuradha was not different. Her face suffused with a strange ecstatic glow, she muttered prayers, made offerings at every possible shrine, thought nothing of the hem if her sari got soaked in dung (135).

Like an alien to himself and the world of enthusiastic pilgrims, he becomes full of jealousy and frustration: "All this preparation, I know was for Krishna" (133). He does not enter the temple on the pretext that it is "too crowded for his taste" (130). In his defiance he looks absurd and silly. He has become jealous of Lord Krishna and Anuradha as well, as she is devoted to Him and not to Som, a degenerate mortal.

Som once carries her to a beautiful valley situated in the shadow of snow-covered hills where there shall be nobody, not even Lord Krishna between the two: "There no one would know her and she would think of none and there would be no one to distract her from her loving of him." (124-25) One evening when the two are drunk, Lord Krishna creeps into their talk:

> "There is a god up there. In those mountains.... There is a temple there. On a hill lined with lepers. You must come with me.... God will cure you." "Cure me of what? A bad heart? Fears? Disappointments?" She said she could not explain. I looked into her drunken eyes and in a way, I understood. Deep inside my heart I know I was a leper, that needed a cure. But I refused to yield ground (126).

She suggests love and divine faith as remedy to his deep-rooted malaise at which he becomes enraged for "dragging God into that room which until that moment had been the stage for satisfying his wildest fantasies" (127). And when he again makes love to her it was as if he were making love to a corpse and not to Anuradha, her self or soul remains elusive to Som. His discontent grows the more, and the more strident becomes his chant "I want, I want, I want" (11) which he is unable to reason out smoothly. As says the *Bhagavadgita:*

dhyayato visayam pumsah
sangas tesu' payayate
sangat samjayate kamah
Kamat krodho' bhijayate (Chapter II, Verse 62)

That is: "When a man dwells in his mind on the objects of sense, attachment to them is produced. From attachment springs desire and from desire comes anger."[11]

And in the next verse:

krodhad bhavati sammohah
sammohat smrtivibhramah
smribhramsad buddhinaso
buddhinasat pransyati (Chapter II, Verse 63)

That is: "From anger arises bewilderment, from bewilderment loss of memory; and from loss of memory, the destruction of intelligence and from the destruction of intelligence he perishes."[12]

These two verses easily sum-up his outlook and conduct in life, besides he is godless which makes his malaise the more grave.

Joshi, in his interview with Sujata Mathai has confessed to having been influenced by Camus and other existentialist writers and also Mahatma Gandhi and the *Bhagavadgita.* Som's confusion results from a contact between the Western and Indian ethos. Godlessness is a common trait of Arun Joshi's protagonists. The symbol of Krishna looms large in the story and the enigmatic elusive Krishna appears and disappears in the novel throughout. It is reminiscent of what Lord Krishna tells Arjuna:

bijam mam sarvabhutanam
viddhi partha sanatanam

(Chapter VII, Verse 10 L1-2)

That is: "Arjuna, know Me as the eternal seed of all beings."[13] Som, like Trishanku, moves to and fro between the Western and the Indian (or Eastern) world. He is very close to the characters of Beckett and Ionesco—absolutely absurd. Ionesco defines absurd as "That which is devoid of purpose... cut off from his religious, metaphysical and transcendental roots, man is lost; all his actions become senseless, absurd, useless."[14]

Although an ardent follower of Darwin with "survival of the fittest" as his motto, he realizes the inadequacy of this theory of Biological evolution to explain the existence of spirit. Like his father, he too is in search of the first cause. As Joshi says, "The son travels farther perhaps, largely it would appear because of the person of Anuradha. But they travel a similar path even though the path itself keeps turning upon itself."[15] He asks Gargi: "Why should Man be equipped, burdened, with this strange...sensibility, or urge or drive? ...What precisely is expected of him, of you and me, of Anuradha of everyone else? Darwin didn't say how we are supposed to evolve further" (131-32). But he is held in surprise when Anuradha says, "Krishna begins where Darwin left off" (132). Som wants to have faith but is unable to have it for want of a sign or evidence. As H.M. Prasad says:

> Som is tormented by his knowledge. Awareness of Spinoza, Freud, Jung, Buddha and Krishna tortures him. Darwin torments. He has gone through the history of

evolution and remembers his Darwin by heart. If Descartes is correct if Freud and Jung and Darwin are correct what should he think of his mother's faith, Geeta's trust?[16]

On yet another occasion, he asks her to accompany her to Bombay. She loves Som and makes the sacrifice against her wishes. But at this climactic stage of their affair, he suffers a nearly fatal heart attack.

But Som had many more mysterious experiences in store. Despite his doctor-friend K's total disappointment he recovers, and with it Anuradha disappears from his life forever. She refuses to meet Som despite his requests, and comes to know from Geeta that Anuradha had told her everything in writing and had sought her forgiveness by which he feels befooled and betrayed and becomes vindictive.

Now Som is bent upon ruining Aftab completely and thereby having full possession of her. He asks Mr. Thapar, his manager, to start buying the shares of Aftab's company once again, but is surprised to know that a block of Aftab's share is lying with Krishna. He says, "There was nothing simple about Krishna. Had it been so, he would not have survived ten thousand years. He would have died along with the gods of the Pharaohs, the Sumerians, the Incas. Krishna was about as simple as the labyrinth of Aftab's Haveli" (173). As Anuradha has sold the shares to Lord Krishna, he decides to "meet Krishna personally," (172) and find some sign of his existence.

Symbolically, Som's journey is the journey of a soul trying to reach out to faith in God. In the course of this journey, he encounters a few characters—a little boy and an old man—that serve as eye-openers to him. The little boy who accompanies the group of men carrying his sick old grand father in a palanquin is a striking contrast to Som. They are carrying the old men from Jaipur to a strange lake in the mountains where he is to die. The boy is desperately looking for a rare pebble in the mountain that he has come to know about from his grand father. On being asked by Som what his reaction would be if he didn't find the stone, the boy nonchalantly says it would affect him the least which is based on the *Karmic* principle in the *Bhagavadgita.* But Som lacks this intuitive wisdom of the boy.

Som's encounter with the old man is his encounter with death itself. Som is astonished to know that he has travelled nine hundred miles to this lake in the belief that this would send him to heaven. Here also a sense of *deja vu* leaves Som dumb and he feels himself an outsider to this world asmuch as he was in the world of Aftab and Anuradha. But a bit of metamorphosis does take place in him. As Som says, "Along with the old man we had all travelled to the other world, haunting, free from fear, you might as well be afraid of a train travelling from one station to another. That black lake, those bronze cliffs, were certainly another station" (194). Actually the boy stands for faith in desireless *"Karma"* where only "*Karma*" was important and not the fruit thereof, and the old man stands for absolute faith in God and his machinations. As H.M. Prasad observes: "Som, like the pilgrim in Bunyan's *The Pilgrim's Progress* passes through the crisscross of agonizing experiences and *The Last Labyrinth* is a drama of a pilgrim's progress of modern times."[17]

But Som is not yet home spiritually. He is still a sceptic like Hamlet about "the undiscovered country, from whose bourn/ No traveller returns." His confrontation with death like Hamlet's when accidental intervention of the pirates makes him realize "there's a divinity that shapes our ends,/Rough-hew them how we will," (V ii, 10-11) teaches him a bit of the spiritual lesson.

At last Som reaches the temple of Krishna at the summit of the mountains, and is surprised to find Gargi there. It is here that K's identity is revealed, as he introduces him to Gargi: "This is Dr. Kashyap. He saved my life" (202). K even discloses the miracle about Som's unaccountable recovery from the nearly fatal heart attack, thereby suggesting Anuradha's role in his life. K divulges the secret that it was not him who had saved Som and that he was as good as dead when Anuradha came to him in the hospital. On the night before, Anuradha had gone on a journey with K to retrieve the missing shares. But seeing his critical condition she straightaway went to Gargi to implore her to save Som. On Gargi's refusal to perform a miracle, Anuradha persisted, begged, wept, and threatened that if she did not save Som she would kill herself. Dr. Kashyap with a choking voice asks Gargi, "I am a medical doctor. I do not believe in things in which Anuradha believes. But I know for a fact that Som had no hope whatsoever and I want to know: Did you save him? Anuradha says you did. And in turn for what you did, she says, you made her promise that she would give up Som. Forever. That to her, Som would be dead, either way. Is this true? Please tell me" (206). To this Gargi only gives him an enigmatic smile of hers, and admits that she has the package of shares, which she will hand over to them next morning.

Love means sacrifice. Absolute love means absolute sacrifice. Anuradha's ultimate sacrifice is reminiscent of Sarah Miles, the saint-sinner-adulteress in Graham Greene's novel, *The End of the Affair.* Sarah prayed to God for the life of her lover, Maurice Bendrix, who had apparently been killed in an air raid while he and Sarah were sleeping together: "Let him be alive, and I will believe, give him a chance. Let him have his happiness. Do this and I will believe.... I will give him up forever" (95). God answered this human prayer. Bendrix returned to life and Sarah instantly but without any explanation gave him up forever.

Gargi's obstinate silence to K's revelation leaves him totally confounded. It was Hobson's choice. He could either take it (the faith) or leave it. As Som says, "Here was this package. I could take it or leave it, she was going to offer me neither explanation nor advice. I had the confused feeling that I was being put on a hook and she was going to do nothing to get me off" (207).

Although he rejects the incident as a "gimmick" and "half-assed rigmarole" (208), he is steadily but surely heading towards faith and trust. Entering the sanctum sanctorum of the temple he sees the man-high flame burning since time immemorial; Som says, "This, then, was Krishna, was it? Kneeling beside that fantastic flame, my heart bursting with sorrow and my old demented love for Anuradha, I vowed.... I was going to get the shares and Anuradha" (208). Even this flame fails to offer him any eternal bliss. Next morning he confesses to Gargi that he is grabbing the shares to avenge Anuradha's betrayal: "I cannot give up Anuradha, you know that. In the absence of evidence I intend to challenge the whole thing. I want to take not only these shares but also Anuradha. It scares me but I have no choice" (213). Gargi passes a note: "There is no harm in believing that God exists" and further "God does not seek revenge. Man's vanity *ahankar* brings him revenge enough" (213-14).

Som takes the shares and returns with Anuradha. Tired he lies down on the bank of a stream with his head on the bundle of shares, and gazes at the impersonal vastness of the sky above him. The thoughts that come to his mind are that of Prince Andrew in Tolstoy's *War and Peace*:

> I was reminded of Prince Andrew, knocked down like a dummy without firing a shot. He had imagined himself to be ambitious. He had hoped Austerlitz would do for him what Toulon had done for the Bonaparte. Lying in the mud, cannon balls flying over him, he had stared at the vast cosmic impersonal dome of the sky and had wondered: My God, where have I been all these years. Why had I never looked at the sky before (214-15).

Now he realizes that the revenge and the bundle of shares actually hold nothing for him and feels utterly defeated. He reflects on the entire episode and realizes that no external system can cure man of the malaise, that the malaise lay within him, and the solution to it should be from within. This is the only truth he had learnt from his journey to the mountains.

Back to Banares he meets Aftab and repeatedly implores him to see Anuradha. His wish is granted but Anuradha asks him to leave the Lal Haveli immediately: " You don't understand. You don't know these people. Things could happen to you in this Haveli and no one would ever know" (279). He leaves the Haveli and comes back the next morning to find that she had gone to the Krishna temple on the night of *Janmashtami* but did not return. Som reports the matter to the police. The place is raided and only a piece of antique clothing is found, perhaps, of hers. Anuradha's leaving Som reminds us of Gerald's leaving Gudrun in Lawrence's *Women in Love.* Gerald wants to break free of Gudrun. As she is domineering and possessive by nature, Gerald wanders off into the snow of the Alps for good. Perhaps, Anuradha too wanders off into the labyrinth of the Lal Haveli and dies. Like Bendrix in *The End of the Affair,* Som seeks God's forgiveness like a defeated existentialist through his intercession:

> Anuradha, listen, listen wherever you are. Is there a God where you are? Have you met Him? Does he understand the language that we speak? Anuradha if there is a God and if you have met him and if He is willing to listen, then, Anuradha, my soul, tell him, tell this God, to have mercy upon me. Tell him, I am weary of so many fears; so much doubtings. Of this dark earth and these empty heavens. Plead for me, Anuradha. He will listen to you (222-23).

This poignant cry suggests that Anuradha has become "the core of his existence, the crystallization of the meaning of his life."[18] Anuradha, to Som, is a living mystery. Her mystery behind her is her unbelievable character, which Aftab sums up thus: "It is just that she can't stand to see anybody fail. It breaks her heart" (39). Her heart is capable of embracing everybody. She is spiritually deep and is not interested in carnal desires. She offers her body to Som when he badly needs it. She is above fear and shame and has become a "*Sthitiprajna*" (a stoic) of the *Bhagavadgita.* She is ever ready to sacrifice. Joshi wroughts her character on the lines of Vedic "*Panchmahakanyas*" who are doubted to be physically impure but mentally chaste. She disappears when his love becomes possessive like the mythical Trishanku. He still dangles between scepticism and faith; the thoughts that colloide like atoms in his skull could be "the harbinger, the pilot escort, of melancholia...of insanity...(or of) faith" (223).

Like Abhimanyu of the Mahabharata, he is still in the labyrinth of existence, lost in the "*Chakravyuha*" where there is an easy way in but an impossible way out. The novel ends where it began. Listening to the roaring hollowness of the void within at night, he puts down in the minute book his thoughts. Unlike the other protagonists of Joshi, he does not progress from alienation to existential affirmation.

Geeta's charactei works as a Dostoevskian mirror to Som that helps the author to lay bare Som's inherent character by contrast or juxtaposition.

In utter frustration Som attempts to commit suicide which is denied him. As he places the revolver on his temple, his wife Geeta shakes him "gently as though rousing a man from sleep" (224). Joshi perhaps suggests that the trusting Geeta will restore the utterly discontented Som to peace and tranquillity. In the closing sentence, Som says, "I hope she understands" (224).

Joshi suggests that an unswerving "trust in the world's mechanisms," can only solve the labyrinths of existence. As H.M. Prasad says:

> Bhaskar's dilemma has crystallized the sociological, psychological and metaphysical dimensions of human existence into Joshi's unique vision of modern man's predicament. Som Bhaskar is an archetype of the new man and *The Last Labyrinth* is a fictional tour-de-force on the chaos of existence and the crisis of consciousness.[19]

Joshi suggests faith as the key to happiness and success. When Som asks the *panda* on the day for vows if people's wishes really get fulfilled, he says, "It depends on their faith. Faith can move mountains." (198) As Som himself later quotes Kierkegaard: "Prayer does not change God but it changes him who prays" (118).

Tapan Kumar Ghosh remarks: "*The Last Labyrinth* is a deep psychological exploration of a lost soul."[20] He is a modern man lost between two worlds, unable to accept or fully reject any of the two contradictory worlds. As H.M. Prasad remarks: "*The Last Labyrinth* is a fictional tour-de-force on the chaos of existence and the crisis of consciousness."[21] His intellectual pride, his great reliance on reason and his faith in science and logic are great impediments to his spiritual realization. Though he is curious to have faith but he wants signs, which reminds us of what Christ said to the Pharisees when they asked him to perform a miracle to prove God's existence. But Jesus gave a deep groan and said, "Why do the people of this day ask for a miracle? No, I tell you!"[22] Only complete faith and absolute surrender to God or Lord Krishna can emancipate Som of his physical and mental problems. As Lord Krishna enjoins Arjuna that:

> *manmana bhava madbhakto*
> *madyaji mam namaskuru*
> *mam evai syasi yuktvai' vam*
> *atmanam matparayanah* (Chapter 9, Verse 34)

That is: "On Me fix thy mind; to Me be devoted; worship Me; revere Me; thus having disciplined thyself, with Me as thy goal, to Me thou shalt come."[23]

Either he should have unconditional faith like his mother's or for that matter, his wife Geeta's, or should have Anuradha-like suffering. He wants faith without any sacrifice. According to Hindu cosmology, it is sacrifice that is at the root of creation. As S. Radhakrishnan writes: "Prayer and sacrifice are means to spiritual life. While true sacrifice is the abandonment of one's ego, prayer is the exploration of reality by entering the beyond, that is, within, by ascension of consciousness."[24] She has an understanding which ordinary women do not possess. But his pride in his so-called education, and especially his desire to possess her render him insane enough not to realize her as the last ray of hope to egress from the blind alley. As Lord Krishna tells Arjuna not to harbour desires that would eventually lead to insanity. It is the strident voice "I want, I want, I want" that is the root of his malaise. But Anuradha's offer to cure Som of his malaise is spurned in a state of total insanity.

Joshi believes that "it is very difficult to steer one's way through life without God, or at least concepts like right or wrong."[25] For Som the understanding born of suffering and humiliation is lost to him, and he remains to the end in introspective solitude.

The influence of the Upanishads may also be expressly seen by the reference of the great Upanishadic sage

Yajnavalkya twice in the work for a particularly poignant question that is addressed to him. In the Brihadaranyaka Upanishad, King Janaka asks, "And when the sun is set, Yajnavalkya, and the moon is also set, and the fire has sunk down and voice is silent, what, then, is the light of man?"[26] Though the novel does not answer this question, but Yajnavalkya replies, "The self, indeed, is his light"[27] But the covetous, proud and insane Som spurns the only hope he could have had. Like Kafka's K in *The Castle* he tries hard to explore the mystery of the divine reality and thereby ascertain the presence of God, but comes out empty handed. As H.M. Prasad opines: "In his quest, in his intent to unravel cosmic mystery, Bhaskar is a modernized, secularized, empiricized, sceptical Nachiketa who has been denied the faith and resolution of the Upanishadic model."[28]

Arun Joshi suggests that the ultimate truth and reality could be realized if only one were to forsake rationalism. Humility, sacrifice and suffering are the three-fold path to exploring Divine truth. Although on closer scrutiny this novel unfolds a conspicuous crisscross of the various Oriental and Occidental literary influences, Arun Joshi's remarkably artistic sensibility has assimilated these influences and rendered the novel a powerful masterpiece revealing his vision of life which is undeniably his own—a Hindu vision of life.

NOTES AND REFERENCES

1. H.M. Prasad, *Arun Joshi*. New Delhi: Arnold Heinemann, 1985, 85.
2. Mukteshwar Pandey, *Arun Joshi: The Existential Element in His Novels*. New Delhi: B.R. Publishing Corporation, 1998, 113.
3. Tapan Kumar Ghosh, *Arun Joshi's Fiction: The Labyrinth of Life*. New Delhi: Prestige Book, 1996, 123.
4. F. Dostoevsky, "Notes from Underground," translated by Constance Garnett, *Norton Anthology of World Masterpieces*. New York: W.W. Norton, 1980, 1885.
5. Jean-Paul Sartre, *Nausea*, translated by Robert Baldick. England: Penguin, 1965, 13.
6. H.M. Prasad, *op. cit.*, 88.
7. Mukteshwar Pandey, *op. cit.*, 116.
8. Tapan Kumar Ghosh, *op. cit.*, 131-32.
9. *Ibid.*, 134.

10. H.M. Prasad, "The Crisis of Consciousness: The Last Labyrinth" in *The Fictional World of Arun Joshi,* edited by R.K. Dhawan. New Delhi: Classical Publishing Company, 234.
11. S. Radhakrishnan, *The Bhagavadgita*: New Delhi: Harper Collins, 1996, 125.
12. *Ibid.*, 126.
13. *Ibid.*, 216.
14. Eugene Ionesco, "Dans Les armes Le la Ville," *Cahiers de la Compagnie Madeline Renaud*, Jean-Louis Barrault, Paris, No. 20, October 1959.
15. Arun Joshi, "Excerpts from a Talk by Arun Joshi at Dhvanyaloka," Mysore, Sept. 1981, IACLALS Newsletter, No. 10 January 1982, 7.
16. H.M. Prasad, *op. cit.*, 90.
17. *Ibid.*, 93.
18. O.P. Mathur and G. Rai, "Arun Joshi and the Labyrinth of Life," *The Fictional World of Arun Joshi,* edited by R.K. Dhawan, New Delhi: Classical Publishing Company, 1986, 152.
19. H.M. Prasad, "The Crisis of Consciousness: *The Last Labyrinth,*" *The Fictional World of Arun Joshi, op. cit.*, 238-39.
20. Tapan Kumar Ghosh, *op. cit.*, 145.
21. H.M. Prasad, *op. cit.*, 108.
22. *The Message of Love*, Bangalore: The Bible Society of India, 56.
23. S. Radhakrishnan, *op. cit.*, 254.
24. S. Radhakrishnan, *The Principal Upanishads*: London: George Allen and Unwin, 1953, 19-51.
25. "A Winner's Secrets: An Interview with Purabi Banerji," *The Sunday Statesman*, February 27, 1983.
26. S. Radhakrishnan, *The Principal Upanishads, op. cit.*, 155-56.
27. *Ibid.*, 256.
28. H.M. Prasad, "The Crisis of Consciousness: *The Last Labyrinth,*" in *The Fictional World of Arun Joshi, op. cit.*, 238.

6

The City and the River

Arun Joshi's *The City and the River* (1990), the fifth and last novel strikes a unique note different from his earlier novels in many respects. In a way *The City and the River is*, "a continuation of and an improvement upon Joshi's major thematic concerns."[1] The nature of the novel is explained on the blurb of the book which reads as under:

> Narrated with humour and a gentle irony *The City and the River* strikes an entirely different theme from Arun Joshi's earlier novels. At one level, it is a parable of the times; at another it deals with how men, in essence entirely free to choose, create by their choice the circumstances in which they must live. It also explores the relevance of God to man's choices and whether all said and done, 'the world indeed belongs to God and to no one else.'

As ever Arun Joshi's *leit motif* remains the same—an anguished man's quest for survival and search for a viable alternative amidst materialism, corruption, cynicism, alienation and dwindling spiritual faith. Unhinged from its cultural heritage and spiritual moorings, his protagonists find themselves lost in a grossly materialistic industrial society. In this quest they are led into the labyrinths of life and death, and sometimes into the labyrinth of the world of spirit. As a matter of fact, in this novel "Joshi has set out on a quest for spiritual commitment for a still centre amidst the turmoil and uncertainty of contemporary life."[2]

While the first four novels are concerned with individual lives, *The City and the River* is a departure from the existing *oeuvre* of Arun Joshi as it is "a commentary on the times"[3] and "a political parable."[4] Joshi has made use of prophesy, fantasy and politics and presented the story in a wider backdrop. The book is a severe commentary on the times, containing echoes of the Indian emergency in the 1970s. Parallels may be found between the Emergency regime of 1974-75 in India and the one portrayed in the novel. The huts of the mud-people are erased in the manner of what the then government did to widen the streets in the name of beautification, "Sundarikaran," of the city of Delhi during the Emergency. Even we find close resemblance between the power structure of the two. The way the Grand Master acquires unlimited powers and leaves no stone unturned to anoint his son to the throne is reminiscent of what the then Prime Minister did. Similarly, the height of sycophancy we find in the novel could be seen then with a view to achieving wider significance and perhaps to avoiding controversy, Joshi has set his book as Amur says, in "a temporal setting which is deliberately confused."[5] In the novel we find coexistence of the two extremes at every level. Hermits, yajnas, sacrifice, primitive people co-exist with electronic surveillance, ultra-modern lasers, helicopters, videos, spying and inquisition. In fact the novel moves on two levels simultaneously. At one level it is a political parable revealing the ruthless governing of the City by the Grand Master and his fawning Council of Advisors. On the other hand are people who struggle and suffer immensely to maintain freedom and liberty of spirit. It is a severe indictment of the corruption and malpractices of political leaders, businessmen, the police and armed chiefs. It is a political novel with a difference fusing satire and philosophical discussion. At another level the novel is a parable of human choice between allegiance to God and allegiance to man. The novel is also suffused with the indigenous sensibility of the novelist, his cultural and spiritual ethos. The Karmic principle of the *Bhaguvadgita* is central. We perceive the influence of Mahatma Gandhi as well.

Tyranny and repression, hypocrisy and deceit, selfishness and corruption, violence and destruction are rampant in the

"City" of the Grand Master. The events portrayed are reminiscent of the emergency in India, as the aftermath in both the cases proved ruinous to the rulers. Although the rulers succeed in doing away with the adversaries, God punishes them for their misdeeds. When human beings fail, it is nature (God) that punishes the wrong-doers. The river is flooded and the king helplessly "gazed at the vast sea in a stunned silence" (257).

It rightly claims a privileged place among the political novels of our literature as it powerfully comments on the political scenario of the past, the present and the future.

Joshi enlarges his canvas, turns his focus from the private to the public, and deals with the socio-political and existentialist crisis of the entire "City" which is every city. He takes up his favourite existentialist issues, but sees them through the spectacles of politics and thereby elevates the novel to the level of political-allegorical satire.

Joshi offers a vision of life that is relevant to both—individual and nation. The metaphysical questions that he seeks to explore in the political context that reflect men's ambition, egoism, selfishness, defiance of Truth, and the suffering consequent upon them. He stresses the need for spiritual commitment and collective responsibility to do away with evils. Concerned with an entire race, the novel turns out to be, as Chatterjee says, "an allegory of Indian history and its mythic truth,"[6] or as Gita Hariharan aptly puts it, "a parable of political society—the endless variations of the relationship between men and power."[7] This metaphysical dimension redeems the novel from being a mere political satire.

The City and the River is divided into eleven sections including a Prologue and an Epilogue. The Prologue strikes a fresh note in Joshi's fiction. Set in an imaginary locale, the scene of action is a Nowhere City. There are two very important characters in it—the teacher, the ageless Yogeshwara, and the disciple, 'the Nameless-One,' that symbolize the processes of regeneration and decay. They have lived together for thirty years in a hermitage amidst snow-covered mountains. In the evening of his thirtieth birthday, the Nameless-One presents himself before his master who recites "a strange sorry tale" (11) and the Nameless-One learns about his own identity. The Great Yogeshwara narrates a tale about the Grand Master who represents the usage to dominate and the boatman who assert their identity. The conflict presented here is an eternal one. Phoenix-like a new city springs on the ruins of the old and the endless cyclic process goes on. Yet another Grand Master and another Hermit of the Mountain appear on the scene to play their respective roles:

> On the ruins of that city, as always happens, a new city has risen. It is ruled by another Grand Master, which, of course, need not always happen, in the new city is another Professor, another Bhumiputra, another tribe of boatmen. There is also another Council and another set of Councilors. The men have other names but the forces they embody remain unchanged (262).

It is this eternal cyclic process that imparts a new significance to his novel making clear the indelible influence of the *Bhagavadgita.*

The dramatic tension stems from the struggle between the Grand Master and the Boatmen. The city and the river in the novel are two opposing symbols. The palace Astrologer, mentor of the Grand Master and the hermit of the mountain are disciples of the Great Yogeshwara. The prophecy about the advent of a king make them choose to interpret it differently, resulting in great struggle and suffering. Boatmen's leader, the Headman, tells the Astrologer: "We have no quarrel with the Grand Master and we have no quarrel with you. It is a matter of allegiance, our allegiance is only to the river and cannot be shared." This accentuates the conflict between the city and the river, between the Grand Master and the Boatmen and lends a vitality and piquancy to the plot. The city's estrangement from the river and all that it stands for leads to death and destruction.

The city, spreading along the river has a three-tier structure:

> First comes the narrow brown band of the mud huts, running from end to end, dotted with the green of many mangroves. Next...on a higher ground, lies the neat rosy

> pink oval of the brick colonies and their special schools, clubs and shopping arcades. Beyond the brick colonies stand the famous Seven Hills ranged in their picturesque formation (12).

The other landmarks are pyramids and the Gold Mines (a huge dungeon) where the state prisoners are confined to undergo inhuman physical and psychological torture. The manner in which individuals are picked up and condemned to live in the huge dungeon is reminiscent of the Emergency in India or, the Moscow trials of the thirties.

Another notable aspect of the City is its unnatural and chaotic atmosphere that reminds us of T.S. Eliot's *The Waste Land*. The City, particularly the Seven Hills and its adjoining area has the dominance of steel and glass and marble and is devoid of vegetation and flowers. Lack of vegetation and flowers has been stressed many a time in the novel. The road linking the palace to the government-houses is well-paved but is "treeless and without flowers" (31). The Professor goes around the city, especially along the corridors of power, in search of his student Bhoma, and is stunned by what he sees: "The Palace lawns, however, leave much to be desired. All brown and yellow. No trees. No flowers. Not a patch of green" (31). The square of the Three Truths with its marvellous fountain also has "so much water and yet no grass or flowers" (36). With the advent of winter, the entire landscape, excepting the palace and its adjoining area, is covered with flowers. Flowers also grow on the river bank and the mango-grove. But, as Arun Joshi says, "in the city's newly laid parks and along its well–straightened avenues and on the Seven Hills...in spite of the chief horticulturist's strenuous efforts and to the Grand Master's great regret, neither grass nor flowers grow" (136). Even the pyramids that preserve the dead bodies of the previous Grand Masters are devoid of flowers. This is the result of the city's severance from the river and consequently leads to corruption and degeneration among the rulers leading to their ruin. To accentuate the conflict, Joshi juxtaposes nature and civilization, the city of steel, glass and marble and the pristine river. Such polarization is an important facet of Joshi's narrative technique and his characterization. The characters are set against one another, and this heightens the conflict between the values and attitudes they stand for.

Joshi's description of the Grand Master's City as being located on the Seven Hills and the manner in which corruption holds its sway over the Seven Hills like a prostitute, seems to be a page from the section "The Revelation to John" in *The Message of Love.* The section is about the time when the Christians were being persecuted because of their faith in Jesus Christ as Lord—the eternal river of love and mercy. A paragraph in this section runs thus:

> The spirit took control of me, and the angel carried me to a desert. There I saw a woman sitting on a red beast that had names insulting to God written all over it; the beast had seven heads and ten horns. The woman was dressed in purple and scarlet, and covered with gold ornaments, precious stones, and pearls.... And I saw that the woman was drunk with the blood of God's people and the blood of those who were killed because they had been loyal to Jesus.[8]

The secret meaning of the woman and of the beast that carries her, the beast with seven heads and ten horns, has been explained in another paragraph that runs thus:

> The seven heads are seven hills, on which the woman sits. There are also seven kings: five of them have fallen, one still rules, and the other one has not yet come; when he comes, he must rule only a little while.[9]

In such unnatural chaotic and spiritually sterile atmosphere, the characters have a sorry tale of their own to narrate. They suffer from alienation, weariness, boredom, rootlessness, and meaninglessness in their lives. The Rallies Master is unhappy and rootless: "His misfortune lay in the fact that instead of teaching him how to row a boat his parents had wanted him to join the ranks of the brick people," (71) and was considered an upstart by the boatmen. The Professor too is tired of his existence and he tells Little Star, "I am tired of being careful, Little Star. I am weary" (87). To Bhumiputra, his life seems to be a mere waste: "Bhoma urged him to stay because he still felt very alone" (157). He was unhappy with "his own ineffective life. A sense of overwhelming futility filled him at such times, so much so that he found no point in living" (174). The Grand Master too is no exception. He is also gloomy and tired. The Minister for Trade tells him: "You are tired. In your weariness you let dark thoughts assail you" (203). Dharma's father suffers from the "Three Truths, Syndrome, statis of the soul, atrophy of the brain and locomotor functions" (135). He confesses: "My insides are rotting. I too am just vanishing" (134). Thus, every character has "a strange sorry tale" (10) of his own to narrate.

Of all the people it is the boatmen who lead an authentic existence in the Hiedeggerian sense. The brick-people and the mud-people can be persuaded, "cajoled, distracted, and, if necessary, threatened" (13). But the Boatmen oppose the Grand Master's plan and refuse to give in to his whims. Though they are simple and poor, but they are far away from being simpletons, they are prepared to pay any price for their authentic existence. They are courageous, honest and bold enough to call a spade a spade. The Grand Master regards them "incomprehensible and stubborn" (14). The Grand Master's father had once advised him: "Boatmen are not as simple as they seem. They consider themselves to be the children of the river, and to the river and river alone do they hold allegiance. They believe, unfortunately with their hearts, and for their belief they are willing to die. And don't let their poverty mislead you into believing that they can be bought" (14). In the face of all odds, they stubbornly oppose the Grand Master to maintain their identity and way of life.

It is the high and middle-class people who lack in authenticity as they never protest and adapt themselves to the changing circumstances. The level of authenticity varies in inverse proportion to the status that varies with the altitude at which they live. The lowliest and the poorest boatmen living in the mud huts are the most superior as they do what they feel like doing. For half of their time "they spend sitting about on the sloping river bank talking, singing, meditating, playing the one-string" (14). The middle class men lack in authenticity as they adapt themselves to the situation and do not practise what they feel like doing. They are unhappy because they have abdicated their freedom to the rulers in the hope of getting a higher position in the administrative hierarchy.

The highest or ruling class lead the most inauthentic lives and impose the same on others. They are the most corrupt, morally bankrupt, utterly shameless hypocrites. The Grand Master, in the name of welfare and prosperity of the city, declares the Era of Ultimate Greatness with the motif of consolidating his own position to become king and pave the way for his son as well.

The Grand Master is "a master of ambiguity" (197). He sets to work only after sunset and works till dawn. He never sees the coming of dawn because wherever he is the first rays of the sun are never allowed to reach. Though he is good-looking and courteous, unlike Plato's ideal Prince, the Grand Master "dislikes music" (48). On the night of the boatmen's blockade in the river, he orders their simple musical instruments to be destroyed with laser-weapons. He and his Ministers practice " Bad Faith." He is a thorough fraud. As per the Professor's last wish, he instructs the Astrologer to issue a decree but not to think of implementing it: "Issuing a decree, Astrologer, does not mean its immediate implementation" (168). The Grand Master and his cringing Council of Ministers fail to look into the nature of their "freedom," freedom to become "for itself" or "in-itself."

To ensure people's allegiance to the Grand Master, the Astrologer carries the message of "the Triple Way or the Way of the Three Beatitudes" to the people. "The Era of Ultimate Greatness" (23) is declared to drum the fear of the palace into them. It enjoins them to follow the Astrologer's Three Beatitudes. But the Boatmen refuse stubbornly to swear allegiance to any human being. They prove the authenticity of their selves in Hiedeggerian and Sartrean terms. For Hiedegger, "genuine existence is existence which dares to face death."[10] Every night a few boatmen are transported to the Gold Mines and are made to undergo physical and mental torture till "the idea of the self is suitably dissolved" (161). The case of Patanjali, who is arrested, as a substitute for Master Bhoma, is exemplary. When Dharma tells: " You only have to apologise and you will be set free," Patanjali boldly asks: "But why should I apologise? I have done no wrong. Rather the Grand Master should apologise for making such absurd rules" (26). The boatmen under Bhumiputra—a scrawny, bearded, mathematics teacher who hails from the mud-quarters—struggle hard to maintain their authenticity in the Sartrean sense of the term. Sartre says, "For the secret of a man is not his Oedipus complex or his inferiority complex: it is the limit of his own liberty, his capacity for resisting fortune and death."[11] A state-sponsored terrorism is let loose and a large number of boatmen, who have spurned the Astrologer's Three Truths and burnt the Grand Master's effigies, are thrown into the Gold Mines. Every effort is made to crush their protest and make them fall in line. The novel seems to have been influenced by the character of Kurtz in Conrad's *Heart of Darkness* who wields great power over natives. A row of severed heads on stakes round the hut give an intimation of barbaric rites by which Kurtz has achieved his ascendancy.

There are some among the brick-people also who are concerned about their own existentialist lives. The professor sacrifices everything including his life, in search of his pupil Bhoma who has been picked up in one of his night operations. In spite of the dire consequences he could meet, he does not shun his search. He too is thrown into the Gold Mines (the huge dungeon) where he gets emaciated and then finally dies. The grand father, Dharma's grandfather, is yet another character who risks his life by giving refuge to Bhoma at his farm. He, along with Dharma, Shailaja and Bhoma, dies in the massive attack by the armed forces of the Grand Master.

Bhumiputra, popularly known as Master Bhoma, is also one of the characters who is ready to sacrifice even his life for the authenticity of his existence. He is considered by the police as the "kingpin of a conspiracy" (43) against the Grand Master, and is arrested for "making subversive propaganda at the university" (43). Unlike other university teachers who side with the Grand Master to ensure his blessing, Bhoma firmly believes that the king is "Naked" (153). Joshi here has used the parable-within-the-parable technique as in Vishnu Sharma's *Panchatantra.* He begins to narrate the parable of the naked king ("The Emperor's New Clothes") to his students and the whole university is taken by storm:

> By the end of the two weeks the whole place was talking about Master Bhoma's parable. "The King is Naked" became a slogan, a cry of revolt. One morning an entire wall was found decorated with it. It appeared on blackboards and in toilets. The authorities started receiving letters that on being opened contained nothing more than a sheet of art paper, "The King is Naked" calligraphed neatly on either side. At the end of the fortnight, the staff secretary called Bhoma and told him to stop preaching his parable, or face serious consequences (154).

Bhoma finds himself in the grips of fear and assures the secretary that he would eschew such acts. But his authenticity makes him restless; he feels ashamed and is moved to tears. But before he has surrendered himself shamelessly to the spineless authorities, the Hermit of the Mountain meets him. Like Lord Krishna, the Hermit helps Bhoma (Arjuna in mythological parlance) as to who he is and the role he is to play in the scheme of things Almighty has predestined. The great Hermit exhorts him: "You have been chosen to speak. The great river has chosen you to speak with the tongue of men what they cannot hear in her troubled lament.... Having spoken you will feel lighter. The weight shall dissolve, the shackles fall" (153-54). Like Mahatma Gandhi, Bhoma again raises himself to the occasion for he knew the rulers were nothing but the shadow of the evil that lurk beneath the Seven Hills. And if men free themselves of the fear of the shadow, and look it straight in the eye, it will "shrivel and creep back into the dungeons from where it came" (155). The Hermit tells despondent Bhoma about his own experience: "I learnt that nothing enfeebled man more than fear, that nothing but fear stood between him and his liberation...and I saw that where men had thrown off this blanket of fear there alone truth had triumphed and great civilizations flourished and man had taken another step towards God" (155-56). In this novel the different characters react in different ways. He further tells Bhoma: " This city, this world, all this is the manifestation of the One, and not the shadow of the Grand Master's ego, as the Grand Master might imagine...and it is He who is the master of all men, including the Grand Master, and it is His will that men follow in every way" (156).

Now Bhoma comes to realize that it was only fear that was to be feared that breeds confusion that leads to inaction. In the words of Hermit, we find reverberations of the *Gita*, and Bhoma chooses to act dutifully in the larger interest of the city: "He was at peace now. There was no choice in him except to go on preaching the king's story" (158). He continues with his recitals that lift the shadow of fear from their souls and infuses hope and courage into them. As Arun Joshi says, "From the realms of a children's story the parable has passed into the lore of a land of sorrow and despair that the boatmen had never known before" (175-76). The Grand Master, threatened by the possibility of a revolt, gets Bhoma arrested but he escapes to the great consternation of the authorities.

Now the Professor, an astronomer of great repute, decides to find Bhoma. Unlike the Astrologer who computes from the movement of the planets the fate of mankind, the Professor, in his "Twenty years of friendship" (27) with the stars has earned "complete freedom" (28). He is so engrossed in his work that he remains totally oblivious of the political developments in the city. The news of Bhoma's arrest disturbs him:

> His balance had been upset because the event did not reconcile with the laws that, according to his beliefs, underlay the working of the universe.... How could men vanish without explanation if stars did not? ...To the Professor the vanishing of Master Bhoma was no different from the unexplained disappearance of a star of the heaven (45-46).

In his search through the corrupt and apathetic administrative machinery, he is assisted by a Gandhi-like figure called the Little Star—a shaven headed brown boy of ten or eleven in loincloth only. When the astronomer says that he seems to know a lot for his age, the little star smiles and says: "I am thousands of years old, Professor.... Everyone is thousands and thousands of years old, tied as we are to the wheel of *Karma*" (42). This again reveals the influence of the *Bhagavadgita.*

The Professor, with the Little Star by his side, searches Bhoma everywhere and is shocked by the corruption, tyranny, degeneration and repression of the City. He fails to find Bhoma and the search leaves him physically and mentally broken. He gives up the search and leaves the city. As Subhash Chandra aptly remarks: "Arun Joshi, therefore, in his novel *The City and the River,* is dealing with the universal predicament of the modern man, besieged as he is by debilitating forces."[12]

The delay in the fulfilment of prophecy makes the headstrong Grand Master impatient. Fear sets in and with it confusion. Mortally afraid of Master Bhoma and his propaganda, he devices a nefarious plan with the Astrologer; to effect an "unquestioning allegiance to the prophecy's goals" (60). But, truly speaking, there is no inevitability in the prophecy. When the politically ambitious Minister for Trade insists on knowing the secret of the prophecy, he says:

> There is nothing inevitable about the prophecy. The hand that made it believes, above all, in man's capacity to change his fate. So even if it speaks of the coming of a king, men can so conduct themselves, so choose, that the king does not come. Or the king that comes is of the right kind (68).

This remark of the Hermit reverberates the influence of the *Gita* which recognizes man's freedom of choice and requires to know what is good and what is evil, to choose good and realize by conscious effort. S. Radhakrishnan writes in his introductory essay on the *Bhagavadgita:* "Our life is mixture of necessity and freedom, chance and choice. By exercising our choice properly, we can control all the elements and eliminate altogether the determinism of nature."[13] Thus a man must gain mastery over himself and overcome his fear and selfish desires. A thorough cleansing of the soul is a must before one receives the vision of truth. According to the Great Yogeshwara, this is true of a nation, a country or a city: "Cities, my children, even as men, make their own horoscopes" (217) But such things are easily said than done, as the dismayed Minister for Trade says ruefully:

> That is where the rub lies—in action. Where one should raise standards of rebellion, one foolishly seeks compromises. Where one ought to call spade a spade, one merely stays dumb—and hopes for the best. Where is the cure. Great Hermit? (69).

Like the great Indian sages, the Hermit replies that the "cure" lay "within oneself" (69). As Mahatma Gandhi says, "the salvation of the people depends on themselves, upon their capacity for suffering and sacrifice."[14] The Hermit also believes that no man is good enough to be a king and that to be a better ruler of the city a man must be "willing to be a better slave" (113). And finally when the minister is baffled by what the Hermit tells about what God is, the Hermit advises him: "Let not the tangle disturb you. Sufficient it always is for a man to mind his own business as truthfully as he can" (70). Here lies the cure and panacea for the ills of life reverberating the very *Karmic* principle of the *Bhagavadgita.*

Like *The Last Labyrinth,* this novel, too, lays emphasis on prayer, faith, understanding and truth. Amid the bitter realities and problems of life, one must offer prayer to God if one is to stay sane. As Kierkegaard says: "Prayer does not change God, but it changes him who prays" (113). Joshi puts forward his ideas through the Astrologer: "Ours is a spiritual civilization. It is through prayer and through vows that a man perfects himself" (100). Mahatma Gandhi, too, put great emphasis on prayers and would conduct public prayers daily at his *ashram* in one of the worst slums on the banks of the Yamuna in Delhi.

The megalomaniac Grand Master is not content with consolidating his position only, but wants his son also to ascend the throne after him. The Astrologer is the Grand Master's tool who advances attractive arguments in order to justify the perpetuation of the rule of a family when he argues:

> No sacrifice is greater than the sacrifice of a young son. But we know we are asking this sacrifice from a family that has for a hundred years sacrificed its men, its women, its children, its wealth, its very all for the sake of this city (101).

The Grand Master exploits the religious feelings of the gullible masses and asks the Astrologer to perform a "*yajna.*" He substitutes the hymn of the sacred river with another composition that speaks of "the greatness of kings and their indispensability to the earth" (97). The blasphemy is protested by the Hermit, which the Astrologer ignores and uses the occasion to swear unquestioning allegiance to the Grand Master, and also to crown his son as his successor. Excepting those who swear allegiance to the Grand Master, the rest are delivered to the Gold Mines. The so-called Bhoma Conspiracy is published to gain public sympathy and thereby "to change the balance of power" (111).

The escalating tyranny of the Grand Master increases the misery of the boatmen. The condition of the city is so unbearable that he decides to complete Bhoma's unfinished work. His search is a " search for some lost bit of himself. For his lost faith in this city, his civilization" (159). He opens a lottery stall and begins to recite the parable of the naked king. One of Bhoma's students relates the story as if he were an ancient bard who had emerged from the depths of the great River to remind the city of a long-forgotten truth (129), which leaves the boatmen hypnotised, and they feel "some of their self respect restored" (132). The Grand Master and his clique are so terrified that they get the Professor, Shailaja's brother and the Headmen arrested and tortured in the Gold Mines. The lottery stall, the symbol of protest and defiance of authority, is pulled down, but the Grand Master fails to contain the resistance.

The Professor is astonished to discover that "men who worshipped the planets and stood in terror of them, had the audacity to bury other men in dungeons of unending night" (163). The inhuman torture that leads to the Headman's losing her eyesight impels the Professor, like Mahatma Gandhi to undertake fast-unto-death. To this the Hermit's reaction is: "This *yajna* of the mud-people, Patanjali, burns only on sacrifice, when the fire is low, when the flame is dying, men must feed it with their lives. And who knows, the gods now call for the Professor's life?" (166). And the Professor also dies in the Gold Mines.

The naked truth is before the Grand Master and his scheming Minister, but they dare not face it for fear of losing face. The disheartened Rallies Master says to Vasu the journalist: "A great city is preparing to immolate itself because its Grand Master and his council dare not lose face. So be it. It is better that the city is destroyed than the Grand Master loses face" (75). They forget their "*dharma*" and "an empire of falsehood is created so someone can become king" (112). Their soul is dead and the physician's only advice to such victims is: "Exercise your soul. Take it for walks. Let it speak when it wants to speak. Let it rip" (134). But they don't exercise their souls and let their authentic selves smother in silence.

Things take an unexpected turn at this juncture. Bhoma comes back. He tells the Hermit: "Wherever I went the shadow was there. I felt its cold grip on my heart and the heart of other men.... It was the city and not the hermitage that would be the stage for the play of my life and that needed to be the goal of my travels" (143). Like Sindi Oberoi in *The Foreigner* Bhumiputra finds the meaning of his life not in escape but in action, and he turns into a dedicated man of action. The Hermit exhorts him to lead the boatmen who, after his escape "felt like orphans in an evil world" (144), to freedom. He excites the boatmen, reminding them that they are the children of the sacred river, and should swear allegiance to none but the river. Under his guidance a campaign is launched for the release of the Headman. The persuasions fail and the boatmen go on strike. The strike moves peacefully when unexpectedly "shock brigade" of the Education Advisor offers unconditional support despite Bhoma's unwillingness and the movement turns violent. Violence mars the hitherto non-violent movement:

> The boatmen watched in amazement as, with breathtaking swiftness, the shock-brigades converted their strike into a general uprising. Within hours the uprising spread from the great river to the pyramids. Shops, schools, buses, telephone exchanges and railway stations were systematically burnt (182).

As Usha Bande aptly remarks: "In its demonic image, the city becomes the city of destruction, a great ruin of pride."[15] Bhoma, seeing this violence and meaningless destruction of properties decides to withdraw the movement. The entire incident is reminiscent of what Mahatma Gandhi did when his peaceful non-violent movement turns violent at Chauri Chaura and he withdrew the entire movement.

While all this is going on, the Grand Master holds a secret meeting in an underground chamber of the pyramids at night. He becomes the King and appoints the Minister for Trade as the new Grand Master of the city. While the Seven Hills celebrate the Grand Master's ascension to the throne, an unequal war rages between the boatmen and the army. The boatmen, Bhumiputra and those who side with him are perished. Before his death, the Hermit performs his last *yajna* of the immortal Time and his consort, the river, to nullify the blasphemy committed by the Astrologer. He is blessed with a vision:

> Just as the Hermit ended his yajna the sun rose lighting up the vast expanse of the river.... High above the palace, the pyramids, the Seven Hills, the peak glowed pink and yellow and, finally, a blinding white that no human eye could stand (249).

And the deluge that follows turns the river into an "ancient sea, like the sea that had first condensed on the whirling planet a billion years ago" (257). And in its "churning whirlpools" (259) is swept away the entire city with its Seven Hills and the Pyramids like it did the Indus Valley Civilization in the 6th century B.C.:

> For seven days and seven nights it rained without a stop. On the eighth day the sun rose and from a clear sky stared down at a vast sea of water. The sea was calm and gave no hint of agitation that had gone into its making. Of the Grand Master and his city nothing remained (260).

Only an illegal child of the boatmen, as Amur remarks "escapes from the deluge to lead, like Shishumar of the Indian myths, another resistance at another point in history."[16] When human beings fail, it is nature that takes its natural course in the name of Divine justice.

Although the city is washed away, the cyclic march of humanity continues. On the ruins of that city, a new city springs up. The river flows on eternally, and the city is ruled by the Seven Hills, by another set of councilors. The conflict is eternal: "The conflict that shall come will also be the same: a matter of allegiance, to God or to man" (262). The city is set for yet another conflict between the forces representing politics and religion over the issue of allegiance. The river is eternal, a new city shall rise from the ruins of the earlier one, and the characters shall also be there to play their roles in this eternal conflict. As Usha Bande aptly remarks: "The river is the life-line of the city. Like blood circulating in the human body, it circulates through the city. Questers turn to it to venture forth on its current."[17] The whole story of the rise and fall of the city reminds one of T.S. Eliot's lines: "In my beginning is my end. In succession/Houses rise and fall, crumble, are extended,/ Are removed, destroyed, restored." The Prologue and the Epilogue join the beginning and the end; and the story ends where it begins and begins where it ends. The Great Yogeshwara explains this phenomenon to the Nameless-One, which speaks of human continuity thus:

> On the ruins of that city, as always happens, a new city has risen. It is ruled by another Great Master, which, of course, need not always happen. In the new city is another Professor, another Bhumiputra, another tribe of boatmen. There is another Council and another set of Councilors. The men have other names but the forces they embody

> remain unchanged. And into all this where you go you will perhaps, be known as another Hermit of the Mountain. And it is possible you will have a disciple whose name will be Little Star (262).

This passage clearly indicates how deeply the *Bhagavadgita* and the Indian mythology in shaping the thematic structure of the novel influenced Arun Joshi. It is this cyclic repetition of things that affords the novel a unique place in Indian English literature. But the significance of the novel lies in the way suggested by Joshi to escape from this endless repetition. As the great Yogeshwara tells the Nameless-One, the illegal child of the boatmen grown to full manhood, on the eve of his departure to the city:

> The main thing is to prevent this endless repetition, this periodic disintegration.... The city must strive once again for purity. But purity can come only through sacrifice. That perhaps was the meaning of the boatmen's rebellion (262-63).

The way is that the city should purify itself "of egoism, selfishness, stupidity" (263). But purification and sacrifice go simultaneously. The "*yajna* of life" "burns only on sacrifice. When the fire is low, when the flame is dying, men must feed it with their own lives" (166). The novel seems to suggest the solution to this malaise. The solution suggested to the malaise in the novel is obviously derived from the *Bhagavadgita*. The cycle of "*Karma*" will move on until the Divine scheme is accomplished. But the same is to be achieved through human instrumentality. Anup Beniwal writes: "The novel...ends on an optimistic note and certainly enlarges the vision of the reader by making him aware of the causes of this eternal conflict and suggesting panacea in the form of Great Yogeshwara's advice to the Nameless-One."[18] The Great Yogeshwara says to the Nameless-One:

> In any case we are only instruments both you and I—of the great God in the highest heaven who is the Master of the Universe. How perfect we are as instruments is all that matters. His is the will, His is the force. But I shall be with you always (264).

We may sum-up with Tapan Kumar Ghosh:

> Indeed, as a re-affirmation of Indian and as an experiment of the parable as a fictional mode to convey mythic truths and political satire, *The City and The River* is a remarkable *tour de force* in contemporary Indian English fiction.[19]

NOTES AND REFERENCES

1. Tapan Kumar Ghosh, *Arun Joshi's Fiction: The Labyrinth of Life*. New Delhi: Prestige Books, 1996, 150.
2. *Loc. cit.*
3. Shubra Mazumdar, *The Book Reveiw*, Vol. XV., No. 1, January-February 1991.
4. Githa Hariharan, "A Political Parable," *Sunday Herald*, July 29, 1990.
5. G.S. Amur, "A New Parable, " *Indian Literature*, Vol. XXXIV, July-August 1991.
6. Kalyan Chatterjee, "More Platitudinous than Profound," *The Telegraph*, 7 June 1991.
7. Githa Hariharan, "A Political Parable," *op. cit.*
8. *The Message of Love*, Bangalore: The Bible Society of India, 318.
9. *Loc. cit.*
10. Marjorie Grene, "Authenticity, An Existential Virtue," *Ethics*, Vol. LXII, No. 4, July 1952, 270.
11. Marjorie Grene, "Authenticity, An Existential Virtue," *op. cit.* 266.
12. Subhash Chandra, "Towards Authenticity: A study of *The City and the River*," *The Fictional World of Arun Joshi*, edited by R.K. Dhawan. New Delhi: Classical Publishing Company, 1986, 271.
13. S. Radhakrishnan, *The Bhagavadgita*. New Delhi: Harper Collins, 1996, 49.
14. M.K. Gandhi, *An Autobiography* or *The Story of My Experiments with Truth*, translated by Mahadev Desai. England: Penguin, 1982, 397.
15. Usha Bande, "Archetypal Patterns in *The City and the River*," *The Novels of Arun Joshi*, edited by R.K. Dhawan. New Delhi: Prestige, 1992, 275.
16. G.S. Amur, "A New Parable," *op. cit.*
17. Usha Bande, "Archetypal Patterns in *The City and the River*," *The Novels of the Arun Joshi*, *op. cit.*, 262.
18. Anup Beniwal, "*The City and the River*: A Critical Review," *The Novels of Arun Joshi*, *op. cit.*, 275.
19. Tapan Kumar Ghosh, *op. cit.*, 173.

7

THE SUMMING-UP

On the contemporary scene of the Indian-English novel, Arun Joshi stands out as a highly significant novelist. He is diametrically different from his Indian or Western counterparts, living or dead, as he has kept the novel form serious. Basically, he is a remarkable thought-provoking novelist with uncompromising propensity towards the moral and the numinous.

Tradition has always had its influence on the literary authors, but every individual author has to exhibit his individual talent and originality. The Indian-English novels are primarily inspired by the modern European and American novels. But they have transmuted the imported material into the racial subconsciousness inherited by them from their tradition.

Arun Joshi belongs to the tradition of existentialist writers like Camus, Sartre, Kierkegaard, Kafka, Marcel, Jaspers, Buber, Paul Tillich, Beckett, Saul Bellow and others. He has himself confessed: "I did read Camus and Sartre, I liked *The Plague* and read *The Outsider*. I might have been influenced by them. Sartre I did not understand clearly or like. As for existential philosophers like Kierkegaard, I have never understood anything except odd statements." Joshi, like other existentialists, is deeply concerned with man's plight and imbroglios engendered by alienation and its concomitant *angst* and agony. But he differs from the Western existentialist writers in the sense that in him the existentialist dilemma, the anguish of alienation and the absurdity of situation never remain the final predicament. His central motif is quest and all his characters are questers and seekers.

Joshi was obviously influenced not only by existentialist writers such as Camus, Sartre and Kierkegaard in the main, but also by a number of other Western novelists and poets such as Thomas Hardy, Joseph Conrad, D.H. Lawrence, Aldous Huxley, Graham Greene, James Joyce, William Golding, William Wordsworth, S.T. Coleridge, Robert Browning, Matthew Arnold, T.S. Eliot, Ernest Hemingway, William Faulkner, Malamud, Ralph Ellison, Arthur Miller, Saul Bellow, Joseph Heller, Proust, Leo Tolstoy and Fyodor Dostoevsky.

But Joshi has taken these influences on his own terms. He has absorbed and assimilated all his influences, oriental as well as occidental, and fused them with the indigenous, transmuting them into organic, well-orchestrated novels with the indelible imprint of his own individuality. The Western writers provide Joshi with a stimulus, a body of suggestions as well as some narrative techniques that have been inconspicuously assimilated, forming an integral part of his native consciousness.

The important narrative techniques are in the nature of a catalyst in Joshi's fiction and his success consists in his remarkable originality. There is a perfect synthesis between the foreign narrative technique and the indigenous content. The influences never become determinant of the texture and structure of the novel to the detriment of the native feel.

The issues that Joshi raises are the ones that concern the post-Independence Indians with Western education. His novels are structured in the immediately socio-cultural situations and are concerned with moral and spiritual problems of the contemporary Indians. The complex stresses and strains in the sensitive minds of his protagonists are the outcome of the dual forces of native ethos and Western influences. They suffer from uprootedness, cynicism, evils of materialism, loss of faith and identity crisis. In this fiction Joshi voices the concerns of the alienated and uncovers deep undercurrent of the agony of the contemporary Indian psyche. Joshi responds to the challenges of his time and the problems resulting from the bi-cultural milieu of the country. Joshi reveals a wholeness of vision by going into the cultural and spiritual problems of his own countrymen.

Unlike the existentialists or his Western counterparts, living or dead, Joshi never accepts alienation as the ultimate condition of life. It is a transitional phase in the protagonist's quest for self-knowledge. Deeply influenced by the techniques of the *Upanishads* and the *Gita*, Joshi looks upon man's life on the earth as apprentice in soul-making.

His fiction is an expression of a distinctly Indian voice where one finds the richness of Indian heritage. Joshi's vision is essentially Hindu. His philosophical leanings are towards Hinduism. In an interview with Arun Joshi, Sujatha Mathai remarks that "Joshi feels that his ethos is essentially Hindu." In *The Foreigner* we find Sindi Oberoi preoccupied with the philosophical problems of involvement and detachment. Billy Biswas's search for his missing self in the mode of the *Sankhya* principle is also essentially Hindu. In an interview with Purabi Banerji he tells: "Hindu is a highly existentialist oriented philosophy since it attaches so much of importance to the right way to live (to exist)." The influence of the *Bhagavadgita* is well marked in *The Apprentice*. Ratan Rathor, the protagonist devotedly follows the *Karmic* principle as enshrined in the *Bhagavadgita*. Arun Joshi says, "I strongly believe that individual action have effects on others and oneself. So, one cannot afford to continue with an irresponsible existence but has to commit oneself at some point." Joshi reposed complete faith in the teachings of the *Bhagavadgita*. He firmly believes that what one sows one reaps. For him, it is not proper to blame God for one's failures, as Sujatha Mathai says, "The *Karmic* law seemed to him to be central." Arun Joshi affirms: "There is no intervening agent between you and God. What you sow you reap."

Existentialism is not a new fad and man's manner of philosophising is as ancient as the history of human civilization itself. Deep existential insight can be found in both, Buddhism and the *Upanishads*. S. Radhakrishnan writes:

> Existentialism is a new name for an ancient method. The *Upanishads* and Buddhism insist on knowledge of

> the self: *atmanam viddhi.* They tell us that man is a victim of ignorance, *avidya,* which breeds selfishness. So long as we live our unregenerate lives in the world of time governed by *Karman* or necessity, we are at the mercy of time. The feeling of distress is universal. A sense of blankness overtakes the seeking spirit, which makes the world a waste and a vain show. Man is not the final resting-place. He has to be transcended. Man can free himself from sorrow and suffering by becoming aware of the eternal. This awareness, this enlightenment is what is called *jnana* or boddhi.

Some of the basic tenets of existential thought are present in Indian philosophical discourse. Man's quest for self-knowledge, meaning and purpose of life as well as his identity in the world where he is ever an alien or a foreigner, has been the preoccupation of Indian philosophy.

Steeped deeply in the Indian tradition, Joshi has imbibed, in a significant way, the essential messages of the Indian religious heritage, the teachings of the *Upanishads,* the *Bhagavadgita,* the *Sankhya* system of Indian philosophy, and also of spiritual leaders and thinkers. However, whatever the alien and indigenous influences, Joshi's stupendous genius, like an excellent alchemist, has transmuted them into an essential component of his craft which has helped him produce powerful original novels one after another bearing the indelible imprint of his tremendous individuality as a novelist.

Thus Joshi is basically a novelist with a broad humanistic outlook demonstrating his moral vision that the Indian-English novel has produced. His novels are essentially reflective of the eternal existential situation of the beleaguered contemporary man, which he has depicted with stupendous artistic finesse. His fiction stands out for the simple reason that he lays remarkable emphasis on the existential situation, and the pragmatic solution he puts forward. The message he patently conveys through his fiction is that man can draw great sustenance from his umbilical cord being unsevered from his spiritual and moral womb even as he lies groaning on the debris of the shattered moral and spiritual values.

With the help of his charismatic genius, Joshi has woven his eloquent message for humanity into the texture of his novels. With a clarity, an intellectual sophistication and an awareness of its relevance to the contemporary context. And he does this in fictional terms without losing sight of the human interest with astounding artistic finesse, dexterity and originality displaying his profound concern for the dire necessity of being good, dutiful and of use to others for the salvation of oneself and the entire humanity as well. Undoubtedly, his novels will have a universal imperishable importance for their affirmative eloquent message for the humanity, and therein lies his inimitable talent and astounding originality.

Bibliography

Abraham, Joy. "Vision and Technique in *The Apprentice*," *The Fictional World of Arun Joshi,* edited by R.K. Dhawan, New Delhi: Classical Publishing Company, 1986.

Abraham, Joy. "The Narrative Strategy in *The Strange Case of Billy Biswas*," *The Novels of Arun Joshi,* edited by R.K. Dhawan, New Delhi: Prestige, 1992.

Amur, G.S. "A New Parable," *Indian Literature,* Vol. XXXIV, 1944, July-August 1991.

Anant, Victor. "The Hypnotised People," *Partisan Review*, 27/2, 1960.

Asnani, Shyam M. "Exploration of the Inner World: A Study of Arun Joshi's Fiction," *The Literary Half-Yearly,* Vol. XIX. No. 2, July 1978.

Axthelm, M. Peter. *The Modern Confessional Novel,* New Haven and London: Yale University Press, 1967.

Bande, Usha. "Archetypal Patterns in *The City and The River*," *The Novels of Arun Joshi,* edited by R.K. Dhawan, New Delhi: Prestige, 1992.

Bandopadhyaya, Manohar. "*The Strange Case of Billy Biswas*," Review, *The Patriot,* 1 August 1982.

Banerji Purabi. "A Winner's Secrets," Interview, *The Sunday Statesman,* 27 February 1983.

Barret, William. *Irrational Man: A Study in Existential Philosophy,* Garden City, 1958.

Baudelaire, Charles. *Selected Poems,* translated by Joanna Richardson, England: Penguin, 1975.

Beniwal, Anup. "*The City and the River*: A Critical Review," *The Novels of Arun Joshi,* edited by R.K. Dhawan, New Delhi: Prestige, 1992.

Bhatnagar, O.P. "Arun Joshi's *The Foreigner*: A Critique of East and West," *The Journal of Indian Writing in English*, 1/2, July 1973.

Camus, Albert. *The Fall*, translated by Justin O' Brien, Penguin, 1963.

——. *The Fall*, Penguin Books, 1957.

Chandra, Subhash. "Towards Authenticity: A Study of *The City and The River*," *The Fictional World of Arun Joshi*, edited by R.K. Dhawan, New Delhi: Prestige, 1992.

Chan, Wing-Tsit and Charles A. Moore. *The Essentials of Buddhist Philosophy*, Honolulu: T.H., 1956.

Chatterjee, Kalyan. "More Platitudinous than Profound," *The Telegraph*, 7 June 1991.

Conrad, Joseph. *Lord Jim*, New York: Doubleday, 1925.

——. *Under Western Eyes*, New York: Doubleday, 1925.

Das, R.J. "Moral Dilemma in Arun Joshi's *The Apprentice*," *Journal of Literature and Aesthetics*, Vol. 1, No. 2, March 1981.

Desai, Anita. *Voices in the City*, New Delhi: Orient Paperbacks, 1982.

Dhawan, R.K. "The Fictional World of Arun Joshi," *The Novels of Arun Joshi*, edited by R.K. Dhawan, New Delhi: Prestige, 1992.

——. (ed.) *The Fictional World of Arun Joshi*, New Delhi: Classical Publishing Company, 1996.

——. (ed.) *The Novels of Arun Joshi*, New Delhi: Prestige, 1992.

Dostoevsky, F. "Notes From Underground," translated by Constance Garnett in *Norton Anthology of World Masterpieces*, New York: W.W. Norton, 1980.

——. *The Brothers Karamazov*, translated by Constance Garnett, New York: Signet, 1960.

Dua, M.R. "An Interview with Mr. Arun Joshi," September 3, 1971.

Eliot, T.S. "Ulysses, Order and Myth," *Selected Prose of T.S. Eliot*, edited by Fronk Kennode, Harcourt Brace, 1975.

——. *Four Quartets,* Delhi: Oxford University Press, 1974.

——. *Selected Poems,* London: Faber and Faber, 1954.

——. *Four Quartets,* London: Faber and Faber, 1970.

Fromm, Erich. *et. al. Zen Buddhism and Psychoanalysis,* New York: Harper and Row, 1970.

Gandhi, M.K. *An Autobiography* or *The Story of My Experiments with Truth,* translated by Mahadev Desai, England: Penguin, 1982.

Ghosh, Tapan Kumar. *Arun Joshi's Fiction: The Labyrinth of Life,* New Delhi: Prestige, 1996.

Grene, Marjorie. "Authenticity, An Existential Virtue," *Ethics,* Vol. LXII, No. 4, July 1952.

Guruprasad, Thakur. "The Lost Lonely Questers of Arun Joshi's Fiction," The *Fictional World of Arun Joshi,* edited by R.K. Dhawan, New Delhi: Classical Publishing Company, 1986.

Hariharan, Githa. "The Book Review," the *Sunday Herald,* July 29, 1990.

——. "A Political Parable," review of *The City and the River,* the *Sunday Herald,* July 29, 1990.

Heller, Joseph. *Catch 22,* London: Corgi Books, 1955.

Hough, Graham. *The Dark Sun: A Study of D.H. Lawrence,* London: Gerald Duckworth, 1956.

Ionesco, Eugene. " Dans Les armes Le la Ville," *Cahiers de la Compagnie Madeline Renaud,* Jean-louis Barrault, Paris No. 20, October 1959.

Iyengar, K.R.S. *Indian Writing in English,* New Delhi: Asia Publishing House, 1973.

Jain, Jasbir. "Foreigners and Strangers: Arun Joshi's Heroes," *The Journal of Indian Writing in English,* 5, No. 1, January 1977.

Joshi, Arun. *The Foreigner,* Delhi: Hind Pocket Books, 1968.

——. *The Strange Case of Billy Biswas,* Delhi: Hind Pocket Books, 1971.

——. *The Apprentice,* New Delhi: Orient Paperbacks, 1974.

——. *The Last Labyrinth,* New Delhi: Orient Paperbacks, 1981.

——. *The City and the River,* New Delhi: Vision Books, 1990.

——. "Excerpts from a Talk by Arun Joshi at Dhvanyaloka," Mysore, Sept. 1981, *IACLAIS Newsletter,* No. 10, January 1982.

Lal, P. "Myth and the Indian Writer in English, A Note," *Aspects of Indian Writing in English,* edited by M.K. Naik, Madras: Macmillan, 1979.

Lawrence, D.H. *Sons and Lovers,* Penguin, 1948.

Machwe, Prabhakar. *Modernity and Contemporary Indian Literature,* Delhi: Chetna, 1978.

Mathai, Sujatha. "I'm a Stranger to My Books," *The Times of India,* July 9, 1983.

Mathur, O.P. and G. Rai. "The Existential Note in Arun Joshi's *The Strange Case of Billy Biswas* and *The Apprentice,*" *Commonwealth Quarterly,* 5/17 December 1980.

Mazumdar, Shubra. *The Book Review,* Vol. XV, No. 1, January-February 1991.

Message of Love, The. Bangalore: The Bible Society of India.

Mukherjee, Meenakshi. *The Twice-Born Fiction: Themes and Techniques of the Indian Novel in English,* New Delhi: Arnold Heinemann, 1971.

Naik, M.K. *A History of Indian English Literature,* New Delhi: Sahitya Akademi, 1982.

Narasimhaiah, C.D. *Awakened Conscience: Studies in Commonwealth Literature,* New Delhi: Sterling, 1978.

Pandey, Mukteshwar. *Arun Joshi: Existential Element in His Novels,* New Delhi: B.R. Publishing Corporation, 1998.

Pathak, R.S. "Quest for Meaning in Arun Joshi's Novel," *The Novels of Arun Joshi,* edited by R.K. Dhawan, New Delhi: Prestige, 1992.

Prempati, D. "*The Strange Case of Billy Biswas*: A Serious Response to Big Challenge," *The Fictional World of Arun*

Joshi, edited by R.K. Dhawan, New Delhi: Classical Publishing Company, 1986.

Prasad, H.M. "The Crisis of Consciousness: *The Last Labyrinth,*" *The Fictional World of Arun Joshi,* edited by R.K. Dhawan, New Delhi: Classical Publishing Company, 1986.

Prasad, H.M. *Arun Joshi,* New Delhi: Arnold Heinemann, 1985.

Prasad, Madhusudan. (ed.) "Arun Joshi," *Indian English Novelists,* New Delhi: Sterling Publishers Private Limited, 1982.

Radha, K. "From Detachment to Involvement: The Case of Sindi Oberoi," *The Novels of Arun Joshi,* edited by R.K. Dhawan, New Delhi: Prestige, 1992.

Radhakrishnan, S. *The Bhagavadgita,* New Delhi: Harper Collins, 1996.

——. *The Principal Upanishads,* London: George Allen and Unwin, 1923.

——. *Indian Philosophy,* London: George Allen and Unwin, 1923.

——. *History of Philosophy: Eastern and Western,* London: George Allen and Unwin, 1953.

Rangachari, S. "T.S. Eliot's Shadow on *The Foreigner,*" *Scholar Critic,* edited by N. Radhakrishnan, January 1994.

Reddy, V. Gopal. *"The Apprentice*: An Existential Study." *The Novels of Arun Joshi,* edited by R.K. Dhawan, New Delhi: Prestige, 1992.

Richards, Vyvyan. *Person Fulfilled,* Cambridge: W. Heffer. Sartre, Jean-Paul. *Nausea,* translated by Robert Baldick, England: Penguin, 1965.

Sewall, Richard B. *The Vision of Tragedy,* New Haven: Yale University, Press, 1959.

Sharma, Susheel Kumar. "Philosophical Reverberations in *The Foreigner,*" *The Novels of Arun Joshi,* edited by R.K. Dhawan, New Delhi: Prestige, 1992.

Srinath, C.N. "Crisis of Identity: Assertion and Withdrawal in Naipaul and Arun Joshi," *The Literary Criterion,* 14/1, 1971.

——. "The Fiction of Arun Joshi: The Novel of Interior Landscape," *The Literary Criterion,* 12/2-3, 1976.

Srivastava, R.K. *Six Indian Novelists in English,* Amritsar: Guru Nanak Dev University, 1987.

Verghese, C. Paul. Problems of the Indian Creative Writer in English, Bombay: Sumaiya, 1971.

Walsh, William. "India and the Novel," *The New Pelican Guide to English Literature,* Vol. 8, edited by Boris Ford, Penguin, 1983.

Index

N

O

P

R

S

THE STORY OF INTEGRATION

A New Interpretation

in the Context of the Democratic Movements in the Princely States of Mysore, Travancore and Cochin 1900-1947

VANAJA RANGASWAMI

MANOHAR
2026

First published 1981
Reprinted 2021, 2023, 2026

ISBN 978-81-943521-1-2

Published by
Ajay Kumar Jain *for*
Manohar Publishers & Distributors
4753/23 Ansari Road, Daryaganj
New Delhi 110 002

Printed at
Replika Press Pvt. Ltd.

To My Mother

CONTENTS

INTRODUCTION

> And I saw a procession of Rajas and Ranis and their satellites and parasites dancing away in a veritable 'danse macabre', for they danced on a seething mass of hungry and famine-stricken humanity, and their dance led to a sudden precipice over which they toppled, and vanished from the scene. They were rather pitiful figures, relics of a bygone age, trying bravely to keep up appearances but doomed to inevitable extinction.—Jawaharlal Nehru to his sister Krishna Nehru Hutheesing, 13 June 1933. *Nehru's Letters to His Sister*, p. 29.

The democratic movement in the princely states of Travancore, Cochin and Mysore is the story of just such 'a seething mass' of humanity—though not so hungry, nor so famine-striken as their brethren in the other states—nevertheless, leading the 'danse macabre' to the precipice and toppling the Maharajas and Ranis to their "inevitable extinction'. Nor were the Maharajas of these three states the 'parasites' comparable to others of the princely order, but enlightened princes bent on giving their states 'good government' and ever assiduous of their title to the status of 'model states'. Again the 'models' they provided were not mere measures of 'bravely keeping up appearances' but were often the best they could provide within the framework of a monarchical order, subservient ultimately to the interests of the paramount power.

The three states I have chosen for my study form not only a contiguous territory, lying as they do in the southern part of India, but were a distinct genre by themselves. They were all ruled by orthodox Hindu monarchs, whose territories were historically and religiously inter-connected and were subjected to the same historical, political, economic and socio-religious forces during the same period. Moreover, these states had, from the very beginning of the twentieth century, acquired a name for their progressive character. Though their efficient governments proved the very basis of their *bona fides* for a continuance of such regimes, by providing the people with the educational, social, economic and legislative amenities, they were themselves instrumental in the initiation of a mass political consciousness. Thus, the democratic movement in these states, though partly affected by events in British India, was independent of the parallel movement for independence in British India, drew its strength from its own roots, and often acted of its own volition.

At this point it becomes necessary that I define the meaning and scope of the term, 'the democratic movement'. The movement in the states ran on two parallel issues at the same time. The first related to a demand of responsible government (with the executive controlled by and responsible to a popularly elected legislature or legislatures), and the second was an extension of the British Indian anti-imperialist struggle. In its orthodox and simplistic sense democratic movement could be defined as the movement on the first issue. However, this movement was not fought in isolation but was interwined with the other movement, though in the earlier stages of the states movement there was a clear demarcation between the two issues. With the entry of the Congress into the States in 1921, this distinction was purposely submerged by a leadershlp within the states which sought to gain a wider base to its cause, and more particularly, all-India sympathies in its favour. The all-India leadership, on the other hand, entered the states sphere mainly to counteract the British machinations which sought to prop up the princes against nationalist forces. Thus, this leadership, though it sought to use the *forces so unleashed* in the states in their ambitions on a democratic programme towards their own programmes of union and integration, did seek to *hold itself aloof* from active involvement in the states peoples' movement on responsible government. This complicated the issues as the aims of the all-India leadership crossed the objectives of the states people on the priorities of issues. The question then arose as to whether the aims of the all-India leadership were to prevail over the others or should the aspirations of the states people for democratic government in the states be supported or brought within the context of the wider movement.

This brings one to a consideration of an allied aspect. Of late, several regional studies have been brought out on the political and social struggle of these states, particularly in Travancore-Cochin and to some extent in Mysore. These studies either treat of the movement in isolation or swerve to the other extreme of making no distinction between the movement in the princely states and the movement in the adjacent section of British India. The first category, while they add to our knowledge by giving depth to the local aspects of the struggle, in my opinion, lacks a perspective as they have not taken into consideration the interaction of the local struggle with the movement in British India and in turn with British policy. The other studies which have made the states peoples' movement as part of the overall freedom struggle, have equally failed by not taking into consideration the contradictions which were thrown up between the states peoples' own ambitions and that of the British Indian nationalists interests. My emphasis has been not so much on details of the course of the movement within, as on the interaction between the states peoples' struggle against the autocratic regimes, with British Indian nationalists anti-imperialist struggle and thus British policy. I have deliberately chosen a comparative study precisely because I think that these aspects—the tripartite interaction between the local movement, the nationalists of India and British policy—need to be examined in some depth.

Thus, in studying the movement one has to take care of not only the internal social, economic, political and religious factors, and the policies of the princes through their agents, their Dewans, but also the external factors which were themselves subject to ambiguities all-around. Thus, it would involve a consideration of the ambiguous nature of the Indian states system, which were supposed to be independent in their internal administration, but, subject nevertheless, to the control of the paramount power. In this, British policy was governed not only by its interests as paramount power of other states but also as governed by its interests in 'provincial' India. Again, as remarked on, it raised the issue of whether representative government was compatible with its concepts of obligations to treaty rights and ideas of intervention. This brought in train their other ambiguities in their dealings with the movement. While on the one hand the paramount power was quick to exhort the princes to read the writings of the time and change their attitude towards this popular movement, on the other hand, it insisted on recognising the princes as the sole authority in the states—even to a eschewing of the word 'representative' in their references to the states nominees. This recognition in effect meant a denial to the state people a representation in all-India matters which made the states people dependent on the British Indian movement for support. In the context of divergent aims there was a constant fear in the minds of the states people that in order to find leverage with the princes--the legally recognised sole authority in the states—the Indian National Congress leadership would ultimately sacrifice theirs. The Indian National Congress leadership, in turn, in their preoccupations with their main aim in the states on integration, while it was ready to use the forces unleashed on the democratic platform to its own purpose, was chary of giving any help to the movement lest it jeopardise its own interests in its dealings with the princes. The Indian National Congress leadership's adeptness in managing to reconcile these conflicting elements is the success story of its achievement on states integration. This changed the very title of the subject which started as the study of the democratic movement in the three states to—*The Story of Integration—A New Interpretation in the Context of the Democratic Movement in the Princely States of Mysore, Travancore and Cochin 1900-1947.*

ACKNOWLEDGEMENTS

For the study of my topic, I have consulted the archival material available at Delhi and other regional centres of Madras, Bangalore and Trivandrum. The research work has primarily been based on the almost untapped material now made available in the AICC and AISPC Papers and the private collections both in microfilms obtained from the India Office Library, London, and as original collections available at the Nehru Memorial Museum and Library. It has been supplemented by the Government of India records of the Foreign and Political and Home Political Departments, the Native Newspaper Reports for Madras States, the Crown Representative Records and the Residency Records (from the India Office Library) and the private collections in the original and microfilms at the National Archives of India. I had hoped to get much material from the regional archives which, with the exception of the Trivandrum Cellar Records Office, proved disappointing.

I have many individuals and organisations to thank for the help given to me. My heaviest debt of gratitude is to my supervisor Dr. Parthasarathy Gupta. He not only read the successive, almost illegible handwritten drafts with patience and gave advice towards its improvement but often went out of his way, even literally, to save me from the long journey to the University. I am also grateful to the Directors and Staff of the Nehru Memorial Museum and Library, New Delhi; the National Archives of India, New Delhi; Karnataka Archives, Bangalore; Tamil Nadu Archives, Madras; Kerala Secretariat Cellar Records Office, Trivandrum; the Theosophical Society Library, Adyar; Secretariat Library, Bangalore; and the Mythic Society, Bangalore. My special thanks are also to *The Hindu* office at Madras for making available a glance at the Subject Index of this paper, to Dr. Kamath of Bangalore University for lending me a short sketch written by Siddalingiah on his life history, and to V.S. Narayana Rao a prominent Mysore Congressman, for elucidating some points. I am also grateful to the University of Delhi, who awarded the Ph.D. degree for this thesis and permitted its publication.

1

The Procrustean Bed of Good Behaviour

Background to the Democratic Movement—Historical, Economic and Social

The three states of my study—Mysore, Travancore and Cochin—came within the ambit of British hegemony during the same period. The Raja of Travancore had entered the British states system as an ally of the East India Company in 1788 when he felt threatened by Tipu Sultan of Mysore 'moving through territories contiguous to the walls of his fort'.[1] In 1789, Tipu's attack on his territory with the object of recovering Cranganur and Ayakota on behalf of his tributary Cochin, involved all three states in a common war. Thus, the areas of the three states were fixed more or less at the same time—that of Cochin in 1791, of Travancore in 1795 at the close of the third Mysore War, and of Mysore in 1799 at the time of the redistribution of territory after the Fourth Mysore War.[2] While Mysore with an area of 29,475 square miles was counted among the premier states of India, second among them as regards population and fifth as regards area,[3] in comparison,

Cochin was a mini kingdom with a total area of 1417 sq. miles,[4] while Travancore occupied the position of a medium state with an area of 7625 sq. miles.[5] The relative importance of these states in the British Indian states system was measured by their gun salutes. In 1867, Mysore was allotted a 21-gun salute, Travancore and Cohin 19 and 17 each respectively.[6]

The beginning of the twentieth century saw these three states emerge as fully fledged 'model states'—in fact, seldom were these states mentioned without their appellation 'model' or 'progressive' affixed to them.[7]

However, it is not my intention here to establish the validity or otherwise of their stature as 'model', but to show that this 'enlightened despotism' was in itself the outcome of two factors, and that the resulting progressive outlook formed the basis for the inception of the democratic movement.

Firstly, it was the outcome of historical factors—a result of the democratic traditions of the people of Travancore and Cochin[8] and in Mysore the result of an interregnum of Muslim good government which had weakened the peoples' personal loyalty to the Hindu kings.

Velu Tampi's rebellion in Travancore which took place hardly a decade after the British intervention was illustrative of this democratic spirit and had two phases. In its first phase in 1802, Velu Tampi, who was summoned by the King and asked to pay Rs. 3000 as his share of the contribution towards a forced loan, asked for three days time during which he convened an emergency Assembly and the 'brass drums of Nanjanad was sounded'.[9] The Assembly which converged before the palace at Eraniel only made its representation against the King's favourite, the forced loans and the salt tax and thus was clearly not antimonarchical. However, though the dynasty did have a legitimacy in the eyes of the people at this period, this legitimacy was however tempered by a democratic spirit.

The second phase of Velu Tampi's rebellion was directed against the imperialist domination brought in by British intervention in the internal affairs of the government. In this second rebellion of 1809, when Velu Tampi set out "to teach a lesson to the Resident",[10] he was joined by the hereditary Dewan of Cochin who was subjected to the same forces.[11]

The Mysore dynasty, tracing its lineage from the thirteenth

century, had exhibited an equal weakness. It had been disrupted by an interregnum of Muslim domination from 1724—1799, under Haider Ali and Tipu Sultan. The able minister of Tipu Sultan, Purniah, who was continued in the same office after the reinstatement of the Hindu dynasty in 1799 had pleaded for the continuation of the old regime, as "the Royal family had long been alienated . . . and the Muslim domination had become a part of the country's political scheme".[12]

In this milieu the state was thrown open to the impact of British suzerainty which involved the payment of twenty-four and a half lakhs of rupees, equal to one-third of her revenue, as subsidy paid in species. The Maharaja's efforts at direct administration and the introduction of a new system of collection—called the 'Sharat' system which tried to convert the Amildar, a mere revenue officer, into an intermediary as guarantor of a specified amount analogous to the zamindars of British India—led to unrest and peasant uprisings in Mysore, Bangalore and Chitaldurg districts.[13] The consequent British intervention in these states following these rebellions vested the government either directly under British administration, as in the Commissionership of Mysore during the period 1831 to 1881 or indirectly under the Residents' influence as in Travancore-Cochin.[14] The period before the Indian Mutiny of 1857 was marked by a policy of vilification of the states system as pretexts for annexation and economic penetration; nevertheless, through the direct influence of its Residents and Commissioners in the administration, it was instrumental in introducing administrative reforms within the states which brought them in line with the administration in British India.

The Indian Mutiny of 1857 brought home to the British administrators the new realisation of these territories as breakwaters during times of danger,[15] and the necessity of befriending the princes as collaborators. From this stemmed the new argument which seemed to realise "the intrinsic merit of Indian polity",[16] on its own ground, replacing the old self-righteous tones of paternalism which held that administration deteriorated once it reverted to Indian rule. This controversy proved of great significance to Mysore. While the Adoption Despatch of 1867 was the triumph of the new school of thought, the restoration settlement—the Rendition Treaty of 1881—was the outcome of a compromise solution between these two schools. Thus, though monarchy was to be restored, it was clearly to be on conditions and guarantees of good government.[17] Among these guarantees for good government, to mention only a few, were the limitations on the civil list,[18] the establishment of an independent judiciary, the observance of established laws,[19] and the submission of expenditure to budget and audit,[20] which were all included in the instrument of transfer signed at the time of the rendition.

The dimensions of these progressive measures can only be realised when compared with conditions in the northern Indian states. Even as late as 1926, many of the states did not even have the facade of a civil list. It was mainly on Irwin's persuasion[21] that the princes moved a resolution in the Chamber of Princes in May 1927, restricting the civil list to not more than 10 per cent of their revenue. However, this was a mere gesture; even while congratulating the princes on their 'progressive inclinations'[22] he frankly admitted to the Secretary of State that this did not mean much as they were likely to wangle their accounts.[23] It was at the same time that the other measures of independent judiciary also raised *vis-a-vis* the northern states.[24]

The period following the 1880s in Mysore (and even earlier in Travancore-Cochin) saw the Resident's interference in the states administration on the wane. Any interference, even if exerted, was only towards promoting its economic interests or in trying to temper the wine of democracy in the states or towards seeing that the states did not provide pockets for the spread of sedition in British India. However, there was one area in which the Residents and British administrators interference was felt—which was in the appointment of the Dewans. The Dewans were now favourites not of the Maharaja but of the Resident. The Residents were often administrators who had served at the Madras Secretariat—the Fort St. George—and were thus partial to those 'able natives' who had proved their ability in the service of the Company or the Secretariat. From the very earliest time of British intervention, we see a number of Mahratta Brahmins[25] monopolising the Dewanship, relieved now and then by the Madrasi Brahmins, the Aiyars and the Aiyangars. This affected the local population which was as well-educated as that of Madras and this sparked off an agitation which combined these three states in a common grievance and was the forerunner of the responsible government movement in the state.[26]

It had been the intention of British policy, at the time of Mysore Rendition, that "the chief authority and ultimate responsibility should rest actually as well as nominally with the ruler of the state".[27] To provide against individual caprice, an executive council as part of the new constitutional machinery had been provided for.[28] However, the first two Dewans, Rangacharlu (1881-1883) and Seshadri Iyer (1883-1894) established the dominance of Dewans "as the natural pattern of Mysore affairs".[29] In this they provided a contrast to affairs in Travancore. During the 1920s, the period of Regency in Travancore, royalty played a more prominent part than the Dewans so that palace politics, intrigues and affairs began playing a prominent part in the politics of the state.[30]

The Dewan's predominance in Mysore and the Maharaja's being kept in the background had one important result. Now any agitation or unpopularity expressed itself against the Dewan rather than the Maharaja. Thus, the agitations depended much on the personal equation between the agitators and the Dewan. Moreover, the agitation in these states was not anti-monarchical, nor for good administration, but mainly against autocratic regime—as personified in that of the Dewans—as it was a movement in demand of a change in the form of government, on their main ideological platform of a democractic ideal of 'Responsible Government'. This lent it a distinctiveness as against those of the northern states which still harped on the abuses of the Maharaja's rule and his personal conduct. Again, partly as a result of good administration and of historical factors the economic set-up provided little fuel for the movement.

The Economic Set-Up

In no other area was the British paramountcy's presence felt in the Indian states as in its economic impact. Thus, a consideration of the economic basis for the democratic movement in the Indian states becomes a more complicated exercise than in the British Indian Provinces. Here we have to take two factors into consideration. Firstly, the economic relationship between the paramount power and the state—where the incidence of the economic policy though ultimately borne by the people was as much a concern of the Maharajas and their government. Under this category would come the question of tribute or subsidy, the paramount power's policy towards the state's finances, borrowing and investment, the impact of British industrialisation on the states, tariff policy, etc. Secondly, the study would involve the consideration of the economic set-up within the states, under which would come an examination of the limitations on the Maharaja's personal expenditure, the policy of the Maharaja towards his own people exhibited in the government's policy towards public expenditure, encouragement of industries, public and private investments, and more particularly, in regard to reforms undertaken by the government to ameliorate distress conditions of the people, the distribution of wealth and influence among communities and government's policy towards these groups.

In examining the above factors we have to decide whether both acted in the same direction to the detriment of the people's condition or ameliorated their conditions, thus providing an economic grievance as basis for the democratic movement against the Maharaja and his administration. We shall also have to consider whether the economic grievance was itself due to the colonial imperialism and not due to the internal set-up of the Maharaja's administration.

The British paramountcy's initial and direct impact on the states was felt in the imposition of the subsidies. While Travancore was made to pay Rs. 8 lakhs and Cochin Rs. 2,40,000, Mysore had to pay a sum of Rs. 24½ lakhs prior to Rendition in 1881 when it was raised to Rs. 35 lakhs[31]—the increase being deferred till 1886 in consideration of the monetary difficulties due to famine conditions which had preceded it.

What hurt Mysore more than the other two states was the mode of payment. While Travancore-Cochin were allowed the option of paying in cash or pepper,[32] Mysore was made to pay in gold specie which entailed a compulsory selling of her crop produce at a low price, the iniquity of which was realised by even the staunchest advocates of British imperialism.[33]

Apart from the payment of subsidy, the Mysore Maharaja

suffered in other transactions with the British paramountcy. An illustration of the discriminatory dealings of British paramountcy is well illustrated in the history of her rail-road construction where her ambitious programme for a state-owned railways in the 1880s was not only obstructed by a refusal from the paramount power to loan the money required, but when constructed from its own resources was compelled into transferring it to the Southern Mahratta Company—to favour British entrepreneurial interests—to the state's financial disadvantage and prestige.[34]

After this first lesson in the paramount power's economic policy, Mysore was rather wary of borrowing for projects not approved by the Government of India. But even so, Visvesvaraya in 1918, in his zeal for an industrialised Mysore, tilted the nicely balanced revenue-expenditure on the side of deficit finance, thus incurring the disapproval of the Government of India for life. His project to develop the iron of the Bhabhabudan Hills—'one of the first large scale industrial enterprises run by the state anywhere in India',[35]—was condemned outright for many a year by the British administrators and his adventurism in having involved the Durbar's finances by embarking on a grandiose and economically unpracticable scheme of public work strongly disapproved.[36]

While this was the attitude of the British Government towards deficit financing in the state, it hardly bothered about the personal debt of the Maharaja, which could be 'compromised' from the public coffers towards the payment of a personal debt.[37]

The same discrimination against the states was prominent in the Government of India's tariff policy. The prohibition and limitations on the manufacture of salt and opium, and the imposition of import duties[38] not only corroded into the tax revenue of the states[39] and made way for the penetration of British imperialism in all its economic aspects, but more importantly, gave a lopsided twist to these states' industrial policy. The powers of fiscal manipulation which are the characteristic of full sovereignty, being absent, these states with no fiscal powers in a country which was largely protectionist, could neither adopt a complete free trade policy nor proceed with its industrialisation with the usual protectionists' confidence.[40] Seen in this context, it is not surprising that the industrial growth—both in the change in the output and in the level of output, between 1901 and 1931—as compared between the states and its adjoining British Indian provinces showed that the princely states did not fare as well as the adjoining provinces with which they were matched.[41]

In spite of these drawbacks with a limited tax base,[42] the low per capita income and the low rate of savings, and the tariff disabilities—these progressive states did industrialise and put up a fight in order to do so. This was mainly because of the fact that in spite of spending on social welfare activities like education, sanitation, irrigation, etc., the government did manage to have a surplus as the revenues increased from year to year. This surplus had to be invested either within the state or in British Indian industries.[43] With the turn of the century these paternalistic states were more keen on investing in industries within their territories than otherwise.

The industrialisation policy of these three states before independence could be demarcated into two stages. In the first phase, the main emphasis was on stimulating private enterprise as a means to develop free enterprise.[44] This phase was marked by a readiness to loan funds and give aid to plantations and entrepreneurs rather than take it up as state ventures.[45]

The convening of the economic Conference in Mysore in 1911 was a turning point. These economic conferences aimed at increasing employment opportunities by diversifying industrial production, laid down the states' policy in regard to industries, particularly to pioneer industries, and gave them advice and assistance. Thus, by 1918 the Conference had given a tremendous stimulus to education and to material advancement of the state and recommended the establishment of large industries, either as private concerns or as concerns financed by the government.[46] By 1929-30 the Mysore Government had aided or set-up as many as 313 concerns with a capital investment of Rs. 2,40,62,751 and a government loan of Rs. 14,18,512.[47] In addition, in spite of a loss of Rs. 36 lakhs during a 10-year period, the government supported the iron and steel works at Bhadravati which, with its disastrously falling demand and declining prices, survived because of the willingness of the government to pour more money into it as a defensive investment.[48]

Cochin and Travancore, though not in sueh a spectacular manner, nevertheless, extended help to promote industry in their own way. They often started enterprises from government funds, but when once it was able to maintain its own they handed it over to private entrepreneurs.

After the 1930s there was a swing towards government-sponsored industries and of governmental projects—as for example, Travancore-Cochin's collaboration in the Cochin Harbour Project with Madras. Thus, these three states developed the characteristics of a truly mixed economy, the very near ideal which an independent India later on aimed at. They could claim more than Bikaner, that they had nationalisation in their state "far more than the Government of India, or even with due respect in England".[49]

Now turning to the agrarian structure in our search for economic grievances as a basis for the historical evolution of the movement one would imagine that the states, denigrated as they were as antiquated semi-feudal structures—as perpetuators of "India of the 18th century or in some cases almost of the middle ages"[50]—they would provide ample evidence of such grievances. But such was not the case with any of these three states as they not only kept in step with British Indian administrative reforms, but tried to ameliorate some of the defects, and thus, in contrast to British India of the adjoining territories, gave even lesser ground for such grievances. This was clearly in evidence in the contrast presented by Travancore-Cochin to that of the adjoining territory in British Malabar, while Mysore was a case by itself.

Gauging the agrarian problem (in the absence of figures regarding the proportion of land cultivated by tenants and other categories) in terms of cultivating owners to that of tenant cultivators, one found that Mysore compared remarkably more than favourably with the adjoining British Provinces and other states. One found on examination that a tenancy problem, let alone one needing any legislation on that behalf, did not exist. A table of comparative conditions in the adjoining provinces of Bombay and Madras, with that of All-India included for a good measure, and that of Mysore, Cochin, Travancore and British Malabar, explains the situation clearly.

TABLE 1.1 : A TABLE ON THE AGRARIAN SITUATION[51]

Provinces	*Non-cultivating owners*	*Cultivating owners*	*Tenant cultivators*	*Agricultural labourers*	*Agricultural labourers as % of agrarian population*
Bombay (1931)	2,47,645	12,12,252	16,36,402	37,37,847	54%
Madras (1931)	3,66,787	47,39,390	14,30,410	50,95,120	44%
All-India (1931)	41,50,758	2,83,97,214	3,62,38,654	3,35,23,423	32%
Malabar (1911)	16,640	21,838	2,52,911	4,57,459	61%
Mysore (1941)	15,804	8,92,972	75,345	1,88,015	16%
Cochin (1941)	10,641	30,321	39,142	90,316	53%
Travancore (1911)	91,305	11,63,974	1,28,523	6,47,534 (including unspecified labourers)	32%

From the above table it becomes clear that in Bombay, Cochin and Malabar where tenancy law had been enacted, as well as in India as a whole, tenant cultivators were more numerous than owner cultivators.[52] The position in Madras, Travancore and Mysore was a study in contrast. The number of owner cultivators was more, being 3 times the number of tenant cultivators in Madras as compared to 9 times in Travancore and the unprecedented figure of 12 times in Mysore. Malabar presented a picture of maximum agrarian grievance. Here the tenant cultivators were fifteen times the cultivating owners, forming as they did 2.88% and 33.43% of the agrarian population respectively,[53] whereas in Cochin, the tenant cultivators were only 1.3 times that of the cultivating owners.

This difference between Malabar and Travancore-Cochin was mainly due to the differences in the percentage of *Janmies.*[54] We find that due to the efforts to create a centralised administrative apparatus in Travancore in 1750 and in Cochin in 1762,[55] 75 per cent of the arable land in Travancore (together with all the fallow, waste land and forest) became government property (or *sarkar pattam* lands, the government being the *janmi*), while in Cochin 50% of the total land was taken over by government.[56] In Malabar, on the other hand, there was virtually no government land, so that the grip of the landlords was far greater than in Travancore and Cochin.[57]

Even of the 50 per cent land which came under *Janmam* tenure in Cochin, only 14 per cent of the cultivated land in the state were leased out to *Kanampattamdars*;[58] thus any legislation *vis-a-vis* cultivating tenants was apt to affect the *Verumpattamdars* directly than the percolation that was needed in British Malabar with the *Kanampattamdars* as intermediaries obstructing it.

As pointed out by K.N. Panikkar in his paper on agrarian relationship, in Kerala the comparison between owner cultivators and tenant cultivators may not be an entirely satisfactory measure, especially when taking into consideration the peculiarities of Kerala, *vis-a-vis* their agrarian set-up, since there was a lot of admixture of categories in the *janmi* system.[59] So the better measure would be to compare the agricultural labourers as a percentage of the total agrarian population in these four categories, to measure the real agrarian problem. Comparison on these terms too finds Travancore and Mysore at a distinct advantage, having a near non-existent agricultural (landless) labourer percentage of 16 per cent in Mysore and 32 per cent in Travancore, as against the very high figure of 61 per cent in Malabar, 54 per cent in Bombay and 53 per cent in Cochin and 44 per cent in Madras.[60] However, it must be added that these figures do not by themselves give a correct picture, especially when comparing Travancore with Mysore. While in Mysore an agricultural population of 12 lakhs was supported in a total state area of 29,475 sq. miles, Travancore's 17 lakhs was supported in 7,625 sq. miles or nearly 1/4th area of Mysore. The greater percentage of landowners to the agricultural population also attested to the dispersal of individual holdings in uneconomic parcels.

Another unique feature characteristic of Mysore's agrarian set-up, as remarked by the Maharaja of Mysore in the Legislative Assembly in 1948, was the near absence of large zamindaris or absentee landlords on a scale sufficient to constitute an economic or social problem, which was again the result of historical factors.[61]

Turning to land legislation in Mysore, the ryotwari system introduced in 1867 based on Bombay Settlement provided for a fixed field assessment and a security of tenure for a period of thirty years.[62] The land tenure in the state was of two kinds, *sarkar* or state and *Inam* lands. In the *sarkar* lands, as long as the ryot paid the state dues, he had no fear of displacement and virtually possessed an absolute tenant right as distinct from that of proprietorship.[63] Making the distinction between the rights of proprietorship as held in *Inam* lands and that of *sarkar* lands where the lands were legally inalienable, was mere casuistry, as in practice, he alienated the right of cultivation. As regards *Inam* lands, an *Inam* Commission determined principles based on that of Madras Commission and treated *Inam* lands as hereditary and alienable property which thus fetched a higher price than *sarkar* lands.

In tenurial reforms the wind was taken out of any grievance in Travancore-Cochin as compared to British Malabar. Travancore in 1865, through the *Pandaravaka* Proclamation declared all *sarkar pattam* lands as private property, hereditable and saleable, thus allowing 75 per cent of the land to come under land-holders in their own right. *The Janmi-Kudiyan* Proclamation of 1867, secured the tenant a protection against ouster. This made the renewal of lease possible only at 12-year intervals which was guarantee enough for the tenant against *janmi* oppression. To allay the oppression of the *kanakkaran* on the sub-tenant the *verumpattakkaran*, court directives were given.[64]

Cochin did one better than Travancore by her legislation in 1912 regarding the same problem. The state not only curtailed the landlord's power of eviction, and in case of eviction, entitled the tenant the full value of improvements made and to a free right to sell such improvements,[65] but also checked some malpractices at the time of renewal of lease, and attached a schedule of the grounds on which eviction was to be considered valid.

In contrast, in Malabar, not only was the greater portion of the land in the grip of the intermediaries, even the land legislation was tardy and in the agitation put up by the intermediate categories on the land legislation issue, the *Verumpattakkaran's* interests were sacrificed.[66]

The absence of any influence of big land-holders in Mysore, and the relatively (as compared to Malabar) small number of *Janmies* and their influence in Travancore-Cochin, had yet another effect in these states' agrarian set-up. Combined as this was with the near absence of not having 'a significant merchant class to exercise influence in the administration'[67] who could act as money-lenders, these states were free from the pernicious pressures of the money-lending class. As the Travancore Government in answer to a member quoting the example of Bhavnagar State, that it had given relief to 25 per cent of debtors, pointed out, in Bhavnagar if one were to get hold of some twenty-five or thirty creditors, one would have got practically all transactions, while in Travancore this could hardly be done as there was no limited class as the money-lending class except in one or two places, and if about twenty lakhs of people were debtors, there were twenty lakhs of creditors also.[68] For what little grievance there could be, the agrarian reforms on loans, etc., enacted were better in scope than similar bills in other provinces and states, both in regard to quantity and quality of debt.[69]

The effectiveness of money-lending enactments in Mysore, Travancore and Cochin is proved from the *Report of the All India Rural Credit Survey* of 1954 which pointed out that while the proportion of borrowings at rates higher than the stipulated maximum (of 12 to 12½ per cent) was around 85 per cent in West Bengal, Bihar, Madras, Orissa and Hyderabad, about 65 per cent in Madhya Pradesh and PEPSU, it was the lowest in Mysore at 10 per cent and Travancore-Cochin at 12 per cent.[70]

Again in its agrarian set-up as in the promotion of industry, these governments took a paternalistic interest. They not only promoted irrigational projects but initiated the institution of Panchayats and local self-government which promoted the involvement of people from the rural areas.[71] In 1917, Mysore increased the non-official elective element in her municipalities and Panchayats[72] and the Travancore Village Panchayat Act of 1925 gave to them a majority of elected members. The Panchayats were charged with the management of local affairs, and given jurisdiction over small civil suits and trying of petty offences. Cochin provided for a greater element of elected members and powers, with even certain powers of taxation, granted to these Panchayat Boards.

Thus, on summing up, one finds that a purely agrarian economic grievance as a basis for democratic movement was non-existent in these three states; especially was it so in Mysore.

Comparing Travancore-Cochin with British Malabar, one finds that excepting the first peasant uprising in Travancore in 1802[73] in response to forced exactions, they presented no counterpart to the economic grievance-oriented, ever recurring Moplah uprisings of British Malabar.[74] Again, while we do find in Travancore-Cochin a social reform movement preceding the political movement and as such forming a basis for it, in British Malabar the rural economic structure leading to the tenancy movement formed the basis of the later political movement.[75] As A.K. Gopalan has pointed out this difference in the tempo of the national movement reflected, as seen, the differences in the historical evolution of the material conditions in those places.[76]

The economic grievance of the states against the paramount power, though it affected the Maharajas, their governments and their people, was borne mainly by the states administration. The persons who came directly into conflict with the paramount power were the Maharajas and their governments. Thus, the economic grievances due to the paramount power's policy became their chief obsessions in their relationship with it. The main controversy of the first two Dewans of Mysore (after Rendition) with the paramount power centred thus around the enhanced subsidy of Rs. 10½ lakhs[77] and over Railway interests and concessions.[78] The subsidy issue as a bone of contention between these two parties is a recurrent feature throughout Mysore's relationship with the paramount power, right up to the end of their talks on federation in September 1939.[79]

In Travancore-Cochin too, the Dewans were no less assiduous in the interest of the state they served, where even in 1907 a Dewan was forced to resign for his non-compliance to satisfy British entrepreneurial interests.[80] Again, the three states' demands in the 1920s centred round customs and other grievances over which they sought a greater intimacy with the British Indian Government and its successors. In this they presented a contrast to the other princely interests which stressed on non-interference of the paramount power in its administration; these interests had sought a codification of rules relating to their relationship with the paramount power and a degree of isolation from the British Indian Government—especially if it were to become one of a democratic nature. As the Viceroy, Lord Irwin, pointed out in 1926 the princes' demand for an enquiry committee into their grievances in this period was representative of two contradictory interests.[81]

Apart from this, in view that the states peoples' movement in their demand for responsible government came into a conflict with the Maharaja and the government, it gave a rather lopsided twist to the economic grievance as a basis for the democratic movement. These states people, especially that of Mysore, though they talked loosely of economic causes, really thought the economic issues were the concern of the Maharajas and not theirs. An illustration of this dichotomy is clear in the speeches of a member prominent in the states peoples movement. Hosakappa Krishna Rao, writing in the *Swaraj Constitution* (approved by and written for the All-India State Subjects Conference in 1928) on the economic issue as a cause of the States Peoples movement, wrote : "until the middle of the Great War the people of the States were comparatively well off. . . . As the war progressed the economic stability of the states became disturbed and revolutionary changes were brought in the economic condition of the people".[82] He relates this with the cost of living going up, which in any case was not a phenomenon of the states alone, but all over India and the world. His charges seem almost trumped up, as no special grievance could be cited by him as specially due to the policies of the monarchy in the south. His charges of the governments showing "no intention to ameliorate hard conditions",[83] seem to fall with a pronouncement which he made in a subsequent year. When it came to the federal issue and the Mysore Government insisted to the paramount power that "Mysore (would) not enter All-India Federation so long as the subsidy or any portion of it was levied from her by British Government",[84] the same Hosakappa Krishna Rao felt, that the "question of subsidy should not be mixed up with that of entering the Federation and . . . had to be dealt with by itself on its own merits".[85]

The dichotomy in the states peoples to this question is easily explicable in that, that while the policies of the paramount power did make the states prone to the economic exploitation of it, the policies of the Maharajas and their governments were not to be blamed.

Again, the economic grievance as a basis for the development of a democratic movement, in the face of an enlightened industrial policy provided little basis for such a movement.[86]

However, there were important qualitative differences on the comparative attitude of these states. The Dewans of Mysore, even from the time of Rengacharlu and Seshadri Iyer (the first two Dewans after Rendition) set a premium in the states subjects' interests and with the policy enunciation of Mysore's economic conferences from 1911, this feature was even more noticeable and revenue considerations were made subsidiary to the larger benefits of industry[87] and the welfare of the people.

Moreover, capitalists from outside were encouraged only so far as they did not affect the industrialists and the interests within the states. In contrast, in Travancore-Cochin, revenue considerations occupied a pivotal position.[88] Thus, while the Dewan of Travancore in 1928 rightly refused to grant any concession to the European planters merely because they had pioneered these industries, nor to the Travancore Cardamom Planters Association (an association of non-Travancoreans established in Madura District to look after their interests in respect of cardamom they grew in Travancore),[89] merely because they were Indians, neither did he extend any concessions to Travancoreans themselves. Thus, when capital and capitalists from outside were allowed on considerations of efficiency and revenue growth, they aroused agitation and jealousies within.[90] Another complication arose when the capitalists—such as factory owners—were Europeans. Any small fracas between management and workers could, and was blown up, into a confrontation with anti-British implications.[91]

Again, success at industrialisation itself, provided the impetus in two ways. Firstly, industrialisation is a product and promoter of an advanced society. As such, the demands for responsible government which was prompted in its first stage by the demands of an intelligentsia was supported by this society. Secondly, with the growth of labour organisations in the 1920s, the state with a greater industrialisation in which the government was a major owner, was vulnerable to the combined demands of labour. Thus, labour with its everyday grievances was only too ready to join the movement which was also against the same government.[92] During the zenith of the movement in the late 1930s and 1940s the major efforts of the state governments lay in satisfying labour union demands as far as possible and separating them from the political agitations. Another complication arose after the Haripura Congress in 1938. How was the I.N.T.U.C. a wing of the Congress to deal with its affiliated labour unions in the state—was not the idea of labour unions supposed to cross frontiers ? Or was it to follow the general Congress policy and disaffiliate itself ?

In its internal agrarian set-up the states were better off than the British Indian territories adjoining them and the states administration in their agrarian policy had tried to ameliorate distress conditions.

In fact, as often quoted by these governments, their very justification for an autocratic government lay in emphasising their comparatively better off position in their economic sphere, not only as a comparison with other states, but with the neighbouring territories of British India and India as a whole.[93]

However, while in Mysore, there was no particular cause for an agrarian grievance at all, Travancore-Cochin presented a small breach.

The economic cause in its social aspects did provide a basis for the movement, for a study of which we would now have to turn to the study of the social set-up, conditions and the policy of the government, leading to a social movement in its turn as a basis for political movement.

The Social Basis

For the understanding of this movement in Kerala, one would, to start at the very beginning, have to familiarise oneself with the caste breakup in these two states.

In the caste break-up particular note has to be taken of the four main communities; Nairs, Ezhavas, the Christians and the Muslims.

In this the most important factor was the castewise distribution of communities in the agrarian set up. As pointed out by Eric J. Miller,

> "Within the village, the caste rank was—and still is— closely correlated with the relationship to the land...Nambudiris and chieftain castes tend to be landowners; the higher Nair sub-castes are either landowners or non-cultivating

TABLE 1.2 : POPULATION OF KERALA BY COMMUNITY[94]

Community	*Percentage of population in Kerala*	*Percentage of population in Travancore*	*Percentage of population in Cochin*
Hindus:			
Brahmins	1.5%	Figure not available	
Nairs	15.4%	17.3%	13.4%
Ezhavas	21.2%	16.7%	24.9%
Other forward Hindu communities	3.4%	30.0%	17.7%
Other backward	10.1%	Individual figures not available	
communities & scheduled castes and scheduled	8.4%		
tribes	1.2%		
Total:			
Hindus	61.2%	64.3%	66.0%
Christians	20.9%	29.3%	27.0%
Muslims	17.9%	6.8%	7.0%
Jains, Jews etc.	.12%	—	—

tenants (*Kanamdars*), the inferior Nairs and some Tiyyas are cultivating sub-tenants either on permanent leases or annual leases (*Verumpattamdars*); the majority of the upper polluting classes are landless labourers, while the lower polluting castes were until recently serfs."[95]

What imparted to the social grievances, its economic and political overtones was the ubiquitous Nair monopoly which was present even in the composition of the legislature. Seventy per cent of the elected members, even after the 1932 reforms, came from this community. To understand the predominance of the Nairs in Travancore in the legislature, we would have to examine the evolution of the constitutional framework, not only with particular reference to the powers and evolution of legislature of the state, but also and mainly, in the light of the peculiar agrarian set-up in Kerala in their castewise distribution. The Chitra Council—the Legislative Council of Travancore convened in 1888[96] with 'not less than 5 nor more than 8 members (in imitation of the wording of 1861 Council Act of British India) as well as the Sri Moolam Legislative Assembly convened in 1904 was based on property qualification and *representative mainly of agricultural interests.* In the context of the distribution of the agricultural set-up quoted earlier, it becomes clear that the Legislative apparatus was representative of only the Nair community as the main holders of land. Neither the Christians who were engaged mainly in the educational field and in European plantations as low salaried employees, nor the Ezhava community engaged mainly as agricultural labourers could obtain any place in the legislature. Even Brahmins in this respect were affected, as constitutionally exempted from the payment of tax, and as a minority in the population, with few possessing an income above the required figure, they could hardly get any representation. Thus, while on the one hand, it led to a scramble for land and a shift in purchases from one communal group to the other (see table below),[97] more importantly it resulted in a coalition of these two communities in order to break the Nair monopoly. As long as property in land was the basis of franchise, the Nair monopoly in the legislature was maintained. The election results, even as late as 1933, bore out the fact that mere lowering of property qualification would in no way solve the problem as nearly 60 per cent of the seats were cornered by this community representing a mere 17.3 per cent of the population.[98]

TABLE 1.3 : SHARE OF DIFFERENT COMMUNITIES IN THE NUMBER OF SALES AND PURCHASE OF LAND IN TRAVANCORE

Community	*1926*		*1930*		*1935*		*1940*	
	Sales	*Purchase*	*Sales*	*Purchase*	*Sales*	*Purchase*	*Sales*	*Purchase*
Brahmin	4.5	2.1	4.3	2.3	3.4	3.2	3.0	2.4
Nair	38.6	29.2	41.6	36.1	44.4	36 2	47.7	27.7
Ezhava	10.2	12.7	13.3	15.8	14.7	17.2	14.2	13.1
Christians	23 3	55.9	19.5	25.5	17.7	22.2	18.3	28.0

The table clearly shows that there was a definite shift in purchases. There were more Nair and Brahmin sellers than buyers, while the Christian community seemed to be buying in a big way. The Ezhavas seem to have fallen in the race after the introduction of adult franchise in 1936.

Seen in the context of the castewise distribution of the agricultural set-up, it is obvious that the Legislative apparatus was not the means of associating the popular elements but a means for coopting a section of vested interests on to the side of the government. Thus any growth in the powers and scope of the legislature, only added to a further aggrandisement of the majority of the population by a minority of caste groups.

In 1892 this clique of vested interests in the Council when it increased its membership did this not through a promulgation or proclamation by the Maharaja but in its own powers; by passing a Bill to amend its own constitution, it conceived a power which only a sovereign legislature like the British Parliament was competent to do.[99] But more than that, the Council made provisions for the Dewan to make regulation in respect of the reserved subjects and submit them to the Maharaja for approval and to make emergency regulations, having the force of law valid for six months. Legally, the Maharaja was the supreme Legislative authority. But the Council "endeavoured to derive a constitutional convention that the Maharaja would not ordinarily exercise his prerogative of legislation".[100] Thus the Council in 1892 had adopted and made pretentions to two momentous rights. Firstly, to amend its own constitution and secondly to enact laws on its own right and to reduce the Maharaja's prerogative to a mere nominal gesture in which position it continued till 1920 and was terminated only on the intervention of British paramountcy.[101]

It was in this background that the thread of communal demands[102] became a part and parcel of Travancore politics. Demands were made by the Ezhava and Christian leaders that when the principle of communal representation in public service was recognised by British Indian Government, the Governments of Baroda and Mysore, it was only proper that the same principle be recognised by the Government of Travancore. As a recognition of this, it demanded that the unrepresented backward communities be given special electorates, and 4 of the 28 seats be set apart for the Ezhavas.[103]

In emulation of the Ezhavas, other communities put forward their demands—the Catholics demanded greater facilities for English education, and representation in the popular assembly[104] and complained that of the 400 revenue officers only one was a

Catholic.[105] The Pulayas asked for free mid-day meals, appointment as peons,[106] and the Parayas asked for access to free education, etc.[107] These characteristics of strife and petitionings by the different communities in regard to favours and distribution of government appointments was compared by *Samdarsi* to a poor man surrounded by four or five fastidious wives,[108] and made a rather irate Dewan remark as early as 1927 that they should stop thinking in terms of 'my community, my community' and should instead take up the burden of 'my country, my country'.[109] But this thinking in terms of community had become a part and parcel of Travancore-Cochin politics that the 'foreign Dewan' movement, which had been the earliest political movement, died a natural death in the realisation that only an outside Dewan could hold the balance between the warring claims of these communities.

Thus it was in the contradictory background of: (i) the combined opposition of the majority of the populace to the vested influence of the Nairs in their monopoly and dominant position in society, government and legislature of the state and government support to its position, and (ii) of their affiliations to their community and community organisations, that Kerala politics, especially that of Travancore, evolved.

There is no doubt that it was the influence of caste organisations and community affiliations which imparted to Kerala politics an instability as in party groupings community affiliations played havoc.[110] An astute Dewan could cut out one community from a coalition by promising them some concessions.

However, to understand the movement in Travancore-Cochin in mere terms of sectarian interests and as a movement of competing elements would be to misunderstand the peculiar nature of Kerala politics. It was in its opposition to the monopolies created by the Nair vested interests that the movement in Travancore gained its democratic character. Underlying the motive of breaking the Nair supremacy lay the realisation that the position of the different caste interests in society could improve only when these interests obtained representation commensurate with the population. Whether these aspirations were truly democratic as they did not cut across localised caste interests and were not based on party ideologies, it is not my point to dispute. It was a democratic movement in the sense of my introductory chapter. It was a movement to get representation on the basis of adult franchise and towards the obtaining of the states' ideal of responsible government where the executive would be responsible to the legislature and ultimately to the people through their representatives. Even the movement of the Ezhavas thus met with considerable Christian support because of Christian sympathies for them against the all embracing character of the vested interests of Nairs. In the political movement—in their demand of 'Civil Rights', of a right to vote and a franchise based on adult suffrage. these movements in 1921 and 1935,[111] unlike in any other part of India, cut across religious animosities. The Ezhavas of the Hindu community joined the Christians against the government, while in 1935 there was a combination of the Muslims, Ezhavas and Christians. Again, while their demand for adult franchise did get channelised into demands for separate electorates, this was only because of the government's plea that adult franchise and territorial constituencies were to be found nowhere in India. Thus the demand for separate electorates was not because of any fear of monopoly of a real majority—as for instance, the Muslim demand for separate electorates in British (North) India because of a fear of Congress-Hindu majority absolutism. Nor was it similar in character to Ambedkar's demand in British India for separate electorates for the backward castes who were in a weak position due to economic and intellectual backwardness and fear of being swamped by the higher caste Hindus. The real demand for reforms in Travancore-Cochin for adult franchise was backed by the knowledge that the Nair supremacy was possible only as it was propped by a repressive government. The communal interests combined with a democratic urge (due no doubt to the phenomenal growth of education) and thus the democratic movement became "an extension and development of the social movement".[112] And, if there were any perversions in the democratic movement it was not so much due to the social set-up alone, but mainly to the perverted actions of the autocratic government with its coterie of vested interests prompting it.

Mysore provided a refreshing change. Here, though the government utilised the caste animosities between the Brahmins and non-Brahmins to safeguard its autocratic position, with the growth of education and the spread of democratic trends in India, a common ideology was able to bridge the chasm to obtain full democratic content. It is in the background of active support to the backward communities by the government that one has to view the communal breakup in Mysore.

TABLE 1.4 : COMMUNAL BREAKUP IN MYSORE[113]

Community	*Percentage in Karnataka*	*Percentage in princely Mysore*
Brahmin	4. %	4.1%
Visvakarma	2.3%	2.2%
Other Forward Hindus	2.5%	1.7%
Vokkaliga (representing the two main Gangadikara and Morasu sects)	13.0%	22.0%
Mahratta	4%	—
Kurubas & Bedars	6.9% and 4.7% respectively	6.5% and 4.6% respectively
Other backward classes	9.6%	8.6%
Scheduled castes and tribes	3.3% and 16.7% respectively	9.6% and 19.1% respectively
Lingayats	15.6%	11.6%
Muslims	10%	6.3%
Christians	2.1%	1.1%
Other tribes, Buddhists etc.	1.1%	0.4%

In this communal breakup, the Christians forming as they did a minute part of the population were of little importance in the political and social make-up of the state. The Muslims, inspite of being a very small community, comprising as they did only 6.3 per cent of the population, often came into conflict with the Hindus over the usual religious issues of taking out processions with music in front of the Jama Masjid. However, these religious tensions leading to riots were confined to particular areas and were sporadic.[114]

Thus, the main communal factions on the political arena was confined to those within the Hindu fold. The castes we have to take particular note of, apart from the Brahmins, are the Vokkaligas and the Lingayats. Population-wise the Vokkaligas in Mysore state representing the agricultural interests were nearly double that of the Lingayats. The Vokkaligas were by tradition a pro-government section. Thus, though the Vokkaliga Sabha presented petitions with a regularity in the Representative Assembly and sought for concessions and favours, they were not tardy in acknowledging them.[115]

The other community, the Lingayats, arose in the eleventh century as a reaction to Jainism which had spread in northern Mysore. This community found its main adherents in the Karnataka part than that of the state of Mysore. Like the Ezhavas of Travancore, perhaps in emulation of their Memorial in 1895, in 1897, the Lingayats prayed for the grant of special encouragement in matters of education and appointment to the public service.[116] Parallel to the S.N.D.P. Yogam formed in 1905, they formed the Lingayat Education Fund in 1909.[117] As an opposition to the hierarchy of caste, they confined their attention not only to their own community but also to those below them. The Government of Mysore, by applauding their efforts of self-improvement removed any animosity that might exist in the community against the government.[118]

However, these communities, perhaps lacking the incentives as the totally suppressed castes in Kerala did, did not respond as well as they. Even as late as 1921, they had not more than half a dozen graduates,[119] in their community and prayed for special privileges and concessions to government posts.

If there was any animosity of the non-Brahmins against the administration it cropped up mainly as a socially backward community lacking in education, which denied them naturally, an access to civil service and in later stages to the legislatures. It is pertinent to remark that even these grievances became prominent only during the period of the Mysore Brahmin Dewans, P.N. Krishnamurthy and mainly Visvesvaraya, which were soon rectified by an administrative policy of sympathetic consideration of these demands and by not having local Brahmins as Dewans.

In view that the Commissioners rule had been imposed mainly due to the opposition of the agricultural community, the Dewans took particular care in their handling of the grievances of this community. Thus the Representative Assembly convened in 1881 by the first Dewan of Mysore after Rendition, more than as a means of affording the people a share in the management of affairs,[120] was conceived as an apparatus to convince them that the interests of the government were identical with those of the people.[121] Thus, the convening of the Assembly at the time of the Dusserah Festival, and the revival of the celebration of the Navarathri (inaugurated earlier by Raja Wadayar in 1610) was with the purpose of affording the people an opportunity of paying their homage to the ruler[122]—a revival of the Durbar in a new setting. In this he was but imitating the British administrators.

The elective principle in the legislature though in a rather embryonic stage, was evident from the beginning. The order convening the Assembly had suggested that the selection be made by the Local Fund Board from the cultivating land-holders in each Taluk and leading merchants in each district. In 1887 the size of the Assembly was determined at 185 and representatives were ordered to meet in Mysore city as distinct groups to select not only their spokesman but also the questions and subjects to be presented.[123] In 1888 each Taluk was asked to list fifteen to twenty nominees from which the Deputy Collector would select. In 1891 the principles of election were conceded[124] and 2,500 increased in 1894 to 8000, were declared eligible to vote on the basis of their tax payment or their standing as graduates. However, this reform had yet to take root even as late as 1901, as is evident from the note written by the Resident which proclaimed that the Assembly consisted of representatives mainly selected by Deputy Commissioners.[125]

Whether it was an elected or selected legislature, and its franchise was based on the tax paid and was limited, unlike the Legislature of Travancore, it was representative of all the communities and interests, thus maintaining a balance within the legislatures.

The Brahmin community, in their Foreign Brahmin movement became opposers of the government. The Vokkaligas and the Lingayats in their caste antagonisms to the Brahmins (who also represented the educated elements) thus became the natural collaborators of the government.[126] This collaboration between the non-Brahmin castes and the government of Mysore was evident in the legislatures of the state from the very beginning. At its very first meeting in the Assembly, the Dewan made a ready response to these agrarian and trading interests which helped in evolving a collaboration and rapport between him and them. In this, they presented a marked contrast to affairs in Travancore, where the educated vested interests representing higher caste Hindus had combined with the government against the majority of the population.

Conclusion

Summing up one finds that a democratic tradition in the states combined as it were with a British intervention coming at an opportune moment, ensured an efficient administration in these states. Guarantees for its continuation was embedded in the Rendition Treaty of Mysore (1881). In this treaty, the Political Department had had the opportunity, to express in terms of an 'Instrument of Transfer', conditions which it considered the ideal in a state's set-up *vis-a-vis* its administration and relationship with the Government of India. In the Political Department's efforts to read the treaties as a whole, this model provided the 'Procrustean bed of good behaviour'.[127] While this model was resented to by the northern Indian princes and their sympathisers like A.P. Nicholson[128] and Leslie Scott,[129] as a contravention of non-intervention policy and their treaties, the willing acceptance of these conditions, not only by Mysore but also by the other two states, ensured good administration in these states and brought them in line with British India. This brought on a qualitative difference of these states as against their north Indian compeers. This, combined as it was with the near absence of any economic grievance in Mysore, with a slight exception in its socio-economic implications in Travancore, confined the states peoples' struggle against the administration mainly at the level of autocratism versus democracy. Thus these states' people in contrast to the other states, complained not so much against the oppressiveness of a feudal order, or *begar* (bonded labour) or against the depredations of the Maharajas, or the personal iniquities and idiosyncrasies of their princes, (examples of which found in the states system in abundance, furnished the Kiplings and the Praver Jhabvalas, the Gaubas, and the Collins-Lapierries with material enough to make the states study, ludicrous illustrations of depravity and pornographic literature!), but for civil liberties and on a democratic ideology. However, this was always a weak ideology when confronted by postures of good government attuned to the welfare of the general populace. While in Mysore the position was further weakened by a government policy of favouring the socially weak community, the grievances of the socially discriminated communities in Travancore against the administration, did provide some leverage for agitation—though on a rather disputed platform of communal grievances as a basis for democratic movement.

2

The Sons of the Soil

The Movement from 1900 to 1919

The states peoples' movement, as mentioned earlier, comprised of two different elements. On the one side was the purely local, political and social movement peculiar to these states, while the second was an extension of the Indian National Congress movement for the freedom struggle in British India.

In the post-independence period, several government-sponsored studies of the freedom struggles in the integrated states taken as a whole[1] have been brought out which also cover the movement in these princely states. These, however, make little or no clear distinction between the two separate movements. This may be because these two movements often converged or coincided at several points. However, for a clear appreciation of the democratic movement in the princely states, it is necessary that we hold the threads of these two movements separate in tracing the course of the movement, and take into consideration the several dimensions the study involves to get a clearer perspective. This involves, as already indicated: (1) a study of the socio-political movement within the states which in its later stages transformed into a demand for responsible government, (2) It also involves a study of Indian National Congress movement in the states and its corollaries, (3) The attitude of the state governments towards it, and (4) The attitude of the Indian National Congress towards the states peoples' movement, which was in turn dependent on, (5) The policy of the paramount power towards native states, taken as a whole.

The Foreign Dewan Movement

The genesis of the democratic movement which was local can be traced to the British policy of bringing in Brahmins from Madras province to head the state administration, especially, as Dewans. In the early stages, there was no premeditated plan to keep out natives, as such, from this high position. Thus, for example, in 1809, soon after the suppression of the Velu Thampi rebellion in Travancore, Omini Thampi, a favourite of the British, was appointed as Dewan Again, after the three-year foreign Dewanship of Colonel Munro (1811-1814), Padmanabha Pillai, a native, was appointed as Dewan. Even as late as 1834, we find a native Dewan of Cochin, Edamana Sankara Pillai, being 'criminally proceeded against' on charges of corruption brought against him as a consequence of a memorial submitted by a deputation of respectable Brahmins, Nairs and native Christians.[2] It was only later, when it was found after these experiments that the Dewanship required an impartiality, a non-involvement with petty state squabbles and an absolute dependence for favours of the British, that the policy of appointing from outside the state adopted. Barring a few exceptions, like Nanoo Pillai in Travancore (1877), there were few native Dewans appointed till the beginning of the twentieth century.[3]

The Rendition of Mysore (1881) came particularly at a time when the policy of appointing Dewans—if the example of Travancore-Cochin were to be followed—had crystallised into a lack of consideration of natives. Moreover, the internal politics of Mysore state at this time made appointment of natives impossible. The Hebbar Iyengars, who were themselves immigrants of the 11th and 12th centuries, and who numbered a mere 2000 in the states population, were distrusted by the Commissioners for their involvement in the efforts to reinstate the Maharaja. Thus, during the Commissionership, foreign Brahmins, mainly from the Madras Provincial Service, had been co-opted in the state services. Rangacharlu (1881-1883), the first Dewan of Mysore after Rendition, had been one such who had attracted the attention of the English administrators while working in Calicut and had been brought to the Commissioner's office at Mysore. Seshadri Iyer, (1883-1896), the next Dewan, had followed the same path, and during his long tenure of Dewanship had to bear the brunt of the agitation—but not without reason. During his Dewanship he had introduced as many as 100 Madrasis into the state administration as gazetted officers of the Mysore Durbar.[4]

That all three states suffered from the same grievance is reflected in the newspapers of this period. A leader published in *Karnataka Prakasika* in 1886,[5] complained of a Dewan in Mysore in whose administration all the evils complained of in that of his brother Dewan of Travancore were repeated. The leading charge against this administration was that it encouraged favouritism; supported as the Dewan was by the British Resident, he did not care for public opinion because there was no one to question his act, not even the Maharaja. While the Dewan of Travancore was not on good terms with the Prince of Travancore, because the latter endeavoured to check the arbitrary acts of the former, the Dewan of Mysore on the most friendly terms with the Maharaja was in even a better position to bring in his favourites. This had allowed the Dewan to appoint Madrasis, who, it claimed, had not even the qualification to subordinate places in the state services and for which intelligent and sufficiently educated Mysoreans could have easily been found. It was felt that the foreign Dewans had become anachronistic and expensive nuisances and that the native princes could do well—to rely for advice and guidance on the members of a well-selected council of all classes of their subjects of which they themselves could be presidents.[6]

These grievances fall under four heads. Firstly came the protest against the unbridled authoritarian rule of the Dewan.

Secondly came dissatisfaction with non-appointment of natives in governmental posts, even when suitable candidates could be found. The third factor was favouritism and fourthly, came the demand for a native Dewan. These complaints occur and re-occur almost as a refrain in all these states—up to 1912 in Mysore and even later in Travancore-Cochin. These complaints against the Dewans were, however, only partly valid for the extent of Dewan's autocratism, in practice, was circumscribed by his personal equation with the Maharaja and the paramount powers' representative, the Resident.[7]

Thus, the main agitation in these three states concentrated mainly on charges of non-appointment of natives in government services. While in Mysore the grievance against 'foreign Dewans' was projected in the press and in the Legislature,[8] in Travancore the grievance was projected in a more dramatic way in the presentation of the Malayali Memorial in 1891.

This Memorial had been preceded by a one-man agitation put up by G. Parameswara Pillai, who under the pseudonym 'Pro-Patra', in an open letter to Lord Connemara, the Governor of Madras in 1887, complained that from 1817 to 1872, the country in the hands of eight Rao Dewans had seen the introduction of relations and friends, and relations' friends, and friends' friends of the Dewans into the high offices of the state.[9]

The mammoth Malayali Memorial signed by 19,038 was an exercise in statistical study which drove home the same point with a greater poignancy and brutality—as all statistically arraigned data do—the iniquity suffered by the natives of the states at the hands of the foreign Dewans.

The ammunition for the charge was inadvertently provided by the then Dewan of Travancore, Mr. Rama Rao himself, in publishing *A Summary of the Returns of the Public Servants in the State*,[10] which for the first time disclosed to the public view the unjust distribution of government appointments among the different castes. The Memorial pointed out that of the 16,167 posts in government service, 3,407 posts with salaries above Rs. 10, 1,444 posts were held by foreign Hindus.[11] If one were to take the higher salaries into consideration, the divergence became more marked, in that the average daily salary earning of the foreign Brahmin was equivalent of Rs. 6.77 ps. as against an earning of 12 ps. for Malayali Sudras and 13 ps. for a Christian.[12]

What emphasised the point even more clearly was the comparative analysis made in the Memorial between the position of the Malayali in British Malabar with that of Travancore State. With a comparable area, population and number of graduates, Travancore had a lower precentage of positions held by Malayalis than in Malabar.[13]

As could be expected, the publication of this Memorial was received with great sympathy in the other two states. The *Karnataka Prakasika* of Mysore ran a four parts serial on this, concluding with the warning that the Memorial ought to teach a lesson to people nearer home.[14]

In spite of the strong plea put forward by the Memorial and the sympathetic agitation in the press in these three states, it was a decade before the paramount power deigned to take note of this irritation. However, the first experiment at a native Dewan, in Dewan P.N. Krishnamurthy in 1901 for Mysore, did not prove successful as it gave rise to charges of corruption and favouritism at non-brahmin hands and so the agitation continued in a virulent form till 1908 when the severity of the agitation was controlled by the passing of the Press Law in Mysore and by the repressive action against the press in Travancore. So till 1908 there were few Dewans in all these three states, who passed unscathed from charges of nepotism, favouritism or of appointing outsiders, overlooking the claims of better educated natives.

Tracing the course of the agitation (against foreign Dewans) from the turn of this century in these three states[15] we see the *Suryodaya Prakasika* in 1900 expressing a hope that the misfortune of Mysore for the past many years in having foreigners as Dewans would now be broken and that a native of Mysore would be made Dewan.[16] The Viceroy, Lord Curzon, on a state visit to Mysore, expressed himself in sympathy with local aspirations and advised the Maharaja to train Mysoreans so that they could be of help in administering the state;[17] as a result of which P.N. Krishnamurthy was appointed Dewan of Mysore on 18 March 1901.[18] The appointment of a native Dewan in Mysore triggered off complaints in the other two states; the *Malayala Manorama* 'disapproved' of the preference shown by the Dewan to persons imported from other districts which, it maintained rendered, the Dewan's name highly repugnant to the subjects of Cochin state.[19]

Dewan P.N. Krishnamurthy's first act as Dewan was to scrap the Civil Service Examination in 1902.[20] This was in response to *Suryodaya Prakasika's* agitation against the examination which was felt was instituted by Seshadri Iyer only to provide for outsiders.[21] But it hardly stopped criticisms against the Dewans. The *Mysore Standard* (whose politics according to the Resident was one of the Bengali type,[22] and had often boasted of its ability to 'unmake' the Dewans) complained on the eve of P.N. Krishnamurthy's retirement that he had been making haste to oblige his relations and friends.[23] The *Suryodaya Prakasika*, which had earlier been so virulent in its attack on foreign Dewans, and particularly of Seshadri Iyer, almost in retraction of its earlier complaint against him, now acknowledged that the administration of the late Dewan Seshadri Iyer had been far better; though he had imported Madrasis into the public services, his policy had created two parties, each trying to expose the fault of the other which had provided a healthy check.[24] However, the term of P.N. Krishnamurthy's Dewanship served to prove that a mere change in the nationality of the Dewan was not enough to provide an answer to the prevalent malaise, but what was really required was a change in the mode of administration to really tone it up.

In Travancore, where the experiment of a native Dewan had yet to be tried, the *Nazrani Dipika* strongly disapproved of the 'importation' of an outsider to fill the post of the Chief Judge when there were competent natives. With the appointment of S. Gopalachari, District Sessions Judge at Tinnevelly, as Dewan, the issue was opened wide again and it was with a sense of injury that *Nazrani Dipika*[25] harped on the same theme in holding that the selection of a Dewan could have been made from a native District Judge. A leader, voicing Cochin's sympathies with Travancore's sentiments also appeared in *Kerala Patrika*.[26]

Mysore's triumph in having a native Dewan was rather short-lived. In 1906, the old policy was reverted to again in the appointment of V.P. Madhava Rao. Thus the refrain was taken up again in these three states and Travancore complained of nepotism and favouritism and Mysore joined to reiterate its regret that the authorities were particularly prone to overlook the merits of the Mysoreans in their anxiety to support the Madrasis;[27] it made a special plea to the Maharaja to make an inquiry personally into the matter.[28] These vituperations in the press against the foreign Dewans often degenerated to personal character vilifications. But it says much for the independence of the press that it spared no one, be he a native or a foreign Dewan.

The Press Act

Till 1905 the States' Governments took little notice of these press vituperations. Thus in Mysore, Seshadri Iyer who had been subjected to the maximum criticism, according to the newspaper *Mysore State*, had allowed them a free course in spite of adverse criticism which had 'even transgressed the bounds of freedom'.[29] His only action against the press was his suspension of the *Desabhimani*, edited by C. Srinivas Aiyangar, for publishing a dialogue between the editor and a mythological king—a clear innuendo against monarchy and derogatory of the Ruler.[30] The press was impounded on the refusal of the editor to pay the fine imposed as a guarantee of future good behaviour.[31] The action obviously was necessitated not because of its being derogatory of the Dewan, but as a clear case of sedition, as against the monarch.

In 1905, the change in attitude towards the press became obvious with the first overt action taken by P.N. Krishnamurthy, a native Dewan. He ordered the representative of the *Mysore Standard* to leave the Durbar Hall, where the Legislative Assembly was in session, on suspicion that this paper was publishing 'fake matters' against the government.[32] This action was condemned as arbitrary by the *Swadesamitram*,[33] *Mysore State*,[34] *Suryodaya Prakasika*,[35] etc.

However, there is little doubt that the actual initiative for gagging the press came not so much from the Dewan, as the Resident in Mysore. In 1906, the Resident, S.M. Fraser in a note to the Political Department, pointed out that the real danger now lay in the "*not less notorious but even more mischievous vernacular newspapers which now unfortunately penetrated the mofussil villages, and. . . spread the poison of sedition to the uninformed masses . . . (The time had thus come for the) Dewans to realise the responsibility which they owed to the British Government* and their own subjects for controlling a native press unparalleled probably for licence in any other native state in India.[36] His sense of chagrin against the press in Mysore is reiterated in yet another note for the subsequent year. "I have made more than one reference to newspapers in this state"[37] he wrote, "because while the character of editors deprives them of influence among educated people, their circulation and power for mischief is steadily increasing among the ignorant and half educated masses; so that the *fact that they appear to be beyond the control exercised*, I believe, over the press in other Native States by the government, is one of unfortunate significances".

Though he was irritated by the 'maliciousness' of the press in its charges against the administration, the Resident's fear of the 'mischievous' nature of the press is more obviously patent in these two notes; thus, though he did rail against the criticism of the Dewan in the press, he was more bothered about the states' 'responsibility which they owed to the British Government'.[38]

The nature of the 'responsibility' became obvious in 1907 when *Suryodaya* published a rumour about a discussion between the Viceroy and the Maharaja on the transfer of certain districts in Kolar to British India.[39] The Mysore Government in April 1907 issued a warning to *Suryodaya* and a general warning to the press against such false rumours.[40] However, when the *Mysore Standard* repeated the same rumour the government felt that the warning had no effect and consideration of the relations existing between the ruler and the paramount power necessitated stronger action. It was this responsibility which the Dewan asserted in his speech emphasizing that the measures had been undertaken to prevent the loyalty of their subjects to the paramount power from being undermined.[41] A clear unequivocal assertion that it was the consideration of the paramount power—(and thus mainly based on the initiative of the Resident) that made the enactment of the law necessary. Seshadri Iyer's action against *Deshabhimani* in 1891 was cited on this occasion mainly to reinforce the government's claim that the government were not creating any new punitive powers, more formidable than that, which was already inherent in the Maharaja's sovereign prerogative,[42] thus claiming that the action taken was nothing more than a gesture. The very fact that the Durbar preferred to deal with it by legislation rather than by the exercise of Maharaja's prerogative[43] showed clearly that the Dewan preferred a sharing of respo sibility for it rather than being held solely responsible for it—which in turn showed an unwillingness towards the measure.

The Bill, consented to by the Viceroy and commended by him in July 1908 "as a wise and patriotic decision",[44] was discussed in August 1908 in the Mysore Legislative Assembly with not even a dissenting voice in the Council[45] and was passed as an Act on 10 August 1908.[46] What surprised public opinion was that while one could condone and expect the official members to side with the government, the non-official members had acted in a surprising manner in shaking off their responsibility by readily giving their assent to the measure.[47]

The first result of the Press Act was the elimination of the *Mysore Standard*, the *Mysore Herald* and the *Jagadguru* from publishing business. Mr. Venkatakrishnayya, the editor of *Mysore Herald*, who had ceased publication of his newspaper as a protest against the Press Act,[48] however, stood as a candidate for election to the Legislative Council from the Legislative Assembly. Madhava Rao who did not want him in the Council had rumours circulated that he was to be deported. Members were pressed to vote for others, the date of the election was postponed,[49] but in spite of these actions, as a triumph to the independent and democratic spirit of the Legislative Assembly in Mysore, he was voted in by a majority as one of the two elected members of the Legislative Assembly to the Legislative Council. The other member elected, Mr. Venkataramayya, was also *persona non grata* with the government. As a culmination of the repressive Press Act, both elections were declared void by the use of the Maharaja's prerogative by the government of Mysore.[50] *The Hindu* proclaimed it "an act of barefaced despotism".[51] From this year there was hardly a year which did not bring a protest in the press against the Press Act of Mysore, or a demand for its repeal in the legislature[25].

The story of press repression and press relations with the Travancore Government was, if anything, even more sordid. Even as early as 1907 the *Malayali* had expressed resentment regarding the barring of the press representative an entry to the State Banquet given in honour of the Governor of Madras. Speeches made at this banquet had been made available only as handouts to the press, which it was held, had been sub-edited by the Dewan and his subordinate officials.[53]

Events came to a head during the tenure of P. Rajagopalachari.[54] His appointment as Dewan of Travancore had been welcomed in the papers as he had been rather popular as Dewan of Cochin and much was expected of him when he declared himself as anxious to associate as much of the popular element as possible in the state's administration. Again, the writings of Ramakrishna Pillai, the editor of *Swadeshabhimani* in Travancore in 1910, was typical of an outspoken press of these three states.[55] His criticism was perhaps couched in a more 'offensive language' when imputations were made on 'the moral conduct of the Dewan'.[56] If there had been any basis for the criticism, the wiser action would have been to ignore it, as had been done by Seshadri Iyer and others, subjected to a similar type of vituperation, or, if otherwise, the Dewan could have prosecuted the editor for defamation.[57]

Instead of this he acted in a foolish manner, when, through a proclamation of the Maharaja on 26 September 1910, Ramakrishna Pillai's paper, the *Swadeshabhimani*, (a tri-weekly) was suppressed, the press and its accessories confiscated, and he was arrested and deported.[58]

Thus, while one could appreciate the Mysore Government's action, which was a mere result of pressure exerted by the paramount power, the action of the Dewan, which was an outcome of a personal vendetta, could afford few excuses. That the Dewan took his cue from British Indian environment, is quite evident. In August 1909, Lord Minto had written letters to the Ruling Chiefs where he had indicated his desire to 'concert measures' and prepare a policy to exclude effectually seditious agitation in the states.[59] The Government of India's passing of the Press Act in January 1910[60] seemed to confer a *carte-blanche* by the paramount power to any repression in the state, provided seditious intent could be traced.

Confident that his action would not be interfered with by the paramount power, the Dewan moved against the editor who had the temerity to criticise the Dewan's conduct in his private capacity.[61] That the editor's conduct did not constitute sedition so long as there was nothing said against the government was a minor matter in the Dewan's opinion. However, his action in forcing a private vendetta only served to pitchfork a run of the mill, outspoken newspaper editor to the position of martyr and a freedom fighter and the Dewan earned for himself the odium of all future historians. The treatment meted out to the editor "was always to remain a stigma on the Travancore Sarkar."[62]

The action of the Dewan was severely condemned in the newspapers of the state.[63] Considerable publicity to the arbitrary action of the Dewan was given, when in 1911, Ramakrishna Pillai the deportee himself, brought out in a Malayali pamphlet the 'brief and connected story of how he came to be sent away from Travancore'.[64]

The subsequent actions of the Dewan tended even less towards his popularity. In a bid towards "emasculating"[65] the Sri Moolam Popular Assembly, he reduced the number of members in the Popular Assembly from 100 to 80 by modifying rules which made ineligible the educated and enlightened section of the population[66] for membership to the Assembly. Moreover, the reservation of the right to veto on the election of any member, as well as any subject brought forward for discussion in the Assembly on pleas of public interest,[67] reduced the proceedings of the subsequent Assemblies to a mere farce. In 1914 the Dewan made ample use of his right of veto of any member to the Assembly and Legislative Council when he ordered the exclusion of entry to the editor of the *Peoples Weekly* first to the Legislative Council and later to the Sri Moolam Popular Assembly. The *Sathianadam* pointed out that to deny him this right was nothing short of an insult to the people.[68]

The Dewan's despotic ambitions were displayed further when he sought to introduce an Official Secrets Regulation in Travancore in 1911. Even as early as 1907 the government had apprehended a clerk of the Hajur Office, passing information to Madras papers, for which offence he had not only been transferred from that office but required to furnish a security as guarantee of further good behaviour.[69] With the growing criticism against him, the Dewan sought permission from the Madras Government to pass this Regulation. He was refused permission as the Regulation envisaged was far more drastic and stringent than the law in force in British India, and on the ground that this draft legislation which tended to take from jurisdiction of the courts matters which were well within their cognisance was likely to diminish the prestige of the courts.[70] The Dewan, on his part, though maintaining that it was not advisable to give to the court's jurisdiction to determine what were matters of state, nevertheless, agreed to drop the proposed legislation.[71] In this he acknowledged that the suppression of the press had made unnecessary such a legislation.

Thus, while in Mysore the Resident's action in forcing the government into a Press Act served to gag a vociferous and inconvenient press in its criticisms against the foreign Dewans, in Travancore, the political climate of British India provided an excuse for the Dewan to take stern measures.[72] The movement which had been brought to a standstill by these Press Acts, was brought to an end in the period following, by a change in the paramount power's policy. In 1912 Lord Hardinge advised the princes, in a speech at Indore, to rely on their own subjects, to give them responsibility and enlist their sympathy in the work of administration.[73] The appointment of a native, Brahmin Dewan in Mysore in Visvesvaraya (1912-1918), of a high caste native in Cochin in Marar (1912-1913) and of a Malayali from Malabar in Travancore in Krishnan Nair (1915-1919) put an end to the anti-foreign Dewan movement. The appointment of high caste Hindus in these states as Dewans now deflected the emphasis on to the parallel stream of the social movement, to which we would now have to turn.

The Brahmin-Non-Brahmin Confrontation in Mysore

The social movement in these states was simultaneous with the foreign Dewan movement and was affected closely by this movement, as the foreign Dewan movement was mainly conducted by the high caste Hindus from within the state.

This confrontation resulted in Mysore in the Madrasi

Brahmin as the head of administration as Dewan, championing the cause of the non-Brahmins against those of the educated and vociferous Brahmins. Thus, the early legislature, though it showed a retrograde facet of Brahmin character in their vociferous demand for caste (Brahmins) compounders in government hospitals (as the high caste Hindus felt a 'repugnance' to take medicines prepared by compounders of lower castes)[74] and for separate third class compartments (as those provided for European and Eurasian passengers),[75] these demands were, however, not upheld by the administration. Again, in 1897, when it was proposed to give preference to Mysoreans in appointment to government posts, Seshadri Iyer, as early as 1892, recorded in a minute the necessity of maintaining a proper proportion of all castes in the services. In this, he took particular care to emphasise that the Brahmin community was already well represented.[76] In turn, when the 1890s saw a vociferous group of Brahmins in the legislature constituting themselves into a Standing Committee,[77] the non-Brahmin elements in the legislature came to the rescue of the government. In this, the opposition of the 'Standing Committee' to the government, even though not entirely motivated by personal animosity to the foreign Dewan but quite often by a genuine desire towards reform, met with opposition from the non-Brahmin, non-English speaking section of the Assembly, which was in a majority. Thus, even the salutary measures proposed in 1888 and 1893 by members representing the Bangalore Rate Payers' Association, for the principle of election in the municipalities and the selection of an Executive Council, (to be elected by the Representative Assembly) met t e same fate at the hands of the non-Brahmin community in the Assembly. They made a counter proposal that the privileges of the educated members be withdrawn and property be made the basis of franchise.[78] It was in such a situation when the Standing Committee, meeting with opposition to even its salutary demands, which in ordinary course should have met with approval from a representative chamber, took up an attitude of confrontation. This role made the Maharaja apprehend that the Standing Committee would ultimately make attempts to curtail his own authority. Thus, the course of the history of the Legislative Assembly in its early days amply proved that if the government held its own against the Standing Committee, it was only with the help of the non-Brahmins in the legislature.[79]

It was during the period of a native Brahmin Dewan in P.N. Krishnamurthy in 1902, that the non-Brahmins fearing a danger to their position now that the support to their position by the foreign Dewans was withdrawn, came into a direct confrontation with the Brahmins. Taking a leaf from the agitational methods of the Brahmin movement itself, *Vrittanta Chintamani* pleading for a due admixture of castes in official patronage, complained that almost all the important officials (Brahmins) were animated by the sole desire, to provide their kith and kin with appointments.[80]

This movement, while it lay dormant during the period of foreign Dewans which followed,[81] gathered momentum and came to a climax again during the period of the native Brahmin Dewan, Visvesvaraya, (1912-1918). Soon after his appointment as Dewan, in December 1912 'a prayer of several associations' urged the Dewan to employ the backward class in proper numbers in public service.[82] The formation of the South Indian Liberal Federation, a non-Brahmin Association in Madras in November 1916, brought this movement of Mysore within the purview of a wider non-Brahmin movement. The Praja Mitra Mandali, claiming to be the 'step sister' (*sic*) of the non-Brahmin organisation of Madras in Mysore, in its Manifesto issued in 1917,[83] reverting to its ever-recurring grievance—the monopoly of Brahmins in the civil service—charged that the community of less than 2 lakhs in a population of 57 lakhs, virtually monopolised the facilities granted for education and the privileges of the public services. It complained that while the agricultural revenue of Rs. 105 lakhs was paid 'almost by classes other than Brahmins', the excise revenue of 60 lakhs by labourers, the system had created two classes of people—those who paid and those who enjoyed. In this, the former unable to escape the grip of the officials, tied to the land as he was, had been made the victim to sustain the other.

As its special plea was for separate communal representation, it was natural that it directed its barrage against the monopoly of the Brahmins even in the legislatures. It asserted that while in the Legislative Council no non-Brahmin had found a footing till 1914, even in the Legislative Assembly, which had originally been called the Association of Representative Ryots and Merchants was now representative only of the Brahmin interests. Complaining against the heavily loaded franchise in the cities, as against the rural parts, it made clear its stand, that in the existing circumstances it could not encourage reforms unless the classes and communities that had stood by the government were granted the right to speak with their own voice. The non-Brahmin community, it took care to explain, was not opposed to responsible government provided it was strictly real and ensured strict communal representation.

In a separate memorandum placed before the Maharaja[84] it demanded that all self-governing councils from the Legislative Council downwards be remodelled so as to secure the principle of communal representation and that government appointments be distributed between the different communities so as to secure a just balance of all interests. To secure the above principle, it even suggested that in case of non-availability of suitable candidates from within the state, outsiders possessing necessary qualifications be brought in to break the existing monopoly.[85]

The non-Brahmins' particular grievance against the Dewan was that he had not published the results of a survey, demanded by a circular in the Legislative Assembly in 1914 into the representation of different communities in the public services with a statement of policy on it. A further interpretation by the Legislative Council in 1917 on the same subject had again been refused.

A series of meetings were held by the Praja Mitra Mandali and other non-Brahmin organisations throughout Mysore in 1917.[86] These meetings projected the situation where the "so-called"[87] representative bodies, the Representative Assembly, the local Boards, Municipal Councils and Legislative Councils were monopolised by the Brahmin elements and were likely to be vested with larger powers, with powers of even raising a special cess, loans, etc., as one of danger to the non-Brahmin community. It feared that unless a protest was made they were likely to be "completely effectively shut . . . from all participation of power not only for the present, but also for the future".

The immediate victim of this non-Brahmin agitation was

Visvesvaraya, the Dewan. In this agitation between the non-Brahmins and Brahmins what has to be taken note of is the fact that the Maharaja himself as a Sudra[88] was likely to be sympathetic to the non-Brahmin position. Even though Visvesvaraya had taken steps to rectify the non-Brahmin position in civil service by constituting an enquiry committee under Leslie Miller,[89] to go into their grievances, his confrontation with the Maharaja, forced on his resignation. The Maharaja, taking advantage of the non-Brahmin charges against the Dewan—of converting Mysore into a "Brahmin colony",[90] sought to break the hitherto held dominant position of the Dewans in Mysore administration.[91] The Maharaja appointed his younger brother as a member of the Executive Council, no doubt as a representative of the Sudras in 1913,[92] and later promoted him as the President of the Executive Council with double votes and precedence over the Dewan.[93] Thus Visvesvaraya's resignation was due not only to the projection of non-Brahmin-Brahmin confrontation, but as Visvesvaraya himself attributed, due to the system under which the states worked.[94]

From this time one objective of the non-Brahmins was achieved in that no native Brahmin Dewan was appointed in the period subsequent. In its immediate impact it isolated the reforms movement as one promoting the powers of a small clique.

Communalism in Travancore-Cochin

The habit of correlating the number of positions held by each section of the populace in government service with sectional and religious discrimination had made its appearance in Travancore-Cochin even earlier than in Mysore. As early as 1882, the *Kerala Mitram* pointed out that there were only twenty-five Syrian Christians among 1424 public servants drawing salaries of Rs. 10 and above in Travancore which was a proof of 'Sarkar's apathy' towards the community.[95] The grievance was all the more genuine as pointed out by its editorial, when one-fourth of the money lying in the coffers of the state was contributed by the Syrian subjects.

The publication of the Malayali Memorial in 1891, while highlighting the Malayali grievance against the foreign Brahmin brought from outside the state, internally showed up more vividly the greater injustice done to the other two communities, the Syrian Christian and the Ezhava than to the Nair. While 61 appointments in government service, with salaries of Rs. 50 and above, were held by the Nairs, the Ezhava community had none, while the Syrian Christian community found a mere 16 appointments. From this stemmed the Ezhava agitation against social, and more importantly, the political discrimination practised by the government which excluded the Ezhavas from government service and from government schools.[96] However, the Ezhava Memorial's petition of 1895, on these grievances to the government, had little effect on the Travancore administration.[97]

The Syrian Christians who suffered a similar lack of government patronage joined their forces with the Ezhavas and from this time started the practice of these two communities supporting each other. Thus the *Nazrani Dipika*, managed by the Syrian National Union Association, usually sponsored the Ezhava cause. In 1900, a leader pointing to the Travancore Government's injustice of keeping away the Ezhava community from government appointments, advised the government that selection be made from all the different castes of the country in filling up appointments in government service.[98] Likewise, the *Manorama* managed by Verghese Mappillai, a Syrian Christian, advised the Ezhavas that the agitation now begun for the removal of their disabilities should not be allowed to rest in its present stage but be carried to the notice of the Government of India and Lord Curzon who was sure to do justice in the matter.[99]

The Ezhava-Christian agitation in the newspapers continued throughout this period. In 1905 the Ezhavas of Travancore forged their new organisation the S.N.D.P. Yogam. Even as early as 1884 the *Kerala Mitram* in a serial had advocated the formation of such associations in Cochin for the social advancement of the people and for the promoting of their education.[100]

The formation of the Ezhava Association in Travancore by Dr. Palpu[101] was not taken by the Nair community quietly. In

May 1905 there was a riot between the Ezhavas and Nairs at Karthikapally.[102] The Ezhavas of Quilon submitted a memorial to the Maharaja complaining of the 'narrow-minded and envious members' of the Nair community who had set fire to the office of *Sujana Nandini*, the newspaper sponsored by the Ezhavas.[103] Demanding a commission of enquiry, it charged that these atrocities were committed with the sanction and support of some of the Nair officials.

Thus from the earliest stages of Travancore's Socio-Political movement, we see the clear demarcation of communal interests and alignment—the Syrian Christian-Ezhava combination against the Nairs and the Nair officials.[104]

In Cochin, though government education and appointments were extended to all its subjects irrespective of caste and was often held up as an example to Travancore Government,[105] it was not free of complaints.[106] The *Kerala Sanchari*, in a leader, reported that at Kattur in the Cochin state, a Tiya was beaten to death by some Nairs as he did not move aside from the public road on the approach of these Nairs. The Leader while deprecating such incidents in the government of a civilised state hoped that the Dewan would take measures to mete out condign punishment.[107]

It was this social disability which projected the movement in Cochin into relief; following a vow taken by a few youths in 1916 in Trippunithura, not to make way on the public roads for the higher castes, a disturbance ensued in August 1918 resulting in a police action of closing certain roads to that community.[108] The Ezhavas, sensing a political motivation in the government's action and fearing that the freedom they had enjoyed hitherto in respect of using public high roads was now being threatened, rose in rebellion. As a result of this agitation, though the authorities withdrew their ban on these roads to the Ezhava community, there was much resentment against it as it neither insisted on such observance nor prohibited it.[109] However, with the change in the Dewanship and a public announcement by the new Dewan, Mr. Vijayaraghavachari, in his presidential address to a Pulaya Congress at Trippunithura that in future, they should consider themselves free from the "trammel of *Theental*"[110] and use all thoroughfares freely as any others, the ruffled feelings of the depressed classes was to a certain extent assuaged.

Thus, though the Cochin Ezhavas and Christians in comparison with those of Travancore suffered no tangible political descrimination, yet their social disabilities provided a bond and made them sympathetic to the movement in Travancore. In fact, a very noticeable and prominent feature is the sympathy exhibited in these two states for each other, based mainly on communal affiliations which transcended state borders and state politics. Thus, we find the newspapers of both states commenting on each others' grievances.

It is only in the background of this Ezhava agitation for equal civil rights in Travancore-Cochin that we can understand the subsequent Indian National Congress movement in these states. It was to be affected much by the caste groupism that had crystallised itself during this period. As the *Keralabhimani* at this period pointed out "the disturbed state of the political atmosphere (presented) . . . two most disturbing factors: (1) the wrong suffered by 26 lakhs of people, Christians, Ezhavas, etc. . . on account of the denial to them of equal rights of citizenship with other classes, and (2) the question of securing a government responsible to the people . . . it would be absolutely vain to try to establish the latter without first securing the former".[111] The line taken was thus analogous to that of the Praja Mitra Mandali in Mysore with this difference; while the Ezhavas could find no representation in the Legislature, barred as they were by possessing no franchise, the Praja Mitra Mandali made demand for concessions due to its economic and social weaknesses. Again, while the Praja Mitra Mandali's position was supported by the government, it was not so in Travancore, in contrast to which, the Cochin Ezhavas found considerable support from the government. Thus, Travancore was to provide a possible ground for Indian National Congress' entry on a 'so-called' non-political issue as that of a social cause, which was however not without its political implications.

On analysing the course of the agitation in both its political anti-"foreign Brahmins" form, and the socio-political Brahmin-non-Brahmin[112] one, what is obvious is the universal character of the complaint and the common course of the agitation in these three states. The other character which becomes noticeable is that both the agitators as well as the administrators seemed to take their cue from British India. There is no denying that the grievance against foreign Brahmins was indigenous; but their obsession with the numbers and proportions of posts held by natives in *Government Service* was but a counter part of the Indian National Congress' agitation for a larger admission of Indians in the higher ranks of the civil service.

The administrators on their part followed the same course, a commonness in policy and method, to counteract the movement. This may have been because, we often find the same Dewans, officiating as such, successively in two of these three states.[113] While this policy after 1908 sought to gag the press in order to maintain their position, it was however the social conditions of a state of confrontation between communities within the states which really brought an end to the foreign Dewan movement. It was in this context of the relationship among the three influential communities—Christians, Brahmins and Nairs—in the states of Travancore and Cochin it was felt that it was not advisable to appoint a local man as Dewan of the State.[114] In Mysore, the period following saw a non-Brahmin Dewan in Kantaraj Urs (1918-1921) and later an outsider in A.R. Banerjee as Dewan (1922-28). Even on the resumption of appointment of a native, the search for one such lay outside these conflicting communities, ending with the appointment of Mirza Ismail in Mysore (1928-1940).

The Indian National Congress in the States up to 1921[115]—Mysore's Involvement with the Congress

While Travancore and Cochin's relationship with the Indian National Congress started mainly after the formal entry of the Indian National Congress in 1921, Mysore's involvement with it can be traced from its earliest days.

Mysore's earliest contact with the Indian National Congress is worth recording in detail, for it brought out not only the Maharaja's and the state's sympathy with it, but was also illustrative of the earliest reaction of the Indian National Congress to this overture, and the paramount power's attitude to this flirting.

The first inkling of its contacts with the Indian National

Congress was made known to the Foreign and Political Department of the Government of India, only through a newspaper item in the *Indian Mirror* in 1887. The newspaper reported that the 'delegates' from the Indian National Congress of Mysore, while participating in discussions of the Congress on questions affecting British India, were also to 'direct the attention' of the Congress to the question of the increased subsidy of the Mysore state and the salt and opium monopolies. Thus for the first time the personal grievance of the Native Princes was sought to be brought to the notice of this public forum. *The Indian Mirror* while remarking on the deep and indisoluble connection between the prince and the people of India[116] hoped that it would evoke sympathy from the people of British India. The Government of India was perturbed not only by the news but the fact that the Maharaja of Mysore had contributed as much as Rs. 1000[117] towards the expenses of the 'so-called National Congress'.[118]

The three delegates who had attended the Congress were not the delegates from the Indian National Congress of Mysore, as there was as yet no such organisation nor were the delegates sent by the Mysore Government. They were delegates attending it in their individual capacity or as delegates of indigenous organisations. Mr. Ramachandra Iyer was a Judge of the High Court of Mysore who attended the Congress as a visitor. Mr. V. Raghavacharlu, a *jagirdar*, represented the Rate Payers' Association and was a member of the Representative Assembly of Mysore, Mr. Srinivasa Iyengar, a Sub-Judge of Mysore was also "appointed a delegate".[119] (It is not clear as to whether he was appointed a delegate by the Rate Payers' Association or by some other agency).

However, as the letter from the Resident pointed out, the delegates from Mysore did not speak. Before attending the Congress the delegates had sought the Indian National Congress' permission to speak on the subject of Mysore problems, particularly the enhanced subsidy, but were told in reply that there was no precedent for discussing the grievances of Native States and that the National Congress was concerned only with British India. In the attitude of the Indian National Congress we find the same equivocation as was its characteristic throughout its relationship with the states. While the money presented by the Maharaja towards the Congress fund was accepted by it readily it refused to involve itself with Native States' politics or grievances on the plea that there was no precedent for discussing the grievances of Native States—this at a time when the organisation had hardly existed for two years and was yet to create its own precedents. The pretext was patently flimsy.

On their part, British paramountcy, as pointed out by the Political Officer in its noting to the Political Secretary, would have found it inconvenient indeed if Native Chiefs aired their grievances in this manner.[120]

To avoid this 'inconvenience' Seshadri Iyer, the Dewan, was summoned to Calcutta and the Viceroy took him to task for having subscribed to the funds of the 'National Congress'. The Dewan admitted the facts but "endeavoured to justify them".[121] At this talk the Viceroy warned the Dewan against the princes' taking part in political agitations going on in British India.[122] He pointed out the difference between a great zamindar living in British India,[123] becoming a member of the Congress, and His Highness the Maharaja who was not a zamindar, but a ***Prince in alliance*** with Her Majesty's Government and such interference was 'something incongruous'.[124]

Though warned off by the paramount power and unsupported by the Indian National Congress in her personal problem, Mysore's relation with the Indian National Congress yet persisted. In 1894 P.N. Krishnamurthy, the future Dewan of Mysore, but at that time a Judge of the Chief Court, attended the Indian National Congress session.[125] In 1895, on the death of the Maharaja, for the first time in Congress history, a resolution with reference to the states was made. The condolence resolution moved by Alfred Webb, the then President of the Indian National Congress, remarked on the Maharaja's wisdom, ability and beneficence and on his constitutional reign.[126] Seshadri Iyer, the other architect of Mysore's close relationship with the Indian National Congress also came in for a share of like praise from the Congress, on his death in 1901.[127]

It was, however, the involvement of a new Maharaja in Congress affairs which again caused a flutter in India Office.[128] The Resident on 15 December 1903 came to know (on his assertion, again only through a newspaper report) and rather late at that, that the Maharaja had consented to the opening of the Congress exhibition on 22 December 1903 at Madras and that the Madras Government had expressed no objection to it.[129]

The Viceroy, while irritated that the Maharaja of Mysore should have been permitted to have any connection with an exhibition that was organized by the National Congress, made it clear to the Resident that he should have strongly dissuaded any such step, but now that matters had gone so far, the only possible course was to reduce the importance of the occasion and speech to narrowed possible limits.[130] Thus, the Maharaja was allowed to open the exhibition and gave a speech that was approved by the Resident and contained no reference to the Congress.[131]

As on an earlier occasion, the Dewan and the Maharaja were warned and asked to keep away from this association of 'discontented pleaders, journalists and graduates without employment.'[132] Though the paramount power was unable to stop the Maharaja from opening the Congress Exhibition, it nevertheless was well in time to see that the delegates from Mysore, Justice Ramachandra Iyer (the delegate who had attended Congress sessions from 1887), Justice Rangaswami Iyengar and V.P. Madhava Rao (the future Dewan of Mysore) who had purchased platform tickets at Rs. 50 each, were prohibited by the Mysore Government from attending the Congress.[133]

Swadeshi Movement in Mysore

From now on the Mysore Government's dealings with the Congress were not to be so direct. But even now the delegates who attended the Congress session in 1905, as pointed out by the leader in *Nadegannadi*, attended the Congress session not because they had any grievance against the Maharaja, the state, or its government, but as complainants against the Resident.[134] It was held that the Resident in interfering with the administration always tried to sacrifice the interest of the state for the benefit of his own community. To remove the consequent discontent among the people it was necessary, it claimed, to represent their grievances.[135] The *Swadeshi* reiterated the same point when it observed that the condition of the Native States was very unsatisfactory on account of the unwholesome restraint exercised by the British Political Officers, who, in fulfilling the functions of a sort of police over these states left little liberty either to their rulers or their subjects.[136]

The post-1907 period saw the involvement of the Mysoreans with the Congress in yet another plane with the 'infiltration' of the *Swadeshi* propaganda in the Native States. In this it was the Resident who complained against the growing tendency of the student population participating in political agitation. The Editor of the *Mysore Herald* was specially marked for the Resident's disapproval, as he had acquired through his paper a position of influence. He was charged of collecting subscriptions for the National Fund, of inciting the students against foreign goods and of organising public rejoicings in honour of the release of Bipin Chandra Pal.[137]

Even Travancore was not left undisturbed by the *Swadeshi* movement. *Kerala Patrika* a pro-government paper attributed a local riot at Trivandrum to the *Swadeshi* lectures that were being delivered.[138]

The result of these activities was seen in the imposition of a Press Law in Mysore State.[139] Further, the paramount power while warning the Maharajas from encouraging sedition in their states, sought to entice the princes as collaborators to 'concert measures' to counteract it. The Viceroy thus cautioned the Maharajas against doctrines which were subversive of internal peace and good government, and emphasized the interests of the Government of India and of the princes in India as identical.[140] As such, he pointed out, it was 'appropriate' that they exchange opinions on the subject with a view to mutual cooperation against a common danger. Thus by emphasizing the attainment of peace and good government as a common goal, British policy sought the collaboration of the princes to put down 'sedition' which was not so much against the princes but endangered the imperial interests of the paramount power.

The Maharaja of Mysore, in an assurance to the Viceroy, declared his resolve to deal promptly and vigorously with anarchy and sedition within the borders of his state. He asserted that no preachers of 'seditious doctrine' would be permitted to 'poison' the minds of his subjects. He promised to repress sedition by either prosecuting them under the criminal law or by expelling them from his dominions; as for seditious writings in the newspapers, he boasted, he had armed himself by means of the Mysore Newspaper Regulation with ample and unrestricted powers. He dismissed the whole agitation as an ebullition on the part of the local press which was the handiwork of a very small irresponsible section of the educated classes.[141] An opportunity soon presented itself to put his loyal professions to the test and to 'out Herod, Herod'!

In August 1911 a series of lectures by V.S. Srinivasa Sastri was organised by the Progressive Union of Bangalore. Two lectures had already taken place, when the third lecture which was due, to be presided over by no less a person than the ex-Dewan of Mysore, V.P. Madhava Rao, was banned by the Mysore Durbar.[142] The innocuous topic—The Hindu Marriage Reforms, on which V.S. Srinivasa Sastri had given his lectures—was as such nothing seditious and was 'vouched' for by V.P. Madhava Rao and Mr. Srinivasa Rao.[143] Moreover, the lectures of V.S. Srinivasa Sastri, belonging as he did to the liberal school of Gokhale was allowed in British India and thus there seemed to be no reason why his lectures should have been banned in Mysore.

What was more surprising than the ban itself was the persecution launched on the sponsors of the meeting. K. Ramachandra Rao, Headmaster of the London Mission School and President of the Progressive Union under whose auspices V.S. Srinivasa Sastri's lecture had been arranged, was asked to resign and K. Srinivasa Rao the Deputy Chief Engineer who was to have presided at the students' convocation warned.[144]

V.S. Srinivasa Sastri who felt that an important right of the people for holding public meetings had been interfered with, approached the Dewan and the Resident for an explanation which however was "not vouchsafed".[145]

The *Daily Post* surmised that there were several causes for the action not the least of them being the singing of *Bande Mataram* at the end of the meeting.[146] Such a severe repression on so innocuous a happening seemed altogether out of character of the Mysore Durbar. As such one would not be far wrong in surmising that the actions were due no doubt to the pressures of the pasamount power and of happenings in Baroda.[147]

In this, the discovery of a secret press in Baroda in August 1911,[148] from which 'seditious literature' was suspected of being printed, and the Gaekwad's personal involvement with the

Congress' extremist movement, seems to have been the main factor.

Thus the Maharaja of Mysore, whose involvement with the Indian National Congress was as such suspect in the eyes of the paramount power, could act in no other manner than as he did, in order to prove his *bona fides*, especially so as it came simultaneous with the excitement of the discoveries at Baroda.

The attitude of Mysore state administration from this time to 1921, was to keep scrupulously away from all activities of the Congress. Thus during the Home Rule Movement when the Doddanna School at Bangalore was placed under the Theosophical Trust, the educational authorities of the state refused to give recognition to it until the Trust authorities assured them that neither the teachers nor the students would associate themselves with political matters or the Home Rule Movement.[149]

The Indian National Congress on its part, during these years, held itself aloof from involvement in the politics of the Indian states; they insisted that the states and British India could not move together and that any attempt at their union would be prejudicial to the interests of both. Their reasons for taking this view were mainly on the count that: (i) by "discussing the affairs of the state on an open platform they might often have to expose the weak and vulnerable points of *Swaraj* or Indian managed government, and (ii) that as most of the states were under the unavoidable influence of the Foreign Office, it could be disagreeable to the Government of India to see the states dragged out of their personal seclusion and meddled with by outsiders"[150] and lead to feel the heavy hand on the states by the Government of India.

Thus by the first argument they made clear their unwillingness to be partisan to the responsible government[151] agitation in the states and thus involve themselves in more than one battle front, in needlessly antagonising the princes, which they euphemistically termed the exposing of 'the weak and vulnerable points of *Swaraj*'.

The second alternative of befriending the princes was tried, as has been narrated, during the early years of the century and found untenable. In a system of government where the paramount power could call its own tune, and the princes, with much to lose and in a position rather vulnerable, events could have taken no other course.

However, by expressing themselves in their first contention in an equivocal manner the Congress only exposed the dichotomy in their thinking. As *The Karnataka* observed, it was a mistake to "think that the cause of the *Swaraj* would suffer even if all the Native States could be proved to be the nurseries of misgovernment, for *Swaraj* did not mean the substitution of an Indian bureaucracy for the existing one. Such *Swaraj*, as was the ideal of the Congress, was not to be seen in its full form in any of the states.... .The fight was chiefly for popular liberty and not merely for gaining a few more appointments for Indians."[152] Was *Swaraj* to mean just the mere driving away of the British from India or was it the establishment of a democratic responsible government? The states' people had no doubt as to what they meant and what they wanted. While they were ready to partake in the first objective of driving away the English, on the Congress programme, nevertheless, their ultimate aim was the establishment of a responsible government. The subsequent years of Congress intervention in the states was to show how these two aims were impossible to reconcile.

This brings us to the consideration of one important aspect. Why did the Congress, having fully realised the futility of its intervention/involvement in the states, enter the states arena in 1921? Was it due to the mere demand of these states people for such an involvement or was it due to other circumstances?

The answer to the above question lay in British diplomacy and policy during these years, which manoeuvred to rope in the princes as collaborators of British imperialism, and sought to create a 'third force' of the princes as a counterpoise to counteract Indian nationalism. In order to do this it even went to the length of creating an unbridgeable border between the princely states and the neighbouring provinces with which it had till then close contacts, and even been controlled by. This policy worked at three levels. Firstly, it worked in the creation of a Princes' Chamber. Secondly, in propounding a policy of reciprocal non-intervention, which however, remained a mere canard, as far as these rights on the side of the princes as against British paramountcy, was concerned. Thirdly, it involved the idea of direct relationship of the states with the paramount power and not through the neighbouring provinces and the

Governor as had been done hitherto. While the first two policies saw the inauguration in this period the third came into action only after 1919. As all these manoeuvres of British policy go as genre I have included it in this section though it belongs to a later period.

Princes as a Counterpoise to Indian Nationalism—The Chamber of Princes

It was with the aim of harnessing princely sympathies to counteract the forces of nationalism that was increasingly becoming apparent during the 1870s in British India, that Lytton utilised the occasion of the Queen's assumption of the title of Empress, to convene a Durbar in January 1877. His subsequent proposal for an Indian Privy Council of Native Rulers was, however, vetoed by the India Council. From this time to the establishment of such a Council the idea was kept alive by several advocates both from the princes as well as the British administrators. The idea was again advocated by the Maharaja of Baroda in 1895. Curzon's interest, according to the Aga Khan, centred in bringing the princes together to consider questions affecting themselves only.[153]

It was Lord Minto who realised shrewdly the potentialities of a Council of Princes as a possible counterpoise to Congress aims.[154] To serve the British purpose as such, the Council required careful handling. To ban this body of princes from any potential mischief, the scope and powers of this Council was to be carefully thought out, so as to obtain different ideas from those of the Congress.[155]

Morley was nearly successful in pulling the council of notables 'out of the cauldron', in the shape the Viceroy desired—as an august and decorative adjunct to the Viceroy, fifty or so in number, to be 'named' by him, to meet once or twice a year at times to be fixed by him and to exchange views with him and with one another on any matter that the Viceroy thought fit or apt at the time.[156]

But in this, the need to be quite sure of the line the princes would run it on,[157] especially in face of the Gaekwad's and Mysore's involvement with the Congress[158] stayed the British administrators' hands.

The first careful experiment was conducted in 1913 when selected princes were invited to Delhi, to discuss proposals for a Chief's College. The conference was a success and met with enthusiastic requests from the princes for a repetition of such conferences.

However, even though the British administrators realised the value of such a chamber "as a great conservative force,"[159] "a great standby . . . in case of any formidable internal troubles in India," and as a "valuable conterpoise to the pseudo-democratic movement,"[160] their constant nagging suspicions as to their ability to fashion this chamber to their requirements,[161] made them postpone the issue till their position was ensured. Thus it was that these administrators had to emphasize constantly the reciprocity involved in their relationship. The Viceroy, in 1916 while answering the chiefs on their demand for such a conference made it clear that while he had no desire to infringe on their position as ruling princes and chiefs, or to interfere in their domestic concerns, they on their part could not be desirous of intervening in the domestic affairs of British India.[162] It was this fear in the British administrators' mind which made Chamberlain await a more opportune moment.[163]

The proposal was again mooted in 1917 when Bikaner, through his special charm supplemented by a timely and munificent birthday present to the King of 2½ lakhs to be disposed of by him for war purposes, had gained the royal favour[164] and consequently a selection to the Imperial War Conference.[165] However, Bikaner by his improvident action in coupling his demand for a Council of Princes with other demands for British India,[166] excited afresh the fears of British administrators of the princes in "their tendency to meddle with the affairs of British India and when collected at Simla to become the tools of the opposition".[167]

Thus the meeting of the princes in November 1917 saw Montagu carefully outline his idea on a Princes' Chamber. He advocated: (1) a Council of Princes—Viceroy suggesting items for the agenda; (2) the Council to sit with the Upper Chamber at invitation of Viceroy to discuss imperial questions, and (3) an advisory Council of four Princes associated with Political Secretary to advise Viceroy on matters concerning the states.[168]

An outline constitution was drafted by the four-men committee of the Princes and submitted for further discussion and opinion in January 1918, to "a heterogeneous group of public figures of the Indian sub-continent",[169] consisting of 10 Indian politicians and 11 state ministers. The princes' efforts, at seeking a wide accord to their Chamber roused again the apprehensions of the British administrators.

The Policy of Non-Interference

Thus one notices that at every turn of the negotiations in conjuring up a Princes' Chamber, there was a persistent fear in the minds of British administrators of a possible collaboration of the princes with the nationalists. It was this fear which on the obverse side of the creation of the Chamber of Princes, involved the propounding of a non-intervention/non-interference policy.

The proposition of non-interference in Indian states was made first by Morley in 1907, when in his budget speech he promised to use his best endeavours to make the Native States in India independent in matters of administration.[170] The policy of non-interference was never clearly defined and hardly ever understood. The early years saw an interpretation of it, entirely different from the interpretation given in subsequent years by the Rajput princes. The advanced states understood it in a different sense from what the Maharajas from northern states interpreted it. As *The Hindu* pointed out, the principle was disregarded even soon after its enunciation when it came in the way of British interests. The retirement of Dewan Gopalachari of Travancore in 1907 was due to his refusal to consent to the Resident's demands, pressed on behalf of the Mundakayam Rubber Planters' Association—British entrepreneurial interests—to build a road to the plantation at government expense.[171] *The Nadegannadi* a Mysore newspaper, looked at these professions in mockery, especially so as even the selection of the Dewan was in the hands of the British administrators. As it taunted, the Maharajas had to entertain the very person nominated by the Madras Government which was indeed a procedure, hardly in consonance with Morley's principle of non-interference.[172] *The Vrittanta Chintamani*[173] also discussed the same fallacy in the non-interference policy. Chamberlain in his talks with Bikaner, in order to guard against a possible collaboration of the princes with the nationalists used it to make it clear, that inasmuch as the princes had expressed their intense dislike for any increased interference by the Government of India in the affairs of the states, non-interference was to be reciprocal.[174] This was interpreted by the Rajput quartette as a *carte blanche* for any type of abuse by the princes in their administration. In later years this demand crystalised itself into a demand for the codification of treaties so as to establish their relationship with the paramount power on clearly indicated lines with areas of interference clearly delineated. But the British administrators' accent on non-interference policy clearly lay not so much in indicating its limitations on paramountcy as much as on giving the princes a protection from criticism in British India in the press and platform. Thus interpreted, it meant that even though they themselves realised the abuses in the native states which needed remedy, they would suppress these criticisms made by 'agitators' from British India showing up princely extravagances, oppression or injustice.[175] Thus the main corrollary of the non-intervention policy was the Press Act of India which emphasized the collaboration of the princes with the British administration in its provisions for the states' protection against disaffection.[176]

Transfer of State's Relationship to the Central Government

Closely allied to the creation of the Chamber of Princes and the non-intervention policy was a third innovation in British policy of transferring the relationship of the states with the provincial governments to that of Government of India. This involved the establishment of a Political Department by the Government of India, to deal directly with the states. The motive for such a measure can again be traced to Chamberlain's momentous talks with Bikaner, following Bikaner's submission of his memorandum of 18 April 1917. Here he explained to Bikaner that no possible Government of India could be "so tender" of the rights of princes as was the present administration; that if and when the wide reforms which he had advocated took place in the Government of India, he would find that the government as it became more popular would also become more interfering, and that if the goal of self-government were reached, it was likely that such a government would claim a right of control and interference in the states, far in excess of anything ever exercised or contemplated under the present system.[177]

The imminence of reforms in British India, leading to a democratisation of the provinces in the following period, projected the problem into greater relief. The problem was not only one of interference—the danger of leaving native states to the mercy of a government's pledged to democratic progress,[178] but also one of tempering and filtering the flow of the new wine of democracy into the states.

Thus when Montagu came over to India in November 1917, along with his proposals for the constitution of the Chamber of Princes, he brought with him a new proposition of direct relationship and the separation of the Political Office from that of the Foreign Office. In the January 1919 meeting of the princes' conference, the princes, prompted no doubt by the Secretary of State's interest in it, supported this measure.[179]

Mysore who had always had direct relationship with the Imperial Government knowing that the proposal was to be driven through by the Rajput quartette in whose favour it was, did not attend the conference.[180] Nor was the proposal, for that matter, in its initial stages received with much enthusiasm by the Viceroy or his Executive Council, as they were frightened by the prospect of the very large increase of work it would throw up.[181] Moreover, as pertinently pointed out by George Lloyd, it could solve no problem as ultimately how was British paramountcy going to insulate the princes when transference to a popular government took place at the centre.[182]

Loundes, a Political Officer, had an ingenious suggestion for it.[183] He suggested the separation of the work in connection with the states into two portions. That which related to British India was to be left, as it was in theory at the present moment, under the Governor-General in Council. The work which had to do with the internal affairs of the states was to be separated and placed directly under the Governor-General as Viceroy. This was the ingenious method adopted in the Butler Committee recommendations[184] which was to provide for a greater degree of insulation between matters of the states and matters of British India on the eve of a British India becoming democratic at the centre with the ushering in of the 1935 Government of India Act.

Thus one can see that the princes' future obsessions with the non-intervention policy and their fears of a democratisation of the government at the provincial level or at the centre, their insistence on safeguards etc., were entirely incited and prompted by the British administrators during this period, and that too, mainly from the 'Home Office'. It was not long before, the Rajput quartette, firmly convinced of the principle of non-intervention and the new theories of their relationship with the Crown took up this cry in the hope not only to eliminate as far as possible any interference by government (especially, if it were of a democratic nuture) with the affairs of the states,[185] but also on a hope that these measures would insulate them from the democratic trends already visible within their states.

George Lloyd, the single opponent of the new policies introduced by the British administration was the only one to realise the dangers inherent in these policies. He warned that if they did not interfere to rectify the maladministration in the states, "agitation against native rule commences both from within and without and the permanence of native state dynasty and system becomes gravely imperilled".[186]

In its immediate impact, neither the creation of the Chamber of Princes, nor the non-intervention policy, nor the transference of government from the purview of the provincial governors to the Government of India made any impact directly or individually on the three states of my study.

The Maharaja of Mysore was very indifferent to the proceedings cf the Chamber and throughout the period of its existence was never a member of it. Cochin was a member of the Chamber for the first year but later pleaded inability to pay its subscription and dropped out of it. Travancore became a member only in the 1940s when to counter the agitation within the states and to consort measures with other princes. C.P. Ramaswami Aiyar led Travancore into the Chamber.

Again these states, as "models" of good administration, hardly concerned themselves with the non-intervention policy. In fact, the states' people believed that the very basis of their stature to being a "model" had been wrought by British intervention and it was hardly conceivable that they would ever countenance such a posture by these princes. In fact, the princes of these three states realising this had nothing to do with this contention and in their grievances with the paramount power concentrated mainly on their economic grievances—which brought about a qualitative difference in their demands of the paramount power, from those of the others.[187]

Again the move of transference of their relationship to the Central Government hardly affected these states. Mysore was, from the beginning, in direct relationship. Travancore and Cochin were brought under the Political Officer who was now called the Agent to the Governor General, Madras State. However as the practice hitherto had been to have a common Resident for Travancore-Cochin, it hardly brought in any change except the change in nomenclature. Ultimately, it hardly mattered whether the Resident reported to the Madras Government or he reported to the Political Secretary of the Government of India.

However, these states were indirectly and collectively affected by these events at the All-India level.

The abuses in the states brought in by the British policy of non-interference caused a closer affinity between the states people and those of British India, who on grounds of humanity, if not of policy, were drawn into a sympathy with them. Though the Congress as an organisation insisted on holding itself aloof from involvement with the states on the responsible government issue, the members of the Congress and other nationalists could not but sympathise with the states people. Thus the sympathies of the British Indian nationalists, and of the sympathies of the states people for each other, served to consolidate them within and a coming together of the states people in general in a central organisation. While within the states it served to consolidate opinion into forming organisations for the redress of the abuses in the states, at the All-India level, it served to organise an All-India States Peoples' Conference to counter and balance the organisation of the princes in its Chamber.

It served another purpose too. The princes nurtured under the illusion of this non-intervention policy and the encouragement given by Montagu to the setting up of a codification committee, demanded that their relationship with the paramount power be defined by some body. A future set of administrators, not so naive in their approach, under the seeming guise of studying this relationship, utilised it towards their own purpose. The committee set up by these administrators in the Butler Committee while guillotining for all time, the policy of non-intervention in their dictum "paramountcy shall remain paramount", gave birth to new theories of the princes' relationship with the paramount power which roused in the minds of the British Indian nationalists a fear that these theories were being propounded towards a creation of 'Ulsters' in India in the states, which in turn gave a new twist to the Congress policy towards the states people.[188]

While this lay in the future, the transference of the states relationship from the democratic control of the provinces to the Government of India roused in the minds of the nationalists, the suspicion of the true nature of British policy. Parallel with the British policy of creating a "third force" in the Princes' Chamber, and of new concepts of their relationship in order to provide an insulation to them from the democratic forces of British India, a new policy was wrought by the Indian National Congress to counter just such a force. For the first time the needs of integration brought home to them the realisation and the necessity of effecting an entry into the states. This they had withheld, even on the most vociferous entreaties of the states people. But Gandhi had to perfect his plan of entry, which he did without offending the princes. It was the invidious demarcations which were sought to be made between the people of the states from their brethren of the contiguous provinces, which ultimately forced the British Indian nationalists to forge a link to emphasise that cultural, linguistic and other affinities bound them with the states peoples. While much propaganda attended the explaining of the Congress entry 'on the constructive programme' no explanations were given as to the real cause of this entry in 1921. The motive lay hidden in an innocuous change—a change in the constitution of the Indian National Congress—which in its affiliation of the states Congress with that of its Pradesh Congress Committees of British India, sought to emphasise the close affinities present in the linguistic provincial areas which the new constitution of the Congress created.

Conclusion

On a summing up, one finds that in these three states an indigenous movement, in an antagonism against foreign Dewans, had become a natural precursor to the movement for responsible government. A parallel movement on the social issue contributed to the alignment of parties within; in Travancore-Cochin it resulted in a Ezhava-Syrian Christian combination against the Nairs, while in Mysore it contributed to a Brahmin-non-Brahmin confrontation. As the antagonism against the foreign Dewans was mainly projected by the high caste Hindus in Mysore, the simultaneous character of these movements had special significance. The government's support to the non-Brahmins, exposed the reforms movement of the Brahmins as that of a small section. Thus, this movement, in order to establish its *bona fides*, had necessarily to seek the support of the Indian National Congress. The Maharajas personal involvement with the Indian National Congress, complicated the issue. More importantly it ushered in a new concept in the evolution of British policy. This policy in the creation of a Chamber of Princes and non-intervention, sought to create a third force to counterpoise the princes against the nationalist forces and to align them with British administration. These manoeuvres and the transference of the states' relationship to a central Political Department in order to keep it isolated from the democratic forces in British India, excited the suspicions of British Indian nationalists. It was the fears of British motives of creating unbridgeable borders between the provinces and the states, which dragged the Indian National Congress into an involvement with the states. This involvement, on a constructive programme, was motivated, mainly, to gain a foothold in the states so as to counter British machinations. It was clearly not to be on the states people's platform of a democratic government, but of union and integration. Thus from the very beginning of its entry in the states, the Indian National Congress' motives being different from that of the states people's pre-occupations on a democratic programme, it was inevitable that it lead to contradictions and to a confrontation. It were these divergences in aims which were responsible for the 'discontinuity' between the local arena and the national arena, remarked on by James Manor (op. cit., p. 188). But his explanation that they were due to Mysore's reputation as 'India's most progressive State' is not adequate, for though it did complicate the issue, the underlying reason for the 'discontinuity' lay in the divergent motives—of a states people on a democratic programme, of British administrators at counterpoising the princes against the British Indian nationalists and of the nationalists in British Indian seeking a Congress entry in the States mainly to counter British machinations and not on a programme to help the states people in their particular movement. It is in the cross currents of differing policies and aims that the states people's movement evolved and it is in this context, viewing it in the light of these divergent motives, that the importance of my study lies.

3

Contradictions to Confrontation

The Movement from 1919 to 1928

Two events in British India proved of great significance to the movement of the states people in this period. The first was the reforms proposal of the Montagu-Chelmsford Reforms of British India. As these talks for reforms were 'in the air' from 1917 itself, we see a parallel demand made in the Indian states for reform, starting almost from this time. The other event was the entry of the Indian National Congress into the states, ushered in, in December 1920, by the resolution of the Indian National Congress at Nagpur. This entry, as already remarked on in the last chapter, was effected not because of the demands of the states people but mainly to counter British policy in counterpoising the princes against the nationalists.

The attitude of princes to reforms within their states was one of extreme caution.[1] British policy—though it publicly acclaimed that measures suitable for British India could not be equally suitable for the very different conditions in Indian states,[2] nevertheless, subjected these princes to some pressure: to put up some form of democratic institutions, the facades which a later Viceroy was to deride.

Thus, inspite of the princes' open avowals not to merge their individual destiny in "arguments on despotism, autocracy, democracy, socialism . . .catchwords ever meaning another form of government called hypocrisy",[3] they were drawn into setting up such institutions in the post 1919 period.[4] These were instituted in sympathy with reforms in British India,[5] and were publicly applauded by the Viceroy.[6]

Cochin, though quite the last among the Indian states to constitute her Legislative Council in 1925, struck out with a boldness. By having an elected majority with wide powers, with rights of interpellation and voting on budget, she warded off much of the agitation that was growing apace in the other two states and confined the movement to the four walls of the legislature and to its social aspects.[7]

Mysore and Travancore had already such bicameral legislative institutions. Thus, the reforms movement took a step further in the reformists' demands of an extension of franchise, scope and powers of these institutions, leading on to their ideal of ministerial responsibility and cabinet form of government, which they were careful to specify as being under the aegis of the Maharaja—the Maharaja playing a role analogous to that of the King of England.

The initial stages of this movement in Mysore—the period of the early years of M. Visvesvaraya's Dewanship (1912-1918)—saw the co-operation of the government in the Assembly with the reformists. In 1913 the number of elected members from the Legislative Assembly to the Legislative Council was increased from 2 to 4 on their demand. The right of discussing the budget and of interpellation was granted to the Legislative Council in 1917.[8]

However, this co-operation was short-lived as a discordant note was introduced by the non-Brahmins. In their confrontation with the Brahmins they projected the growth in the powers of the legislatures as one of danger to the non-Brahmin community unless the imbalances within the legislature between these two communities were rectified by forming separate electorates for the weaker community.[9]

The Government of Mysore, though partial to the non-Brahmins on the communal problem, dismissed their proposal to bring in candidates from outside Mysore so as to maintain a balance between communities. It recommended that in government departments which did not require a high standard and in departments where practical and technical skill could be imparted, candidates from backward communities be taken, on the basis of absolute minimum qualifications specified, instead of on a competitive basis.[10]

It was against this background of non-Brahmin demands that the reformists in the legislature put forward their proposals in 1920, for the right of discussion and vote of the budget in the Legislative Assembly. The resolution pointed out that the retention of this right in the Legislative Council alone was not enough as that Council was only a minor body which could not be said to represent the peoples' voice.[11] This demand was reiterated yet again in the Legislative Assembly in the October session of 1921.[12]

The implications of responsible government were spelt out for the first time in the press in August 1922 in their advocacy of a government by an executive responsible to an elected Assembly, the Maharaja taking the role of a constitutional monarch. However, such 'extreme proposals' which could give to the Brahmin majority inordinate powers was, much to the jubilation of the Resident, not liked by the non-Brahmins.[13]

It was as a concession to non-Brahmin elements that a redefinition of responsible government attempted. This resolution stipulated that subject to a 'fixed percentage', the resolutions passed by this Assembly be made binding on the Executive, subject of course to the veto of His Highness the Maharaja.[14]

Another proposal demanding rights to vote on taxation, etc., again conceded that it was to be on the agreement of a 'prescribed majority'.[15] These proposals clearly exhibited the fact that the Brahmins in the legislature were not insistent on brute majority as the decisive factor, but were willing to cater to the non-Brahmin minorities' interests and weaker position.

The Dewan, while professing himself in sympathy with the natural aspirations of the people in this matter, dismissed the reformists' demands on the plea that conditions in Mysore were not on all fours with those in British India.[16] Thus, it is not surprising that neither the terms of reference nor the decisions spelt out in the Constitution Committee appointed by the Mysore Government in October 1922, under Brajendranath Seal,[17] could please the reformists. A Conference convened to discuss the question of reforms on 15 November 1922, described the reforms proposed as utterly inadequate and demanded that complete power over finance and legislation be conferred on the Legislative Assembly.[18]

The demands of the reformists for budgetary control was likewise, dismissed by this committee on the plea that specific money grants could not be dealt with by two sets of people's representatives, in two different Houses—perhaps in a contrary way.[19]

On the communal issue, the Seal Committee Report brushing aside the non-Brahmin demand for plural or communal constituencies on the plea that it would be no remedy to plant a minority or minorities perpetually in a stronghold from which they could overthrow or abstruct the will of the majority, suggested other means to rectify their problem. In the absence of universal suffrage, it proposed adjustments of the franchise, to bring about an equitable distribution of interests *vis-a-vis* rural and urban elements. In a solution to the communal problem, it proposed to reserve 35 seats through nomination, to secure protective representation to communities not *qua* communities but only *qua* minorities, to any community, standing in need of it (which was to be decided after election results were known), not by virtue of its being a social segregation group but as likely to be swamped at the polls. In this manner, on the pretext of safeguarding itself from discrimination in favour of or against any particular community, it safeguarded its own position.[20]

It is important to note that the minute of dissent by the non-Brahmin members of the committee emphasized not so much their dissatisfaction at the numbers allotted to the minorities but to the fact that their competency of representation had to depend on the efficiency[21] and on whether the faculty was alive,[22] or a duly registered association. The Brahmin members took care to emphasize their entire agreement with the solution and conceded that if the representation secured through the general electorates was not *adequate* then the best course was to give such minorities representation;[23] for while communal electorates were likely to make the divisions between communities too rigid and perpetuate them,[24] an absolute brushing aside of the communal demand would only aggravate the grievance.

Thus, the Seal Committee Report while it salved the communal tensions, it provided no answer to the aspirations of the reformists. In June 1923, a conference was convened by the reformists to discuss the Seal Committee Report. The meeting condemned the report and resolutions were passed demanding responsible government. These conferences on constitutional reforms were the beginning of the States Peoples' Conferences and are as such, of importance in the framework of constitutional agitation. The first conference of the states peoples held in 1927 enunciated a proposal of responsible government on the lines laid down in these early conferences. They demanded an executive of the government which was to be dependent on the will of the Legislative Assembly.

However, the non-Brahmin elements were not yet ready to join hands with the reformists which isolated their movement as that of a small section of educated, urban elements. In order to rectify its isolation from the masses the reformists movement, observing the success of the untouchable movement in Travancore,[25] tried to enlist the backward communities by espousing their cause. In May 1926 a *satyagraha* movement was organised by the Mysore Congress on behalf of the Kaniyars for securing entry into the temple of Sri Gunja Narasimhaswami temple in Narasipur.[26] The Mysore Government, frightened by the growing popularity of the reformists after the entry of the Indian National Congress in the states,[27] became patently hostile to the movement. It refused permission to Tagadur Ramachandra Rao to bring out a paper on behalf of the Kaniyars called the *Kaniyar Patrika*. Questions were asked in the Legislative Assembly as to why when permission had not been denied to other communities like the Vokkaligas and the Devangas to bring out their own papers, permission for a similar request on behalf of the Kaniyars should now be denied.[28] Questions on temple entry on behalf of Kaniyars found repeated mention in the Legislative Assembly Proceedings of 1928. However, this movement failed mainly because of the lack of any real enthusiasm from the discriminated community itself and because the government in turn espoused the Harijans' cause and stopped it from gaining much ground.

It is only against this background of isolation of the reformists' movement by the activities of the non-Brahmin movement that we can understand the later Congress movement in the state. Lacking any real economic grievance, or a broad base, the reformists' movement for responsible government could find a broader base only when it identified itself with the wider movement based on the ideology of Indian nationalism of British India. This led to its association in later years with the Congress as an organisation and its obsession with the name "Congress" and its use of the Congress flag in all its agitations.[29]

The Constitutional Problem in Travancore

The reform movement carried on mainly by the Nairs in Travancore was agitated, not so much by the measures of reforms, but by the question of agency. Here the problem was whether regulation was to be passed through the existing Legislative Council or whether it should be promulgated by the prerogative of the Maharaja.[30] In 1918 the opinion of S. Srinivasa Iyengar, the Advocate-General, who had till recently been an active Congressite, was taken on this issue. He gave his opinion that while according to sound constitutional theory there was no representative legislature in Travancore, the Maharaja by purporting to part with his legislative powers, subject to specified exceptions, had deliberately established a convention and given an assurance that without the consent of the Legislative Council he would neither over-rule or exercise its power. So he thought it fit that the reforms be carried through the Legislative Council, with, however, expressions of the legal right of the sovereign emphasized.[31]

The Government of India objected to such a course; it felt that its concurrence in such a course would make openings for attacks in the future, on other princes. So it expressed a rather dangerous theory, that as trustees to the heirs and successors of the Maharajas it could not allow the Ruler of an Indian state to think himself competent to divest himself, and incidentally his successors, of their inherited rights. In order to vindicate the sovereign's prerogative publicly, it asked the Maharaja to make the Council 'present a dutiful address' accepting the constitution, making it clear that it had no greater right than those accorded by promulgation.

More important than the reforms granted by the Travancore Government,[32] it becomes necessary to examine the questions that British paramountcy aroused by its interpretations, in terms of future reforms. Did it not mean that the ultimate recognition of a 'responsible government', even if granted by the Maharaja, depended on the Government of India's attitude as 'Trustees' to the Maharaja's heirs and successors? Again, even if the Maharaja did grant such a government, would it not be incumbent on him to do so only after reserving the rights to rescind it at a future date by himself or by his successors? Again, if a right of the Legislature, recognised by the Maharaja and enjoyed by it for so long could be withdrawn, in such a peremptory manner, what was the guarantee that the Legislature, in itself the product of a mere promulgation by the Maharaja, would not be withdrawn by him or his successor? If one were to build up these propositions, one would come to the same conclusion as C.P. Ramaswami Aiyar did, in Shanmugham Chetty-Winterton-Ramaswami Aiyar controversy—that responsible government was incompatible with the conception of the states as they existed in British India—in spite of Winterton's pronouncement to the contrary.[33] Thus, even if such 'responsible government' were brought into being, it was hardly conceivable that they could be anything more than 'carefully camouflaged autocracy', without a guarantee to its continuation except on the whims of the autocracy. It is possible that it was this aspect of the states' position that made Jawaharlal Nehru remark in November 1933, that the State Peoples Conferences had seldom faced the issue directly. The time had come, he asserted, for the people of the Indian states to take up a definite and clear attitude on the subject and work with the rest of India for the realisation of the common goal of full freedom.[34] Did such an assertion mean that the immediate goal of the states people should be getting rid of the 'British raj' in order to realise their ultimate aim of responsible government?

While these questions were left to a later date, in its immediate application the Political Department now issued directives to these states that there was good ground for holding that for some time to come *no* further advance was to be made and that any step calculated to detract from the powers now possessed by the Maharaja was to be countenanced.[35]

In accordance with this directive, in the June session of 1929 the resolution in Mysore Assembly for responsible government was disallowed by the government on the pretext that it was a subject of no practical interest to the government at that moment. However, such an attitude of the state governments only whetted the appetite of the states' people which had already been aggravated further by the reforms in British India. In this, the entry of the Congress into the states in 1921 and the states' participation in the Congress movement served further to strengthen their own movement.

The Indian National Congress Activities in the Native States 1921—1928

As remarked on earlier, it was with its need to find a foothold in the states to counter British schemings at balancing the princes against the nationalists, that the Indian National Congress stepped in with an extension of their organisation into these states, in December 1920-January 1921. The Working Committee resolution passed on 1 January 1921, giving the Indian states people the right of sending their delegates to the Indian National Congress from this year,[36] significantly assigned these states to contiguous Congress provinces based on linguistic affiliations.[37] An illustrative list was given by which Travancore-Cochin were allotted to Kerala Pradesh Congress Committee and Mysore to Karnataka Pradesh Congress Committee. It was also provided in the same resolution that the All-India Congress Committee could, from time to time, assign particular Indian states to particular provinces and a Provincial Congress Committee could, in turn, allot particular Indian states assigned to it by the AICC, to particular districts within its jurisdiction.

It is interesting to note that at the very time the paramount power in its transfer of relationship of the states from the provincial governments, to the Government of India, was trying to delink the close relationship that existed between these Indian states and their adjacent provinces,[38] the Indian National Congress stepped in to forge that very link on a more stronger basis of peoples' sentiments to a contiguous territory and linguistic affiliations. Whether the measure was a mere coincidence or the outcome of an intentional policy was never clear in Mahatma Gandhi's writings or other writings of that period.

However, the very fact that the Congress organisation in the states was to be started as mere affiliated adjuncts of the headquarter organisations in the provinces, makes one suspect that, even though no publicity was given to the fact, the main aim was to link the states with their contiguous area. So in this light the entry of the Indian National Congress in the states was a measure towards integration of the states with India—a recognition of the unity of India at the very time that British policy was trying to demark them on an invidious basis. To safeguard itself from involvement in the states peoples' programme of responsible government, article VIII of the new constitution clearly stipulated that the inclusion of Indian states in the electorate was not to be taken to include any interference by the Congress with the internal affairs of such states.[39] The resolution on responsible government passed by it, calling on the princes to take immediate steps to establish full responsible government in the states, was used merely as a sop to the states people to counter provisions of article VIII. Interpreting this proviso in his article 'The Congress' in *Young India*, Mahatma Gandhi wrote:

> there was dissent when Article eight was reached. It referred to non-interference by the Congress in the internal affairs of the Native States. The Congress would not have passed the proviso if it had meant that it could not even voice the feelings of the people residing in the territories ruled by the princes. Happily the resolution suggesting the advisability of establishing responsible government in their territories enabled me to illustrate to the audience that the proviso did not preclude the Congress from ventilating the grievances and aspirations of the subjects of these states, *whilst it clearly prevented the Congress from taking any executive action in con-*

nection with them; as for instance, holding a hostile demonstration in the Native States against any action of theirs.[40] This stance of his and the reasons for it were well explained in his speeches and writings of 1920, where he even went further in holding that the states' people could not possibly participate in the Congress movement of the provinces. In July 1920, Mahatma Gandhi, referring to the expulsion of sixty students by Junagadh administration, for taking part in the Non-Co-operation movement wrote: "If the Nawab Saheb has taken the step on his own, it is plain that the subjects of Native States are worse off than people under British rule. Our princes are in a sorry plight. They are in the position of subjects themselves, their power and their wealth depend entirely on the British Empire and are safeguarded by it. The people living in dependencies being subjects of subjects are doubly dependents."[41]

The same point was reiterated by him as late as October 1920, when he affirmed his feelings against starting such agitations in the states mainly out of consideration for the awkward condition it might put the princes into.[42] It was this consideration of the princes which, according to the Resident of Mysore writing in August 1920, necessitated a good deal of pressure to be brought to bear on Gandhi to induce him to visit Bangalore on 21 August 1920. Even in his address, Gandhi emphasized this point when he reiterated that he did not consider the states a suitable field for his gospel of non-co-operation because of their subjection to British influence.[43]

The Congress in its new relationship with the states, purposely left vague the policy it was to follow towards them. The Working Committee resolution on 22-23 November 1921 states: "thereafter there was some discussion on the policy of the Congress towards the states and it was the sense of the meeting that it was not desirable at this stage to enunciate any such policy".[44]

This policy of leaving the Indian National Congress policy towards the states vague and un-enunciated led to much confusion in later years. However, what was obvious was that the states' peoples were, from now on, to be included as delegates to the AICC, and secondly, the Congress could express its sympathies with the states peoples' aspirations but could take no part in its politics or agitations. Thus in its active phase, it could confine itself mainly to constructive programme of the Congress such as collection of funds for Congress, khadi, social uplift and Harijan work and temperance programme.

The entrance of the Indian National Congress in these three states and their course in the first few years, provide three interesting case studies of their involvement in Congress-state politics and the impracticability of such involvement.

Khilafat Repercussions in Cochin

The first state to be brought into the arena was Cochin. The Kerala Pradesh Congress Committee had hardly organised its branch committees in Cochin in the first week of February and C. Rajagopalachari delivered his speech on 'The Congress and the Native States' in inaugurating branch committees, on 18 February 1921, when troubles started. On 20 February 1921, the Congress Committee, 'under Nair auspices'[45] organised a congratulatory welcoming to the Khilafat leaders of Calicut, when an anti-non-cooperators gang broke up the meeting by throwing stones.[46] On 25 February 1921, the Christian and Ezhava anti-non-co-operators wanted to have a procession with music and to have a meeting condemning the non-co-operation movement. The Ezhava procession stopped the music under the order of the police on approaching the mosque, but the Christian procession insisted on going by the mosque with music and the Muslims got ready to oppose it.[47] This open provocation, needless to say, ended in a communal riot. The Christians, who according to the Resident, during this period, were ardent supporters of the British connection, decided that no meeting purporting to be representative of the general public should be allowed to pass unchallenged, and had prepared in advance for a showdown. The Nairs sent emissaries to their collaborators the Moplahs of Malabar, while the Christians received reinforcement from their co-religionists from outlying parts. What actually happened was, according to the Residents' report, still in doubt; apparently, the Christians burst the barriers and made a rush for the Hindu positions of the town.[48]

Thus the very beginning of Congress entry into Cochin was marked by the passions of communalism. The Nairs, at this period being pro-Congress, the Christians and the Ezhavas took the offensive against the Nairs. Thus, the encounter was a mere projection of their earlier Civil Rights Movement. In this encounter the state was not the object of the attack, since there was no statutory discrimination between the several communities. On the other hand, according to the Resident, the Christians recognising that the Durbar, as 'guided' by the paramount power, was bound to 'see justice done' between castes, and castes were the most loyal party in the state and wished for the continuance of the British connection and the assurance thereof at an impartial Durbar.[49]

Students Agitation in Travancore

The case of Travancore in 1921 illustrated yet another aspect. The enhancement of fees by the Maharaja's College, Trivandrum, led to a strike and subsequent involvement of the Congress on behalf of the students. This agitation seemed like a mere opportunism on the part of the Congress,[50] and an effort to rope in the student elements to its side.

These two early movements showed clearly the dichotomy present in the states people's mind as to the party against whom they were to agitate. The movement in Cochin became a purely indigenous communal fracas between erstwhile antagonists, while the movement in Travancore which was as a result of enhanced fees was mainly the blowing-up of a local grievance against the administration into something else. Neither of these movements were against the paramount power.

Such agitations made obvious to the Indian National Congress the necessity of explaining clearly its stand in the states peoples participation of the non-co-operation movement. Motilal Nehru, whom we can take as fairly representative of the Indian National Congress view, declared in an address to the Rajputana, Central India, Ajmer and Marwar Political Conference that there was no reason for the Maharajas to be alarmed at the non-coperation movement; he declared that it was directed only against the British Government and not against them. In this, he even went to the length of warning the delegates who came from the states, that the true happiness of both rulers and the ruled lay in a hearty co-operation between them and that nothing could lead to a more disastrous result than the application of the Congress programme of non-co-operation in the states.[51]

The Congress Movement in Mysore

The movement in Mysore was most in keeping with Motilal Nehru's intention. However, it fully proved the effectiveness of British policy in converting even an unwilling Maharaja into a collaborator of British imperialism.

The Congress entry into this state came at the very fag end of the *Khilafat* movement. While the Mysore Congress' early programme centering round this movement was not very effective, it gained momentum in June 1921.[52] The prime movers in this agitation were Setlur (originally a Judge of the Chief Court of Mysore who had been removed from his position, again through the interference of the Resident for carrying 'seditious' correspondence with Aurobindo Ghose), and Kharpur (a retired Chief Engineer of Mysore).

The programme of Congress agitation centering round the *charkha*, boycott of foreign cloth, wearing of Gandhi caps, etc., ending in a students' agitation and *hartal* on Tilak's birthday, 17 November 1921, was effectively stopped by the interference of the Resident. The Executive Council of the Maharaja while unwilling to take drastic action, was forced into ejecting the agitators from outside, prohibiting political meetings and warning the Congress.[53]

The action of the Durbar in practically muzzling the Congress activities was criticised in an article in *The Hindu* where it was clearly hinted that the Durbar was acting under the pressure of the Resident.[54] The Mysore administration, ever sensitive to this paper's criticism as it reflected the British Indian Nationalist views, to demonstrate itself as free from the Resident's pressures, took an independent stance in a matter of press censorship,[55] and furthermore allowed the resumption of Congress activities in June 1922 on an explicit understanding with the Mysore Congress that it would confine itself to the economic side of the programme.[56] However, even these activities landed it in difficulties, when S. Srinivasa Iyengar and particularly Jamnadas Mehta from British India, in a speech at

Mysore criticised the Viceroy and the British Prime Minister on a foreign policy matter– the Turkish succession in Anatolia—in what the Resident considered, "offensive language". While the Mysore Government's action in warning the Bangalore DCC (much to the chagrin of the Resident who deprecated this tendency of the Mysore administration in having "great faith in warnings"!) and Bangalore DCC's apology for the 'seditious' speech of Jamı adas Mehta was in keeping with its now set pattern, the remedy proposed by the President of the Bangalore City Congress Committee proved revealing. Setlur, in a letter published in *The Hindu* of November 1922, proposed that the Congress organisation should change its nomenclature—to call itself Gandhi Ashram or something similar—so as to avoid British officers taking fright at the name 'Congress'. Such a course, he held, would relieve the pressures of the Reside ıt on an administration which had no desire to interfere, and in turn, relieve the consequent troubles of the Mysore Congress.[57] It is interesting to note that faced with the same problem—in an unwillingness of a state organisation to embroil itself directly in the British Indian programme at this time,[58] and in a situation which happened to be reversed at a later period, the solution proposed seemed to be the same. However, while in Haripura in 1938, the issue was forced through to the advantage of the British Indian position and to the discomfiture of the states people,[59] in 1923 the Working Committee of the Indian National Congress evaded the issue in ruling that the existing Congress Committee continue to be worked in the Native States as hitherto, unless the Provincial Committees concerned decided otherwise.[60]

The resumption of political activities in November 1922 once again brought on the interference by the Resident, in which the Durbar taking cover under legal opinion ruled that the 'inflammatory' speeches complained of by the Resident were in no way dissimilar to those made in British India.[61] On the other side it made an informal attempt at requesting the Mysore Congress to desist from political agitation and getting of political agitators from outside, which the Mysore Congress refused.[62]

The Mysore Government thus was forced to take extradition action against outsiders, which brought a near end to all political activities in the state. As a result of these bans on political meetings the projected visit of C. Rajagopalachari in April 1923 had to be abandoned.[63]

Thus, what started in Mysore as a great movement petered out by the middle of 1923 when even a *hartal* organised in celebration of Gandhi Day proved a complete failure.

Hindered in all their activities on the All-India movement, the states people in May 1923 organised a Mysore State Congress to reactivate the other part of their programme on internal reforms. Thus, there came into being two organisations of the Congress, the Mysore State Congress with its programme on internal reforms and responsible government, and the Mysore Congress as an extension of the Indian National Congress.[64] The Mysore State Congress held meetings on its programme for responsible government from July to September 1923.[65] Its plan to get a footing in the civil and military station of Bangalore in starting an organisation in the 'guise of a sangam',[66] however, was frustrated by the Resident acting under "a moral obligation to support the Durbar".[67] The Mysore Congress resumed its British Indian activities in July 1923. It was in usual difficulties with the Mysore Government when it broke its so-called pledge in sending its volunteers to participate in the Nagpur *satyagraha* and was allowed to carry on its activities only after apologising.[68] In the process the volunteers sent out to participate in the Nagpur flag agitation were given no support and left to their own resources, which led to open recriminations by the volunteers against the Congress.[69]

Thus we see that the Indian National Congress in the states could not successfully carry on much agitation. The activities of the Mysore State Congress in its agitation for responsible government was suspect in the eyes of the state administration, while any other activity by the Mysore Congress, other than in its constructive phase, was barred by the pressure of the Resident.

The post-1924 activities of the Mysore Congress were confined to mere imitating of the activities of the Indian National Congress. The Mysore Congress organised a Rashtriya Seva Samithi on 30 March 1924, which was a counterpart to the Hindustani Seva Dal of British India.[70] The Mysore State Congress instituted a new political society on the lines of the Swarajya Party of British India called the Bangalore Swarajya

Society or Party.[71] The main objective of this party was to capture seats in the Legislative Council, the Representative Assembly and the local boards and to educate the masses on the subject of their rights and liberties in the governance of the state.[72]

More important than this programme, on Motilal Nehru's suggestion, this party declared that its main intentionwas to work for national unity as it was the first aim of Swarajya Party to absorb Indian states into the future constitution of the country,[73] which emphasised yet again the real motive of Congress entry in the native states.

The course of Congress movement in Mysore proved amply the difficulties of the states' people carrying out an active struggle on behalf of the Indian National Congress. The Congress by its uncompromising attitude towards a participation in the states peoples' movement on responsible government, seemed to demonstrate the impossibility of conducting any movement on the political arena, by this organisation.

It was in this context that Gandhiji defending the policy of non-interference, at the Kathiawad Political Conference in January 1925, explained that it was dictated by its impotence. He told them that as much as the Congress could not have any effective voice in the relations between Indian states and the British Government even less could its interference be effective in the relations between the Indian states and their subjects. He asserted that as long as British India did not obtain *Swaraj*, so long would India, British as well as Native, remain in a disturbed condition; they could put their houses in order only when British India had attained *Swaraj*.[74] Expanding on the same theme he held that the non-interference policy by the Congress was as much "a virtue of necessity (as) a matter of policy. It was both and perhaps a little more. It was to be admitted that the Congress possessed no authority for enforcing its will in Indian states even to the extent it did in British India proper. Prudence therefore dictated inaction whence action would be a waste of effort if not folly".[75] But he took care to clarify that abstention by the Congress did not mean absence of any effort on the part of Congressmen. Those who were interested in the states were to use their effort to influence the state's administration. The local committees were to help and guide the distressed people so long as they did not come into clash with authority. But when they acted they were to do so not as Congressmen, but in their individual capacity. The position of the Congress was not to be compromised [76]

The Congress activities thus circumscribed by Gandhiji's injunctions hoped to achieve two prominent aims. First, as already reiterated so often, was the aim of integration. Secondly, in its present non-involvement it reserved for itself the role of an intermediary as between the states people and the states administration. The Congress performed this role several times before independence, especially during the height of the movement in 1937-1939. However, its involvement with Travancore during the period 1924-1928 was to prove the first experiment on it. The exploratory test was carried out in Travancore, albeit on a so-called social programme.

Vaikom Satyagraha—A Carefully Conducted Experiment

The Congress agitation in Travancore was an experiment conducted under the personal supervision of Gandhiji. The agitation was apparently non-political; Gandhiji characterised it as a 'socio-religious movement'. As Gandhiji explained, it was certainly part of *satyagraha*, but was not a part of the political movement as conducted in British India. He was personally averse to Congressmen creating directly or indirectly any complication in the Indian states, where the Maharajas were no better circumstanced than British Indian subjects. He asserted that it had no immediate or ulterior political motive behind it, it was not directed against the Travancore Durbar, but purely against an age-long 'intolerable, sacerdotal prejudice' and the Travancore Durbar was not the target of the agitation. The Durbar's intervention was purely in the interest of peace and it was the duty of the leaders on the spot to keep the movement within proper bounds and prevent it from becoming anti-Durbar.[77] The Durbar on its part, at least in its initial stages, acted according to the rules of civilised politics as befitted a model state, especially in its treatment of the arrested leaders.[78] As such, the agitation exhibited comparatively little of the rancour and barbarity which marked the agitations of a later date, when the movement was plainly political and directed against the Durbar. There was one complainant, however, and it was partly in that sense that I used the word "apparently non-political". Even here, as in Mysore, the Resident took objection to the movement, as it was organised and controlled by Congress volunteers, the daily processions headed by the Congress flag and every movement punctuated by the cries of *Vande mataram* and *Mahatma Gandhi ki jai.*[79] But the movement being avowedly socio-religious, the Resident could not interfere, as had been the case in Mysore. However, as the movement gathered momentum the camouflages of its non-political character soon wore thin and the government became openly antagonistic to it.

The site of the agitation, the public roads leading to an important temple at Vaikom in north Travancore, was well chosen. The road was maintained on public funds, access to which was freely given to Christians, Mohammedans and caste Hindus, while the Ezhavas, Parayas and Pulayas, belonging to the Hindu fold were expressly denied access through public notices maintained by the government.[80]

The rules for conducting the agitation[81] were laid by Gandhiji himself, who stipulated that only a limited number were to participate, there was to be no show of force or defiance, and that the demonstration was to be postponed or even abandoned, if it did not comply with the conditions laid. He warned that caution was specially necessary as the opponents for reforms had not been convassed enough.[82]

The *satyagraha* started as scheduled on 30 March 1924,[83] after a duly advertised appeal, sent among others by Gandhiji and C. Vijayaraghavachariar, appealing to the Maharaja to open the road.[84] A ritual fast was observed by the satyagrahis before entering the prohibited area. They were duly arrested and according to Kesava Menon, the secretary of K.P.C.C., "their dignified behaviour greatly impressed public, conduct of the police (was) praiseworthy".[85]

Gandhiji, in spite of his misgivings of a possible dearth of volunteers to carry the fight to the finish, stipulated that it be confined to those of the Hindu fold and that too by the local populace alone. He even prohibited any help from outsiders in supplying of funds.[86]

Thus, by 11 April 1924, the *satyagraha* "undoubtedly

arrived at a delicate state",[87] not because of a dearth of volunteers as feared earlier, but because of a dearth of leaders as they had all been picked up by the authorities.

In this it was aggravated by a more aggressive stance now taken by the state authorities when they prevented the volunteers by physical obstruction, starving them into submission in the blazing sun rather than allow them to cross the barrier and court-arrest.[88]

The lack of leaders to conduct the movement raised an important issue—that of converting a local Indian state movement into one of All-India application, by the participation of the Indian National Congress in it. Gandhiji had his own reservations. He felt it was a difficult, if not an impossible task, to concentrate the energies of leaders from different provinces in a single movement.[89] These reservations were thus the outcome of the ambiguous role of the Congress in a state's arena. In this the main factor to be borne in mind was, that if the Indian National Congress as an organisation were to participate in the states on a local issue, precedence could well be established which could entail the Congress espousing the cause of local grievances of 562 other states. Thus, the dichotomy in the views of the states' people against that of the Indian National Congress was once again made obvious even in this so-called non-political movement.[90] Under such limitations the *satyagraha* limped on till September 1924, when a change in the regime made possible a compromise.[91] As a first measure, the Maharani Regent ordered the release of the prisoners and the satyagrahis on their part suspended the agitation.[92]

In February 1925, on the initiative of the Travancore Government, the question was put up for discussion before the Legislative Council and was defeated by a narrow majority of 22 against 21 votes.[93] Subsequently, Gandhiji himself visited Kerala to solve the deadlock on 8 March 1925 and had discussions with the Maharani Regent, the Dewan and the orthodox elements. His proposals for an arbitration body—composed of learned Shastris or *suvarna* Hindus, or a panel nominated by the orthodox elements, the satyagrahis and the Dewans—was refused, on which, the Durbar as a measure of compromise, agreed to the removal of the government board banning entry, while the satyagrahis on their part agreed to call off their agitation and not cross the line.[94] The compromise was analogous to that arrived at between the Cochin Civil Right agitators and the administration in 1917[95] and was in no way much of an improvement.

At best, the result may seem a small concession gained at the end of a thirteen-month agitation. As Gandhiji saw it, it was neither a defeat nor a victory. All the experiments conducted in these three states, during this period, may be characterised (in a conversion of terms) as pyrrhic defeats. Considered in retrospect, it is clear that these experiments had gained for the states' Congress a definite advantage.

In this respect, it is necessary to point out that had the movement been really non-political, as made out by Gandhiji, the site chosen for such a demonstration could well have been in the British Indian part of Kerala where the social disabilities complained of—against which the demonstration was avowedly carried—were quite as prevalent. In the British Indian part of Kerala, though there were no government maintained boards demarcating limits of entry to the *svarnas*, even here, social customs imposed its own limits. Thus, the demonstration was clearly political and motivated as means of gaining a footing in state politics—be it even so, on the so-called social platform or otherwise. In Kerala, by championing the cause of the Ezhavas, the Vaikom *satyagraha* gained for the Congress cause a wider base, which hitherto, as seen at the time of the Trichur agitation (1921), and the students' agitation at Travancore, had been lacking. The All-India sympathy exhibited towards the Vaikom *satyagraha* made the states also a part of Congress agitation, though on a different plane. Mysore on its part had flexed her limbs on Congress agitational programme and had found the advantages of fighting for her own programme of responsible government with a prominently displayed Congress badge. The Indian states were now prominently on the Congress agitational map. The next few years were to really decide how far the two differing aims—that of the states people on their responsible government platform, and that of the Indian National Congress on integration—were reconcilable. In this yet another development had taken place during the years 1921 to 1928, which was to focus the problem—that of the irreconcilable nature of the two aims—into clear relief, when the

Indian States Peoples' Conference and its allied bodies were brought into being.

The Birth of the Indian States Peoples' Conference

The same period which saw the entry of the Indian National Congress into the state[96] (December 1920) also saw the entry of yet another organ, forged for collective action, on their particular programme of responsible government in the states, in the Indian States Peoples' Conferences. The simultaneous entry of these two organisations, more or less at the same period, brought on a close connection and collaboration between the 'Subjects Conferences' and the Indian National Congress, in spite of Indian National Congress' disclaimers to the contrary.

The Bhor Subjects' Conference convened in December 1920 and the Deccan Native Subjects' Conference (Dakshini Sansthan Hitavardhak Sabha) convened in 1921,[97] were the first of their kind in India. At the second session of the Deccan Native States Subjects' Conference held in May 1922, the President of the Conference 'despaired' of getting anything for the subjects either from the rulers, or the Government of India, and in keeping with the practice at that time, recommended the taking of 'an influential deputation' to England to lay their case before the Prime Minister of England and Parliament.[98] This proposal exhibited the independent attitude of the states subjects' conference at the initial stages, as an organisation distinct and apart in every way from the Indian National Congress, ready to act of its own volition with a clear recognition of the Indian National Congress stand of not embroiling itself with the states subjects' programme of internal reforms in the governance of the Indian states.

However, this independent stance of the states peoples' conferences was short-lived. The first meeting of the nature of an all-India character was held in Belgaum in December 1924 to synchronise with the Indian National Congress session at the same place. At this meeting attended by Mahatma Gandhi, N.C. Kelkar, the President of this session complained of the condition of the Indian states people suffering from a threefold neglect: firstly, at the hands of the British Government on the technical and plausible ground of inability to interfere in the internal matters of the states, again at the hands of the subjects of the Indian states themselves as they came face to face with repression within very close limits, and lastly, at the hands of the Indian National Congress which was "yet more inexcusable".[99]

However, these all-India States Subjects' Conferences and individual States Subjects' Conferences, (barring the political conferences in the south) were of a sporadic character and thus the need was felt for a central organisation to represent the views of the people of the states generally, and to speak on their behalf.[100] At the same time, in the southern states where subjects' agitation (as corroborated by the Political Department itself), in their demand for responsible government was more 'than elsewhere' and was 'sustained' and not 'sporadic' as in other parts, decision was taken to arrange just such another meeting.[101]

The Indian States Peoples' Conference (ISPC) met simultaneously at two centres in Bombay and Madras in December 1927, and was attended by 700 delegates from all important states in which 70% of the salute states were represented.[102] Representative as it was of so many states the ISPC claimed that the conference occupied the same position to the people of the Indian states as the Indian National Congress and other political organisations in relation to British India.[103]

The northern meet became the nucleus of the ISPC and the southern meet became a branch of the above body and called itself the South Indian States Peoples' Conference (SISPC). This conference (SISPC) at Madras, coinciding as it did with the Indian National Congress session at Madras in December 1927, evoked the sympathies of this session to the ISPC programme. Thus, the Indian National Congress for the first time expressed itself with the political movement within the states.

The southern states people had been active in taking the initiative on this issue. The Kerala Provincial Conference in April 1927 had exhorted the Indian National Congress to actively participate in the internal affairs of the native states, and appealed to the Indian National Congress to alter its constitution, if necessary, to this end.[104] A part recognition to this demand was given by the Madras session of the Indian National Congress, when it expressed itself as "emphatically of opinion that in the interests of both the rulers and the people of the Indian states, they should establish representative institutions and responsible government in the states at an early date".[105]

A resolution of this character for the first time brought before the Congress was hailed by Satyamurti, who seconded the resolution, as "a symbol of comradeship and of support in the struggle which they may have to go through in the Indian states".[106] However, this support promised so generously at this historic session at Madras, was to see a retraction even before the programme of support had been in force for a year-and-a-half. The natural evolution of these two organisations in a common programme was to meet a check yet again in the machiavellism of British policy at its old game of counter-poising the princes against the forces of nationalism in British India, which was yet again to have its repercussions on the Indian National Congress policy towards the states.

The Princes' Fears and British Policy to Their Rescue

As in 1917, it was proposals for reform in British India which proved the catalytic agent. It was in the wake of a crop of states subjects' conferences and states peoples' organisations, the entry of the Indian National Congress into the states' arena in 1921, the states peoples' involvement in the Congress programme and *vice versa* (though on a so-called social programme), that the repercussions of a federal greater India, with a democratic government at the centre, realised. The main problem centered round the transfer of paramountcy to an Indian Parliament. The *Swaraj Constitutions* proposed by the Congress protagonists, as that of Srinivasa Iyengar in 1927,[107] and that of the All Parties' Conference sitting in session from 1927[108] made clear claims for a transfer of paramountcy to a democratic Indian Parliament. It is not surprising that such proposals naturally roused the concern of the princes to the question of the future of Indian states in the event of a democratisation of the Government of India. While this concern of the princes had been brushed aside by Reading in 1925, as "it not being profitable to discuss in detail the future relations of the princes at this time,"[109] the proposals for constituting a Parliamentary Committee to examine the question of further reforms in British India, made the princes' anxiety even more prominent. As early as April 1926, Irwin wrote to Birkenhead of the "various uneasiness of the princes"[110] and of Alwar proposing to consult Simon on the constitutional position of the princes towards a Government of India that was gradually moving in the direction of democracy. The princes expressed themselves on the same anxiety in May 1927 at a conference convened specially to give them an opportunity of expressing their views.[111] Their discussions showed that they were concerned in two problems; the first of adjusting some fiscal and administrative matters and the second of finding means by which their position *vis-a-vis* British India could be secured in the event of British India attaining a greater measure of responsible government.[112]

The Butler Committee which was thus the result of the princes' wish for an enquiry into their position was constituted in September 1927 to give an authoritative decision/assurance to allay the fears of a princely order to a future democratic Government of India.

The ISPC and the SISPC coinciding as they did with the formation of the Indian States Committee in 1927, makes it clear that their origin owed not a little to the formation of the Butler Committee to enquire into the grievances of the princes. This is corroborated by Hosakappa Krishna Rao (one of the founding members of the SISPC), according to whom, the constitution of a separate committee "ostensibly for determining the future relationship of the princes of the Indian states with British Government but really to strengthen the British position in India",[113] forced the states people "to prove their dissociation",[114] with the princes and to declare their desire to come into a closer union with British India, which made them oganise two conferences.

The end of 1927 thus saw a number of forces converging on the same issue with differing interests. It was inevitable that the next phase would bring the several organisations promoting these divergent causes—the ISPC on a democratic programme for the states, the Indian National Congress on its own programme of integration with claims for the transfer of paramountcy to a popular government at the centre and the British paramountcy in its Indian States Committee promoting its own position, *vis-a-vis* the princes, into a collision.

Conclusion

Summing up the arguments thrown up in this chapter, one finds in the states, a situation of contradictions. These contradictions appeared to run through the very fabric of its system.

The dismissal of the reformists' demands by a Mysore administration, on the plea that conditions in the states were not in concord with British India, and the ruling by British paramountcy on the rights of Travancore Legislature, brought into relief the very contradictory nature of the states peoples' aspirations in the existing states system. If the very rights of a Legislative Council, enjoyed by it and accepted by the states' administration ever since 1892, could be summarily withdrawn by a British paramountcy, on the plea that they could not regard a ruler of a state to be competent to divest himself or his successors of their inherited rights, what was the guarantee for the continuance of a legislature (let alone one enjoying the powers of a responsible government), except as on the whims and fancies of the Maharajas and that of the paramount power?

The entry of the Indian National Congress in the states on a programme of integration and as on an extension of an anti-imperialist struggle, presented an equal contradiction.

The first experiment in Cochin ended in the usual communal fracas between the Ezhava-Christians against Nair elements. Mysore tried to project the movement in keeping with Congress intentions as one against British imperialism. However, the movement proved fully the effectiveness of British policy, when through the Resident's pressures on its administration it prohibited not only speeches which were allowed without hindrance in British India, but even forced a Bangalore District Congress Committee to apologise for speeches made by outsiders against British policy in Anatolia.

The third experiment in the states peoples' socio-religious issue in Travancore, proved inasmuch as full of contradictions as that in Mysore. As Gandhiji explained, the movement was definitely part of *śatyagraha* but was not part of the political movement in the states. However, when the very boards barring entry to the roads to the Ezhavas were put up by the government and maintained by it, it could hardly prove to be one without its political implications. Even the question when referred to the legislature was defeated only because of the government bloc and its nominees voting against it.

In this, with proposals for a democratic government at the centre, the period saw a number of forces converging on the same issue with differing interests. The Indian States Peoples Conference had its own ideas of projecting the democratic programme of the states, the Indian National Congress had its primary objective of integration with claims to a transfer of paramountcy, the British administrators were engaged in the entrancing game of counterpoising the princes against the nationalist forces and propounding new theories in their Butler Committee enquiry to do so, and the princes with a programme of safeguarding their autocratic position against the democratic forces within, it was inevitable that these forces came into collision.

4

The Fears of Federation

The Movement from 1928-1933

The main political activity in India, both in British India as well as in the princely states, during this period revolved round proposals for constitutional reforms. Prior to the 1920s, as pointed out by S. Srinivasa Iyengar in his introduction to his proposals for a *Swaraj Constitution*, few proposals for constitutional reforms, *vis-a-vis*, British India and the individual states had taken into consideration the 'formidable problem' of the position of the Indian states, either with or in relation to the constitution of free India.[1]

With proposals for constitutional reform leading to a greater democratisation at the centre, this matter came into consideration both at the hands of British Indian politicians as well as the princes and their subjects.[2] The crop of 'swaraj constitutions' and 'schemes' proposed is illustrative, not so much of the differing variations on schemes for constitutional reforms, but were mainly indicative of how these interests sought to treat this issue.

The *Swaraj Constitution* of S. Srinivasa Iyengar by emphasising the consent of the princes to the mode of choosing representatives to the Central Legislature, sought to trade a recognition of the rulers as sole authority in the states for a reciprocal recognition of free India's right to paramountcy[3]—which was the crux around which all constitutional proposals of this period, in relation with the states revolved. The All Parties Conference meeting in Delhi in February 1928 reflected more or less the same views.

The South Indian States Peoples Conference found the nationalists' obsession with the transference of the rights of paramountcy to itself, and for this purpose its willingness to come to terms with the princes, disconcerting. It felt that a negotiation with the princes on the above terms would sacrifice the interests of the states people and would only mean the mere "substitution of King Stork for King Log".[4] Hence, clearly affirming their desire to preserve the individuality of their respective states and their loyalty to the ruling houses, they asserted that they did not hanker after unity but desired only union with British India.[5] A further elucidation of this phrase is to be found in the constitutional proposals spelt out by them. The greater India of their conception was a federal constitution with fuller autonomy for the individual states and provinces, except in so far as matters of common interests which were to be dealt by a central government. The states, though retaining their hereditary rulership, were to have responsible government as the British Indian provinces. The bicameral legislatures of the central government, to which the executive was to be responsible, was to be made up of elected members both from the states and the provinces, the number of members from each area being determined on the basis of population. Thus, the linking of British Indian provinces and Indian states was to be on the basic principle of equality as in the USA, where questions of paramountcy did not arise. On the coming of this constitution into force, the arrangements, treaties, etc., hitherto entered into were to 'become null and void'.[6]

The cause of the divergence between the nationalists' approach and that of the states people is to be traced again to the differing aims of these two bodies. The nationalists of British India were mainly concerned with the establishment of a greater India with a powerful nationalist central government, preferably in a unitary structure, in which the powers of government of India, as at present, were to be transferred intact to it. The States Peoples Conference, especially the southern wing of it, whose main aim was the establishment of a responsible government in the states and the abolition of autocracy, found in the nationalists, exaggerated respect of the treaty rights of the states, a disregard for the particular interests of the states people. They feared that ultimately the nationalists would sacrifice the states peoples' interest in order to gain their aim. This fear was not altogether ill-founded as the Indian National Congress' dealings with the princes showed.

The Nehru Report—the product of the All Parties Conference, published in August 1928, showed an equal willingness to bargain with the princes at the cost of the states people. In an effort to entice the princes to their conference[7] and in evidence of its accommodation for a consideration, it asserted, that it was possible for "even a democratic India" to sympathise with the legitimate grievances of the princes and that "it was by no means impossible or impracticable" to define the limits within which the Government of India could seek to interfere. It was as an extension of the same theory that the Report proclaimed that the expression 'Indian State' could only be taken to mean the individual ruling prince of the state concerned, and as such negotiations had necessarily to be carried on with them.[8]

The only concession made to the democratic ideals of the states people was a warning to the princes that a federal union would necessitate, perhaps in varying degrees, a modification of the system of government and administration in the state.[9] Here it did not spell out the nature of the government as responsible government for which the southern states peoples were now striving,[10] but admitted rather vaguely that it was inconceivable that the people of the states who were fired by the same ambition and aspirations as the people of British India, would "quietly submit to existing conditions for ever or that the people of British India, bound by the closest ties of family, race and religion to their brethren on the other side of an imaginary line"[11] would never make common cause with them. The stress on the 'imaginary line' only went further to emphasise its own position on integration and its championing the states peoples cause as a threat to bring the princes into line.

The British administrators, in their turn, were now to give yet another twist to the paramountcy question, in their publication— *the Report of the Indian States Committee.* The Butler Committee, constituted mainly to allay the fears of the princes,[12] was asked to give its opinion, not so much on the position of the princes, *vis-a-vis*, the paramount power (as avowed in its terms of reference) but to restrict itself to two questions, viz., whether the British Government's treaty obligations could be delegated to a future dominion government or whether the Viceroy should take the place of the Governor-General in Council.[13]

The Butler Committee, tailoring its pronouncements to the required needs, proclaimed its dictum that paramountcy was to remain paramount in order to fulfil its obligations arising out of 'imperial necessity';[14] to satisfy the demand of the princes, it declared that the relationship of the states was a relationship to the Crown.[15] In order to provide an insulation for the states from a future democratic central government, the Committee proposed that the Viceroy act in a dual capacity—the Viceroy as an agent of the Crown in dealing with matters pertaining to the Crown in relationship with the princes, and as the Governor-General in Council in dealing with matters of British India. Butler could hardly claim originality in this ingeneous scheme as it had been proposed earlier by another Political Officer, Lowndes, to Chelmsford in 1920.[16]

A further blow was aimed at the states peoples when this committee refused to give a hearing to them under the plea that their terms of reference did not cover an investigation of their 'alleged grievances'. An added injury was inflicted in their reference in the Report to the States Peoples Association by the use of the words "persons purporting to represent them"—which even questioned the *bona fides* of these associations to represent the states people.[17] From this time we can trace the practice of the princes and the British Government to prefix the term 'so-called' in all references to the states' organisations.

Thus, by refusing them any recognition, the very *raison d'etre* of these organisations ceased. In this, the Nehru Report, in its emphatic pronouncement that the Indian state was to be taken to mean the individual ruling prince of the state concerned,[18] helped not a little in the British contention that the rulers and their accredited delegates were the only ones capable of negotiating on behalf of the states. It was an extension of this same theory which denied the states people a representation even at the Round Table Conference in October 1929.[19]

On this issue the parties invited to the Round Table Conference had taken up specified positions. The Congress, except for a desultory enquiry through Vithalbhai Patel of Irwin, whether the subjects of the states would be represented, had exhibited no stronger a view.[20] Even if the Congress did insist, or attach importance to representation of the Indian states people, Irwin and the Secretary of State had agreed that they were to reiterate the constitutional position that the peoples' representative would have no *locus standi* in a conference which was to discuss questions of constitutional policy, in regard to which the accredited governments of states were the only people who could speak with authority. In this they were ready to assure them that whatever the outcome of the conference, the existing protection which the states' subjects now enjoyed in the shape of British intervention in case of misrule would not be impaired.[21] The Congress did not insist, and the opportunity did not arise for even this reiteration.

The princes on their part, inspired as they had been by the political department earlier, to an opposition—to the inclusion of the subjects' representative, naturally now assumed the states would be represented purely by the princes or their ministers. The Viceroy decided to uphold the princes, for in addition to the constitutional merits of the question, he on his part decided to presume, that the princes would not play on other terms.[22] The Secretary of State agreed as their prime objective was to make the conference a success, he thought it would be fatal to alienate the princes merely on the ground of tactics quite apart from other considerations.[23]

With the princes now in a dominant position, the Maharaja of Bikaner took the earliest opportunity in an interview to the press and a speech extending to about twenty printed pages to proclaim the princes objection to sit and negotiate on an equal basis with the 'so-called' representatives of the peoples of the state as a separate and independent party. Such a demarcation, he said, implied a complete misconception of the relations between the ruler and the ruled, as the rulers were the natural representatives of the people of the state.[24] These instances of outright condemnation by Bikaner of the ISPC saw the beginning of a wordy duel between him and the Indian States Peoples Conference.[25] But more importantly, it deflected the energies of the ISPC into an argument with the paramount power, in its efforts to wrest for itself a representation to the constitutional confabul ations now going on in England. The period between October 1928, when the Butler Committee refused to give a hearing to the states people and the final irrevocable decision taken in April 1931, to give no representation to them at the Round Table Conference, a continuous agitation was put up by them on the issue of representation, both in England and in India.[26] The ISP Copened an office in England in September 1929. Due to its efforts, a question was raised in Parliament on this matter[27] and a personal plea was made to the Labour Party Prime Minister, Ramsay MacDonald, in December 1929, emphasising that the states peoples' exclusion was against his own proclaimed views of summoning the Round Table Conference for purpose of permitting free representation of all points of view.[28]

The All-India States Subjects Committee, meeting in Cochin in June 1930 and the General Secretary of the SISPC in a letter to the Viceroy, made a special plea to revoke the British decision.[29] Even as late as 15 November 1930, G.R. Abhyankar, in a petition to the Viceroy, pleaded that the views of the states peoples, especially on questions of intervention and transfer of paramountcy, should not be allowed to go by default.[30] He petitioned that Ramachandra Rao, a resident of British India, be co-opted even at this stage to give the states peoples' case, even if not the people, a representation. The Political Department, while agreeing that there was a great deal of truth in what Abhyankar wrote, rejected the appeal as too late now for any more representation to be included even if it were desirable to do so.[31] Moreover, it declared that it was not clear how 70 million could be represented by one or two persons, specially when the problems and difficulties in the states differed so widely. The argument put up by the Political Department was spurious. Firstly, the nomination to the Round Table Conference was not representative of the population or area but was based on parties and views. Secondly, even on their own assertion, the internal condition of the states was not in question, and in this context, the allusion to size and differing problems of the various states was hardly pertinent where the ISPC wanted to represent only on issues affecting the Indian states peoples as a whole.

A last effort was again made by the ISPC before the second Round Table Conference, at obtaining representation when Lord Snell was asked to use his influence towards this purpose, which was however again denied.[32]

It was this denial of a place for the states people at the Round Table Conference, in spite of the strong plea put up by them, by setting a precedence for such denials even in future, struck in turn, at the very root of a collaboration or joint action of the states peoples as against their princes or the paramount power. It was thus not lack of credibility[33] which weakened the states people's voice but British policy which denied any recognition to this organisation. This it did, as seen above, by affixing the term 'so-called' in all its references to this organisation and secondly, by denying them any representation to all conferences convened to discuss India's Constitution. An organisation for collective action in such circumstances could hardly retain its vigour. Repudiated as the ISPC was by the princes, and rejected by the British administrators, it was to meet yet a more severe punishment at the hands of the British Indian nationalists themselves, which was again, the result of the Butler Committee's decisions. The Indian National Congress on its part, seeing the decisions given by the Butler Committee were contrary to the previous thinking—in holding that paramountcy was not transferable—began to suspect the *bona fides* of the British Government. They feared that the new concept of personal relationship between the states and the Crown was mainly evolved to drive "further the wedge between the states and the rest of India".[34] A feeling grew among the nationalists that "at one stroke of the pen, the states were delinked from the Governor-General in

Council and pegged to the British Crown", in order to forge "for the Imperial political armoury another formidable weapon, the problem of the states".[35] This fear of the nationalists had found place even earlier than the publication of the Butler Committee Report; the Nehru Report had asserted that the statements made by the Butler Committee left little doubt that attempts were being made to convert the Indian states into an Indian Ulster by pressing new constitutional theories into service.[36]

These fears of the Indian National Congress of the intentions of the British in India had its most marked repercussion on the relationship of the Congress with the states peoples' organisations. The predominant problem of the Indian National Congress *vis-a-vis* the states was one of ensuring that the rights of paramountcy were transferred to a nationalist government and that the integrity of India as a unit was safeguarded. In this, the new theory of the princes' relationship as that with the Crown meant that British Government's treaty obligations could not be delegated to a future dominion government and that any successor government would have to base its new relationship with the states only on the basis of a new contract—may be through an instrument of accession. The princes being the legally recognised party with whom the successor government would have to entertain negotiations, the Congress was wary of declaring themselves on the side of the states people in the confrontation between the states people and the princes—lest their main aim on integration be jeopardised. Thus' in this confrontation the Congress now took its seat firmly on the fence, just as much as some of the enlightened princes now pretended to occupy a similar seat in the confrontation between British Indian nationalists and British Imperialism. Consequently, while the Congress decided to have a foot in the states, as a possible instrument to bring about integration, it could hardly declare itself on the side of the states people in its internal reforms issue; in fact, it was to its advantage to see that their demand was not satisfied lest their leverage through it on their interest of integration be weakened.

The result of these considerations was immediately apparent following the Butler Committee decisions published in March-April 1929. Earlier, in the Madras session of 1927, the Indian National Congress had expressed itself unequivocally in sympathy with the states peoples' aspirations.[37] In October 1928 the Committee appointed by the AICC to revise Congress constitution under the presidentship of A. Rangaswami Iyengar, with Shiva Prasad Gupta and Jawaharlal Nehru as the other committee members, had suggested the deletion of Article VIII of the Congress constitution, banning it from interfering with the internal affairs of the Indian states. It held that there was absolutely no reason why the constitution should prevent interference in the states if they at any time desired it, as it was wholly impossible not to interfere in some way or the other.[38] The deletion was mainly proposed on the suggestion of the southern states, as the Kerala States Conference held in May 1928,[39] and the Karnataka Pradesh Congress Committee, in its suggested amendments, had felt that the princes were consolidating their power,[40] and it was best that the Congress took up the cause of the subjects of the states.[41] The Indian National Congress session at Calcutta in December, 1928-January, 1929 marked yet another step when this amendment was adopted without discussion.[42] Moreover, the resolution on the states urged, not only for the introduction of responsible government based on representative institutions in the states, but also exhorted the states administration to issue immediate proclamations or enact laws guaranteeing elementary and fundamental rights of citizenship, such as rights of association, free press and security of person and property. It marked a further step in assuring the people of the Indian states of its "sympathy with and support in their legitimate and peaceful struggle for the attainment of full responsible government in the state".[43]

But this marked the furthest limits of the Indian National Congress' concession to the states people. The publication of the Butler Committee Report in March-April 1929 brought on a retraction in policy or at best a freeze on the rapprochement which was evident in the earlier years between the ideals of the Congress and that of the states people. Even the deletion of clause VIII, restricting the Indian National Congress from intervening in the states, as Vallabhbhai Patel pointed out, helped in no way, following Butler Committee's decision, in its working interpretation; there was not a single instance in which the Congress did interfere with the states affairs after that change had been effected.[44]

The acceptance of the Viceroy's invitation to the Round Table Conference without emphasising the necessity of a proper and adequate representation of the people of the states, in the Delhi Manifesto of October 1929, was the first intimation of a change in policy of the Indian National Congress towards this organisation, following the decisions of the Butler Committee.[45] The disillusionment which followed on being treated as the "real untouchables",[46] and the confrontation of the ISPC with Mahatma Gandhiji which was to follow, is part of the history of this organisation of a later period.[47] However, at this time they could hardly antagonise the nationalists and so made excuses for this lapse on the nationalists part as "done through inadvertence".[48] They hoped the leaders would rectify it by taking an early opportunity of making it clear that there would be no practical and final decision of the constitutional problem of the relations of the states with British India, without an effective participation of the representatives of the peoples of the states in them. However, these importunities were to fall on deaf ears, for the Indian National Congress meeting at Lahore in December 1929 went back to the 1927 position in its relation with the states in expressing a mere opinion that the time had arrived for the ruling princes in India to grant responsible government to their people. At this Congress there was no mention of the sympathy and support promised so generously earlier.

Thus, on summing up, one can see that the Butler Committee decisions had two important results. Firstly, by denying the states people a representation at its enquiry it set a precedence for all future conferences, called to discuss India's Constitution. This robbed the states peoples organisation for collective action of its very right to existence. Secondly, by arousing the fears of the Congress on its own position *vis-a-vis* integration, it successfully withdrew British Indian nationalists support to this organisation. Thus, the ISPC meeting little support from the Indian National Congress to its cause was now deflected into a confrontation with the Indian National Congress.

This confrontation between the states people and the Congress resolved itself into a question of priorities. The Indian National Congress firmly believed that their involvement in the states peoples cause would not only serve to disperse their energies (quite often on local issues), but that as long as the imperial power remained to guard the princes' position, the fight carried on by the states people against the princes would prove fruitless. It was this analysis of their position which confirmed the Indian National Congress, which had its reservations even earlier, to a non-involvement with the states peoples movement, so as not to jeopardise their position on independence and integration. In furtherance of this hypothesis, it even advised the states people not to force the issue with the princes, but to concentrate their energies in their struggle against imperialism. The states people on the other hand were reluctant to accept this position. They felt that while they were willing to participate in the wider movement, their ideal could act as no obstruction to the interests of the Congress. They believed that their movement itself could prove of help to the cause of integration and thus their cause was in itself a part of the overall struggle for freedom, towards which the Indian National Congress should help. With these divergences in the aims and priorities, it was inevitable that these two organisations should come into a confrontation. The breaking out of the civil disobedience movement in British India postponed these issues.

Princes on Federation

Before dealing with the movement in these states, carried on in the shadow of British Indian politics, it becomes necessary that we touch upon one other aspect of the states—the princes' attitude towards federation, their bargaining on it, and differences of these three states, especially Mysore, in their approach to the same question.

The British administrators, by giving the princes one-third representation in both houses of the federal legislatures, had relied upon the Indian states, with their monarchic polities, to contribute to the "necessary elements of stability and experience",[49] in other words, to balance the British Indian nationalists, with their allies, the princes. In this, the British Government, by its insistence in tying up the federal proposals for all-India, with granting of responsible government to British India, made itself open to pressures of princes bargaining.[50]

The princes, on their part, had hoped to do away with paramountcy in exchange for dominion status for British India.[51] Their initial enthusiasm and the "generous and patriotic response",[52] made by them at the first Round Table Conference soon floundered in the disenchantment of the several Committee Reports submitted at the second and third Round Table Conferences.

In the face of a rejection of their proposals their main accent lay on 'safeguards'. On the publication of the White Paper in March 1933, the Special Committee of Ministers[53] gave its opinion that the safeguards regarding interference were "too vague" and that the wide discretionary authority placed at the disposal of the Governor-General for ensuring adequate standards of administration in federal subjects left the way open for serious interference.[54] Their special complaint was the inclusion of Fundamental Rights in the constitutional proposals with no provisions for the princes to contract out of it.[55]

In these three states, especially that of Mysore, the differences with the paramount power arose not so much on issues of constitution, as much as on personal grievances peculiar to them. Their special *bete noire* was their long standing grievances over the subsidy and custom's issues. Thus, in contrast to the proposals of the northern Indian states, and especially of Hyderabad, which harped on safeguards and demanded segregation of affairs of British India from those of the states—Mirza Ismail opted for an organic relationship between a federal senate or Upper House dealing on all-India affairs and a Lower House dealing with British Indian affairs.[56] This was in keeping with the Mysore Government's attitude made clear even earlier, to the Butler Committee, in holding that the question of paramountcy need exercise the state's government less and less as these governments became constitutional. It gave as its opinion that the paramountcy interference in states could "cease to exist". once a fully constitutional government had been established.[57]

The inclusion of the subsidy question with the federal negotiations came about in June 1932 when the Mysore Legislative Assembly passed a resolution recommending to the Government of Mysore the proposal that they do not enter the All-India Federation so long as the subsidy or any portion of it was levied from her by the British Government.[58] This resolution which was government inspired was opposed by Hosakappa Krishna Rao (an active Mysore Congress member and of the SISPC) who pleaded that the question of subsidy should not be mixed with that of entering federation and that the latter had to be dealt with by itself on its own merits.[59]

In October 1932, the Davidson Committee[60] examining the question of federal finance, while declaring that in a federal constitution tributes could have no place, gave little remission to Mysore. It recommended that for the time being only that portion of the subsidy be paid by a state which exceeded five per cent of its annual revenue.[61] The remission of the balance was to be spread over a period of twenty years. It was in this context that Mirza Ismail "practically put a pistol"[62] at the British Government's head and declared to the Viceroy that unless subsidy was remitted in full and the civil and military station at Bangalore retroceded, Mysore would decline to enter the federation.[63]

Even on the question of the retrocession of Bangalore Cantonment, the state's people had distinctly different views, not only from that of the Mysore Government, but even from that of the Indian National Congress. In October 1937, when the question of the assigned tract was decided in favour of the state by the British Government, the Bangalore Cantonment Congress Committee, (BCCC) which was affiliated to the Karnataka PCC, without making any references to the AICC waited on deputation on the Resident and expressed their opposition to the proposed retrocession. In this their avowed fear was that such a retrocession would curtail even the few rights and privileges they possessed.[64] The main question that agitated the Indian National Congress members was whether, they who were fighting for independence against British rule, could now countenance "such a reactionary attitude".[65] The Congress high command was hardly "inclined to agree"[66] with the Bangalore CCC. However, the BCCC in making their opposition to retrocession were motivated not so much by their fears of curtailment of their few rights as much as the fear that the haven, which the Bangalore Cantonment Congress organisation had provided for the Mysore State Congress and Mysore Congress at times of severe repression within the state, would now be lost.[67] Thus, the BCCC was motivated not so much by the AICC's position and principles as it was by local interests.[68]

Cochin presented little contradictions on the Federal issues. Once its financial interests in the Cochin harbour and customs were settled, the people were in favour of joining the federation and the Ruler himself had no individual views.[69]

Travancore, with the entry of C.P. Ramaswami Aiyar as its legal adviser, demanded an allocation of seats based upon population.[70] This demand for multiple representation was a matter of *izzat* and arose mainly out of its resentment at being bracketted with states like Cochin, Rewa and Bhawalpur, and putting it in a position of inferiority to states like Baroda, Gwalior, and Kashmir.[71] On this issue the states people were neutral, while they favoured federation; the Travancore Government till 1935 being "susceptible to the force of public opinion in the state",[72] expressed its willingness to settle the issue by mutual agreement.[73]

With this background in mind, where the aims of the Indian National Congress proved different from that of the states people and where the administrations of these three states showed an enlightened approach to the Indian constitutional problem—in tallying their demands to the needs of the nationalists as far as possible, even to proposing an 'organic relationship' in a federal chamber—let us see how the states people's movement was affected by the British Indian nationalists' approach to it. This problem was further complicated by the Mysore administration's sympathy towards the British Indian movement and its treatment of their leaders as state guests.

The Movement within the States—The Movement in Mysore (1928—1932)

The period 1928-1932 in Mysore saw the participation of the states people in two simultaneous movements—one purely on behalf of the states people and the second on behalf of the Indian National Congress. To promote these two distinct activities of the state, as already noted earlier, there were technically two bodies, the Mysore State Congress and the Bangalore District Congress Committee as a branch of the Indian

National Congress. While the personnel of these two bodies were quite often the same, the Mysore Government drew a clear distinction in its dealings with them. While it was sympathetic to the All-India movement promoted by the Bangalore District Congress Committee, it was clearly antagonistic to the activities of the Mysore State Congress. The Bangalore District Congress Committee was allowed to organise *hartals* on the wider movement—as for example the *hartal* observed on Lala Lajpat Rai Day on 29 November 1928.[74] In reciprocation, there was a tacit understanding on the part of the Indian National Congress not to transgress the bounds of this 'favoured' treatment. Even a meeting to condemn the Butler Committee's decision was abandoned by the Bangalore District Congress Committee on a friendly warning that the Mysore Government would not welcome the proposal.[75]

As an extension of the Mysore Government's partiality to the wider movement in British India, the British Indian nationalists were often received as state guests. In reciprocation, the nationalist leaders eschewed state politics and confined themselves to safe topics like the promotion of temperance or khaddar,[76] and were even sometimes openly antagonistic to the movement of the Mysore State Congress. Thus, Vallabhbhai Patel, addressing a meeting on 12 September 1929 (to note after the Butler Committee decisions were made known) of the 'Mysore Peoples Congress' (denoting the Mysore State Congress), while laying stress on the Brahmin and non-Brahmin movement in South India refused to speak on local politics of the state. He regretted to see that there should have been some little ill-feeling between the government and the people. He further praised the Mysore state's people for being very lucky in possessing a model ruler, and clinching the argument in favour of the prince, ended with an opinion that if the Maharaja did not pay heed to the people, the fault seemed to lie with the latter and not with the ruler.[77] Again, Dr. M.A. Ansari, on a visit to Bangalore, treated as a state guest of the Government of Mysore, was on 2 October 1929, met by a few 'local agitators' who invited him to go in procession through Bangalore City, but he refused. Addressing a Youth League of Bangalore, he said that the Mysore State had *Swaraj*, praised the ruler and his broad vision and statesmanship. The 'local agitators' of

Bangalore City of course were dissatisfied with the views expressed by him.[78]

The Dewan, on his part, was openly sympathetic to the Indian National Congress. Referring to events in British India on the breakdown of the concord reached in Delhi Manifesto—leading to the decision of the Congress not to participate in the Round Table Conference—he talked of the 'great and patriotic soul', who represented the spirit of India and voiced their sentiments as probably no one else could do, 'giving passionate expression' as he did to the growing feeling of "national self-consciousness which had lately swept over the country like a flood tide".[79]

This rather very curious personal feeling towards Gandhiji on the part of the Maharaja and Mirza Ismail, and their "taking to their bosom" a gentleman who was still the head of the civil disobedience movement and treating him as a state guest, irked Willingdon and Company.[80] Especially was it irritating as they received a good many communications from other rulers to say that it made it extraordinary difficult for their own position.

It is in the context of these conflicting interests that one has to study the Mysore State's people's movement. Firstly, there was the the paramount power which tried to isolate the British Indian movement from any contact with the Maharajas and their governments. Secondly, there was the state government's overtures to the British Indian leaders in order to isolate the Mysore State Congress movement. Thirdly, an Indian National Congress tried to maintain the balance between these two bodies—that of the states peoples and the Maharaja—and in its efforts to exhibit its so-called fairness, tended to side with the Maharaja; in this their ulterior motive not only lay in isolating the Maharaja from becoming active collaborators of the British but also to ensure its interests on integration. It is only in the crucible of these conflicting elements that one can understand the later complications leading to the Haripura decision in 1938. In its immediate consequence, in the wake of the heightening movement of the civil disobedience movement in British India, the conflict between the states people's movement and the Congress leadership was postponed for the time being, in a show of solidarity.

It was in this background that the administrators of Travancore and Mysore came into a confrontation with the states people in 1927-1928 over a matter of press censorship. Mysore sought the help of British India to stop what the Dewan called 'malicious attacks' on his administration, made by papers in British India. In order to give them protection, British India, in addition to its provisions under the Princes Protection Against Disaffection Act, now brought into operation a new Indian Post Office Act to ban entry to 'undesirable journals'.[81] Travancore banned the entry of two newspapers—the *Sreevazhumcode* and *Veerakeralam*, originating from Tangaseri, a British Indian enclave within the boundaries of Travancore—by bringing into operation the Sea Customs Regulation, the legality of which procedure was open to question.[82]

The two states people, who had a long history of struggle for the freedom of the press, now mounted an agitation in the press from within the state and even reprinted some of the articles prohibited entry.

In Mysore, the *Prajamitra*, 'the main vehicle of the Brahmins' was the first to succumb to the retaliatory actions of the autocratic government and was muzzled in October 1928. This was followed in January 1929 by further bans imposed by the Mysore administration on the newspapers, the *Mysore Patriot*, *Sampadbhyudaya* and the *Sadhvi*.[83]

The role of the Bangalore District Congress Committee in the agitation which followed these repressive acts of the Mysore administration was of great significance in the history of this state's people. This body, which as a subordinate branch of the Indian National Congress, was to engage itself only in its 'constructive activities', now involved itself in the state's political programme on behalf of press freedom. The prosecution of two of Mysore journalists for sedition made the Bangalore District Congress Committee invite T. Prakasam, the editor of *Swarajya* of Madras, for consultation in regard to the kind of propaganda to be carried in the state, in order to make the Mysore Government cancel the order,[84] and in case the propaganda was not successful to even threaten civil disobedience.[85]

The involvement of the Bangalore District Congress Committee in what was purely a state's issue demonstrated quite clearly, that subjected as the state's people were in the simultaneous course of two movements in which the personnel of both was one and the leadership the same, the artificial divisions, which the Indian National Congress tried to emphasise, could hardly persist. This relationship was complicated further by the flag demonstration which played a prominent part in this state's peoples' movement and was purposely adopted by them to demonstrate the same point.

The flag demonstration owed its orgin to N.S. Hardikar, a leader from Dharwar, in British India. The Hindustani Seva Dal organised by him in emulation of those in British India, started camps of exercise for the youth in April 1929[86] and initiated the practice of a ritual National Flag hoisting in the last week of every month.[87] In spite of notice being served on him banning him from delivering any speeches, the flag hoisting as a monthly ritual was continued throughout 1929, though he, in obedience to the ban, made no speeches.[88]

The Mysore State Congress which had elected as its president, Mr. Venkata Krishnayya (the editor and owner of many newspapers which had been recently banned),[89] now through a resolution, adopted the Congress Swaraj flag as the flag for the Mysore State.[90] From now on was started the ritual flag hoisting of the Congress flag in all its functions as if to stress that interests of the states peoples were one with the British Indian movement.

The youth movement conducted under the aegis of the Bangalore District Congress Committee on its part now involved itself in state politics. It organised a meeting on 7 February 1930 in Bangalore, in order to congratulate Sitarama Sastri who had been convicted on an offence under a Press Regulation.[91] On his release, Mr. Sitarama Sastri appealed to the youth of the state to be ready to agitate for a responsible government and also to participate in the *satyagraha* which was to be launched by Gandhiji in order to gain independence for India.[92]

On 4 March 1930, at a meeting organized by the Bangalore District Congress Committee, Hosakappa Krishna Rao made an appeal that as independence for India was equally important both to the state subjects and to British Indians, the people of the Mysore state and other states, should shoulder the burden with British Indians.[93]

It was in the face of such complete intermingling of both movements in Mysore state that the national flag became the target of Mysore prohibitory orders. In March 1930, for the first time, the Mysore Government prohibited processions with national flags. This order was defied by Tagadur Ramachandra Rao and others of the Bangalore District Congress Committee.[94]

The declaration of the civil disobedience movement in British India, much to the relief of the states administration, now deflected the states peoples movement to its parallel course. In this it was the Resident who complained of the state government's inactions in allowing the wider movement to gain ground within the state. In April 1930, 40 volunteers of the Hindustani Seva Dal participated in the Karnataka salt disobedience campaign.[95] On 16 April, four volunteers left for Hubli and Khaddar caps were now more in evidence in Bangalore City than ever before.[96] Meetings were organised and attended by 3000 to 4000 people in the city, where the arrest of Mahatma Gandhiji was condemned and a strong appeal made for boycott of foreign cloth.[97]

Till May 1931, activities on the national cause were allowed within the state with little hindrance.[98] It was only at the time of the Gandhi-Irwin (Pact) truce period that the state government came down heavily on all political activities, especially over the 'flag issue' which was to prove a prickly issue not only for the Mysore Government but also for the Indian National Congress, from this time to its ultimate solution in 1938.[99] Immediately following the Gandhi-Irwin Pact, on 5 May 1931 the Mysore Government prohibited the President of the Mysore Youth League and prominent State Congress leader K.T. Bhashyam from delivering a speech and his defiance led to arrest.[100]

At the time of Jawaharlal Nehru's visit to Bangalore in June 1931, a ceremonial flag hoisting was conducted on the bed of a tank known as 'Gandhi Sagar'.[101] A majestic pole, sixty feet high, was specially erected for this function, which, it was asserted, was to remain a permanent fixture. While the function which was honoured by Nehru had been allowed, on 28 June 1931 on the visit of K. Bhashyam (a Congressman from Madras) the police Inspector threatened to put an end to all such flag hoisting functions. The next day the imposing flag staff was found hacked to pieces, guy wires cut with pliers, the pole bent and broken into parts and the place desecrated.[102] The police were "suspected to be the culprits". To counter this "great dishonour to Congress and country",[103] a decision was taken by the Bangalore District Congress Committee to conduct a fast and start a *satyagraha* to avenge this desecration.

A huge public meeting was held the next day when workers from railways and mills gathered, merchants supplied the necessary things,[104] and a more impressive flag staff was made and a decision taken by the Bangalore DCC to observe 7 July 1931 as flag day, with usual propaganda for hawking khaddar, prohibition, etc. Even before the movement could gather any momentum, the Mysore Government passed an order on 4 July 1931 prohibiting the flying of the national flag for a period of six months.[105]

The main question now was whether a flag, the symbol of not only an august body like the Congress, but a symbol of the aspirations of India as a whole for freedom, could be thus allowed to be desecrated or banned by an Indian state. A special deputation was sent to confer with Mahatma Gandhiji on the question.[106] Gandhiji promised to write to Mysore Government.[107] While the negotiations between Gandhiji and Mirza Ismail were carried on with little effect till December 1931, efforts were made by the Bangalore District Congress Committee to take on lease the area of the flag pole from the municipality (dominated by Congressmen) at an annual rent of Rs. 6.[108] The Government frustrated this programme by trying to wrest the whole tank area from the municipality.

On this flag issue, both the government and the Bangalore DCC took uncompromising attitudes. Mirza Ismail, as Dewan, while accepting the aspirations and ideals associated with the Indian National flag yet opposed its being publicly hoisted. He was prepared to allow the flag to be displayed in private. His ambiguous ruling while it gave occasion to the Mysore Congress' ridicule that an action considered as derogatory could not cease to have that meaning when hoisted on private premises, open directly to public view,[109] showed up the real intent of the ban. The efforts of the government to frustrate the Mysore Congress' plan to buy the plot and make it private, showed clearly that its main objection lay in the efforts of the Bangalore DCC to play up the national flag to gather public support to its own cause.

The Bangalore DCC on the other hand thought the question was of "almost international importance".[110] They wanted to bring this issue out into the open arena of the AICC so as to elicit from the Congress a clear-cut enunciation of Congress policy on their attitude towards the states. For, they held that if it was decided that the national flag had no place in Mysore, i.e., in an Indian state, it would follow that the Congress had no place in the states at all. But neither the Congress nor Mahatma Gandhi were ready to express themselves on this issue at this time. Mahatma Gandhi equivocated on this issue by holding that it was not possible for him to advise from a distance and asked them to act as their 'inner voices' dictated to them.[111] Jawaharlal Nehru while 'entirely' sympathising with them, asked them to wait, till a decision came out of Mahatma Gaudhi's talks with Mirza Ismail and not to 'indulge' in *satyagraha* so long as there were other ways of obtaining redress.[112] The main plan of the Indian National Congress at this time was to postpone decision on this issue as by this time it was obvious to them that in case of failure of talks at the Round Table Conference they would have to start civil disobedience. As Jawaharlal Nehru wrote, they had tried their best to come to some terms with the Mysore administrators on the matter in dispute and had given them every chance to alter their policy without any loss of prestige. They could do no more. However, in this they were not ready to "wind-up Congress activities anywhere".[113]

And there the matter ended, only to raise its head again and again in flag agitations several times till it was once and for all settled in 1938 by Vallabhbhai Patel.[114]

The stalemate in the Bangalore DCC arguments with the Indian National Congress strengthened the hands of the Mysore Government. On 20 July 1931, the state's administration followed up by a ban for three months on volunteer organisations[115] as a result of which even the Indian National Congress' activities, like picketing foreign cloth shops in the city, was given up.[116] The venue of political activity thus was shifted and there was an increase of Congress activities in the Civil and Military Station of Bangalore[117] right up to the resumption of the civil disobedience movement in January 1932.

The ban had another effect. As there was a ban only on political activities and not on labour movement, the movement was directed towards organising this section. As a result on 18 July 1931, in Binny Mills, conducted by British interests, 3000 workers entered the mills, and downed their tools. The leader of the strike was K.T. Bhashyam, the President of the Bangalore DCC. The police firing which followed the strike resulted in three being killed, and several wounded.[118] An unofficial enquiry was instituted which established, to their own satisfaction at least, the high-handedness of the police and the apathy of the government.[119]

The growing popularity of Congress movement among the Trade Unions, led to the imposition by the Mysore Government of a novel order which prohibited the vice-president of the Textile Labour Union from entering certain specific areas, like the mill area and so on.[120]

Thus, during the truce period of the duration of the Gandhi-Irwin Pact, political activity was not only kept going in spite of the Mysore administration's ban on it, as the Resident acknowledged, it was idle to disguise the fact that the local Congress Committee was steadily increasing in influence and holding numerous meetings.[121]

The arrest of Mahatma Gandhi in January 1932 saw the Mysore authorities issue a warning that no further Congress activities would be tolerated in the state and that it was useless to try to hold processions or political meetings.[122] The movement after the arrest of as many as 119 by March 1932[123] lay in giving surreptitious help to the movement in British India in money, and in helping the underground movement, in which the Mysore Government if not openly sympathetic, was nevertheless, much to the chagrin of British administrators, not aggressive in countering it.

The police account compiled by J.L. Collins, District Superintendent of Police, Kanara, gives a clear picture of this phase of it.[124]

According to this report, on the resumption of civil

disobedience in January 1932, volunteers and workers who had gained experience in the first civil disobedience movement now extended help secretly. With the Congress Committees in British India being declared illegal in January 1932, the Karnataka Pradesh Congress Committee office was shifted to Bangalore. They also gave help and shelter to active workers working secretly in the border of Mysore state. The Congress workers moved about in these villages, supplied information and acted as coordinating units for disseminating the reports sent from the different *Kendras*. The educated Mysoreans prepared well worded drafts for Kanarese bulletins, printed in Bangalore and sent to newspaper correspondents. The lack of censorship arrangements in Mysore state helped not a little as the Congress correspondence could be conveniently sent and received.[125]

The British Indian administrators' request to Mysore Government for providing some means by which they could have direct control over the printing of bulletins or of enacting laws analogous to the Criminal Law Amendment Act of India, was brushed aside.

The Mysore Government, moreover, expressed themselves as not being prepared to repress the Congress movement unless the Congress resorted to unlawful activities within their state limits.[126] Neither was it ready to take any step to prevent the Congress people of the state from offering resistance outside the state limits.

The allegations by the British Indian police of Mysoreans complicity in British Indian movement was profusely substantiated by intercepted letters, newspaper extracts and bulletins.[127] These letters showed that the President of the Bangalore DCC, Venkatapatayya, had even agreed to bear all expenses of the no-tax campaign.[128]

Representations made by the Bombay Government were given rather evasive replies by Mysore Government.[129] As the noting of the Political Secretary pointed out, the Dewan was very diffident of taking drastic action for fear that it might give the people a pretext for starting an agitation within which was at present non-existent.[130] It was in this context that the Mysore Government was subjected to the strictures by the Political Department which called on the Dewan to discourage effectively any movement in their territory and advised that the line of action might be easier to follow if he were more 'guarded in his own reference to Mr. Gandhi'.[131]

Any serious confrontation of British Government in India with the state authorities over this issue was avoided only because of the civil disobedience movement being held in abeyance in British India itself, following this note at the end of 1933.

Constitutional Movement in Cochin

In Cochin the main attack on the administration was in the Legislative Council. By 1927, a group calling themselves the 'Progressive Party' was, according to the Resident, "causing the government some embarrassments" and with a stray independent vote or too had even effected one or two substantial cuts in the budget.[132] Again in 1929, the same party as a means to show its dissatisfaction at the Durbar's rejection of its resolutions, now moved for omission of the allotment made in the budget and the resolution was carried by a majority of 24 against 16. The Durbar no doubt did restore this grant but had, according to the Resident, sustained a bad moral defeat.[133] Similarly, a Bill to regulate the Nambudiri Brahmins, passed by the Legislative Council was withheld by the Maharaja's veto. There was so much comment in the newspapers[134] that the Maharaja thought it necessary to issue a communique explaining his reasons; as the Resident pointed out, this created a condition which one could hardly imagine possible in any state in north India.

Thus, the presence of a non-official majority in the Council confined the movement entirely to the Legislature, where demands for responsible government were also made.

The Regency Movement in Travancore (1926—1932)

Political activity in Travancore during this period was mainly confined to its internal aspects. The wider movement of British India, in contrast to Mysore, found little support, and what little was extended was only when it did not cross their own interests internally.

The movement in Travancore in the period between 1926 to 1931 revolved round the termination of Regency[135] or in its allied aspects—in a demand for the establishment of a Regency Council. Its connection with the responsible government movement lay in the fact that no reforms could be introduced during a Regency.[136] Thus, it was quite often as an extension of their demands on responsible government that resolutions and memorials demanding the termination of Regency were made.

Like all other political activities in Travancore, it also had its communal slant. It was alleged to be the handiwork of the Nairs.[137] This communal issue was to a certain extent complicated by palace politics.

As early as 1927, the Junior Maharani (the mother of the minor Maharaja) was implicated in what was called the Brooke Bond agitation. A scheme promoted by the Resident to grant the Brooke Bond Company 25,000 acres of land, met with an opposition from the Syrian Christians who were already in Tea business. In this agitation figures on the area of acreage granted to the Company were exaggerated and the opposition assumed anti-imperialist tones. However, the Nair elements, the chief signatories of the memorial demanding Regency Council, promised to support the Resident, provided he supported theirs.[138]

The junior Maharani's rival—the Valia Koil Tamburan—the consort of the Maharani Regent, was often accused by the Nairs of favouring the Syrian Christians.[139]

It was against this background that the state was made open to the British Indian movement. Involved as this state was in communal palace politics within, in contrast to the spectacular participation of Mysore state's people in the civil disobedience movement and their sympathy to the movement for freedom in British India—Travancore proved patently indifferent. This was also partly because prior to April 1930, little enthusiasm had been shown by leaders in the Kerala Pradesh Congress Committee in organising the movement in the states. This was in direct contrast to Mysore where even as early as 1928 it had not only a very active organisation in the Bangalore District Congress Committee, but the leaders from the Karnataka Pradesh Congress Committee had taken an active part in organising and setting up Seva Dals, etc., and created an enthusiastic volunteer corps. In fact, in Travancore, it was only on 23 March 1930 that a meeting was held to "resuscitate"[140] the now moribund local Congress Committee to concert measures for the enlistment of volunteers.

One would not be far deceived in accepting the account of the Resident that even the celebration of Independence Day on 26 January, 1930 in Travancore was marked by little interest except amongst a few of the students,[141] or that the announcement of Mahatma Gandhi's decision to break salt law in March 1930 elicited very little interest, although two Travancoreans took part as Gandhiji's companions.[142]

On the commencement of civil disobedience on 6 April 1930, a public meeting was held by the now resuscitated Trivandrum Congress Committee and brave resolutions were passed supporting salt tax campaign, congratulating the two Travancore men who were with Gandhiji's column and demanding the establishment of an All-Travancore Volunteer Corps.[143] A volunteer corps of 31 satyagrahis was enrolled for *satyagraha*. On 2 May 1930, a party of eleven satyagrahis started on their march (which number increased to twenty-four), from Travancore to Alwaye. The party reached Calicut and the salt was broken when K. Kumar the leader of the party was arrested.[144]

Apart from this single instance of participation by the states in the civil disobedience movement, even the AICC files present little evidence of any great enthusiasm on the part of the Congress from the states part of Kerala, in the civil disobedience movement.

Thus, the starting of *satyagraha* on the old issue of their social grievance at Suchindram in May 1930[145] and again in January 1931 for the opening of roads to the public,[146] may be attributed to efforts of the Congress to rouse the waning enthusiasm of the people in the state. The Gandhi-Irwin (Pact) Truce period was utilised by the Congress to reactivate the Travancore State Congress. In December 1930, Taluk Sabhas and branches[147] were formed to rouse the enthusiasm of the state's people on the programme of responsible government, so as to involve both the movements as in Mysore. Another device adopted was the invitation to leaders from British India to the states. Jawaharlal Nehru's visit to Travancore in May 1931 aroused enough enthusiasm and the crowd was so enormous that, that his car hemmed in was brought to a standstill.[148]

As a result of this propaganda, affairs in Travancore in

August 1931 picked up enough enthusiasm to be described by the Resident "as rather disquieting".[149] The Congress was now supporting labour and encouraging the move for a strike, and there was an underground movement to organise a youth league,[150] in all of which one can see the emulation by the Travancore Congress of Mysore Congress tactics.

However, on the resumption of the civil disobedience, with the arrest of Mahatma Gandhi on his return from the Round Table Conference in January 1932, the members of the Congress Committee in Travancore published their resignation in the papers and even declared that they had not got enough courage to continue the movement.[151] By August 1932, political activity in Travancore appeared to be as dead as it was in Cochin.[152]

Cochin, which had a more active Congress Party, was able to put up some show of an agitation and called a largely attended public meeting at Trichur on 12 March 1930, to lend support to Gandhiji, and to start an Ashram at Trichur to train volunteers.[153]

The general unpreparedness in the two states and on the part of the Kerala Pradesh Congress Committee was accounted for, by K. Madhava Menon, in his report to the AICC, as "due to the losing of 'credit' in Malabar of the Congress". This, according to the same report, was due to the Moplah rebellion of 1929. The "atmosphere was not at all congenial to civil disobedience and many Congressmen were diffident in starting the campaign"[154] even in Malabar, let alone in the states part of Kerala.

This lack of enthusiasm in Travancore was, as already noted, partly due to the internal politics of the state. With the termination of the Regency on 6 November 1931, expectations of reforms were rather high on the part of the people as the legal ban to such reforms had now been removed. Declarations of impending changes in 1932 moderated political activities to the presentation of memorials pleading for special or joint electorates with reservation of seats, without prejudice to their right to contest for general constituencies.[155] In this, even the early irritant which was provided in the appointment of C.P. Ramaswami Aiyar as legal adviser failed to provide any impetus to a movement.[156] The protest agitation against the appointment of C.P. Ramaswami Aiyar organised by

G. Sankaran Nair,[157] soon fizzled out by the end of November. Even the people's resentment against C.P. Ramaswami Aiyar for running the state, along with the Junior Maharani, with the Maharaja in the background and Austin the Dewan almost out of the picture,[158] were almost assuaged by the legal adviser's several lengthy conversations with the Resident where he promised that the communal situation would receive His Highness' very early and serious attention.[159] C.P. Ramaswami Aiyar even held out a promise of a scheme which he was to submit to the Maharaja's consideration, which would remove the grievances of Christians, Nairs and Ezhava communities, *vis-a-vis*, employment in proper numbers in government service. While the shortfailings of the reforms proposed subsequently spearheaded an agitation in these states by the discriminated communities, at this time the expectations raised served to keep this state out of the general movement of British India. In this, the Congress policy towards the states—especially on the federal issue—seems to have been partly the reason for the general lack of response from the Kerala State to the civil disobedience movement.

The extent of the disenchantment of the Kerala State to the movement of British India and its irritation can be gauged from the proceedings of the All-India State Subjects Committee meeting in Cochin on 2 June 1930. This meeting expressed irritation at the British Indian leaders not championing their cause and warned them that any constitution drawn up without the participation of the representatives of the people of the states would stand condemned by a-third of India, and that if they did meet in any conference with the voice of the people of the states excluded from evolving a constitution for India, it would be considered as a gross and ungrateful betrayal of their brethren in the states.[160]

These threats of these States Subjects Committees, nor the sly efforts of the Mysore Congress—as in the flag issue—to involve the Indian National Congress in its movement, or failing it, to get a clear-cut enunciation of policy on the place of the states people in the wider Indian movement or *vice versa*, seem to have had any effect. Nor were their efforts to rope in the Indian National Congress' support to their cause to prove in any way successful; for the decision to sacrifice the states peoples interest had already been taken. Thus, though Jawarharlal Nehru, in February 1931, in a draft appeal to the Congress, had stipulated among other conditions, that the Congress work for "freedom and protection of the fundamental citizen rights of the people of the Indian states"[161] and that adequate representation be granted in any federal legislature that may be evolved, these proposals found no resonance in any Congress pronouncements or resolution.

It was in this background that the Kerala Provincial Conference convened in May 1931 demanded that the Congress enunciation of fundamental rights be made applicable to the people of the native states as well,[162] and that the Indian National Congress accept no scheme of federation without definite provision for immediate establishment of full responsible government in the Indian states as well as in British Indian Provinces. It insisted that it include provisions for elected reprsentatives (to the Federal Assembly) of the people of the state.

It was in view of the final disallowance of the ISPC to the Round Table Conference by the British administrators and in view of the rather unhelpful attitude of the Indian National Congress, that the ISPC issued a manifesto making known their views on the several issues.[163] It demanded that entrance by the states to the federation be made conditional on fulfilment of certain minimum conditions guaranting, among others,

(a) federal citizenship and Fundamental Rights for the people of the states, embodied in the new constitution;

(b) federal judicial machinery to protect these Fundamental Rights to the people of the states;

(c) the linking of the judiciary in the state to the federal supreme court; and

(d) direct representation to the people of the states in the central legislature by the same system of election and power of voting as may prevail at the time for the people of British India.

In a special appeal to the people of British India it enjoined that for the sake of some power for themselves, they should not permanently sacrifice the interest of 80 millions of the states people. In a special plea to Mahatma Gandhi it exhorted him to "take care of the interests of the people of the states as distinguished from those of the princes"[164] and ensure that the stipulations made in the manifesto be taken care of in the making of a federal constitution.

Mahatma Gandhi did make a personal appeal to the princes at the Round Table Conference. Citing the friendly spirit which had existed between the Congress and the rulers, he pleaded that the rulers should allow the fundamental rights of the states peoples to be included in the federal constitution "to be tested by the court",[165] and that the princes should introduce "elements, only elements of respresentation on behalf of their subjects".[166] However, the manner of the presentation of the states peoples case by Mahatma Gandhi at the Round Table Conference was a cause of complaint in subsequent years by the states peoples' organisation. They felt he had not made it clear whether the election of the states people' and Declaration of Rights in their interest was merely "a desirable feature, or an essential condition".[167] This contention of the states people may seem mere casuistry to those who have not understood the basic divergence of the Congress policy and that of the states people. If it had been acknowledged as an 'essential condition', by an extension of it as a theory—an ideology—it would have included the arena as inclusive of the structure within the state. This in turn would have taken the states' people a step further in the inclusion of their demands on responsible government. If it were a mere concession, it may be only held as a particular instance of the relationship of the Indian National Congress with the Maharaja and his administration. Another feature also had to be taken care of in the Congress-states people relationship. The Congress concessions to the elective principle in a federal chamber would not necessarily have helped the states peoples in their movement for responsible government, unless the federal chamber had been given more powers to interfere in the units of the states. Without such developments, such an introduction would have helped the Congress mainly, for it would have allowed it to play with more votes in the federal chamber, as it was possible that elected members from the states would be more amenable to Congress interests. However, this took the states peoples in their internal struggle for responsible government little further. This dichotomy in the states-Congress relationship was to become more prominent with the enunciation of federal proposals and their crystallisation in the next period.

The failure of the talks at the second Round Table Conference, leading to a civil disobedience movement in British India, the arrest of the nationalists and the ban on the Congress organisation, postponed any settlement of these issues for the time being. They were taken up only in June 1934, on the resumption of Congress activities, the course of which will be dealt in the next chapter.

Conclusion

The differing interests of the Indian National Congress, the states peoples and the princes, were spelt out in their constitutional proposals during this period. The independent postures of the states people, however, met a check in the pronouncements of the Butler Committee. While its pronouncements, that the relationship of the princes was with the Crown, affected both the British Indian Nationalists' aspirations on their claims to paramountcy, and the states people on their democratic programme, it dealt a more severe blow on the state peoples position when it refused to entertain their views in their committee. This set a precedence for similar refusals to the states people to any future conference convened for consultation on constitutional reforms. This, more importantly, robbed this central organisation of its very *raison d'etre*. Combined as this was with the new concept of personal relationship of the prince as between the states and the Crown, it, by arousing the fears of the nationalists of British motives, had its chain repercussions on the Indian nationalists' relationship with the states people. The two organisations, the ISPC and the Indian National Congress, which had been moving closer, were now arrested on their tracks and from this time one could trace a further disengagement of the Indian National Congress from the aspirations of the states people on responsible government (on which, it had had reservation even earlier).

In this, denied as the states people were any say in the constitutional conferences or meetings convened by British administrators for all India, the collective organisation of the states people was now dependent on the INC. Meeting an unsympathetic attitude from them, they existed solely as an organisation in confrontation with the Indian National Congress.

The Butler Committee decisions thus were to further the confrontation, which was already apparent in the relationship of the states people, *vis-a-vis*, the British Indian nationalists. However, the breaking of the civil disobedience movement in British India and the states peoples participation and involvement in it, though in varying degrees, postponed the issue to the subsequent period.

But what was clear, even now, was that the participation of the states people in a nationalist programme was to be reciprocal. It was this which made it impossible for a branch of the Indian National Congress to withold itself from an active involvement in a purely local issue. The Bangalore District Congress Committee (a body which as a subordinate branch of the INC was to promote only the British Indian objective and engage itself in the 'constructive' work alone) was to involve itself in a purely local issue on press freedom. The Mysore State Congress' ritual of flag hoisting seemed to press the same point. It was in this context that a dishonour to the Congress flag (a hoisting of which by Jawaharlal Nehru, just a few days prior to it, was attended by much pomp and ceremony) became an issue of "almost international importance". But in this, the subordination of the states programme, in Mysore, to the British Indian nationalist movement, in its active phase of Civil Disobedience, seemed to emphasise the priorities accepted by this states people.

Tranancore exhibited an altogether different facet. The disenchantment of the local populace, in the face of INC policy, was clearly evident in the inability of a Congress leadership to enthuse them into an active participation on the national programme of Civil Disobedience. Even the resuscitation of the 'untouchability' issue at Suchindram was not able to promote any enthusiasm for it. Here, it was made abundantly clear that the national programme was subordinate to the local issue—at this time the interests of the Regency movement—and could only be on a reciprocal basis.

5

Confrontation to Climax

The Movement from 1933 to February 1938

The ISPC-Indian National Congress Confrontation (1933-1936)

As already noted in the last chapter, following the Butler Committee decisions, one could trace a disengagement of the Indian National Congress from the aspirations of the state's people on a democratic programme.[1] The state's people, agitated by this facet of Congress policy, had postponed bringing their grievances to the open forum of the INC only due to the nationalists own pre-occupation with the Civil Disobedience movement. In this, they had hoped that their active participation in the Civil Disobedience movement of British India would make for a reciprocal sympathy to their cause. However, Congress policy, based as it was on the objective of an Indian union, proved to be not very sympathetic to it. The evolution of the peculiar federal proposals which emerged out of the Round Table Conferences in the White Paper of 1933 strengthened Mahatma Gandhi's appreciation of the value of a non-aligned policy as between the princes and the states' people, in order to obtain a leverage in the political negotiation.[2] Thus the Congress was willing to make no further accomodation towards the states peoples' cause beyond what was adopted in 1928. The pleadings by the states people which followed this unsympathetic treatment of their cause by the Indian National Congress, only served to bring the ISPC up against Mahatma Gandhi as the real policy maker of the Congress. The rise of the Socialist Party during the same period (1933-34), as a party within the Congress, brought to the front differences between groups within the party on the question of support to the states people and this complicated the issue further.

This confrontation between the ISPC and the Indian National Congress brought home a realisation within the states that the constructive work of the Congress by itself could find little support, unless the Congress was willing to make some concession to the states peoples' view. This conflict, though carried on at an All-India level, had its significant effect on these states, and as such, has to be studied in detail as part of these states peoples' movement. Moreover, it was events in Mysore which really accelerated the confrontation from a mere verbal slanging argument to its active phase of the passing of a resolution in favour of the states' people in the Calcutta Congress. This brought on a direct intervention by Mahatma Gandhi, leading in its turn, to the momentous Haripura decision in February, 1938 which ultimately brought an end to this confrontation.

Thus, it was in the background of this encounter between the ISPC and the Indian National Congress that the late 1930s saw the main thrust of the democractic movement in these three states. In this, the three Dewans, Mirza Ismail in Mysore (1928-40), Shanmukham Chetty in Cochin (1937-41) and C.P. Ramaswami Aiyar in Travancore (1931-1936, as legal adviser and 1936 to July 1947 as Dewan) by their close connection with the Congress leaders[3] and individual approaches in reacting to the movement, left their indelible mark on it. In this, through their close personal relationship with the Maharajas, they were able to assert an absolute domination over the administration.

The announcement of an Indian National Congress session scheduled for October 1934 at Bombay, brought out the long deferred question of Congress policy towards the states' peoples movement, again, into the open. Preceding this session, in June 1934, a deputation of the ISPC, headed by N.C. Kelkar, waited on Gandhiji at Poona to obtain his views. Gandhiji suggested that the deputationists may draft a resolution to be adopted by the Working Committee, on which he agreed to give his opinion.[4]

The draft resolution proposed by the ISPC,[5] and a separate questionnaire presented to Gandhiji, by this deputation, demanded that the Congress should reaffirm the resolution pledging its support to the state's people's cause passed at the AICC sessions at Madras and Calcutta in 1927 and 1928 respectively.[7] Citing the active support given by the people of the states to the civil disobedience movement, it requested that the Congress in a spirit of good comradeship and reciprocation would insist on elected representation for the states in the Constituent Assembly that it was demanding and in spelling out its rejection of the White Paper scheme, emphasize that it was so because of the provisions concerning the states.

The substitution of the word 'pledge' for the earlier 'assurance' was clearly a demand for a more active participation of the nationalists in the state movement. Secondly, the stipulation of popular representation from the states to the Constituent Assembly was to ensure that no agreement would be arrived at with the Indian states' governments above the heads of the states' people by the Congress.

Mahatma Gandhi's reply reiterated, yet again, the old arguments on the legal position of the states as independent entities under British Law where the Congress had no more power to shape the policy of the states than it had that of Afghanistan.[8] He explained that it was not "want of appreciation or will", that compelled Congress policy to one of helplessness, but a conviction that any attempt on the part of Congress at interference (except an attempt at conversion of rulers through petitions), would only damage the cause of the people in the states. In this, while taking care to emphasize that the states were undoubtedly an integral part of geographic India, he brushed aside their demands on Federation, explaining that the

Congress entering the Federation had to depend upon mutual adjustments and many other circumstances beyond the attitude of the princes or their subjects.[9]

These rigid attitudes adopted by Mahatma Gandhi (and through him the Congress) and the Indian States Peoples' Conference emphasised, yet again, clearly the divergent issues that were involved. As Mahatma Gandhi asserted, he was "well aware of the general abuses in the states" and detested "corruption, high handedness, unbridled autocracy",[10] as much as they did. Though his sympathy was for the reform of these abuses his cause could not be compromised. His main concern was for the unity of India which overrode other considerations; the need of the Congress was to keep its hands free, as a federation would depend on mutual adjustments,[11] mainly with the rulers who were in the legal sense the recognised authorities in the states.

With viewpoints so different, as Gandhi pointed out, there seemed to be no meeting ground. Therefore it was best to agree to differ as to the methods of approach.[12]

Having failed to convince Mahatma Gandhi, the Indian States Peoples' Conference decided to take the issue to the forefront of Congress politics.[13] In order to do the needful propaganda for the purpose, a manifesto emphasizing their demands on Fundamental Rights, of the principle of election of states representatives, and a change in Congress creed so as to include the states people in their goal of *swarajya*, was issued by the ISPC in October 1934.[14] Rajendra Prasad, the President of the Congress, was requested to place it before the Subjects Committee meeting of the Bombay session scheduled for 24 to 26 October 1934.

However, the states people were out-manoeuvred by Mahatma Gandhi. His proposed counter resolution redefining Congress policy, made a deliberate reaffirmation of the non-interference policy in its very opening sentence.[15] While such a resolution revising the clause that had been deliberately deleted in 1928, would have retarded the position of the states people (*vis-a-vis* their special interest of responsible government) in the Congress, neither his subsequent appeal to the rulers for granting responsible government and civil liberties, nor his statement emphasizing the geographical unity of India "notwithstanding the fact that it was cut up into parts governed under different systems,"[16] would have gained much for the states people. Rather than have such a resolution reviving the non-interference policy, Balwantray and other states representatives requested Mahatma Gandhi to drop the resolution, to which request Gandhiji ultimately agreed.[17] No resolution on the states people was ultimately passed at the Congress session at Bombay. In the face of this opposition from Mahatma Gandhi, the states people did not even dare to bring their question to a discussion at the open forum for fear that Mahatma Gandhi's resolution be ultimately passed.[18]

The question of the states came up again for discussion in June 1935, brought about this time by the rather imprudent remarks of one of its prominent members Mr Bhulabhai Desai, the Leader of Congress Party in the Assembly. In his speech before the Mysore Bar Association on 10 June 1935, emphasising the rulers' legal position in the states polity he advised the states subjects, as a desirable policy, to be friendly with them. He held that the concept of abolition of the princes was psychologically wrong for it only drove the princes to become the allies of Great Britain.[19] The *summum bonum* of his contention was that it was not good policy for the states people to make an issue of responsible government at this juncture.

The controversy[20] which raged over Bhulabai's speech achieved what the repeated petitions of the ISPC had been unable to do; the question of the Indian states came to be included in the agenda of the Congress Working Committee meeting held at Wardha on 29 July 1935.[21] The redefined policy of the Congress in July 1935, accepted the proposition that people of the states had an inherent right to *Swaraj* no less than the people of British India and that it stood by the declarations made earlier. While emphasising, that the responsibility and burden of carrying on that struggle within the state would necessarily have to fall on the states' people themselves, and that the Congress could only exercise moral and friendly influence upon the states, it gave them an assurance that the Congress would never be guilty of sacrificing their interests in order to buy the support of the princes.[22]

While this assurance went a long way towards assuaging the state people, at the AICC meeting in Madras on 17 October

1935, when the Working Committee resolution passed at Wardha was made open for debate, the states people, with the help of the socialists in the Congress, made a concerted move to gain a further assurance of representation in the Constituent Assembly on the same basis as in British India. They demanded that the acceptance of the constitution by the Congress be made conditional on inclusion of elementary rights of citizenship in it for the states people.[23] In a bid to involve the Congress participation in the states people's movement, Kamaladevi Chattopadhyaya, belonging to the socialist camp, charged that "expressions of helplessness and impotence on the part of Congress . . . had been working the imagination of the Congress too much and should be given up for active participation".[24]

Though the amendments of the socialists was defeated by 31 votes to 10, that the question had caused an acrimonious debate and the fact that the voting had been divided was itself of importance. From this time, the states question was made an issue of a party faction within the Congress with the Socialist Party staunchly coming out in support of the states people. The states peoples activities with the Indian National Congress lay in exploiting this factionalism to their advantage into prodding them on to a change of policy[25] in giving them active help in their political activity. The only bone of contention now between the states people and the Congress was the ban on active participation of the Congress in the states and the matter of representation to the future Constituent Assembly, being confined solely to the states people and on the same basis as in British India.

The Congress assurance to the states people that it would not sacrifice the states people's interest "to buy the support of the princes", had put a stop to all charges and suspicions of Congress treachery. In a further extension of this assurance the Congress in its session at Lucknow in April 1936, proclaimed unequivocally that in its opinion the people of the states should have the same right of self-determination as those of the rest of India and that now Congress stood for the same political, social and democratic liberties for every part of India.[26]

It was this constant bickering which had become a part and parcel of the Indian National Congress' relationship with the states people which made a section of both parties realise the necessity of a new organisation to evolve for a better relationship. Thus, *a new chapter in the progress of the states peoples politics*[27] was begun when the states people met in an All-India Conference in July 1936 at Karachi to organise a body on *lines closely analogous to those adopted by the Congress.* This body, though it arose out of the ashes of the earlier one, was different from the ISPC and worked on a different basis.

The ISPC had adopted an independent posture as a distinct body from that of the Indian National Congress.[28] The new body—the *All India States Peoples' Conference*—was evolved as a link association (though theoretically absolutely independent from the INC) more or less under the tutelage of the Indian National Congress. Thus it took its cue, not so much from the states peoples' interest, but obeyed the behests made known from behind the curtains of the Indian National Congress. This organisation, so as to avoid controversies over their relative position on political issues being brought to the open sessions of the INC, chose members prominent in the INC and avowed sympathisers of the states people's cause as the President of the new body. Thus Sitaramayya and later Jawaharlal Nehru became its president in its early years. It is the confusion in the understanding of the aims of the earlier organisation and that of the later one that has lent itself to misstatements.[29]

Prominent as these three states had been in the activities of the ISPC which represented their views more closely than the later organisation the AISPC, these three states were wary of joining the new organisation. In October 1937, Travancore, Cochin and Mysore were approached by the AISPC to become affiliated members. However, in spite of repeated requests from it, these states, suspicious as they were of this new organisation, did not join the organisation till 1940.[30] Thus the policies, the postures and the attitudes of the AISPC affected these states, which took their direction after 1938 directly from Mahatma Gandhi, only peripherally.

Course of the Movement within the States—Travancore (1933-36)

The confrontation of the ISPC with the INC, during the years 1933-36, in its immediate impact, found the subjects of Travancore exhibit little interest in Indian National Congress activities. In fact, during the period 1933-37 there was not even an active Congress organisation or branch within the state.[31] The movement within state, lay outside Congress interest or intervention.

It was the impending constitutional changes promised in 1932, along with C.P. Ramaswami Aiyar's promise of reforms in civil service leading to equitable distribution of communities, which held the state peoples' movement in Travancore under leash. Added to this was an announcement by the Government of Travancore, in November 1932, of a Committee on Temple Entry.[32]

However, little was it realised that this measure of the Travancore Government was mainly motivated by tactical considerations. Realising the explosive nature of the situation in Travancore, where the social issue did provide a base for a political agitation, the government of Travancore's tactic lays in separating the social issue from the political.

The reform constitution published in December 1932, by insisting on property qualification and by providing no special electorates, provided little advantage to the demands of the discriminated communities. The non-official majorities which it provided for in both the legislatures thus only went towards the entrenching of the Nair vested interests.[33] Thus it was realised from the very day of its promulgation that there was likely to be a good deal of unrest and trouble, unless the Travancore Government saw their way to afford some concessions.

Travancore Government explained its action on the plea that adult franchise had not been adopted anywhere in India, and that in British India reservation of seats had been allowed only for minority communities and not for seats whose voting strength to population was considerable. This when studied in the context of Mysore and Cochin concessions in like contingencies—only lent itself to the realisation that issues were being purposely confused.

On 25 January 1933, twelve different associations of Christians, Mohammedans and Ezhavas of Travancore held a joint conference at Travancore at which it demanded representation in the Reformed Council in proportion to the population; they threatened to boycott the council unless their demand was satisfied.[34] This joint Political Conference saw the forging of the Samyukta Party and the beginning of an organised movement in Travancore.

Several meetings were held in February and March 1933, with the press taking an active part in it. As a result the government was forced into holding informal discussions[35] with these communities, when the Dewan came to an understanding to dissolve the legislature in case of any injustice resulting from elections.[36]

Elections were held in June 1933 which returned a majority of Nairs to both Houses. The government tried to satisfy the discriminated communities by distributing the 'nominated seats' at their disposal among them. However, even after the distribution, the Nair majority in both councils as a total against the combine of these three communities was still maintained.[37]

The agitation which followed, adopted the boycott of legislature tactics as had been done by the swarajists in British India, against the Montagu-Chelmsford reforms. The impending visit of the Viceroy in December 1933 and the continuance of an active campaign of agitation against the reformed legislatures,[38] compelled the government to open negotiations to try to come to some terms. The abstentionists suspended the movement in December 1933[39] when the Dewan and C.P. Ramaswami Aiyar expressed the government's willingness to redress their grievances, if they would approach the government and the Maharaja in a 'proper spirit'.[40] The Travancore Government in turn followed up in February 1934, on receiving the report of the 'Temple Entry Committee' constituted earlier, by issuing orders to abolish unapproachability and to throw open all roads, tanks and wells to all classes of people. The orders were issued before Mahatma Gandhi's arrival at Trivandrum and was acclaimed by him in his speeches.[41]

In March 1934 the abstentionists waited in a deputation on a new Dewan and reminded him of his predecessors and C.P. Ramaswami Aiyar's earlier promise to redress their grievances. C.P. Ramaswami Aiyar, however, denied having given any such promise. The Dewan only gave them "a patient hearing".[42]

The Dewan, with C.P. Ramaswami Aiyar as legal adviser,

subjected as he was to his criticism, worked under an additional restraint than other Dewans had done hitherto.[43] This was especially irksome as while the Dewan was blamed for resultant action, the legal adviser was able to interfere with impunity.

The sustained agitation carried on by these communities for a period of two and half years,[44] forced the administration into a scheme for reforms of the two legislatures in August, 1935 which tried to satisfy the discriminated communities. This was followed up in August 1936 by another scheme which went further towards amending the existing franchise and constituencies of the two State Assemblies, and modified the Nair predominance.[45]

Before we move on to the course of the subsequent peoples movement in this state, it becomes necessary that we should analyse some of the general features in their first confrontation in the Abstention Movement. This movement had a genuine grievance which was peculiar to this state alone. In Cochin, though the Nairs had a social predominance, this was not carried on to the political plane.[46]

Secondly, the movement was characterised by a spirit of give and take by both parties. The agitators during the time of the Viceregal visit were ready to suspend the movement, so as not to embarrass the government, and the Dewan was also ready to consider their grievances with a sympathy and a genuine effort towards an amelioration of it. And, again, the government was moved by a desire to establish its *bona fides* in the eyes of the outside world, as for example, its social reforms to coincide with Gandhiji's arrival. Thirdly, even if there was sometimes a sense of bitterness it was against the legal adviser; thus the stage was set for a direct confrontation when the hated legal adviser himself became the Dewan in the next round. In the context of a despotism, which was the characteristic of the state's administration, the personal relationship between the Dewan and the people was often a prominent factor. Another important factor, than the one enumerated above, was that their first success over the government in gaining their objective, of changing the franchise, whetted the states peoples' appetite to go all out for their ultimate millenium—responsible government—in the subsequent period. It is important to note, however, that while in their Abstention

Movement the Indian National Congress played no part (as at this period with the resignation of the Congress members in 1932 the Congress organisation in the state lay moribund), the movement which followed in 1936 after C.P. Ramaswami Aiyar's appointment as Dewan, was affected and conditioned by the events in other states and by Congress policy in general towards the states. More important than all these factors was that this movement provided the very base to the states peoples' movement which the civil disobedience movement, unlike in Mysore, had failed to provide. Again, it was the Samyukta Party forged by this movement, which formed the core round which the Travancore State Congress was built, and forming as it did the forerunner of the Congress movement in this state, it changed the very character and personnel of the Congress in Travancore.

Apathy in Mysore Congress (1933-1936)

The same period from 1933 to the end of 1936, in Mysore, was marked by a near total lack of interest in any political activity. As Hardikar in a letter to Jawaharlal Nehru remarked in August 1936, the people who were once prominent in the Congress movement, had now become very lukewarm towards the Congress organisation and there was not a single representation on the Karnataka Pradesh Congress Committee from the state of Mysore.[47] There was a general grievance that the British Indian leaders had not cared to sympathise with the people of the state in their Congress activities, and they saw no reason why the states people should participate in any Congress propaganda.

Earlier in August 1935, soon after the Wardha resolution, attempts had been made to revive political activity on its old programme of flag demonstrations. However, a government order banning not only such demonstrations but all political activity,[48] now resulted in an altogether unexpected turn.

The near apathy in the Mysore State Congress during the years 1933-1936 had resulted in the stepping up of activities of the rival organisation of the non-Brahmins. The Peoples Federation which was a coalition brought about in 1934 between the Praja Mitra Mandali[49] and of the Peoples Party—

formed in 1930 with responsible government as its goal[50]—now found itself in the same boat as the Mysore Congress. The Peoples Federation had planned to hold several raiyat conferences in the state from 20 March to 20 April, 1935, thus even earlier than the flag demonstrations planned by the Mysore Congress. The Mysore Government's ban on all political activity or conferences of the raiyats[51] led to a realisation of the unity of interests and made possible a further evolution of the merger principle. Thus, at the time of the discussions in the Legislature on the ban on meetings of the Peoples Federation, K.T. Bhashyam (a Brahmin and a prominent Mysore State Congress member) in the Legislature, had come to their support. This was the first step which made possible a merger between the Mysore State Congress and the Peoples Federation. Such a merger was not without a precedence. The Karnataka non-Brahmin Conference had merged with the Indian National Congress at Belgaum in May 1930.[52]

Though in March 1936 election the Mysore State Congress and the Peoples Federation had contested the elections against each other, even then, according to Chengalaraya Reddy, the President of the Peoples Federation, they had realised that a situation would soon arise when it would be necessary to carry on the political struggle under the direct auspices of the Congress.[53] The Peoples Federation, according to him, stood out of the Congress only because of the official Congress policy of non-interference in the internal politics of the state.[54]

The 'situation' awaited by the Peoples Federation arose much too soon. In December 1936, the Mysore State Congress had roused itself from its apathy to constitute a Mysore Parliamentary Board from the various District Congress Committees in the state, for the purpose of contesting the elections to the Representative Assembly and the Legislative Council,[55] which were scheduled to take place in March 1937. The Mysore State Congress Parliamentary Board, at its inaugural meet on 16 January 1937 had invited Mrs. Kamaladevi Chattopadhyaya, a staunch supporter of the states in the Congress, to inaugurate the campaign. However, the Government of Mysore served an order on her prohibiting her from making any speeches in Bangalore City within a radius of five miles, for a period of six months.[56]

Now a series of repressive actions of the Mysore Government gave a basis for an active movement. On 17 January 1937, the Town Hall where meeting of the Congress was to be held was not made available and the two main speakers, T. Ramachandra Rao and D.P. Karmarkar barred from making speeches for one month. On 24 January 1937 the celebration of Independence Day and holding of public meetings, demonstrations etc. were prohibited. On 25 January 1937 the Bangalore City Congress Committee President, Shamanna and G.R. Swami and 14 others were arrested. On the same day the hoisting of the National Flag was prohibited for one year within a 7 mile radius of Mysore City. On 29 January 1937, T. Ramachandra Rao was arrested.[57]

In June 1937 the city Magistrate of Bangalore prohibited the holding of meetings within the limits of the city without obtaining previous licence. K.T. Bhashyam tried to take the issue to the Legislature but was frustrated by the Dewan who banned this discussion relating to the matters applicable to the High Court.[58] In July 1937 M.R. Masani, the then General Secretary of the All India Socialist Party, who had been invited by the Mysore State Youth League—a branch organisation of the Mysore State Congress—was prohibited from making any speeches or in taking part in the Conference. Again, the Mass Awakeners' Union, another branch of the Mysore State Congress was prohibited from holding a procession on 19 July 1937.[59]

It was not as if these repressive actions were directed against the Congress mainly because the government could not permit activities of outside agitators in the state;[60] the Dewan of Mysore who prohibited activities of outside Congress agitators, had himself invited Shri Bhai Parmanand, the Vice-President of the Hindu Mahasabha, to pay a visit to Mysore during Moharrum and the Holi holidays from 11 to 17 March 1937[61] just prior to the elections.

It was in the background of these repressive actions that the movement in Mysore built up into a crescendo. However, before continuing with this account leading on to the Calcutta Congress resolution and its aftermath, it becomes necessary that we shift our perspective to the movement in the other states to bring the narration of events on a parallel sequence.

Cochin Congress Movement

In Cochin, though its government had proceeded quite far towards the amelioration of the communal problem and, according to Mahatma Gandhi, provided an example which other states would do well to copy,[62] its political situation during 1935-37 was not so happy.

Soon after his appointment as Dewan in 1935, Shanmugham Chetty found himself opposed by the vested interests and the people of the state because of a series of actions which made him open to charges of corruption and nepotism.

The Central Bank of India which had till then no branches in Cochin, was made the state's bank and the States' balances transferred to it from the National Bank of India which had hitherto held it.[63] This action was doubly suspect as the Dewan's brother had been provided with an appointment in the Central Bank of India. His next action in revoking the licence of the Trichur Electric Company and giving the contract to Chandrie & Company of Madras, brought the vested interests of the state into a confrontation with him. To cap it all, the *West Coast Review* which complained of the Dewan's action was prosecuted on charges of sedition and convicted by the chief judge, who had himself owed his position to the Dewan's favours and had been a mere dismissed sub-Inspector of Travancore State.[64]

Apart from the prosecution of the *West Coast Review*, other local newspapers as *Gomati* and *Cochinite* were also proceeded against,[65] and Cochin, which had till now prided itself on having no press regulation, had a press Act rushed through in the Legislature. The temper of the Legislature was made obvious when it threw the Act out, by a majority. An Emergency Press Regulation was then passed by Proclamation and the Independent Party in the Legislative Council staged a walk-out to voice its protest.[66]

In May 1937, the spirit of the people was ruffled yet a little more by the arrest of Mr. Cheriyan Manjuran, a prominent labour leader, on charges of sedition. The arrest caused wide-spread resentment among the labour circles throughout Kerala, resolutions criticising the actions of the Cochin Government were passed at meetings held at various places within the states of Travancore, Cochin, Calicut and Canannore in British Malabar.[67] Thus events in Cochin just as much in Mysore seemed to be marching towards a crisis.

Travancore (1936-37)

In contrast to affairs in Cochin and Mysore, the political situation in Travancore presented a picture of calmness. C.P. Ramaswami Iyer, with the assumption of office as the new Dewan, in October 1936, showed a really conciliatory spirit. He assured a deputation of the All-Travancore Joint Political Congress (the Samyukta Party)[68] that the Government would not show any distinction between one faith and another and that the question of Temple Entry was engaging the anxious attention of the Maharaja and the government. Moreover, he took this opportunity to make a melodramatic appeal to the deputationists, "not as a favour (but as) an appeal" to them, as patriotic citizens of Travancore, that however strong their feelings might be, however emphatically they did have to express those feelings, never to give the impression to the world outside that there was any form of tyranny or oppression in Travancore, or that the administration was essentially at fault.

In keeping with this promise on 12 November 1936, a Royal Proclaimation was issued throwing open all state owned temples to all Hindus irrespective of caste or community.[69]

In April 1937, the second election under the reformed constitution was held without tension. There seemed to be perfect accord between the Dewan and the people. In the reconstituted chamber of the Travancore Legislature held on 21 May, 1937 T.M. Varghese, the Christian leader of the Joint Political Congress Party, was elected Deputy President and thus the Dewan according to the Resident had won over the opposition *en bloc.*[70]

In September 1937, some of the Congress ministers from the Madras Province made a visit to the state when K. Santhanam, a prominent Congress member, exhorted the administration, that in keeping with the Temple Entry Proclamation, Travancore would give the lead in the matter of removing disabilities on civil liberties, and extend absolute freedom of speech and expression and establish responsible government in the state.[71] C.P. Ramaswami Aiyar was seen, much to the chagrin of the Resident, in the company of Congress ministers and even entertaining C. Rajagopalachari at a party at his house in Mylapore.[72] On the 25th birthday of His Highness, the state guests included P.S. Sivaswami Iyer and Madras Congress ministers.[73]

In the words of the Resident "now that the rulers of the state themselves had begun to flirt with the Congress, the public was not slow to note the change in attitude".[74] On 12 September 1937, a committee was formed to revive the Congress movement in the state.[75]

With affairs in Travancore running so smoothly, especially in contrast to affairs in Mysore and Cochin, given the character of C.P. Ramaswami Aiyar, it was inevitable that, Jack Horner like, he would harp on the 'what a good boy am I' theme, which was to bring him into a confrontation with the administrators of the other states. It was in this context that Mirza Ismail complained to the Political Secretary of C.P. Ramaswami Aiyar's "lack of good neighbourliness"[76] in his references not only in the public utterances and in the press, but in official correspondence, of missing no opportunity of putting other states and statesmen in the wrong and of 'telling the world' how he and Travancore shone by comparison. He trusted that in future references, direct or indirect, to the state, if any were made at all, it would bear some relation to the facts and would at all events, be in a happier vein.[77]

The dispute between the administration of Travancore and Cochin was complicated further by the animosities of the Maharajas themselves that arose out of the Temple Entry Proclamation in Travancore. Here, in a temple situated in Cochin,[78] the Maharaja of Travancore by long historical precedent, had the right of appointing the *Kaimal* or chief priest. The controversy arose, when in April 1937, on representation made by some *yogakars* to His Highness the Maharaja of Cochin, he declared the temple polluted because a *Tantri* who officiated in a Travancore temple which was open to *svarnas*, had officiated in the temple. The Maharaja of Cochin held that purificatory ceremony was necessary before a festival (at which the Maharaja of Cochin took a prominent part) could commence. What tickled British mirth was that a Dewan of Cochin, a prominent member of the Justice Party, was to defend the orthodoxy of a Maharaja in fighting indirectly the Temple Entry Proclamation, while a Brahmin of Madras, the Dewan of Travancore fought on the side of Temple Entry.

It was at this time when this controversy was at its height that C.P. Ramaswami Aiyar complained to the British Government of attacks against the Maharaja of Travancore in the press of Cochin.[79] In support of this he sent a copy of a pamphlet brought out by a Cochinite called "Namgulate Prasthavana". As the pamphlet contained merely speeches delivered by the authors in Madras, Shanmukham Chetty answered that it would be more appropriate for Travancore to complain to Madras Presidency than to Cochin. He, in turn, complained against the Travancore Government allowing attack against the Government of Cochin in support of which he sent extracts from the newspapers which criticised Shanmukham Chetty's policy of importing foreigners and foreign companies.[80]

These accusations not only contributed to a feeling of bitterness between the administrators of these two states, but also had an important bearing in that, that at the time of the height of the movement in Travancore, when public agitation was banned and the moment had to go underground, Cochin territory proved a convenient asylum and centre for this movement. A characteristic which is evident in the movement of these three states, especially that of Kerala, was that it was not confined to the limits of the states territory but overflowed into British Malabar, and each other's territory. Thus there was a cooperation among the agitators of these states which was in direct contrast to the relationship existing between the heads of administration in the states, on the eve of the gathering of momentum of the movement.

Events in Mysore Leading to Calcutta Congress Resolution

The immediate cause which precipitated a confrontation in Mysore between the states administration and the states people took place in August 1937, when the Mass Awakeners Union, announced a public meeting in the labour quarters of Bangalore and the authorities banned all public meetings in the city for a period of six months.[81]

On 8 August 1937, at a meeting of the various representatives from all parts of Mysore and of the members of the Mysore Congress Board,[82] decision was taken to start a peaceful non-violent 'Direct Action' demonstration as the only means of combatting the repressive measures.[83] A Direct Action Council consisting of three members—T. Siddalingiah, M. Seetharama Sastri and Tagadur Ramachandra Rao—was constituted at the same meeting[84] and decision taken to start the campaign 'not later than 10 October 1937 and not earlier than 1 September, 1937', so as to give them time to start negotiations with the government with a view to the withdrawal of the ordinances. It was decided at the same meeting to approach the Indian National Congress and Jawaharlal Nehru to bless the campaign.[85]

In view of the later controversies of complicity and involvement of the Indian National Congress in states peoples' movement, it becomes necessary to emphasise here the polnt that the movement in Mysore was thus not instigated directly or indirectly by the Indian National Congress or its members. Nor was active support of that organisation asked.[86] The letter from Siddalingiah to Jawaharlal Nehru emphasized this point, yet again, in his assertion, that the decision, conduct, credit and discredit, success or failure would be theirs, and theirs the sole responsibility in the matter; only blessings of an elder was sought.[87]

Jawaharlal Nehru in his reply reiterated the same point. He warned that, while it was not their wish to come in the way of any legitimate steps that might be taken, they were to consider such steps in all their bearings, and in any action they did take, the responsibility was to rest on the Board.[88]

In such a context the important question of the attitude to be adopted by the Karnataka Provincial Congress Committee had to be determined.[89] The anomalous nature of the body was made obvious in the instructions set out to it for its conduct by Jawaharlal Nehru. The later misunderstandings of the Karnataka Provincial Congress Committee (KPCC) with the Mysore Congress Board lay in its inability to perform a double role. As agent of the Indian National Congress it was deputed to act as intermediary and interview the officials there, while as a superior authority over the District Congress Committees of the Mysore State, they were asked to work in agitating public opinion and informing it of the repressive activities of the government. If in the carrying on of this work any arrests were made, well and good. But a deliberate breach of orders was to be avoided.[90]

In response to the first instruction, Hukkerikar, the General Secretary of the KPCC was asked to interview Mirza Ismail on 22 September 1937. Misunderstandings arose because the Mysore Congress Board demanded that he be accompanied by Shrimati Kamaladevi or the Secretary of the Mysore Congress Board, both of which were refused. Again, immediately after the interview the Mysore Congress Board pressed him to give publicity to the results of the interview through the press,[91] which he refused to do before getting the permission of his superior, the President of the KPCC.[92] In the meantime, Mirza Ismail took the initiative and had published his account of the interview.[93] This account published by the Associated Press of India made out that the Mysore government was morally in an unassailable position and the government attached very little importance to the activities of what was after all a small section of agitators.[94] Thus the efforts of the KPCC only went to discredit the local Congressmen. This was all in keeping with Mirza Ismail's established policy of keeping in with the Indian National Congress by maintaining personal good relations with them, while making out that the state Congress members were a set of hooligans. The apparent success of this policy, during this period, was partly the reason for the Travancore Maharaja and C.P. Ramaswami Aiyar hobnobbing with the Madras Provincial Congress members in late 1937.

The failure of the KPCC made Jawaharlal Nehru take up the role of the intermediary directly through his correspondence with Mirza Ismail. However, the direct approach[95] dialogue between a Jawaharlal Nehru who was personally convinced that the Indian states system was entirely out of date[96] and a Mirza Ismail who asserted that the demand for immediate responsible government was in itself a subversive act,[97] was bound to prove infructuous.

Throughout August and September 1937, several meetings were held in the state protesting against prohibitory orders.[98]

The Mysore Government retaliated by police raids on the premises of the Congress offices, arrests of the members of the Council of Action and the demand of security for persons arrested as surety of good behaviour.[99] The Council of Action refused to defend themeselves and a series of 'dictators' were listed in case of arrests. On 13 October 1937, 'Repression Day' was observed in Bangalore and Mysore and K.T. Bhashyam was appointed dictator and was arrested.[100]

On 16 October 1937, the much awaited for merger between the Peoples Federation and the Congress took place at a special conference held at Mysore with only three dissenting.[101] No longer could the movement be condemned as that of a handful of agitators or of a section. All the parties now in Mysore had combined towards one goal. A demonstration of this solidarity was expressed even in the Legislature when the elected members, as a protest against the repressive measures adopted by the government, staged a walkout.[102] On 19 October 1937, the government which till then had evaded such a motion,[103] admitted an adjournment motion to discuss the high-handedness of the police.[104] The answering speech of the government spokesman was conciliatory. After explaining the government's position regarding the flag issue, that the government could not permit the display of the flag in a spirit of hostility to the Mysore flag or in a manner which could cause provocation, or annoyance, to those who were not members of the Congress Party, he emphasized the government support to the normal activities of the Congress such as Khadi, etc. The motion was withdrawn on the assurance given by the government to take notice and redress of police excess which came to the notice of the government.[105]

Till now the activities of the agitators as well as the government had obeyed the well recognized norms of non-violent behaviour. However, on 24 October 1937, the first police firing took place as an aftermath of the gagging orders passed against Mr. Nariman.[106] According to the President of the Civil Liberties' Union, the crowd took to indiscriminate pelting of stones, hurling of shoes, and attacks against police officials and the police authorities too did not act with sufficient restraint.[107]

The government followed up this action by press restrictions which was always a sore point with the public of Mysore.

Janavani, a Canarese journal, and *Prajamata*, an English daily, were suspended and the editor of *Prajamata*, B.N. Gupta, served with a notice to quit the state within 24 hours.[108] On 26 October 1937, a motion to discuss the press law on merits, so that it might be liberalised to the extent possible,[109] was disallowed.

It was in this situation when the momentum of the agitation had built up to a seeming crescendo that the Indian National Congress session of the AICC was held at Calcutta on 29, 30 and 31 October 1937. The resolution passed at this meeting shifted the scene of activity from the internal agitation in Mysore to the controversy within the Indian National Congress and with the states people, on a question of policy of the Indian National Congress, *vis-a-vis*, the states.

The resolution drafted by some members, and circulated for signatures,[110] had received the assent of 84 members. The resolution was proposed by the socialist member, Shrimati Kamaladevi Chattopadhyaya, and seconded by Nariman. The resolution expressed its emphatic protest against the ruthless policy of repression in Mysore State[111] and sent its fraternal greetings to the people of Mysore. It wished them all success in their legitimate non-violent struggle and appealed to the people of Indian states and British India to give all support and encouragement to the people of Mysore in their struggle against the state for right of self-determination.

The passing of the resolution had not been smooth and had met an opposition from Vallabhbhai Patel group. However, that the involvement and complicity of the Mysore representatives to the AICC, in the drafting of the resolution was minimal, is made obvious on a consideration of the events.

Chengalaraya Reddy, the President of the Mysore State Congress on its merger with the Peoples Federation, and the General secretary of the KPCC, Mr. Hukkerikar, had gone to Calcutta to place the case of Mysore before the Working Committee, if called upon to do so.[112] However, till the afternoon of the third day (31 October 1937) they had not been called, and even when they were, they were merely asked whether Nariman or Kamaladevi had given them an undertaking, on which the Working Committee arose.[113]

The resolution had been taken up first before the adjournment for lunch and had been passed by the AICC by a majority.

However, Chengalaraya Reddy, finding Vallabhbhai Patel declare himself ready to "oppose the resolution tooth and nail"[114] had suggested that the latter portion of the resolution, promising all support and encouragement be completely dropped. But Vallabhbhai Patel "would not agree to any proposal".[115] Frightened, Chengalaraya Reddy had requested some of the members to propose an amendment, which was however rejected. Vallabhbhai Patel, nor Bhulabhai Desai who had been present brought any amendment of their own.[116]

That the representative of Mysore had not himself wanted such a resolution, nor had he sought the active participation of the Congress in the state's agitation is corroborated by a letter from Jawaharlal Nehru to Mirza Ismail. He wrote:

> That resolution was a non-official one, pressed by a large number of members. Many of us had no desire to take any steps which might perhaps make it more difficult to end the friction which is developing in Mysore. I might add that even a gentleman from Mysore, who had come to tell us of what was happening there, was not particularly desirous that the AICC should pass a resolution. But the feeling of members was so strong that it found vent in the resolution that was passed.[117]

The resolution, thus, was clearly the outcome of a long history of in-fighting within the Congress on the issue of its participation in the states peoples movement, carried since 1933. It was mainly the handiwork of the socialist element in the Congress which ultimately had little to do with the pressure or otherwise brought in by the Mysore people or other states people. Again, if it was passed without amendments it was because of the passive acceptance of the right wing Congress members. Thus it is obvious the Mysore states people were mere scapegoats utilised by these two parties for a fight within the Congress. Again a careful examination of the resolution, made in its interpretations, makes it clear that the resolution was not all that revolutionary or radical. As Jawaharlal Nehru interpreted it (just before the controversy on this issue broke out), the resolution was meant to denote not much of a change from erstwhile policy. Their fundamental policy was to continue as in the past. This policy was of every sympathy and help but no deliberate law breaking on their part.[118] He further stipulated that the Mysore states peoples action in carrying on the agitation was to be on their own responsibility.

As Balwantray pointed out, the resolution only carried out the assurance given in 1928 and since reiterated at subsequent sessions of the Congress. On the face of the earlier resolutions which asserted that in the very nature of things the fight would have to be carried on by the people of the states, no active assistance of the people had been contemplated by the Congress, though it had not forbidden it either.[119] Thus if active support had not been solicited by the states people (as evidence of Chengalaraya Reddy's efforts at Calcutta Congress) nor had it been meant by the Indian National Congress, it was not the wording of the resolution which was at fault but a resolution on the states itself.

The strongly worded denouncement of Mahatma Gandhi in the *Harijan* of 13 November 1937 made clear his objection to the resolution. In view of the momentous change it wrought in the relationship of the Indian National Congress with the states, it is important that we quote Gandhi's view on the resolution extensively and analyse the real issues behind it. Gandhi, wrote :

> Much more offensive in my opinion,[120] was the Mysore resolution; and the pity of it was that it was carried with practically nobody to speak out for truth. I hold no brief for Mysore. There are many things I would like the Maharaja to reform. But the Congress policy is to give even his opponent his due. In my opinion the Mysore resolution was *ultra vires* of the resolution of non-interference, this so far as I am aware, has never been repealed. On merits, the AICC was not out to deal with the states as a whole. It was dealing only with the policy of repression—the resolution did not set-fourth the correct state of affairs, and the speeches made were full of passion and without regard to the facts of the case. The AICC should have appointed, if it was so minded, a committee of even one person to ascertain the facts before proceeding to pronounce judgment. The least it can do in such matters, if it has any regard for truth and non violence, is to let the Working Commitee to pronounce its judgment on them, and if necessary, review them in a judicial manner.[121]

Couched as the statement was in the usual Gandhian innuendos it becomes necessary to analyse the charges made to get at the real meaning of the criticisms of the resolution made by Gandhiji.

While the latter part referring to the resolution on Mysore repression—that it had not been made after a duly conducted inquiry into the facts of the case—is rather peripheral to his main criticism, the first part provides the clue to his real censure of it. His first sentence, that nobody had spoken out for the truth and that Congress was 'to give even his opponent his due', is to be seen in the context of a speech made by Mirza Ismail, on 16 October 1937, at the Mysore Legislative Assembly. Mirza Ismail while proclaiming that Mysore was one of the first to stand up for the ideal of all India unity,[122] had warned the Congress indirectly that :

> Nationalism ought not to mean the self-immolation of the component entity. Federation is not merger....In a word we must render unto Mysore the things that are Mysore's and unto India the things that are India's. ...We cannot concede to any body of persons who are not subjects of His Highness the Maharaja, the right to interpose in matters that lie strictly between the people and the Government of Mysore. It is a recognition of the justice and reasonableness of the principle that the wise and high-souled Mahatma Gandhi uniformly and consistently held that Congress should refrain scrupulously from attempts to meddle with the domestic concerns of the Indian states.[123]

Seen in this context, where Mysore had proclaimed itself as willing to federate,—in view of the greater ideal of the Indian National Congress to preserve the integrity of India as a whole —the AICC resolution had defaulted on the merits of its policy. Only in this context did he proclaim that the resolution had not treated the 'States as a whole'.

His contention that the resolution was *ultra vires* was wrong.[124] In 1928 the non-interference clause in the Indian National Congress constitution had deliberately been dropped.[125] Thus though it had not been legally repealed, dropping the clause from the constitution, for all practical purposes, meant that this provision was to be left undefined and unasserted. Thus as Jawaharlal Nehru proclaimed in his unpublished rejoinder to the criticisms made by Gandhiji, he was unable to discover any basis[126] for Gandhijis's definite charge of the resoution being *ultra vires*. The Congress constitution in no way prohibited or barred such a resolution. Nor had any Congress or AICC resolution, so far as could be quoted, come in the way. Mahatma Gandhiji himself acknowledged that the Congress had been guilty of intervention in the past but his criticisms now lay in the fact that he knew "that it was not proper and he (would) not have written the article if he did not feel it imperative to cry a halt".[127] Thus the emphasis was not on its being *ultra vires* as the need of a policy to cry a halt.

Mahatma Gandhi's censure is to be traced not only to his preoccupation on the interests of preserving the integral unity of India but partly also to the fact that the states problem had been made a matter for infighting within the Congress and had provided grounds for "artificial combinations within the Congress"[128] where the main problem of integration had been allowed to be sacrificed in an alignment with the states people against not only the Maharajas, but the ultimate interests of the Congress.

Gandhiji by his dramatic denunciation of the resolution as *ultra vires* captured the interest of the public, both in the states as well as British India, which was ultimately, as one can see, the purpose of such a denouncement. Thus at the time of Gandhiji's criticisms the motives underlying Gandhiji's censure not being made clear, it gave rise to considerable misunderstandings. Datar writing to Balwantray Mehta even conjectured that Mahatma Gandhi's motive could have been due to the resolution having been moved by a socialist and supported by Nariman.[129] Like Balwantray Mehta did, we could dismiss this theory as unfounded for Mahatma Gandhi was never moved by these personal piques, but had his own views on the matter of the states, which unfortunately one was unable to see as his views were not shared by the rank and file of Congressmen.[130]

Even Gandhi's own trusted lieutenant, Jawaharlal Nehru, at his most impetuous, wrote out a statement to the press as a rejoinder to this criticism which showed clearly his misinterpretation of Mahatma Gandhi's censure. His statement written on 26 November 1937, which was ultimately withheld from publication, while dismissing the main objection to Gandhiji of the resolution that on merits the AICC was not out to deal with the states as a whole, on the plea that "on the merits of a resolution opinions could differ and as chairman"[131] he had no business with them, he picked on the other peripheral points for his defence. He wanted substantiated Mahatma Gandhiji's charge, which laid "stress on this that truth and non-violence were violated and the resolutions on Mysore was *ultra vires*."[132] He personally could not "recollect anything that (could) be described as violation of truth or non-violence. So far as the working of the resolution was concerned (there was) nothing in it which could in any way be described as a departure from truth or non-violence". Here Jawaharlal Nehru erred in holding that Gandhiji categorised the wording of the resolution as such. His criticism laid stress on the pronouncement by the AICC on repression before any inquiry had been conducted in which it had departed from 'truth and non-violence'.

The withdrawal of this statement from publication by Jawaharlal Nehru is eloquent testimony to his acceptance of the real basis for the charges made by Gandhiji. And this basis lay in his criticism that the AICC had not dealt with the question of the states as a whole, which was the only plane—on that of preserving the integrity of India—on which the AICC could involve itself in the matter of the states.

Whatever be the rights and the wrongs of Gandhi's criticism or the several interpretations of his motives, there is no denying that one article of Mahatma Gandhi's expressing disapprobation of the AICC resolution on the states, was enough to annul the very resolution passed by a majority on it. As Balwantray Mehta pointed out, the states people could make no headway in this affair, unless Gandhiji's blessings was assured, or at least, his benevolent neutrality. With Bapuji in the opposition even the Congress support was not likely to avail much and it was imperative that they carried Gandhiji with them as far as they could.[133] However, subsequent to the Calcutta resolution it was not the states people who carried Mahatma Gandhi with them, but Mahatma Gandhi who carried the states peoples movement.

The immediate result of Mahatma Gandhi's denouncement was that political agitation against the government of Mysore received a set back[134] and there was little hope of any political activity.[135] Even the usual flag hoisting and Congress pledge taken on 26 January, was prohibited by a Government Order.

Till the definition of Congress policy at Wardha on 3 February 1938, there was a confusion in the Mysore State Congress camp.[136] Chengalaraya Reddy, visiting Bombay in January 1938 and meeting the Working Committee members, felt that the Mysore Congress Party could not expect any help from the Congress headquarter.[137] Mysore State Congress met in this atmosphere of utter despondency on 14 January 1938 at Chitaldrug. This meeting authorised the President of the Mysore State Congress to seek some compromise with Mirza Ismail. However, Mirza Ismail, with a new found confidence with an extension of service as Dewan by the Maharaja "as a public expression"[138] by him of confidence in Mirza Ismail and his "present political policy in the state",[139] even threatened to refuse recognition of the Congress in Mysore and to ban it if necessary,[140] in which he claimed "he had the support of Mahatmaji, Vallabhbhai Patel and Bhulabhai Desai".[141]

Before moving on to a description of the states movement which followed in the shadow of the Haripura resolution, it becomes necessary that we turn our attention to the other two states and developments at the all-India level.

While in Cochin political activity had come to a standstill because of expected reforms in the Legislature, in Travancore the movement which had gathered momentum in October 1937, was now to be, in turn, affected by the pronouncement of Mahatma Gandhi.

On the occasion of his birthday in October 1937, the Maharaja of Travancore released political prisoners who had been imprisoned during the Abstention Movement. A mammoth reception and procession headed by gaily decorated elephants and accompanied by numerous musicians was taken out at Alleppey to commemorate Mr. C. Kesavan, the Ezhava leader's release.[142] This reception caused considerable nervousness to Travancore Government.[143]

On Gandhiji's denunciation of the Calcutta Congress resolution, the government moved against T.M. Varghese, the Deputy president of the Sri Moolam Assembly. He was removed by a resolution of no confidence, instigated from the government benches, for having participated in the reception given to C. Kesavan at Trippunithura in Cochin. C. Kesavan had "annoyed" the Travancore Government by paying a glowing tribute to the Dewan of Cochin *vis-a-vis* his policy towards untouchables.[144] C.P. Ramaswami Aiyar's annoyance was doubly compounded by the announcement of reforms in Cochin in January 1938, which promised to that state people their millenium of responsible government.

Compatibility of Responsible Government in the States System

At the All India level, January 1938 saw talks being held between Mahatma Gandhi and Lothian on the federal issue. At this meeting with Lothian, Mahatma Gandhi made it clear that while the goal of the Congress was to supplant the present Act, by a constitution prepared by a Constituent Assembly, in its present acceptance of the federal proposals, he would personally insist on only two conditions. The princes, or enough of them, were to concede the elementary civil liberties to their people and right of election, at least of some portion of the states people, to the federal parliament. In this the precise 'degree' of such concessions could be a matter of discussion.[145] If these conditions were agreed to by the princes and the paramount power he promised to press the Congress to agree to allow the Act to go into operation without alteration.[146] The conversation of Gandhi with Lord Lothian makes it clear that Gandhiji was ready to sacrifice all other opposition of the Congress to the federal scheme for this one concession to the states people's demand made earlier in their manifesto of 1934 in their stipulation that Congress insist on an insertion of a Declaration of Fundamental Rights in the White Paper on reforms and election of states representatives to the Federal Legislatures.[147]

Gandhi's insistence on this point was not entirely altruistic in its motives. As Zetland, the Secretry of State, in a memo to the Cabinet surmised, while the Right Wing of the Congress condemned the Federal Provisions of the Act equally with the Left Wing they were willing to enter the federation if they were satisfied that they could secure an immediate majority in the federation.[148] Thus Gandhiji's demand for elements of representation and his subsequent tactics in the state in 1939 in bringing pressure on the states through agitations could have been motivated by this necessity.

His solution was however, better than that of C. Rajagopalachari, who in spite of remarking "that the states people were the real untouchables, they had no rights they had only duties",[149] behaved towards them on the federal issue with the callousness of a Brahmin. He, in his turn in a conversation with Lothian, proposed that the federation be allowed to go forward under the Act for British India alone so far as the Assembly was concerned, but constitute an all India Council of State—composed of nominees of the provincial governments and princes, which could act as a second chamber; the right of any of the state to adhere to the Federal Assembly was to be granted as soon as its representatives were elected by the people.[150]

As Lothian remarked, this scheme would mean that Congress could secure an immediate and absolute majority in the Assembly.[151] On the other hand, it would have also meant a constant and irreconcilable quarrel between a British Indian Lower House and a Council of State, dominated by the princes' nominees.[152] But more importantly, which Lothian did not care to mention, it would have meant an end, for all time, to the aspirations of the states people, not only internally but even on the federal issues. So the advantage would have been to the Congress and provincial India alone. There was an added danger that in order to get concessions in the Council of State, as then constituted, the interests of the states people would have been entirely sacrificed.

Mahatma Gandhi's proposal was supported by the Aga Khan who thought this was the only way out for the princes also, towards which, he wanted the British administrators to encourage the princes.[153] However, the Viceroy was not ready to add to the problems on federation, endangered as it already was, by the 'safeguards' and conditions stipulated by the princes. When negotiations had been opened in 1937 on federal limitations, Patiala had suggested 40 and Bikaner been unable to content himself with less than 116 in a total of 159 items. As the Viceroy pointed out, His Majesty's Government were not concerned so much with Congress acceptance or otherwise of the federal proposals as much as the princes acceptance.[154]

It was in this background of his talks with Mahatma Gandhi and other leaders, that Lothian on 24 January 1938, issued a statement which indicated a change in British policy of momentous significance. In this statement he made clear that paramountcy could certainly not be interpreted to mean that Great Britain would support a ruler in denying his own subjects the very rights which had been granted to British India.[155] In further elucidation of this statement, he pointed out that "when the movement for responsible institutions in the state.. reached fruition, it would automatically remove the principal objections now raised to an All India Federation, and other anomalies in the Act.[156]

Influenced by these two events, the announcement of Reforms in Cochin,[157] and the statement of Lord Lothian which seemed to spell out a new Magna Carta for the states people, an adjournment motion for discussing responsible government was moved by T.M. Varghese, the Congress leader in the Sri Moolam Assembly in Travancore, on 2 February 1938.

C.P. Ramaswami Aiyar, grasping the nettle with both hands, in his characteristic manner, in an obvious, direct and belligerent reference to reforms in Cochin, took this opportunity to denounce dyarchy as of little significance. He maintained that a Legislature which did not have complete responsibility over finances became a purely advisory body and did not get any responsibility. The appointment of an Executive Council or a minister for helping the Dewan in the administration, was not responsible government. Responsible government involved government of the country by accredited representatives of the people and not by a particular person, or persons, who were allowed liberty to do what they liked as long as they did not come into conflict with the wishes of the ruler. In answer to Lothian's plea for granting rights to the states people, analogous to those granted in the provinces of Brilish India, he came out with his legal theory that it was impossible, without the active concurrence of the British Government, for the Ruler to divest himself of his undivided authority and jurisdiction over the governance of his state in favour of any other authority, for the Maharaja would constitutionally be unable to fulfil his obligations to the paramount power. Thus the maintenance of treaties was inconsistent with the grant of real responsible gavernment.[158]

C.P. Ramaswami Aiyar's contention was not a new political theory propounded in the relationship of the states and the

Government of India. K.M. Panikkar, writing as early as 1927, had held the same view when he wrote :

> If an Indian ruler today decided to establish constitutional government in the state, he would find that the paramountcy of the British Government stands as an insuperable objection. If a legislature is given all the powers which nominally exist in the ruler, it will become vested with full sovereignty of the state, and automatically the limitations which are now accepted by the princes as a result of political practice would be scrapped...(while) the powers of a ruler can beexercised by the Government of India...a Legislature cannot be deposed or placed under tutelage. The result is that the Government of India can at no time permit the introduction of a complete system of responsible government within the states.[159]

C.P. Ramaswami Aiyar's monoeuverings at shifting the blame on to the shoulders of the paramount power, boomeranged. Not only did it give rise to a controversy in the papers on the issue,[160] and his criticism of reforms in Cochin brought on a rejoinder from Shanmukham Chetty,[161] thus aggravating the already simmering enmity between the Dewans of these two neighbouring states, but more importantly these controversies brought about an authoritative statement from the British Government in India, on the issue. "This absurd contention",[162] the "silly suggestion put forward by Ramaswami Aiyar", was disposed of by means of an answer to a question in the House of Commons which proclaimed that it was not the policy of the paramount power in ordinary circumstances to intervene in the internal administration of full powered states and that the paramount power would certainly not obstruct proposals for constitutional advance initiated by a Ruler.[163]

Thus aborted in his attempt to shift the blame for not establishing responsible government on to the paramount power, C.P. Ramaswami Aiyar had to explore other avenues. In this, the Congress decision to disaffiliate the organisations in the states in the existing communal milieu in Travancore, proved opportune.[164]

The Haripura Resolution and its Repercussions on these States

The draft resolution of the INC drawn under the direct guidance of Gandhi at Wardha, on 6 February 1938, proclaimed that it stood for the same political, social and economic freedom in the states as in the rest of India and assured them of its "vigilant interest and sympathy" with their movement in the states. But it made it clear that in the face of its "inability...to give protection or effective help, due to numerous limitations and restrictions imposed by the rulers or by British authority...such movements were likely to develop more rapidly.. if it did not rely on extraneous help and assistance or on the prestige of the Congress name". Thus it directed that *no Congress Committees be established within the states and that they do not undertake any internal struggle in the name of the Congress, but start independent* organisations for this purpose. However, it allowed individual Congressmen to render assistance in their individual capacity, where the struggle could develop without committing the Congress organisation and name, and could act unhindered by other considerations.[165]

Thus the main clause that was inimical to the states people was the banning of Congress Committees within the states and the use of the Congress name in their particular struggle. As Pattabhi Sitaramayya pointed out, at the Haripura Conference, such a clause affected only "some of the states like Mysore, Travancore and Cochin where the Congress had become an established institution with its tradition as in the provinces .. where the people were likely to feel hurt...that their long standing rights had been abridged".[166]

For the main part of the Indian states where no movement or organisation had taken effect, the Haripura assurance making it "obsolutely clear that when freedom comes, it must be not only merely for those in British India but...for the people of the Indian states as well",[167] proved beneficial. Again the clause which allowed individual Congressmen in their personal capacities to offer assistance, made it possible for these Congressmen to initiate and spearhead such movements within the states where, as yet, no such organisations or movement had taken place. Thus the Haripura session, under the guidance of Mahatma Gandhi laid the master plan for the integration of the numerous small and petty principalities and other backward states in the eventuality of freedom for India.

By snapping the connection between the states people and the Indian National Congress it brought to an end the continuous bickering which had been carried on since 1928 between the states people and the Indian National Congress. As Pattabhi Sitaramayya pointed out :

> the States Peoples Conference and the Indian National Congress had been running on parallel or even divergent lines. They had been suspecting each other...The Congress (due to a suspicion) that the states people were trying to exploit the name of the Congress...and the states people because the Congress was not assisting them...and that they were even on better friendly terms with the princes than the people themselves".[168]

From now on, what Sitaramayya did not emphasise, but became clear in the subsequent period, was that while the Indian National Congress banned the states people from using their 'trade mark' the states peoples grievance was to be freely used by the British Indian leadership to further their cause on integration.

In its present application it hurt the states people of Mysore most, as it had been carrying on its agitation mainly in the name of the Congress from the very beginning of its movement. It was particularly inconvenient as, at this moment, the members of the Mysore Congress in the legislature had as a protest against the repressive policy of the government and to show that the country was behind their movement, resigned their seats and sought re-election.[169] To rectify this temporary difficulty, Subhas Chandra Bose in his ruling,[170] allowed their functioning as they had done so far till the elections of 5 March 1938. In the meantime, the Mysore Congress came out with a very ingenious idea to extricate themselves from this difficulty. The Mysore Congress Board, at a meeting on 28 February 1938, decided that for carrying on political work, a separate organisation—to be called the Mysore Congress—be inaugurated and that a convention of the same be called in April. The condition of membership to the new organisation was to be a dual membership, to the Mysore Congress and the Indian National Congress, for which enrolment was to take place simultaneously.[171]

As C. Rajagopalachari the master of apt phrases put it, it was like the term 'vegetable ghee' which did not deceive more than Mysore Congress.[172]

While Travancore interposed the word 'state' in its organisation in calling it Travancore State Congress, Mysore and Cochin by calling their organisation the Mysore Congress and Cochin Congress, carried on a long correspondence on this issue with the Working Committee of the Indian National Congress and was subjected to its strictures in its resolution of 15 May 1938, for not giving effect to the letter and spirit of the Haripura Congress resolution.[173]

Cochin had a particular problem on this issue which, as was usual in Kerala politics, was tangled with the communal. At the time of the constituting of the new party, a splinter group within the Cochin Congress demanded that they adopt as one of their chief planks in their platform proportional representation of all communities in the state service and legislature[174] which amendment was lost by 26 votes to 21. The splinter group formed themselves into the Cochin State Congress in order to exploit the communal feelings of the people;[175] the Cochin Congress found it impossible to cooperate with this organisation's ideals and programme of work. As the real heir to the Congress name, the Cochin Congress was not ready to take another title, as it was loath to give up the name 'Congress' to the Cochin State Congress. Thus faced by adamancy on this issue by these Congress organisations within the state, and with the support of Mahatma Gandhi on this issue who did not find anything wrong in the name being used,[176] the Indian National Congress' grievance against the states organisations in calling it after the 'Congress' was allowed to lapse.

The real ramifications of the Haripura decisions camouflaged as it was in the controversy over the retention of the name Congress to their internal organisation, lay ultimately in the issues which had been ever present—even from the very day of Congress entry within the states. The Haripura decision gave an emphatic, categorical 'no' to the long drawn states peoples endeavours to involve the Indian National Congress in its own movement. This 'no' decided the priorities on which the states movement was to be governed—which meant it had to 'kow tow' to the Congress line ultimately. By staying outside the states peoples movement the British Indian leadership had reserved for itself the right of criticism through which it retained complete control over the states movement. The 'Congressmen' incited movements which were to follow during the later 1938's to 1940's were thus not genuine indigenous movements of the states people or carried out to futher their aspirations, but were motivated by Congress interests on integration and were mere exercises to show the power of the Congress in the states, which could be vital instruments if necessary and were there merely to further its interests. In such a context, the ploy of Mysore Congress—of retention of the word 'Congress', or of double membership mattered little ultimately, where the responsible government movement had been given a death blow in the retraction of any support by the Congress. Their millenium could only be achieved after Indian independence.

In this, the ramifications of the Haripura Congress decisions was even more far reaching in the politics of Kerala. From the time of the genesis of the Socialist Party within the Indian National Congress in 1934, the Malabar area of Kerala, which had a long history of an economic grievance in its agrarian structure, had come under the influence of the Socialist Party. The Malabar District Congress Committee was dominated by this section. However, a balance between the Right and the Left Wing of the Kerala Pradesh Congress Committee was maintained by the presence of the members from the two states of Travancore and Cochin. The consequent bickering between the Right and the Left Wing of the KPCC had necessitated the intervention of the AICC in KPCC matters.

By 1935 the Left Wing had gained a popularity in the political conference[177] and thus could get most of their resolutions passed at these meetings,[178] though the Kerala Pradesh Congress Committee had a majority of the Rightists within it. In this anomalous position, to effect a compromise, Brelvi presiding at the 1935 political conference, had suggested the conceding of some seats to non-socialists in return for which the peasants and labour department of KPCC was given to the socialists.[179] Again in 1936, the KPCC dominated by Rightists came into a confrontation with the Leftists over their refusal to support the workers of the Malabar Spinning and Weaving

Company over a strike and over some financial issues involving a sum of Rs. 200, when the KPCC even decided to disaffiliate the Malabar District Committee which spearheaded the socialist opposition. E.M.S. Nambudiripad complained to the AICC of the KPCC's decision to crush the leftist tendency which was developing in the movement.[180]

Even though a compromise and settlement was patched up by the AICC between the KPCC and the Malabar District Congress Committee, the confrontation between these two parties remained a feature of Kerala politics.

Thus when the Haripura decision banned the Congress committees from within the states from taking part in any political programme, the support which the Right Wing received in the Kerala Pradesh Congress Committee from the members in the 'states' area and the nice balance between the Right and Left Wings of the KPCC which was maintained in it, was now completely disturbed. Unlike Mysore, where membership to the Mysore Congress and the Indian National Congress was simultaneous, in Travancore and Cochin the membership to the Travancore State Congress and to Cochin Congress was distinct.[181] Thus by 1940 the number enrolled in the Indian National Congress in Travancore dropped to about 500 members and in Cochin to about two thousand.[182] Thus the Rightist's influence exerted from the states part of Kerala was entirely eliminated from the Kerala Pradesh Congress Committee. The amendment of the Congress constitution at Bombay in June 1939, aggravated the situation further when the number of representatives to the KPCC was based on population and constituencies. It gave rise to a lopsided distribution of seats, when membership to the Indian National Congress bore no relationship with the population in these areas. Based on population, Travancore with 52 lakhs, Cochin 12 lakhs, and Malabars 39 lakhs the seats allotted to them in the KPCC would have been respectively 52, 12 and 39 to each of these areas. But Travancore with a membership of 500 based on membership constituency could be allotted merely one seat, while Cochin could have 4.[183] Instead of allowing the rest of the seats to lapse, Malabar DCC dominating the KPCC now decided to redistribute the seats to various other constituencies, purporting to act under a clause [G-(2) Article 10] of the

Congress constitution. This gave rise to a lot of gerrymandering when the socialists strongholds were allotted more seats.[184] The Leftists who gained a predominance in the KPCC, now utilised this opportunity to strengthen their position.[185] Thus the Haripura Congress decision was the main factor which strengthened the influence of the socialists-communists in Kerala within the organisation.[186]

However, the subsequent reversion in 1942 in allotting seats based on mere population, irrespective of the members, and allotment of 51 seats to Travancore, 11 seats to Cochin and 39 to Malabar, was not fair, for the Congress activities in these states were at a standstill.[187] The reconstituted KPCC with a Rightist majority, alienated as it was from the general rank of the members in Kerala who came mainly from the communist areas of Malabar, only aggravated the situation further, and gave a lopsided turn to the growth and development of the Congress party in Kerala as a whole.[188] Thus one could trace the phenomena of a constitutionally constituted communist government later on in the fifties to the Haripura Congress resolution disaffiliating the Congress organisations carrying on political activity from the Indian National Congress. The other phenomena in Kerala, of a communal influence in a communist dominated regime, can again be traced to the same Haripura decision.

Hitherto, the balance between the communities within the Kerala Congress taken as a whole, had been maintained by the significant prominence of the Nair element from British Malabar and the Kerala Congress representing as it did all the communities, was exempt from charges of communalism. Now the Travancore State Congress, by itself, with its nucleus made up of the Joint Political Conference which had been forged mainly on the communal grievance of the three communities—the Syrian Christians, the Ezhavas and the Muslims—was prone to charges of communalism. Even the 'old guard' of the Indian National Congress in Travancore was unable to decide whether to join the new organisation, the Travancore State Congress, or to forge a rival organisation. This group felt that the Joint Political Conference had taken opportune advantage of the disaffiliation decision of the Haripura session and engineered a state Congress to exploit the name of the Congress. They held it "nothing less than blasphemy",[189] to allow this pact of communalists who had their faith in communal aims, and little faith in the Congress' programme of untouchability, khaddar and prohibition, to take its name. However, this group, in contrast to the Cochin Congress, commanded little following in Travancore, and thus finding a common plank in the aim of responsible government, made common cause with them. The Travancore Committee of the Indian National Congress resolved by an overwhelming majority of (28 for, against 4) to suspend the activities of that committee and to amalgamate with the Travancore State Congress.[190]

The presence of this communal chink in the make up of the Travancore State Congress proved of great significance to C.P. Ramaswami Aiyar for he was able to utilise this to perfect his strategy for combating the movement for responsible government put up by this organisation. The very beginning of the confrontation between the Travancore government and the Travancore State Congress (in 1938) saw C.P. Ramaswami Aiyar charge the Travancore State Congress of being no national party as communal consciousness overrode national sentiment in the state.[191] He maintained that the government had come into conflict with the organisation as the Travancore State Congress had 'pinned' its faith in communalism in Travancore.[192]

To obviate charges of such a nature, the 'old guard' proposed double membership—membership to the Indian National Congress as a necessary condition for membership to the Travancore State Congress—as was practised in Mysore. But such a device, even in Mysore, was protested by the Indian National Congress and as such could not be adopted in Travancore where the Travancore State Congress also had ideas of marking out its own course independent of the control of the Indian National Congrees.

Not realising the manoeuverings of C.P. Ramaswami Aiyar, in not only discrediting the Travancore State Congress on this count, but to use that very communalism to his own advantage, the All India States Peoples Conference played into his hand.

Pattabhi Sitaramayya's acknowledgement of this communal consciousness in Travancore only went towards a public acknowledgement of the weakness in the Travancore State

Congress, and was utilised by C.P. Ramaswami Aiyar to entirely discredit this organisation; in this, Pattabhi Sitaramayya's jejune efforts, (in writing to the Travancore Durbar) pleading for grant of responsible government took this state no further. Again, his pleadings that these "communal distempers", "were in the nature of pathological phenomena met with in groups not fully alive to the wide interests of the masses", and were "to be viewed in the right perspective",[193] went unheeded, for C.P. Ramaswami Aiyar had viewed the problem in his own "perspective" and discovered innumerable possibilities in it to counteract the Travancore State Congress.

His strategy lay thus in reinforcing his policy of repression and bans by playing up the communal differences, through them creating a rival party to the State Congress, inciting *goondas* to overawe and bring confusion at Congress meetings, making all these in turn the cause of further bans on such meetings on grounds of averting a clash between antagonistic sections.

This overall plan met its first check in January 1938 in an article written by A. Narayana Pillai exhorting the different communities of Travancore to sink their petty differences and unite.[194] Coupled as this article was by another criticising the irregularities of the Dewan President in the Legislative Assembly,[195] C.P. Ramaswamy Aiyar thought it fit (while proclaiming aloud that Travancore was not fit for responsible government because of the communal problem), to institute a case against Narayana Pillai on charges of sedition, for transgressing in these articles the limits of legitimate criticism and promoting feelings of enmity and hatred between communities.[196]

The subsequent period was to show the clever handling of the communal situation by the Dewan to his own purpose even to a breaking up of the Travancore State Congress.

Conclusions

The long drawn conflict between the Indian National Congress and the States people during the period 1933 to 1936 showed up clearly the divergence in the aims and priorities of the states from that of the British Indian leadership's. This conflict came to a head with the denunciation by Mahatma

Gandhi of the Calcutta Congress resolution which had committed itself, as of sympathy to states peoples struggle in Mysore. The disaffiliation of the states organisations from the parent body—the Indian National Congress—which followed at the Haripura Congress, settled the question of priorities once for all. As far as the British Indian nationalists were concerned, the states peoples cause was now to subserve the Indian National Congress' aims. To further Congress aims on the states, another development had taken place when a 'new chapter in the progress of states politics' was initiated at the Karachi Conference in July 1936. This new body, the AISPC, was to prove the spokesman not of the states people, but was to project the Indian National Congress' aims on the states.

Within the states, while the Haripura decision had its effect only on immediate events in Mysore (as in a need to fight the election in the name of the Congress), it was to leave its lasting mark in Kerala—in a strengthening of the communist wing and in being open to charges of communalism.

By the end of February 1938, a rather frightened, disclaimed, discredited, dishonoured and bedraggled organisations in these states were seemingly left to mark out their course in the coming years, independent not only of the help and support of the Indian National Congress but of the leash and control of its leaders. However, the subsequent year was to prove how different was the situation which was to develop, and how the organisations which had to fight for its very name in attaching the name 'Congress' was to come completely under the wily Mahatma and his able adjutant, Vallabhbhai Patel.

6

The Movement Betrayed

The Movement from February 1938 to 1940

In contrast to affairs in Cochin, events in Mysore and Travancore, following the Haripura resolution, led up to a crisis. While the movement in Mysore was a continuation of the earlier phase, the building up of the tempo of the movement in Travancore in 1938-39 was due not to any particular grievance indigenous to the state (in contrast to the earlier 'Abstention' phase), but mainly due to repercussions of events outside. The Travancore State Congress members themselves attributed it to the advent of popular ministries in the provinces of India, which they claimed, stimulated the desire of the people for a like form of government.[1] In this the reforms proposed in Cochin, as already seen,[2] had its repercussions. The Travancore administration on its part attributed it to the "inopportune manoeuvres"[3] on the part of Mysore Government, particularly the inclusion in the terms of reference to the Constitution Reforms Committee of Mysore, the method of selecting states representatives to the central legislature.

The motives attributed by these different parties are of some importance. The Travancore Government's analysis emphasised the Indian National Congress' interests in the states and exhibited the administration's tendency to see in the struggle, interference from outside parties. The British administrators taking their cue from these readings characterised the movement in the states under a blanket term as 'Congress, inspired',[4] which the movement in the south, especially in Travancore and Mysore, definitely was not.[5] The state Congress' motive emphasised their particular interest—their avidity for a democratic form of government. To understand the divergence in the emphasis, one has to study the Haripura resolution in a new perspective—in the context of the movement in the states subsequent to that resolution. This analysis would show that contrary to all previous notions—that it was motivated by a relaxation of Congress interference in the states—the underlying motive behind Haripura resolution was to gain manoeuvreability in shaping the movement within the states to the Congress needs. In this it was to act in a double capacity; where the movement was indigenous and on the programme of responsible government solely, it effected its control through moral pressures (handled mainly by Gandhi) and through British Indian leaders in their capacity as intermediaries. Where the movement was incipient, it gave entry to British Indian leaders to states politics which was utilised to arouse enthusiasm, with the ultimate aim to promote British Indian interests on integration.[6] In this the Haripura resolution saw to it that by making non-interference in the states as part of Indian National Congress policy, the leadership itself was insulated from pressures within the body of the Congress. These pressures by the British Indian leadership were exerted, as surmised shrewdly by the Dewans of the states meeting at Bombay[7] in November 1938, by the needs of capturing power at the federal level. In a memorandum presented to the Viceroy they pointed out that with 125 seats out of 375 allotted to the Indian states in the federal assembly, failing at attempts to reach any agreement with the Muslims, the Congress party could obtain a majority only if the states agreed to send in elected representatives to the federal legislature. Thus under the 'avowed' object of agitating on immediate responsible government, the Dewans surmised, the Congress sought to exert pressure on the Indian states to alter their systems of government and method of choice to the federal legislature. To counteract the Congress move, the memorandum sought an authoritative declaration from the paramount power that it was not their policy to insist on the grant of partial, or complete, responsible government, or to fetter the choice of their representatives to the federal legislature. By this manoeuvre they hoped, the movement, propped up as it was by the main interest of the Congress, would completely collapse. Mahatma Gandhi countered this move by issuing a threat of interference from the provinces in respect of the people of the states. The Working Committee of the Congress taking its tone from Mahatma Gandhi, warned the state administration that if the Congress "felt a call" for interference, it would do so; it proclaimed that the Haripura decision was never conceived as an obligation, thus by innuendo reserving for itself the right to rescind it at a later date, while at present it asserted its right and duty to guide the people of the states and lend them its influence.[8]

It was the atmosphere of conflicting interests which prompted the paramount power, at the beginning, to declare its policy as one of complete indifference as to the direction chosen on internal reforms by the princes,[9] and later, in face of the nationalists direct participation, as at Rajkot, which it considered was under improper pressure,[10] to align itself with the princes. It was then that it decided to give all help to them even if it precipitated a crisis in the provinces in the calling off of ministries by the Congress.

In this, while Mahatma Gandhi conceived of the states peoples movement as an integrated whole and looked at it from the interest of All India, these two states people were moved by local considerations and by their programme on responsible government. These divergences in viewpoints, again brought these parties to a confrontation within the movement itself, as partisans of the wider movement amenable to all India leadership or as affected by the exigencies of local politics.

As these events affected Cochin least, it becomes necessary that we take that area first, and then, as events in Mysore was to precede the movement in Travancore on which it exerted its own pressures, Mysore next, before proceeding to Travancore.

Calm in Cochin (1938-1939)

The new constitution for Cochin, proposed in January 1938,[11] obviated or at least, minimised any need for an agitation. The constitution proposed joint responsibility and a dyarchical form of government with the minister in charge of transferred subjects being dependent for his continuation in office on the popular vote of the Legislature.[12] Explaining away the safeguards proposed in the constitution, Shanmugham Chetty, as Dewan, promised that the working of the new constitution would be more liberal and democratic than the wording would seem to imply.[13]

The delegating of the department of uplift of depressed classes to the popular minister was of significance in the context of communal politics in Kerala. Following Haripura, the Cochin Congress was split on the issue of communal policy and a splinter group based its demands on the 'communal cry',[14] of representation in the legislature and services on basis of population, community-wise. The Cochin administration by delegating this department to the popular minister preserved itself from the wrangles of the conflicting elements.[15]

The advantage of the Cochin constitution to the Cochin Government was obvious in its very first session when the new minister was able to obtain for the government the passing of the budget in toto, with only 2 or 3 dissents from the ranks of the independent members.[16] In October 1938, to further the appearance of a popularly constituted constitution, an assembly called the Durbar (consisting of invited nominees and members of the Legislative Council) was asked to frame a constitution Act laying down clearly the existing form of administration, the mutual rights and responsibilities of the rulers and the ruled.[17]

These measures confined the movement for an extension of reforms and for responsible government to the Legislature. In December 1938, the pattern was set, when a motion for reform was tabled and discussion allowed.[18] Cochin's involvement in the responsible government movement now lay mainly in extending its help to its sister state of Travancore.[19]

The Mahatma, Mirza Ismail and the Mysore Congress (1938-39)

For the acceleration of the movement and the turn that it took in Mysore, Mirza Ismail was mostly to blame. Claiming that it was his request for assistance of Congress leaders in British India which was partly responsible for the Haripura resolution,[20] he made a rather provocative speech at the Karnataka Sahitya Parishad. While deprecating the "campaign of misrepresentation and vilification", carried on by the "meaner minds"[21] (in an obvious reference to the Mysore politicians) he professed a desire to convince other "unjust critics" (obviously his friends from British India). The Mysore Congress members saw in this speech of the Dewan a motive to "wean them from the parent body".[22]

It was as a measure of convincing the Indian National Congress leaders of his good intentions that the Dewan announced the release of the political prisoners and the appointment of two committees, one for reforms and the other for federal affairs.[23] The Political Affairs Committee whose proceedings were to be in camera was to make its recommendations relating to federation.[24] The Constitution Reforms Committee was to concern itself with the composition, functions and powers of the legislatures, with special regard to extension of franchise. But more importantly, it was to include among these questions the method of appointment of representatives to the federal legislature and their relations with the government and the legislative bodies in the state.[25] The inclusion of this clause in this committee was not so much to placate the state's people, as the Right Wing leadership in the Indian National Congress whose attitudes towards the states people movement was mainly motivated by their interests in the federal legislature. With three seats in the Council of State and seven in the Legislative Assembly, this insertion to captivate British Indian leadership's interest, was of significance. Thus it was not surprising that while Mysore Congressmen saw in it attempts at 'political tinkering'[26] in order to stop agitation without giving anything away, *The Hindu*, which had always adopted a pro-Mysore Government stand and was pro-Indian National Congress, now commented rather favourably and commended its terms as being "wide as could be desired".[27]

The Mysore Congressmen's chief complaint against the terms of reference of the committee was that it contained no declaration of responsible government as their ultimate goal. Other irritants were provided in the non-recognition by the Mysore Government of the Mysore Congress, as an extension of which its reiteration that Congressmen nominated to the committee were to represent in their personal capacity and not as members of that organisation. It moreover excluded in the committee most of the prominent Congressmen and allotted to them a mere 4 places in a committee of 20.[28]

Within the Mysore Congress itself serious rifts were becoming apparent. The inclusion in the Reforms Committee of T. Ramachandran, (who was in the confidence of Mahatma Gandhi) and of K. Chengalaraya Reddy (who had till recently been the head of an opposition party) and the exclusion of other prominent members in the Mysore Congress was not without reason. Soon the Resident was reporting rather gleefuly of differences within the Mysore Congress and of K. Chengalaraya Reddy "accused of playing a double game".[29]

It was in this situation that decision was taken by the Mysore Congress Working Committee to refer the question of cooperation, or otherwise, with the Reforms Committee to an open session scheduled to be held at Sivapura on 11 to 13 April 1938. At the same meeting the idea of consulting Mahatma Gandhi on this issue was pressed forward by T. Ramachandran and was accepted. However the decision to consult Mahatma Gandhi was not unanimous; H.C. Dasappa, a prominent member of the Mysore Congress deprecated the fact that it had to be guided by men "of the morality of T. Ramachandran", and saw the acceptance of Ramachandran's idea by Mysore Congressmen as falling "victim to (his) machinations".[30]

Thus from the very beginning of the movement after Haripura, whether the Mysore Congressmen desired or not, or whether Gandhiji himself was personally willing or not, Mysore Congressmen were pushed into obtaining his help and guidance and thus his advice was to predominate. Mysore set the pattern and instead of the states peoples movement being free, after the Haripura decision, to direct its own course, it was to become more and more dependent on Mahatma Gandhi's direction.

Till now Mirza Ismail playing up to the Indian National Congress had been able to dominate the political scene. The Mysore Congress, on the eve of the meeting at Sivapura on 11 April 1938, marked as it was by suspicion and dissensions within its ranks, had been in no very happy state of mind. However, the series of repressive acts which followed in the wake of the Sivapura convention, mainly due to the precipitate action of the Mysore administration, soon reversed these roles and drove the main issue of cooperation or otherwise in the Reforms Committee to the background.[31]

On 9 April 1938, two days before the Sivapura convention was due to meet, anticipating that the national flag hoisting would be played up by the Mysore Congress, Mysore administration imposed its usual ban on such ceremonies.[32] Making capital out of the order, with intentions to make the defiance of this order the central theme of demonstrations at Sivapura session, the Mysore Congress reiterated its contention that the flag was meant in no way as derogatory to the Maharaja and affirmed that it stood for "the freedom and honour of India as a whole including the Indian states"[33] by which it sought to emphasise the Indian National Congress' interest in the movement. Special preparations were thus made at the Sivapura session to focus attention on the flag demonstration, with the dictator designate guarding the honour of the flag by a sitting vigil at its foot.

The end of Sivapura session saw the beginning of flag demonstrations all over Mysore. The defiance by Mysore Congress of a government order prohibiting flag demonstrations at the site of an annual *jatha* in Viduraswatha, on 25 April 1938, led to a *lathi* charge and a shooting incident by a police party 37 strong, against a crowd of twenty thousand.[34]

This incident ranks in the annals of this states people on a comparable position as Jalianwala Bagh. The official count of the casualties estimated it at 10 killed and eight injured, while the unofficial estimates ranged to 32 killed and 48 injured.[35]

While, as Mahatma Gandhi pointed out, one could never know with absolute certainty, whether it was forced on by circumstances as the police evidence maintained,[36] or was the outcome, as claimed by Mysore Congressmen, of a premeditated design on the part of the administration,[37] there was little doubt, as pointed out by a member of the Enquiry Committee, the attempt to disperse such a huge crowd by a small police force was nothing short of 'midsummer madness' which could have easily been avoided.[38]

In establishing the guilt or otherwise of a 'premeditated design' of Mysore administrators, it is pertinent to remark that only 5 days prior to the shooting incident, C. Rajagopalachari (who had been deputed by Mahatma Gandhi to mediate on the issue at Mirza's insistence)[39] had in a note to Mirza deprecated the use of the flag by Mysore as a 'symbol of battle' in celebrating flag hoisting "creating the impression that the INC was challenging the Mysore Government".[40] He even advised Mirza Ismail not to grant any additional nominations to members of the Mysore Congress in the Constitution Reforms Committee as no principle was involved.[41]

Premeditated or otherwise, the firing incident served to pitchfork the states peoples cause to the notice of the outside world. Within the state large gatherings of villagers enquired about their next session, while, outside the states, British India rallied to the Mysore Congress support. The Karnataka Pradesh Congress Committee giving its opinion that the firing at Viduraswatha was "unjustifiable, unnecessary and indiscriminate", hoped that the consciousness and the strength that had been generated would result in the solution of the greater question of responsible government.[42] Jayaprakash Narain and M.R. Masani of the Socialist wing of the Congress, urged for an action such as was taken in connection with the Nagpur flag satyagraha when volunteers from all over the country went to Nagpur and participated in defiance of a similar ban.[43] The Madras Congress socialist party urged the Indian National Congress to abandon its policy of non-intervention in the affairs of Indian states and to actively associate itself with the struggle of the states people.[44] But the Mysore Congress was wary of accepting the profferred help of the socialists as it had often proved a broken reed in Congress politics, as the Calcutta Congress resolution and its aftermath had so conclusively proved.

Thus the fact that Sir Mirza Ismail who had always shown great deference to Mahatma Gandhi,[45] and the Mysore

Congress (which according to Rajaji "constantly pretended to act under Gandhiji's instructions")[46] by looking for assistance from the same quarters, complicated, (as the Resident characterised) "the domestic problem".[47]

Mirza Ismail, in his telegrams to Mahatma Gandhi pleaded that the firing was resorted to in sheer self-defence, that a proper judicial enquiry would be held, and that Mahatma Gandhi should "please keep an open mind".[48] Mahatma Gandhi stipulated that the tribunal contain outsider of unimpeachable impartiality, approved by Congress, and advised the government to recognise the awakening in Mysore and to agree to a transfer of responsibility to the people.[49]

Vallabhbhai Patel offered to be an intermediary between the state Congress and the administration,[50] the offer was accepted by the Dewan who felt confident that he could bring round Congress leaders, such as Patel, to his own point of view.[51]

Thus, Mysore formed the first test case for the acting out of the role of intermediary envisaged by Mahatma Gandhi in separating Indian National Congress activities from the affairs of the states. But here it has to be noted that the role of the intermediary in this case, where Mahatma Gandhi had his own aims on the states and Vallabhbhai acting as his agent was partial ultimately to those interests, was a double edged weapon which could cut both the interests of the Mysore Government as well as that of the Mysore Congress. The British administrators with their own interest in mind, feared that it would be in a dangerous position, for if Patel refused to be convinced the Dewan would be led into "granting any concession"[52] which in the interests of "his beloved master"[53] he would subsequently find impossible to defend. But it was equally likely that this interference could act as the restraining influence on the Mysore Congress against the Mysore Government and ultimately prove detrimental to its cause. Congress intervention in the states soon subjected both—the states people as well as the state governments—to these lacerations.

Mahatma Gandhi's statement on the Viduraswatha firing issued on 29 April 1938, in the role of a potential intermediary thus pleased neither party. His assumption that there could have been some provocation for the firing "though the information received... on behalf the public was to the contary",[54] was commented upon by the socialists supporting the states people as an exhibition of the "halting and apologising attitude of the high command".[55] On the other hand his advice to the states administration to divest the government of its autocracy[56] was resented by Mirza Ismail as a "surrender to hooliganism",[57] who put the blame for the tragedy at Mahatma Gandhi's door in proclaiming that had he (Mirza Ismail) not treated the agitation with leniency (which he claimed was done on Gandhi's advice) all this trouble would not have arisen.[58]

With the Dewan in a belligerent mood, the speech of Patel's was necessarily conciliatory. He accused the state Congress of having acted in an unwise and undisciplined manner and exhorted them to cooperate with the Mysore government 'the model state'. He further admitted that the Indian National Congress looked at the state people's struggle with a great deal of suspicion,[59] and that their policy was not to encourage the struggle for the flag in Indian states as their struggle for freedom was a fight for the freedom of Indian princes also. However, he added, more as an aside, that once India was free they would settle their accounts with the princes without the intervention of a third party! Here he did not make it clear who the third party was, the British Government or the states people!!

The speech was significant in that he made a deliberate declaration that the British Indian leaders were not prepared to help the Mysore Congress against the government, nor was it ready to allow the flag to become a matter of contention in their struggle.[60]

The settlement proposed by him was spelt out in two memorandums. For the negotiations on the flag issue (which had started even as early as 20 April 1938, and thus preceded the shooting) Vallabhbhai Patel come with a solution proposed by Gandhi, which was to hoist both flags—Mysore flag as well as the Congress flag—on all ceremonial occasions, care being taken that nothing was done to imply the superiority of one over the other.[61]

The other terms of the agreement proposed that in return for the withdrawal of civil disobedience by the Mysore Congress, the government release political prisoners, withdraw prohibitory orders, recognise the Mysore Congress as a political organisation, add 3 members to the Constitutional Reforms Committee selected by the Mysore Congress and give an explicit statement that the Reforms Committee was open to recommend responsible government.[62]

In its immediate effect the settlement seemed to give the victory to the Mysore Congress.[63] It was felt by the British administrators that the Mysore Government had been forced to accept this position against their will by the strong pressure of the British Indian leaders.[64] Their indignation lay not so much at the 'humiliating capitulation', of the Mysore Government, as that Gandhi and a political organisation of British India should have been permitted to associate so closely with details of the internal administration of the state,[65] so as to even claim to regulate its affairs.[66] Its irritation was against the Dewan for having allowed them to establish such a hold over him,[67] for which state of affairs the Dewan 'could not be held to be wholly innocent';[68] Mirza Ismail, it was held by the British administrators, by his mishandling had not only prejudiced the Maharaja and his government but had paved the way for trouble in other states.[69]

In spite of the alarming view taken by the British administrators on the settlement, the settlement in the long run did not prove as disadvantageous to the administration as feared. Firstly, it gave a respite to the government to gather its forces. Secondly, the solving of the flag issue lost for the Mysore Congress the propaganda value on which it had made capital ever since 1931. Thirdly, the addition of 3 members to its existing 4 to the Reforms Committee gave them no majority in a committee of 26.[70] The explicit statement that the committee was open to recommend responsible government proved ultimately of little value to the Mysore Congress.[71] More importantly, the Mysore Congress was forced by the British Indian leaders to hold its hand till the publication of the Reforms Committee decision, which was judiciously deferred by the Dewan till November 1939.[72]

In the meantime the administration was not above giving a few pin pricks to the Mysore Congress over which, restrained as it was by the British Indian leadership, it could take little action except complain vociferously. The curtain was up on this drama even from the very day of the settlement in May 1938.

On 10 May 1938 the government indirectly, through an article in *The Hindu*, floated its intention to refer the settlement to the Political Affairs Committee, before finalising it.[73] The Mysore Congress objected to the subordination of the position of the Congress to this Committee which could create a precedence of referring all matters to it in future.[74] To avoid further mischief, Vallabhbhai Patel asked the Dewan to formulate the settlement, emphasising the exact details of the terms dictated by him.[75] In this the Mysore Government was able to score a small triumph through the machinations of the Resident where the government instead of issuing a bilateral agreement, signed by both parties as decided by Sardar Patel, issued a unilateral communique drafted by the Resident. The communique changed the tenor of the terms by making it out that it was not out of compulsion or the mediation of Patel (which the Resident was careful to see was not "openly admitted") that the agreement was arrived at, but as due to the "generous attitude", of the government towards the Mysore Congress. The Resident in this took credit for saving "the face of the Mysore Government in their somewhat humiliating position ... (and) to come out of the settlement with considerably more dignity."[76]

Other irritations soon piled up on the Mysore Congress. On 26 May 1938, two weeklies published from Hubli—The *Prajamata* edited by B.N. Gupta and *Praja Sakti* by N.S. Hardikar were banned entry and their Bangalore editors extradited.[77]

Complaints by the Mysore Congress to Vallabhbhai Patel and other leaders related of intimidation by government officials to force witnesses to give evidence at the Ramesam Enquiry Committee, enquiring into the Vidhuraswatha tragedy, that the demonstrations there were marked by violence.[78] Disciplinary action, it was alleged, was also taken against some village officials for participating or showing sympathy with Congress activities.[79]

In July 1938, the office of the Mysore Congress was raided, their office records seized and sent to this Enquiry Committee.[80] Knowing that the decisions of the Ramesam Committee were being rigged by the Mysore Government, the Mysore Congress sought to make even non-rescinding of the deportation order served on the editors of *Prajasakti* and *Prajamata* a "normal if not a real issue",[81] and to withdraw its nominees from the Reforms Committee and their counsel from the Ramesam Committee. However, Patel advised them not to break with the Mysore Government on the present comparatively minor issue which had no bearing on the main constitutional reforms.[82]

The movement in harness, it was not surprising that the state Congress leaders complained of the "offensive and insinuating remarks"[83] made by the chairman of the Viduraswatha Committee against the Congress witnesses, and of Mirza Ismail indulging in "slow and repressive methods in the calm produced by the Patel settlement".[84] On the other hand, by September 1938, Mirza Ismail was in such a dominant position as to boast to the Political Secretary that due to his policy, he did not anticipate any further trouble from the Congress party in the near future, and if there was any, he was fully capable of suppressing disturbances firmly.[85] In this new found confidence of Mirza Ismail the Viduraswatha Enquiry Committee findings, published on 19 November 1938, not only laid the responsibility for the firing on the "campaign of unparalleled violence"[86] indulged in by the State Congress (which even the Resident, expressed in an understatement found "most interesting"),[87] but made the report itself the instrument for further repression in the committee's suggestion that a Criminal Amendment Act be introduced and that the High Court table notice of professional misconduct on the part of legal practitioners engaging themselves in movements of civil disobedience.[88]

The Mysore Congress Working Committee was thus justified in expressing its opinion that the Enquiry Committee had only functioned as a costly machinery which through "flimsy casuistry" shifted the blame on the Congress even while admitting "that the initial prohibitory order itself was imperfect and illegal . . . that the crowd was non-violent before the police lathi charge . . that the authorities would have been wise if they had withdrawn . . . and that the government officers bungled from the very beginning."[89]

The deliberations of the Constitutional Reforms Committee published in November 1939, was to prove as much a long drawn out farce as the enquiry on the Viduraswatha shooting.[90] The realisation even from the beginning that the deliberations of this committee, where the "reactionary elements were having their full sway",[91] was unlikely to bring them any nearer their goal, only made the state Congressmen more restive.

Thus little incidents proved to be a fair ground for grievances where even the naming of a building after a British police officer—a Mr. Hamilton—proved cause for an agitation.[92] A motion was moved in the Legislative Council urging the removal of the name, following which a Satyagraha was staged in front of the police station, led by Tagadur Ramachandra Rao.[93]

However, these demonstrations helped little to further the movement as the British Indian Congressmen had the movement firmly under leash. The growing disparity in the direction from the top, from the British Indian leaders, and the forces from below in the movement within the state, brought on a rift within the ranks of the State Congress. Things came to a head when Mr. Bhupalam Chandrasekharaiah, advising constitutional agitation, resigned from the Congress but refused to vacate his place in the Constitutional Reforms Committee. The refusal of the Mysore Government to appoint another Mysore Congress member in his place proved the signal for a call for dissociation of the Congress members in the Reforms Committee.[94] At a special meeting convened by the All Mysore Congress Committee on 22 February 1938, a section of the Congressmen demanded that the representatives demand an immediate declaration from the government its intentions regarding responsible government and, in the event of a refusal, to resign. As against this radical demand the Mysore Congress Working Committee which feared to prejudice their cause in the eyes of the wider public, chiefly in the eyes of Mahatmaji,[95] felt that it should continue in the Reforms Committee to give proper lead. The sensation of the day was provided when there was a tie in the resolution and was decided by the casting vote of the President who moved with the radicals—leading to a walkout by the Working Committee.

Subsequently, a compromise was arrived at which allowed the members in the Reforms Committee to continue without a formal resignation while dissociating themselves from its proceedings. A non-cooperation programme was chalked out entailing resignations of Congressmen from the legislatures and local boards. But support for this programme was rather partial[96] as the decision on resignation not being unanimous, a splinter group formed a new party called Praja Parishad, under Bhupalam Chandrasekharaiah, with its object of attainment of responsible government through constitutional means.[97]

The State Congress convention meeting at Viduraswatha from 14 to 17 April 1939 was rather undecided about its future programme except in so far as to declare that any constitution falling short of their demand for full responsible government would be resisted by them.[98] But even this proved an empty threat as Mahatma Gandhi had discouraged any civil disobedience even in other states[99] and Mirza Ismail was found busy at his old game of courting the British Indian leaders,[100] in spite of the Viceroy's personal injunctions to him "to sup with a very long spoon",[101] with them. Thus while Mysore administration disallowed even peaceful picketting, and arrests were the order of the day,[102] and it was openly known that the recommendations of the Reforms Committee were likely to be nothing near the demands of the Mysore Congress,[103] Mahatma Gandhi was "loath" to give an interview to the Mysore Congress leaders, and even when he did so, it was only in order to give "them a bit of his mind". Vallabhbhai Patel warned them that "in going to Bapu who had . . advised them to pitch their demands in a lower key they were going to the wrong man",[104] and that their rival Bhupalam would be called if necessary in case of defiance of Gandhi's orders.[105]

It was not surprising that Mirza Ismail well aware of the fact that the British Indian leaders had given no promise of support and little encouragement to the Mysore Congress movement, now even repudiated the earlier agreement[106] as "no pact or anything of the kind",[107] but a mere concession to representation made by them.

Meeting as the Mysore Congress Commttee did in this atmosphere in July 1939 at Arsikere, its authorisation of the working Committee to approach the Government with a view at negotiation was necessarily weak. In case of failure in its endeavour, resolutions to apply all sanctions against the government were modified by clauses deleting the time limit etc.[108]

The Dewan in a dominant position, requests of the leaders of the Mysore Congress for an interview was refused.[109] On 14 August 1939, 13 Congress leaders were arrested for defying a government ban on meetings, following which, decision was taken, in view of the attitude of the government, to start satyagraha from 1 September 1939. The Working Committee was dissolved on that date and the first dictator T. Siddalingiah and 8 others broke the prohibitory orders and were arrested and convicted. By November 1939, more than 11 dictators and 1747 volunteers were put under detention.[110] Jayaprakash Narain and Jawaharlal were understood to be taking an interest in the agitation.[111] But even now, as in the earlier instance, Mirza Ismail by seeking an interview with Gandhi reversed the process. In December 1939, the President of the State Congress and 11 Working Committee members were released, and proceedings set afoot to allow for the nominee of Gandhi, Mahadev Desai, to come to Mysore and report on the situation to him.[112]

On 12 December 1938, Mahadev Desai arrived at Bangalore. As was usual he was treated as a state guest, taken round the state by the Dewan personally, made speeches to the Congress gatherings on the pattern of Vallabhbhai Patel,[113] complimented the Maharaja and the Dewan's governance, advised the Mysore Congress not to start agitations but develop the constructive side of Congress work, mentioned with great approbation the fact that Mirza was to open a khadi exhibition at Madras, and compiled his report for Gandhi.[114]

The report refuted the Dewan's contention that the movement was purely non-Brahmin, or inspired by selfish ends and personal animosities, but attested to Desai's personal conviction that the Congress in Mysore had acquired a firm hold on the mass mind.[115] It also remarked that unlike the struggle on the part of the Mysore Congress, conducted absolutely on non-violent lines, the conduct of the government officers had been marked by repressive treatment, especially of detenues in lockups awaiting trial where they had been coerced in order to extort apologies. However, the report acknowledged, within prison walls, once the detenues had been charged and convicted there was generally speaking no humiliation imposed on them.[116]

Mirza Ismail's proposal to initiate enquiry into the charges made by Desai[117] was countered by Gandhi who proposed an honourable settlement with Mysore Congress, or failing that an enquiry by outsiders (he proposed C. Rajagopalachari). While the proposal is of little importance to the movement,[118] what is significant is that even after charges of the nature made by Mahadev Desai, Gandhi advised the suspension of the movement and forced the state Congress to his proposal.[119] Though its popularity was vindicated in January 1940 when it took part in the local Board elections, contesting 133 seats out of 173,[120] and capturing 119, with the directive from Gandhi the active phase of the movement came to an end.

There was however one point of significance. For the first time Gandhi acknowledged to "a wide divergence",[121] between the views of Mirza and himself, in that Mirza Ismail did not trust the leaders and he did. This was the prelude to Ramgarh resolution on the states which declared for the first time that the struggle for Indian independence was for the freedom of the whole nation including the states;[122] this could be taken as a promise to the states people that their problem would be solved on independence.

From the beginning of the movement in Mysore after the Haripura decision, one sees the tight hold maintained by Gandhi on the movement. The movement was never allowed to come to a crisis. The sending in of emissaries and mediators was not so much to solve the problem as to relieve tensions and bring about peace. The sole idea of Gandhi seems to have been not to instigate the movement as made out by the British administration, but to tone down the movement itself. One could discern the same trend of affairs in Travancore too, where the first opportunity to make a breach in an interference in the state Congress affairs, was utilised by Gandhi to bring down the pitch of the movement. However, there was a qualitative difference in the approach of Travancore administration from that of Mysore. While Mysore's Dewan pretended to be amenable to Gandhi's directions, Travancore took a more belligerent attitude and took advantage of the suppression by Gandhi of the movement in the state to the full. Again, while Mysore Congress Working Committee was more amenable to Gandhi's instructions (mainly because of the close association of Mysore Congress with INC from the beginning) Travancore Congress, a relatively new organisation, outgrown from the

Samyukta Party owing little allegiance to the old organisation did defy his directives, though ultimately with little success.

Travancore (1938-39)

The Dewan's hand was considerably strengthened in April 1938 by the extension of his term of office for another five years. The idea, as C.P. Ramaswami Aiyar himself characterised it, was to "stabilise the position and obviate ill-directed manoeuvers and agitation".[123] The Resident saw in the announcement a clear indication to the popular party that the Maharaja was behind the Dewan in his disapproval of the Travancore Congress movement. With such a mandate from the ruler, C.P. Ramaswami Aiyar made ready his strategy to use the communal set up of the state to his advantage.

While banning meetings of the Travancore State Congress,[124] rival parties and meetings to it were engineered by the Dewan. These meetings protested against the agitation for responsible government and congratulated, His Highness the Maharaja for having extended the services of the Dewan. Thus a 'States Peoples League' was proposed at a meeting at Changanacherri on 28 April 1938 with C.M. Joseph and Mannath Padmanabha Pillai (the president of the communal organisation —the Nair Service Society) as its committee members.[125] A similar meeting of the Kananite Syrian Catholics was held at Ettumanoor.[126] The All-Kerala Nair Conference meeting in May 1938 proved the prelude to the convening of a new organisation, the Travancore National Congress, in Augu t 1938.

These Nair conferences convened under Mannath Padmanabha Pillai, expressed their opinion that it was not advisable for the members of the Nair community to join the agitation carried on by the State Congress[126] and resolutions were passed by the Travancore National Congress requesting the government to change the present system of franchise and to revert to to the old system which favoured the Nairs.[127] However, "Nairs of advanced views" dissociated themselves from these conferences and even staged a walkout of the first Travancore National Congress meet and started parallel meetings protesting against this organisation.[128]

The result of the mushrooming of these parties and organisations was that even when the ban on meetings of the Travancore State Congress was lifted,[129] their meetings were subjected to a great deal of heckling and interruptions from hostile elements in the gatherings.[130] Such meetings were quite often broken up by *Goonda* elements simply walking up to the platform and hustling the speaker off it.[131] The Travancore State Congress accused the police of involvement in organising such rowdyism.[132] Whether there was any truth in their charge or not, there was no denying, as commented on by the Resident himself, that the Travancore police failed to bring home assaults by hooligans on sympathisers of State Congress. Two of these assaults were on editors of newspapers who had shown hostility to the Dewan and the government.[133]

It was thus that such seemingly paltry incidents like that of a burglary, in the house of one of the Working Committee members of the Travancore State Congress — Anne Mascarene (an advocate of Trivandrum Court) — became important enough to find inclusion in a memorandum submitted by the Congress to the Maharaja on 30 May 1938.[134]

This memorandum charged the Dewan of black and tan methods in his treatment of political opponents, of hostility towards freedom of speech and press,[135] of nepotism in public service, and by innuendo, of corruption in his dealings with big business in giving extraordinary concessions to capitalists and contractors from outside. Citing specific cases it charged the Dewan of handing over the Travancore Sugars and Trivandrum Rubber Company to agencies "financed by outsiders", in which transaction, it alleged the involvement of the Dewan's son.[136] The memorandum marked for special reference the nationalised state transport system;[137] it charged that in the purchase of chassis and ordering of bodies, preferences had been shown to non-Travancoreans. The long list of complaints against the Dewan ended with charges of a top-heavy administration, distribution of appointments as personal favours and purchase of public men and party leaders through the mechanism of appointments.[138] It demanded the dismissal of the Dewan, an enquiry into his administrative acts and financial transactions and immediate grant of responsible government as the only remedy.

To counteract charges of communalism, the majority of the signatories of the memorandum happened to be Nairs, consisting as it did of 10 Nairs, 7 Christians and 4 Ezhavas — the

Nairs representing those who had walked out of the All Nair Conference. As the Resident pointed out some of the criticisms contained in the memorandum were undoubtedly justified, but the instances quoted of black and tan methods were "trivial to a degree and the innuendos regarding corruption ... based on the flimsiest evidence".[139] This personal indictment of the Dewan was caused by several factors, not the least of which was the intense, almost hysterical hatred shown by the educated classes for him, due to his "domineering and contemptuous"[140] treatment of them; it was also due to the introduction of a state banking system, and state transport system arousing the hatred of the vested interests. The Dewan had on his part, in retaliation of these attacks by the vested interests, perpetrated (what the Resident called) an act of 'alleged frightfulness'[141] in engineering a run on the Travancore National and Quilon Bank. The Directors of this bank had for years identified themselves with the opposition parties in Travancore and had excited the Dewan's personal enmity. The Dewan maintained that the collapse of the bank was due to the mismanagement of the Directors who had now successfully transferred the odium of the crash on to the administration.[142] It was mainly in this context, especially as the memorandum lowered the movement to that of a personal vendetta against the Dewan promoted by vested interests, that Mahatma Gandhi effected his breach into the movement through his insistence that the memorandum be withdrawn.

The intervention of Mahatma Gandhi in Travancore affairs followed the personal invitation by two prominent members of the Travancore State Congress to intercede and bring about a negotiation on Mysore lines.[143] Mahatma Gandhi sent Rajkumari Amrit Kaur to solve the political tangle, and was, according to C. P. Ramaswami Aiyar, shown the papers relating to contracts and other transactions with which she professed herself satisfied.[144] In spite of Rajkumari Amrit Kaur's warning that a civil disobedience movement would not be supported by the AICC a campaign was launched on 26 August 1938 by the Travancore State Congress; countered by, in turn, the promulgation of a Criminal Law Amendment Regulation.[145]

The demonstrations in Travancore were not so well organised on non-violent lines as the ones in Mysore. At one of its earliest meetings on 29 August 1938, at Shangumugham beach, after the arrest of leaders, a small police party was manhandled by the mob and a police car overturned and burned.[146] This was the first indication of the violent turn these demonstrations had taken. On 31 August 1938, at a similar demonstration at Neyyatinkara, after the arrest of the dictators of the day, a *melee* ensued and resulted in the first baptism of fire when five villagers died in the police shooting.[147] Similar events followed at Attingal,[148] Quilon,[149] Pudupallee[150] etc., when on 3 September 1938, Mahatma Gandhi issued a statement charging the Travancore administration of repression and the State Congress of making serious charges unsupported by any evidence against the Dewan in their memorandum.[151] A temporary lull in the agitation now shifted the venue to the press with C. P. Ramaswami Aiyar and Gandhi indulging in a lively exchange of communiques[152] where Gandhi insisted that the Travancore administration declare a general amnesty and appoint an outsider of integrity to enquire into the shooting. The Resident agreed to this, but his idea was to have an enquiry by outsiders in which "Travancore Government might seem to be defendants",[153] while it was in actuality to be a sedition and rebellion trial in which the State Congress leaders were to be tried by a High Court Judge of British India, selected at Travancore Government's request to the Crown Representative. Thus, even if Gandhi's idea had been accepted it would have been as much a farce as the Ramesam Enquiry on the Viduraswatha tragedy in Mysore.[154]

However, with the government's cancellation of the licence of a newspaper—the *Malayala Manorama* owned by the chairman of the Travancore National and Quilon Bank,[155] the agitation was again resumed resulting in shooting incidents at Trivandrum beach, Attingal, Shertallai and rioting at Chengannor.[156]

On 11 October 1938 the Travancore State Congress organised a lightning strike among the boatmen of Ambalapuzha, Mavelikara and Karunagapalli, which brought the backwater traffic almost to a standstill.[157] It was this spread of agitation among the labour organisations that forced the Travancore administration to offer amnesty to political prisoners, and repeal emergency legislation in return for withdrawal of the memorandum and the corruption charges made against the Dewan. This offer was rufused by the leaders in the jail in spite of the intervention of Captain Nimbalker, President of the Madras Civil Liberties Union,[158] and a reiteration from Gandhi on it.[159]

On 22 October 1938, on the occasion of the Maharaja's birthday, an amnesty was declared, 189 prisoners released and the emergency legislation was suspended by the Travancore Government, which the State Congress repudiated as no concession. On 23 October 1938, the State Congress leaders were summoned to consult Gandhi and Vallabhbhai at Kohat, and Gandhi advised them strongly to withdraw the memorandum.[160]

However, the resolution passed by the Travancore Congress on 30 October 1938 showed little signs of obedience to the Mahatma's commands. It adopted what C. P. Ramaswami Aiyar called a "completely intransigent attitude".[161] It declared the amnesty as "unwarrantable and regrettable",[162] and declared its intention to undertake a fresh programme of direct action.[163] It appointed Anne Mascarene and T.K. Naryana Pillai in charge of a volunteer corp to express sympathy with the boatmen's strike and labour strike,[164] and planned for the holding of an All Travancore Conference at Trivandrum, and a fresh collection of funds, significantly authorising J. Kuruvilla of Trichur (in Cochin territory) to be in charge of it.[165]

The Travancore Government instigated by the Resident decided in November 1938 to prosecute the signatories of the memorandum before a special court, examining specially the various disturbances from 28 July 1938, leading to rioting in each case.[166]

At the same time, the State Congress leaders were again recalled to Wardha and at a meeting on 13 and 14 November 1938, were told "to act according to the commandments of Gandhiji. Messrs Patel, C. R. Pattabhi Sitaramayya and G. Ramachandran . . requested Gandhiji to insist State Congress people for the withdrawal of the memorandum and Gandhi told them that his personal view was to withdraw the memo" so as to resume correspondence towards an easy and "tangible solution".[167] In this G. Ramachandran's action in sending a note to Gandhi without the knowledge of the Working Committee of the State Congress, exasperated them not a little and there was even a move to ask him to resign. At this meeting Gandhi told them that while they were free to take his advice or otherwise on the memorandum question, they were bound to suspend civil disobedience.[168] He warned them that if it resulted in violence, even if it were instigated by the authorities or otherwise, he would hold them responsible. Here he made it clear that he would not be a party to a struggle in pursuit of a personal matter to "the exclusion of the most important one of swaraj".[169]

In face of such a warning, while Pattam Thanu Pillai, N.K. Pillai and some others were for withdrawal of the memorandum, it was opposed by the Ezhava leader V.K. Velayudhan, and the Christian T. M. Varghese. T. M. Varghese openly asserted that his position and interests were at stake, representing as he did the Marthomites who were against the withdrawal and his connection with the Travancore National and Quilon Bank to whom he was indebted. He felt that even after withdrawal it was unlikely that the Dewan would stop prosecuting them.[170]

On 13 December 1938, a proclamation was issued by the Maharaja instituting criminal prosecution against the signatories of the memorandum.[171]

Yet another reminder had to be sent by Gandhi to Pattam Thanu Pillai, insisting that they withdraw the memorandum even if prosecution proceedings were taken by the administration,[172] before the State Congress decided at its meeting on 22 December 1938, at Vattiyoorkavu, to authorise the President to take decision on the conduct of the movement in any manner he deemed fit.[173]

In spite of the brave statement by R. Sankar, the acting President of the Travancore State Congress, that the withdrawal was the result of a realisation among the committee members that the struggle had reached "a stage of such depth, strength and proportions,"[174] where the personal allegations against the Dewan were of no consequence, and that it was not the result of threats that the memorandum was withdrawn, there were few who could deny that it was solely the result of the pressures exerted by the British Indian leadership. The withdrawal of the memorandum clearly signified the passing of the movement from the hands of the state leadership to that of British Indian leaders, and that it was to subserve the Indian National Congress' interest. Thus after Haripura resolution, we find as in Mysore, the direction of the Travancore agitation come completely into the hands of British Indian leadership. The protests and indignation expressed at the private meeting on G. Ramachandran's 'apostasy' in wiring to Gandhi soliciting his decision on the memorandum,[175] the railings of H.C. Dasappa against another Ramachandran in Mysore,[176] or the commiserations and advice of T. Siddalingiah (of Mysore) to Pattam Thanu Pillai that they stop going in deputation to Gandhi,[177] were the mere lashings of a fish on hook. The subsequent period in Travancore was to see it landed neatly by Mahatma Gandhi and his coterie. Thus, as in Mysore, the states people's movement in Travancore was soon to be caught in a trap, partly the making of Mahatma Gandhi and partly the result of the policy of the Travancore administration. In spite of T. Siddalingiah's exhortation to the Travancore Congress that they ought to concert measures to organise themselves and adopt a dynamic programme for realising their objective,[178] the movement was to fail singularly.

In its immediate effect, there was a move by the more radical members to repudiate the leadership of the State Congress and prepare another memorandum.[179] There was still an expectation that the movement freed from charges of personal vindictiveness against the Dewan, would now build up, even to a civil disobedience agitation on purely ideological grounds. In this, even the dropping of the charges of sedition against the memorialists by the administration,[180] was not regarded in any sense as motivated at a political settlement, as the Travancore administration soon followed it up by disqualifying 19 elected members to the legislature (all on Travancore State Congress ticket) on account of conviction under Criminal Law Amendment Regulation for political offences.[181] The Travancore State Congress pleaded in a statement that their plan for direct action was not of their seeking, that if they did resolve on it they should be fully supported not only by the people of Travancore but also by the "sympathies of the world outside."[182] Their pleadings were mainly directed at Mahatma Gandhi from whom they expected opposition.

In view that there were more than 300 volunteers still in

the lockup, on 17 January 1939 the State Congress declared its intention to launch direct action in six weeks unless negotiations were opened by the government on proposals put forward by it. These proposals stipulated, among other conditions, a general amnesty, the repeal of Criminal Amendment Regulation, recognition of the State Congress for negotiations, restoration of licences to newspapers, and withdrawal of prosecution against labour strikers[183] etc. But more importantly their concern was concentrated on government manoeuvres to reopen the communal issue in a repeal of the franchise concessions granted after the Abstention Movement.[184] This move was particularly aimed at the Ezhava group in the State Congress who were already disgruntled by the State Congress attitude in stepping up the constructive activities, specially on prohibition, which with their main profession as toddy tappers, hurt their economic interests.[185] Thus the stage was set for the breaking off of the Ezhava community from the Travancore State Congress, if its particular interests were jeopardised by the State Congress withdrawal to agitate on the issues of Ezhava interests. As pertinently pointed out by G. Ramachandran, the Travancore State Congress was now forced into a position to fight "or permit the steady destruction of its organisation"[186] under the adroit handling of the Dewan.

The AISPC realising the difficulties under which the Travancore State Congress laboured, passed a resolution on Travancore, drafted by Jawaharlal Nehru himself, which proclaimed that the State was justified in starting the satyagraha.[187] Gandhi first advised the postponement of the date of ultimatum,[188] and on the very eve of satyagraha, when Travancoreans hopes were raised high on rumours that he was to personally conduct the agitation "repeating tactics employed at Rajkot",[189] he ordered a suspension of the movement, which thus came as an anticlimax.

There was good ground for the high hopes of the Travancore State Congress. On Gandhi's advice to postpone date of ultimatum issued on 25 February 1939, the Travancore State Congressmen had met Gandhi and apparently persuaded him enough to have got his agreement to their elaborate plan of satyagraha drawn at a meeting on 6 and 7 March 1939, constituting a shadow cabinet of seven members to take charge of the struggle even if it had to go underground.[190] To this plan he had seemingly given acquiescence in an article in *Harijan*; Gandhi had elaborated here his conditions on the conduct of the agitation where he stipulated that there was to be no violence, disobedience was to be undestructive, participation of the largest number to be ensured and the student element kept out of it.[191]

In ordering the suspension on 23 March 1939 Gandhi's avowed reason was the "inhumanities perpetrated by a number of hirelings recruited as special police by the Travancore authorities to deal with the Congress".[192] In this he proclaimed himself as well aware of the "heart burning and disappointment",[193] caused by the suspension, leading even to desertion and disbelief, but dismissed these as of little consequence as he felt the movement would be better without them, as it was to him a sign that the deserters did not know what satyagraha was.

In spite of the suspension, attacks by *goonda* elements on Congressmen continued. On 31 March 1939, a party of 11 Congress workers under T.M. Varghese were assaulted and robbed, in which the Travancore government's involvement was suspected.[194]

On 22 April 1939, Gandhi declared that he was "not likely easily to advise resumption of civil disobedience"[195] and in June 1939 issued a statement that mass civil disobedience was to be suspended indefinitely,[196] and adviced the State Congress to open negotiations with the Dewan, with a will to negotiate pitching their demands on a lower key. Here he emphasised that the condition precedent to any civil disobedience was their coming under the discipline of the State Congress, even to their taking up constructive programme as a measure of the test of such discipline.

His advice to the State Congress to pitch their demand on a lower key,[197] his emphasis on Congress discipline and the remark that with the exception of Aundh nowhere were the princes ready to give full responsible government nor were the paramount power anxious for the people of the states to receive it,[198] all went to reiterate his old contention that the state peoples agitation on responsible government could only prove infructuous. As such, a mere awakening of the states people without realising the price—in the realisation that their aim was only realisable on the attainment of swaraj for India—was not enough. So all these agitations of the state's people during the late 1930's went again towards the same realisation, reiterated yet again, on the question of priorities. Was the states peoples objective possible without gaining the Congress objective—Gandhi's opinion went again to give a final negative to the states peoples cause.

However, even Gandhi's own objective, in negotiations, leading to some type of concessions on the federal issue was to prove abortive at the hands of the Dewan who made it clear to the negotiators[199] that any negotiation would be opened by him only on the clear understanding that "no intervention of outside persons however exalted or influential with regard to political activities",[200] would be countenanced. His second condition stipulated that they give up the idea of civil disobedience for all time and that they understand clearly that the Travancore Government while ready to discuss settlement on matters of controversy, had no intention of establishing responsible government in the sense of responsibility of the executive to the legislature. Such a demand, as pointed out by Mahadev Desai to Glancy, the Political Secretary, was, to say the least, unfair. Thus Gandhi, though reluctant to advise a struggle, saw that if the Dewan insisted on "robbing the people of their self-respect there was nothing left for them but to engage in fight for honour, however hopeless and unequal the fight".[201] With C.P. Ramaswami Aiyar picking up the gauntlet, even to a "conflict with a world figure"[202] like Gandhi, the Travancore State Congress on the guidance of Mahatma Gandhi issued a pathetic statement reserving its right to seek advice and guidance of persons outside Travancore, and a declaration that while the State Congress was ready to work any scheme arrived at by mutual consent, they would always have responsible government as their ultimate end in view.[203]

On 6 September 1939 the State Congress in a resolution proposed the reactivisation of the Congress on moderate lines, declaring as their ultimate aim, the establishment of a responsible government. It decided to take up countrywide propaganda and agitation on constitutional lines as it proclaimed it had no desire to come into conflict with the government. In pursuance of this moderate attitude they gave up a procession, with flag hoisting ceremony etc., in obedience to a government communique banning them.[204]

Making the declaration of war and the break off of federal negotiations by the paramount power, the pretext, the Dewan on 23 September 1939, declared that no conversations were possible with any party on constitutional reforms until normal conditions were restored.[205] It is relevant to note here that soon after, in November 1939, Gandhi 'absolved' the State Congress from any restraint[206] on his part, showing clearly the close connection between federal negotiations and his interference in the state. But this absolution came very late in the day. With war as the pretext the states administration came down heavily on the State Congress with a Defence of Travancore Proclamation which made even innocuous meetings of the State Congress[207] an offence and had the leaders of the Congress behind bars in no time.

It was invitable that the Ezhava organisation with hardly any interest on the constructive programme of the Congress, and with the additional threat of a change in the system of franchise, would now dissociate themselves from the State Congress. In November 1939, the President of the SNDP Yogam advised the Ezhavas to dissociate themselves from political agitation and confine themselves to social and communal needs. Thus what had been threatened from May 1939, from the time of Gandhi's orders to suspend agitation[208] was given its final stamp when on 23 December 1939, the Ezhava leaders in jail, Gopala Panikkar, V.K. Velayudhan, and R. Sankar, appealed for conditional release and were released.[209]

There was one other important effect of Gandhi's policy on Travancore. Prior to the withdrawal of the memorandum, the labour organisations had been completely under the control of the State Congress Right Wing leadership. In fact the boatmen's strike of October 1938 was partly a response to the vested interests fears of nationalisation of the backwater traffic. But after the withdrawal of the memorandum one sees a marked change. Thus a meeting organised by A.K. Gopalan, immediately after the withdrawal of the memorandum, under the presidentship of S.C. Banerji, President of the All India Trade Union Congress, was boycotted by the Right Wing local leaders as they felt the meeting had been arranged by A.K. Gopalan "to spite the local leader."[210] At the meeting S.C. Banerji was bent on exploiting the states peoples grievances consequent on the Haripura resolution and Gandhi's handling and asserted that while the Indian National Congress could make distinction between the British Indian provinces and the Indian states, the Trade Union could make no such distinction.[211]

Thus with the Gandhian leadership discredited, the radical wing, especially from British Malabar, found ready material in Travancore.[212] As E.M.S. Namboodiripad in a letter to Jaiprakash Narain wrote, the Forward Block tendency in Travancore was on the rise and even a Forward Block Conference was mooted, with a programme for direct action.[213] A meeting organinised by K.A. Joglekar, President, Bombay Kirni Kamgar Union, resolved that the State Congress workers had failed through over dependence on Gandhian leadership and proposed a more radical line.[214] These manoeuvres and participation of left wingers from outside is of importance, as in the post 1939 period, with the arrests of most Congress members and the complete rout of this party at the hands of the Dewan, it was this wing which was to gain ascendancy. The period subsequent saw mainly the activities promoted by these agitators from outside, especially from their radical compatriots of British Malabar. Thus Gandhian leadership and his emphasis on British Indian interest, reinforced the trend already established after the Haripura resolution in the changes wrought in the constitution,[215] to turn Kerala into the stronghold of communism and communalism, the very traits which are to be discernible even today.

Conclusions

Seen in the perspective of events subsequent to Haripura, the analysis of the states peoples movement in these states show, contrary to previous notions on it, that the Haripura resolution was motivated not by a relaxation of Congress interference in the states but was effected as a means of gaining complete control over the movement through moral pressures. In this the Haripura resolution saw to it that by making non-interference in the states a part of Indian National Congress policy, the leadership itself was insulated from pressures within.

The breach in the movement of the states people was effected through suggestions pressed forward by confidants of Gandhi prominent in the states movement, to consult Gandhi. A real handle was provided when the Mysore administration, following a shooting incident, sought the intervention of Gandhi. This provided the British Indian nationalists the moral stature to control the movement in its position as intermediaries and as emissaries. Through them, and through direct threats of supporting a dissident section, Gandhi forced the states people into an initial postponement of a satyagraha and subsequently to its withdrawal.

The divergence in impositions from the top and the movement from below, led to a split in Trancore politics. The Ezhava section, threatened in its position by the Dewan's move to revert to the earlier system of franchise which was to its disadvantage, now in a position rather vulnerable, broke off from the Congress. A section disillusioned with the British Indian leadership's imposition, went to swell the communist movement which had already gained support organisationally by the Haripura decision on disaffiliation.

Parallel with its efforts at gaining control over the movement in these states, the nationalists had been active in organising and promoting movements in other states so as to further their interests on federation at this time and on integration ultimately. These exercises of the 1938's gave them the confidence of controlling the entire states peoples movement to their needs. The question of priorities—on integration versus responsible government—was thus settled for all time. From now on, while the British Indian leadership was made free to utilise the states peoples movement to its needs, the cause of the states people on responsible government on its own was pushed into a position of secondary importance.

7

Prometheus on Leash

The Movement from 1940 to October 1947

Incompatibility of Treaty Rights with Independent British India

Seen in the context of the 1938-39 strategy of Gandhian policy, dealt with in the last chapter, it is not surprising that the question of the states and their problems, important as it was, as Jawaharlal Nehru acknowledged in his letter to Sheikh Abdullah, had now receded into the background.[1] The tendency now was to concentrate on the 'minority issue' of British India almost to a total exclusion of the problem of the states. Thus, while the Reforms Commissioner, H.P. Hodson, complained of the very small part which the problem of the states seemed to play in the British Indian politicians 'approach' to the constitutional issue, and of their new tendency to leave it out of the picture,[2] the British administrators were no less guilty in their approach to these questions.

The August Offer of 1940 was concerned with British India

alone—this in spite of the British administrators' sympathies for the princes who had demanded a more positive declaration, that any revision of the 1935 Act would be undertaken only in consultation with them.[3] This, non-consultation of the princes, or their representatives, had irked C.P. Ramaswami Aiyar and had even prompted him to suggest to Mirza Ismail and Hydari[4] a joint consultation to discuss and make some representation to the Viceroy on behalf of the larger states.[5] Mirza Ismail declined to be a party to such a conference.

The reason for this callous treatment of the princes was due to the growing realisation, during this period, in the British administrators own minds, of the incompatibility of maintaining their treaty obligations to the princes with their promises for a self-governing British India. As Wylie rightly remarked "the vision"[6] of an Indian Union was inconsistent with the maintenance of the princes treaty rights and obligations. The British administrators, in spite of all their sympathies for the princes, were caught in the "unenviable position" of reconciling their "past promises with present day realities",[7] especially in face of the states peoples demonstration during the period 1938 to 1940. The *Transfer of Power* volumes dealing with this period from 1942 to March 1946 show clearly the evolution of the above realisation.[8] It is in this context that the importance of the states peoples movement to be considered.

The May 1941 memorandum of Amery's to Linlithgow mainly emphasised the weakness of the small and petty states Durbars to maintain themselves against "subversive activities" or successfully to negotiate for a firm footing in a new Indian structure without the help of Britain.[9] As such, the main problem was of grouping the majority of these principalities to withstand these pressures, or to liquidate them by absorption in either other states or with British India. In order to keep their hands free for such a course it was increasingly necessary that the British Government refrained from any new pronouncements stressing the sanctity of rights and had to impress upon the Durbars the need to adjust themselves to their claims for their continuation being considered on their own merits. It was in this context that the Cripps proposal though it made generous concessions to the princes,[10] hurt their susceptibilities[11] by cdeviating from the earlier constitutional proposals in making no mention of the treaty position of the princes *vis-a-vis* the Crown.[12] Likewise, it was the British administrators efforts at grouping of the Western Indian states,[13] by rousing their suspicions of British motives on their position, which lead in turn, to a show of hysterics by the princes in their 'Chamber Crisis'.[14]

It was only on the eve of the Cabinet Mission Plan when Corfield, as spokesman of the princes, demanded a clear indication of the British position *vis-a-vis* the treaties,[15] was the real implications of British Indian independence on the position of the states irrespective of their size, and willingness of the British administrators to give such a promise, spelt out.

It was in this context that it was now clearly acknowledged, at least at the Cabinet meetings, that paramountcy itself *was essentially derived from the fact that they were paramount in British India*—which in fact of British Indian independence would "clearly no longer admit it of being discharged".[16] The accent on paramountcy in British India was of particular importance in carrying out of British obligations to the states. For while other paramountcy obligations—on personal and dynastic affairs, on economic and fiscal provisions, and even against external aggression could be contrived at, there could be no guarantee "in respect of the ruler against insurrection of his own subjects or incursions from neighbouring Indian territories".[17] Hitherto, the Crown had carried out these obligations by the use of troops in control of the Governor General (through section 286 of the 1935 Act) by the use of the special responsibility of the Governors in the provinces for the protection of the states rights. Under an independent British India these provisions could naturally not be brought into operation. This brought into question the possibility of having British troops under their control[18] and of free passage for them through British India to these non-adhering states and a guarantee by provincial governors to restrain its people from incursions into neighbouring non-adhering states—the obvious use of the Protection of States Against Disaffection Act as hitherto exercised. The Viceroy had to acknowledge, with an Indian government in British India, the demands of the princes was out of question—which ultimately boiled down to an abandoning of their position on obligations regarding treaties.

Such an acknowledgement led to a realisation that there was "no secure future in isolation for even the minor powers, much less for the Leichensteins and Monaccos with which India was garnished".[19] The requiem thus sung on the small states, and the danger to even the big states realised in the absence of the props of British military power, it was not surprising that the princes, in the 1946 Cabinet Mission confabulations, were consigned to the ante-chamber.

However, the British administrators endeavour to soft pedal the issue and to let down the princes rather gently, again penalised, in its immediate implication, the states peoples cause. The Cabinet Mission Plan of 16 May 1946, as the resolution of the Working Committee of the Indian National Congress criticising it did point out, left its provisions regarding the states rather 'vague'.[20] It was purposely made 'vague' so as to give the Rulers a chance at what the Cabinet Mission hoped, would be a fair and just arrangement with the leaders of British India as to their future relationship.[21] It was this hope which after long confabulations on the drafting of a warning note to the princes, frankly pointing out the definite limits in honouring of treaty obligations,[22] made them withdraw from such a position and scrap the very idea of a warning.[23]

It was this vagueness which contributed much to a sense of insecurity of not only the rulers but also of the states people. The Cabinet Mission while stipulating that paramountcy would neither be retained nor transferred, left the 'precise form' in which their cooperation was to take place with British India, to negotiations and the princes discretion and suggested that the void created by the cessation of paramountcy be filled either by the states entering into a federal relationship,[24] with successor government or governments, or into 'particular relationship,' with it or them. Thus the states confabulations with British India was to be at two levels, one for entry into the Constituent Assembly involving discussions on the number and mode of selection to the same, and secondly on relationship with British India—federal or otherwise. The British provisions regarding both were vague, except in suggesting that it be taken up by negotiating committees of both parties. Here the British administrators did not specify whether talks on both these proposals were to precede and take place outside the Constituent

Assembly or otherwise, or to be carried on collectively by the Maharajas or individually.

In the negotiating committee's confabulations itself, the princes sought to widen the talks to an inclusion of discussions and acceptance of their 'fundamental points', guaranteeing their position as sole authorities in the states and in the selection of representatives, with rights to withdraw from the confabulations if the decisions in the Constituent Assembly did not meet their approval.[25] On B.N. Rau's suggestion,[26] the Congress leadership leaving the fundamental points—to a discussion at a full forum, insisted that preliminary talks by the negotiating committees be confined only to the other two basic points, of distribution and mode of selection to the Consambly.

The princes counter demand to make the acceptance of their 'fundamental points' a pre-condition to their entry into the Constituent Assembly[27] failed, with Bikaner, Patiala and Baroda deciding to join the proceedings independent of the decisions of the Princes Chamber; this broke up the common front put up by them.

What was pertinent in this to the states people was that while they could find no place on the British Indian side of the Negotiating Committee, as it was drawn from members of the Constituent Assembly to which they had as yet no entry, it was inconceivable that the states negotiating committee of the princes would ever agree to an inclusion of states peoples representatives on their side. Thus in these talks, as in earlier instances, the states people were once again left out, with the dubious championship of the British Indian leaders talking on their behalf. With two issues before them, viz. cooperation in the union and the other of enforcing democratic principles in selection of members to the Constituent Assembly, the question was not only that of their position in the Constituent Assembly but how far were their demands on responsible government likely to be looked after in the larger context of British Indian interests ?

The fears of the states people were particularly relevant at the time when no final decision had been taken on partition, and the princes were therefore in a strong bargaining position in the event of a loose federal structure being set up.

The States people on this issue thus had their own doubts

and it was D.V. Gundappa of Mysore who once again expressed their misgivings. He wrote :

> As to the Congress, the feeling among many of the workers for the peoples cause in the states, is frankly, that the sympathy of the bulk of the Congress leaders for the cause is of a passive variety; they are no doubt willing to help; but when the critical occasion comes, they are apt to say to themselves—'British India First'—and make compromises too readily over states questions. Of course, they protest that freedom cannot be halved and that real freedom must be for all. If the Congress high command had been actively interested in the cause, they could well have made it a condition of their accepting the Cabinet Mission's Plan . . . conditional on the inclusion of a good majority of the states representatives being returned from the states people and that the representatives (were) enabled to join the Assembly at its inception.[28]

However, the problem of British Indian leaders, bent on their vision of a united India was not so much on making conditions for the entry of the states into the Constituent Assembly as much as enticing them to take a part in their confabulations. What was required, as Bikaner adumberated, was "goodwill, confidence and trust on both sides", which meant in his terms a repudiation of "credence attached by leaders outside to the malicious allegations made by . . few disgruntled persons"[29] from within the states. In face of such a declaration, even the speech of Nehru, the champion of the states peoples cause, speaking on behalf of the AISPC on the eve of the Cabinet Mission, was necessarily constrained and vague. While deprecating that the states problem had not been taken into consideration—as "other problems were supposed to have priority", and could only be considered in the context of an independent India—he touched rather lightly on the necessity of adoption of democratic principles in the representation to the Constituent Assembly and recognition of a democratic structure in the states while emphasising mainly the civil liberties issue in the states.[30] Thus it is not surprising that the British Indian leadership, again expressing itself through the voice of Nehru, in order to safeguard its main interest on some form of union, made it clear that the Constituent Assembly discussions were to be confined to only union matters; he asserted that the discussions would not include the "question of monarchical form of government in the states",[31] nor would the Assembly wish to interfere in the internal arrangements of the states.[32] The AISPC (to which the three States Congress' of our study had become affiliated only in December 1945)[33] taking its cue no doubt from the British Indian leaders, while disputing the 'princes fundamental points' of 29 January 1947, on the question dear to the states peoples heart,—on details of internal administration, wished not "to express any opinions at this stage".[34]

The same British Indian leadership's interests on union, foisted on the AISPC meeting at its Gwalior Conference in April 1947, the policy of promoting trauquility and forbidding active movements against state authority on the eve of the transfer of power by Britain to Indian hands,[35] lest, no doubt, their chances of enticing the princes into the Constituent Assembly were jeopardised. Thus it was that even on the eve of Travancore declaring its 'independence', Rajendra Prasad visiting Travancore, in reply to a question put by Pattam Thanu Pillai in regard to the Indian National Congress' help to their movement, prevaricated on the issue. Without answering in any way the states leaders question he dealt mainly on his belief that it was not possible "at any time for Travancore to think of a separate existence of its own"[36]—thus dealing only with the issue that predominated in the British Indian leaders mind—on that of union.

However, the dilatory tactics adopted by these states (with the exception of Cochin), in spite of these assurances in joining the Constituent Assembly and the Indian Union, and the stance on independence of Travancore[37] forced the British Indian leadership into championing the cause of the people. It was only in this context that Mahatma Gandhi declared that the states "belonged to their people",[38] and that if the rulers had the right to exist it was only as trustees and servants of the people. Again, while emphasising that the union was not inimical to the princes, he declared that his erstwhile policy "to leave the states alone"[39] had now changed with the reins of the government passing into the peoples hands. In this he asserted, the people of the states were with the British Indians, as, "if the princes were allowed to become independent, it could only be at the cost of the freedom of the people of the states."[40] Thus the states people were once again called to work on the British Indian programme so as to serve their own interest. It was then that the AICC, taking its tone from Mahatma Gandhi, declared, at its meeting on 14 June 1947, that it was of vital importance that progress leading to responsible government take place rapidly in the states.[41] Yet this did not mean in any way a support to the states peoples programme, as how was one to reconcile this with Vallabhbhai Patel's politic assurances to the princes[42] and to Hari Singh, the Maharaja of Kashmir, ending in a note of rhetoric "is it necessary to assure you that in your domestic affairs the Congress has no intention whatever of intervening?"[43]

Thus while British Indian interests were always ready, at least outwardly, to repudiate the states peoples cause, the states people were once again made to serve the British Indian interest on union, though this time it was emphasised that it would serve their interest in the process. It is important to note at this point that the contradictions that were apparent were only of British Indian leaders making and not of the states people. However, the constant repudiation of the states peoples cause in their reiteration that they were not going to interfere in the states, served, as Sarat Chandra Bose pointed out, to sabotage to some extent the demands of the states people.[44] It was this factor which prolonged the issue of the states peoples demand—especially in Mysore—even after the Maharaja's conceding on the 'Union' issue.

It is not my contention here that the British Indian leadership was entirely oblivious of the interests of the states people. Ultimately they did help unobtrusively, and did declare on 16 November 1947 that whatever "the legal implications of accession and lapse of British paramountcy, the moral result of independence of India was undoubtedly the establishment and recognition of the power of the people, as distinguished from that of the princes and feudal or other interests hostile to natural popular aspiration".[45] But this declaration came after all three states, covered by my study, had achieved their ends and in the process of achieving it, passed through not only fears and doubts about Indian National Congress' motives towards them, but in order to serve the larger interests, suffered a loss—especially in Travancore—of popularity due to the divergence and consequential gap due to policy instructions from above and the forces from below. Again the declaration was motivated not so much for the promotion of the states peoples cause, as it was merely the next step to achieve the British Indian objective on integration so as to bring the Indian states, whether under the princes or under democratic regimes, under central control of the All India leadership.

The final stamp on the inevitability of complete cooperation and the rubbing out of any distinction between these units—as from British India and from the states—was given, when in order to ensure uniformity of responsible government in all the states, contrary to its earlier promises not to discuss on internal administrations—even this question was taken up by the Constituent Assembly in March 1949 in giving the states a uniform model constitution.[46] This constitution more importantly left the recognition, deposition etc. of the rulers not in the hands of the states legislatures but in the hands of the central government,[47] thus providing for the supremacy of central leadership in all matters. Thus, in fact, British India became the inheritors of British paramountcy, whether willed by the British or not. As put so aptly by the *Round Table* a "Transmigration of Paramountcy"[48] had taken place and for this achievement of the British Indian leadership the help of the states people was more considerable than that of the British Indian leaders to their cause. But this was inevitable with the British Indian leaders holding the whip hand *vis-a-vis* the states, especially so following Haripura.

Seen thus in this broad framework of British policy towards the states and of the policy of British Indian leadership of the Congress, it is not surprising that the Praja Mandals and State Congress lost its earlier glory—except as a threat for possible insurrections and danger to the states administrations and that too mainly to promote the programme of the Congress High Command on union and integration. Thus the movement of the states peoples in this period—1940 to 1947—falls mainly in the nature of an epilogue.

Cochin (1941 to 1947)

The movement in Cochin, as in the earlier phase, was carried out mainly in the legislature and centered round demands for further reforms. transfer of more departments to the popular ministers and on the extension of franchise.[49] These demands met with fluctuating reception at the hands of successive Maharajas and Dewans. The government though regretting its inability to oblige, was particularly sympathetic to these demands in the earlier phase—in the period of Shanmugham Chetty's tenure. These demands were not so well treated, in the period following, under the European Dewan.[50] It was only after another change in the regime in a new accession in January 1946, and the imminence of constitutional changes in British India, that it met with some favour.

The course of the movement, within the legislature was marked by petty factional wrangles, leading to splits, coalitions and formation of new parties.[51] Claiming, as all these parties did, an allegiance to the Indian National Congress and its programmes, there were no clear-cut distinctions between party programmes; nor did they fight on issues. Even the two original parties, the Cochin Congress and the Cochin State Congress which differed on communal issues—now candidly agreed that their "ideals did not differ from those of the other parties".[52] Reduced to mundane terms it was the mere jockeying of rival factions to capture power on vague charges and counter charges of non-fulfilment of expectations. Their *bona fides* were all the more suspect in their efforts at prolonging the life of the legislature when in power within.[53] As the Maharaja of Cochin rightly remarked, these "bewildering changes of party labels by members of the Council showed a lack of political education and laxity of principles, which augured ill for the future".[54]

Disgusted with these antics within the legislature, a new party, claiming a closer association with the aims of the Indian National Congress, was formed in 1942 in the Cochin State Praja Mandal, with a programme of standing outside the legislature "to build up an organisational background among the masses".[55] As a more radical party it came into a confrontation with the government from its very inception and on its affiliation with the Cochin Karshaka Sabha, a kisan organisation, its annual meeting scheduled to be held on 10 and 11 January was banned and its leaders arrested.[56]

The August 1942, Quit India Movement, found its adherents mainly from this party. As the Resident reported, of these three southern states, Cochin, under the Cochin State Praja Mandal Party, showed itself more 'inflamed' in staging protest meetings and processions on this score, in spite of government's ban on it.[57] These meetings were held in almost every town or place of importance in the state, the most prominent of these localities being Ernakulam, Mattancheri and Trichur.[58] The breaking up of these meetings by lathi-charges, especially at Trichur on 15 August 1942, led to a demand for the instituting of an enquiry on the conduct of the police and to a calling of the state Minister for Rural Development (the leader of the coalition of Cochin State Congress and the New Progressive Party, in the Unionist Party) to dissociate himself from the government. It did seem an anomaly that a party claiming allegiance to the Indian National Congress should side with the state government in repressing the activities taken on behalf of the Indian National Congress. While the party in opposition, the Cochin Congress, resigned both inthe legislature and the Trichur Municipality, the Cochin State Congress found few to obey the Praja Mandal's behests.[59]

On 31 August 1942, the government of Cochin ordered an indefinite blanket ban on all meetings.[60] Thus while the Cochin State Praja Mandal in the period subsequent, concentrated on improving its organisation (without defying the ban or coming into any open confrontation with the government), the movement reverted back to the legislature in its incipient demands for further reforms. The growth of communist activities in the other two areas of Kerala, in this period, had its natural repercussions on Cochin. The Cochin District Karshaka Sangha, which published handbills urging agricultural labourers to organise themselves, and the Athikad Toddy Tappers Union were given particular attention to by the government, and were banned in April 1944.[61]

The resignation of the Cochin Congress members in the legislature in sympathy with the State Praja Mandal Party in 1942, led in its turn to a coming together of these two organisations.

In June 1945 general elections in the state, the Cochin Praja Mandal secured 12 of the 38 seats open for election and claimed a position as the biggest popular party within. However, it decided not to accept office but to act as an opposition from within.[62]

The Cochin State Praja Mandal Party was now associated even more closely with the Congress agitations of the other states. Its annual meet of July 1945 was presided over by Pattam Thanu Pillai of Travancore.[63] In its September 1945 meet, in common with the Mysore Congress and Travancore State Congress, it made a plea for popularly elected representatives to the Constituent Assembly.[64] In contrast to affairs in Travancore and Mysore, its relations with the government during this period proved smoother, and it was not surprising that a combined conference of the South Indian States People, with the participation of the Mysore Congress, the Travancore State Congress and the Pudukkottai State Congress, was held at Trichur in December 1945.[65]

This close association of the Cochin Praja Mandal with the movements in other states had its repercussion within. In March 1946, a black flag demonstration by students of Ernakulam against C.P. Ramaswami Aiyar, who had been invited to open a primary school, flared up into a riot and police action.[66] The government's action in placing M. Mathew Varkey, the editor of *Malabar Mail* and his associate and chief representative of the paper, Cheriyan Manjuran, a labour leader, under restrictive detention (as the chief instigators in their criticism of the Travancore Dewan's education policy),[67] led in turn to a demand for an enquiry on it. The subsequent adjournment motion pressed in the Legislative Council by P. Govinda Menon, the leader of the Cochin State Party proved the prelude to a successful manoeuvering of a no-confidence motion against the party in power and capturing of power by the Praja Mandal as a coalition government.[68] However, even the Cochin State Praja Mandal's career in this legislature, due to its involvement with the outside movements, was not without its embarrassments. A students' demonstration in support of the Travancore movement had to be suppressed on the complaints of the Travancore Dewan.[69] The government, with the agreement of the party in power was forced into issuing a statement that even though in sympathy with Travancore movement it could not acquiesce in such demonstrations.

Cochin Government's action clearly proved that as long as the British Government remained as guardians of the princes, even popular ministries were to be ultimately governed by central policy—proving clearly the hollowness of a democratic government in the prevailing imperialistic structure.

The passage of Cochin State into an Indian Union was one of the smoothest. The appointment of a Franchise Committee in January 1946,[70] and the further reforms in the extension of powers in transferring all departments, barring finance and relationship with the Crown, to popular control and the appointment of an additional minister with powers of joint collaboration with the Dewan,[71] allowed the ministry to evolve into a future cabinet. But more important than these was His Highness', announcement of his agreement to a merger of his state into the linguistic province of Kerala in order to allow it to function as a separate and cohesive unit in the greater federation of India.[72] Towards a realisation of this he even proposed talks with Madras and Travancore to give shape to the people's aspiration,[73] which as Jawaharlal Nehru pointed out, was in complete contrast to that of the other states.[74] Again, in the State peoples other demand for popularly elected representation to the Constituent Assembly, Cochin was the first State to declare that selection to the Consambly would entirely be by election by the Legislative Council with official members abstaining from voting.[75] She was among the first to sign her entry to the Constituent Assembly, and on accession to an Indian Union.

In March 1947, a native-born Dewan, C.P. Karunakara Menon, was appointed, replacing Sir George Boag. The Franchise Committee Report recommending adult franchise was published in October 1946;[76] the Constitutional Committee recommendations[77] were promulgated in the Government of Cochin Act bringing a fully responsible government, with the transference of all administrative control to a council of elected ministers into effect from 29 August 1947 with Panampalli Govinda Menon as its first premier.

Repression in Travancore (1940-47)

The movement in Travancore, especially that under the leadership of the Travancore State Congress, during these years, subjected as it was to the double control of a tight rein of Mahatma Gandhi's and the severe repressive policy of C.P. Ramaswami Aiyar's 'reign'—found itself at a low ebb. These suppressing influences made the movement, in its initial stages, go underground, and, in its later stages, into a tangenital course of part of its wing to an affiliation with communism—leading in turn to a hasty uprising engineered by the communists in 1946 and consequent severe repression at the hands of the Dewan; this lost for the Travancore State the deterrent value of a 'direct action' at the opportune moment, thus allowing the Dewan his postures on an 'independent Travancore'.

C.P. Ramaswami Aiyar's strategy during the period 1940 to December 1941, lay not so much in declaring the Travancore State Congress as illegal, but making it impossible for it to hold even ordinary public meetings, let alone carry on constitutional agitation. This was accomplished by the complete muzzling of the press, the arrests and conviction of Congress sympathisers—ostensibly for non-political offences, but really because of their support to the Travancore State Congress programme—and a reign of terror by a body of special police whose 'special' job was to appear in mufti at every Congress meeting to break it up by acts of *goondaism.*[78]

It was in this situation that Gandhi scotched any move at a resumption of the satyagraha by ruling that the resumption of civil disobedience in British India could not, and ought not, to apply to the states.[79] The removal of such a ban on participation by individuals was of little interest to the states people as it stepped up their cause no further.

With such a decision from the High Command it was not surprising that C.P. Ramaswami Aiyar, who had as late as 3 April 1940 solicited an interview with Gandhi—with no doubt the idea of utilising his intervention to hold the State Congress on leash—did now refuse, on the extraneous plea that the leaders of the Travancore State Congress had connections with communist activities.[80] In this, Gandhi's contention that he would not allow the Travancore State Congress to start agitation as he discerned "violence in the air",[81] helped C.P. Ramaswami Aiyar considerably as with his 'special police' he could always be sure to give any agitation, a violent twist. Thus with C.P. Ramaswami Aiyar making any movement in Travancore impossible it was driven to take refuge in the columns of the *Harijan* and in Ernakulam, in Cochin State, which became the propaganda centre for it.

The 'apogee' of autocratic action was reached when the Dewan initiated prosecution proceedings against State Congressmen for publishing a statement in the *Harijan* on the Dewan's refusal to meet Gandhi and for 'hoping'[82] through them to "force an outside enquiry and mediation upon the states".[83] A. Achutan was arrested in August 1940 under the Defence of India Rule, while G. Ramachandran evaded arrest by working from Ernakulam and British India.[84]

Cochin's Part in Travancore Movement

C.P. Ramaswami Aiyar who had complained against Shanmugham Chetty even earlier[85] now accused him of involvement in giving help to what C.P. characterised as a "dozen malcontents . . some of whom were avowed communists."[86] He complained of Ernakulam rendering financial help to the agitators, giving encouragement to the organisation and march of *jathas* into Travancore from British India and Cochin State,[87] allowing newspapers within the state to devote more space to Travancore affairs than to Cochin news, and thus providing a "vantage ground for agitation against Travancore".[88] There was no gainsaying the fact that press statements of the Travancore State Congress agitators were often published in Cochin State newspapers before their ceremonial courting of arrest.[89] Shanmugham Chetty's defence was patently weak. He asserted that he could discover no communist cell in the state,[90] and that there was no law in the state under which the Travancore agitators could be expelled[91] unless shown that they were acting against Cochin State itself. His demands for a clear directive from the paramount power[92], proclaiming himself even ready to resign on the score[93]—only made the Political Department realise their blunder in having political rivals for the past 25 years,[94] like C.P. Ramaswami Aiyar and Shanmugham Chetty as Dewans of neighbouring states. It was mainly this realisation and his open championing of the political movement of British India which in a measure was responsibie for the forced resignation of Shanmugham Chetty in 1941.

Shanmugham Chetty's intransigence served little purpose; C.P. Ramaswami Aiyar, with the Political Department applying its pressure on him, was able to smoke out the Travancore State Congress from its burrow in Cochin. In October 1940 the Travancore State Congress centre at Ernakulam was wound up and the volunteers ordered to return to Travancore, to give up for present their political programme and concentrate on the working of the constructive programme and alleviation of economic distress prevailing in the state.[95] Gandhi's decision, at this time, to step down the movement in Travancore, was to some extent, the result of events in British Malabar.[96] However in doing so Gandhi replying to the usual claims put up by C.P. Ramaswami Aiyar on the incompatibility of responsible government with the treaty position of the Indian states, warned that these "extravagant claims"[97] on the position of the Indian states would "have no validity" nor make the slightest difference when the British were ready or compelled by events to recognise India's independence—a guarantee to the states people that Indian independence would see their objective also realised.[98]

In January 1941, a rapproachment between the Travancore Government and Travancore State Congress was brought about through the intermediation of Pattabhi Sitaramayya which favoured, on the whole, the Dewan's position. The Dewan while releasing the detenues and allowing the State Congress to reopen its office at Trivandrum, made it clear that he would under no circumstances tolerate a recrudence of civil disobedience, or subversive activity against the government. In this he asserted that it was the decided policy of the state government not to grant responsible government nor to create ministries in the sense of an Executive removed by or on the instance of the Legislature.[99]

After such a capitulation it was mere form whlch made Pattam Thanu Pillai declare that it was still the State Congress' objective to work peacefully and constructively towards their goal of responsible government.[100]

The Gandhian wing of the movement after this, in any active political agitation barring participation in the general elections of 1944, came to a standstill, till the eve of British Indian constitutional changes and independence. Activities in support of British India was made taboo by the Dewan, in that even the traditional observance of 26 January as the Day of Independence, was not allowed.[101]

By August 1941 the police reports proclaimed that the speeches of the State Congress were "restrained in tone",[102] and that there was no passage in the speech that could be taken exception to. The same reports gleefully reported the State Congressites as "disheartened and disillusioned"[103] as contrary to expectations of a dissolution of the legislatures and new elections, the Dewan announced the extension of the present legislature to June 1942.[104]

It is not surprising that parallel with this disappointment and the restraints placed by the Travancore administration on even legitimate activities of the Congress, we find activities among labour organisations becoming prominent. The centre of this radical movement, which became active from April 1940, converged round Alleppey, the convenient centre to the excitation of discontented labour, with leaders of Alleppey playing a prominent part.[105] The leaders were asked to maintain secrecy, move incognito and organise volunteers.[106] In December 1941 the President of the Conference of the Shertallai Coir Workers Union, K. Janardhanan Nair, proclaimed that labour movement could not be any longer divorced from politics and exhorted the Travancore State Congress to intensify its campaign for responsible government.[107] At the annual meeting of the Quilon Workers Union, resolutions were passed promising support to any political organisation in the state which stood for responsible government,[108] (which showed the growing divergence between the Gandhian leadership and the states movement) and suggested that a more comprehensive scheme than the individual satyagraha of Gandhi be adopted for the attainment of India's freedom. At the same meeting a move for coalescing of all Trade Unions in an All-Travancore Labour Federation was mooted and in January 1942 the body was inaugurated around a core of prominent unions in Travancore[109] with Srikantan Nair, the labour leader, as its President.[110] This Federation reiterated its view that the establishment of responsible government was an "urgent necessity".[111]

These resolutions precipitated C.P. Ramaswami Aiyar into issuing a warning on the "dangers of mixing up political issues with problems arising out of the relations between capital and labour".[112] Orders were passed by him, under the ubiquitous Defence of Travancore Act restraining Srikantan Nair, K.P. Janardhanan Nair and T.V. Thomas from participating in any meeting. In April 1942, Pattam Thanu Pillai and G. Ramachandran were also put under confinement for their participation in the All-India States Peoples Day on 19 April 1942.[113]

In spite of these restraining orders, the Cellar Records of the Kerala Secretariat furnish overwhelming evidence of an active labour movement in Travancore during this period in the staging of strikes[114] and protest meetings,[115] eliciting from the government repeated warnings.[116]

The declaration of Quit India resolution on 8 August 1942 proved an opportune signal for the Travancore government to clamp down on all activities, including those of the trade unions. Barring such "mild"[117] demonstrations by the student community and individual defiance of the ban after a ceremonial notice by leaders of the State Congress, there were few big demonstrations put up in this state on the Quit India movement.[118]

Following the release of leaders in May 1943 on an understanding that they would cooperate with the government in the economic crisis over food shortage, the ban on the activities of the Travancore State Congress was lifted in June 1943.[119] This compromise was effected mainly because of Congress expectation of fresh elections in the imminence of a dissolution of the legislature in March 1944.

The lifting of the ban proved the signal to a recrudence of labour activities;[120] communist classes were held at the Coir Factory Workers Union at Alleppey where communist members from British India, like E.M.S. Namboodiripad, K.K. Warrier, and K.C. George attended.[121] This was of special significance in that there was a growing divergence between the socialist wing and the Gandhian wing within the Kerala PCC in British Malabar. While this came to a head only in August 1945[122]

C.P. Ramaswami Aiyar perfected his plans to utilise these divergences to his particular use in Travancore. While on the one hand, he cautioned the Travancore State Congress that he would reject nomination slips of communists entered on Travancore State Congress tickets,[123] he warned, on the other hand the Trade Union leaders, T.V. Thomas and Janardhanan Nair (as President and members of the Executive of the All-Travancore Trade Union Congress) that grant of nominated seats as conscessions to labour (two seats in the Legislative Assembly and one in the Legislative Council)—would be withheld if they collaborated or helped the Congress in the elections.[124] As a result of these manoeuvres the Parliamentary Board of the Travancore State Congress[125] meeting in March 1944 expressed itself as unwilling to include communist or 'Trade Union' candidates among its nominations. The communist wing of the State Congress while agreeing to step out, expressed their willingness to cooperate without contesting the seats.[126] Even this was banned them after the Dewan's talks with the Trade Union leaders. The State Congressites and the communists meeting at a conference on 10 June 1944 drew up a statement declaring that the Travancore State Congress and the Trivandrum Communist Party were two independent organisations, unconnected with each other.[127] Thus the Dewan by his intrigue was able to effect the first breach on the solidarity of right and left wings of Travancore State Congress.

However, in a body which till now contained both the 'left wingers' as well as the 'right wingers' with quite often the shades of grey being indistinguishable from both, there was always a difficulty in making out, who was what. The Travancore Government utilised this as the pretext to reject a number of Travancore State Congress nominations (including that of Pattam Thanu Pillai) on the score of being communists and on the ground that they had been convicted before criminal courts and had not sought condonation of the government.[128] Again he utilised the same pretext, after elections, to declare that the Trade Unionists had rendered help to the State Cougress and thus had forfeited their claims to the nominated seats.[129] Apart from these tactics, to stop the Congress from obtaining any hold at the elections, he made the mourning for the death of the infant heir presumptive, the pretext for prohibiting any meetings during the theee months preceding the elections.[130] It was not surprising that under these disabilities the Travancore State Congress, at the elections fared not too well and gained a mere 11 seats in a Legislative Assembly of 72, though by its presence it did add some liveliness to the hitherto dull proceedings.[131]

The communist wing of the Travancore State fared even worse in its relationship with the government. Not only were they given no representation in the legislatures, their activities were scrutinised with the greatest suspicion. On 2 July 1944, the labour leaders met at a conference to reactivate their organisation and in August 1944 they started 32 branches of the their organisation in the state, with Alleppey as headquarters.[132] Their attempt to hold an agricultural conference to inaugurate All-Travancore Karshaka Sangam, started in September 1944 with affiliation to the All-India Kisan Sangha, was vetoed by the Dewan.[133] The State Communist Party was prohibited from holding a conference by the Dewan on charges that they had taken part in "provocative demonstrations".[134] Following the ouster of the 'Left Wingers' from the KPCC in August 1945, the communists from Malabar attempted to wean labour in Travancore from the Congress hold on trade unions into communist hands, and Alleppey and Kottayam became the centre of these activities.[135] The Travancore Government's heavy handling of communist activities made them in turn declare in April 1946 that they were determined to establish national government and a change in the present system of administration by revolution, if necessary.[136] The Travancore State Congress while deploring these "undesirable happenings",[137] and attributing it to the "evil result of Dewan's rule",[138] decided to sever its connections with communists in May 1946. However even here, C. Kesavan, the Ezhava idol—considered by the Dewan as a communist—was allowed to fraternise with the communists while remaining within the Congress fold.[139]

To understand the psychology of the communists who talked in terms of revolution one has to take several factors into consideration; not the least important of this was the feelings of outcasteism apparent in Travancore State Congress policy in cutting the communists off from the parent body. This also resulted in an equal severance of the restraining influence which the Congress had hitherto exercised. The repressive acts of the Dewan in resiling from his promise to allot three seats in the legislature to the trade unions, his ban on their participation in the elections etc. added to the list of grievances already existing in the state. This was added to the Christians' fears on the Primary Education Bill and Dewan's recently introduced Constitutional Reforms in the American Model Constitution.[140]

There were other factors also which made for a sense of disillusionment and for a 'hankering' for a rebellion. These centered round the states peoples fears on their position arising out of the Cabinet Mission talks in their application to the states. The non-transference of paramountcy to a central government made them 'apprehend' the states being used as British military enclaves from where "seeds of conflict will be spread in India".[141] In this, the Travancore State Congress feared, that even if elected representations were granted to the Constituent Assembly, it could prove of little use in the question relating to the internal administration of the state.[142]

Thus it was increasingly realised that it was demonstrations from within which was likely to promote their objectives on responsible government. The realisation that the Cabinet Delegation was in itself necessitated by the enthusiasm of the INA trials, and by the strike of the Royal Indian Navy,[143] only added to their fervour for a revolution which was influenced further by the return of some INA heroes of the locality and their support to the communists.[144] In these circumstances the food crisis provided the right handle for the uprising.[145] The imminence of this revolution was obvious even as early as September 1946 to E.M.S. Namboodiripad. He referred to the situation in Travancore as being on the brink of a fight on the scale of 1938 demonstrations—with a prominent difference in that the earlier one had "*vakils* and other people"[146] in the first rank but now was to be that of the labourers.

The site chosen for this "organised insurrection",[147] engineered mainly by the younger generation with the help of the Communist Party,[148]—centered round Shertallai and Ambalapuzha, the areas most industrialised in Travancore and where the proportion of labourers and landless people in the population was the largest in the state;[149] labour in this region had for the last few years come under the influence and control of the Communist Party.[150] The Communist propaganda among them to appropriate the paddy grown and 10% of the coconuts picked for themselves,[151] was made thus the pretext for action by the government against the ring-leaders and in turn a signal by the communists for a confrontation between the *Janmis* in the area and the labourers. On 13 August 1946, a big communist jatha was excited into raiding the houses of these landlords, and manhandling them. Following the security proceedings taken against some leaders, a secret conference of the representatives of the Travancore Trade Union Congress was held on 25 September 1946 when repressive policy of the government was discussed and it was resolved to consolidate the workers and prepare for a struggle.[152] Training centres were opened at Punnapra, Vayalar, Muhama and Kalawankoodam, all situated within the Taluks of Ambalapuzha and Shertallai, with Vayalar as headquarters, which they called the Moscow. Each of these training centres consisted of not less than 2,000 workers. Trenches were dug in Vayalar and collection of spears, sticks, knives etc. were got ready and the trainees were taught to lie flat during firing and impressed that in this position the bullet could not hit them, allowing them to tackle with long spears.[153]

It was not as if the government were entirely unaware of the trouble brewing. On 30 September 1946 an Emergency Ordinance was promulgated vesting in the executive and the police, extensive and arbitrary powers. These included provisions to arrest and search house without warrants, detain persons without trial, ban of meetings generally, and provided for proscribing newspapers and political organisations.[154]

Following the banning of the Travancore Trade Union Congress and the Communist Party, a general strike was declared by them on 23 October 1946, the day of the Maharaja's birthday. This proved the start of an agitation at Shertallai, Vayalar and Alleppey where buses and boat services carrying rice proved the convenient targets.[155] On 24 October 1946 there was a clash between the reserve police and the agitators (who included demobilised members of the Malabar police)[156] at Punnapra where the police party was overpowered and four of them killed. The insurrectionists cut telephone and telegraph wires, demolished bridges and small culverts. The 'rioters' held the day till the rushing in of state troops during late in the day.[157] Martial law was proclaimed in the area,[158] with the Dewan dramatically appointing himself the Supreme Commander. He requested the paramount power to rush help from their stores equipment and troops stationed at Bangalore.[159] In the retaliatory firing by the state forces which followed, more than 2000 workers were killed; in order to bring down the statistics on those killed they were burnt by petrol being poured over them. The punitive action taken by the state forces and the declaration of martial law confined the movement to the Shertallai-Punnapra, Vayalar area and did not allow it to spread to other centres in the state or to the frontier districts.[160] This was of particular significance in that this underground movement had taken its direction mainly from the Malabar Communist Party leaders, before and during the riots, and there was always the danger of their communist brethren from across the border participating in the movement directly.[161] The British Indian wing confined its activities to inciting them to continue the struggle till all repressive measures were withdrawn, the leaders released, the ban on the Trade Union Congress removed and the demands of the workers granted. The Dewan took full responsibility and blame for the military action which he said had been taken "deliberately" as he had seen "no point in going piecemeal".[162]

As rightly observed by the Report of the Criminal Intelligence Department "the communists in their haste to lead all struggle",[163] had exploited the situation of grievances and had unleashed a rebellion, even before the time was really ripe. The grievances, as the Dewan himself, apportioning an amount of blame on Travancore State Congress, 'indirectly' acknowledged, stemmed from "the great political discussions and decisions ahead in the country involving British India and the Indian states".[164] On these decisions the state government as well as the British Indian parties themselves had as yet to declare their intentions. The manoeuvers of the Travancore State Congress in making speeches attacking the government and urging the people to direct action against it,[165] were merely in the nature of preparations to meet the coming eventuality they foresaw.

The communists thus in their miscalculations not only

queered the pitch so carefully prepared by the Travancore State Congress in their hastiness, but in addition, contrary to their expectations that the Travancore State Congress and other parties would line up with them in the struggle, were left unsupported.[166]

The Travancore State Congress on this issue thus took an altogether independent line. While supporting the government in its upholding of the low figures on casualities, (of 94 persons killed at Vayalar, 37 at Manancheri and 40 at Punnapra, amended to a total of 190 later)[167] it ended on a note warning the government against repression and proclaimed that a government which could not protect its own people without resort to martial law had no place in governance.[168] On the other it hand deplored the violent methods adopted by a section of labour, under the guidance of communist leaders whose activities were dictated and controlled by a 'foreign party'; it expressed itself on the side of labour to whom it appealed to free themselves from the communist leadership responsible for their troubles. It took this opportunity to warn the industrialists and landlords, in turn, that their relationship with their employees could no longer be that of the master to a servant but one of cooperation.[169] The Dewan characterised this attitude of the Travancore State Congress as "unhelpful, obstructive",[170] and as one of hunting with the hounds and running with the hares.

The Travancore State Congress' policy though partly dictated by its jealousy of communist leadership's (from British Malabar) hold over Travancore labour (which the Dewan was quick to taunt demonstrated the "negligible character of the influence exercised by the Travancore State Congress on the industrial population of the State")[171] was dictated to a greater extent by the needs of British Indian leadership which imposed a "policy of promoting tranquility and forbidding active movements against state authority on the eve of transferring power by British to Indian hands".[172] Thus in its policy of 'wait and see', the Travancore State Congress' position had been made difficult by the hasty action of the communist uprising, the serious nature of which repercussion was soon to be made clear in the strategy of the Dewan which followed in the wake of the insurrection.

The communist uprising, on the Dewans own assertion, was completely suppressed in a matter of four days. In spite of this the martial law in the affected areas was allowed to continue.[173] In the mopping up operations which followed, 17 Trade Unions were banned, every member of the Travancore Trade Union Congress was arrested, leading writers and literary critics in any way connected with the socialist programme,[174] along with 5 out of 11 members of the Travancore State Congress Working Committee were put under detention. The emergency Act with its powers to detain, intern or extern, on suspicion of their acting, or with intentions to act, against the government, was all comprehensive. Even areas outside the boundaries of the Martial Law were not exempt from its sphere.[175] But what was significant was the novel method adopted by the government in impounding all ration cards of the 'suspects' and allowing only those with the Tahsildar's permit to draw rice and textile.[176] The success of this measure is at once obvious in his repetition of the same threat to coerce signatures on his 'independence'[177] stand, taken just subsequently. As usual, there was one other area from which he sought an insulation— in plugging the hole created by the extension of help from Cochin to the Travancore movement.[178] This he achieved, as in the earlier instance, with the asistance of the Political Department[179] which in the process of forcing a reluctant Cochin Dewan[180] (though this time an Englishman and expected to kowtow to the Political Department's behests) to its wishes, landed him and the 'popular government' of the Cochin State Praja Mandal in some embarrassment.[181] But it was a matter of question whether with a fully responsible government in Cochin and an independent British India this lacuna in suppressive tactics could be plugged in future.

As a result of these repressive measures, Travancore was not only made free of any demonstrations for the Dewan to make his next move,[182] but more importantly, his success in dealing with the insurrection made him lose all fears of any threats of a deterrent nature in the threats of 'direct action' by the Travancore State Congress. It was in this sense that the hasty action of the communists in their insurrection, before the time was ripe, had proved impolitic in wasting its force in coming even before the support of the arms of the paramount power to the states administration had been withdrawn.

On 3 June 1947, the Mountbatten plan for the future of India was declared and on 7 June 1947 the Joint Sub-Committee of the Negotiating Committee sent its request to Travancore to send its names for selection of representatives to the Constituent Assembly.[183] "Our megalomaniac friend C.P."[184] who in his visions of playing the champion of princes had even sent his resignation of his position in 1946 in order to have a "free hand and detached and untrammelled position"[185] to speak the prince's cause, now announced Travancore's refusal, on 11 June 1947, to participate in the work of the Constituent Assembly and declared that Travancore was to maintain independent state after the transfer of power by the British Government and the lapse of paramountcy.[186]

British Indian leadership which had till then equivocated on giving help for the state people's movement,[187] now that its own position on integration was threatened, was forced into align ing itself on the side of the state people. While Mahatma Gandhi declared that C.P. Ramswami Aiyar's declaration was "tantamount to a declaration of war against the free millions of India,"[188] the Madras Government in withdrawing the services of a police officer lent to the Travancore Government declared that its action "was full of significance" and its "first reaction to the Travancore Government's declared attitude to the Indian Union."[189]

The declaration of 'independence' by C.P. Ramaswami Aiyar proved the signal for the resumption of the struggle on the part of Travancore State Congress, which declared on the same day its decision to celebrate 13 June 1947 as Constituent Assembly Day.[190] Congress meetings were held in spite of the bans imposed by the Travancore Government at Alwaye, Kottayam, Palai, Karunagappally, Alleppey, Kanjirapalli, Trivandrum and Neyyatinkara.[191] These meetings held in defiance of the ban proved to the administration the necessity of different tactics. Removing his ban on meetings and resorting to his old tactics of disrupting them through the use of *goondas*,[192] the Dewan now with a clear conscience stoutly denied that there was any suppression of liberties, issued strict instructions to editors of all dailies and weeklies in Travancore not to publish any news about State Congress activities in the state, engineered statements from retired government officials supporting his stance on independence[193] and made arrangements to collect signatures in support of his 'independence' decision by resorting to intimidations of all kinds, including the deprivation of ration cards for food and textiles.[194] On 7 July 1947, the Dewan referring to the sound financial position of the state pleaded that Travancore was eminently fit to be independent and that it was best to remain so.[195]

While these postures of the Dewan elicited from Dr. S. Radhakrishnan an appeal to the British to persuade the princes to a union so as to evade an epitaph on British rule that "British found this country strong, suspicious and disunited and left her weak, poor, brutish and disunited"[196] and from Mahatma Gandhi "to leave no cause for anybody in India to say that the British were mischievous",[197] mischievous Britishers of the ilk of Sir John Anderson, ex-Governor of Bengal and member of the Conservative Party, found it excellent opportunity to fish in these troubled waters and to declare that Britain should "be willing to enter into new relationship with such states".[198] His Majesty's Government, as reflected in Attlee's and Mountbatten's statement, on its part, while repeating their desire that all Indian states should identify themselves with one or the other, left its provisions on the states as vague as could be in its lapse of paramountcy clause in the Government of India Act of 1947.

In these circumstances the Travancore State Congress in preparation for a long struggle shifted a part of its office to Ernakulam in July 1947.[199] Though suffering from a lack of funds[200] it was however augmented by the joining of Mannath Padmanabhan with the Nair Service Society in train and his organisational zeal.[201] In face of these enthusiasms and the growth of the movement, the Dewan reimposed a restriction on meetings in making it obligatory to get prior permits.[202] A definance of this ban led to the arrest of several leaders and the taking over of the Bar Association premises for holding a meeting within.[203] On 18 July 1947 the Maharaja in a broadcast to his people made clear his intention to have an independent Travancore.[204]

The sudden capitulation of the Dewan on the 'independence' issue on 29 July 1947 and his subsequent resignation, makes it necessary that we take a day-to-day account of the events leading to it. In this the non-availability of authentic records, from all sources, the AICC Papers, the British Crown Representative Records, or those from the National Archives of India makes our task rather difficult as one has to stick to the rather unsatisfactory accounts of the newspapers which allow no glimpse into the mechanics of the intriguing situation.[205] Chronologically reviewing the situation one finds that on 20 July 1947 C.P. Ramaswami Aiyar met Mountbatten and, later, V.P. Menon, when he seems to have stated that he would not agree to accession but to some form of agreement on the subjects indicated in the Instrument of Accession.[206] On 21 July 1947 he was recalled for another discussion by Mountbatten; while there is no indication as to what transpired at this conference he did seem to have carried a copy of the Instrument of Accession with him.[207]

On 24 July 1947 the State Congress held a meeting at Alleppey to review the situation.[208] On the same day the Tinnevelly District Congress Committee in British India appointed a sub-committee to chalk out a programme in consultation with the State Congress leaders to aid it in their present fight.[209] On 25 July 1947 the princes were called to a meeting by the Viceroy at which he made a special plea for the princes joining the Constituent Assembly and the Indian Union.[210]

The speech of Mountbatten was of particular significance. British sympathisers of the princes felt that the Viceroy's address warning the princes that terms after 15 August would not be favourable and financial burden could well be made so heavy as to jeopardise the states,[211] was inconsistent with what was said in Parliament[212] and reflected the 'honour of labour government'.[213] Salisbury considered this statement tantamount to going down in history with a "badge of betrayal". That the move was entirely the Viceroy's, is clear in his letter to Pethick Lawrence, for while asserting that no pressure was being applied, that he was only making them "see advantage of offer received"[214] he confessed to trying his "best to create an integrated India, which while securing stability"[215] would ensure friendship with Great Britain, and that if he were allowed to play his own hand he would no doubt succeed.

On 25 July 1947 the Dewan returned to Travancore to be

attacked by an assailant with a sword stick, while returning from a public concert where the electric lights as part of a pre-meditated plan had been put off at the right moment for the assailant to make good his escape.[216] While the arrests of Congress leaders followed,[217] on 29 July 1947, the government announced its decision to join the Union[218] and a report of the Dewan's resignation followed soon after.

A rather indirect evidence on the role of Mountbatten in the integration problem is vouchsafed in his message to C.P. Ramaswami Aiyar, on his injury, in his reference to "his profitable talks with the Dewan of Travancore"[219]. There can be little doubt that Mountbatten's speech did have something to do with the capitulation of the Dewan, which even his detractors can do little to belittle.

In this, other factors such as Gandhi's support in getting funds for the Travancore Congress movement[220] and the rallying of British India and Cochin to its cause[221] could have played their part.

With the state's capitulation, the State Congress objective was soon achieved. On 30 July 1947 Pattam Thanu Pillai and all others who were arrested in connection with the Direct Action Campaign were released.[222] As Pattam Thanu Pillai pointed out there was a sense of relief in that the necessity for a direct action was averted[223] in the announcement of reforms following soon after. On 4 September 1947 the government announced its decision to grant responsible government and to constitute a Constituent Assembly for the state, made up of a representative body consisting of persons elected on the basis of adult franchise. They were to submit a draft for the revision or modification of the Constitution Act with a view to the establishment of responsible government. For deciding the rules for this representative body a small committee consisting of 15 members, in which half of them were Travancore Congress members, was constituted.[224] In this she had the distinction, as remarked on by Hanumanthaiya, leader of the Congress Party in the Legislature in Mysore, to be the first Indian State to frame a constitution by the peoples representatives.[225]

The collapse of princes autocratism with the very withdrawal of British paramountcy can best be expressed in the words of C.P. Ramaswami Aiyar's epitaph on these princes. Apropos of the Travancore State Congress resolution to remove all statues and memorials raised to him and the demand for an enquiry regarding financial commitments entered into during his regime on which he wanted Vallabhbhai Patel "to bring these people to their senses", he referred to 'the poor Maharaja' who seemed to have lost heart completely and displayed a lack of stamina and courage which deeply hurt and annoyed him. The Maharaja's behaviour, he opined, was in keeping with the "great Kshatriya rulers—descendants of sun and moon (who behaved) like mendicants and sycophants and (had) no more spirit than a parcel of frightened rabbits or sheep. They deserved their fate."[226]

Mysore (1940-47)

In its resolution of February 1940 the Mysore Congress now candidly acknowledged that "like most organisations in India, the Mysore Congress too"[227] had come under the general influence of Gandhi and that under his guidance and advice they had decided to suspend civil disobedience movement indefinitely. The bone of contention between the states people and the Indian National Congress settled amicably, with the Congress declaration at Ramgarh promising 'freedom of the whole nation' including the states,[228] H.C. Dassapa, the then President of the Mysore Congress assuaged his flock that when India obtained independence they in Mysore would also obtain responsible government, "since the Mysore Congress was a branch of all India National Congress".[229] (This much for the Indian National Congress resolution at Haripura!)

Thus with Gandhi soft-pedalling the states peoples issue, the movement in the state entered a period of 'drift' where the only aim of the State Congress lay in keeping the organisation active and alive for a future possible eventuality. In this the Mysore Government's policy of repression in making even constitutional agitation, let alone civil disobedience, impossible, it helped to provide them with grievances to keep the movement alive. Prominent among the repressive acts was the Legal Practitioners Act, which, by striking at the most 'intransigent elements' within the states, sought to ban 19 practitioners from practising in the Mysore High Court on the score of their being 'prison goers.'[230] A prominent Congressman and lawyer was convicted under this Act for inciting others against giving evidence in a judicial enquiry on police excesses. Other lawyers were proceeded against, in turn, for protesting against this judgment.[231] A motion tabled in the Mysore Legislative Council on it was disallowed by the Dewan and the Mysore Congress decided to observe 7 August 1940 as the day protesting against it.

Mahatma Gandhi, while protesting from the wings on the autocratic action of the state administration and pointing out that such action was to be witnessed nowhere in British India—where Bhulabhai Desai, Rajgopalachari and Munshi had achieved even ministership in analogous situations[232]—nevertheless advised the Mysore Congress to avoid coming into a confrontation with the administration on this issue and even asked them to participate in the elections, due soon. The Mysore Congress acting on this advice decided to contest elections to strengthen the movement from within it.[233] The state administration frightened by the preparations, postponed the elections to March 1941,[234] before which a confrontation within the administration itself—in a personal tussle now developing between the new Maharaja (on his accession on 3 August 1940) and the Dewan—seemed to promise a new orientation by the administration to its dealings with the Mysore Congress.

For the first time the President of the Mysore Congress, K.T. Bhashyam was invited to a public government ceremony—*Pattabhishekam*—the investiture ceremony of the Maharaja in September 1940. The Mysore Government released 136 political prisoners who were taken out in a mammoth procession.[235] In keeping with this spirit, a case pending against a prominent Congressman, H.C. Siddiah, under the Legal Practitioners Act, was dismissed, though the judge was not above expressing certain views on sedition while doing so.[236] Mirza Ismail's manoeuvers to create a government sponsored party—the Rashtriya Mahasabha—was deprecated by the Maharaja who feared that the Dewan's hand may not be clean in his open partisanship of it, even to a rigging of the election to "secure a majority pledged to support the government".[237] The Maharaja sought to break the predominance of the Dewan in the administration by reviving the powers of the executive council.[238] While these actions of the Maharaja were hailed by the Mysore Congress leadership as the dawn of a new era,[239] the Political Department of the Government of India expressed its fears that these bickerings between the Dewan and the Maharaja could go towards the encouragement of the Mysore Congress.[240]

In the municipal elections held in November 1940, the Mysore Congress by winning all the 23 seats frightened the Dewan into rejecting the nomination slips of the Mysore Congress members to elections in the Legislature. The rejections, the Mysore Congress complained, were made on "frivolous and in some cases ridiculous"[241] pretexts. The Maharaja made these complaints against the Dewan the pretext for declaring his loss of confidence in him.[242]

In spite of these hindrances, the Mysore Congress came out in the elections as the biggest party whithin the legislature by winning 101 seats out of 303 in the Legislative Assembly and 16 out of 68 in the Legislative Council.[243] However, with Mahatma Gandhi unable to give a clear cut decision on office acceptance,[244] the Mysore Congress while deciding to keep its options open—to cooperate "to advance popular cause", or to obstruct "when that may be necessary",[245]—made it clear that no settlement was possible unless responsible goverment was declared as the goal of constitutional development in Mysore.

It was not surprising that the Maharaja with the resignation of the Dewan, saw no reason to comply with these demands. The Maharaja constituted his Executive Council from other members in the Legislative Assembly, on which the Mysore Congress Party in the Legislature to express its dissatisfaction, staged a walkout.[246] The administration in turn, banned public meetings, and even prohibited the entry of the President of the Mysore Congress into the city limits of Mysore.[247] Mahatma Gandhi, however, restrained the Mysore Congress from coming into a direct confrontation by banning them from any form of direct action.[248] The defiance of government bans by individual Mysore Congressmen led to a series of arrests throughout 1941-42.

The declaration of the Quit India resolution in August 1942 had its repercussions in the state. The government arrested those leaders who had attended the Bombay session.[249] A village in Shimoga district earned its rights to martyrdom when under the influence of the Quit India resolution the villagers of Isoor, forced the village officials to resign. The Patel, as head in charge of the village, refused, resulting in a fracas when children and school students teased him. The next day, the police posse which entered the village bent on repercussions, was met by a board banning admission to government servants. The villagers in opposition to the police, cut off telegraphic wires, pulled down a bridge and barricaded the roads. The government in order to put down the resurrection called in the military troops. In the trial which followed, 11 people were sentenced to death and 23, including 3 women, to transportation for life.[250] Other incidents—a police action in Bangalore when 5 were killed and 35 wounded,[251] arson and explosion cases, the observance of 'Quit India Day' on 6 September 1942 —and as 'Leaders Day' on 9 September 1942—saw the Mysore Congress banned as an unlawful association in spite of its disclaiming all connections with these incidents. Throughout 1943, with the Mysore Congress banned and the prominent leaders in jail no agitation was put up.[252] In early 1944, on the pleadings of a few Congress members to allow them to participate in the District Board elections, they were released. In the elections which ensued, the Mysore Congress in spite of the ban on its organization won 126 of the 177 seats in it.[253]

In view of the obvious drift in political activity, differences arose on the lines of future policy which crystallised itself into questions of aims—on a 'popular government' on a programme of cooperation with the administration or on 'responsible government' of non-cooperation. Though the shades of opinion between these aims did not seem too clear cut it showed that a wing of the body was not too satisfied with the local Congress policy, under the direction of Gandhi. The statement issued by K. Hanumanthaiya on 5 October 1944 pointing out that the government defeats in the Board elections showed a lack of confidence in the ministry was merely a device to deflect these divergences within the Mysore Congress on to a concrete programme.[254]

A refreshing change from these bickerings within the Mysore Congress was provided by the attitude of the Mysore State Muslim League which took an altogether independent note from that of the All India Muslim League. It, in April 1945, refused to celebrate 'Pakistan Day' as the issue did not concern Indian states.[255] Thus all the elements within the states, on the eve of British Indian constitutional changes seemed to be concentrating on one programme that seemed to concern them to the exclusion of all other problems in British India.

In spite of the bans on Congress committees and prohibitory orders a session of the Mysore State Congress was held on 16 and 17 June 1945 under the presidentship of Nijalingappa. This conference in addition to a demand on responsible government, expressed dissatisfaction at the exclusion of Indian states at the Simla Conference and demanded that the Viceroy appoint an elected representative from the states at the centre in the proposed interim government.[256] Rather a tall order, in that the Wavell plan had concerned itself with the constituting of an Executive Council from British India alone, to which it had not even called in consultation of the princes, let alone a representative of the states people.

With the imminence of constitutional changes in British India, a deputation left Bangalore to consult Gandhi on the future programme, following which the propaganda wing of the Congress seemed to become active.[257] Constituted under Thimma Reddy, it sought to coordinate the efforts of all the political organisations in the state for the establishment of responsible government and to agree to a common plan of action.[258]

The close connection between action in British India with a quick reaction in the states showed clearly the close link that was to provide for an insurrection in the states with the imminence of a British withdrawal. In order to coordinate work with the Indian National Congress, dual membership—simultaneous membership in Mysore Congress and the Indian National Congress which had been its policy in the early post Haripura period, and given up later—was again made a part of the State Congress programme.[259] A resolution was passed by the Mysore Congress in July 1946 demanding that the State Congress representatives be included in the Constituent Assembly from the very beginning of its deliberations so that they could take part in it on the question of civil liberties and fundamental rights and on the "vital matters as the setting up of a commission to determine the provincial boundaries on linguistic basis".[260] The linking of this question with their own preoccupations on their problem of responsible government was made on two counts. Firstly, the states people hoped that a discussion on Karnataka unification—an important consideration in the INC preoccupations on integration—would ensure their inclusion in the Constituent Assembly from the very beginning, and secondly, and more importantly, it was to counter the efforts of the Deccan princes in forming a Deccan States Union which included areas of Karnataka; these princes were actively wooing the INC leaders to their programme by promising a form of responsible government in this Union.[261] In this the pronouncement by Jawaharlal Nehru and the British Indian leadership that questions of monarchical form of government was not to be at issue at the Constituent Assembly debates,[262] made this state's people even more avid to ensure that the question of linguistic provinces —which could ultimately lead to their interest—would at least be included in the discussion in the Constituent Assembly. It was these considerations which made them emphasise that unless this "vital demand for the formation of linguistic province was accepted and given effect to, there would be no peace in the public life of Karnataka and would even result in grave consequences".[263] It is necessary to point out that while the members of Mysore Congress in the Karnataka Pradesh Congress Committee were assiduous in the promotion of this, the members of the Travancore State Congress in an analogous situation were partly lukewarm to that ideal which was due to the contradictions that exisisted between the Malabar Pradesh Congress Committee leadership and the Travancore State Congress leadership in Kerala.

In view of the constitutional developments in British India, the Mysore administration lifted its ban on the Mysore Congress in September 1945.[264] The Mysore Congress meeting at Bangalore in its open session at Subhas Nagar on 3 November 1946, authorised its Working Committee to take "all necessary steps including satyagraha",[265] to press for their demands on responsible government. A memorandum was submitted by it to the Maharaja seeking a reply on the above demand.[266] On 8 January 1947 the Maharaja announced his consideration of further constitutional advance, towards which he directed his Dewan to submit proposals after consultation with political bodies.[267] The Dewan's evasive tactics in calling for opinions from all sections in Mysore and his departure on a two months assignment to the United States of America, as Chairman of the UNESCO, forced the Mysore Congress, meeting on 24 January 1947, to declare that only an authoritative announcement in clear and definite terms on their demands at a very early date, would satisfy them.[268] As an earnest of the government's promise on it they demanded that an interim ministry be appointed composed of leaders of public opinion capable of securing the support of the legislature, failing which they declared their intention to launch a satyagraha. The government retaliated by introducing a cumulative voting system for District Board elections[269] to prevent the Congress from retaining its hold on it. Prohibitory orders were also passed all over the state on pretext of communal tensions where none existed.[270] As a result of these repressive tactics the decision on the date for starting satyagraha was fixed to be taken at the Working Committee meeting on 6 March 1947 to be placed before the All Mysore Congress Committee meeting on 8 and 9 March 1947.[271] Before this, the decision of Attlee, expressed in February 1947, to transfer power into responsible Indian hands by a date not later than June 1948 and his decision not to hand over their powers and obligations under paramountcy to any government of British India[272] made them "apprehensive of the disposition"[273] on the part of the princes not to join the Constituent Assembly on some pretext or the other. In view of the disappearance of paramountcy, immediate establishment of responsible government, they declared, was an imperative necessity and threatened that any transitional arrangement that Mysore made with the Crown without the consent of the people would be repudiated if it were found harmful to the interests of the people.[274] However, active agitation on this issue or that of their objective of responsible government was stayed by the directives of the AISPC in April 1947 in imposing a ban on any agitation in the states at this time. In this, the Dewan of Mysore also assured them of considering a programme of reforms.[275]

The declaration of 'independence' by C.P. Ramaswami Aiyar in Travancore on 11 June 1947, galvanised the British

Indian leadership into action and the AICC meeting on 14 June 1947 once again made responsible government a part of the British Indian interest on integration, and declared that in consideration of the changes taking place in the transfer of power it was of vital importance that progress leading to responsible government take place.[276] Seeing now the combination of the British Indian leadership with the State Congress the Government of Mysore following the AICC declaration of 14 June 1947, made haste to declare its decision to enter the Constituent Assembly on 17 June 1947,[277] though on accession to the Union it proclaimed its reservations as subject to decisions at the Constituent Assembly. On 5 July 1947 it agreed to the signing of a standstill agreement.[278]

With actual accession by the Mysore Government deferred till practically the eve of the departure of the British, the Mysore Congress by emphasising its demand that all seven members of Mysore's quota in the Constituent Assembly be elected by popular votes,[279] hoped to retain the involvement of the Indian National Congress on its programme. The Mysore Government with hopes of placing the subject of constitutional relations with the Dominion of India outside the purview of popular control,[280] on 2 July 1947 declared that only 4 of the seats were to be elected through the Legislatures on transferable vote—which could give the Congress only 2 seats as against the five of the government.[281]

The initial distinction made by the Mysore Government, as H.C. Dasappa pointed out, between joining the Constituent Assembly and joining the Union, was evidently intended to drive a bargain with the centre—especially on non-interference in the internal governance of the state.[282]

In this the delaying tactics adopted by even the 'sagest of the princes and their advisers' was in the hope that the developing tactical situation between the British Government and the rival Indian communities would favour them in the terms they could make.[283] The Congress while keeping the states peoples uprising as an ultimate threat, was rightly willing to come to some type of terms with the princes in order to realise their main point on accession. The overtures of Vallabhbhai Patel and the persuasion of Mountbatten, with all the prestige of the Crown Representative, "including scarcely veiled threats of trouble if they failed to act",[284] acted as a decisive factor and the turning point. With the capitulation of Travancore, causing almost a "political landslide among the states in favour of accession",[285] with Mysore trailing in its wake in its accession to the Indian Union on 9 August 1947,[286] these states peoples cause—especially in Travancore and Mysore with a politically conscious public—was soon achieved. While Travancore, with its capitulation on accession, succumbed with little show of fight on the responsible government issue, taking it as almost synonymous with accession, Mysore did hope to play its erstwhile tactics of separating the internal movement from the external. However, with accession assured, all the advantages, even without the active help of the British Indian leaders, lay with the states people. A successful conclusion was inevitable as a result of the strategic weakness of the states system which was realised even earlier by British administrators in their notings on the impossibility of maintaining their obligations, with a British India in the hands of an Indian Government.[287] The lapse of paramountcy brought in its corollary the lapse of the States Protection Act, and accession successfully removed one of the main props on which the states autocratic structure had been built. The '14 days satyagraha' of Mysore proved the significance of this weakness involved in the withdrawal of the British from erstwhile British India.

With the independence of India on 15 August 1947, the Mysore Congress stepping up its long deferred demand for a popularly elected Constituent Assembly to frame its constitution and for an interim government before it came into effect, declared its intention to launch a 'direct action' on 1 September 1947. The Mysore Government while clamping down with a Pre-Censroship of News Ordinance,[288] hoped to stem the struggle by promising a responsible government and popular administration of subjects on other than those specified in schedule II.[289] This schedule barred from the purview of popular control, among other state subjects, those dealing with the states relationship with the dominion government, military, the summoning and dissolving of the legislature, direction and control of election, residuary and emergency powers in case of breakdown of the constitution. The Dewan before laying these proposals before the

Maharaja was asked to obtain the advice and counsel of a committee elected by the legislature and of such other experts. This constitution was to come into effect on or before 1 July 1948. However, the days of such truncated reforms were over. As the editorial in *The Hindu* pointed out, the reforms promised did not even go as far as did the 1935 Act of the British Indian Provinces. As it declared, popular opinion had every reason to "view with suspicion a constitution framed by a functionary (the Dewan) whom it considered otiose and whose elimination it looked forward to".[290]

Dismissing these proposals, the Mysore Congress proposed to stage a satyagragha in front of the palace on 14 September 1947. K. Chengalaraya Reddy and 40 other top ranking leaders were arrested under the Mysore Public Security Act.[291] A series of dictators, as its practice in the 1938-39 agitation, were appointed to take charge of the agitation. The government while declaring that it was not its intention to suppress the legitimate activities of any party, banned all processions and meetings. The defiance of these orders led to a series of firing incidents taken in order to disperse crowds.[292] This time the arrest of leaders hardly helped at all, as the agitation had spread among all sections of the population. The Pre-Censorship Ordinance was the signal for the editors to launch a satyagraha from 30 September 1947. Apart from the students,[293] the trade union cooperatives, especially in Kolar area proved very active. In fact the workers of the Kolar Gold Field were the first to go on a strike in support on 1 September 1947.[294] 14,000 workers belonging to Mysore Champion Reef Mines downed their tools from 22 September 1947 to 30 September 1947.[295] On the declaration of the Mysore Railwaymen's strike[296] the government tried to buy off their participation by promising to raise their salaries to that of other class I Railways, and yet failed in its bid. The merchants went out on a hartal from 30 September 1947.[297] While the government was almost paralysed by these what proved of significance was the participation of agitators from outside. The small state of Kadur,[298] in Karnataka, sent its participants as equally did Travancore[299] and Cochin.[300] Satyamangalam and Coimbatore contributed their share as did the Karnataka areas from outside Mysore.[301] The Madras

Government sent a novel complaint to the Mysore Government that its police's practice of dumping these satyagrahis on to the border towns of Madras gave rise to rationing difficulties![302]

This proved clearly the difficulties of a state when the States Protection Act was completely removed. The Mysore Government brought to its knees by these demonstrations sought terms, this time with the leaders directly.[303] This was in contrast to the earlier practice of the Mysore Government seeking the interventions of British Indian leaders, or their help as intermediaries which showed now the disinclination of the nationalists to interfere in states affairs once their objective on them had been achieved. On 12 October 1947 the satyagraha was called off. An agreement was arrived at between the Dewan and the Mysore Congress on the night of 11 October 1947.[304] This agreement established an interim ministry of nine members, of whom not less than six were to be from the Mysore Congress party and three recommended by it after consultation with other parties.[305] This ministry was given the powers to set up a Constituent Assembly of elected members to frame their constitution[306]—bringing to a successful close the movement in the state.

Conclusions

The correspondence in the *Transfer of Power* papers during the period 1942-47, brings out clearly the British administrators realisation that it was impossible for them to carry out their treaty obligations once they quit British India. It was now clearly realised that the concept of paramountcy itself was essentially derived from the fact that they were paramount in British India, which in point of British Indian independence could no longer 'admit of it being discharged'. However, the British administrators endeavours to soft pedal the issue, again penalised (in its immediate application) the states people. Thus instead of giving a warning to the princes, which had been advised by Wavell, the India Office left the provisions regarding the states purposely vague so as to give the princes a better bargaining position *vis-a-vis* British India. This left the confabulations preceding the entry of the states to the Constituent Assembly, to negotiating committees from which the states people were excluded. With the two issues—one of some form of cooperation in the Indian Union and the other of safeguarding the states people's position on a democratic government, there was always a fear in the states people's mind of their interests being sacrificed.

With Mahatma Gandhi in full control of the movement, during this period, it is not surprising that the states people's movement lost all volition to act of its own. Gandhi played down the states peoples issue and the movement entered a period of drift—characterised by a desultory participation in the elections of the states and acceptance of terms offered by the states administration. Mysore, in her fears of a probable repudiation of her cause by the Indian nationalists, took up the cause of Karnataka unification as a second thread. In Travancore the disillusionment with Gandhian leadership led to a decline of State Congress popularity. More importantly, a section swerved towards communism. An abortive rising in 1946 under British Malabar leadership by the communist wing, lost for the State Congress the deterrent value of a 'direct action' threat at the opportune moment and made possible the Dewans postures on an 'independent' Travancore.

It was C.P. Ramaswami Aiyar's declaration on 11 June 1947 of Travancore's intentions, which reactivated the British Indian leadership—which had equivocated till then on the states peoples cause—into championing their cause. It was, again, the states peoples cause which provided the necessary leverage for British Indian nationalists, to prise the princes from their position and forced them into signing in on accession at this period, and integration later.

The stance of 'independence' of C.P. Ramaswami Aiyar, as well as the last ditch efforts of the Mysore administration to maintain its position, even after British Indian independence, seems to show a lack of appreciation of their position, by even so called intelligent princes and their administrators. The fall of these states like the proverbial nine pins in the bowling alley, in the dextrous handling of the maestros, Gandhi and Vallabhbhai Patel (not to mention the timely warning given to the princes by Mountbatten) fully vindicated Mahatma Gandhi's contention that the states peoples movement could prove successful only on the withdrawal of the British. The fears and suspicions of the states people, of a possible Congress betrayal seem exaggerated and ludicrous.

But it is pertinent to remember that one tends to judge from facts *post facto* which followed mainly from the establishment of strong unitary governments in British India, following partition. The study of this movement thus has given rise to three pertinent questions. The first two are in the nature of hypothetical ones. The first calls for an examination of the states peoples chances at achieving their objective, had their hands not been stayed by Mahatma Gandhi. The second involves the question of the position of the states people in a loose federal structure as envisaged in the Cabinet Mission Plan. These two questions relate to the third one—was the cause of integration at variance with the states peoples objective and was Gandhi's policy one of active sabotage of the states peoples cause and, if so, was he justified ? These questions in fact are not only confined to this chapter but runs as a central theme throughout this study. So these questions will necessarily have to be dealt with in my next chapter summing up the conclusions of the study as a whole.

8

The Movement Analysed

The democratic movement in the Indian states met a check at every point. While one can understand these checks at the level of confrontation between the states people and the administration in the states which were directly threatened by this movement—and at the level of paramount power's policy, (whose interests on a continuation of their regime lent a natural support to the autocratic rule of the princes), what is inexplicable, or needs an elucidation, is the lack of sympathy of the Indian National Congress High Command. It was clearly obstructive from its very initial stages. It was an anomaly, which the states people were quick to point out, that the Indian National Congress fighting for self-determination, should be so callous of the states peoples aspirations.

The democratic movement in these three states was indigenous and sprang of its own roots. The 'foreign Dewan' movement initiated this movement in the states which was, no doubt, inspired by the parallel movement in British India. However, this movement was independent of the movement in British India, and the states people were more importantly preoccupied with this than even the parallel movement on the wider arena. This was more obviously so in Travancore where its participation in the non-cooperation movement of 1921, or that of 1931, was nominal, while it hardly concerned itself with the Quit India Movement of 1942 at all. Cochin, who gained her aims most often with ease, had few contradictions. Mysore took up the mantle of the British Indian movement partly because the reforms movement in the states was isolated as that of a small section and to gain a wider base it, necessarily, had to involve itself on the freedom struggle of British India.

The movement in the states though independent of the wider movement in British India was, nevertheless, not fought in isolation; the states people's movement, more often as not, was not only fought simultaneously on both points but was more importantly affected by the Indian National Congress' policies and attitudes towards it. In this, while the states people were ever ready to align themselves with the Indian National Congress in their struggle and towards the promotion of their motives, the Indian National Congress refused to involve itself with the democratic struggle on its own, at any time. The post-Haripura involvement of the Congress leadership in the states people's movement at Rajkot, Jaipur, Orissa states etc., obscured the issues and have led to wrong conclusions, of a sympathy of the Indian National Congress' leadership to democratic movements' in the Indian states. However, the British Indian nationalists intentions on it are made more than clear in its treatment of the movement in Travancore and Mysore where these peoples movement was indigenous and had acquired enough thrust to carry out their programme on their own without Indian National Congress' help. What was asked of the Indian National Congress over here was not the active help to its movement, as was made out by the Calcutta resolution, but the moral blessings to it to carry out their programme. It was here that the British Indian leadership showed their antagonism and in order to bring this movement to heel, made an invidious breach through manipulations in acting as intermediaries. The Indian National Congress High Command's treatment of these states, more than its involvement with those of the northern ones, shows the real measure of its policy towards a democratic movement in the Indian states.

The Indian National Congress had to enter the states arena due to machinations of British policy. It was the British administrators' efforts at counterpoising the princes against the nationalists, and more importantly, their policy of creating an invidious boundary between the states and the neighbouring provinces (in their efforts to secure the princes from the influence of a democratised government in the provinces, projected in the Government of India Act of 1919) that raised the necessity of Congress entry (to counter British machinations at creating spheres of British influences in the states), on a programme of integration. To understand Congress obstructionists' attitude towards the movement in the states one would have to analyse how their interests on integration could have run counter to the aspirations of the states people on a democratic programme. From the very beginning of its entry into the states, the Congress High Command, though it obscured its interest in the states under a blanket of constructive programme, nevertheless, was consistent throughout of making it absolutely clear that it was *not* entering the states arena on the states peoples' programme of responsible government.

Was this reluctance merely the result of a recognition of the legal position of the princes as the ultimate authority in the states (which it candidly and to the cost of the states people recognised in its All Parties Constitution), antagonism with whom could put the Indian National Congress' interests on Union and integration in jeopardy ? Or was it the result of a realisation that the states peoples struggle was in vain and a wasted effort till the withdrawal of British from India was assured ? If that were solely the reason why its involvement in the northern Indian states? Or was it due partly to a realisation that the states people's achievement or success—even partially so, could itself encourage regionalism and prove a possible danger to their own aspirations on integration?

In its initial stages, its own recognition of the legal position of the princes in the states and the Butler Committee's pronouncements in their non-recognition of the states people—in allotting no position to them even in an enquiry *vis-a-vis* the states—did seem to confirm the Indian National Congress to put a premium on the legal position of the princes. While upto 1938 this position of the Indian National Congress did seem a valid excuse, the leadership's approach to the states in the post-1938 period, in their involvement in personally spearheading such movements in the other states, did show that their earlier position had been robbed of its significance. This showed that when its own interests on federation and integration demanded it, it was not chary of using the states people's movement as a lever to prise the princes from their position.

Gandhi's own assertions was at the level that British paramountcy was the ultimate contender and that till its withdrawal the movement could gain nothing except allow it to pervert affairs in the states.

Gandhiji defending his own case, in refuting charges apropos of Rajkot[1]—that but for his 'bad handling' of the situation, the people of Rajkot would have got what they wanted—pointed out that it would be most misleading to think that before his entry and 'mishandling' "the princes were so trembling in their shoes that they were about to abdicate their powers".[2] What they were doing, he asserted, was conferring among themselves on ways and means of countering the menace—as they thought it to be. As a result of the confabulations, he pointed out, they planned to arraign the forces of communalism to their side. As such the problem resolved itself into the the necessity of Congressmen or satyagrahis gaining control over these forces before they could take the agitation to the climax.

Applying the above argument to the states of our study we find that with little communal rancour in Mysore after 1938, this contention falls through. In Travancore there is little doubt that C.P. Ramaswami Aiyar was, in accordance with the strategy of the Dewans, using communalism in Kerala to antagonise the Nairs and the Ezhavas. Had the movement been allowed to run its course there was the possibility that these antagonisms would have been aggravated and, in addition, entrenched the State Congress in its communal bias and served to add to charges of hooliganism. It was in this sense that Gandhi was 'callous' of the State Congress fears of Ezhava dissociation from the movement which he felt would leave the body better for the leaving of this communal faction

However, his solution hardly helped, as their withdrawal helped little in allaying the forces of communalism, and it only served to weaken the body and made way for its replacement by a different ideology which seemed to be favourable to its cause.

This brings one to a related aspect of the problem in a consideration of the attitude of the paramount power towards these agitations for responsible government and of reforms for full responsible government, granted by states administration even without agitations. The policy of the paramount power, as enunciated in its parliamentary answers, pronouncements of the Viceroy and the Secretary of State,[3] avowedly proclaimed that while the paramount power would not stand in the way of introduction of changes in the form of governments in the states, the nature of these changes was a matter for the rulers themselves, and that in case of pressures from popular agitation, while the rulers were required to remedy mis-government, they would be given protection to which they were entitled under their treaties against violence and disorders.[4] However, in practice it was otherwise.

Zetland himself confessed in a letter to Linlithgow, apropos of Rajkot, that the "apparent *volte face* in connection with the personnel of the committee",[5] to which the Rajkot Durbar had agreed to in their negotiations with Patel, was due to some extent, at any rate, to pressures from the British administrators and that he was not certain that in this particular case he "*could say conscientiously*"[6] that they had not attempted to stand in the way of the decisions of the rulers to takes teps to liberalise the form of government in the state. In Rajkot, the intervention of the British administrators could have been, to a certain extent, a result of two reasons. One, because it was a British Political officer against whom the movement worked in its initial stages and secondly, because it was their main antagonists, the British Indian nationalists, who had entered the fray. But examining the question a little further in the context of our three states one finds that even had the nationalists withheld themselves from any involvement in these states and allowed the states people to have had a straight fight, the evidence shows that the states peoples position would not have been very promising. British policy in the matter of intervention in the states, due to pressures to reform, subjected themselves to only one exception which was to the favour of the states people. They stipulated that while supporting the Maharaja "they were to secure the abolition of abuses and raise the standard of administration".[7] And in these three states which were held up as paragons of good administration, it is doubtful if the British administrators would have allowed the states people to have had a free hand. At best, had the hands of the states administration been forced, there would have been efforts at playing at reforms without giving the substance, as was done by Mysore in her Reforms Committee proposals of 1939 and by C.P. Ramaswami Aiyar in his American Model Constitution in 1946 (which had, in any case, been prepared by him as early as 1939 for just such an eventuality), and by the constitutional proposals put forward by Mysore even as late as September 1947.

Thus the movement in the states would have been infructuous in the end, resulting in the meantime, quite possibly, in shooting incidents without achieving their objective; as long as the states had the protection of the paramount power and the backing of the States Protection Against Disaffection Act there was little chance of the states people obtaining their objective. The abortive nature of any agitation till the withdrawal of the British was proved even more clearly in the violence exhibited by C.P. Ramaswami Aiyar in putting down the communist uprising in 1946, in Travancore.

While this was the attitude of the paramount power on pressures towards reforms, their attitude to reforms even when granted without these pressures, in spite of their avowals that they would not stand in the way of such reforms,[8] was, with the imminence of war, actually antagonistic. Even when a small state like Aundh did grant responsible government, the Maharaj Kumar of Aundh has warned against the move.[9]

Thus analysed, the real fight in the matter of reforms in the states was not between the people and the states administration alone—which was in a sense mere shadow boxing—but between the paramount power and the people of the states, in which the paramount power was ready to resist any pressure brought to bear upon them from the leadership in the provinces, even were it to result in "a serious political crisis."[10]

As Mahatma Gandhi correctly diagnosed, it was only the conversion of rulers, through peaceful means, which could bring about reforms and not by forces and agitations. With the Dewan and the Maharaja against the movement, the administration could, by using the forces of communalism at their command, always project even peaceful agitation as creating violence and disorder and get the paramount power to its help. Thus, Gandhi was correct in his view of priorities. Unless the paramount power itself was removed, there was little chance of attaining the states peoples ideal through pressures; even otherwise the Maharaja himself should have been willing not only to divest himself of autocracy but himself spearheaded such reforms; agitations could serve little purpose.

In such a situation, one cannot find fault, if the astute mind of Gandhi did project to stop the states people from a wasted endeavour—a *harakiri*—and tried to put their energies to some use in accepting the bargain implied by Mirza Ismail, in his offer of election of states people to the central legislature, in return for Gandhi's muzzling of the movement in Mysore.

This master-stroke in policy which Gandhi imparted to his policy *vis-a-vis* the states did push the British administrators into a difficult corner, in that their nefarious plans to project the princes as a counterpoise to popular forces in the federal legislature was put to a tight squeeze. Again this was Gandhi's peculiar bombardment of the "network of friendly fortresses in debatable territory" on which British imperialism in 1931 had put so much trust as to assert that because of it "it would be difficult for a general rebellion against the British to sweep India",[11] counterpoised as they were by the loyal native states. Thus, in 1938, while the Viceroy did proclaim to the Secretary of State that he would not be a party to an endeavour which would give any understanding to the Congress that would in "practice amount to a variation from the strict interpretation"[12] of the federation proposed, he was through Gandhi's policies forced into holding talks with Mahatma Gandhi in April 1938,[13] when pressed by him, the British administrators had to accept "that some element of popular choice as distinct from nomination should enter into the selection of states representatives".[14]

While the British administrators in a subsequent period,

did, in order to allay the fears of princes "of a violent onslaught upon the state",[15] give an ambiguous ruling in December 1938,[16] they could hardly give a concrete assurance to their plea for the Viceroy's backing as against Congress.[17] He had to emphasise that while they were willing to extend support to their difficulties against the Congress, he "could not undertake to put an effective fence against the march of ideas"[18] for "at root, this movement was not dependent upon federation (but was) fundamentally a part of a great upsurge of political activity which one could trace right across the face of Asia from the Nile to the Yellow River in China. . . directed towards a liberalising of political institutions and towards the progressive recognition of the individual subjects".[19]

The British Government on its own acknowledgement was, now, due to the policies of Mahatma Gandhi, caught in a cleft stick. The princes who had been coopted into a federation to act as a counterpoise to the popular representatives at the centre were themselves now being subjected to the same popular forces from which the British Government could hardly give them any protection. The British administrators themselves, though they realised the inadequacy of a federation to protect their interests, could not throw federation overboard for fear of ridicule from Conservative quarters. It was in such a situation that Zetland confessed to their position as one "on the horns of a dilemma"[20] and on the eve of Second World War Linlithgow confessed to "a certain sneaking fondness for the idea of saying rather more definitely that [they were] putting federation into cold storage".[21]

The war delivered them and the states administrations out of a sticky situation. The Viceroy remarking rather sanctimoniously that the princes would have "bitter cause to rue their failure to seize federation when it was at their disposal",[22] made the outbreak of war the pretext for throwing overboard the inconvenient federation, in spite of having by then nearly "2/5th in their pocket, Baroda, Mysore and Kashmir almost in the net, Gwalior as good as caught and Indore the same".[23]

Seen in this context of British difficulties on federation it becomes clear that even in a loose federation as proposed by the Cabinet Mission, the hands of the Congress leadership would have been strong enough, were it willing to do so, to hold the central leadership from active interference in the states on behalf of the states administration. Thus given an active movement from within the states and the States Protection Against Disaffection Act in abeyance, with the independence of British India, as the British administrators did realise, the chances of a state administration holding their own as against the states people was heavily loaded against the princes. While they may not have capitulated as quickly as they did, following partition, in face of a unitary government, they would, nevertheless, have been forced to come to terms with the states people. In this the Congress leadership would have been forced to help them as a popular administration in the states returning all members to the central legislature as elected was certainly to the Congress nationalist's advantage; and it would have been inconceivable, that after independence, be it a federal or a unitary structure, the Congress would have, or even could have, put a fence against the state peoples ambitions.

Granted that the Congress High Command after independence would not, and could not, have betrayed the states people, was it really necessary for Gandhi in the meantime to have forced these states peoples organisation, in the period subsequent to Haripura, not only to stop the movement but to accept the humiliating conditions imposed upon it by the states administrations—which was again solely due to the embargo placed on it by Mahatma Gandhi? Left to themselves, there is little doubt, that but for Gandhi, the states people could have got, if not a full responsible government, better terms than they did.

In such a contingency could not the State Congress, strong as it was from within, have flouted the leadership from without? As it was, the states movement was pitted against two strong forces, that of the princes with almost unbridled powers for repression and of a paramount power willing to support it through its military forces. Were the moral support of the nationalists also to be withdrawn there was little possibility of its thrust being effective. In this, in Mysore, Gandhi in order to bring the Mysore Congress to heel threatened to even support the dissident Congress against the main body,[24] while in Travancore he issued an oblique warning that he would not be a party to a stru gle in pursuit of a personal matter to "the exclusion of the most important one of swaraj".[25] Here though he could hardly spell out clearly whether the states peoples intransigence was against swaraj in their non-withdrawal of the memorandum, or in a continuation of their struggle, the subsequent course showed clearly that he was not ready to countenance the states peoples struggle even on the platform of responsible government. These equivocations of the Congress High Command was due to their rather ambiguous position. For, while their position on integration demanded a states peoples awareness and political consciousness to use them as levers for obtaining British Indian interest on integration, the same political consciousness could not be misdirected to an assertion of an independent position *vis-a-vis* the Congress leadership in the provinces. Thus the assertion of Mahatma Gandhi shows that, apart from a realisation of the impossibility of the states people achieving their goal prior to independence, one could not rule out an ulterior motive present in the actions of the British Indian nationalists *vis-a-vis* the states peoples movements, which may have been due to their apprehensions that the states peoples success, even a partial one, itself could present an eventual danger to their own aspirations on integration. Such fears could not be ruled as out of context as there is confirmation *post facto* in the postures of a Sheikh Abdullah, on an independent Kashmir following independence and the establishment of a popular government. The states organisation of Travancore and Mysore did have modified versions of such ambitions. Mysore, which had till independence thought of a united Karnataka as a 'vital necessity' made a *volte face* following the achievement of her ambitions. The states peoples proposals on the disbandment of AISPC was that Congress organisations in the state be treated as separate provinces and not as part of Karnataka.[26] Travancore Congress which had never made any bones on this issue even earlier, made a like demand.

Again Hanumanthaiyya's dissent note in the 'Model Constitution Committee' of the Constituent Assembly of 1949[27] was for a retention of greater powers by the states—even to a power vested on the states legislature for the deposition of the Maharaja, etc., which exhibited a clear adherence to the states peoples earlier stand against a transference of paramountcy. The states peoples demand, it is clear, given a chance, and the centripetal tendencies ever present in India, was quite likely to be against, in its extreme proposals, if not integration, at least against making the centre all powerful. Thus the confrontation in the states *vis-a-vis* the Congress High Command ultimately resolved itself into the British Indian nationalist's obsessions on central control as against the states peoples ambitions of marking an independent path. Seen in this perspective it becomes clear that the British Indian nationalists did have an imperative need to stay the hands of the states people in their course till their own position at the centre was secured to bring the states people under their direct command. This position was explained rather obliquely by the AISPC, speaking of course not on behalf of states peoples aspirations, as much as, that of the British Indian nationalist's. It was Nehru who naively proclaimed "what is the nature of conflict today? This must be clearly understood. It varies from state to state but the demand is everywhere for full responsible government. *Yet the Conflict is not at present to enforce that demand but to establish the right of organising people for that demand* . . . the freedom of the people of the states is a big enough thing, yet it is part of the larger freedom of India and till we gain that larger freedom it is a struggle for us".[28]

Thus at every stage the needs of integration did cross the aspirations of the states people and there could never have been a meeting of purposes till independence for British India was achieved. The states peoples struggle was at every stage in contradiction and confrontation with that of the nationalists, except in so far as it promoted the nationalist's interests on integration. As such, though the fight did seem a contradiction in terms, it was not a mere fight of priorities of democracy versus integration, but in another and more important aspect, an assertion of a prospective central government against possible centripetal forces. Thus to treat of the states peoples struggle as part of the wider movement, especially as in these states where the movement was more strongly on the democratic platform, seems to me an erroneous appreciation of the states people's movement. Again,[15] the AISPC contribution to these three states movements, fighting as they were on their own programme of responsible government, was minimal. For here these states people having established an organisation to promote their demand, and mainly motivated as they were for enforcing that demand for responsible government, the AISPC could hardly concern itself with this programme, involved as it was in the other states in 'organising people for that demand',[29] towards a promotion of Indian National Congress aims on integration.

Seen in the perspective of 25 years of Mahatma Gandhi's manoeuvrings, it is clear, that the story of the integration of the states was not the mere result of a *tour de force* of Vallabhbhai Patel and V.P. Menon or the result of the naive outpourings of a Nehru as President of the AISPC but the fruit of Gandhian *real politik* whose figure alone stands out as a colossus in his clear manipulation of a states peoples movement as a force towards his main objective on integration. In this Vallabhbhai Patel with a quick appreciation of underlying motives helped him ably to wipe out the six hundred and odd states with all their "petty princelings, and their courts, and their privileges, and their pomps, and their armed forces, and their pedigree and all"[30] as was done in Germany, with not even a relic left as a trace in an Almanac de Gotha.

If this integration was achieved at the price of a small dislocation in the states—as in Travancore in its deflection to communism and communalism—it was a small price indeed, in the face of an achievement of welding 562 states in the making of a united India. The states peoples movement is thus again a new version of the story of integration with its central theme of achieving a transfer of paramountcy on the British withdrawal, this time not so much over the Maharaja's, who were in any case a spent force, but over the popular, but regionally oriented forces in work in the states, so as to ensure a united India.

CHAPTER 1

NOTES

1. Letter from Raja of Travancore to Governor of Madras, 19 June, 1788. C.U. Aitchison, *A Collection of Treatise, Engagements and Sanads*, Vol. X, p. 224.
2. G.R. Josyer, *History of Mysore and Yadava Dynasty*, p. 4.
3. D.V. Gundappa, *All About Mysore*, p. 2.
4. C. Achyuta Menon, *Cochin State Manual*, p. 1,
5. C.U. Aitchison, op. cit., Vol. X, p. 207.
6. Ibid., Vols. IX and X.
7. A few random examples could testify to their claim to 'models'. Sir Harcourt Butler enumerated these 'South Indian States' amongst 'the most progressive'. Amiya Kumar Bagchi praised them for setting up state enterprises and helping Indian capitalists to setup factories within their territory. Even H.H. the Maharaja of Bikaner testified to the advanced stage which subjects of states such as Mysore, Travancore and Cochin had reached. See Sir Harcourt Butler, *India Insistent*, p. 1; Amiya Kumar Bagchi, *Private Investment*

in India, 1900-1939, p. 214, Bikaner's speech at the Bikaner Legislative Assembly, 19 December, 1929, File No. 193-R/1929, Foreign and Political (F & P) National Archives of India (NAI).

8. The very first Chera king, from whom the Rajas of Travancore Cochin traced their lineage had been chosen by an oligarchy of Brahmins. Cantervischen has remarked on the assemblies which acted as checks on the king's arbitrary powers. See Cantervischen—*Letter from Malabar*, pp. 76-78; Achyuta Menon—*Cochin State Manual* p. 497.
9. See V. Nagam Aiya, *The Travancore State Manual*, p. 420 and T.K. Velu Pillai, *Travancore State Manual*, Vol. III, p. 449.
10. Ibid., p. 473.
11. Velu Tampi's rebellion is illustrative of the two phases of the struggle of the states people—one against the government for reforms and in its later ideals for 'responsible government' and the second against the imperialist domination as part of the movement in British India on the wider issue, as struggle for freedom.
12. G.R. Josyer, *History of Mysore and the Yadava Dynasty*. p. 68.
13. G.R. Josyer, op. cit., p. 140.
14. From 1811 to 1814 the Resident himself acted as the Dewan in Travancore-Cochin.
15. Rawlinson in Parliament, *Hansard*, Vol. CLXXXV, pp. 827-833, quoted by Donavan Williams, *The Adoption Despatch of 16 April 1867, its Origin and Significance, Collins Davies Memorial Volume*, p. 238.
16. Ibid., p. 235.
17. The initiative in respect of the restoration of monarchy had been entirely with the deposed Maharaja who had made his repeated representations with every change of Viceroy or the Secretary of State. Thus, the role of the champion of the people was adopted by the outgoing Commissioner himself who stipulated a series of conditions. See Donavan Williams, op. cit. and J.D, Gordon's despatch to India Office, 10 February 1879 quoted by D.V. Gundappa, *All About Mysore*, op. cit., p. 44.
18. In 1831, the Commissionership fixed the civil list arbitrarily at Rs. 10 lakhs. From time to time, the Maharaja did petition for a raise, and at the time of accession in 1947 amounted to Rs. 23 lakhs (as compared to the Nizam's 50 lakhs) which constituted less than 4 per cent of the state's revenue. Travancore-Cochin voluntarily agreed to a very modest list of Rs. 6 lakhs and Rs. 35,000 respectively which at the time of accession in 1947 amounted to Rs. 15 lakhs and Rs. 1,74,000 respectively.
19. Travancore set the precedence in this; as early as 1832, the Maharaja ceased to interfere in decisions of cases except those of capital punishment and had from 1836 drawn a code of civil and criminal procedure. The administration could never be sure of the decisions of the judiciary which acted very often in an independent manner. In

comparison, Mysore did not have such a good reputation.

20. This provision made impossible the juggling with accounts or getting money apart from the civil list, which was the accepted practice among quite a few Maharajas of the North.
21. Letter from Irwin to Birkenhead, 17 November 1926. Halifax Collection, 10L, Vol. II, pp. 152-153, Roll 1, NMML.
22. Letter from Irwin to Birkenhead, 11 May 1927. Halifax Collection, 10L, Vol. II, p, 94, Roll 1, NMML.
23. Letter from Irwin to Birkenhead, 17 November 1926. Halifax Collection, 10L, Vol. II, pp. 152-53, Roll 1, NMML.
24. See letter from Irwin to Birkenhead, 11 May 1927, Halifax Collection, Vol. II, p. 94, Roll 1, NMML.
25. These were settlers from Bombay Presidency who had come to Tanjore in the wake of Mahratta influence. The other possible reason for appointing outsiders was to do away with local intrigues.
26. See *post* pp. 29-34.
27. Letter from Secretary of State to Government of India, 12 August 1880, Parliamentary Papers, 1881, LXX, pp. 525-527, quoted by Gustafson, *The Making of a Model State*, p. 89. An unpublished thesis from the University of Wisconsin, U.S.A., available in microfilm at NMML.
28. Gundappa, *All About Mysore*, op. cit., p. 44.
29. Gustafson, op. cit., p. 106. This feature persisted till the ouster of Mirza Ismail in 1941 when the Maharaja in order to revive his powers reactivated the Executive Council. See *post*, pp. 223-24.
30. See *post*, pp. 116-17.
31. This was a particular sore point with Mysore; for while a number of States were exempted from paying any tribute, Mysore's share constituted 40 per cent of the GOI total amount of Rs. 92 lakhs, gained from this source.
32. These two states gained a respite as a result of rise of the price of pepper in the world market. For Treaty provisions on this, see C.U. Aitchison, *A Collectian of Treaties, Engagements and Sanads*, Vol. X, p. 225.
33. See *Despatches of the Duke of Wellington*, pp. 498-500, published as an appendix by Thompson and Garatt, op. cit., pp. 656-57.
34. By the hypothecation agreement, the Company was allowed to buy the built railways at cost price and to extend it further; the Durbar was allowed to possess it after a period of fifty years, thus losing the interest on the loan raised. To add injury to hurt, the Government of India pocketed the sum paid by the Company (Rs. 68,60,508) towards famine relief extended lavishly by the Commissionership earlier, which would in any case, according to the prior agreement, have been defrayed by a 5 per cent interest on the loan. For greater details see Gustafson, op. cit., pp. 95-98.
35. Amiya Kumar Bagchi, *Private Investment in India, 1900-1939*, op. cit., p. 324.

36. Letter from Birkenhead to Irwin, 25 November 1926, Lord Halifax Collection, MSS, EUR, C, 152, Vol. II, p. 134, available in microfilm Roll 1, NMML.
37. The Maharaja of Mysore's debt, incurred prior to Rendition was liquidated to the tune of Rs. 80 lakhs in this way.
38. These import duties, in which the states had no say, increased almost six times during the period 1914 to 1926. Visvesvaraya was sent as a special delegate of the Durbar to petition the Secretary of State to a reduction of the subsidy. See Vivesvaraya's Memorandum to Birkenhead, 21 October 1926. Halifax Collection, Vol. II, pp. 134-37 Roll 17, NMML.
39. Mysore paid to the central coffers, a subsidy of 35 lakhs, Travancore was given a sum of Rs. 40,000 in lieu of restrictions placed on levying import duty, subject to the condition that it would be offset against any import duty allowed at her ports not exceeding Rs. 13,000. As this sum did exceed the stipulated amount no money was given. Cochin came off the bargain better. It was allowed not less than 1 lakh as her share of customs and Rs. 10,000 in lieu of import duties lost. See Dewan Raghaviah at the Round Table Conference, December 1930. *Indian Round Table Conference Proceedings of the Sub-Committee, I*, p. 203.
40. John Hurd, *Some Economic Characteristic af the Princely States of India, 1901-1931*, an unpublished thesis for the University of Pennysilvynia. Available in Microfilm, NMML. See also R. Balakrishna, *Industrial Development of Mysore*, pp. 295-96.
41. Amiya Kumar Bagchi, op. cit., pp. 77-78.
42. While the average revenue of Mysore between 1911-1918 was Rs. 280 lakhs, Travancore's was 157 lakhs in 1915 (see *Indian Review*, January, 1915, p. 185), thus showing that the revenue of Travancore was just a little above half that of Mysore. But more importantly, even with this limited tax base, 1/4th her revenue was credited to the Government of India.
43. Travancore had saved by 1903 an aggregate of 90 lakhs of which 60½ lakhs were invested in Government of India and other securities, bringing an interest of Rs. 2,60,000, *The Imperial Gazetteer*, Vol. XXIV, p. 18.
44. S. Subramaniah, *The Economics of Public Enterprise in India with Special Reference to Mysore*, p. 290. Ph.D. Thesis, Madras University (1956).
45. In Travancore in 1862, the first British planter Munro was given land in Peermade hills to start a coffee plantation for which social overheads in the form of roads, etc., were provided by the state. In 1881, James Darah was allowed to start a cotton mill. (See A.K. Gopalan, *Kerala Past and Present*, p. 46). Similarly, Mysore allotted land to Emerson a British planter, and to the Anglo-Indian Association on very favourable tenures for cultivation of coffee. See Hayavadana Rao, *Mysore Gazetteer*, Vol. IX, p. 327.

46. A request for the establishment of an Industrial Association and placing of one-fifth of the government's revenue at its disposal was made in the Mysore Legislative Assembly as early as 1897, which, however, had been brushed aside by the Dewan on the grounds that it was not possible to take the initiative to spend public money when the people themselves did not come forward to invest any capital. See *Legislative Assembly Proceedings*, October 1897, p. 75.
47. *Indian Review*, August 1918, p. 560. See also Gundappa, *All About Mysore*, op. cit., p. 75.
48. Address of Mirza Ismail, Dewan of Mysore, at the Representative Assembly, October 1931, *Mysore Representative Assembly Proceedings*, p. 1.
49. H.H. The Maharaja of Bikaner at the Round Table Conference, 4 December, 1930. See *Proceedings of Sub-Committee I, Round Table Conference*, p. 100.
50. R. Coupland, *The Indian Problem, 1853-1935*, p. 15.
51. The figures for Bombay, Madras, India, Mysore and Cochin are as given in the *Report of the Committee for the Revision of the Land Revenue System iu Mysore* (1950), (Karnataka Act) appointed by the Mysore Government on 13 August 1948, pp. 144-145. The figures are according to differing census years, but it hardly matters as the proportion in each category are only in question. The figures for Malabar have been taken from K.N. Panikkar, *Agrarian Legislation and Social Classes in Malabar*. p. 5, paper read at the History Conference, Calcutta, December, 1974. The figures for Travancore have been taken from *Census Report, 1911*, pp. 280-81.
52. *Report of the Committee for the Revision of the Land Revenue System in Mysore* (1950).
53, According to figures given by K.N. Panikkar, op. cit.
54. The three tenurial categories in the Janmam System were: (1) The *Janmi* as sole legal proprietor of land. His holding, the *Janam*, was absolutely exempt from tax so long as they remained with the original proprietors. However, circumventing this clause, alienation took place by *Kanampattam* tenure which gave rise to category, (2) *Kanakkaran* who had land pledged to him in security for the interest of money advanced to the *Janmi*, at the commencement of the tenancy. This lease was renewable every twelve or stipulated period of years. The *Kanakkaran* in turn subleased it to a category, (3) The *Verumpattakaran*, See *Imperial Gazetteer of India*, Vol. XXIV, p. 18.
55. A.K. Gopalan, *Kerala Past and Present*, op. cit., p. 38.
56. See E.M.S. Namboodiripad, op. cit., p. 140.
57. Ibid. Actually 56 per cent of land representing 270,000 acres was held by *Janmies* in Cochin. Out of this 1/6th was covered by Sircar Devaswam lands—belonging to temples and under the control of government. Of the rest only '30 per cent or 70,000 acres were held under *Kanam* tenures and constituted but . . . 14 per cent or 1/7th of the cultivated lands in the state'. A minute in the question of Land

Legislation in Cochin State, File No. 373, 26 June 1912, Political Department, Tamil Nadu Archives.

58. A minute on the question of Land Legislation in Cochin State, File No. 373, 26 June 1912, Political Department, Tamil Nadu Archives (T.N. Archives).
59. The *Kanakkaran* himself was quite often a *Janmi* who in relation to another of a lower category returned himself as such or *vice versa*. See K.N. Panikkar, op. cit.
60. *Report of the Committee for the Revision of Land Revenue System in Mysore* (1948), pp. 144-45, Karnataka State Archives.
61. The polygars or small chiefs who had studded the state in the early period had been quelled by Haider Ali as he suspected their favouring the English. Thus, there were few families in Mysore which could claim hereditary wealth with the exception of Yelandur Taluk conferred on Purniah, the Dewan at the time of reinstatement in 1799. G.R. Josyer, *History of Mysore and the Yadava Dynasty*, p. 85.
62. C. Hayavadana Rao, *Mysore Gazetteer*, Vol. IV, p. 29.
63. *Imperial Gazetteer*, Vol. XVIII, p. 232.
64. See T.K. Velu Pillai, op. cit., p. 603.
65. A minute on the question of Land Legislation in Cochin State File, No. 373, 26 June, 1912, Political Department, T.N. Archives.
66. For a greater elucidation on this point, see K.N. Panikkar, op. cit., p. 9.
67. Bowring, *Eastern Experiences*, p. 16, quoted by Gustafson, op. cit., p. 60.
68. Additional Head Sircar Vakil, 17 November 1936. *Proceedings of the First Assembly of Reformed Parliament*, Vol. IX, p. 74.
69. Ibid.
70. *All India Credit Survey Report of the Committee of Directives*, Vol. II, published by the Reserve Bank of India (1954), p. 174.
71. The Hesarghatta tank, Krishnaraja Sagara and Sivasamudram dams in Mysore and Periyar, Kodayar and Annamalai Projects in Travancore-Cochin were some of the outstanding projects.
72. *Indian Review*, July 1917, p. 491. The Panchayats in these states were most often government-sponsored. This was mainly to counter the demands of the ideologies of responsible government. Here the government could often hold that it had a democratic set-up at the grass-roots level.
73. See *ante* p. 2.
74. The ninteenth century uprisings in British Malabar, though attributed by the British to the fanaticism of the Moplahs, is discounted by modern research and have been classified as peasant movements due to agrarian discontent.
75. The very small pocket of *Janmi* influence in Travancore was no doubt utilised by Communists to raise an uprising in Shertallai-Vayalar. But here too, more than agrarian economic grievance, it was the Communist's influence over the trade unions which was primarily

responsible for it and at best could only be treated as an over spill of Communist activities from British Malabar. See *post* pp. 212-215.

76. A.K. Gopalan, *Kerala Past and Present*, op. cit.. p. 38. E.M.S. Namboodiripad in his book *Kerala, Yesterday, Today, Tomorrow* makes no distinction between the movement in British Malabar and that of the states. After quoting an injunction of the Travancore Maharaja to the Appeal Courts to see that while the *Janmis* received their dues, their tenants possession right was not to be curtailed, he proceeds on to the agitation in British Malabar. He proceeds from the Maharaja's injunction which is clearly non-partisan to a description of the movement in Malabar, thus plainly confusing the issues. See Namboodiripad, op. cit., pp. 117-18.
77. The Rendition Treaty Settlement of 1881 raised the subsidy from Rs. 24½ lakhs to Rs. 35 lakhs.
78. See *ante*, p. 7.
79. See *post* p. 103.
80. See *post* p. 57.
81. See *post* p. 88.
82. Hosakappa Krishna Rao, *Swaraj Constitution*, published in March 1928, pp. 10-11.
83. Ibid.
84. *Mysore Legislative Assembly Proceedings*, 11 June 1932, p. 236.
85. Ibid.
86. Except in so far as in Travancore-Cochin where emphasis on revenue considerations made possible the import of capital and capitalists from outside and aroused jealousies within. See *post* pp. 181-182.
87. S. Subbramaniah, op. cit., p. 291.
88. See George Kristoffel Lieten, 'Nature of Travancore's Economy Between the Two World Wars', *Journal of Kerala Studies*, Vol. II, March 1975.
89. See *Sri Mulam Popular Assembly Proceedings*, 1928, p. 16.
90. See *post* p. 181 and p. 136.
91. See *post* p. 112.
92. See *post* p. 112 pp. 190-191.
93. At the height of the movement in Mysore in 1937-38, Mirza Ismail in his correspondence with Jawaharlal, reiterated repeatedly that the Mysore Government stood for economic democracy above the political. See *post* p. 141 Again C.P. Ramaswami Aiyar in his stance on 'independence' emphasised again the economic viability of the state to maintain its own position. See *post* pp. 219.
94. Table as shown by Oren Stephen, *Religious Groups at Political Organisation*, unpublished thesis for the University of Columbia, p. 46. According to Census figure of 1921.
95. Eric J. Miller, *The Economic Weekly*, 9 February 1952. The general acceptance of this pertinent quotation is realised in finding it quoted by the *All India Rural Credit Survey* (1954)—Survey Report of the Committee of Directives, Vol. II, p. 75, published by the Government of India.

96. The convening of the Legislative Council in Travancore was prompted mainly by the success of Legislative Assembly convened in Mysore in 1881. As an experiment in 1885, at the time of proclaiming his Revenue Settlement, the Maharaja at a meeting of 'leading citizens', put forward this proposal.
97. Table presented by George Kristoffel Lieten, op. cit., p. 103.
98. *Communitywise Breakup of Positions Held in Legislature, 1933 Elections :*

Community	In terms of population percentage	Seats won in Assembly by Election	Seats won in Council by Election
Nairs	17.3%	25 (nearly 60%)	10 (7 high castes Hindu other than Nairs)
Christians	29.3%	8	2
Ezhavas	16.7%	3	0
Muslims	6.8%	1	2
		Total seats open for election 43	Total seats open for election 16

Table prepared from data supplied by *Fortnightly Report*, 3 July 1933.

99. Report of the A.G.G. Madras states on the evolution of the constitution of the state. File No. 525-P/1927, F&P NAI.
100. Ibid.
101. In 1898, the validity of the promulgation brought before the Travancore High Court was upheld though not as a judicial decision but as an *obiter dicta*. The Madras Government also upheld this position in advising the Durbar as "neither necessary nor expedient to make any public declaration of the right" at that moment.
102. These demands were in the nature of appeals, as lacking a sizeable backing in a Legislature monopolised by the Nair elements, any agitation within it was impossible.
103. *Sri Moolam Popular Assembly Proceedings*, 1925, p. 140.
104. Appeal by Cheramans, *Sri Moolam Popular Assembly Proceedings*, 1928, p. 146.
105. *Sri Moolam Popular Assembly Proceedings*, 1930, p. 300.
106. *Sri Moolam Popular Assembly Proceedings*, 1928, p. 285.
107. *Sri Moolam Popular Assembly Proceedings*, 1930, p. 336.
108. *Samdarsi*, 13 July 1918, NNRMS, NAI.
109. *Sri Moolam Popular Assembly Proceedings*, 1928, p. 138.
110. One would have to anticipate events to illustrate this point. In 1921, with the Nairs propagating the Indian National Congress cause, the

Christian and Ezhava communities were in opposition in their anti-non-co-operation movement, in Cochin (see *post* pp. 75-76). In 1935, in its 'Absentionists' movement, the Ezhavas, the Christians and the Muslims (who later on were to form the Travancore State Congress) joined in their demand for adult franchise against the Nair interests in the legislature in Travancore (See *post* pp. 130-133). However, in 1939, the Dewan was able to weed away a section of the S.N.D.P. Yogam from the Travancore State Congress. (See *post* p. 190). In 1947, just prior to independence, the Nair community was led into the Congress fold by its leader Mannath Padmanabhan. (See *post* p. 219). Even today, the caste affiliations as the basis of party affiliations in Kerala can hardly be denied.

111. See *post* pp. 130.
112. E.M.S. Namboodiripad, op. cit., p. 2.
113. Table as shown by Oren Stephen, op. cit., p. 54. The figures as given by the *Report of the Backward Class Committee* (1961), p. 41, published by the Government of Mysore and *Backward Class Commission Report*, Vol. II (1955), Appendix VI, published by the Government of India.
114. A long standing dispute between Mohammedans and Hindus of Molakamaru on the above issue in 1912, resulted in riots and was to remain a troubled area and cause of riots in 1916, 1917 and 1920. The riot of 1928, resulting in 120 injured in Bangalore, acquired its political overtones mainly due to the appointment of a Muslim as Dewan in Mirza Ismail. See *Report on the Administration of the Police Department (Mysore) for the years 1911-1921*, NAI. Fortnightly Report, August 1928, CRR, IOL, ACC 4, NAI, and letters from Resident to Political Secretary, 1928, File No. 357-P/1928, NAI.
115. As an example, see the Vokkaliga Sabha's address in the Legislative Assembly leading the government memorandum on education as a means of 'democratising knowledge', and the Miller Committee Report as the *Mitakshra* (last word) of official patronage as it had recognised the fundamental right of all communities to be represented in government office. See *Mysore Legislative Assembly Proceedings*, October 1921, p. 182.
116. *Mysore Legislative Assembly Proceedings*, 9 October 1897, p. 72.
117. *Mysore Legislative Assembly Proceedings*, October 1921, p. 108.
118. It acclaimed the Lingayat Education Fund's efforts as one of philanthropic interest 'for spreading its activities outside its own community to that of other depressed classes'. See *Review of Progress of Education in the Mysore State, 1911-1916*, p. 91. Available in Karnataka State Archives.
119. *Mysore Legislative Assembly Proceedings*, October 1921, p. 108.
120. Note by Resident on Constitutional Reforms in Mysore, 1901, CRR, IOL, ACC 5, NAI.
121. Address at the Representative Assembly by Dewan A.R. Banerji, 7 October 1922. Official Papers connected with the Constitutional

development in Mysore (1924), Karnataka State Archives (KSA).

122. Note by Resident, 1901, CRR, IOL, ACC 5, NAI.
123. Gustafson, op. cit., p. 175.
124. Address at the Representative Assembly by Dewan A.R. Banerji, 7 October 1922. Official Papers connected with the Constitutional Development in Mysore (1924), KSA.
125. Note by Resident, 1901, CRR, IOL, ACC 5, NAI.
126. Added to this, as James Manor pointed out, by not interfering with the local power systems created by these two communities in the rural area, the government of Mysore successfully separated the local level politics from the state level politics and created difficulties for the state level politicians to co-opt these elements into their movement. (See op. cit., p. 9). This gap could be bridged only after 1937 when the non-brahmin organisation joined the mainstream of .he movement.
127. From Procrustes, the legendary Greek robber, who to fit his prisoners to his bed of torture had them stretched or sawed off their limbs. The term was used by A.P. Nicholson, in his book *Scraps of Paper* in his defence of the princes, against the political department's imposition of these conditions on those of the northern states.
128. Author of *Scraps of Paper.*
129. The lawyer engaged by the North Indian princes to represent them at the States Enquiry Committee.
130. One is delightfully reminded of Kiplings allusions to the Native Princes and the 'Supreme Government's' exhortation to them to refrain from kidnapping woman or filling offenders with pounded red pepper and eccentricities of that kind and to his ditties.

> Rustam Beg of Kolasai,
> Slightly backward Native State,
> Lusted for a C.S.I.,
> So began to sanitate.

only to find that when

> The Birthday Honours came,
> Sad to state and sad to note,
> Stood against the Rajahs name,
> Nothing more than to C.I.P.

See Kiplings *Departmental Ditties and Other Works* and 'consequences' in *Plain Tales from the Hills.*

CHAPTER 2

NOTES

1. The books of G. S. Halappa, *History of Freedom Movement in Karnataka* (1965), P. K. K. Menon, *The History of Freedom Movement in Kerala* in 3 volumes (1964-72) and R. L. Handa, *Struggle for Freedom in the Indian States* are among some of these publications.
2. M. J. Koshy, 'The History of the Legislature of Travancore-Cochin upto 1956' A Ph. D. thesis for the University of Kerala, p. 113-114.
3. Mr. Marar in 1912 in Cochin and Nagam Aiya in 1924 in Travancore are the few exceptions in Travancore-Cochin even after the turn of the century. In Mysore the turn of the century saw the appointment of P. N. Krishnamurthy (1901-1906), M. Visvesvaraya (1912-1918), Kantaraja Urs (1918-1922) and Mirza Ismail (1928-40) as native Dewans.
4. For an account of the confrontation of the Hebbar Aiyangars against foreign Brahmins and the Dewan, see Gustafson, 'Mysore 1881-1902; The Making of a Model State' unpublished thesis for the University of Wisconsin, U.S.A.

5. This Mysore daily, one of the earliest newspapers (started in 1865) was the chief organ of the Mysore Brahmins.
6. *Karnataka Prakasika*, 30 Auguss 1886. From the *Native Newspaper Reports Madras State* (NNRMS) for the year 1886, NAI. I have quoted from this passage extensively as it epitomises all their grievances and raises the first demand for a greater say of the people. See also *Karnataka Prakasika*, 26 September 1886, NNRMS, NAI.
7. To cite only a few examples in Cochin, the deterioration of personal relationship between Dewan Venkata Rao (in 1908) and the Maharaja was the cause of the Dewans removal. The Dewan had been supported by the Resident but however, a popular insurrection against him and in support of the Maharaja led to his dismissal. The inability of Dewan Ramiangar to get on with the Travancore Maharaja led to his subsequent dismissal. Even as late as the 1940's, the deterioration in the personal relationship of Mirza Ismail and the Maharaja of Mysore led to the Dewan's resignation though he had served ably during the most difficult times in Mysore.
8. For the agitation in the Legislature, see *post* p. 40-41.
9. The letter by *Pro-Patra*, the Malayali Memorial, the newspaper reviews on it, the Counter Memorial, etc. have been published as appendices to the book by M.J. Koshy, *Genesis of Political Consciousness in Kerala.*
10. See *The Western Star*, 19 January 1891, published as an appendix by M.J. Koshy op. cit. However from this time even the census reports were wary of declaring either the castewise distribution of the populace in individual employment or in agriculture and industry. It was again the refusal of the Mysore Dewan to produce a likewise data which precipitated his resignation in 1918. See *post* p. 42.
11. See M.J. Koshy, op. cit.
12. The figure for Malayali Sudras (Nairs) has been grossly exaggerated by the inclusion of the Exhavas, excluding their representation it would be in a position better than that of the Christians.
13. The Memorial pointed out that the two areas were almost equal in area and population. Inhabited by the same class of people, with 50 Malayali graduates to a population of 2,401,158 and area of 6730 square miles in Travancore, to that of 57 Malayali graduates in a population of 2,365,033 and 5,765 square miles in Malabar and with comparable literacy rates, while in Malabar 66% of the appointments in Revenue Department and 51 per cent were held by Malayalis, in Travancore only 60 per cent in Revenue Department and 41 per cent in the Judicial Department were open to them.
14. *Karnataka Prakasika*, 19 January 1891. See also *Mysore Herald*, 24 January 1891, *The Bangalore Post*, 14 January-May 1891, *The Kerala Nandini*, 23 January 1891, *Bangalore Spectator*, 14 January-May 1891, etc., published as an appendix by M.J. Koshy, op. cit.
15. As the agitation was common to all the the three states, I will be dealing with the account in a purely chronological order. As events

in one state were well known in the other two, it was often some occurrence in the one which triggered off the other two. Thus my treatment of the account, I hope, will not be *de trop*.

16. *Suryodaya Prakasika*, 14 November 1900. *Native Newspaper Reports, Madras* State NNRMS, NAI.
17. *Suryodaya Prakasika*, 12 December 1900, NNRMS., NAI.
18. *The Nadegannadi*, 19 March 1901 and *Vrithanta Patrika*, 21 March 1901 hailed the appointment, NNRMS., NAI.
19. See *Malayala Manorama*, 2 March 1901 and 17 August 1901, 21 September 1903 NNRMS., NAI. and Malayali 29 June 1903, NNRMS NAI.
20. The examination was introduced in 1891 by Seshadri Iyer to counter charges of favouritism. However as it was open to the Madrasi also to compete, the early years of the examination returned mainly Madrasi Brahmins and thus became in itself an additional grievance. The grievance was all the more felt as Natives of states were not allowed to compete in the British Indian Civil Service Examination.
21. *Suryodaya Prakasika*, 11 September 1901, NNRMS., NAI
22. A note on the Maharaja and officials of Mysore State 1905-1906, sent by Resident, CRR. IOL, ACC5, NAI.
23. *Mysore Standard*, 8 May 1905, NNRMS., NAI. Dewan P.N. Krishnamurthy had his own supporting paper, the *Mysore Herald*, see 'A note on the Maharaja and officials of Mysore 1905-1906, CRR, IOL, ACC5, NAI.
24. *Suryodaya Prakasika*, 12 July 1905, NNRMS, NAI.
25. *Nazrani Dipika*, 14 June 1905, NNRMS,, NAI.
26. See *Kerala Patrika*, 30 June 1906, NNRMS., NAI.
27. *Malayali*, 12 January 1907, and *Suryodaya Prakasika*, 17 June 1907, NNRMS., NAI.
28. *Vrittanta Chintamani*, 19 June 1907, NNRMS., NAI.
29. *Mysore State*, 16 October 1905, NNRMS., NAI.
30. See *Statement of Object and Reasons*, to *the Mysore Press Law*, File No. 135/1908, Deposit 1, Foreign and Political Department, NAI.
31. Ibid.
32. *Swadesamitram*, 17 October 1905, NNRMS., NAI.
33. Ibid.
34. *Mysore State*, 16 October 1905, NNRMS., NAI.
35. *Suryodaya Prakasika*, 25 October 1905, NNRMS, NAI.
36. Extracts from 'A note on the Maharaja and officials of the Mysore State 1905-1906'. Crown Rep.esentative Records, (CRR) India Office Library (IOL), available in Microfilm, ACC 5, NAI. Emphasis supplied by the author.
37. Extracts from 'A note on the Maharaja and officials of the Mysore State 1906-1907', CRR, IOL, ACC 5, NAI. Emphasis supplied by the author.
38. Mysore's involvement in the British Indian movement of *Swaraj* was thus the main reason for the enactment of the Act. For an account

of their involvement and the necessity of the Press Act in that context see *post* pp. 50-51.

39. Of special significance, as Kolar was the main repository of Mysore's gold mines *Suryodaya*, 4 February 1907, NNRMS., NAI.
40. Statement of 'Subjects and Reasons' written by the Dewan while explaining and soliciting permission from the Government of India. File No 135/August 1908, Deposit 1, Foreign Department, NAI.
41. Dewan's speech in Legislative Council while introducing Bill, File No. 135/August 1908, Deposit 7, Foreign Department,NAI.
42. Ibid.
43. Note by Resident to Secretary, Foreign Department, 13 March 1907 CRR.,IOL,ACC 5, NAI.
44. Letter form Political Secretary to Resident 12 July 1908. File No. 135/ August 1908, Deposit 1, Foreign Department, NAI.
45. *Swadesamitram*, 11 August 1908, NNRMS., NAI.
46. The Bill prohibited the publication of any newspaper without the prior permission of the government. The permission could however be withdrawn by the government at any given time. For contravention of government rules, the editor could be punished with extradition and confiscation of the press.
47. *Jagadguru*, 9 August 1908, NNRMS., NAI.
48. *The West Coast Spectator*, 15 October 1908, NNRMS., NAI.
49. Ibid.
50. The discussions on the Press Law in 1908 was illustrative of the character of the two legislatures in Mysore. The Legislative Council enacted the law without a single dissenting vote—with even the non-official members voting with the government; on the other hand the Legislative Assembly showed an independent spirit in voting the two members in spite of government's action.
51. *The Hindu*, 15 October 1908; see also *Bharati*, 7 August 1908, *Jagadguru*, 9 August 1908, *The Kesari*, 12 August 1908, *The North Arcot Patriot*, 15 August 1908; *Vrittanta Chintamani*, 26 August 1908, NNRMS., NAI., *The Wednesday Review*, 12 August 1908, pointed out that in some respects, the clauses regarding punishment of offending editors and confiscation of the printing presses were much more stringent than those of the recent enactment of the Government of India.
52. During the tenure of Mr. Visvesvaraya as Dewan, the Act was amended in 1916, so as to permit the offender to have the privilege of a judicial enquiry. In 1922, the Dewan with the idea of repealing the Act and placing a milder regulation, placed it before the Legislative Assembly. The motion for repeal was however defeated. In 1929, the government acknowledged 'that there were some drastic provisions in it' and that they intended to introduce another enactment containing suitable modification. However, the Act remained as part of Mysore Statutory till the states integration in 1947.

    For a demand for repeal of this Act through the years, see *Patriot*,

12 December 1911, 1 March 1912, *Dhanwandhari*, 30 October 1913, *Sampadabhyudaya*, 29 March 1915, *The Indian Review*, 1920, p. 403. See also *Legislative Assembly Proceedings* May 1920, p. 114, October 1920, May 1921, October 1921, October 1927, p. 230, 18 October 1929, pp. 277-78.

53. *Malayali*, 9 February 1907, NNRMS., NAI.
54. He was Dewan of Cochin from 1896-1901 and of Travancore 1908-1914.
55. *Wednesday Review*, 27 November 1907. See also *Malayali*, 28 September 1907 NNRMS., NAI.
56. *Malabar Herald*, 8 October 1910, NNRMS., NAI.
57. *Kerala Patrika*, 15 October 1910, NNRMS., NAI.
58. *Malayali*, 28 September 1910, NNRMS, NAI.
59. Letter from Lord Minto to certain Ruling Chiefs. The Gazette of India Extraordinary 22 January 1910. Harcourt Butler Papers, India Office Library. Available in microfilm Roll 13, Sr. No. 66, NMML. Emphasis supplied by me.
60. This Act declared the security deposited as guarantee of good behaviour forfeit if any paper in British India contained, directly or through inference any allusion which was against His Majesty's government or any native prince.
61. *Kerala Patrika*, 15 October 1910, NNRMS., NAI.
62. Ibid. See also *Malabar Herald*, 7 March 1914, NNRMS., NMML.
63. See *Malayali*, 28 September 1910, *Malabar Herald*, 8 October 1910, *Kerala Patrika* 15 October 1910, *United India and the Native States*, 5 November 1910, NNRMS, NAI.
64. *United India and Native States*, 13 May 1911, NNRMS, NAI.
65. *United India and Native States*, 17 December 1910, NNRMS, NAI.
66. *Malayali*, 3 December 1910, NNRMS, NAI.
67. Ibid.
68. See *Sathianadam*, 3 April 1914. NNRMS, Available in microfilm, NMML.
69. *Swadeshamitram*, 16 November 1907, NNRMS, NAI.
70. Letter from Chief Secretary, Madras Government to Acting Resident, Travancore and Cochin, July 1911, G.O. No. 547/26 July 1911, p. 5, Tamil Nadu Archives (TNA)
71. Letters from the Dewan to the Resident, Travancore and Cochin States, 4 July 1911. G.O. No. 547/26 July 1911, p. 6, TNA.
72. In Cochin during these years, the presence of an outsider (in the sense that he was not from the Province of Madras) in A.R. Banerji made the enactment of a similar Press Act unnecessary. A Press Act was passed in this state only in 1921 following communal riots in Trichur.
73. See *Sadhvi*, 19 November 1912, NNRMS, NMML.
74. *Mysore Legislative Assembly Proceedings*, October 1888, p. 18.
75. *Mysore Legislative Assembly Proceedings*, October 1897, p. 73.
76. *Mysore Legislative Assembly Proceedings*, May 1921, p. 12. Dewan in an exposition of government support to backward castes.

77. The self-appointed Standing Committee of 22 members—12 from Bangalore city (from the Bangalore Rate Payer's Association), 8 from the districts and 2 Europeans, representing as it did a majority of urban elements and dominated by educated Mysore Brahmins, projected the Mysore Brahmin versus Madrasi Brahmin confrontation, already carried out in the press, on to the Assembly floor. Prominent among these members were M.C. Rangaiangar, an advocate from Mysore city, M. Venkatakrishnayya, a school master of Mysore and C. Srinivasa Rao a coffee planter. See note by Resident 1901, CRR, IOL, ACC 5, NAI.
78. *Mysore Legislative Assembly Proceedings*, 17 October 1888, p. 13.
79. The Regency administration of 1895 fearing that the standing Committee's virulence of attack was due to the personal animosity of the foreign Brahmin Dewan in Seshadri Iyer, had him replaced by a non-Brahmin Dewan. The new Dewan came to an understanding with the Standing Committee. In 1897, no elections were held in Mysore due to a virulent epidemic of plague, and ultimately, as the jubilant note of the Resident remarked, the plague intervened and swept off a pernicious movement, sweeping off all the most troublesome members. For a description of the Legislative Assembly Proceedings and Brahmin-non-Brahmin confrontation during this period, see the note by the Resident, 1901, CRR, IOL, ACC 5, NAI.
80. *Vrittanta Chintamani*, 1 August 1904, NNRMS, NMML.
81. During the period of foreign Dewans, V.P. Madhava Rao (1906-1909) and T. Ananda Rao (1909-1912), the old agitation against foreign Dewans came back into prominence.
82. *Mysore State*, 16 December 1912, NNRMS, NMML.
83. *Manifesto Issued by the Praja* Mitra *Mandali*, (undated, presumably December 1917). A copy of the Manifesto is available in file No. 48, p. 19, C.R. Reddy Papers (Private Collection list) NMML.
84. Memorandum placed before his Highness, the Maharaja of Mysore by Praja Mitra Mandali (undated, presumably late 1917 or 1918), File No. 10/1919, C.R. Reddy Papers, NMML.
85. Showing quite clearly the existence of cross communal alliances with British India.
86. Prominent among these meetings were those held in Bangalore on 30 May 1917, 18 November 1917, in Mysore on 2 November 1917, at Narasimharajapuram on 26 November 1917 Devangare (by the All India Lingayat Conference) on 28 November 1917.
87. Speech by Basaviah at a meeting in Bangalore, November 1917. File No. 48, C.R. Reddy Papers, NMML.
88. The Mysore Maharaja was often referred to as the 'Sudra' Maharaja and decision was taken only in 1928, after a voluminous correspondence on the issue, not to describe him as such in any official correspondence. For documents on this issue see file No. 60-P (Confdl.)/ 1928, Sr. No. 69, CRR, IOL, ACC 4, NAI.
89. Refer Government Order No. EAG-308, 23 August 1918. A copy of

the order is available in File No. 48, C.R. Reddy Papers, NMML. For actions taken by the Seal Committee on this Committee's recommendations, see post pp. 67-69.

90. M. Visvesvaraya as Dewan of Mysore, editorial *Justice*, 14 January 1918. Cutting available in C.R. Reddy Papers, NMML.
91. The same policy was adopted by a later Maharaja in 1940 in trying to get out of the hold of Mirza Ismail, when the Maharaja projected himself as sympathetic to the Congress cause. See *post* p. 223.
92. See *Sadhvi*, 17 January 1913, NNRMS, NAI.
93. Quoting from 'an extremist paper of Bombay', the *Justice* in an editorial, 11 December 1920.
94. *Daily Post*, 10 December 1918, quoting Visvesvaraya in its editorial. Cutting available in File No. 45, C.R. Reddy Papers, NMML.
95. *Kerala Mitram*, 1 February 1882, NNRMS, NAI.
96. *Malayali*, 9 March 1901, NNRMS, NAI.
97. The Ezhavas could find few representation in the legislature as the franchise was based mainly on property and thus favoured mainly the Nairs. See *ante* p. 19.
98. *Nazrani Dipika*, 7 February 1900, NNRMS, NAI.
99. *Malayala Manorama*, 10 February 1900, NNRMS, NAI.
100. *Kerala Mitram*, January 1884 and March 1884, NNRMS, NAI.
101. The promotion of such an association by Dr. Palpu reinforces the adage that personal grievances are the busiest promoter of popular causes. Dr. Palpu, while given a personal grant of Rs. 50 to prosecute his studies in medicine by the then Dewan, V.P. Madhava Rao and by the Travancore Maharaja, was not yet treated as a *bona fide* government sponsored scholar lest it became mandatory for the government to take him into its service. Denied employment in the medical department of the state he found service in Mysore and worked from that state to promote the Ezhava cause. For details see Jeffrey (Robin) '*Decline of Nair Dominance* (1847-1908)' (1971) p. 178, Ph. D thesis, University of Sussex (1973).
102. *Satyavadi*, 22 May 1905, NNRMS., NAI.
103. Ibid.
104. As yet, the government headed by a foreign Dewan had not aligned itself with either party. During the Nair agitation against Dewan Rajagopalachari in 1910 the Ezhava organisation held scrupulously away from any support to the agitation against the Dewan. For a greater elucidation on this see Jeffrey—*op. cit.*, It was only after the Congress declared itself as one with the Ezhavas that the combination of the government with Nair interests crystallised itself.
105. *Sujana Nandini*, 5 July 1905, NNRMS, NAI.
106. *Nazrani Dipika*, 25 April 1900, NNRMS, NAI.
107. *Kerala Sanchari*, 17 October 1900, NNRMS, NAI.
108. *See Swadeshamitram*, 9 August 1918, NNRMS, NMML and *Samadarsi*, 3 August 1918, NNRMS., NMML.
109. *Swadeshamitram*, 9 August 1918, NNRMS, NMML.

110. *Theental*, untouchability. See *Samadarsi*, 31 May 1919, NNRMS, NMML.
111. *Keralabhimani*, 5 November 1918, NNRMS., NMML,
112. For non-Brahmin substitute Ezhava-Nair for Travancore-Cochin.
113. To cite a few examples—P. Rajagopalachari was Dewan of Cochin (1896-1901) and of Travancore (1908-1915), V.P. Madhava Rao of Travancore (1904-1906) and of Mysore (1906-1909), A.R. Banerji of Cochin (1907-1914) and of Mysore (1922-1928).
114. *Chakravarti*, 2 October 1915, NNRMS, NMML.
115. I have extended the period upto 1921 in th's section of the chapter (though this chapter chronologically stops at 1919), mainly because there was no activity of the Congress in the states in the period 1914 to 1921, either in relation with the Maharaja or the states people or vice versa. If any inclusion or mention has been made of the post 1914 period, it has been done only to explain the reasons and motive of that policy.
116. *Indian Mirror*, 18 December 1887. Paper cutting CRR, IOL, ACC 5, NAI.
117. Letter from Sir H.N. Prendergast, Resident, Mysore State to W.J. Cunningham, Political Secretary, Government of India (GOI) 11 January 1888, CRR, IOL, ACC 5, NAI.
118. Noting by Political Office marked to W.J. Cunningham, Political Secretary, GOI, along with the paper cutting mentioned above, CRR, IOL, ACC 5, NAI.
119. Letter from Sir H.N. Prendergast to W.J. Cunningham, 11 January 1888, CRR, IOL, ACC 5, NAI.
120. Noting by Political Office marked to W.J. Cunningham, Political Secretary, alongwith paper cutting of the *Indian Mirror*, CRR, IOL, ACC 5, NAI.
121. Note from Sir Mackenzie Wallace, Secretary to the Viceroy, to W.J. Cunningham, Political Secretary, GOI, on H.E.'s, talks with Seshadri Iyer. The note is undated, CRR, IOL, ACC 5, NAI.
122. Ibid.
123. An obvious reference to Raja of Darbhanga.
124. Note from Sir Mackenzie Wallace, Secretary to Viceroy, to Political Secretary W.J. Cunningham, on H.E's talks with Seshadri Iyer. The note is undated; CRR, IOL, ACC 5, NAI.
125. *Vrittanta Chintamani*, 17 January 1894, NNRMS, NAI.
126. A.I.C.C. File No. 1/1885-1920, p. 55, Resolution No. 10, NMML.
127. See G.R. Josyer, *op. cit.*
128. Maharaja Krishnaraja Wadeyar (1902-1940). (1895-1902, the throne was managed under a Regency.)
129. Telegram from Resident, Mysore State, to H.E. the Viceroy, 15 December 1903, CRR, IOL, ACC 5, NAI.
130. Telegram from H.E. the Viceroy to Resident, Mysore State, 22 December 1903, CRR, IOL, ACC 5, NAI.
131. Telegram from Resident, Mysore State to H E. the Viceroy, 15

December 1903, CRR IOL, ACC 5, NAI.

132. Telegram from Resident, Mysore State to H.E. the Viceroy, 22 December 1903 CRR, IOL, ACC 5, NAI.
133. *Vrittanta Chintamani*, 17 January 1904, NNRMS, NAI.
134. *Nadegannadi*, 22 December 1905, NNRMS, NAI.
135. Ibid.
136. *Swadeshi*, 5 January 1907, NNRMS., NAI.
137. Letter from Resident, Mysore State to Political Secretary, 1 July 1908, File No. 135/August 1908, Deposit 1, NAI.
138. *Kerala Patrika*, 13 June 1908, NNRMS, NAI.
139. See *ante* pp. 34-37.
140. Letter from Lord Minto to certain Ruling Chiefs, 6 August 1908, Harcourt Butler Papers, Roll 13, Sr. No. 66, available in microfilm, NMML.
141. Letter from H.H. the Maharaja of Mysore to H.E. the Viceroy, 11 November 1909. Harcourt Butler Papers, Roll 13, Sr. No. 66, NMML.
142. *Madras Standard*, 29 August 1911, NNRMS, NMML.
143. Letter from V.S. Srinivasa Sastry to the Editor, *The Hindu*, 7 September 1911, NNRMS, NMML.
144. *Madras Standard*, 30 August 1911, NNRMS, NMML.
145. V.S. Srinivasa Sastri in a letter to the Editor, *The Hindu*, 7 September 1911, NNRMS., NMML.
146. *The Daily Post*, 6 September 1911, NNRMS., NMML.
147. According to G.R. Josyer, the Dewan's plea to his confidential Assistant who criticised his action, was a pitiable "if the Assistant knew all the facts of the banning he would agree with the action". (See G.R. Josyer—*op. cit.* pp. 249-250). A file indexed at NAI, with the intriguing title 'Circumstances under which Srinivasa Sastri's lectures in Mysore were prohibited' is unfortunately unavailable. (See Index F & P, October 1911, File No. 91, Deposit NAI).
148. Subsequent to the discovery of the secret press, the Gaekwad, (who had retained Aurobindo Ghose as his Secretary earlier) confessed to his relations with Madame Cama and Bipin Chandra Pal. The British administrators sought to deal firmly with him so as not to encourage the same 'spirit of disloyalty' elsewhere. The Maharaja was made to recant his association with the Congress publicly, and to express his disapprobation of sedition and seditious writing. Through a Hajur Order he was made to assert that the interests of the native states was bound irrevocably with British India and that all persons who conspired to subvert the government in one, equally offended against the other. See letter from Hardinge to the Secretary of State, 14 September 1911 and 21 September 1911. See also Hajur Order, 27 February 1912, [*The Statesman*, 5 March 1912, Hardinge Collection, items No. 59 and 162 respectively, IOL Roll 15, NMML.
149. *Sampada Abhyudaya*, 19 July 1917, NNRMS, NMML.

150. *Karnataka*, 1 September 1915, reporting a discussion with Congressmen, NNRMS., NMML.
151. V.S. Srinivasa Sastri—*The Future of Indian States.*
152. *Karnataka*, 1 September 1915, NNRMS., NMML.
153. The Aga Khan writing in the *Pall Mall Gazette*, 1920. Reprinted in *Indian Review*, February 1920, p. 139.
154. Letter from Minto to Morley, 28 May 1906. *India, Minto and Morley*, 1905-1910, Correspondence of Minto compiled by Mary, Countess of Minto, pp. 28-29.
155. Letter from Minto to Morley, 28 May 1906, *India, Minto and Morley, op. cit*, pp. 28-29.
156. Letter from Morley to Minto, 26 July 1907 and Minto to Morley, 31 July 1907, *India, Minto and Morley, op. cit.*, p 157.
157. Letter from Minto to Morley, 30 November 1908. *op. cit.*, p. 255.
158. See *ante* pp. 47-50 and p. 52.
159. Even the King approved of the plan. Refer letter from Lord Stamfordham (Private Secretary to the King) to Chelmsford, 22 August 1916 and 21 November 1916, Chelmsford Collection, IOL, Roll 1, NMML.
160. Letter from Chamberlain to Chelmsford, 24 November 1916. Chelmsford Collection, IOL, Roll 1, NMML.
161. The Governors of Punjab and Bombay opposed the plan. They felt that they were calling into existence a "formidable power", a sort of "Trade Union" of princes, likely to intrigue with political leaders in British India. See Chelmsford to Montagu, 29 January 1919, Chelmsford Papers, Vol. 3, p. 246, Roll 1, NMML.
162. The Viceroys speech, 30 October 1916, *Indian Review* November, 1916 p. 802.
163. Letter from Chamberlain to Chelmsford, 24 November 1916. Chelmsford Collection, IOL, Vol. 2, p. 315, NMML.
164. His friendship with the king dated from 1902 when he had been appointed as his A.D.C. As the King's protege he was subject to the King's badinage and favour. As for example, he was given the highest rank and seated next to the Queen; or again, had sent word through the Secretary of State to tell him that he much preferred him in his *pugree* than in his bowler hat adopted by him. See letter from Chamberlain to Chelmsford 23 March 1917, letter from Stamford to Chelmsford 14 April 1913, Chelmsford Collection, Vol. 12 and 1, p. 10 and p. 1 respectively, IOL, Roll 1, NMML. See also Karni Singh—*Relation of the House of Bikaner with the Central Powers* 1465-1949, p. 199.
165. His direct selection by the King created quite a few problems to the Secretary of State, for it had not only made his own position untenable, but the Nizam as the premier prince and as natural representative had to be given an explanation of some kind. A heavy price was paid for this open favour, as the Nizam feeling slighted refused to join the subsequent conferences of the princes. See letter from Chamberlain to Chelmsford, 10 January 1917. Chelmsford Collection, IOL, Vol. 3, p. 1, Roll 1, NMML.

166. In his memorandum submitted to the Imperial War Cabinet on 18 April 1917 Bikaner along with this request for a Council of Princes had urged for a formal and authoritative declaration of self-government for British India. Karni Singh and K.M. Panikkar make much of this memorandum but the underlying motive, as explained by Bikaner to Chamberlain, seems to have been not so much to promote the cause of the Indian nationalists as much as to establish his and other princes' *bona fides* in the eyes of British Indian Nationalists. Refer Karni Singh—op. cit. pp. 206-211. See Memorandum of Bikaner, 18 April 1917. Chelmsford Papers, IOL, Vol. 3, p. 80 and 104, Roll 1, NMML.
167. Letter from Chamberlain to Chelmsford, 8 May 1917. Chelmsford Collection, Vol. 3, p. 104, Roll 1, NMML.
168. Barbara Ramusack—*Indian Princes as Imperial Politicians*, p. 100, unpublished thesis for the University of Michigan, U.S.A., available in microfilm, NMML George Lloyd, the Governor of Bombay in criticism of Montagu's proposals, pertinently pointed out that such a Princes Council, whose functions were solely advisory and confined to matters of common concern was redundant, for apart from questions of honours and salutes they had hardly anything in common.
169. This conference among others, included Manubhai Mehta, Keshava Rao Jadhava, M Visvesvaraya, Daya Kishen Kaul, C.Y. Chintamani, Malaviya, V.S. Srinivasa Sastri, Chandavarkar, Sapru and others. Barbara Ramusack - *op., cit.* pp. 102-104.
170. *The Hindu*, 12 August 1907, NNRMS, NAI.
171. Ibid.
172. *Nadegannadi*, July 1907, NNRMS., NAI.
173. *Vrittanta Chintamani*, 21 August 1907, NNRMS, NAI.
174. See Chamberlain to Chelmsford, 8 May 1917, Chelmsford Papers, IOL, Vol. 3, p. 104, Roll 1, NMML.
175. See letter from George Lloyd, Governor of Bombay to Montagu, 19 May 1921, Montagu Collection, IOL, Vol. 26, pp. 39-42, NMML.
176. This Act passed in 1910, immediately after the Gaekwad's fiasco, made reciprocal provisions for the compulsory deposit being made forfeit for exciting disaffection towards any native prince or vice versa against British India. In 1921, while the provisions of the Press Act dealing with British India was repealed, the guarantees for the states was provided in a new States Protection Against Disaffection Act. This Act pressed for by the princes, (except for Gwalior, Dewas and four Bombay states) was passed, (with Sapru in the Press Committee dissenting) on 26 September 1922 and remained a part of British Indian statutary till Indian independence.
177. Letter from Chamberlain to Chelmsford, 8 May 1917, Chelmsford Collection, Vol. 3, p. 104, Roll 1, NMML.
178. Letter from George Lloyd to Montagu. 28 February 1918, Montagu Collection, Vol. 24, p. 29, NMML.
179. *Indian Review*, February 1919, p. 110.

180. Letter from Chelmsford to Montagu, 29 January 1919. Chelmsford Collection, Vol. 5, p. 17, Roll 1, NMML. See Letter from George Lloyd to Montagu, 2 July 1920, Vol. 25, pp. 55-65 and Montagu to George Lloyd, 24 November 1921, Vol. 23, pp. 83-90, Montagu Collection, NMML.
181. Letter from Chelmsford to Montagu, 31 March 1920, Chelmsford Collection, IOL, Vol. 6, p. 75, Roll 2, NMML.
182. Letter from George Lloyd to Montagu; 2 July 1919. Montagu Collection, IOL, Vol. 25, pp. 55-65, NMML.
183. Letter from Chelmsford to Montagu, 31 March 1920. Chelmsford Collection, IOL, Vol. 6, p. 75, Roll 2, NMML.
184. See *post* p. 94.
185. Letter from George Lloyd to Montagu, 2 July 1920, Montagu Collection, Vol. 2, pp. 64-65, Roll 1, NMML.
186. *Ibid.*
187. With this exception; C.P. Ramaswami Aiyar did, in the late 1930s and 1940's invoke the help of British paramountcy on this count mainly to stop Cochin providing a take off ground for agitations. See *post* p. 184, pp. 207-208, p. 217.
188. See *post* pp. 97-101.

CHAPTER 3

NOTES

1. Chelmsford to Montagu, 11 December 1919. Chelmsford Collection, IOL, Vol. 11, p. 485, Roll 4, NMML.
2. Pratt on behalf of Montagu in reply to a question by Terell, 25 June 1919. *Parliamentary Debates, Commons, Official Report,* Fifth Series, Vol. 117, p. 163.
3. His Highness the Maharaja of Alwar, July 1919. *Indian Review,* July 1919, p. 643.
4. To cite only a few, Baroda established a Legislative Council in 1908 and a Legislative Assembly in 1917, Bikaner a Legislative Council in 1917, Nawanagar and Hyderabad an Advisory Council in 1919. After 1919 Government of India Act, Dewas established a representative Assembly in 1922, Bhopal a Legislative Council in February 1922, Kashmir and Scindia, Legislative Assemblies in July and December 1922 respectively.
5. Chelmsford to Montagu, 11 December 1919. Chelmsford Collection, IOL, Vol. 11, p. 774, Roll 4, NMML.

6. Reading at a banquet given by Scindia of Gwalior, December 1922. *Indian Review* 1922, p. 82.
7. The Legislative Council consisted of 45 members, 30 elected and 15 nominated, with broad franchise, though based on properity qualification. However, to correct the imbalances of the backward communities, special representation was given to them. The Report on Constitutional Reforms in the Indian states sent by AGG Madras States (1927) File No. 585-P/1927, NAI.
8. Address by A.R. Banerji, 7 October 1922 recapitulating the course of reforms. Official Papers Connected with Constitutional Development in Mysore (1924), Karnataka State Archives (KSA).
9. Leslie Miller Committee Report, July 1919. See also annexure 3 to G.O. 1827-80, 16 May 1921, KSA.
10. See *ante* p. 42.
11. *Mysore Representative Assembly Proceedings*, October 1920.
12. Resolution proposed by N. Krishnia Sastry, October 1921. *Mysore Representative Assembly Proceedings*, October 1921, p. 119.
13. Resident's report to the Political Department, 30 August 1922 CRR, IOL, ACC 4, NAI.
14. Resolution passed by K.T. Seshaiya, October 1921. *Mysore Representative Assembly Proceedings*, October 1921, p. 121.
15. Resolution passed by C. Narasimhaiya, October 1921, *Mysore Representative Assembly Proceedings*, October 1921, p. 122.
16. Dewan's reply October 1921. *Mysore Representative Assembly Proceedings*, October 1921, p. 216.
17. See terms of Reference, Report of the Committee appointed to work out the details of the scheme for Constitutional Development in Mysore, (Published 15 March 1923).
18. At the same conference, as an overture to gain the support of the Maharaja, it was proposed that even the treaty rights and relations with British Government be brought under the purview of the Legislative Assembly. This was a clear offer to make the Rulers' grievances on the subsidy as their own. Fortnightly Report, 2 December 1922 CRR, IOL, ACC 4, NAI.
19. *Report of the Committee Appointed to work out the Details of the Scheme for Constitutional Development in Mysore*, p. 31, KSA.
20. *Ibid.* p. 53. Doing away with the secondary franchise of municipalities, Boards etc. which were the strongholds of Brahmins, it proposed primary election with franchise distributed on different scales. The strength of the Assembly was reduced from 288, urban constituencies getting 37 seats as against 163 for the rural. Special interests were given 15 while 35 seats were reserved for the minorities. The franchise worked up to 1 representative for every 33,000 in rural constituencies, while in the urban area it varied from 1 in 30,000 in Bangalore, 1 in 21,000 in Mysore to 1 in 8,000 from the 29 other town constituencies. The main point was Bangalore and Mysore, the stronghold of educated Brahmin elements were allotted only 4 seats each.

21. Minute of Dissent by Messrs. K. Chandy and K Matthan, Ibid. p. 207.
22. Ibid.
23. Note by Messrs. S. Venkatesayya and C. Srinivasa Rao, Ibid, p. 235.
24. Minute of Dissent by Messrs. K. Chandy and K. Matthan, Ibid. p. 208.
25. See *post*, pp. 81-85.
26. *Representative Assembly Proceedings*, Mysore, June 1926, Question 15.
27. See *post*, pp. 77-80.
28. *Representative Assembly Proceedings, Mysore*, October 1927, p. 128.
29. See *post* pp. 108-111.
30. Report of AGG., Madras States, 1927. File No. 525-P/1927, F & P, NAI, See *ante*, p. 20 for the powers which had been appropriated by the Legislative Council and the controversy over it.
31. Ibid.
32. The Maharaja's promulgation of 2 December 1920 enlarged the non-official elements to not less than 2/5ths with rights of interpellation, discussion of budget etc. However, the franchise was still based on property which still confined it to the Nair interests. While Mysore was on the right path of solving her communal problem on an equitable basis the reforms in Travancore Legislature only served to aggravate the exisling communal malaise.
33. See *post* pp. 150-153.
34. Letter from Jawaharlal Nehru to the Provincial Secretary, Indian States Peoples Conference, 2 November 1933. Jawaharlal Nehru Correspondence (JN Papers) Vol. 34, NMML.
35. Lynch Blosse to Residents, 1927. File No. 527-P/1927, NAI.
36. Answers to queries made by Captain Lal Awadesh Pratap Singh, Member, AICC. File No. G-27/1934, pp. 5-7, AICC Papers, NMML. Earlier too, the states people, had attended Congress meetings. (See *ante* pp. 48-50) But they had done so in their individual capacity and not as accredited members of Congress organisations from within the states.
37. Indian National Congress Resolution, 1920, clause VIII, Act V, File No. G-27/1934, AICC Papers, NMML.
38. See *ante* pp. 57-61, for British policy towards the states which prompted Congress to step in from 1921.
39. *Collected Works of Mahatma Gandhi*, December 1920, Vol. XIX, p. 192.
40. *Collected Works of Mahatma Gandhi*, 5 January 1921, Vol. XII, pp. 198-199. Emphasis supplied by me.
41. *Collected Works of Mahatma Oandhi*, 11 July 1920, Vol. XVIII, p. 36.
42. *Collected Works of Mahatma Gandhi*, 20 October 1920, Vol. XVIII, p. 36.
43. Letter from Resident, Mysore State to Political Secretary 25 August 1920. CRR, IOL, ACC 5, NAI.

44. Answers to queries made by Captain Lal Awadesh Pratap Singh, member, AICC. File No. G-27/1934, pp. 5-7, AICC Papers, NMML.
45. Resident to Chief Secretary, 25 June 1921, G.O. No. 302, 21 July 1922, Political Department, Tamil Nadu Archives (TNA).
46. *New India*, 28 February 1921. Paper cutting in G.O. No. 302, Political Department, 21 July 1922, TNA.
47. Ibid.
48. Resident to Chief Secretary, 25 June 1921, G.O. No. 302, Confdl Political Department, dated 21.7.22, TNA.
49. Ibid.
50. The later agitation of the Congress in Travancore in the period 1924-25 provides one with yet another example. However, coming as this did chronologically at a later date, it is narrated in subsequent pages. See *post* pp. 81-85.
51. *The Indian Review*, April 1921, p. 267.
52. See reports of the Resident on the Khilafat and non-cooperation movement in Mysore State upto middle of January 1922 dated 4 February 1922. CRR, IOL, ACC 4, NAI.
53. Ibid. See also the Resident's reports for second half of April 1922, CRR, IOL, ACC 4, NAI.
54. I have been unable to locate the article in *The Hindu* among the microfilm copies available at Madras. The reference is mainly from the Resident's report for the second half of March 1922 and April 1922, CRR, IOL, ACC 4 NAI.
55. Three paper's of Mysore, the *Sampada Abhyudaya*, the *Hilal* and the *Mysore Patriot* had been made in March 1922 a subject of a quasi-judicial enquiry on the Resident's complaint against them for print ng what he termed 'seditious articles against British Government'. *The Hindu* article had specially resented the confiscation of the pension of Venkata Krishnayya, the editor of *Sampada Abhyudaya*. The Government orders on the enquiry while holding that it would be justified to suppress these papers, nevertheless decided to take no action against them, which the Resident irritatedly characterised as evidence of a "lack of nerves". Refer *The Hindu*, March 1922, Residents Reports for March 1922 and 18 October 1922, CRR, IOL, ACC 4, NAI.
56. Resident's report, second half of June 1922, CRR, IOL, ACC 4, NAI. See also the account of the publication of Mysore Conference.
57. Letter to the editor from Setlur, President, Bangalore City Congress Committee, *The Hindu*, 20 November 1922. See also Residents report for first half of December 1922. CRR, IOL, ACC 4, NAI.
58. When Setlur asserted that "in Mysore . . . there can be no question of non-cooperation" he meant that the extension of a British Indian aqitation on a non-cooperation programme in the states was not workable. Even Gandhiji and Mohtal Nehru had their reservations on it (see ante p. 74 and pp. 76-77). James Manor, has misunderstood this ass(rtion of Sethur's as an unwillingness of a patrician gentlemen

to engage himself in the rough and tumble of an active programme! (See James Manor op. cit. p. 75).

59. See *post* pp. 154-156
60. Resolution of the Working Committee, AICC with reference to S. Setlur's letter in *The Hindu* of November 1922, 1 January 1923. File No. G-27/1924 AICC Papers, NMML.
61. The Dewan in November 1922 was forced into giving an assurance to the Resident that steps would be taken to make it impossible for British Indian 'seditionists' to address political meetings. However, the administration was unable to stop these meetings and was the cause of the Resident's complaints. See Resident's reports for December 1922 and D/O letter of the Dewan to the Resident, December 1922, CRR, IOL, ACC 4, NAI.
62. The Mysore Congress in a resolution passed at this time, while expressing itself as ready to co-operate with the authorities in avoiding all causes of embarrassment to the administration, affirmed its right to call publicists from British India for carrying on their constructive programme. See Resolution passed by the Mysore Congress, 9 September 1923. File No. 62/3 R VIII, Collection of the History of Freedom Movement Unit, NAI.
63. Resident's report for April, May 1923, CRR, IOL, ACC 4, NAI.
64. It is James Manor's misunderstanding of the nature of the two organisations which has led him into erroneous assertions – firstly, that there were several organisations in Mysore, antagonistic to each other and secondly, to have misunderstood the INC resolutions on the name 'Mysore Congress' following Haripura resolution on the states. There would have been no objection from the INC had the word 'state' been interposed in the name 'Mysore Congress' working on the state's people's programme of responsible government. See James Manor, op. cit., p. 74 and p. 108, and for my explanation, see *post*, pp. 155-156
65. See Resident's Report, July 1923, August 1923 and September 1923, CRR, IOL, ACC 4, NAI.
66. The Civil and Military Station was under the control and jurisdiction of the Resident. For accounts of the Mysore Congress and Mysore State Congress in this phase when they carried on political activities under guise of Bhajan parties see account of a Mysore Congressman available in File No. 60/3 R VIII, Collection of History of Freedom Movement Unit, NAI.
67. Resident's report, July 1923, CRR, IOL, ACC 4, NAI.
68. As a result of this apology the Mysore Congress was allowed to observe Gandhi Day on 18 September 1923. See Resident's report, September 1923, CRR, IOL, ACC 4, NAI.
69. Resident's report, second half of October 1923, CRR, IOL, ACC 4, NAI.
70. Resident's report, second half of April 1924, CRR, IOL, ACC 4, NAI.
71. Resident's report, first half of October 1923, CRR, IOL, ACC4, NAI.

72. Resident's report, first half of October 1924, CRR, IOL, ACC 4, NAI.
73. Ibid.
74. Gandhiji at the Kathiawad Political Conference, January 1925. *The Indian States Problem* by M.K. Gandhi, pp. 8-9, published in *Young India* of January 1925.
75. Gandhiji in a personal explanation to Jamnalal Bajaj, in *Young India* on 23 July 1925. Jamnalal Bajaj had proposed a motion at the Working Committee meeting, to form an Inquiry Committee feeling that it was unwise to break the tradition of non-interference. *The Indian States Problem*, by M.K. Gandhi, pp. 47-48.
76. Ibid. It is pertinent to remark that there was an element of consistency in this policy up to 1947.
77. Gandhi in an interview to *The Hindu*, 15 April 1924, published in *The Hindu*, 17 April 1924. See *Collected Works of Mahatma Gandhi*, Vol. XXIII, p. 440.
78. See K.P. Kesava Menon's letter to Gandhi, 24 April 1924, where he wrote "we are treated as state prisoners. A separate block is set apart for us . . . books and newspapers are also allowed . . . we receive from the (police) the same polite treatment as we received from the police officers at Vaikom". Published *Young India*, see The *Collected Works of Mahatma Gandhi*, Vol. XXIII, p. 477. See also letter of G.W. Sebastian to Mahatma Gandhi, quoted by him, Vol. XXIV, p. 50.
79. Report of the Agent to the Governor General (AGG Madras) to Secretary, Foreign and Political Department, 21 April 1924, File No. 77 Political/1924, NAI.
80. See letter from K.P. Kesava Menon (Secretary KPCC) to Mahatma Gandhi, 12 March 1924. *Collected Works of Mahatma Gandhi*, Vol. XXIII, Appendix IX, p. 561. See also Report of the AGG Madras to Political Secretary, File No. 77-Pol./1924, NAI.
81. The local unit conducting the agitation was the Untouchability Committee of the Kerala Pradesh Congress Committee which held its inaugural meeting on 29 February 1924 and was attended by K.P. Kesava Menon, A.K. Pillai, T.K. Madhavan, and other prominent members of the S.N.D.P. Yogam.
82. Letter from Gandhi to Kesava Menon, 19 March 1924, *Collected Works of Mahatma Gandhi*, Vol. XXII, p. 272.
83. Originally, at the meeting of 29 February 1924 it had been proposed to start the demonstration on 1 March 1924, which was, however, postponed at the request of some members in order to canvas public opinion.
84. Letter from AGG to Political Secretary, File No. 77-Pol/1924, NAI.
85. Telegram from K.P. Kesava Menon, 1 April 1924. The *Collected Works of Mahatma Gandhi*, Vol. XXIII, text as a footnote. See also letter of AGG to Political Secretary, File No. 77-Pol/1924, NAI.
86. This he explained on the score of untouchability being the sin of the Hindus; it was only their suffering which could convert the hearts of

orthodoxy. The only exception to this rule was made in the case of George Joseph who led the agitation on 6 April 1924 even before Mahatma Gandhi's instructions on this had reached. See letter from Gandhi to K.M. Panikkar 10 April 1924, Gandhi to George Joseph, 6 April 1924. *The Collected Works of Mahatma Gandhi*, Vol. XXII and XXIII, p. 410 and p. 391 respectively. See also Vaikom Satyagraha, *Young India*, 1 May 1924, *op. cit.*, Vol. XXIII, pp. 66-68, and 20 May 1924, op. cit., Vol. XXIV, p. 94.

87. There were over a 100 on the waiting list for martyrdom according to the Resident. See letter from AGG Madras state to Chief Secretary, Madras, 10 April 1924 and 21 April 1924. G.O. No. 151, 30 August 1924, Political Department, TNA. See also Gandhi's interview to API, 13 April 1924. *The Collected Works of Mahatma Gandhi*, Vol. XXIII, p. 437.

88. Gandhi suggested a way out to counteract Travancore police tactics. He suggested that they drop fasting and conduct the agitation in relays. See telegram from George Joseph to Gandhi, 11 April 1924, telegram from Gandhi to George Joseph 11 April 1924. *The Collected Works of Mahatma Gandhi*, Vol. XXIII, p. 419.

89. Interview to *The Hindu*, 15 April 1924, published on 17 April 1924.

90. See T.K. Ravindran, *Vaikom Satyagraha and Gandhi*, p. 87 for appeals by the satyagrahis and Gandhi's refusal. Gandhi did depute C. Rajagopalachari who advised fasting as a measure of compulsion which was, however, refused by Mahatma Gandhi who had his own reservations. He felt that fasting used against a Maharaja in a native state would compel him to yield which he did, not because he was convinced of the evil but because he could not bear to see the death of a subject. The same conditions however did not stop him from fasting at a later period, against Rajkot! See Gandhi to C. Rajagopalachari's telegram, 15 April 1924, op. cit. Vol. XXIII, p. 443, and Interview to Vaikom deputation 20 May 1924, op. cit. Vol. XXIV, p. 90.

91. The Congress camps met a series of setbacks when smallpox broke out in the Congress satyagraha camp and the long stalemate made the KPCC lose its initial enthusiasm, especially so, through a lack of funds. See letter from Vaikom satyagrahis, quoted by Gandhi in *Young India*, 19 February 1925, op. cit., Vol. XXVI, p. 158.

92. Gandhi in an article in *Young India*, September 1925, op. cit., Vol. XXV, p. 115.

93. Of the 35 non-officials, 21 had voted with the Congress, 2 stood neutral, 7 against and the rest had been absent. Thus, the measure had been defeated mainly with the help from government nominees, of which a member of the depressed class himself had voted against entry. See Mahatma Gandhi quoting a letter of a satyagrahi, 19 February 1925 and 21 February 1925, op. cit., Vol. XXVI, pp. 158, and 198 respectively.

94. See *The Hindu*, 14 March 1925, op. cit., Vol. XXVI, p. 304. See also

the Dewan's speech at Vaikom, reprinted as an Appendix, op. cit., Vol. XXVI, p. 579.

95. See *ante* p. 45.
96. See *ante* pp. 72-84 for the Indian National Congress entry into these states and their activities.
97. The first session was convened at Poona by N.C. Kelkar and A.V. Patwardhan, See a "Short Report of the Daxini Sansthan Hitavardhak Sabha", 25 May 1921. File No. AP 29/1928, pp. 121-125, AICC Papers, NMML.
98. The President's speech at the Deccan Natives States Subjects Conference, May 1922. Reported in the *Indian Review*, June 1922, p. 417.
99. Speech by N.C. Kelkar at the Indian States People's Conference, December 1924. See *Indian Quarterly Register*, compiled by Mitra, December 1924, Vol. II, Mahatma Gandhi in the post 1924 period did take an active interest in such conferences, especially that of Kathiawad at which he presided and addressed (See M.K. Gandhi—*The Indian States Problem*, pp. 8-9 and pp. 49-52.)
100. Memorandum presented by the deputation of the Indian States Peoples Conference to the Indian States Committee, 19 November 1928. File No. 62-Spl/1931, F & P, NAI.
101. Political Department's noting to the Political Secretary, 7 November 1928. File No. 62-Spl/1931, F & P, NAI.
102. Memorandum presented by the deputation of the ISPC to the Indian States Committee, 19 November 1928. File No. 62-Spl/1921, F & P, NAI.
103. Ibid.
104. Article 14, resolution passed at the Third Kerala Provincial Conference, 26 April 1927. *The Indian Quarterly Register*, Vol. 1, p. 409.
105. Resolution proposed by Manilal Kothari and carried unanimously at the Indian National Congress Session, Madras, 28 December 1927. *The Indian Quarterly Register*, Vol. II, p. 411.
106. Satyamurti's speech, see *The Indian Quarterly Register*, Vol. II, p. 411.
107. For the *Swaraj Constitution* proposals see *post* p. 92.
108. For the All Parties Conference proposals see *post* pp. 93-94.
109. Letter from Lytton to Birkenhead, 2 July 1925. Quoted by him from Birkenhead's report of the Proceedings of his eighth conference with Reading on 29 May 1925. Birkenhead Collection, IOL, Vol. 3, Roll 1, NMML.
110. Letter from Irwin to Birkenhead, 28 April 1926. Birkenhead Collection, IOL, Vol. 4, p. 28, NMML.
111. Letter from Irwin to Birkenhead, 26 May 1926. Birkenhead Collection, IOL, Vol. 4, p. 47, Roll 1, NMML.
112. Letter from Irwin to Harcourt Butler, 22 May 1927. Harcourt Butler Collection IOL, Vol. 61, Roll 13, NMML. The three states of my study were mainly concerned with the economic problem. The problem of 'safeguards' played a minor part, as was clear in their

demands at the Round Table Conference as well as in their conditions for entry into a federation. See *post* pp. 101-104.

113. Hosakappa Krishna Rao, *Swaraj Constitution*; Introduction to the Constitution, was approved by the All India Subjects Conference, Madras, and published on 8 May 1928. (Copy available in AICC Subjects File, File No. 101/1924-32, NMML). The report was published before the publication of the Indian States Committee Report, and had its own interpretation of the Indian States Committee. *Report of the Indian States Committee* claimed that it was set up to examine the relationship existing between the state and the paramount power, but was in truth otherwise. See *post* p. 94. See also the above Report, p. 5.

114. Ibid.

Chapter 4

NOTES

1. S. Srinivasa Iyengar, *Swaraj Constitution*. See introdution to the book, p. x. Available in Theosophical Society Library, Adyar, Madras.
2. The constitutional proposals for the states followed one upon the other in 1928-29. S. Iyengar's proposal was followed by that of Hosakappa Krishna Rao's Written on behalf of SISPC it was an answer to the above proposal and the *Report of the All Parties Conference*, (giving the Indian National Congress' view). Visvesvaraya's proposals, giving the SISPC amendments on the earlier proposal was published in January 1929 and that of the Butler Committee in March-April 1929. There were various schemes proposed by the princes themselves, prominent among which were, Akbar Hydari's scheme on behalf of Hyderabad, Mirza Ismail's on behalf of Mysore, Patiala-Dholpur scheme on behalf of a faction of the Princes Chamber, Nawanagar's on behalf of the other faction, etc., which came up in the wake of proposals for a federation in the 1930s.
3. S. Srinivasa Iyengar, op. cit., introduction, p. x. See also p. 4 and

pp. 27-28.

4. Hosakappa Krishna Rao, op. cit., introduction, p. XIV.
5. Ibid., p 16.
6. The interesting solution to the question of paramountcy supplied by the SISPC was the very one adopted by the British Government on the eve of the transfer of power in its declaration that paramountcy lapsed on the British leaving India.
7. The princes under the tutelage of the Political Department, however, refused to participate in the conference. The Political Department, which feared for the 'intellectual capacity of the Princes' in dealing with British Indian politicians, camouflaged its sentiments well in a note to the princes where it was merely pointed out that the princes could in no way curtail their dignity or agree to sit as equals to their subjects in a conference. See letters from Wilberforce Bell to Glancy, 30 August 1928, Glancy to Wilberforce, 31 August 1928. File No. 193-R/1929, F & P, NAI.
8. While making these lavish concessions to the princes, it however took care to safeguard its particular interests. It asserted that it could not accept any one sided arrangement by which the princes could hope to influence the policy of legislation in the Indian legislature without submitting themselves to common legislation, nor would it accept the position that it was obligatory for the British Government to remain in India, to protect the prince's Treaty Rights. See *Report of the All Parties Conference*, pp. 72-73 and pp. 85-86.
9. Ibid., pp. 83-84.
10. It was as a result of the recognition of the princes as the sole legal authority in the states that Visvesvaraya's constitution amended its definition of responsible government. To bridge the gap between the now legally accepted, irremovable executive it proposed that the chief minister be selected by the prince and be responsible to him. The other ministers, chosen by the legislature, were to be appointed by the ruler, on the chief minister's recommendation. The Dewan was to be 'responsive' to the other ministers ruling, A report of the SISPC under Visvesvaraya's Presidentship, sent by A. Padmanabha Iyer, 22 January 1929, Mirza Ismail Papers, NMML.
11. Ibid., p. 72,
12. For the origin of this committee see *ante* pp. 87-88.
13. For a greater elucidation on this point see the article by the author on *The Butler Committee Report—A Reappraisal.* For a cross correspondence to illustrate this issue see, among others, letters from Irwin to Harcourt Butler, 22 May 1927, Harcourt Butler Collection, IOL, Vol. 61, Roll 13, NMML; Irwin to Birkenhead 25 May 1926, 30 June 1926, Birkenhead Collection, IOL, Vol. 4, p. 47 and p. 72 respectively, Roll 1, NMML; and Irwin to Birkenhead, 15 September 1927 and 29 February 1928, Harcourt Butler Collection, IOL, Vol. 5, p. 114, Roll 2 and Sr. No. 85, Roll 16, NMML, See also Birkenhead to Irwin, 15 December 1927, Halifax Collection, IOL, Vol. 2, pp. 138-139, Roll 1;

and 23 March 1928, Harcourt Butler Collection, IOL, Sr. No. 85, Roll 16, NMML.

14. *Report of the Indian States Committee*, p. 31.
15. In this, both the Viceroy and Harcourt, frankly acknowledged in their private correspondence, that this new theory was hardly in accordance with practice. As Butler pointed out, when the princes were deprived hitherto, of their powers, they had been deposed by an order of the Governor General in Council. See Harcourt Butler to Irwin, 30 October 1927, Harcourt Butler Collection, Vol. 61, Roll 13, NMML. For Irwin's agreement with Butler, see letter from Governor General in Council to Birkenhead, 15 September 1927, Harcourt Butler Collection, Sr. No. 85, Roll No. 16, NMML.
16. See *ante* p. 59.
17. *Report of the Indian States Committee*, p. 7.
18. *The Report of the All Parties Conference*, p. 86.
19. Letter from J. Simon to the Prime Minister, 15 October 1929, and amendment by Irwin, 31 October 1929. File No. 193-R/1929, F & P, NAI.
20. Letter from Irwin to Secretary of State, 5 November 1929, File No. 193-R/1929, F & P, NAI. For reasons of this callous treatment of the states people by the Indian National Congress, see *post* pp. 97-101.
21. Letter from Secretary of State to Irwin, 13 November 1929, File No. 193-R/1929, F & P, NAI.
22. Letter from Irwin to Secretary of State, 5 November 1929, File No. 193-R/1929, F & P, NAI.
23. Letter from Secretary of State to Irwin, 15 November 1929, File No. 193-R/1929, F & P, NAI.
24. Interview to the Associated Press of India by Maharaja of Bikaner, 2 November 1929, *The Times of India*, 3 November 1929. See also speech by Maharaja of Bikaner at Assembly, 19 December 1929, File No. 193-R/1929, F & P, NAI.
25. See Mani Shankar Trivedi's reply to Bikaner, *The Hindustan Times*, 6 January 1930. The Working Committee resolution of ISPC, 16 November 1929, File No. 193-R/1929, F & P, NAI; and letter from K.T. Mathew, General Secretary SISPC to Viceroy, 2 June 1930, File No. 62-Spl/1929, F & P, NAI.
26. Telegram from K.T. Mathew to Viceroy, 23 October 1928 and 5 November 1929, Files No. 193-R/1929 and 62-Spl/1931, F & P, NAI. See also the pamphlet, *The Work Done by the ISPC in England*, and printed pamphlet issued by the ISPC in September 1929, *The London*, 4 September 1929.
27. Question by Rennie Smith, 2 December 1929. Parliamentary Debates, Commons, Official Report, fifth series, Vol. 232, Question 10, pp. 1893-94.
28. Letter from Mani Shankar Trivedi to Ramsay MacDonald, 7 December 1929, File No. 193-R/1929, F & P, NAI. See also memorandum submitted by Abhyankar on behalf of the ISPC to the Government

of India, where he pointed out the dichotomy in British approach. Here a conference convened to carry out a pledge to grant responsible government, sought to exclude the peoples representatives while including the princes, who were not even concerned with the term responsible government, File No, 62-Spl/1931, F & P, NAI.

29. The southern states had a proliferation of these organisations during this period. The All India States Subjects Conference—a branch of the ISPC—and the SISPC merged to form an Indian States Peoples Federation in Bangalore in September 1930. See letter from K.T. Mathew, 8 September 1930. For the resolution passed by these organisations see resolution passed by All India States Subjects Committee, Cochin, 2 June 1930; and letter from K.T. Mathew, general secretary to the South Indian States Peoples Conferences, 25 June 1930. All are available in File No. 62-Spl/1931, F & P, NAI.
30. Letter from G.R. Abhyankar to Viceroy, 15 November 1930, File No. 62-Spl/1931, F & P, NAI.
31. Note by Political Secretary, 23 November 1930, File No. 62-Spl/1931, F & P, NAI.
32. See letter from W.D. Croft, India Office to Cunningham, Private Secretary to Lord Snell, 16 April 1931, File No. 62-Spl/1931, F & P, NAI.
33. James Manor by attaching importance to the word 'so-called' has inferred that the states organisation lacked credibility in its initial stages, op. cit.
34. *White Paper on the Indian States*, published by the Ministry of State, Government of India (1930 , p. 16.
35. Ibid.
36. *The Report of the All Parties Conference*, p. 73.
37. Report of the Committee appointed by the AICC to revise Congress constitution, 25 October 1928. File No. G-27/1928, p. 2, paragraph 8, AICC Papers, NMML. See *ante* p. 87.
38. Report of the Committee appointed by the AICC to revise Congress constitution, 25 October 1928. File No. G-27/1928, p. 2, paragraph 7, AICC Papers, NMML.
39. Letter from K.T. Mathew, Secretary of All India States Subjects Committee, 14 May 1928. File No. G-27/1928, p. 87, AICC Papers, NMML.
40. Suggested amendments by Karnataka Pradesh Congress Committee on Article VIII, 20 April 1928. File No. G-27/1928, pp. 129-130, AICC Papers, NMML.
41. Ibid. See also letter from Hosakappa Krishna Rao to Jawaharlal Nehru, 1 April 1928, File No. G-27/1928, pp. 191-193, AICC Papers, NMML.
42. See resolution passed at the Indian National Congress, 1 January 1929 The *Indian Quarterly Register*, Vol. II, p. 372. For a full text, see letter from Kothari, Secretary, Indian States Subjects Association to K.T. Mathew, Secretary, Indian States Subjects Conference, 23 January 1929. File No. G-110/1929-30, p. 5, AICC Papers, NMML.

43. Ibid.
44. Sardar Patel defending the resolution on the states proposed at the Working Committee of the AICC at Wardha, 17 October 1935, *The Indian Half Yearly Register*, Vol. II, pp. 277-278.
45. Resolution passed by the Working Committee of the Indian States Peoples Conferences, 16 November 1929. File No. 193-R/1929, F & P, NAI.
46. C. Rajagopalachari referred to the states people as "the real untouchables, they had no rights, they had only duties". Yusuf Meherally's speech, Madras session of the INC, 17 October 1935. *The Indian Half Yearly Register*, Vol. II, p. 277.
47. See *post*, pp. 125-128.
48. Resolution passed by the Working Committee of the Indian States Peoples Conference, 16 November 1929. File No. 193-R/1929, F & P, NAI.
49. Statement of the Chancellor of the Princes at the meeting of the Chamber of Princes, 25 March 1933, file No. 89-R/1933, F & P, NAI.
50. As early as November 1931, the Viceroy had suggested that the Secretary of State give the "*hookum*" on a "general advance on British India alone". This the Secretary of State refused as he felt that the princes were the "only safe body" who could "steady the ship of federation" and unless there was an all-India Federation "any hope of British Indian federation was out of question". See Willingdon to Samuel Hoare, 30 November 1931, Samuel Hoare to Willingdon, 30 November 1931 and 28 January 1932, Templewood Collection, IOL, Vol. V, p. 36 and p. 72, Roll 2, NMML.
51. These demands revolved round Leslie Scott proposals (a) relations to be conducted by the Viceroy, (b) not reading the treaties as interrelated whole, (c) succession to be settled by dynastic laws, and (d) the desputes between the princes and the paramount power to be settled by arbitration. The variations on the princes schemes were conditioned by the position they occupied in 'Indian India' as a whole. Hydari, on behalf of Hyderabad, proposed that the Chamber of Princes be replaced by a Council of Princes with one vote to each of the princes up to 17 guns and segregation of the activities of British India from the states. For joint consultations they were to meet in a federal council of 72, consisting of 36 British Indian representatives, 24 state representatives and 12 Crown nominees. Bikaner proposed individual membership at the Federal Chamber. These proposals infuriated the smaller princes and Patiala-Dholpur on behalf of them proposed "collective bargaining" by an elective standing Committee of Princes. See R.J. Moore, op. cit., pp. 227-228. See also letter from Viceroy to Samuel Hoare, 21 January 1935, Templewood Collection, Vol. 18, pp. 625-626, Roll 3, NMML.
52. Tej Bahadur Sapru, quoted by R. Coupland, op. cit., p. 118.
53. The Special committee of ministers was appointed by the Standing Committee of the Chamber of Princes and had as its Chairman C.P.

Ramaswami Aiyar. The other members were Prabhashanker Pattani, K.M. Panikkar, Rushbrooke Williams and Maqbool Mahmood. Mysore and Cochin do not seem to have exhibited much interest in this committee.

54. The report of the special Committee of Ministers, 27 March 1933. File No. 89-R/1833, F & P, NAI.
55. The White Paper had stipulated that while no statutory expression to any large range of declarations towards fundamental rights was needed, some provisions, as respect due to personal liberty, rights of property, eligibility of all for public office, etc. could and should find a place in the constitution Act. Refer *The White Paper Proposals for Indian Constitutional Reform* (1933), p. 29. See also statement of Bikaner as Chancellor of the Chamber of Princes, on White Paper Proposals at its meeting on 25 March 1933. File No. 89-R/1933, F & P, NAI.
56. See R.J. Moore, op. cit., pp. 138-139.
57. Refer views of Durbars and Political officer's on the question of intervention. File No. 2-Spl/1933, F & P, NAI.
58. Even as early as 1887 its irritation over the subsidy issue had made it seek the Indian National Congress collaboration. See *ante* p. 48. *Mysore Legislative Assembly Proceedings*, 11 June 1932, pp. 236-245.
59. Ibid.
60. Davidson Committee appointed by the Round Table Conference was instructed to report on the obtaining of contribution to Federal finance from its different units on a uniform basis as far as was possible.
61. Dewans address to the Mysore Legislative Assembly, 10 October 1932. *Mysore Legislative Assembly Proceedings*, October 1932, pp.3-5.
62. Letter from Willingdon to Samuel Hoare, 5 February 1933. Templewood Collection, Vol. 6, p. 240, Roll 2, NMML.
63. Telegram from Resident to Viceroy, 24 January 1933. CRR, IOL, ACC 4, NAI. The question of retrocession of the ceded territories had followed Hyderabad's bargaining on the Berar question.
64. *The Hindu*, 30 October 1937.
65. Letter from R. Krishna Aiyar to the President Indian National Congress, 2 November 1937. File No. G-88/1937, p. 387, AICC Papers, NMML.
66. Letter from Jawaharlal Nehru to R. Krishna Aiyar, November 1937. File No. G-88/1937, p. 389, AICC Papers, NMML.
67. See *post* p. 110, p. 112 and note 101.
68. Letter from R. Krishna Aiyar, 2 November 1937. File No. G-88/1937, AICC Papers, NMML.
69. Dewan's address, Cochin Legislative Council, 29 July 1935, *Legislative Council Proceedings*, Cochin, 1935, p. 3. See also report on the attitude of the Indian states towards federation, sent by AGG, Madras State, 4 June 1936. File No. 64-Spl/1936, F & P, NAI.
70. Minutes of the Informal Conference of Rulers and Representatives

held at Viceroys House, 14 March 1933. File No. 89R/1953, F & P, NAI.

71. Letter from the Maharaja of Travancore to Willingdon, 8 February 1935. See also letter from C.P. Ramaswami Aiyar to Willingdon, 1 April 1935. Templewood Collection, Vol. 8, p. 644, 706 respectively, Roll 3, NMML.
72. Report on the Indian States to Federation, Report by AGG, Madras State, 4 June 1936. File No. 64-Fed/1936, F & P, NAI.
73. Letter from Samuel Hoare to Willingdon, quoting the *Times* report, 24 May 1935. Templewood Collection, Vol. 4, p. 1301, Roll 2, NMML.
74. Resident's report, December 1928, CRR, IOL, ACC 4, NAI.
75. Resident's Report, 7 April 1928, CRR, IOL, ACC 4, NAI.
76. Harindranath Chattopadhyaya in December 1928 and Gangadhararao Deshpande in November 1928, though invited by the Mysore State Congress, confined their speeches to Congress' constructive activities, See CRR. IOL, ACC 4, NAI.
77. Resident's report quoting Vallabhbhai Patel's speech, 1 October 1929. File No. 17/Poll/1929, H & P, NAI.
78. Resident's report quoting Vallabhbhai Patel's speech, 8 October 1929, File No. 17/1929, H & P, NAI.
79. Speech by the Dewan, *Mysore Legislative Assembly Proceedings*, 13 June 1930, p. 13.
80. Letter from Willingdon to Samuel Hoare, 17 December 1933. Templewood Collection, Vol. 7, p. 433, Roll 3, NMML.
81. See note handed to the Resident by the Dewan of Mysore, 17 August 1927. File No. 197-R/1927, F & P, NAI.
82. Notification issued in the Travancore Gazetteer, 10 January 1928. File No. DR 2/1928, H & P, NAI.
83. Resident's Report, 18 January 1929, File No. 17/1929, H & P, NAI.
84. Resident's Report, 31 January 1929, File No. 17/1929, H & P, NAI.
85. In December 1929, in face of the open sympathies of the Bangalore District Congress Committee to the states people's agitation against the Press Regulation, the old press Regulation "which was so stringent" was modified, allowing the editor to appeal to a chief Court.
86. Resident's report, 19 April 1929, File No. 17/1929, H & P, NAI.
87. Resident's report, 17 October 1929, File No. 17/1929, H & P, NAI.
88. Resident's report, 21 May 1929, File No. 17/1929, H & P, NAI.
89. See Resident's report, 21 May 1929, File No. 17/1929, H & P, NAI.
90. Resolutions passed by the Mysore State Congress, 5 May 1929.
91. Resident's report, 13 February 1930, CRR, IOL, ACC 4, NAI.
92. Resident's report, 2 March 1930, CRR, IOL, ACC 4, NAI.
93. Resident's report, 4 March 1930, CRR, IOL, ACC 4, NAI.
94. Resident's report, 20 March 1930, CRR, IOL, ACC 4, NAI.
95. Resident's report, April 1930, CRR, IOL, ACC 4, NAI.
96. Resident's report, 1 May 1930, CRR, IOL, ACC 4, NAI.
97. Resident's report, 16 May 1930, CRR, IOL, ACC 4, NAI.

98. The State Government allowed the meetings, hartals and other propaganda on Gandhi's arrest, Jawaharlal Nehru's arrest, on the death of Bhagat Singh, etc. See reports of 2 December 1930, 17 April 1931, CRR, IOL, ACC 4, NAI.
99. See *post* p. 172.
100. See letter from K.T. Bhashyam and N.S. Ramaswami, general secretaries, Bangalore District Congress Committee on special deputation to Mahatma Gandhi, 7 July 1931 File No. G-145/1931, pp. 51-57, AICC Papers, NMML.
101. This venue was chosen mainly to beat the ban on such ceremonies within the city limits. These gimmicks, as well as its endeavour to open a branch of the Bangalore DCC in the cantonment area, was to provide for alternative sites in case of bans on Congress activities. (For such instances see the Resident's report for July 1930 and 29 August 1931, CRR, IOL, ACC 4, NAI). It was this importance for a base in the cantonment area which made the states people take an anomalous position in the retrocession issue. (See *ante* pp. 103-104.)
102. Ibid. A photograph of the pole can be found in File No. G-135/1931, pp. 51-57, AICC Papers, NMML.
103. See telegram from Bangalore District Congress Committee to Jawaharlal Nehru. 2 July 1931, File No. G-145/1931, pp. 61-62, AICC Papers, NMML.
104. Letter from K.T. Bhashyam to Mahatma Gandhi, 7 July 1931. File No G-145/1931, pp. 51-57, AICC Papers, NMML
105. Resident's report, 17 July 1931, CRR, IOL, ACC 4, NAI. See also copy of Mysore Government Order (undated 1931) available in File No. G-145/1931, pp. 11-13, AICC Papers, NMML.
106. See Letter from K.T. Bhashyam and B.S. Ramaswami Iyengar to Jawaharlal Nehru, 7 July 1931 and letter from same to Mahatma Gandhi, 7 July 1931. File No. G-145/1931, p. 49, AICC Papers, NMML.
107. Residents report 17 July 1931, CRR, IOL, ACC 4, NAI.
108. Letter from B.S. Ramaswami Iyengar, Bangalore DCC to Jawaharlal Nehru, 15 July 1931. File No. G-145/1931, pp. 29-39, AICC Papers, NMML.
109. Letter from B.S. Ramaswami Iyengar to Jawaharlal Nehru, 15 July 1931. File No. G-145/1931, pp. 29-31, AICC Papers, NMML.
110. Letter from V.S. Narayana Rao, Secretary, Bangalore DCC to Jawaharlal Nehru, 5 September 1931. File No. G-145/1931, pp. 7-9, AICC Papers, NMML.
111. Ibid.
112. Letter from Jawaharlal Nehru to B.S. Ramaswami Iyengar, 24 July 1931. File No. G-145/1931, p. 27, AICC Papers, NMML.
113. Letter from Jawaharlal Nehru to the Secretary, Bangalore DCC, 18 September 1931. File No. G-145/1931, pp. 3-5, AICC Papers, NMML.
114. See *post*, p. 133, p. 135, pp. 169-170 and p. 172.
115. Report report 3 August 1931, CRR, IOL ACCG, NAI. See also

copy of Mysore Government Order, File No. G-145/1931, pp. 11-13, AICC Papers, NMML.

116. Ibid. See also File No. G-145/1931, pp. 11-13, AICC Papers, NMML.
117. See reports for activities of the Mysore Congress in the C & M station of Bangalore, for 3 August 1931, 17 August 1931, 29 August 1931, 18 September 1931, 21 October 1931, 26 November 1931, CRR, IOL, ACC 4, NAI.
118. Resident's, report, 3 August 1931, CRR, IOL, ACC 4, NAI.
119. Resident's report, 17 August 1931, CRR, IOL, ACC 4, NAI.
120 General remarks on government repression by V.S. Narayana Rao, Secretary, Bangalore DCC to AICC, 5 September 1931. File No. G-145/1931, pp. 15-17, AICC Papers, NMML.
121. Residents' report 10 October 1931, CRR, IOL, ACC 4, NAI.
122. Residents' report 15 January 1932, CRR, IOL, ACC 4, NAI.
123. Residents' report 1 March 1932, CRR, IOL, ACC 3. NAI.
124. Police report sent by J.L. Collins, District Superintendent of Police, Kanara, to I.G. of police, Presidency of Bombay, (undated 1932). File No. 228-P/1932, F & P. NAI.
125. Police report sent by J.L. Collins, District Superintendent of Police, Kanara to I.G. of Police, Bombay Presidency, 1932 (undated), File No. 228-P/1932, F & P. NAI.
126. Ibid.
127. See enclosures to letter from Deputy Secretary, Foreign and Political Department, to Metcalfe, Resident, Mysore, 12 March 1932. See also letter from C.W.C. Turner, Political Secretary, Bombay Presidency to Resident, Mysore, 24 March 1932. File No. 228-P/1932, F & P., NAI, pp. 8-10.
128. Intercepted letter from Gundappa Hathikeri, Bangalore, to S.G. Kulkarni, meant for D.P. Karmarkar, 10 March 1932. File No. 228-P/1932, F & P, NAI. See also circular from KPCC Office Ankola 13 March 1932 in same file.
129. These pointed out that agitators were not doing much harm, and asserted that the Congress organisations commanded little following and that there were few Mysoreans who had gone across the border. Letter from Secretary, Government of Bombay, to Hallett, Political Secretary, 5 August 1932, File No. 228-P/1932, F & P., NAI.
130. Noting of Hallett, Political Secretary, Government of India on letter from Secretary to Government of Bombay, 5 August 1932. File No. 228-P/1932, F & P., NAI.
131. Note by Glancy, Political Secretary, Government of India, 23 December 1933, File No. 172-P (Secret)/1932, CRR, IOL, ACC 3, NAI.
132. Resident's report, 3 August 1927, File No. FR-32/1932, Home Political, NAI.
133. Report of the AGG Madras State, 15 August 1929, File No. FR 32/1929, H & P, NAI.

134. Fortnightly Report, 31 March 1930, File No. 18/3 (Political) H & P. NAI
135. Regency was imposed under the Proclamation of 1924 and was to continue to be in effect till the minor Maharaja attained majority on November 1931.
136. This principle governing minority administration rules had been enunciated by George Lloyd and was an accepted maxim of British policy. The acceptance of this principle is reflected in the resolution passed by the South Indian States Peoples Conference meeting on 28 September 1929 at Trivandrum, which demanded the termination of regency mainly on that score. Similar resolutions were passed at Pandalam, Punalur, Chengannur, Vadakkedathukavu, Adoor, Ezhamkulam, Venmani, Chirayankil, Neyyatinkara and Quilon. See Memorial to H.E. the Viceroy presented by the States Peoples Conference September 1929. Copy available in the Theosophical Society Library, Adyar, Madras.
137. See Resident's report, 28 September 1929, File No. 17/1929, October, H & P, NAI.
138. For agitations on this issue inside the Sri Moolam Popular Assembly and outside, see *Srimoolam Popular Assembly Proceedings*, 1927.
139. See note by Political Department on Memorials to terminate Regency in Travancore and on establishment of a Regency Council, 11 October 1930. See also correspondence of G. Sankaran Nair, advocate of Calicut to Resident, on same theme, CRR, IOL, ACC 138, NAI.
140. Resident's report, 31 March 1930, CRR, IOL, ACC 138, NAI.
141. Resident's report, 15 February 1930; CRR, IOL, ACC 138, NAI.
142. Resident's report, 31 March 1930, CRR, IOL, ACC 138, NAI.
143. Residents's report 15 April 1930, CRR, IOL, ACC 138, NAI.
144. A short history of satyagraha in Kerala sent by the KPCC File No. G-107/1930, AICC Papers, NMML.
145. Resident's report, 31 May 1930, CRR, IOL, ACC 138, NAI.
146. Resident's report, 17 January 1931, CRR, IOL, ACC 138, NAI.
147. Ibid.
148. Resident's report 1 June 1931, CRR, IOL, ACC 138, NAI.
149. Resident's report, 18 August 1931, CRR, IOL, ACC 138, NAI.
150. Resident's report, 4 September 1931, CRR, IOL, ACC 138, NAI.
151. Resident's report, 31 January 1932, CRR, IOL, ACC 136, NAI.
152. Residents report, 2 August 1932, CRR, IOL, ACC 136, NAI.
153. Resident's report, 13 March 1930, CRR, IOL, ACC 138, NAI.
154. Report sent in by K. Madhava Menon General Secretary, Kerala Pradesh Congress Committee to AICC, 13 April 1930. File No. G-107/1930, AICC Papers, NMML.
155. Of these, the Ezhavas presented two memorials, in March 1932 and July 1932, the Mohammedan Association on 21 August 1932 and the Latin Christian Mahajana Sabha on 4 September 1932. (See Data collected by P.C. Joseph on the *Joint Political Congress and Abstention Movement in Travancore*, p. 5).

156. C.P. Ramaswami Aiyar was appointed as legal adviser in November 1931, (which coincided almost with the end of Regency) on a pay of Rs. 3000 for work "totally incommensurate with this high figure". (see Fortnightly Report, 15 October 1932, CRR, IOL, ACC 136, NAI) This appointment was specially resented as in the legal fight between the tenants of Malabar and the Jenmies, C.P. Ramasami Aiyar had sided with the Jenmies. The Congress in Malabar and G. Sankaran Nair as "champions of the tenants of Malabar" naturally resented the appointment.
157. Resident's report 3 December 1931, CRR, IOL, ACC 138, NAI.
158. Resident's report 15 October 1932, CRR, IOL, ACC 136, NAI.
159. Resident's report 10 November 1931, CRR, IOL, ACC 138, NAI.
160. Letter from K.T. Mathew to Viceroy, 2 June 1930. File No. 62 Spl/1931, F & P., NAI.
161. Draft appeal by Jawaharlal Nehru for consideration of the Congress Working Committee, 16 February 1931. Jawaharlal Nehru Miscellaneous Papers, NMML.
162. Resolution passed at the Kerala Provincial Conference, 2 to 4 May 1931. *The Indian Half Yearly Register*, Vol. 1, p. 333.
163. Manifesto issued by the ISPC, June 1931. File No. AP-29 (Miscellaneous)/1931, pp. 49-51, AICC Papers, NMML,
164. Resolution passed by the ISPC on 9,10,11 June 1931. File No. 62-Spl/1931, F & P., NAI.
165. Speech by Mahatma Gandhi on the national demand at the Federal Structure Committee September 1931. Indian States Problem, an anthology of Mahatma Gandhi's letters, speeches, articles, etc. on the Indian states, pp. 54-57.
166. Ibid.
167 Questionnaire issued by N.C. Kelkar on behalf of the deputation of the ISPC to Mahatma Gandhi, 22 June 1934. File No. G-27/1934, AICC Papers, NMML.

CHAPTER 5

NOTES

1. The South Indian States Peoples Conference after the Round Table Conference merged with the ISPC.
2. Apart from recognising the Maharajas as the sole authority vis-a-vis the states, conceding thus to them the principle of nomination to the central assembly, it recognised the princes' contention that the range of authority in their territories was to differ from that over British India and was to be determined on principles that were "expedient and possible", and agreed upon by the rulers. See *White Paper on Proposals for Indian Constitutional Reforms*, 1933, p. 2.
3. All three leaders maintained some type of connection with this body. Mirza Ismail and Shanmugham Chetty were included in the Congress ministry in the post-independence period. C.P. Ramaswami Aiyar was an ex-secretary of the Home Rule League (1917-1918) and of the AICC (1917-1918) and had even contested the election of 1920 on the Congress ticket. For a career sketch see *A Sketch* published by the C.P. Ramaswami Aiyar Foundation, Madras.

4. Notes taken by Mahadev Desai (?) of the meeting between Mahatma Gandhi and a deputation of the ISPC, 20 June 1934. File No. G-27/1934, AICC Papers, NMML.
5. Draft resolution suggested by the ISPC deputation headed by N.C. Kelkar to Mahatma Gandhi, 22 June 1934, File No. G-27/1934, AICC Papers, NMML.
6. Questionnaire drafted by N.C. Kelkar on behalf of the deputation of the ISPC to Mahatma Gandhi, 22 June 1934. File No. G-27/1934, AICC Papers, NMML.
7. See *ante* pp. 98-99.
8. This pronouncement has to be considered in the context of British proposals spelt out in the White Paper. This had emphasized categorically that the states though under the suzerainty of the Emperor was not a part of His Majesty's dominion. Thus parliament could not legislate for it and federation was to be determined on agreement with the rulers. See answer by Mahatma Gandhi to the Kelkar questionnaire, 22 June 1934. File No. G-27/1934, AICC Papers, NMML, and *White Paper on Proposals for Indian Constitutional Reform*, 1933, p. 2.
9. Answer by Mahatma Gandhi to N.C. Kelkar questionnaire, 22 July 1934. File No. G-27/1934, AICC Papers, NMML.
10. Letter from Mahatma Gandhi to Amritlal Sheth, General Secretary ISPC, 30 July 1934. File No. G-27/1934, AICC Papers, NMML.
11. Mahatma Gandhi in reply to N.C. Kelkar questionnaire, 22 July 1934. File No. G-27/1934, AICC Papers, NMML.
12. Letter from Mahatma Gandhi to Amritlal Sheth, 30 July 1934. File No. G-27/1934, AICC Papers, NMML.
13. Resolution for the Working Committee meeting of the Indian States Peoples Conference 1934 (undated) File No. G-27/1934, AICC Papers, NMML.
14. The Manifesto of the Indian States Peoples Conference, October 1934. File No. G-27/1934, AICC Papers, NMML.
15. For the resolution drafted in Mahatma Gandhi's handwriting see File No. G-27/1934, AICC Papers, NMML.
16. Ibid.
17. See letter from Balwantray Mehta to Datar, 6 December 1937. File No. 18, Group I, All India States Peoples Conference Papers, (Private Paper Collection), NMML.
18. They did make an attempt, though with little success, in December 1934 to bring the issue before the AICC. See statement of Babu Rajendra Prasad, President of the Indian National Congress, at the Working Committee meeting, Patna, 5 December 1934, File No. G-27/1934, AICC Papers, NMML.
19. Speech by Bhulabhai Desai to the Mysore Bar Association, 10 June 1935, as reported by *The Servant of India*, 27 June 1935.
20. Gandhi supported Bhulabhai in his views, but asked him to clarify his point by making it clear that he did not support the princes in

their pomp and autocratism. An open letter to Vallabhbhai Patel was issued by Bhulabhai, clearing this and other issues. See Bhulabhai Desai to Vallabhbhai Patel, 6 June 1935. See also Amritlal Sheth to President, INC, 17 July 1935, File No. G-27/1934, AICC Papers, NMML.

21. Statement issued by the Indian States Peoples Conference reviewing the resolution passed by the Congress Working Committee at Wardha, 16 August 1935. File No. G-27/1934, AICC Papers, NMML.
22. Statement issued by the Congress Working Committee, 29 July 1935. File No. G-27/1934, AICC Papers NMML.
23. The above resolution discussed at Wardha on 29 July 1935. Ibid.
24. The *Indian Annual Register*, 17 October 1935, p. 277.
25. On the obverse side, at the Calcutta session the socialists used the controversy to assert their hold on popular mind, in spite of the states people being ready to withdraw their resolution. See *post* pp. 143-144.
26. Resolution passed at the open session of the Congress at Lucknow, April 1936. File No. G-35/1938, Part VII, AICC Papers, NMML.
27. Pattabhi Sitaramayya, *History of the Indian National Congress*, Vol. 2, p. 78.
28. Even earlier, K.T. Mathew, on behalf of the several states peoples organisations that he represented, had, in maintaining the distinctiveness of the ISPC from the INC, categorically asserted, that "serious attempts" were being made by some British Indian politicians to create an impression that they were "the custodians of the rights and interests of the people of Indian states", while some others "were endeavouring to create an organisation for the states people under the auspices of the Indian National Congress." The new organisation thus represented the triumph of the British Indian nationalists endeavour. Refer letter from K.T. Mathew to Viceroy 5 May 1931, file No. 62-Spl/1931, F & P, NAI. I have made a distinction between the ISPC and the later body, the All India States Peoples Conference (AISPC) by consistently deleting the word 'All' in the earlier organisation. There is an element of consistency in my doing so as the word 'All' was never stressed in the earlier one.
29. Urmila Phadnis, the author of *Towards the Integration of the States*, has, without making a distinction between the earlier organisation the ISPC and its later evolution into the AISPC, observed "although the leadership of the AISPC was in the hands of Congressmen, Congressmen as a body was disinclined to play an active role in the States", op. cit., p. 97. The leadership of the ISPC was not necessarily, as stated above, in the hands of congressmen or leaders of the movement in British India. It was so only in the later organisation, the AISPC. The contradictions remarked on were only seemingly there in the AISPC, for in actual fact there was no contradiction between it and the British Indian nationalists. These contradictions were there only with the ISPC when it held independent postures from that of the INC.

Again James Manor's statement (in his book *Political Change in an Indian State*, pp. 80-81) that Mysore was not a member of the AISPC till 1940, is open to ambiguous interpretation, as he has made no distinction between the two organisations. Mysore was a member, and a prominent one at that, of the SISPC. Two of its meetings in May 1929 and 1931 were held at Bangalore. Again, it was Hosakappa Krishna Rao, a subject of Mysore and a prominent member of the SISPC, who drafted a constitution for the states people.

30. See letter from Achyuta Menon to Balwantrai Mehta, 9 October 1937, File No. 5, Group 1, Balwantrai to B.N. Gupta, 31 March 1938, File No. 13, Group 1, Achyuta Menon to Balwantrai, 2 April 1938, File No. 5, Group 1, etc. of the AISPC Papers, NMML.
31. In Travancore, with the resignation of the Congress Members in 1932 (see *ante* p. 117) the Congress organisation in the state lay moribund.
32. Resident's report, 10 November 1932, CRR, IOL, ACC 138, NAI.
33. The Sri Moolam Popular Assembly was to consist of 72 members, 62 of whom were to be non-officials—43 of them elected from general constituencies, 14 nominated from minority communities and the rest by interests. The Sri Chitra Legislative Council was to consist of 37 members, of whom 27 were to be non-officials, 16 from general territorial constituencies, 5 nominated and 6 from special interests. Property franchise was to be higher in the council than in the Assembly. See Resident's report, 16 January 1932, CRR, IOL, ACC 134, NAI.
34. Resident's report, 1 February 1933. CRR, IOL, ACC 134, NAI.
35. Resident's report for 15 February 1933, and 16 March 1933, CRR, IOL, ACC 134, NAI.
36. M.J. Koshy, op. cit., pp. 289-293.
37. For table of caste/religious categories in legislature see *ante* p. 19 and *Note* 98, Chapter 1.
38. See Resident's report for 3 July 1933 and 2 August 1933, CRR, IOL, ACC 134, NAI.
39. Resident's report, 2 January 1934, CRR, IOL, ACC 134, NAI.
40. Resident's report, 16 May 1934, CRR, IOL, ACC 134, NAI.
41. Resident's report, 3 February 1934, CRR, IOL, ACC 134, NAI.
42. Resident's report, 16 May 1934, CRR, IOL, ACC 134, NAI.
43. For the Dewans Austin and Habibullah's complaint to the Resident, see letter from AGG, Madras States, 2 January 1935 and Resident's report, 3 September 1934, File No. 415-P(S)/1935, CRR, IOL, ACC 134, NAI.
44. Resident's report, 30 August 1935, CRR, IOL, ACC 133, NAI.
45. Resident's report, 31 August 1936, CRR, IOL, ACC 134, NAI.
46. See C. Kesavan's speech at Tripunithura, December 1937. Fortnightly Report, 16 December 1937, CRR, IOL, ACC 133, NAI.
47. Letter from Hardikar, Secretary, Karnataka Provincial Congress Committee to Jawaharlal Nehru, 28 August 1936. File No. G-27/1936, AICC Papers, NMML.

48. Ibid.
49. See *ante*, pp. 41-42 for this organisation's activities from 1912-1918. See also Report submitted by Pattabhi Sitaramayya and Balwantray Mehta, President and General Secretary respectively of the All India States Peoples Conference, on tour of Mysore from 19 to 29 December 1937. File No. G-38/1937, AICC Papers, NMML.
50. The Peoples Party had agitated on the same programme as the South Indian States Peoples Conference, and had demanded representation of the states people at the Round Table Conference and advocated Visvesvaraya's constitutional proposals. Thus, its programme had been hardly distinguishable from that of the Mysore State Congress. However, as a party favoured by the government in 1930-31, it had been allowed to hold many conferences of the raiyats under its auspices (See *Mysore Legislative Assembly Proceedings*, 17 June 1935, p. 68)
51. *Mysore Legislative Assembly Proceedings*, 13 June 1935, pp. 14-17.
52. The Karnataka non-Brahmin Conference Proceedings, 11 May 1930. *The Indian Annual Register*.
53. Speech of Chengalaraya Reddy, inaugurating the merger of Peoples Federation with the Mysore State Congress, 16 October 1937. Quoted by Pattabhai Sitaramayya in his report submitted to the AISPC, 19 to 29 December 1937. File No. G-88/1937 AICC Papers, NMML.
54. Ibid.
55. The Secretary of the Karnataka Pradesh Congress Committee reporting on the formation and history of the Mysore Congress Board, 28 August 1937. File No. G-88/1937, AICC Papers, NMML.
56. Resident's report, 3 February 1937, CRR, IOL, ACC 1, NAI. See also a report of repression in Mysore sent by Mysore Congress Board, August 1937. File No. G-88/1937, AICC Papers, NMML.
57. Resident's report, 15 February 1937, CRR, IOL, ACC 1, NAI and the Diary of Repression sent by Mysore Congress Board, August 1937. File No. G-81/1937, AICC Papers, NMML.
58. *Mysore Legislative Assembly Proceedings*, 20 June 1937, p. 150.
59. Resident's report, 31 July 1937, CRR, IOL, ACC 1, NAI and also Diary of Repression sent by Mysore Congress Board, August 1937, File No. G-8/1937, AICC Papers, NMML.
60. Resident's report, 31 July 1937, CRR, IOL, ACC 1, NAI.
61. One of the strategies adopted by the princes administrations to counteract agitations within, was to invite communal strife and hold that up as a bogy for justifying their repression (for invitation to Savarkar see V.D. Savarkar Papers, dated 6 March 1937, p. 189, Roll 1, NMML). Even in Travancore under the general blessings of the administration and of the Kerala Nair Conference an All Travancore Hindu Mahasabha was organised. See resolution passed by the Kerala Nair Conference, on 1 May 1937. CRR, IOL, ACC 133, NAI.
62. Mahatma Gandhi writing in the *Harijan*, 20 July 1935, p. 183.
63. Two petittons from M.P.K.R. Menon and Trichur Electric

Corporation, 1936. File No. 328-P(S)/1936, CRR, IOL, ACC 135, NAI.

64. Ibid.
65. AGG's Report on Shanmukham Chetty, 22 April 1936, CRR, IOL, ACC 133, NAI.
66. Resident's report, 2 December 1936, CRR, IOL, ACC 133, NAI.
67. Resident's report, 15 June 1937, CRR, IOL, ACC 133, NAI.
68. For their earlier activities on the Abstention Movement see *ante* pp. 130-133. File No. 1845/1936, Cellar Records, Kerala Secretariat.
69. Resident's report, 16 November 1936, CRR, IOL, ACC 134, NAI.
70. Resident's report, 2 July 1937, CRR, IOL, ACC 133, NAI.
71. Resident's report, 1 September 1937, CRR, IOL, ACC 133, NAI.
72. Ibid.
73. Resident's report, 16 November 1937, CRR, IOL, ACC 133, NAI.
74. Resident's report, 17 September 1937, CRR, IOL, ACC 133, NAI.
75. Ibid.
76. Letter from AGG, Madras States to Corfield, 13 July 1937. File No. 318-P(S)/1937, CRR, IOL, ACC 1, NAI. The constant bickerings and complaints among the Dewans against each other was a prominent feature of this period. This was in direct contrast to the early 1930s when Mirza Ismail, the Dewan of Mysore, had represented all the three states at the first Round Table Conference and had called a meeting of the southern states administrators before his departure to London in August 1930 (refer *The Hindu*, 21 August 1930) or again, as, had Raghaviah, the Dewan of Travancore represented both Travancore and Cochin at the Federal Finance Committee of the RTC.
77. Letter from Mirza Ismail to C.P. Ramaswami Aiyar, 3 July 1937. File No. 318-P(S)/1937, CRR, IOL, ACC 1, NAI.
78. See Koodalmanickam Temple dispute case, details available in CRR, IOL, ACC 134, NAI. Refer also Resident's report on the dispute, 14 May 1937. CRR, IOL, ACC 134, NAI.
79. Letter from Shanmukham Chetty to AGG, Madras State, 27 May 1937. CRR, IOL, ACC 134, NAI.
80. *Malayali*, 21 March 1937, *Bharat Patrika*, 10 March 1939 and 31 March 1937. Extracts sent by Shanmukham Chetty to the Resident, 27 May 1937, CRR, IOL, ACC, 134, NAI.
81. A Report of Repression in Mysore sent by the Mysore Congress Board, August 1937. File No. G-88/1937, AICC Papers, NMML.
82. The Mysore Congress Board, originally called the Mysore Central Board was constituted after the elections held in March 1937 and consisted of the members elected to the Legislatures and the representatives of the district Congress Committees. (The Karnataka Provincial Congress Committee Reporting on the Mysore Congress Board, 25 August 1937. File No. G-88/1937; AICC Papers, NMML).
83. Report of the resolutions passed by the Mysore Congress Board of its meeting, 10 August 1937. File No. G-88/1937, AICC Papers, NMML.

84. Report issued by the Mysore Congress Board, 12 January 1938. File No. G-88/1937, AICC Papers, NMML.
85. Report of the resolution passed by the Mysore Congress Board at its meeting, 10 August 1937, File No. G-88/1937, AICC Papers, NMML.
86. The resolution suggested to the AICC by B.N. Gupta, the editor of *Prajamata* a paper often persecuted by the Mysore Government is illustrative of the nature of help that was sought. He suggested that no member of the Working Committee of the Congress should consent to be a state guest without the previous approval of the local Congress Committee. This resolution brought out the real handicap suffered by the states people through the hobnobbing of prominent members of the Congress with the states administration. (See also *ante*, p. 105), Letter from B.N. Gupta to AICC, 10 August 1937. File No. 7/1937, P & I, AISPC Papers, NMML.
87. Letter from T. Siddalingaiah, President Congress Board to Jawaharlal Nehru, 13 August 1937. File No. G-88/1937, AICC Papers, NMML.
88. Letter from Jawaharlal Nehru to Siddalingaiah, 27 August 1937. File No. G-88/1937, AICC Papers, NMML.
89. See Letter from President, KPCC to Jawaharlal Nehru, 16 August 1937. File No. G-88/1937, AICC Papers, NMML.
90. Letter from Jawaharlal Nehru to Secretary, KPCC, 2 September 1937. File No. G-88/1937, AICC Papers, NMML.
91. Letter from V.S. Narayana Rao to Jawaharlal Nehru, 25 September 1937. File No, G-88/1937, AICC Papers, NMML.
92. Letter from Hukkerikar to Jawaharlal Nehru, 4 October 1937. File No. G-88/1937, AICC Papers, NMML.
93. Letter from V.S. Narayana Rao to Hukkerikar, 28 September 1937. File No. G-88/1937 AICC Papers, NMML.
94. *The Associated Press of India Report*, 23 September 1937, *The Times of India*, 25 September 1937.
95. Letter from Mirza Ismail to Jawaharlal Nehru, 8 October 1937. File No, G-88/1937, AICC Papers, NMML.
96. Letter from Jawaharlal Nehru to Mirza Ismail, 19 October 1937, JN Correspondence I Category, p. 167, NMML.
97. Letter from Mirza Ismail to Jawaharlal Nehru, 29 October 1937. File No. G-88/1937, AICC Papers, NMML.
98. See Fortnightly Reports for 14 August 1937, 1 September 1937, 15 September, CRR, IOL, ACC 1, NAI.
99. Letter from V.S. Narayana Rao, Secretary, Mysore Congress Board to Jawaharlal Nehru, 7 October 1937. File No. G-88/1937, AICC Papers, NMML.
100. Resident's report, 30 October 1937, CRR, IOL, ACC 1, NAI
101. Letter from Chengalaraya Reddy to Jawaharlal Nehru. File No. G-88/1937, AICC Papers, NMML.
102. *Mysore Legislative Assembly Proceedings*, 16 October 1937, p. 1.
103. See *ante* p. 135.

104. *Mysore Legislative Assembly Proceedings*, 19 October 1937, p. 83.
105. *Mysore Legislative Assembly Proceedings*, 19 October 1937, pp 95-96.
106. Situation in Bangalore, a press note issued by L.S. Raju, President Civil Liberties Union, 26 October 1937, File No. G-88/1937, AICC Papers, NMML.
107. Situation in Bangalore, a press note issued by the President Civil Liberties Union, 29 October 1937.
108. Situation in Bangalore, a press note issued by the President, Civil Liberties Union, 29 October 1937.
109. *Mysore Legislative Assembly Proceedings*, 26 October 1937, p. 143.
110. Letter from Hukkerikar to Jawaharlal Nehru, 14 November 1937. File No. G-88/1937, AICC Papers, NMML.
111. The resolution passed at the AICC session at Calcutta, 31 October 1937. File No. G-35/1938, Pt. VII, AICC Papers, NMML.
112. Hand chit given by Chengalaraya Reddy to Jawaharlal Nehru (camp Calcutta), 31 October 1932. File No. G-88/1937, AICC Papers, NMML.
113. Letter from Hukkerikar to Jawaharlal Nehru, 14 November 1937. File No. G-88/1937, AICC Papers, NMML.
114. Ibid.
115. Ibid. The merger of the Peoples Federation Party with the Mysore Congress had excited in Vallabhbhai Patel's mind a suspicion that the "neo-Congressmen", of Mysore were exploiting the name of the Congress towards their own purpose. Pattabhi Sitaramayya was asked by Vallabhbhai Patel to investigate this "specific point", when on his tour to Mysore in December 1937. This may, to some extent, explain his antagonism to the Mysore Congress support in the Calcutta AICC session. However, Pattabhi Sitaramayya in his report completely absolved the new Mysore Congress organisation from such permeditated machinations. (Refer letter from Pattabhi Sitaramayya to Vallabhbhai Patel, 28 December 1937. File No. 7/1937-42, pp. 115-121, AISPC Papers, NMML.
116. Letter from Hukkerikar to Jawaharlal Nehru, 31 October 1937. File No. G-88/1937, AICC Papers, NMML.
117. Letter from Jawaharlal Nehru to Mirza Ismail, 4 November 1937. JN Correspondence, Vol. 34, p. 173, NMML.
118. Letter from Jawaharlal Nehru, as President Indian National Congress to Secretary, KPCC, 11 November 1937. File No. G-88/1937 and G-35/1938, Pt. VIII, AICC Papers, NMML.
119. Letter from Balwantray Mehta to Datar, 6 December 1937. File No. 19, Group I, All India State Peoples Conference Papers (AISPC) (Private Papers Collection) NMML.
120. Mahatma Gandhi in the *Harijan* of 13 November 1937. Also reprinted in the *Indian States Problem*.
121. Ibid.
122. Address by Mirza Ismail to the Mysore Legislative Assembly, 16 October 1937. *Mysore Legislative Assembly Proceedings*, p. 11.

123. Ibid.
124. It was held by some prominent members of the Congress that the resolution was *ultra vires* as it went beyond the Congress position and policy of giving sympathy and support when it called on the people of the states and British India to give all support and encouragement to the people of Mysore. There was another view that it transgressed the limits of legality when it made pointed reference to a particular state and had not treated the states in general. For views on the Mysore resolution, see letters from Mahadev Desai, 19 November 1937 and 2 December 1937, Vol. No. 17, from J.B. Kripalani, 18 December 1937, Vol. 40, from Vallabhbhai Patel 12 December 1937, Vol. 81, from Achyut J. Patwardhan 10 December 1937, Vol. 82 and Rajendra Prasad 24 December 1937, Vol. 85, all addressed to Jawaharlal Nehru, JN P. pers, NMML.
125. See *ante*, p. 99 and pp, 126-127. In 1934, Gandhi had made a deliberate to attempt reintroduce the clause but the whole motion was suspended on the states peoples' agreeing not to press the issue.
126. Unpublished Press statement by Jawaharlal Nehru on Mahatma Gandhi's views on Calcutta resolution, 26 November 1937, File No. G-88/1937, p. 277, AICC Papers, NMML.
127. Mahadev Desai to Jawaharlal Nehru giving the gist of Gandhi's opinion as stated to him, 19 November 1937.
128. See D.G. Tendulkar, *Mahatma—Life of Mohandas Karamchand Gandhi*, Vol. 4, (1934-38), p. 206.
129 Letter from B.N. Datar to Balwantray Mehta, 28 November 1937, File No. 19, Group 1, AISPC Papers, NMML.
130. Letter from Balwantray Mehta to Datar, 6 December 1937, File No. 19, Group 1, AISPC Papers, NMML.
131. Unpublished press statement by Jawaharlal Nehru on Mahatma Gandhi's views on Calcutta resolution, 26 November 1937, File No. G-88/1937, p. 277, AICC Papers, NMML.
132. Ibid.
133. Letter from Balwantray Mehta, 6 December 1937. File No. 19 Group 1, AISPC Private Papers, NMML.
134. Fortnightly report, 1 December 1937, CRR, IOL, ACC 1, NAI.
135. Fortnightly report, 13 January 1938, CRR, IOL, ACC 1, NAI.
136. Statement by Chengalraya Reddy, January 1938. File No. G-88/1937, AICC Papers, NMML.
137. Fortnightly report, 13 January 1938, CRR, IOL, ACC 1, NAI.
138. Fortnightly report, 15 December 1937, CRR. IOL, ACC 1, NAI.
139. Ibid.
140. Chengalaraya Reddy's report to Jawaharlal Nehru of his interview with Mirza Ismail on 2 February 1938. File No. G-88/1937, AICC Papers, NMML.
141. Telegram from editor *Sadhvi*, to Congress Working Committee at Wardha, 5 Februrary 1938. File No. G-88/1937, AICC Papers, NMML.

142. The crowd was estimated at a lakh. See Resident's report, 2 October 1937, CRR, IOL, ACC 133, NAI.
143. Resident's report, 13 October 1937, CRR, IOL, ACC 133, NAI.
144. Fortnightly report, 16 December 1937, CRR, IOL, ACC 133, NAI.
145. Gandhi's statement for 'Lord Lothian and Responsible Statesmen Only', 20 January 1938. Zetland Collection, Vol. 15, p. 38, Roll 5. NMML.
146. Ibid.
147. The manifesto of the Indian States People's Conference, October 1934. File No. G-27/1934, AICC Papers, NMML, See *ante* p. 119 and p. 126.
148. Memo by the Secretary of State to the Cabinet, Cabinet Papers, 9 February 1939, Zetland Collection, IOL, Vol. 25, Roll 9, NMML.
149. See Yusuf Meharally's speech at the Congress Session at Madras, for his reference to Rajaji on the states people, 17 October 1935. *The Indian Annual Register*, Vol. 2, p. 277.
150. Memorandum submitted to the Viceroy by Lothian on his conversation with leaders, 20 January 1938. Zetland Collection, Vol. 15, pp. 36-37, Roll 5, NMML.
151. Ibid. An analogous proposal had been mooted by Willingdon in November 1931 in a letter to the Secretary of State. Seeing the princes (especially Bikaner) weaken 'very considerably in his enthusiasm for the princes entering a federal scheme', he had proposed that the secretary of State fall 'back on to a general advance in British India alone . . and to give his *hookum* both on the minorities question and the matter of safeguards'. (See letter from W llingdon to Samuel Hoare 19 November 1931, Templewood Collection, Vol. 5, p. 36, Roll 2, NMML.) But this *hookum* the Secretary of State was unwilling and unable to give hemmed in as he was by the conservative party's opposition to the federal scheme and their own obsession in thinking that the princes were needed as a party 'to steady the ship of federation'. (See S. Hoare to Willingdon, 28 January 1932 and 8 February 1932, Vol, 5, p. 72, Roll 2, NMML).
152. Ibid.
153. Memorandum submitted by Lothian to the Viceroy, 20 January 1938, Zetland Collection Vol. 15, pp. 36-37, Roll 5, NMML.
154. See Report by C.F. Wylie to Glancy, 8 January 1937. Zetland Collection Vol. 13, p. 20, Roll 4, NMML. Letter from Linlithgow to Zetland, 28 January 1938. Zetland Collection Vol. 15, Roll 5, NMML.
155. Lord Lothian's statement issued to the Associated Press of India, 24 January 1938. Document in *Travancore Today Her Struggle for Freedom*, published by the Working Committee of the Travancore State Congress, July 1938.
156. Ibid.
157. Shanmukham Chetty in his reforms proposals for Cochin, outlined in January 1938, proposed a form of dyarchy where the Dewan was to administer certain departments under the 'reserved subjects' while

the 'popular minister' answerable to the legislature, was to be in charge of the 'transferred' subjects such as the department of agriculture, industries, panchayats, uplift of depressed classes etc. As these reforms were promulgated in June 1938 and became effective only later, I have dealt with this development in the next chapter, see *post* p. 166.

158. Report of C.P. Ramaswami Aiyar's speech in the *Sri Moolam Assembly*, Travancore, 2 February 1938. *The Times of India*, 5 February 1938.
159. K.M. Panikkar—*The Indian States and the Government of India*, pp. 46-47.
160. V.K. Krishna Menon on the "Travancore Dewan's Fallacies" *The Indian Express*, 12 March 1938. Also published in the pamphlet brought out by Travancore State Congress, *Travancore Today Her Struggle for Freedom*, p. 48. See also *The Hindu*, 4 February 1938.
161. Shanmukham Chetty maintained that even full responsible government 'could be worked without infringing Treaty rights or offending the provisions of the law'. His argument followed *The Hindu*, reasoning that the treaty provisions had at no point stipulated on the Maharaja's personal administration. To say that the 'Cochin Reform was not a step in the direction of respoosible government was to ignore the scope of its working'. See Shanmukham Chetty's reply, *The Times of India*, 5 February 1938.
162. Letter from Zetland to Linlithgow, 20 February 1938. Zetland Collection, Roll 3, Vol. 7, p. 38, NMML.
163. *Parliamentary Debates*, *Commons*, *Official Report Fifth Series*, Vol. 332, p. 4. Winterton in answer to a question by Captain Heligers on statement of Dewan of Travancore.
164. See *post* pp. 159-161.
165. See Draft Resolution for Haripura passed at Wardha by the Working Committee of the AICC, 3 to 6 February 1938. File No. G-6/KWI (Part I)/1938, AICC Papers, NMML.
166. Pattabhi Sitaramayya at the Haripura Congress, 20 February 1938. File No. 30/1938. R-1, AICC Papers, NMML. The Wardha resolution as amended at Haripura, in an effort at conciliation of the members from the states, allowed Congress Committees within the states. However, as Gandhiji pointed out at a subsequent interview with the states people, it was a useless concession as these committees in the states were to be allowed to do nothing. See notes by Mahadev Desai of Mahatma Gandhi's interview with state Congress members. *Harijan*, 5 March 1938, Vol. 6, (1938-39), p. 31 and Haripura resolution, 20 February 1938, File No. G-6 KWI (Part I)/1938, AICC Papers, NMML.
167. Speech by Pattabhi Sitaramayya at the Haripura Congress, 20 February 1938, File No. 30/1938, R-1, AICC Papers, NMML.
168. See Bhulabhai Desai's speech at the Subjects Committee discussions Haripura, 18 February 1938, as reported in the police report of the

proceedings, Jodhpur, File No. 53/3 RIV&V, p. 24, History of Freedom Movement Unit collection, NAI.

169. The members had resigned in December 1937, before the trend of the Haripura resolution had become known. Out of the total 18 elected representatives from general constituencies in the Legislative Council 13 belonged to the Congress Party. Of these 11 resigned their seats and 2 had just recently been elected through bye-elections. Six of the 11 were returned uncontested, while 5 faced election in March 1938. See letter from T. Siddalingiah, President, Mysore Congress Board, to Subhas Chandra Bose, President, INC., 21 February 1938. File No. G-6 KWI (Part I)/1938, AICC Papers, NMML.
170. See Subhas Chandra Bose's ruling marked in the above letter.
171. Letter from President, Mysore Congress Board, General Secretary, Indian National Congress, 1 March 1938, File No G-88/Pt.I/1938, AICC Papers, NMML.
172. Letter from C. Rajagopalachari to Vallabhbhai Patel, 8 March 1938, File No. G-88/1938, AICC Papers, NMML.
173. Working Committee resolution passed at Bombay 15 to 19 May 1938. *Harijan*, 28 May 1938, Vol. 6 (1938-39), p. 31. See also letters from J.B. Kripalani to General Secretaries Cochin and Mysore Congress, 14 March 1938, 15 April 1938 and others in File No. G-88/(Pt. I)/1938, AICC Papers, NMML.
174. Fortnightly report, quoting resolution proposed, 4 April 1938, CRR, IOL, ACC 133, NAI.
175. Letter from Kurur Nilakantan Nambudripad, President, Cochin Congress, to General Secretary, AICC, 14 April 1938. File No. G-35/ Part IV, 1938, p. 85, AICC Papers, NMML.
176. V.S. Narayana Rao, in his letter to the General Secretary, AICC, giving an account of the Mysore Congress presidents interview with Mahatma Gandhi at Delang, 17 April 1938. File No. G-88/1938, AICC Papers, NMML. However a letter of Abul Kalam Azad to J.B. Kripalani asserted that at their interview at Delang they had consented not to use the name Congress. See letter of A.K. Azad to J.B. Kripalani, 12 April 1938, File No. G-88, Pt. 1, p. 95, AICC Papers, NAI.
177. The growing dominance of the Left Wing in the Kerala Pradesh Congress Committee was directly related to the near inactivity of Indian National Congress organisation in the Travancore State, where with the resignation of the Congress members in 1932, there was hardly any Congress organisation worth its name till 1937. See *ante*, pp. 116-118.
178. Report by E.M.S. Namboodiripad to General Secretary AICC, on deadlock in Kerala Congress, 9 August 1936, File No. P-15/1936, AICC Papers, NMML.
179. Ibid.
180. Ibid.
181. The effect of this was felt in subsequent years. To understand the

remifications of this disaffiliation effected at Haripura, one would have to transgress the limits of strict chronology and project it to the later years to understand it.

182. See Dr. Subbarayan Committee's Report and recommendation to AICC on Kerala Pradesh Congress Committee, 8 October 1940. This Committee was appointed following the KPCC's contravening of AICC's orders calling on all Congress Committees to condemn the Viceroy's and Secretary of State's rejection of the proposals made by Congress at Ramgarh. The AICC had issued specific instructions not to mix any other issues with these meetings. Following a ban on meetings imposed by the Government of Madras the KPCC in defiance of the AICC's order resolved to observe 15 September 1940 as a protest day

183. At the time of the elections in December, the KPCC found that with a membership of 43 or 44 members it was entitled to a mere 5 members at the AICC. See report of Dr. Subbarayan Committee, 8 October 1940. File No. P-11/1942-46, p. 257, AICC Papers, NMML.

184. Some constituencies even obtained as many as 13 and 11 seats each. Ibid.

185. The primary Congress membership in Kerala which was a mere 5,638 in 1936, was by 1940 raised to 50,000 which came mainly from the Malabar area. Though the General Secretary of the Left Wing dominated KPCC denied any connection between Kisan and Labour organisations, the Rightists alleged a close connection between them and the KPCC. See evidence of K. Damodaran, Secretary, KPCC, 2 October 1940 and of K. Kelappan, 25 September 1940 before Subbarayan Committee, File No. 48/1940, AICC Papers, NMML.

186. During the predominance of the Kerala Congress Socialist Party in the KPCC, C.P. Ramaswami Aiyar alleged the infiltration of communists under this party in Travancore agitation for responsible government. See note on the connection between state Congressites and communists, sent by C.P. Ramaswami Aiyar to Resident, Madras States and Polindia, 1940. CRR, IOL, ACC 134, NAI.

187. Following recommendation of Dr. Subbarayan Committee, a committee of 3 members under Nandakeolyar was appointed by the AICC to manage affairs of the KPCC in 1940, which continued till May 1942. See File No. P-11/1942-46, AICC Papers, NMML.

188. See Memorandum submitted by Calicut Taluk to AICC and letter from KPCC to General Secretary 19 March 1942. File No. P-11/1942-46, AICC Papers, NMML.

189. Refer letter from K. Kumar, Ex-President of the Travancore District Congress Committee to AISPC, 21 April 1938. File No. 5, Group 1, p. 11, AISPC Papers (Private Collection), NMML.

190. Press statement issued by Pattam Thanu Pillai as a refutation to Pattabhi Sitaramayya's statement of April 1938, 4 May 1938. File No. 4, Pattam Thanu Pillai Papers (Private Collection), NMML.

191. Refer Pattabhi Sitaramayya's appeal to the Travancore Durbar to

introduce responsible government in the state. *The Indian Express*, 30 April 1938.

192. Refer Pattam Thanu Pillai's statement refuting Pattabhi Sitaramayya's statement upholding Travancore Government's charges of communalism in Travancore State Congress, 4 May 1938. File No. 4, Pattam Thanu Pillai Papers (Private Collection), NMML.
193. Letter from Pattabhi Sitaramayya to the Travancore Durbar, April 1938. *The Indian Express*, 30 April 1938. See also File No. 5, Group I, (1937-42) p. 5, AISPC Papers, (Private Collections), NMML.
194. The article directed particularly at the Nairs pleaded from them a recognition of the discriminated communities demand for communal representation—for 'if between communities a pact' was made, popular rights and popular influence could gain ground. See translation of Shri Narayana Pillai's article 'The Problem of Representation in the Public Service and Nairs' published as Appendix 1 of Appendices Part II in *Travancore Today Her Struggle for Freedom*, pp. 92-93, a pamphlet published by the Travancore Congress in 1938-39.
195. The article criticised particularly the disallowance by the Dewan of discussions in the Legislature of attacks made on two editors by *goondas* and the non-action of police on it. *Travancore Today Her Struggle for Freedom*, op. cit., pp. 94-96.
196. See Notice issued by Travancore Government on A Narayana Pillai, 28 January 1938, op. cit., p. 97.

CHAPTER 6

NOTES

1. The memorandum submitted to His Highness the Maharaja of Travancore on 31 May 1938. See *Travancore Today, Her Struggle for Freedom*, p. 6.
2. See *ante*, p. 152
3. Noting by Polindia of an interview with G.P. Pillai and N. Kunju Pillai of Travancore, on Travancore situation, 9 May 1938. CRR, IOL, ACC 137, NAI.
4. See memo by the Secretary of State to Cabinet, 2 February 1939. Cabinet Papers, 44 (39), Copy No. 12, Vol. 25 B, Roll 9, Zetland Collection, NMML.
5. Though the Congress in the states was inspired by the democratic principles now in work in the provinces and by its achievements it was not instigated from outside, in which sense the British administrators used it.
6. The period 1938-39 saw several demonstrations in the states where Congressmen took part directly or acted as intermediaries to bring

about a settlement. The first of these was of course in Mysore, where Vallabhbhai Patel brought on an agreement between the administration and the Congress in April 1938, (see *post*. pp. 171-173). A similar agreement was brought on by him in June 1938 at Mansa; he, Kasturba Gandhi and subsequently Gandhi himself took an active role in the agitation in Rajkot State (January 1939) and Jamnalal in Jaipur (January 1939), etc. Other agitations, to mention only a few took place in Orissa (January 1939) Ramdurg (March 1939), Hyderabad (February 1939) Mewar (February 1939), Limbdi (February 1939), Talcher, (April 1939) etc.

7. Among the Dewans meeting at Bombay on 18 November 1938 were C.P. Ramaswami Aiyar, V.T. Krishnamachari of Baroda, Sardar Angre of Gwalior, Surve of Kolhapur etc., as also some Kathiawar rulers who were consulted. The Memorandum was drafted by C.P. Ramaswami Aiyar. For covering letter from Skrine, AGG, Madras State, and the memorandum see 18 November 1938. Vol. 15, p. 548, Roll 5, Zetland Collection, NMML.
8. Gandhi in an editorial "States and the People", December 1938. *Harijan*, Vol. 6, 1938-39, p. 360. Here it is important to note, it was only misrule that was emphasised and not responsible government. See also, the Working Committee resolution passed at Wardha, 11 to 16 December 1938, *Harijan*, 17 December 1938, Vol. 6 (1938-39), p. 382.
9. Carl Health, the Chairman of the Indian Conciliation Group, characterised the answer given by Muirhead at the House of Commons as a 'purely negative one'. See Carl Heath to Zetland, 17 December 1938. See also Zetland's answer to Carl Heath, 19 December 1938, Vol. 8, pp. 176-179, Roll 3, Zetland Papers, NMML, and Parliamentary Debates, 16 December 1938, Vol. No. 492. 1138-39, item No. 2352
10. In Rajkot, the oppointment of a retired civilian—Patrick Cadell as Dewan was resented by the Thakore Saheb who in collaboration with his ex-Dewan Virawala, entered into an agreement with Sardar Patel, that on the Dewan's ouster he would be amenable to reforms in the state. By this agreement of 26 December 1938, 7 members of the Sardar's choice were to be appointed to a Reforms Committee of 10. The Thakore Saheb's resiling from his promise proved the signal for an agitation against the Durbar, in which Vallabhbhai Patel. Kasturba Gandhi and Gandhi himself took an active part. As a result of Gandhi's fast the Viceroy intervened and Maurice Gwyer was nominated as arbitrator to go into the clause of the agreement, and the decision was given in favour of Patel. However, the states administration with the active collaboration of the paramount power (who had been irritated earlier by the ouster of the British Dewan) staged a communal problem by fomenting trouble between the Hindus, Muslims and the Bhayyats. With Jinnah and Ambedkar entering the fray, Gandhi acknowledged his failure to solve the problem and withdrew in April 1939. For an account see *Rajkot Fiasco* by

Prof. Devaprasad Ghosh, *India Tomorrow*, 30 April 1939. File No. G-12/1937-39, AICC Papers, NMML. See also Gandhi in *Harijan*, April 1939, Vol. 7 (1939-40), p. 104, 6 May 1939, p. 113, 24 June 1939, p 169. See also Memorandum by the Secretary of State to Cabinet, 9 February 1939. Cabinet Papers 44(39), Vol. 25, Roll 9, Zetland Collection, NMML.

11. Cochin which had an elected majority from 1925 was granted a wide franchise in 1932, with separate electorate for the discriminated communities (the demand of the Joint Political Conference in Travancore during the same years) and an elected Deputy President in the legislature.
12. The 'reserved' subjects under the Dewan included the departments of Finance, Law. Police, etc., and the 'transferred' subjects under the 'popular' minister was confined to the departments of Agriculture, Industries, Panchayats, Cooperatives, uplift of the depressed classes etc. Any no confidence motion against the popular minister was to be confined to the 58 elected members, the government bloc of 20 nominated remaining neutral. See *Cochin Constitutional Reforms Committee Report* (January 1938) and the Residents, report on Cochin Reforms, 3 June 1938, CRR, IOL, ACC 133, NAI.
13. In a subsequent period Shanmugham Chetty even went further in proclaiming his belief in democracy as the most suitable form of government for India. See speech of Shanmugham Chetty at Maharaja College, Ernakulam, February 1940, CRR, IOL, ACC 134, Resident's report, 11 April 1938, CRR, IOL, ACC 133, NAI.
14. Letter from K.N. Namboodiripad, President, Cochin Congress, 24 June 1938, File No. G-35/Part IV/1938, p. 85, AICC Papers, NMML.
15. A peculiar problem did arise when the SNDP Yogam organisation contemplated the initiation of direct action against the government, as a protest against the orthodoxy of the Maharaja in his position against the untouchables and Temple entry. With a popular ministry in charge of the department for the uplift of backward classes, a near farcical situation seemed imminent, with a splinter group within the same party working for its own downfall. See letter from E.M.S. Namboodiripad to General Secretary, AICC, 11 June 1939, File No. G-12/1937—39, AICC Papers, NMML.
16. This was significant for prior to these reforms, Cochin Congress acting as an opposition to the government had always, as a measure of exhibiting its dissatisfaction, moved for cuts in the budget, See *ante* p. 144 See also 31 July 1938, CRR, IOL, ACC 133, NAI.
17. Resident's report, 18 October 1938, CRR, IOL, ACC 133, NAI.
18. *Cochin Legislative Council Proceedings*, 8 December 1938. A similar discussion was allowed in December 1940 when a discussion demanded additional portfolios in charge of the popular minister. See also Resident's report for November 1940, CRR, IOL, ACC 134, NAI.
19. In this Shanmugham Chetty was a special target for C.P. Ramaswami Aiyar's complaints. The Cochin Dewan not only invited the radical

Youth League leader of Travancore, John Kuruvilla, to a party given to the Viceroy in January 1939 on his visit, but also introduced him. Glancy, as political Secretary had to haul up the Dewan for allowing articles attacking the Travancore Government in his state papers. For later help, see *post* pp. 207-208, p. 219 See Residents reports for 24 January 1939, 26 January 1939, CRR, IOL, ACC 177, NMML.

20. See letter from Resident to Polindia on settlement following Vidurasswatha firing 3 May 1938. File No. 296-P(S)/1938, CRR, IOL, ACC 3, NAI.
21. Reference was to Jawaharlal Nehru's and Sri Krishna Sinha's (a minister from Bihar) criticism on repression in Mysore. Speech by Mirza Ismail at the Karnataka Sahitya Parishad, Bangalore 27 February 1938, File No. G-88 (Part I)/1938, AICC Papers, NMML.
22. Letter from H.C. Dasappa to Jawaharlal Nehru, 2 March 1938, File No. G-88 (Part I)/1938, AICC Papers, NMML.
23. Letter from H.C. Dasappa to Jawaharlal Nehru, 24 March 1938. File No. G-88 (Part I)/1938, AICC Paperes, NMML.
24. Resident's report, 29 March 1938, CRR, IOL, ACC 1, NAI.
25. Mysore Government Order No. G-2691-2751 on Constitutional Reforms, 1 April 1938. File No. S 99-P/1938, Political Department, NAI.
26. Resident's report, 13 April 1938, CRR, IOL, ACC 1, NAI.
27. *The Hindu*, 6 April 1938.
28. Letter from H.C. Dasappa to Jawaharlal Nehru, 24 March 1938. File No. G-88 (Part I)/1938, AICC Papers, NMML.
29. Resident's report, 29 March 1938, CRR, IOL, ACC 1, NAI.
30. A parallel situation where a party favoured consultation with Gandhi and others opposed it is to be seen in Travancore movement also. See See *post* p. 184. There is little evidence to show whether it was Mahatma Gandhi himself who manoeuvred into such a position through his confidants. Letter from H.C. Dasappa to T.T. Sharma, editor, *Vishwa Karnataka*, 5 April 1938. T.T. Sharma Collection, KSA.
31. Nothing is known from reports on the conference as to the decision taken on the question of their cooperation with the Reforms Committee. For reports on this conference, see report sent by Mysore Congress to AISPC, 10 to 14 April 1938. File No. 13, Group I, pp. 491-495, AISPC Papers, NMML. See also Residents report on Sivapura convention 13 April 1938. CRR, IOL, ACC 1, NAI.
32. Order under section 31 of the Mysore Police Act issued by District Magistrate on 9 April 1938. See also letter from Narayana Rao to Jawaharlal Nehru, 17 April 1938. File No. G-88/1938, AICC Papers, NMML.
33. Statement issued by H.C. Dasappa, April 1938. See also letter from V.S. Narayana Rao to AICC, 17 April 1938. File No. G-88 (Part I)/1938, AICC Papers, NMML.
34. For a description of the scene of disturbance see *Proceedings on the*

Report of the Committee of Enquiry of the Disturbances at Viduraswatham, 19 November 1938, p. 4, KSA. The Committee was appointed by the Mysore Government on 5 May 1938 and was made up of official nominees. See also *Madras Mail,* 26 April 1938 and the government communique issued on 28 April 1938, CRR, IOL, ACC 1, NAI.

35. Press Communique issued by the Government of Mysore, 28 April 1938. CRR, IOL, ACC 1, NAI. See also *Madras Mail*, 26 April 1938 and the Report of the Resident 1 May 1938, CRR, IOL, ACC 1, NAI.
36. Gandhiji's statement, 29 April 1938, "Price for Gaining Liberty," *Harijan*, 7 May 1938. The Police account claimed that it resorted to lathi charge only under duress of hooliganism. Report of the witness examined by L.S. Raju, the Public Council, at the Viduraswatha Enquiry Committee. *Proceedings on the Report of the Committee of Enquiry of the Disturbances at Viduraswatha*, pp. 8-9, KSA.
37. Congressmen charged that the local authorities had ample signs of the coming trouble and that in violation of an assurance given to them at the time of their arrest to allow the crowd to disperse peacefully, they had lathi charged with intent to discredit such gatherings. See statement by R R. Gundappa Gouda at the unofficial informal Enquiry Committee appointed by the Working Committee of the Mysore Congress immediate to the shooting incident, 28 April 1938. File No. G-88 (Part I)/1938, p. 135, AICC Papers, NMML.
38. De Souza in his dissenting note on the necessity of firing maintained that the crowd would have quietly dispersed had the police party been more circumspect He found confirmation for this view *expost facto* in the behaviour of the crowd which assembled on 3 May 1938, even armed with sticks, which melted away on its being left alone. See the *Report of the Viduraswatha Disturbances*, published on 19 November 1938, p. 85, G.O. No. 1571-1621, KSA.
39. Siddalingiah had in an interview with Mahatma Gandhi at Delang stressed the necessity of the flag "to feel our national unity and also symbol of worship of the mother land". To this Mahatmaji acceded. See letter from V.S. Narayana Rao to the Secretary AICC 24 April 1938. File No G-88/Part I, 1938, p. 129, AICC Papers NMML. See also *A Short History of My Life* by Siddalingaiah, Series 1, p. 13, available in the personal collection of Dr. Kamath of Bangalore.
40. Note by C. Rajagopalachari sent to Mirza Ismail through Brahmachari Ramachandra 20 April 1938. File No. 266-P(S)/1938, CRR, IOL, ACC 3, NAI.
41. Even Gandhi proclaimed himself as unaware of the wide awakening in Mysore. See "Price for Gaining Liberty", by Gandhi, 29 April 1938. *Harijan*, 7 May 1938.
42. Statement by H.B. Gowda, 28 April 1938. File No. G-88 (Part I)/ 1938, p. 135, AICC Papers, NMML.
43. Karnataka Pradesh Congress Committee's resolution on Viduraswatha 1 May 1938. File No. G-88/1938, AICC Papers, NMML. See also

letter from Jayaprakash Narayan and Mr. Masani for circulation among members of AICC, 1938. File No. G-11 (Part 2)/1938, AICC Papers, NMML.

44. Resolution passed by the Madras Congress socialist party 1 May 1938. File No. G-88 (Part I)/1938, AICC Papers, NMML.
45. Refer letter from Resident to Polindia, 3 May 1938. File No. 296-P (S)/1938, CRR, IOL, ACC 3, NAI.
46. Note from C. Rajagopalachari to Mirza Ismail, 20 April 1938. File No. 296-P(S)/1938, CRR, IOL, ACC 3, NAI.
47. Letter from Resident to Polindia 3 May 1938, File No. 296-P(S)/1938, CRR, IOL, ACC 3, NAI.
48. Telegram from Mirza Ismail to Mahatma Gandhi, 28 April 1938. File No. 296-P(S)/1938, CRR, IOL, ACC3, NAI.
49. Telegram from Mahatma Gandhi to Mirza Ismail 28 April 1938, File No. 296-P(S)/1938. CRR, IOL, ACC 3, NAI.
50. Telegram from Vallabhbhai Patel to Mirza Ismail 29 April 1938. File No. 296-P(S) 1938, CRR, IOL, ACC 3, NAI.
51. Letter from Resident to Polindia, 3 May 1938, File No. 296-P(S) 1938, CRR, IOL, ACC 3, NAI.
52. Letter from Resident to Polindia, 3 May 1938, File No. 296-P(S)/1938, CRR, IOL, ACC 3, NAI.
53. Comments of Political Secretary in letter from Resident to Polindia and enclosures, 16 May 1938. File No. 296-P(S)/1938, CRR, IOL, ACC3, NAI.
54. Gandhiji's statement on Viduraswatha, 29 April 1938, *Harijan*, 7 May 1938, Vol. 6, 1938-39, p. 104.
55. Letter from K.F. Nariman to K.P. Neelakanta Pillai, Secretary, KPCC, File No. 1, p. 87, Pattam Thanu Pillai Papers, NMML.
56. Gandhiji's statement 29 April 1938, *Harijan* 7 May 1938, Vol. 6/1938-39, p. 104.
57. Letter from Mirza Ismail to Mahatma Gandhi, 1 May 1938. File No. 296-P(S)/1938, CRR, IOL, ACC 3, NAI.
58. In this connection it is interesting to note that T.B. Sapru resented Congress interference in the states as he saw "not the slightest reason why the Congress should be multiplying its battle front". He was critical of the dictatorial tone adopted by the Congress High Command, which he proclaimed "with the trappings of democracy" with no organised party to oppose, it acted in the most dictatorial manner which would ultimately "be its internal rot". See letter from T.B. Sapru to C.Y. Chintamani 6 May 1938. Mirza Ismail Collection, NMML.
59. He seems to have forgotten that he came as a mediator in his personal capacity. Extensive quotation of Vallabhbhai Patel's speech of 8 May 1938 in the Residents reports of 14 May 1938. CRR, IOL, ACC 1, NAI.
60. For the Government's declaration on the flag issue prior to Patel's arrival, where it expressed its resentment at such demonstrations as

expressing an allegience to an authority outside the state, see Proceedings of the Mysore Government, May 1938. G.O. No. 3516-3524, KSA.

61. Resolution passed by the Mysore Congress, 10 June 1938, after a reading of a letter from the Indian National Congress President, Subhas Chandra Bose, of 20 May 1938, File No. G-88 (Part 2)/1938, p. 205, and p. 279, AICC Papers, NMML.
62. Ibid.
63. Comments of Home Department on Mysore's dlfficulties, 20 May 1938, File No. 296-P(S)/1938, CRR, IOL, ACC 3, NAI.
64. Letter from Resident to Polindia on settlement of Mysore Government with Mysore Congress, 17 May 1938, File No. 296-P(S)/1938, CRR, IOL, ACC 3, NAI.
65. Comments of Secretary, Political Department, 16 May 1938, File No. 296-P(S)/1938, CRR, IOL, ACC 3, NAI.
66. Noting by Thorne Smith Secretary, Home Department 20 May 1938, File No. 296-P(S)/1938, CRR, IOL, ACC 3, NAI.
67. Letter from Viceroy to Secretary of State, 24 May 1938, File No. 296-P(S)/1938, CRR, IOL, ACC 3, NAI.
68. Comments of Secretary, Political Department, 16 May 1938, File No. 296-P(S)/1938, CRR, IOL, ACC 3, NAI.
69. Ibid.
70. The earlier committee of 20 had been augmented not only by the additional members from the Congress Party but another 3 nominated by the government.
71. The Constitutional Reforms Committee Report subsequently brushed aside this proposal on the plea that passing as the country was through rapid changes, it was impossible for anyone to foresee the trend of political activities a decade ahead, let alone pronounce that their ultimate aim was responsible government. See *Report of the Committee on Constitutional Reforms in Mysore*, 1939 p. 29.
72. Resident's Report, 28 July 1938, CRR, IOL, ACC 3, NAI.
73. *The Hindu*, 10 May 1938.
74. Letter and telegram from V.S. Narayana Rao to Vallabhbhai Patel, 10 May 1938. File No. G-88 Part 2/1938, p. 167, AICC Papers, NMML.
75. Letter from Resident to Political Secretary, 17 May 1938. File No. 296-P(S)/1938, CRR, IOL, ACC 3, NAI.
76. See letter from Siddalingiah to Vallabhbhai Patel 14 July 1938. File No. G-88 Part 2/1938, p. 277, AICC Papers, NMML. See also letter from Resident to Political Secretary, 17 May 1938, File No. 296-P(S)/1938, CRR, IOL, ACC 3, NAI.
77. See Government Order No. P. 6731-9. of 26 May 1938, and G.O. No. 21-29 of July 1938, Proceedings of the Mysore Government, KSA See also Working Committee resolution of the Mysore Congress, 27 and 28 June 1938. File No. G-88 Part 2/1938, AICC Papers, NMML. Even earlier vernacular papers had their licence cancelled for comparing the income of the Maharaja with that of a poor man,

See Resident's report3 May 1938, CRR, IOL, ACC 3, NAI.

78. Letter from V.S. Narayana Rao to Vallabhbhai Patel 10 May 1938. File No. G-88 Part 2/1938, AICC Papers, NMML.
79. Working Committee resolution of the Mysore Congress, 27 and 28 June 1938. See also letter from V.S. Narayana Rao to Secretary AICC, 1 July 1938, File No. G-88 Part 2/1938, AICC Papers, NMML.
80. Letter from Siddalingiah, President, Myore Congress, to Vallabhbhai Patel, 14 July 1938, File No. G-88 Part 2/1938, p. 277, AICC Papers, NMML.
81. Letter from Siddalingiah, President, Mysore Congress to Vallbhbhai Patel 14 July 1938. File No. G-88 Part 2/1938, p. 277, AICC Papers, NMML. See also letter from Siddalingiah to Chief Secretary Government of Mysore, 12 July 1938. File No. G-88 Part 2/1938, AICC Papers, NMML.
82. Quotations from the letter of Vallabhbhai Patel by the Resident in his report of 28 July 1938, CRR, IOL, ACC 1, NAI.
83. Statement issued by Chengalaraya Reddy on Viduraswatha Enquiry Committee Chairman's behaviour, 3 August 1938. File No. G-88 Part 2/1938, p. 295, AICC Papers, NMML.
84. Letter from Siddalingiah to Vallabhbhai Patel 14 July 1938. File No. G-88 Part 2, 1938, AICC Papers, NMML. He complained of Mysore Government's persecution of Congressmen for offences that were age old and petty, mainly to frighten capitalists from extending any support to its movement.
85. Note by Glancy, Political Secretary, Government of India on his conversations with Mirza Ismail, 20 September 1938. File No. 299-P(S)/1938, CRR, IOL, ACC 3, NAI.
86. See conclusions of the Report of the Enquiry Committee on Viduraswatha firing 19 November 1938. KSA.
87. Resident's report, 29 November 1938. CRR, IOL, ACC 1, NAI.
88. Apart from the conclusions of the report cited above, see also Working Committee resolution of the Mysore Congress on the Viduraswatha firings, 21 November 1938. File No. G-35/Part 1/1938-39, AICC Papers, NMML.
89. Working Committee resolution of the Mysore Congress on Ramesam Committee, 21 November 1938. File No. G-35 Part 1, 1938-39, p. 43, AICC Papers, NMML.
90. The Mysore Reforms Committee proposals, in lieu of Cabinet responsibility, proposed an Executive Council jointly responsible to the Maharaja, consisting of not less than 5 members, including the Dewan. Two concillors were to be selected by the Maharaja from among the elected members of the Assembly and Council. However there wos no guarantee that even these two members would be chosen from the majority party. In the name of joint responsibility what was sought was an irremovable executive even in case of an adverse vote in the Legislature. For Reforms proposals See *Report of the Committee on Constitutional Reforms*, 6 November 1939, KSA. The

Residents Supplementary Report on Constitutional Reforms Committee, 16 November 1939, CRR, IOL, ACC 1, NAI, and the article by K.T. Bhashyam—The 'Mysore Struggle' published in the *Indian Express* January 1940, a copy of which is available in File No. 13, Group 1, p. 613, AISPC Papers, NMML.

91. Letter from H.C. Dasappa to Jawaharlal Nehru, 7 February 1939. File No. G-35 Part 1 1938 39, p. 29, AICC Papers, NMML. See also R.R. Diwakar's speech reported by the Resident 15 February 1939, CRR, IOL, ACC 1, NAI.
92. Mr. Hamilton, it was alleged by H.C. Dasappa in the Council, had remarked that he would even shoot fifty persons if necessary to maintain law and order. Coming as this declaration did, soon after the Viduraswatha shooting, naturally irritated the Mysore Congressmen's susceptibilities. See Legislative Council Proceedings, January 1939, also see Resident's report 1 February 1939, CRR, IOL, ACC 1, NAI.
93. Resident's report 1 March 1939, 15 April 1939, CRR, IOL, ACC 1, NAI. See also Mysore Congress resolutions passed at Viduraswatha on 17 April 1939. File No. 13, Group 1, p. 417, AISPC Papers, NMML.
94. According to the pact entered into with Vallabhbhai Patel the Mysore Government had agreed to having 7 members as its quota from the Reforms Committee. Its refusal to consider the appointment of a fresh member was regarded by the State Congress as breaking of the pact. See Resident's report 1 February 1939, CRR, IOL, ACC 1, NAI. See also letter from H.C. Dasappa to Nehru 7 February 1939, and *Report of the Committee* (published on 6 November 1939), pp. 1-2. KSA.
95. Report of the Congress in Karnataka, compiled by D. Narasingh for the AICC of the INC, 13 July 1939, File No. G-28/1938, p. 21, AICC papers, NMML.
96. Only 8 out of the 13 members in the Legislative Council, 49 out of 140 in the Representative Assembly and 5 out of 7 in the Reforms Committee withdrew from these bodies.
97. Resident's report 31 March 1939, CRR, IOL, ACC 1, NAI.
98. Resident's report 30 April 1939 and 1 July 1939 CRR, IOL, ACC 1, NAI. See also Report of the second phase of satyagraha issued by State Congress, 4 October 1939. File No. 13, Group 1, p. 337, AISPC Papers, NMML.
99. Resident's report, 30 April 1939. CRR, IOL, ACC 1, NAI.
100. Mirza Ismail issued a personal invitation to Mahatma Gandhi and Vallabhbhai Patel to come and rest at Mysore as state guests. This was soon after Rajkot fast of Mahatma Gandhi. He praised Mahatma Gandhi's moderation and 'practicalness' in the subject of reforms and the British Indian leaders were not far back in this game of back scratching. While Pattabhi Sitaramayya, the ex-President, of the AISPC praised the industrial policy of Mysore, C. Rajagopalachari attended the Mysore Representative Assembly from which the Congress leaders had resigned. See Resident's report 15 May 1939, and 15 June 1939, CRR,IOL, ACC 1, NAI.

101. Impressions of the Viceroy on Mysore in a report to the Secretary of State 17 January 1939, File No. 46 (24)-P(S)/1939, CRR, IOL, ACC 3, NAI.
102. During this period, Siddalingiah and 11 other Congressmen were arrested for making speeches in spite of there being no official ban on it, see File No. G-12/1937-39, AICC Papers, NMML.
103. In May 1939 a leading article was published in *The Hindu* giving a version of the recommendation of the Reforms Committee and criticising it as being too cautious. This article was not refuted by the Mysore Government which showed that the decisions of the Reforms Committee were to be on same lines. See *The Hindu*, May 1939, and also Residents report, 1 June 1939, CRR, IOL, ACC 1, NAI.
104. Intercepted letter from Mahadev Desai to Ramachandran, 13 June 1939, CRR, IOL, ACC 1, NAI.
105. Bhupalam Chandrasekharaiya did interview Vallabhbhai Patel in June 1939. (See Resident's Report 1 July 1939, CRR, IOL, ACC 1, NAI) This was to counteract the plan of Mysore Congress leaders to work in conjunction with Travancore Congress on parallel lines (see Resident's report 15 June 1939, CRR, IOL, ACC 1, NAI)
106. Entered into with the help of Vallabhbhai Patel, see *ante*, pp. 172-173.
107. Nehru remarking on this denial as 'significant of the new mentality' pointed out that if Mirza Ismail had his will the last year and more would have to be 'scratched out of the pages of history'. Quoted in *The Mysore Struggle*, op. cit. File No. 13, Group 1, p. 337, AISPC Papers, NMML. See also Mirza Ismail at the Legislative Council on budget discussions, 17 July 1939, and Residents report, 1 August 1939, 15 June 1939, CRR, IOL, ACC 1, NAI.
108. Residents report 15 July 1939, CRR, IOL, ACC 1, NAI. See also *The Mysore Struggle*, a report published by Mysore Congress to AISPC, 4 October 1939. File No. 13, Group 1, p. 338, AISPC Papers, NMML.
109. The private interview of K.T. Bhashyam with the Dewan requesting him to grant an interview to the Mysore Congress and not to judge them by their belligerent speeches which he disclaimed was for the public, was purposely leaked out to the press. See Resident's report, 1 August 1939, CRR, IOL, ACC 1, NAI.
110. This in spite of novel tactics adopted by the state administration, when instead of arresting volunteers it took them in lorry loads and dumped them in out of the way spots. See letter from Second Dictator, Mysore Congress to Resident, AICC, 5 September 1939, File No. G-12/1937-39, AICC Papers, NMML.
111. Resident's report, 17 October 1939, 16 November 1939, CRR, IOL, ACC 1, NAI. See also intercepted letter from Jawaharlal Nehru to Mysore Congress (undated) sent along with Resident's letter to Polindia 20 October 1939. CRR, IOL, ACC 1, NAI.
112. There is little documentary evidence to show on whose invitation Mahadev Desai was sent as Gandhi's emissary. A spurious report

purported to have been given by H.C Dasappa alleged that Gandhi had given them advice 'to manoeuvre the situation' to force the Dewan to come to a settlement. When confronted by this statement by the Dewan, Mahadev Desai denied any such interview having been given. (See enclosure to Desai's Note 11 December 1939. File No. 46(24)-P(S)/1939, CRR, IOL, ACC 2, NAI.

113. See *ante* p. 172.
114. Resident's report, 15 December 1939, CRR, IOL, ACC 1, NAI.
115. A copy of the report was sent to Mirza Ismail on 31 December 1939. In between, Mirza Ismail who had made a trip to Shegaon to see Gandhi on 29 December 1939, had K.T. Bhashyam and other members of the Mysore Congress clapped in jail. (See letter from Mirza Ismail to Gandhi, 31 December 1939, CRR, IOL, ACC 2, NAI. Residents report 3 January 1940, CRR, IOL, ACC 1, NAI., and report by the Mysore Congress to AISPC 29 January 1940, File No. 13, Group 1, p. 229, AISPC Papers, NMML.
116. This was corroborated by V.S. Narayana Rao, a long time secretary of the Mysore Congress, in a personal interview with the author.
117. The Nageswara Rao Enquiry Committee was constituted by the Dewan to go into the question of police excesses. But in view of Gandhi's advice to the State Congress members not to give evidence, its judgement that there was no instance of torture or ill-treatment was proved puerile. See Resident's report 2 February 1940, CRR, IOL, ACC 1, NAI. See also report to the AISPC by the State Congress 29 January 1940, File No. 13, Group 1, p. 229, AISPC Papers, NMML & article by Gandhi, 'A One Sided Enquiry,' 11 May 1940, *Harijan*, Vol. 7, p. 121.
118. For Gandhi's correspondence with Mirza Ismail on the issue, see telegram from Gandhi to Mirza, 18 January 1940, 31 January 1940. CRR, IOL, ACC 2, NAI.
119. Resolution on suspension of civil disobedience undated February 1940, File No. G-72/1940, p. 1155, AICC Papers, NMML. See also 15 March 1940, CRR, IOL, ACC 2, NAI.
120. Report by K. Pattabhi Raman "What the Mysore Congress has achieved", 1940, File No. 13, Group 1, p. 213, AISPC Papers, NMML.
121. See letter from Gandhi to Mirza Ismail, 31 January 1940, CRR, IOL, ACC 2, NAI.
122. API Report on the proceedings of the Subjects Committee open session, 20 March 1940. File No. G-24/1942, part 4, p. 248, AICC Papers, NMML.
123. Refer letter from AGG, Madras State to Polindia, 5 April 1938, for the gist of C.P. Ramaswami Aiyar's letter to the Resident, 3 April 1938, File No. 197-P(S)/1938, CRR, IOL, ACC 1, NAI.
124. Prohibitory orders were issued at Trivandrum, Chengannur, Alleppey, Quilon, Shertallai, Kottayam, Neyyatinkara etc. on 7, 9, 16, 24 March 1938, and 9 April and 8 May respectively.

125. Police Report, 28 April 1938. File No. 2701/1944, Cellar Records, Kerala Secretariat.
126. Police Report, 25 April 1938, File No. 2709/1944, Cellar Records, Kerala Secretariat.
127. Resident's reports to Polindia on the All Kerala Nair Conference, 3 May 1938, 13 May 1938, 3 June 1938, CRR, IOL, ACC 133, NAI.
128. Resident's report 3 June 1938, CRR, IOL, ACC 133, NAI. See also Police Reports of the meetings of the Travancore National Congress, 1 August 1938 and 8 August 1938. File No. 130/1945, Cellar Records, Kerala Secretariat.
129. Ibid. See also Resident's report 3 May 1938, 13 May 1938, 3 June 1938, CRR, IOL,ACC 133, NAI.
130. In view of the ban imposed in Travancore at several places, the Travancore State Congress had tried to hold meetings at Madras in April 1938. In this C. Rajagopalachari as chief minister of Madras seems to have had his reservations in allowing such a meeting here and allowed it only on promise by the Travancore State Congress that they would say nothing incompatible with his position as premier. See letter from Pattam Thanu Pillai to C. Rajagopalachari 14 April 1938 and 19 April 1938. File No. 1, p. 61, Pattam Thanu Pillai Papers, NMML, See also Resident's report, 3 May 1938, CRR, IOL, ACC 133, NAI.
131. Resident's report of the Travancore State Congress meeting at Neyyatinkara 8 May 1938, dated 16 May 1938, CRR, IOL, ACC 133, NAI.
132. See Press Note issued by Travancore Government, 2 July 1938, CRR, IOL, ACC 133, NAI.
133. Resident's report, 16 May 1938, CRR, IOL, ACC 133, NAI.
134. Even at a later date the Resident reiterated yet again that there was 'no doubt' that the responsibility rested on Travancore police for their failure to deal effectively with these attacks by hooligans on individuals. See Resident's report, 16 May 1938, CRR IOL, ACC 133, NAI.
135. See *Travancore Today Her Struggle for Freedom*, p. 20. See also Appendices to same volume, part IV, pp. 170-186 for statement and press references on it. The Memorandum complained of the stringency of licensing system under the newspaper regulations to add to which extra-legal methods had been adopted to 'correct' their criticisms. See *Travancore Today Her Struggle for Freedom*, pp. 17-19, and the suppression orders served on *The Kaumudi*, daily and weekly 16 and 24 March 1938, *The Malabar Herald*, 14 February 1938, the note by the Travancore State Congress on the "Freedom of Press in Travancore" published in *The Prabodhini*, 17 May 1938, published as Appendices, Part III, items, XIX, XX, XXIII respectively.
136. Ibid., pp. 21-24.
137. This was of significance as it was fears of nationalisation of the backwater traffic which made for a strike among the boatmen. See *post* p. 183.
138. Even at the time of C.P. Ramaswami Aiyar's resignation in 1947, a

demand was made that these charges be examined by an independent tribunal.

139. Resident's report, 17 July 1938, CRR, IOL, ACC 133, NAI.
140. Resident's report on affairs in Travancore, 11 October 1938, File No. 739-P S)/38 of 1938, CRR, IOL, ACC 137, NAI.
141. For reports on the controversy, see Resident's report for 1st half of May 1938, 3rd July 1938 and 11 October 1938, CRR, IOL, ACC 138, NAI.
142. According to the Resident, the directors of this bank, Messrs Mammen Mappillai and Mathen, fearing a crash, had as early as 13 May 1938, through an intermediary, intimated to the Dewan and the Resident, the nature of the memorandum under preparation and had promised to prevent its publication if the government would give them the required help. It was only on the Dewan's refusal to oblige that the memorandum, which had been printed at Cochin at the cost of Travancore National and Quilon Bank, been circulated in July. See letters from Resident to Polindia, 11 October 1938, and of C.P. Ramaswami Aiyar to Resident, 31 October 1938. File No. 739-P(S)/38 of 1938, CRR, IOL, ACC 137, NAI.
143. G. Ramachandran, whose son was married to Gandhi's granddaughter was one of those who requested intercession. See Resident's report 17 July 1938, CRR, IOL, ACC 133, NAI.
144. See letter of C.P. Ramaswami Aiyar to AGG, Madras, 31 October 1938, CRR, IOL, ACC 137, NAI.
145. Rajkumari Amrit Kaur's advise to the State administrators to lift the ban on meetings was in turn refused by the administration which insisted on the withdrawal of the memorandum. See Resident's report 2 September 1938, CRR, IOL, ACC 133, NAI.
146. See Police Report, 30 August 1938, File No. 3/1945, Cellar Records, Kerala Secretariat, and also telegram from AGG, Madras State to Polindia 1 September 1938, CRR, IOL, ACC 137, NAI.
147. See Colonel Wathis' report on firing at Neyyatinkara, 2 September 1938, CRR, IOL, ACC 137, NAI. See also Police Report, September 1938, File No. 50/1938, Cellar records, Kerala Secretariat.
148. Resulting in 3 dead, 5 injured. Police report 1 September 1938, File No. 4487/1944, Cellar Records, Kerala Secretariat.
149. Two Killed, several injured, telegram, 3 September 1938, CRR, IOL, ACC 137, NAI.
150. Resident's report, 19 September 1938, CRR, IOL, ACC 137, NAI.
151. Statement to the press on Travancore situation, 3 September 1938. The *Harijan*, 10 September 1938. Vol. 6, (1938-39), p. 252.
152 See *Harijan* 6 September, 24 to 26 September 1938, Vol. 6 (1938-39), p. 278, p. 252, and 17 September 1939, p. 258, See also Resident's report 16 September 1938, CRR, IOL, ACC 133, NAI.
153. Residents report 7 September 1938, CRR, IOL, ACC 133, NAI.
154. See *ante* p. 175. The political Department demurred to such a suggestion as it could raise doubts as to the independence of the Travancore

judiciary. The popularity of the movement can be gauged by the fact that the Resident felt that the Judges of Travancore, with no exception, could be relied upon to be unaffected by popular clamour against the Dewan and police and would probably acquit state Congress leaders. This was in contrast to affairs in Mysore where in reply to Gandhi's objection against an enquiry by a Mysore judge, in the Nageswara Rao enquiry against police excesses, the Dewan protested that it would reflect on the integrity of the judiciary in Mysore. see Telegram of Resident to Polindia, 10 September 1938, and 11 September 1938, CRR, IOL, ACC 137, NAI.

155. Resident's report, 16 September 1938, CRR, IOL, ACC 133, NAI and 10 October 1938, CRR, IOL, ACC 137, NAI.
156. Police Report, 2 October 1938. File No, 1/1945, Cellar Records, Kerala Secretariat.
157. One of the gimmicks introduced at these meetings among boatmen was to organise them on floating platforms, created on boats tied together. More importantly this strike was the signal for the spread of the movement among labour organisations. In this the Travancore Coir Factory Workers Union organised a general strike on 19 October 1938 and a general strike was organised at Alleppey. See Resident's report 10 October 1938, 17 October 1938, 19 October 1938, CRR, IOL. ACC 137, NAI.
158. Resident's report, 6 October 1938, CRR, IOL, ACC 133, NAI.
159. Press Statement by Gandhi 8 October 1938. *Harijan* Vol. 6 (1938-39), p. 279.
160. Resident's report 26 October 1938, CRR, IOL, ACC 137, NAI. See also Gandhi's statement to the Press, 29 October 1938, *Harijan*, Vol. 6, (1938-39), p. 312.
161. Letter from C.P. Ramaswami Aiyar to Skrine, AGG, Madras State, 30 October 1938, CRR, IOL, ACC 137, NAI.
162. Resolution 4, of the Working Committee meeting of 30 October 1938. Copies available in CRR, IOL, ACC 137, NAI.
163. Resolution 10, of the Working Committee meeting of 30 October 1938. Ibid.
164. C.P. Ramswami Aiyar's letter to AGG, Madras State 30 October 1933, CRR, IOL, ACC 137, NAI; See also Police Report 29 November 1938, for strikes organised among boatmen, file No. 1970/1944, Cellar Records, Kerala Secretariat.
165. A characteristic of this phase of the movement was the help given by the other two areas of Kerala to it, both in men and money. A *jatha* of thirty volunteers participated in the movement from Malabar and Cochin. See Resident's report, 18 September 1938, 23 September 1938, and 8 November 1938, File No. P. 36/1938, CRR, IOL, ACC 137, NAI. See also resolution passed by the Workers Union, Calicut, 25 September 1938, File No. G-35 Part VII, p. 138, AICC Papers, NMML, and the account of a meeting of Keralites at Delhi, 20 September 1938, *The Hindu*, 20 September 1938.

166. Resident's report, 2 November 1938, CRR, IOL, ACC 133, NAI.
167. Informer's report of Travancore State Congress meeting of 27 November 1938, dated 29 November 1938, File No. 2762/1944, Cellar Records, Kerala Secretariat. See also *Harijan*, 17 September 1938. Vol. 6 (1938-39) p. 382.
168. See Mahatma Gandhi's statement to the press, 10 December 1938 *Harijan*, 17 December 1938, Vol. 6 (1938-39), p. 382.
169. Ibid. This statement was appropos of withdrawal of memorandum and not of responsible government versus *swaraj*.
170. Police report of an informer's report of talks of Travancore State Congress 30 November 1938, File No. 2762/1944, Cellar Records, Kerala Secretariat.
171. Copy of Proclamation issued by H.H. the Maharaja of Travancore, 13 December 1938, File No. 1, p. 237, Pattam Thanu Pillai Papers, NMML. See also 16 December 1938, CRR, IOL, ACC 133, NAI.
172. Gandhi advised that the statement withdrawing the memorandum clearly stipulate that the allegations made by them were made with a full sense of responsibility, that their belief in the truth of those allegations still persisted and that they withdrew it only on a realisation that these allegations would harm the greater struggle for responsible government. See Telegram from Mahatma Gandhi to Pattam Thanu Pillai, 15 December 1938 and telegram from Gandhi to Pattam Thanu Pillai, 18 December 1938. File No. 1. pp. 254-55, Pattam Thanu Pillai Papers, NMML.
173. A small triumph was allowed the Dewan when he prevented the meeting of two converging processions to meet at a common site and this important resolution had to be read at two different points. For an account of the meetings. see Resident's report, 6 January 1939, CRR, IOL, ACC 133, NAI.
174. Statement issued by R. Sankar, 31 December 1938, CRR, IOL, ACC 137, NAI.
175. See *ante* p. 182.
176. See *ante* p. 168.
177. In a letter to Pattam Thanu Pillai on 9 November 1938, T. Siddalingiah wrote "I read in the papers that your state Congress are going on a deputation to Mahatmaji. I hope we stop such a move now". See File No. 1, p. 173, Pattam Thanu Pillai Papers, NMML.
178. Letter from Siddalingiah, President Mysore Congress, to Pattam Thanu Pillai, 6 January 1939, File No. 9, pp. 1-3, Pattam Thanu Pillai Papers, NMML.
179. The second memorial was drafted by John Kuruvilla of Cochin and printed and broadcast in Ernakulam in Cochin territory. See Residents reports, 5 January 1939, and 15 January 1939, CRR, IOL, ACC 135, NAI.
180. The Government's gesture was motivated not so much on grounds of reciprocal clemency but through a realisation that as the charges would not be defended, judgment as *exparte* decisions would be made

capital of by the state Congress. See C.P. Ramaswami Aiyar's letter to Skrine, 2 January, 1939, CRR, IOL, ACC 137, NAI,

181. Travancore Bulletin No. 2, 8 January 1939. *Harijan*, 18 February 1939, Vol. 7 (1939-43), p. 19. See also Resident's report 15 February 1939, CRR, IOL, ACC 135, NAI. See also Ramachandran's speech quoted in the same issue, p. 19.

182. Statement issued by Pattam Thanu Pillai, 14 January 1939. File No. 2, Pattam Thanu Pillai Papers, NMML.

183. Statement issued by the Working Committee of Travancore State Congress, 17 to 21 January 1939. *Harijan*, 25 February 1939, Vol. 7, (1939-40), p. 31.

184. The demand for such a move came from the government sponsored Travancore National Congress. Muslims waited on the Dewan and made a representation that their position be not jeopardised by this move, to which the Dewan commended their loyalty with appreciation and referred them to the so called majority party in the legislature—the Travancore National Congress. See Resident's report March 1939, CRR, IOL, ACC 145, NAI. For Working Committee resolution of 17 to 21 January 1939 see the *Harijan*, 25 February 1939, Vol. 7, (1939-40), p. 32, See also Resident's report, 30 January 1939, CRR, IOL, ACC 137, NAI. for a copy of the resolution passed.

185. Picketting of toddy shops commenced as early as November 1938, but was never taken up seriously till after the withdrawal of the memorandum in January 1939. Even now K.C. George the Secretary of the Travancore Youth League pointed out that the prohibition programme did not appeal to the masses as it threw out of employment "about one and a half lakh of skilled labourers", for whom while it was easy to say alternative jobs were to be provided, in practical terms was impossible to do, See File No. 1167/1944, Cellar Records, Kerala Secretariat and letter from K.C. George to Pattam Thanu Pillai, 3 February 1939, File No. 2 (1939-40), p. 37, Pattam Thanu Pillai Papers, NMML, See also Resident's report, 15 January 1939, CRR, IOL, ACC 135, NAI.

186. Travancore Bulletin by G. Ramachandran 28 January 1939, *Harijan*, 25 February 1939, Vol 7 (1939-40), p. 30.

187. See letter from P.K. Ramakrishna Pillai, delegate AISPC to Pattam Thanu Pillai, 22 February 1939, File II, p. 53, Pattam Thanu Pillai Papers, NMML.

188. Gandhi's editorial on *Travancore Again*, 25 February 1939, *Harijan*, Vol. 7, (1939-40), p. 29.

189. The Dewan proclaimed his intention to the British administrators that in such a contingency he be allowed to prohibit his entry and if disobeyed even arrest him. To which the British authorities had agreed. Telegram from AGG, Madras state to Polindia, 23 March 1939, and reply from Polindia, to AGG Madras State, 26 March 19 9, CRR, IOL, ACC 137, NAI.

190. The plan of agitation was projected in several stages. The first

commencing with picketing of liquor shops, manufacture of salt, opening of volunteer camps distribution of banned literature etc., leading to the next stage of disobedience of forest law, ending with the final stage of non-payment of taxes.

191. *Harijan*, 18 March 1939, Vol. 7 (1939-40), p. 53. See also his telegram to R. Shanker, 20 March 1939 and from Philipose 21 March 1939 where the only direction from Gandhi was that they commence satyagraha only when they received an intimation from him. Otherwise they had no inkling that he would advise for a total suspension. See File No. 2, p. 79, and 51, Pattam Thanu Pillai Papers, NMML.

192. These hirelings turned up at the meetings of the Travancore State Congress completely drunk and under the supervison of regular police men in mufti, abused them and created a melee. C.P. Ramaswami Aiyar repudiating these charges maintained that the irregular force was in no way less trained than the volunteers of the Congress. See statement issued bp N.S.K. Pillai, acting President, Travancore State Congress, 23 March 1939, File No. 4, p. 42, Pattam Thanu Pillai Papers, NMML and letter from C.P. Ramaswami Aiyar, 24 March 1939, *The Hindu*, 24 March 1939.

193. The statement to the Press by Gandhi, API version, 23 March 1939, *The Hindu*, 23 March 1939.

194. See Gandhi on *Repression in Travancore*, 4 April 1939, the *Harijan*, 8 April 1939 Vol. 7 (1939-40), p. 81, see also Travancore State Congress Working Committee resolution, 17 April 1939, the *Harijan*, 22 April 1939

195. *Unhappy Travancore* Statement by Gandhi, 17 April 1939, *Harijan*, 22 April 1939.

196. Gandhi's editorial, *New Technique in Action*, 4 June 1939, *Harijan*, 10 June 1939 Vol. 7 (1939-40) p. 153.

197. With the aim of promoting the federal ambitions possibly--though this was not exactly spelt out.

198. See Gandhi's editorial *New Technique in Action*, 4 June 1939. *Harijan*, 10 June 1939 Vol. 7, p. 153.

199. A committee of three under Pattam Thanu Pillai with T.M. Varghese and V.K. Velayudhan was to act as negotiators under the direction of Gandhi. See file No. 2763/1944, Cellar Records, Kerala Secretariat.

200. For correspondence on negotiations see letter from Gandhi to Pattam Thanu Pillai, 24 June 1939, from Pattam Thanu Pillai to C.P. Ramaswami Aiyar 26 June 1939, File No. 2, pp. 273-74, Pattam Thanu Pillai Papers, NMML. See also Resident's report 15 July 1939, CRR, IOL, ACC 135, NAI, Gandhi to C.P. Ramaswami Aiyar, 10 August 1939, Note by Glancy on talks with Mahadev Desai 19 August 1939, File No. 6(50)P S/1939, CRR, IOL, ACC 137, NAI.

201. Letter from Gandhi to C.P. Ramaswami Aiyar 10 August 1939, File No. 5(50)-P(S)/1939, CRR, IOL, ACC 137, NAI.

202. Letter from C.P. Ramaswami Aiyar to Gandhi 15 August 1939, File No. 6(50)-P(S)/1939, CRR, IOL, ACC 137, NAI.

203. See letter from Gandhi to Pattam Thanu Pillai 31 August 1939 and Pattam Thanu Pillai to C.P. Ramaswami Aiyar 24 August 1939. File No. 2, pp. 299-305 and p 295 respectively, Pattam Thanu Pillai Papers, NMML.
204. Resident's report, 15 September 1939, CRR, IOL, ACC 135, NAI. See also resolutions passed at State Congress meeting 6 September 1939, File No. 62/1939, Cellar records, Kerala Secretariat.
205. See extracts of Travancore Government communique of 23 September 1939, published in the *Harijan,* 7 October 1939, Vol 7, pp. 297-98. See also telegram from Travancore State Congress to Gandhi, published in *Harijan,* 14 October 1939, Vol. 7, p. 305, and Resident's report 30 Septem ber 1939, and 3 November 1939, CRR, IOL, ACC 135, NAI.
206. See 'Travancore Again', by Gandhi, 6 November 1939, *Harijan,* 11 November 1939, p. 333.
207. These meetings were organised to protest against the 60th birthday celebrations of the Dewan as a state ceremony.
208. In May 1939 the first signs of Ezhava disgruntlement was seen in the interview by Yogam Secretary with the Dewan, and there were frantic telegrams sent on the resignation of some Ezhava leaders. See telegram from Mathew to Pattam Thanu Pillai, Pattam Thanu Pillai Papers, NMML.
209. Police report 16.4.115 M.B., corresponding to December 1939, File No. 1462/1944 Cellar Records, Kerala Secretariat.
210. Police Report of meeting at Kidangamparambur 1 December 1939, File No. 197/1938, Cellar Records, Kerala Secretariat.
211. Police transcript of S.C. Banerji's speech at Alleppey, 1 December 1938, File No. 197/1938, Cellar Records, Kerala Secretariat.
212. A.K. Pillai under whom it was organised, tried to do some propaganda in Mysore also, but here, in spite of the disenchantment with the Gandhian leadership, the masses remained still with the right wing.
213. See intercepted letter of E.M.S. Namboodiripad to Jaiprakash Narain, 20 July 1938. File No. 376/1939, Cellar Records, Kerala Secretariat.
214. Police Report of K.N. Joglekar's speech, 7 June 1939, File No. 320/1939, Cellar Records, Kerala Secretariat.
215. See *ante* pp. 157-161.

CHAPTER 7

NOTES

1. Letter of J. Nehru to Sheikh Abdullah, 7 January 1942, Jawaharlal Nehru Papers (JN Papers) Vol. 48, pp. 114-15, NMML.
2. Note on the tour of the Reforms Commissioner, 8 November 1941 to 7 December 1941, Annex to Document 30, para 4, p. 65, *Transfer of Power* (1942-47), Vol. 1, edited by Nicholas Mansergh and E.W.R. Lumby (1970).
3. See Aide Memoire presented by the Chamber of Princes, 25 January 1940 and also letter from Linlithgow to Zetland, 12 March 1940, Vol. 19, Reel 6, pp. 78, and p. 175, Zetland Collection, IOL, available in microfilm at NMML.
4. At this time the Dewan of Hyderabad.
5. See supplementary Report of the Resident Madras States, to Political Department 7 July 1940, CRR, IOL, ACC 2, NAI.
6. See Wylie's views on British policy towards the states as narrated by Wavell in his letter to Amery 29 December 1943. Document No. 287, para 3, p. 578, *Transfer of Power*, Vol. IV.

7. Wavell to Amery, 20 April 1944. Document No. 467, pp. 901-903, *op. cit.*, Vol. IV.
8. Only eight volumes consulted.
9. Linlithgow to Amery, recapitulating Amery's Memorandum of May 1941 in his letter of 13 September 1943. Document No. 111, p. 237, op. cit., Vol. IV.
10. The Cripps offer vis-a-vis the states dealt only with the long term plan. It conceded to the princes their right to 'appoint' representatives (replacing the words 'invited to send' in the original draft). The states were given the option to adhere to the states at the federal or individual union level or not at all. A concession granted to the princes as a "bargaining point, to teach the congress what it would have to face if it insisted on a separation from the Empire". The Congress objections to the Cripps proposal (apart from its being a post dated cheque) lay chiefly in the fact that these provisions struck at the very conception of Indian unity. See Draft Declaration, Annex to Document No. 265, pp. 357-58, Amery to Linlithgow, 1 March 1942, and 10 March 1942 and 24 April 1942, Documents No. 200, 296 and 683 p. 273, 396 and 844 respectively, and Cripps notes on his interview with Gandhi, 27 March 1942, Document No. 397, p. 498, op. cit, Vol. 1 and AICC resolution, **2** April 1942, File No. G-26/1942 (Part III), p. 167, AICC Papers NMML,
11. A part irritation of the princes against Cripps lay in the fact that he had accorded Pattabhi Sitaramayya an interview so as to give the states people a representation. For complaints of the princes on this score and the one cited in the text, see Jam Saheb's complaint to H. Craig, 1 June 1942, Document No. 115, pp. 165-75, and Linlithgow to Amery, 25 May 1942, Document No. 86, p. 190, op. cit., Vol. II.
12. Cripps proposition vis-a-vis the non-adhering states, that it was impossible to grant them protection in an independent India, had been disputed by Amery, who, on the analogy of South Africa thought it possible to continue such a relationship. See Amery to Linlithgow 26 March 1942, Douments no 386 end 410. p. 683 and p. 843 op. cit, Vol. I.
13. Two schemes for grouping were introduced during this period. The co-operative scheme sought to force the smaller states to come together of their free will, while the Attachment Scheme transferred certain police functions, hitherto exereised for them by the Political Department, to larger neighbouring states. The legality of this order was questioned by a Ruler and a ruling against the Government order on 6 December 1943, necessitated the passage of the Bill through the House of Commons on 8 February 1944.
14. The princes' efforts at getting a clear eommitment to their position from the Viceroy in September 1944 having failed, they strove to move a resolution on this in the Chamber of Princes. The Viceroy's disapproval to the discussion of 'so delicate a topic' in the Chamber, led to the Standing Committee of the Chamber of Princes resignation.

Wavell's refusal to be pressurised by these tactics led ultimately to the withdrawal of these resignations. See Bhopals letter to princes 14 December 1944 and enclosure to Document No. 157 pp. 320-324, Bhopal to Wylie as reported to Wavell, Wavell's letter to Amery 4 December 1944, Document No. 131, pp. 265-266, Griffin to Bhopal, 26 November 1944. Document No. 112, pp. 235-236, draft letter by Wavell to princes, which was however withdrawn, 21 January 1945, Documents No. 221, p. 437, and Bhopal to Wavell 9 February 1945, Document No. 225, p. 532. *op. cit.* Vol. V, Bhopal to Wavell 15 July 1945, Document No. 617, p. 1255.

15. See Colville to Wavell, 3 September 1945, Document No. 86, para 6, p. 119, op. cit. Vol. VI.
16. Cabinet discussions by India-Burma Committee 1 September 1945 and 11 September 1945. Document No. 101 and 105, p. 239 and p. 253, op. cit., Vol. VI respectively.
17. Proposed redefinition of His Majest's Government's obligations to the Indian Princes, Memorandum by Secretary of State of India, 9 October 1945. Document No. 137, pp. 326-29, op. cit., Vol. VI, emphasis supplied by me.
18. In this connection, there was one interesting point raised by Sir William Barton. The question was, who was to finance it? The princes for their part would contend that they had assigned territory to meet the cost of the military guarantee—a territory now included in the provinces. It was hardly conceivable that the new dominion would agree to finance those states which stood out from it—unless the defence system of the whole of India were to remain in the hands of a commonwealth! See "Princes in Politics in India", by Sir William Barton, in the *American Review*, Vol, 141, pp. 359-60,
19. Amery to Wavell. 26 October 1944. Document No. 72, pp. 155-156, *Transfer of Power*, Vol. V, op. cit.
20. Resolution of the Working Committee of the Indian National Congress, 24 May 1946. See *Speeches and Documents on the Indian Constitution* (1921-47) Vol. 2, p. 593, edited by Sir Maurice Gwyer and A. Appadorai. This vagueness it must be admitted in fairness, also penalised the princes. As Sir Evan Jenkins, the private Secretary to the Viceroy, pointed out, representation to these states had been granted without indicating their subsequent rights as units. Memorandum and Minutes by E. Jenkins and Wavell, 22-28 August 1945. Document No. 53, p. 123-24, op. cit., Vol. VI.
21. Shiva Rao advocated "the adoption of a more menacing tone" towards the princes and that the new proposal coming as from a "purely Labour Government" should encourage democratic and socially progressive forces in India, while encouraging small states to merge in British India it should ask the bigger states to send elected representatives to the proposed Constituent Assembly. See Shiva Rao's note on India, 20 August 1945, Document No. 16, pp. 100-105. *Transfer of Power* Vol. VI, op. cit. See also Gibson and Patrick's note

on Shiva Rao's proposal, 25 August 1947 and 27 August 1945, Documents No. 56 pp. 135-136 op. cit. Vol. VI.

22. Wavell advocated such a warning being issued and even drafted a note on it. See Cabinet discussions on the necessity for drafting of such a note and the draft documents No. 105 and 197, p. 254, and pp. 451-460 respectively, *Transfer of Power*, Vol. VI, op. cit.
23. As Pethick Lawrence pointed out while it was time to show the princes the 'red light' such a warning would "thoroughly unsettle them . . . (and) weaken their tactical position when the discussions were open." See Pethick Lawrence to Wavell 21 December 1945, Document No. 306, p. 670. *Transfer of Power*, Vol. VI, op. cit.
24. Statement by the Cabinet Mission to India, 16 May 1946. Command Paper 6821, Maurice Gwyer and Appadorai, op. cit., p. 580.
25. C.P. Ramaswami Aiyar was the main instigator on this issue. The States Peoples Negotiating Committee convened by Pattabhi Sitaramayya disputed the rights of representation of the princes of the Chamber of Princes itself and thus in its turn the states Negotiating Committee's proposals. See copies of notes prepared by Consambly, 8 January 1947. The Constituent Assembly's Negotiating Committee's views on it see File No. 29/1947, p. 17 and18/1947, pp. 497-507, AICC Papers, NMML and Shiva Rao, op. cit Vol. 1, for States Peoples Negotiating Committee's views, p. 612. See also Ramaswami Aiyar's interview to the API, 12 January 1947. File No. 18/1947, p. 267, AICC Papers, NMML.
26. B.N. Rau's Note Regarding Negotiations Between the States Committee and the Corresponding Committee of the Princes, 8 February 1947. Shiva Rao, Ibid., p. 618. See also note prepared by Shiva Rao, 28 January 1947, File No. 29/1947, pp. 29-36, AICC Papers, NMML.
27. See Resolutions passed at the princes meeting of 2 April 1947. Shiva Rao op. cit., p. 632.
28. Memorandum by D.V. Gundappa on the Constituent Assembly and the states given to the AICC and the Constituent Aseembly, 5 December 1946. File No. 18/1947, pp. 377-403, AICC Papers, NMML.
29. Bikaner's appeal to the AICC and AISPC, "the Indian Constitution and the States" Address delivered at Bikaner, 12 February 1946. *Asiatic Review*, Vol. 143, pp. 161-62.
30. Statement issued by Jawaharlal Nehru on major changes and Praja Mandals, 29 March 1946, File No. SPI/1945-48, pp. 104-105. AICC Papers, NMML.
31. See Nehru's speech moving the report of the States Committee in the Constituent Assembly, 28 April 1947, Shiva Rao, op. cit., Vol. 1, p. 738.
32. In this, Nehru's incidental reference that it was for the people to decide on internal administration of the states led to protests by C.P. Ramaswami Aiyar individually and the Chamber of Princes collectively. The Karnataka PCC in turn entered a note on it protesting

that 500 odd rulers and their henchmen could never represent the states. See note by KPCC, undated, presumably April-May 1947, File No. SPI/1945-48, p. 95-97, AICC Papers, NMML.

33. In this connection the paper prepared by Kachru on the possible role of the states peoples movement on integration is rather interesting. See AISPC—*A Brief History*, 1947. File No. 17/1947, pp. 7, AICC Papers, NMML, resolution passed by South ISPC, Trichur, 23 December 1945, File No. G/1942-45, pp. 311-312, AICC Papers, NMML. See also resolutions passed at the Jaipur session of AISPC, 23 October 1945. File No. 24/1946-47, p. 105, AICC Papers, NMML.
34. For States Peoples Negotiating Committee resolutions See Shiva Rao, op. cit., p. 612.
35. Statement by Pattabhi Sitaramayya, President, AISPC, 13 January 1948. File No. SPI/1945-48, AICC Papers, NMML. See also the Travancore Government's Police Reports on the Gwalior Conference, 10 May 1947. File No. 205/1947, Cellar Records, Kerala Secretariat.
36. See Police Report of Pattam Thanu Pillai's question and Rajendra Prasad's answer to the Working Committee of the Travancore State Congress, 10 May 1947, File No. 224/1947, Cellar Records, Kerala Secretariat.
37. See *post* p. 218.
38. S.N's summary of Gandhi's post prayer speeches, 13 June 1947, *Harijan*, 22 June 1947, Vol. XI, p. 197.
39. Gandhi at the AICC meeting, 14 June 1947, *Harijan*, 22 June 1947, Vol. XI, p. 197.
40. Ibid.
41. Resolution moved by Pattabhi Sitaramayya on the states, AICC on 14 June 1947.
42. Statement by Sardar Vallabhbhai Patel on Indian States, 5 July 1947. Refer Maurice Gwyer and A. Appadorai, op. cit., Vol. II, pp. 770-72.
43. Letter from Sardar Patel to Hari Singh, 3 July 1947, *Sardar Patel's Correspondence* (1945-50), Vol. 1, p. 33.
44. Sarat Chandra Bose opening the procedings of the Madras DCC, 15 December 1947. *The Hindu*, 16 September 1947.
45. Resolution passed by the AICC, Delhi, 16 November 1947. File No. 13, Group I, AISPC Papers, NMML.
46. See Shiva Rao, op. cit., Vol. IV, pp. 547-64.
47. For dissenting note of Hanumathaiya on this issue where he held that this para be vested with the states legislature see, Report of the Committee for the drafting of Model Constitution for the Indian States, 22 March 1949, paragraphs 5, 7, 9, 11, 14 and 18, Shiva Rao, Vol. IV, op. cit., pp. 552-53.
48. "A Revolution of the Indian States—A Transmigration of Paramountcy", *Round Table* (1948-49), Vol. 39, pp. 36-43.
49. See the Resident's reports for first half of February 1941, October 1941, December 1941, August 1943, December 1945, and second half of July 1942, November 1942, March 1943, January 1945, March

1945, CRR, IOL, ACC 134, 135 and 136 NAI and the *Cochin Legislative Council Proceedings* for those periods.

50. Mr. Dixon was dewan from June 1941 to November 1943 and Sir George Boag till March 1947, when a native-born Dewan, C.P. Karunakara Menon, took over.
51. The splinter groups from the original two parties, the Cochin Congress and the Cochin State Congress, coelesced to form a third party in a New Progressive Party. A no-confidence motion tabled by the Cochin State Congress against its rival, the Cochin Congress was defeated in April 1940 by this party abstaining from voting. See Resident's report, April 1940 CRR, IOL, ACC 133, NAI. In 1942, yet another party was forged when the Cochin State Congress formed a coalition with the New Progressive Party to form a Unionist Party with the rather mundane aim to confine their coalition "to the present working of the transferred subjects", and to an immediate defeat of the party in power—the Cochin Congress. See Resident's report, 28 February 1942, CRR, IOL, ACC 134, NAI.
52. See K.T. Bhashyam presiding at the Cochin Congress convention in May 1940 and the Raja of Nilambur presiding at the Cochin State Congress in June 1940. See also Resident's report from May 1940 and June 1940, CRR, IOL, ACC 134, NAI.
53. See the Resident's report for March 1941, December 1941 and February 1944. CRR, IOL, ACC 133, and 136, NAI.
54. The message of His Highness the Maharaja of Cochin to the Legislative Council 29 July 1946. File No. 39, p. 66, AISPC Papers 2nd instalment, NMML.
55. See manifesto issued by the Cochin Praja Mandal on "Why the Cochin Praja Mandal" 23 February 1942, File No. 39, pp. 92-99, AISPC Papers, 2nd instalment, NMML.
56. See Resident's report for second half of January 1942, CRR, IOL, ACC 134, NAI. See also resolution passed by the Working Committee of the Cochin State Praja Mandal 25 May 1942, File No. 5, p. 123, Group I, AISPC Papers, Private Collection, NMML.
57. Resident's report for 15 August 1942, 31 August 1942, 10 September 1942, 15 September 1942, CRR, IOL, ACC 134, NAI.
58. Resident's report 28 August 1942, CRR, IOL, ACC 134, NAI.
59. There were totally eight resignations in the legislature on this score. Six from the Cochin Congress, one from the Cochin State Congress & one independent member. The Trichur Minicipality resigned enmasse. See Resident's report September 1942, and October 1942. CRR, IOL, ACC 134, NAI.
60. Resident's report, September 1942, CRR, IOL, ACC 134, NAI.
61. The same period saw strikes organised at the Tata Oil Mills, Burmah Shell, Sitaram Spinning and Weaving Mills etc. See Residents reports for December 1943, 30 April 1944, and July 1944, CRR, IOL, ACC 133, NAI.
62. Resident's report, 15 June 1945, CRR, IOL, ACC 133, NAI.

63. Resident's report, 31 July 1945, CRR, IOL, ACC 133, NAI.
64. Resolution passed by the Cochin State Praja Mandal, 30 September 1945, File No. G-20/1942-45, pp. 311-12, AICC Papers, NMML.
65. Resolutions at this conference pleaded for a closer affiliation with the Indian National Congress and elected representatives to the Constituent Assembly. See SISPC resolutions, 22 and 23 December 1945. File No. G-20/1942-45, pp. 53-55, AICC Papers, NMML.
66. See Cochin Government Press Note 12 March 1946 File No. 39, pp. 72-87, AISPC Papers, second installment, NMML. For Travancore Governments unpopular education policy, see *post* note 131.
67. Government Order against M.M. Varkey, Cheriyan Manjuran etc. 6 April 1946, See File No 39. AISPC Papers, NMML.
68. Statement issued by the Cochin State Praja Mandal 9 September 1946, File No 39, p. 68, AISPC Papers, NMML.
69. For details on it see *post* p. 217.
70. Resident's report, December 1945, CRR, IOL, ACC 133, NAI.
71. Cochin Government's Gazette Extraordinary, 31 January 1946, CRR, IOL, ACC 133, NAI.
72. Cochin Government Gazette Extraordinary, 21 March 1946, File No. 39, AISPC Papers, NMML.
73. The message of His Highness the Maharaja of Cochin to the Legislative Council, 29 July 1946, File No. 39, AISPC Papers, NMML.
74. Statement to the press, issued by J. Nehru, 17 August 1946, File No. 39, p. 59, AISPC Papers, NMML.
75. On this score, and on score of having 1.48 million as its population, the Cochin administration asked for two seats to the Consambly but was refused demand. See telegram from the Maharaja of Cochin to the President of the Constituent Assembly Negotiating Committee, 18 February 1947. See Shiva Rao, op. cit., Vol. 1, p. 625.
76. See the *Indian Review*, October 1947, p. 38.
77. On the presentation of a Joint Memorial in the Legislature, a constitutional Committee had been appointed by the Maharaja in September 1946 consisting of a majority of elected members, see letter from President, Cochin State Praja Mandal to President, AISPC, 15 September 1946 and Proceedings on the appointment of a Constitutional Advisory Committee, 23 September 1946. File No. 39, AISPC Papers, NMML. and *Indian Review*, 1947, p. 559.
78. See report of K. Santhanam's speech at Madras and statement issued to the press by the Travancore State Congress, 27 March 1940. File No. 5, p. 67, AISPC Papers, Group I, (Private Collection) NMML. See also Travancore State Congress's Manifesto, written by A. Achutan, president of the Travancore State Congress, 27 July 1940, *The Harijan* 28 July 1940, Vol. 7, p. 225.
79. See Mahatma Gandhi in his 'Question Box' *Harijan*, 13 April 1940, Vol. 7, p. 9 and 283. See also Police report of State Congress activities sent by C.P. Ramaswami Aiyar to Resident, 28 March 1940. File No. 11/35-P(SEC)/1940, CRR, IOL, ACC 134, NAI.

80. Gandhi's editorial on "Ban on Congress activities in Travancore", 17 July 1940 *Harijan*, 21 July 1940, Vol. 7, p. 216.
81. Gandhi in a letter to Subhas Chandra Bose wrote that he had stopped civil disobedience in the states wherever he had influence--Travancore and Jaipur were examples of it—as he "breathed" "violence in the air" and saw "no atmosphere for non-violent action". See letter of Gandhi to Subhas, 10 April 1939, Vol. 9, p. 247, JN Correspondence, NMML.
82. Comment by G. Ramachandran on C.P. Ramaswami Aiyar's refusal to meet Mahatma Gandhi 17 July 1940 and Congress manifesto written by A. Achutan, *Harijan*, 28 July 1940, Vol. 7, p. 225, and statement issued by A. Achutan, 25 July 1940. File No. 5, p. 73, AISPC Papers Group I, NMML.
83. Travancore Government's press note, 29 July 1940. Published in the *Harijan*, 18 August 1940, Vol. 7, p. 256.
84. See Resident's report for August 1940, and September 1940, CRR, IOL, ACC 134, NAI.
85. See *ante* p. 139.
86. Among these 'mal-contents' were T.M. Verghese and G. Ramachandran, who worked mainly under the direction of Gandhi. See letter from C.P. Ramaswami Aiyar to Glancy, 23 March 1940 Police Intelligence Reports, for 5 April, 18 May 1940, and Residents report of 2 April 1940, File No. 11/35-P(SEC)/1940, CRR, IOL, ACC 134, NAI.
87. C.P. Ramaswami Aiyar's letter to Glancy, 1 May 1940 and enclosed police reports, File No. 11/35-P(SEC)/1940, CRR, IOL, ACC 134, NAI. See also police reports 27 April 1940, File No. 639/1946, Cellar Records, Kerala Secretariat.
88. Letter from Glancy to Resident (Undated, presumably March 1940) CRR, IOL, ACC 134, NAI.
89. See Resident's report, 5 April 1940, CRR, IOL, ACC 134, NAI.
90. Letter from Shanmugham Chetty to Resident, 8 June 1940. File No. 11/35-P(SEC)/1940, CRR, IOL, ACC 134, NAI.
91. Letter from Shanmugham Chetty to Resident, 6 July 1940. File No. 11/35-P(SEC)/1940, CRR, IOL, ACC 134, NAI.
92. Residents report of his interview with Shanmugham Chetty, 13 July 1940. File No. 11/35-P(SEC)/1940, CRR, IOL, ACC 134, NAI.
93. Letter from Shanmugham Chetty to Resident, 6 July 1940. File No. 11/45-P(SEC)/1940, CRR, IOL, ACC 134, NAI. On 3 May 1940 he even had the 'audacity' to publish a press communique stating that the newspaper reports that Travancore State Congressites were ordered by the Police Commissioner of Cochin to leave the state was absolutely unfounded. See Resident's report to the Political Department, 20 August 1940, CRR, IOL, ACC 134, NAI.
94. Shanmugham Chetty was a candidate for the post of Dewan Travancore when C.P. Ramaswami Aiyar was appointed. C.P. Ramaswami Aiyar accused Shanmugham Chetty's actions as promoted by feelings

of jealousies. See letter from Resident to Glancy, 10 April 1940, CRR, IOL, ACC 134, NAI.

95. Travancore State Congress Resolution meeting at Ernakulam, Residents report for second half of October 1940, CRR, IOL, ACC 135, NAI.

96. The accent on the alleviation of economic ills in the resolution of the Travancore State Congress showed clearly the connection between this and Morazha riots of British Malabar. At Morazha, near Cannanore, the convening of a peasant conference on 15 September 1940, the 'protest day' scheduled by Kerala Pradesh Congress Committee to protest against the prices and economic depression, proved the signal for a lathi charge and a riot. K.P.R. Gopalan, the President of the North Malabar Youth League, the executive of the All Kerala Karshaka Sangam and members of the Kerala Congress Socialist Party were, as a result, sentenced to death and seven others to transportation by the Madras Government. See Subbarayan Report on the growth of communism in Kerala, File No. 11/1942-46, p. 133, AICC Papers, NMML.

97. The 'extravagant claims' put up by C.P. Ramaswami Aiyar in the Legislative Assembly was mainly to impress Sir Francis Wylie, the Political Adviser, on a visit to Travancore. This proclamation not only brought on a frank statement by Wylie that the "paramountcy plea was in fact the merest execuse and the real reason, because he did not believe in it on quite other grounds", also brought on a rejoinder from K.N. Katju and of unequivocal support from Gandhi. See notes by Sir Francis Wylie on his visit to Mysore, Travancore and Cochin, 1941. File No. 267-P 41(SEC), CRR, IOL, ACC 135, NAI. See also Resident's report August 1940, CRR, IOL, ACC 134, NAI.

98. This was the only time a clear warning was given to the states on their position Vis-a-vis a future British India. At a slightly later date when he was asked to give a 'plain declaration' on it he equivocated by saying that such a declaration was contrary to the spirit of non-violence. Gandhi's reply to Sir C.P. on his statement on the position of the states, 30 July 1940. *Harijan*, 4 August 1943, Vol. 7, p. 233, and also see *Harijan*, 14 June 1942, p. 189, and 2 August 1942, p. 249.

99. *The Hindu*, 23 January 1941. See also the Resident's report, January 1941. File No. 5(7)/P-41(SEC)/1941, CRR. IOL, ACC 136, NAI.

100. See Resident's report 1 February 1941. File No. 5(7)-P 41(SEC)/1941, CRR, IOL, ACC 136, NAI.

101. Government Order, 24 January 1941. File No. 786/1941, Cellar Records, Kerala Secretariat.

102. Police Report on Pattam Thanu Pillai's speech, 19 August 1941. File No. 365/1941, Cellar Records, Kerala Secretariat.

103. Police Report, 21 October 1941, File No. 3185/1944, Cellar Records, Kerala Secretariat.

104. Resident's Report, 15 September 1941, CRR, IOL, ACC 136, NAI.

105. Several labour meetings were held at Alleppey, Quilon and Shertallai during the period 30 April 1940 to December 1940 under labour leaders like K. Kunchu Pillai, Srikantan Nair, Pothan Joseph, K.S. Joseph, T.V. Thomas, S. Narayana P llai, E.V. Kesavan, R.N. Krishna Pillai etc. For information on these meetings see File No. 2025/1944, 2026/1944 to 2035/1944, Cellar records, Kerala Secretariat.
106. See Police report sent as enclosures, to C.P. Ramaswami Aiyar's letter to Resident, 28 March 1940, CRR, IOL, ACC 134, NAI. See also Intelligence Report regarding Madras States, 2 April 1940, File No. 11/35-P(SEC)/1940, CRR, IOL, ACC 134, NAI.
107. Resident's report, 1 December 1941, CRR, IOL, ACC 136, NAI.
108. See Resident's report for November 1941 and January 1942, CRR, IOL, ACC 134, NAI.
109. The original members of this federation were (a) Navika Thozhilali Sangam (b) Coir Factory Workers Association, Shertallai, (c) Mineral Workers Union, Travancore (d) Punalur Paper Mills Union (e) Professional Motor Workers Union, (f) All Travancore Estate Workers Union (g) Quilon Factory Workers Union, (h) Travancore Cashewnuts Workers Union (i) Alleppey Karitta Workers Union etc. showing the wide nature of the body. See File No. 469/1944 Cellar Records Kerala Secretariat.
110. Srikantan Nair, Janardhanan Nair and T.V. Thomas were labaur leaders, with connections to the Travancore State Congress, and were members of the Travancore Congress Parliamentary Board.
111. See Police report, File No. 539/1904, Cellar Records, Kerala Secretariat.
112. Press communique issued by C.P. Ramaswami Aiyar on 27 February 1942, File No. 469/1944, 424/1944, the report of the IG of police on labour movement.
113. See Resident's report for 2nd half of April 1942, CRR, IOL, ACC 134, NAI.
114. The strike sites chosen for demonstrations were quite often companies under British nationalists management or government management. For accounts of strikes in Harrison & Crossfield, Willam Goodacre and Thomas Stephen & Company, etc., see File No. 424/1944, Cellar Records, Kerala Secretariat. For strike at Kundara Ceramic Factory, Goodacre and Company, Empire Coir Works, Punja Cultivation Labour Strikes (in which Ezhava women workers with broomsticks as weapons obtained their demands on enhancement of their rates) See File No. 443/1944 and the report of the Inspector-General of Police on labour and Residents report for April 1942, CRR, IOL, ACC 134, NAI.
115. Right upto 13 August 1942 we see several meetings staged at Alleppey, Shertallai, Quilon, Chavara, Karunagappally and Punalur. For records of these meetings under T.M. Varghese, K.K. Warrier, Suganthan, B.K. Nair, P.N. Nair, T.V. Thomas and K.P. Janardhanan Nair, see File No. 2401, 2404, 2410, 2416, 2422-25. 2427, 2431, 2433, 2434,

2445 and 2586/1944, Cellar Records, Kerala Secretariat.

116. Resident's Report first half of July 1942. CRR, IOL, ACC 134, NAI. On 19 August 1942, the Travancore Government while declaring the INC, the AICC, the KPCC and other such allied bodies as unlawful imposed on the Travancore State Congress a ban on holding meetings, which was extended from time to time till June 1943. Resident's report for July 1942, September 1942, January 1943, March 1943 and June 1943, CRR, IOL, ACC 135, NAI.

117. Resident's letter to Polindia, 28 August 1942, File No. 12(12)-P/1942, CRR, IOL, ACC 134, NAI.

118. The First to inaugurate this satyagraha was E. John Philipose, following which leading members of the Travancore State Congress, numbering over 20 courted arrest. See the Residents report for 3 September 1942 and 18 September 1942, CRR, IOL, ACC 134, NAI.

119. See the Resident's report for January 1940, May 1943, June 1943 and July 1943 and August 1943. CRR, IOL, ACC 135, NAI. See also report of the Inspector-General of Police interview with Pattam Thanu Pillai in jail on 4 August 1943. File No. 290/1944 and 5 August 1943, File No. 513/144, Cellar Records, Kerala Secrretariat.

120. See File No. 300/1944, 418/1944, 321/1944, 3571/1944 for meetings in Alleppey, Quilon, Shertallai, and Trivandrum during the period 1943-44, Cellar Records, Kerala Secretariat.

121. See Police Report of the meeting of the Travancore Coir Workers Union under the presidentship of T.V Thomas, on 28 November 1943, and of a communist class being opened at the same union at which E.M.S. Namboodiripad was to give instructions for 3 days from 22 November 1943, File No. 260/1944 and 238/1944, Cellar Records, Kerala Secretariat. See also Resident's report November 1943, CRR, IOL, ACC 135, NAI.

122. A resolution passed by the KPCC on 31 August 1945 demanded that the left wingers be expelled from the congress as it was against their organisational unity to have political parties with different creeds owing allegiance to different ideals. See File No. P-11/1942-46, p. 69 AICC papers, NMML.

123. Press communique of the Travancore Government, 24 March 1944. File No. 636/1944, Cellar Records, Kerala Secretariat. See also Residents report, second half of March 1944, CRR, IOL, ACC 133, NAI.

124. See letter from T.V. Thomas to Chief Secretary 1 April 1944, letter from Chief Secretary to C.P. Ramaswami Aiyar, 7 June 1944, Inspector General of Police to T.V. Thomas, 14 June 1944 and letter from Chief Secretary to T.V. Thomas 16 June 1944. File No. 1621/1944, Cellar Records, Kerala Secretariat.

125. This board was consituted of T.M. Varghese, Pattam Thanu Pillai, C. Kesavan, Sivan Pillai, and A.J. John.

126. This decision was taken at a secret meeting of the Travancore State Congress in March 1944. See Police report. File No. 1991/1945 and

report of the secret meeting of the Travancore State Congress, 24 March 1944. File No. 539/1944, Cellar Records, Kerala Secretariat.

127. Police report of the Travancore State Congress meeting of 10 June 1944, dated 11 June 1944, File No. 1456/1944, Cellar Records, Kerala Secretariat.

128. See Resident's report of 30 April 1944. CRR, IOL, ACC 133, NAI.

129. See Police report, File No. 3257/1944, Cellar Records, Kerala Secretariat.

130. See Resident's report, 15 April 1944, CRR, IOL, ACC 133, NAI,

131. Its main thrust in the Legislature was against the Dewan's compulsory education scheme. It felt that as an otherwise laudable move was being used to create communal differences. For reports on its proceedings and other Congress activities see Police Report, 26 July 1944, File No. 2593/1744 and 2252/1944. cellar Records, Kerala Secretariat. See also File No. 47, pp. 141-153, pp. 161-171, AISPC IInd instalment NMML and Resident's report from 31 July 1944, 31 August 1944 and 31 January 1945, CRR, IOL, ACC 133, NAI.

132. Police report, File No. 3257/1944, Cellar Records, Kerala Secretariat.

133. Police Report 18 September 1944, File No. 2896/1944, Cellar Records, Kerala Secretariat.

134. Residents report, 15 August 1945, CRR, IOL, ACC 133, NAI.

135. See Police Reports, December 1945, File No. 168/1946, Cellar Records, Kerala Secretariat.

136. Police Bulletin of speeches made at a meeting of Cashew Factory Workers Union, 5 April 1946. File No. 394/1946, Cellar Records, Kerala Secretariat.

137. Police report on Congress reaction to the above statement, File No. 394/1946, Cellar Records, Kerala Secretariat.

138. Ibid

139. The Dewan on his part tried to exploit this disengagement between the communists and the Congress in a provocative statement in the Legislative Assembly where he proclaimed that the communist party would be consulted as much as the State Congress in the matter of future constitution making. See A.K. Pillai's memorandum to Corfield, 28 November 1946, CRR, IOL, ACC 133, NAI. Police reports dated 7 May 1946 and 30 May 1946, File No. 541/1946, Cellar Records, Kerala Secretariat.

140. These reforms proposed in January 1946, while promising adult franchise to elections to legislatures provided no provisions to bind the executive to decisions of the legislature—reducing it thus to a mere debating society. The legislature was to act through sub-committees in respect of their control over administration and its policy, with the Dewan the irremovable executive given the right to veto its suggestions. See communique issued by the Travancore Government on Constitutional Reforms, 16 January 1946. File No. G-20/1942-46, pp. 35-39, AICC Papers, NMML. For criticisms on it, see meeting of Cashew Factory Workers Union under the presidenthsip of

K.P. Nanoo, 5 April 1946, Travancore State Congress meeting on 1 April 1946, presided by N.V. Chacko, File No. 394/1946. Cellar Records, Kerala Secretariat and the Dewan's statement on it, and K.A. Mathew's arrest, 24 March 1946, File No. 468/1946, Cellar Records, Kerala Secretariat.

141. See circular issued by the Communist Party on the observance of Anti-Empire Day on 7 July 1946. File No. 592/1946, Cellar Records, Kerala Secretariat.

142. See intercepted letter of Pattam Thanu Pillai (writing from Delhi) to C. Narayana Pillai, 21 April 1946, File No. 375/1946, Cellar Records, Kerala Secretariat.

143. See circular issued by the Communist Party of Travancore on the observance of 7 July 1946 as Anti-Empire Day. File No. 592/1946, Cellar Records, Kerala Secretariat.

144. There was a growing gap between the Travancore State Congress leadership and the labour unions as a result of the British Malabar communist activities in these areas. In July 1946, a demonstration was held against T.M. Verghese of the Travancore State Congress by labourers from the A.D. Cotton Mills and released INA men, for the Travancore State Congress' non-observance of hartal on the arrest of Jawaharlal Nehru earlier. See Police Report of State Congress meeting at Kavanad, 27 July 1946. File No. 657/1946, Cellar Records, Kerala Secretariat.

145. 1944-45 had been a particularly bad period for Kerala as a result of scarcity of rice. As the District Relief Committee and Servindia Travancore Relief Committee remarked, nearly 30 per cent of the population was subjected to starvation. See File No. 47, pp. 163-165, AISPC Papers, NMML and Memorandum submitted by above Committee, 26 September 1944, File No. 47, pp. 151-60, AISPC Papers, NMML.

146. Observations of E.M.S. Namboodiripad in *Deshabhimani*, 2 October 1946. File No. 231/1946, Cellar Records, Kerala Secretariat.

147. C.P. Ramaswami Aiyar in an interview to the Associated Press of America, 5 November 1946, CRR, IOL, ACC 133, NAI.

148. Ibid.

149. Pattam Thanu Pillai in a speech, *The Hindu*, 31 October 1946.

150. Report sent by the Intelligence Bureau of the Criminal Investigation Department Office Madras (1946) CRR, IOL, ACC 133, NAI. See also Pattam Thanu Pillai in a statement, *The Hindu*, 31 October 1946.

151. Ibid. See also activities of the Catholic Youth Congress and arrest of Mr. Cheriyan J. Kappan for asking "cultivators to forcibly occupy forest lands belonging to the government and to cultivate them, promising support to such cultivators". Cutting of API news, 26 October 1946, CRR, IOL, ACC 133, NAI.

152. Ibid. See also observations of E.M.S. Namboodiripad, 20 October 1946, File No. 231/1946, Cellar Records, Kerala Secretariat.

153. The only contemparary comprehensive account of the preparation

for the movement and the course is to be seen in the report of Intelligence Bureau of the Criminal Investigation Department Office, Madras (1946) which has been the main source utilised. See CRR, IOL, ACC 133, NAI.

154. See Travancore Government Gazette Extraordinary, 30 September 1946, File No. 47, p. 99, AISPC Papers, 2nd instalment, NMML. See also Memorandum presented by A.K Pillai to Conrad Corfield, 28 November 1946, CRR, IOL, ACC 133, NAI. K.C George, describing this period, would have us believe that it beat that of the NVD and that of the Gestapo's fascistic methods! See K.C. George, *Immortal Punnappra Vayalar*.
155. Report of the Intelligence Bureau of the Criminal Investigation Department Office Madras (1946), CRR, IOL, ACC 133, NAI.
156. Telegram from the Crown Representative to Secretary of State, 29 October 1946. File No. 343-P/46, CRR, IOL, ACC 133, NAI.
157. A party of processionists, trained and equipped with "wooden spears, axes and locally available weapons", made a planned attack on a police party encamped in a house in Punnappra. See report of the Intelligence Bureau, op. cit. and 25 October 1946 report in *Statesman*, 26 October 1946. For statements and accoonts of participants see K.C. George, op. cit., pp. 72-90.
158. Ibid.
159. Resident to Polindia, 24 October 1946, File No. 343-P/46, CRR, IOL, ACC 133, NAI.
160. See Intelligence Bureau Report, op. cit.
161. It does not redound to the communist movement in Kerala much, that while making the Travancore people the cat's paw of their agitation, at the moment of struggle they extended little help.
162. C.P. Ramaswami Aiyar in an interview to the Associated Press of America on the disturbance at Travancore. *The Tribune*, 5 November 1946.
163. See Intelligence Bureau Report, op. cit.
164. C.P. Ramaswami Aiyar at the inaugural address of the Agricultural Society, immediately after the police action, 26 October 1946, reported on 29 October 1946. CRR, IOL, ACC 133, NAI.
165. Ibid.
166. The projected meeting on 11 October 1946 of the Travancore State Congress did not take place though according to communists, C. Kesavan had on their behalf promised the All-Travancore Trade Union Congress help in their general strike on 24 October 1947. See K.C. George, op. cit., p. 167.
167. See State Congress Committee report, after their investigations at Vayalar, on 16 December 1946, Punnappra on 18 December 1946 and 2 February 1947 at Manancheri, File No. 12/1948, Cellar Records, Kerala Secretariat. See also Pattam Thanu Pillai's statement that the numbers of casualities in the riots as published by Government was correct. File No. 15/1947, Cellar Records, Kerala Secretariat and

Resident's report of Travancore Government's communique on it, 15 December 1946, CRR, IOL, ACC 133, NAI.

168. In its private report (as reported by a police officer) it had declared that "but for the declaration of martial law the situation would have gone beyond control". There is no other report of this committee's findings consisting of T.M. Verghese, A. Sankara Pillai and A.J. John except in this police record. See File No. 12/1947, Cellar Records, Kerala Secretariat.
169. Pattam Thanu Pillai's speech, 29 October 1946, *The Hindu,* 31 October 1946.
170. C.P. Ramaswami Aiyar on Pattam Thanu Pillai's statement of 29 October 1946. *The Hindu,* 31 October 1946.
171. Ibid.
172. Statement issued by Pattabhi Sitaramayya on AISPC policy, 13 January 1948. File No. SPI/1945-48, pp. 48-49, AICC Papers, NMML. See also report of the AISPC meeting at Gwalior in April 1947, according to which this decision had not been liked by the members of the delegates from Travancore to AISPC. See File No. 205/1947, Cellar Records, Kerala Secretariat.
173. Memorandum by P.K. Pillai to Corfield, 28 November 1946, CRR, IOL, ACC 133, NAI. See also article by Miss Anna Mascarene in *Malabar Herald* under title "Labour Struggles in Travancore", 9 November 1946. File No. 47, AISPC Papers, NMML. Martial Law was removed on 9 November 1946, even then the troops continued to stay in these areas and arrests were effected without warrants as precautionary measures. See Resident's report, November 1946, CRR, IOL, ACC 133, NAI.
174. Among the writers arrested were Ponkunnam Varkey, P. Kesava Dev, Thakazhi Sivasankara Pillai, K. Ramakrishna Pillai, Professor Kuttipuzha Krishna Pillai, etc. Ibid.
175. On 1 November 1946, the reserve police effected several arrests at Kottayam and Koothatukulam. See article by Annie Mascarene, *Malabar Herald,* 9 November 1946, File No. 47, AISPC Papers, NMML.
176. Ibid.
177. On 11 June 1947 in view of the lapse of paramountcy declared by His Majesty's Government, the Dewan opted for Travancore to stay 'independent' as from the date of British withdrawal on 15 August 1947.
178. For his complaints on Cochin providing a centre for the "issuance" of pamphlets, monetary help, bomb and explosives, and in giving asylum to agitators, etc., and for failing to take measures "which ought to be expected of a friendly neighbour state", see C.P. Ramaswami Aiyar to Sir George Boag, 28 October 1945, Resident to Polindia, 29 October 1946, Resident to George Boag, 7 November 1946 and C.P. Ramaswami Aiyar to Resident, 31 October 1946, CRR, IOL, ACC 133, NAI.
179. The Resident and Political Department supporting C.P. Ramaswami

Aiyar felt that the states would be in a "sad position indeed if they were to combine just now on a policy of unrestrained toleration of criticism". For the Political Department's strictures on George Boag, see Resident to Boag, 7 November 1946, 10 November 1946 and 11 November 1946. CRR, IOL, ACC 133, NAI.

180. The Cochin Dewan while dismissing C.P. Ramaswami Aiyar's complaint as "grossly exaggerated", reiterated that the communists had given no help and that it was not expedient "to provoke them by taking any action which was not made necessary by their conduct", and asserted that "nor was it called upon to suppress all criticism of Travancore State. He reacted to the charges of the Travancore Dewan exactly as his Indian predecessor had done ! See Boag to Resident, 30 October 1946, 7 November 1946, CRR, IOL, ACC 133, NAI.
181. A proceession from Calicut to support Travancore cause, passing through Cochin was stopped on the specific injunctions of the Political Department. The State Praja Mandal which was the government in power was blamed for the lathi charge which ensued. See Resident to Boag, 11 November 1946, CRR, IOL, ACC 133, NAI and Annie Mascarene's article in *Malabar Herald*, 9 November 1946. File No. 47, p. 63, AISPC Papers, NMML.
182. In this, the decision of the Gwalior Conference of the AISPC to stay the hands of the states people from starting any agitation also helped. See File No. 205/1947, Cellar Records, Kerala Secretariat.
183. See File No. 238/1947, Cellar Records, Kerala Secretariat.
184. K.M. Panikkar to Sardar Vallabhbhai Patel, 15 June 1947, *Sardar Vallabhbhai Patel Correspondence*, edited by Durgadas, Vol. 5, p. 386.
185. He was made to withdraw his resignation only on the advice that it might in effect weaken rather than strengthen his position. See statement given by Travancore Government to the press on C.P. Ramaswami Aiyar's resignation, 5 December 1946, telegram from Resident to Political Secretary, 5 December 1946 and Dewan's official letter from Resident to Political Secretary, 23 December 1946. CRR, IOL, ACC 133, NAI.
186. Government Press Note 11 June 1947, File No. 268/1947, Cellar Records, Kerala Secretariat.
187. See *ante* p. 199.
188. Travancore delegates interview with Gandhi on his day of silence, 29 June 1947, *Harijan*, 29 June, 1947, Vol. 11, p. 214.
189. C.P. Ramaswami Aiyar to Avinashalingam Chettiyar, 1 July 1947, File No. 331/1947, Cellar Records, Kerala Secretariat.
190. State Congress President's appeal to observe 13 June 1947 as Constituent Assembly Day, 11 June 1947, File No. 268/1947, Cellar Records, Kerala Secretariat.
191. Ibid. See also Police Reports, 14 June 1947, and other reports of agitation till 7 July 1947. File No. 268/1947, Cellar Records, Kerala Secretariat.
192. On 7 July 1947, K.A. Mathew, leader of the Travancore State

Congress Party in the Assembly was stabbed while addressing a meeting at Tiruvalla. See *The Hindu*, 11 July 1947. Again at Pettah an unnecessary fracas was created by a police officer intruding with a question at the State Congress meeting which proved the signal for the interference of the police and lathi charge. See statement by Pattam Thanu Pillai, 14 July 1947, *The Hindu*, 15 July 1947.

193. These pointed out the dangers of aligning with British Malabar, the centre of communist activities, see joint statement by G. Parameswaran Pillai, E.J. Philipose etc., 30 June 1947, *The Hindu*, 2 July 1947.
194. Letter from T.M. Varghese to Hiralal Sastri, 4 July 1947, File No. 47, pp. 39-40, AISPC Papers, NMML.
195. C.P. Ramaswami Aiyar at the Travancore Legislative Council, 7 July 1947, *The Hindu*, 8 July 1947.
196. Dr. S. Radhakrishnan in a speech in Madras, 2 July 1947, *The Hindu*, 3 July 1947.
197. Mahatma Gandhi's appeal to Britain, 8 July 1947, *The Hindu*, 10 July 1947.
198. Sir John Anderson in a speech, 11 July 1947, *The Hindu*, 13 July 1947.
199. Letter from T.M. Varghese to Hiralal Sastri, 4 July 1947, File No. 47, pp. 39-40, AISPC Papers, NMML.
200. Police Report on State Congress position, 10 May 1947. File No. 203/1947, Cellar Records, Kerala Secretariat. See also Police Report for first half of June 1947 for Congress failure on its "three lakhs fund" collections. File No. 364/1947, Cellar Records, Kerala Secretariat.
201. Mannath Padmanabhan and Gangadharan Nair joined the Travancore State Congress in April 1947 "to induce the public to take part in the direct action proposed to be started by the Travancore State Congress". See Police report 21 April 1947, File No. 234/1947 and 1 June 1947, File No. 364/1947, Cellar Records, Kerala Secretariat.
202. This measure was imposed by the Dewan on the plea that now that the paramount power had washed its hands off its obligations, it became necessary for the states administration to maintain a calm atmosphere. See government press note 15 July 1947, File No. 467/1947, Cellar Records, Kerala Secretariat.
203. See *The Hindu*, 20 July 1947 to 23 July 1947.
204. See Royal Message on Independent Travancore, 18 July 1947. See R. Ramakrishnan Nair, *Constitutional Experiments in Kerala*, a collection of documents on Travancore Reforms, pp. 102-103.
205. The Crown Representative Records stop with 1946, while the AICC Papers are made open only to August 1947. The papers from the National Archives of India for post 1945 is not available to ordinary scholars.
206. See V.P. Menon, *The Story of the Integration of the States*, pp. 114-15.
207. Ibid. p. 116.
208. Report in *The Hindu*, 16 July 1947.

209. Police Report, 24 July 1947, File No. 301/1947, Cellar Records, Kerala Secretariat.
210. Viceroy to open conference of states, 23 July 1947, *The Hindu*, 25 July 1947. See also address of H.H. the Viceroy Lord Mountbatten to a special full meeting of the Chamber of Princes, 25 July 1947, Maurice Gwyer and Appadoorai, Vol. III, *op. cit.*, pp. 772-775. At this meeting 4 points of significance were made by the Viceroy: (1) That of the 565 states the majority were irretrievably linked geographically with the Dominion of India—negotiation with each state separately was thus out of question; (2) Vallabhbhai Patel's statement of 5 July 1947 had asked them to join the Constituent Assembly only in respect of three subjects—Defence, External Affairs, and Communication—with no financial commitments; (3) These subjects had to be handled for the states. for its own convenience and advantage by a larger organisation; and (4) that the draft Instrument of Accession prepared for their signatures included explicit provisions that in no other matters would the central government have authority to encroach on the internal autonomy or the sovereignty of the states. For a description of the impact of this meeting see also V.P. Menon, *op. cit.*, p. 108.
211. Telegram from Richardson Barring to Attlee, 29 July 1947. Box 7, Attlee Papers available in microfilm in NAI.
212. Secret telegram of Pethick Lawrence to Viceroy, 1 August 1947. Box 7, Attlee Papers, NAI.
213. Telegram from Richardson Barring to Attlee, 29 July 1947. Box 7, Attlee Papers, NAI.
214. Letter from Viceroy to Secretary of State, 4 August 1947, Box 7, Attlee Papers, NAI.
215. Ibid.
216. 'Attempt on C.P. Ramaswami Aiyar', 25 July 1947, *The Hindu*, 27 July 1947.
217. See reports for 28 July 1947, *The Hindu*, 29 July 1947 and 29 and 30 July 1947.
218. 'Travancore to Join Union', 29 July 1947. *The Hindu*, 30 July 1947.
219. See Interview of the correspondent of *The Hindu*, with Chandrasekhar Aiyar, the acting Dewan, 29 July 1947, *The Hindu*, 30 July 1947.
220. A rather dubious source, Lapierre, maintained in a speech at India International Centre, Delhi, that Mountbatten disclosed to C.P. Ramaswami Aiyar that Mahatma Gandhi had asked Dalmia to contribute to the Travancore State Congress Funds. There is no mention of this in his book *Freedom at Midnight*, or any other source that I have come across.
221. That there was considerable nervousness due to the projected help of Madras and Cochin is made obvious in a noting of the Travancore Government. On 31 July 1947, with its capitulation, it remarked that Sardar Patel be asked to order Madras and Cochin to keep "hands off Travancore" in its revised position. See note by Government,

unsigned draft, 31 July 1947, File No. 467/1947, Cellar Records, Kerala Secretariat.

222. Government Press Note, 30 July 1947, File No. 467/1947, Cellar Records, Kerala Secretariat.
223. Statement of Pattam Thanu Pillai, 12 September 1947, *The Hindu*, 14 September 1947.
224. See Proclamation of H.H. the Maharaja of Travancore, 4 September 1947 and Government Press Communique of 4 September 1947, Documents No. 10, 11 and 12, published by R. Ramakrishnan Nair, *op. cit.*, pp. 103-11.
225. Extracts from speech by Hanumanthaiya, 3 November 1947, File No. 512/1947, Cellar Records, Kerala Secretariat.
226. Letter from C.P. Ramaswami Aiyar to Tricumdas, enclosure to a letter from Vallabhbhai Patel to Nehru, 27 March 1948. *Sardar Patel Correspondence*, Vol. 6, p. 373.
227. Resolution of the Mysore State Congress passed at Shimoga in February 1940, File No. 12/1940, p. 15, AICC Papers, NMML. See also Resident's report for March 1940, CRR, IOL, ACC 2, NAI.
228. Proceedings of the Subjects Committees open session, 17 March 1940, See report of United Press of India, available in File No. G-26/1942 (Part 4) p. 248, AICC Papers, NMML.
229. Resident's report of H.C. Dasappa's speech, 15 September 1940, CRR, IOL, ACC 2, NAI.
230. See resolution passed by the Mysore Congress, April 1940 and Mysore Law Associations meeting on it, 7 July 1940. CRR, IOL, ACC 2, NAI.
231. Resident's report, 30 July 1940, CRR, IOL, ACC 2, NAI.
232. Mahatma Gandhi's editorial 'Mysore Lawyers', the *Harijan*, 13 July 1940.
233. See resolution passed at the Working Committee of the Mysore Congress at Nanjangud, 26 May 1940 and Bulletin issued by Mysore Congress to AISPC, 13 June 1943. File No. 13, Group I, p. 207 and p. 221, AISPC Papers (Private Collection) NMML.
234. Resident's report, 30 July 1940, CRR, IOL, ACC 2, NAI.
235. Resident's report, 15 September 1940, CRR, IOL, ACC 2, NAI.
236. Resident's report, 15 October 1940, CRR, IOL, ACC 2, NAI.
237. See telegram from Resident to Polindia, 16 October 1940, CRR, IOL, ACC 2, NAI.
238. Resident's report, 24 February 1941, May 1941 for the Maharaja's complaints against the Dewan and Mirza's own against the Maharaja. CRR, IOL, ACC 2, NAI.
239. K.T. Bhashyam at a Congress meeting at Viduraswatha on 12 September 1940. See Resident's report, 30 Septembe 1940, CRR, IOL, ACC 2, NAI.
240. Resident's report, 28 October 1940, CRR, IOL, ACC 2, NAI.
241. Among others, a common ground for rejection was that the date of birth had been indicated in words instead of in figures, that the word

'female' had been struck off bearing the word 'male' without noting the same in the space provided for it! Out of 120 rejections, 80 belonged to that of the Mysore Congress members. See the Amildar Bangalore's orders, 23 January 1941, printed in *The Hindu*, 25 January 1941. Statement published by K.T. Bhashyam, 11 January 1941, *The Hindu*, 14 January 1941.

242. See Resident's report, 31 January 1941 and 24 February 1941, CRR, IOL, ACC 2, NAI.
243. It was a considerable triumph as the seats were dispersed among different elements with only 227 seats open for general constituencies in the legislative Assembly and 28 for general constituencies, out of 44 open for election in the Legislative Council. See note on Constitution of Mysore prepared by Wylie, 12 August 1941, CRR, IOL, ACC 2, NAI.
244. See Resident's report, April 1941, CRR, IOL, ACC 3, NAI.
245. See Resident's report, April 1941 and May 1941, CRR, IOL, ACC 3, NAI.
246. Resident's report for June and August 1941, CRR, IOL, ACC 3, NAI.
247. See the Working Committee of the Mysore Congress resolution, 10 November 1941. File No. 13, Group I, p. 3, AISPC Papers (Private Collection) NMML. See also Resident's report, November 1941, CRR, IOL, ACC 3, NAI.
248. A deputation of K.T. Bhashyam, Dasappa and Siddalingiah waited on Gandhi to get directions from him (and were advised by him to approach the government in a quiet manner and to deprecate against the issue of such government orders). See Resident's report, December 1941, CRR, IOL, ACC 3, NAI.
249. Resident's report, August 1942, CRR, IOL, ACC 2, NAI.
250. For an account of the Isoor satyagraha see an unmarked pamphlet in R.R. Diwakar Papers, Mysore State Archives, see also the pamphlet "Revolt in Karnataka" from 9 August 1942 to 8 April 1943, issued by the Karnataka Congress Committee, available in File No. 8/1942, AICC Papers, NMML.
251. Resident's report, 17 August 1942, CRR, IOL, ACC 2, NAI.
252. For a report on the political situation in Mysore in this period see letters of Resident to Fitze Patrick Polindia, April 1943. File No. 12(3)-P(S)/1943, and Resident's report, 2 September 1942, 2 November 1942, CRR, IOL, ACC 2, NAI.
253. Resident's report, August 1942, CRR, IOL, ACC 2, NAI.
254. See Resident's reports dated 3 October 1944, 10 October 1944, 18 November 1944, CRR, IOL, ACC 1, NAI.
255. Resident's reports January 1945 and 5 April 1945, CRR, IOL, ACC 1, NAI.
256. Report of the Mysore State Congress session held on 16 and 17 June 1945, 2 July 1945, CRR, IOL, ACC 1, NAI.
257. See statements issued by N.C. Thimma Reddy on 8 July 1945, 29 July 1945, 15 August 1945, and 18 August 1945, File No. 10/1945, AICC

Papers, NMML.

258. See letter from Nijalingappa to J.B. Kripalani, 24 August 1945, File No. P-10 (Part 2)/1942-46, p. 221, AICC Papers, NMML.
259. On this, Pattabhi Sitaramayya wrote to the Mysore State Congress President not to rescind the Haripura resolution but to strive to achieve their aspirations through their own efforts. See Resident's report, 3 September 1945, CRR, IOL, ACC 1, NAI.
260. Even earlier, in October 1945, the Mysore Congrees had appointed a sub-committee to examine the question of Karnataka unification. See Resident's report of Mysore Congress resolutions passed on 13 and 14 October 1945, 18 October 1945, and 2 November 1945, CRR, IOL, ACC 1, NAI. See also report of the activities of the All Karnataka Unification League, September 1945, File No. P-10 (Part 2)/1942-46 pp. 2-3, AICC Papers, NMML and Resolution passed by the Working Committee of the Mysore Congress, 28 July 1946, File No. G-15 (KWI)/1946, p. 237, AICC Papers, NMML.
261. See statement by S. Nijalingappa, President of the Karnataka Pradesh Congress Committee on Deccan States Union, 26 July 1946, File No. G-15, (KW-1)/1944, p. 285, AICC Papers, NMML, and letter of R.R. Diwakar to J. Nehru, 18 July 1946, File No. G-15(KW-1)/1946, pp. 207-213,. AICC Papers, NMML. See also letter of U.N. Dhebar to H.H. Dhrangadara, 7 February 1947, File No. 2/1947, pp. 99-100, AICC Papers, NMML.
262. See *ante* p. 199.
263. See resolution passed by the Karnataka Provincial Congress Committee and Mysore Congress on 18 January 1947 and 7 February 1947. See also letter from V.T. Magadi to the President, Indian National Congress, 18 February 1947, File No. P-9(KW-1)/1946-49, pp. 235-37, AICC Papers, NMML.
264. See Resident's report, 3 October 1945, CRR, IOL, ACC 1, NAI.
265. Resolution passed at the open session of Subhas Nagar, Bangalore, 3 November 1946, see resolution of Mysore Congress 16 February 1947 for a recapitulation of this resolution, File No. 18/1947, pp. 423-425, AICC Papers, NMML.
266. Memorandum by the Mysore Congress to the Maharaja, reference to which made in its resolution of 16 February 1947, File No. 18/1947, pp. 423-25, AICC Papers, NMML.
267. Proclamation by His Highness on 1 January 1947. See also Proclamation of His Highness, the Maharaja of Mysore 18 September 1947, File No. 2/1947, pp. 71-72, AICC Papers, NMML.
268. Recapitulation of events, Mysore Congress resolution of 16 and 17 February 1947, File No. 18/1947, pp. 423-25, AICC Papers, NMML. Also published in *Sardar Patel Correspondence*, Vol. 5, p 410.
269. Only 3/5 of which membership was open for election.
270. Letter from K. Chengalaraya Reddy to Sardar Patel, 10 February 1947. *Sardar Patel Correspondence*, Vol. 5, p. 403.
271. Letter from Chengalaraya Reddy to Pattabhi Sitaramayya, 26 February

1947, File No. 18/1947, pp. 421-22, AICC Papers Papers, NMML.

272. Prime Minister Attlee's statement, 20 February 1947. The *Framing of India's Constitution* by B. Shiva Rao, Vol. 1, pp. 515-517.
273. Resolution passed by the Mysore Congress, 8 and 9 March 1947. *The Hindu*, 10 March 1947.
274. *Ibid.* See also H.C. Dasappa's statement to the AISPC on affairs in Mysore, 16 June 1947, File No. SPI/1945-48, p. 59, AICC Papers, NMML.
275. Statement of Ramaswami Mudaliar, 29 April 1947, *The Hindu*, 30 April 1947.
276. Resolution moved by Pattabhi Sitaramayya on the states, AICC meeting on 14 June 1947.
277. Dewan at a press conference on 17 June 1947, *The Hindu*, 18 June 1947. See also letter of H.C. Dasappa to Vallabhbhai Patel, 16 July 1947, *Sardar Patel Correspondence*, Vol. 5.
278. Dewan addressing a joint session of the Mysore Legislature, 5 July 1947. *The Hindu*, 6 July 1947, The *Indian Review*, p 437.
279. If election were left to the Legislature, the Mysore Congress with only 120 out of 310 seats in the Legislative Assembly and 24 out of 68 in the Legislative Council could hope to obtain only 2 or 3 seats. See letter of H.C. Dasappa to Vallabhbhai Patel, 23 June 1947, *Sardar Patel Correspondence*, Vol. 5, p. 414
280. As it did in its reforms proposals mooted in its proclamation of 4 September 1947. See proclamation of H.H. the Maharaja of Mysore, 4 September 1947, File No. 2/1947, pp. 71-72, AICC Papers, NMML.
281. See letter from H.C. Dasappa to Vallabhbhai Patel, 16 July 1947, *Sardar Patel Correspondence*, Vol. 5, p. 416. See also *The Hindu*, 10 July 1947.
282. Letter from H.C. Dasappa to Vallabhbhai Patel, 23 June 1947, *Sardar Patel Correspondence*, Vol. 5, p. 414.
283. "Valediction to India", article in the *Round Table* (1946-47), Vol. 37, p. 33.
284. "The revolution in Indian States: A Transmigration of Paramountcy", article in the *Round Table* (1948-49), Vol. 39, pp. 36-43.
285. "India and Pakistan, Accession of the States", article by a Special Correspondent in the *Asiatic Review*, (1947), pp. 323-27.
286. Press Communique issued by the Mysore Government on 10 August 1947. *The Hindu*, 10 August 1947.
287. See *ante* p. 195.
288. This Ordinance required editors of local dailies to submit for scrutiny all matters "relating to incidents, speeches, comments, activities or anything whatsoever, either actual or proposed connected indirectly or directly" with the satyagraha movement in Mysore. Orders were served on selected newspapers which had been partial to the Congress cause. *The Hindu*, 2 September 1947.
289. Proclamation of H.H. the Maharaja of Mysore, 4 September 1947, File No. 2/1947, pp. 71-72, AICC Papers, NMML. The constitution

proposed on the lines of the above proclamation were laid before the Maharaja and published on 24 September 1947. See Proclamation of H.H. the Maharaja of Mysore, 24 September 1947, File No. 2/1947, p. 71, AICC Papers, NMML.

290. 'Mysore Reforms', editorial in *The Hindu*, 24 September 1947.
291. 'Arrest of Leaders' 4 September 1947, *The Hindu*, 5 September 1947.
292. Starting from the firing on a workers demonstration at Kolar Gold Fields on 1 September 1947 (see *The Hindu*, 2 September 1947) to a students' procession on 4 September 1947 (see *The Hindu*, 4 September 1947) in front of the palace on 5 September 1947 to the firing incidents at Bhadravati on 29 September 1947 (see *The Hindu*, 10 October 1947), Chikhabellapur 30 September 1947 (see *The Hindu*, 20 October 1947), there was not a single day till the declaration of peace talks that passed without a demonstration or firing.
293. For account of students strikes, see *The Hindu*, 4 September 1947.
294. 'Hartal at Kolar Gold Field' 1 September 1947, *The Hindu*, 2 September 1947.
295. See accounts of the strike in *The Hindu* from 22 September 1947 to 30 September 1947.
296. See *The Hindu*, 2 October 1947. The strike continued till 9 October 1947.
297. See 30 September 1947. *The Hindu*, 1 October 1947.
298. A police firing took place on a first batch of volunteers from Kadur who tried to stage a satyagraha in front of the palace, as scheduled earlier from 14 September 1947. See *The Hindu*, 14 September 1947.
299. Travancore's help was specially mentioned by K.C. Reddy in a message of thanks, after Mysore had won her agitation. He wrote, "it was a grand gesture that Travancore made by sending a satyagraha jatha to Mysore carrying the message of sympathy and support from Pattam Thanu Pillai"—21 October 1947, *The Hindu*, 23 October 1947.
300. A similar *jatha* to that of Travancore was sent by Cochin on 1 October 1947. See *The Hindu*, 1 October 1947.
301. Karnataka claimed to have sent more than 2,000 volunteers to help the Mysore satyagraha. See *The Hindu*, 11 October 1947.
302. 7 October 1947. *The Hindu*, 9 October 1947.
303. On 6 October 1947, the leaders of the Mysore Congress were released and on 8 October 1947 were invited to meet the Dewan.
304. 'Peace Settlement' 11 October 1947. *TheH indu*, 13 October 1947. See also H.H. the Maharaja of Mysore's Proclamation, 13 October 1947, File No. 24/1946-47, AICC Papers, NMML.
305. The Mysore Congress ruled that any person against whom there was the least suspicion of their having acted against the satyagraha were to be barred from the ministry even though otherwise qualified. Thus getting rid of possible insubordination to its interests from other parties it sought to make it a cabinet. See *The Hindu*, 21 October 1947.
306. Agreement between the Mysore Congress and Government, 13 October 1947, File No. 23/1946-47, AICC Papers, NMML.

CHAPTER 8

NOTES

1. See *ante*, p. 165 and Notes, Chapter 6, Note No. 10.
2. Editorial by Gandhiji, "How Far", 24 June 1939, *Harijan*, Vol. 7 (1939-40), p. 169.
3. The major pronouncements were - Wintertons' answer in House of Commons, 21 February 1938, Zetlands speech, 27 May 1938, Colonel Muirheads answer in House of Commons, 16 December 1938, Viceroy's speech at Calcutta on 19 December 1938 and the Viceroy's speech to the princes at an informal meeting at the Viceroy's House, 13 March 1939.
4. See Memo to the Cabinet from the Secretary of State, 9 February 1939. Cabinet Papers 44(49) Zetland Collection, Vol. 25B, Roll 9, NMML.
5. Letter from Zetland to Linlithgow, Vol. 11, p. 36, Roll 3, Zetland Collection, NMML.
6. Letter from Zetland to Linlithgow, 12 February 1939, Vol. 11, p. 36, Roll 3, Zetland Collection, NMML.
7. Ibid.

8. See *ante* p. 153.
9. See letter from Apa Pant to Jawaharlal Nehru (undated 1938), Vol. No. 78, pp. 103-105, JN Correspondence, NMML.
10. Letter from Zetland to Linlithgow, 12 February 1939, Vol. 11, p. 36, Roll 3, Zetland Collection, NMML.
11. Rushbrooke Williams, quoted by J. Nehru in his speech at the Udaipur session of the AISPC, 31 December 1945, File No. 104, Part II, pp. 110-19, JN Papers, NMML.
12. Letter from Linlithgow to Zetland, 16 April 1937, Vol. 13, p. 94, Roll 4, Zetland Collection, NMML.
13. Letter from Linlithgow to Zetland, 15 April 1938, Vol. 15, p. 277, Roll 5, Zetland Collection, NMML.
14. Speech by Secretary of State, 27 May 1938. Enclosures to policy on states, Vol. 25 B, Roll 9, Cabinet Papers File (39), Zetland Collection NMML.
15. Letter from Zetland to Carl Heath, 19 December 1938, Vol. 8, pp. 177-79, Roll 3, Zetland Collection, NMML.
16. See Colonel Muirhead's answer in House of Commons, *ante* p. 165.
17. Letter from Linlithgow to Zetland, 8 November 1938, Vol. 15, p. 499, Roll 5, Zetland Collection, NMML.
18. Ibid.
19. Viceroy's speech to the princes at an informal meeting at the Viceroy's House, 13 March 1939, Vol. 7, p. 120, Roll 5, Zetland Collection, NMML.
20. Letter from Zetland to Carl Heath, 19 December 1938, Vol. 8, pp. 177-179, Roll 3, Zetland Collection, NMML.
21. Letter from Linlithgow to Zetland, 31 August 1939, Vol. 18, p. 85, Roll 6, Zetland Collection, NMML.
22. Letter from Linlithgow to Zetland 14 December 1939, Vol. 18, p. 120, Roll 6, Zetland Collection, NMML.
23. Letter from Linlithgow to Zetland, 27 November 1939, Vol. 18, p. 238, Roll 6, Zetland Collection, NMML.
24. See *ante*, p. 177.
25. See *ante*, p. 185.
26. See letter from Nijalingappa on KPCC Mysore Congress merger, 29 August 1948, File No. P-9(KW-i)/1946-49, AICC Papers, NMML.
27. Shiva Rao—op. cit., Vol. IV, pp. 551-552.
28. J. Nehru's Presidential Address to AISPC, Ludhiana, 8 February 1939. Emphasis supplied by the author, File No. 104 part II, Subject Files, pp. 48-60, JN Papers, NMML.
29. Here it is the later states peoples organisation in the AISPC which is referred to and not the earlier ISPC. For a greater elucidation on this point see *ante* p. 129.
30. Wavell visualising the states position on British withdrawal in a letter to Amery 20 April 1944, *Transfer of Power*, Vol. V, Document 467, pp. 901-02.

Bibliography

ORIGINAL SOURCES

Government Records

(1) National Archives of India

Foreign and Political Department Records (1900-1947)
Home Political Records (1900-1947)
Fortnightly Reports (1922-47)
Crown Representative Records, available in microfilm
Accession No. 1-5 Mysore
,, 297-341 Mysore Residency lists
,, 133-140 Madras States
Mysore Residency Records, NAI
Madras States Residency Records, NAI
Native Newspaper Reports, Madras States (1900-1928) (available in Tamil Nadu Archives up to 1933)

(2) **Tamil Nadu Archives**

Proceedings of the Political Department and Government Orders on it 1900-1938

(3) **Karnataka State Archives**

Official Papers of the Viduraswatha Enquiry Committee (1938)

Report of the Administration of the Police Department of Mysore 1911-1921

Proceedings of the Home Department, Government of Mysore (open only up to 1938)

(4) **Kerala State Archives**

Proceedings of the Home Department, Government of Travancore

Cellar Records of the Kerala Secretariat Archives

PRINTED MATTER—GOVERNMENT PUBLICATIONS AND RECORDS

(a) **General**

Indian Political Practice—A collection of the decisions of the GOI in political cases by C.L. Tupper, compiled in 1895 in 4 volumes

Imperial Gazetteer, Vol. XVIII, published by GOI

Memoranda on the Indian States—1926, 1930, 1932, 1934, 1936, 1937 and 1940

Report on Indian Constitutional Reforms (1918) (Montagu Chelmsford Reforms—Chapter X, pp. 191-198 relevant) GOI Publications.

Papers Relating to the Sixth Despatch on Indian Constitutional Reforms (1919) (Chapter X in 1919 Act)

Report of the Indian States Committee (1928-29), published by GOI

Report and Evidence of the Indian States Committee (1927), available in 4 volumes (1927-29)

Report of the Special Committee on Economic and Financial Relations Between British India and Indian States—Report of W.W. Nind (1930)

Constitutional Reforms—Indian State Enquiry Committee Report by J.C. Davidson (1931)

Views of Indian States: Correspondence relating to a meeting of States Rulers held at Bombay to discuss GOI Bill and Draft Instrument of Accession (1935)

Round Table Conference Proceedings, India Office Stationery:

(*i*) *Indian Round Table Conference Proceedings*, 12 November 1930 to 19 January 1931

(*ii*) *Indian Round Table Conference Proceedings of Sub-Committee I* (on Federal Structure) 12 November 1930 to 19 January 1931

(*iii*) *Indian Round Table Conference Reports*—Refer Reports of Committee on Federal Structure, Reports I, II, III and IV.

(*iv*) *Indian Round Table Conference, Second Session Proceedings of the Plenary Session*, 7 September 1931 to 1 December 1931

(*v*) *Indian Round Table Conference, Second Session, Proceedings of Federal Structure Committee*, 7 September 1931 to 1 December 1931

(*vi*) *Indian Round Table Conference*—Second Session, Federal Finance Sub-Committee—Stenographic notes on the meeting of the Sub-Committee at St. James Palace on 28 September 1931 (no mention of this meeting in other proceedings)

Joint Committee of Indian Constitutional Reforms—Report 1933-34—Proposals for Indian Constitutional Reforms, White Paper, 1933

Secretary of States Evidence Before the Joint Committee on Indian Constitutional Reforms, 2 volumes (1933)

Debates on Indian Affairs, House of Commons Session, 1935

Parliamentary Debates Official Report (1936)

Government of India Act 1935

Report of the Committee Appointed to Negotiate with the States Negotiating Committee (1946-47)

Indian Independence Act (1947)

Ministry of States on Indian States Finance Enquiry Committee Interim and Final Reports in 2 parts by V.T. Krishnamachari (1948)

White Paper on the States, published by the Ministry of State, Government of India (1950)

Special Assistance to Part B States—Ministry of States Enquiry by N.V. Gadgil (1953)

All India Credit Survey—Survey Report of the Committee of Directives, Vols. I, II, and III (1954)

Parliamentary Dabates, House of Commons for relevant periods

(b) Mysore

Mysore Administration Report 1880-1886 in 3 volumes

Mysore Census Reports for the years 1871, 1881, 1891, 1911, 1921, 1931, 1941

Mysore Civil List for 1880-1935

Mysore Gazette 1872-1925 and also *Index to Mysore Gazetteer 1872-1925*

Review of Progress of Education in Mysore State 1911 to 1916

Mysore Police Report on Administration from 1877-1921 in 15 volumes

Mysore Statistical Abstracts for years from 1923-24 to 1947-48

Summary of Material and Moral Progress and Condition in Mysore (1898-99)

Proceedings of the Assembly of Rayats of the State of Mysore (1895)

Mysore Government Order—Index 1811 to 1915

Review of Progress of Education in the Mysore State (1911-1916)

Agriculture in Mysore (1928)

Mysore Legislative Assembly Proceedings (1881-1947)

Mysore Legislative Council Proceedings (1908-1947)

Mysore Committee of Enquiry for Further Encouragement to Members of the Backward Communities in the Public Service (1921)

Mysore Committee on Constitutional Development, B.N. Seal Report (1922)

Constitutional Development in Mysore—Report of the Committee—Chairman Rajkumar Banerji, (1923)

Official Papers connected with *Constitutional Development in Mysore* (1924)

Committee of Enquiry into Bangalore Disturbances—Chairman M. Visvesvaraya (1928)

Mysore Retrenchment Committee (1931)

Committee for Examining Condition and Prospects of Tenants in Inam and Jodi Villages—Chairman S. Hiriannaiya (1932)

Mysore Agriculture Relief Committee—Chairman N. Madhava Rao (1935)

Mysore Committee on Constitutional Reforms—Chairman K.R. Srinivasa Iyangar (1939)

Viduraswatha Disturbances Enquiry Committee—Chairman Vepa Ramesam (1938)

Mysore Legislative Council Selection Committee on Money Lenders Bill—Chairman N. Madhava Rao (1938)

Mysore Legislative Assembly Select Committee on Bill to Amend Mysore Land Revenue Code—Chairman N. Madhava Rao (1938)

Mysore Committee on Prison Reforms in Mysore—Chairman K.S. Chandrasekhara Iyer (1941)

Report of the Committee for the Revision of the Land Revenue System in Mysore (1950) appointed by Mysore on 13 August 1948

Karnataka Through the Ages (1968)

(c) Travancore

Native States—Madras—An Account of Travancore-Cochin Pudukottai Banganapalle

Travancore Before and After—Parliamentary Delegation and Travancore, January 1946

Travancore Census Administrative Reports for 1907 (Part I), 1911 (Part IV Administrative), 1921 (Part V)—1931 (Part I)

Travancore Excise Committee Report—Chairman K.A. Krishna Aiyangar (1933)

Travancore Unemployment Enquiry Committee (1926)

Travancore Banking Enquiry Committee—Chairman Vaidhyalingham Pillai (1929)

Travancore Public Service Recruitment Committee—Chairman V. Subba Iyer (1931)

Travancore Economic Enquiry Committee Report (1931)

Travancore Cooperative Enquiry Committee—Chairman C.K. Devadhar (1932)

Travancore Education Reforms Committee (1932)

Travancore Temple Enquiry Committee—Chairman V.S. Subramania Aiyar (1932)

Travancore Administration Report for the year 1936-37

Travancore Debt Relief Enquiry Committee Report—Chairman V.S. Subramania Aiyar (1939)

Sri Moolam Popular Assembly Proceedings (1905-1947)

Sri Chitra Council Proceedings (1888-1947)

(d) Cochin

Cochin Administrative Reports and Census 1901, 1911, 1921, 1931

Cochin State Progress of Education—The Book On It (1917)

Cochin Nair Relation Committee Report—Chairman T.S. Narayana Iyer

Cochin Christian Succession Bill Committee (1919)

Cochin Economic Depression Relief (1934)

Cochin Legislative Council Select Committee on Debt Conciliation Bill—Chairman A. Sankara Menon (1936)

Cochin Franchise Committee Report—Chairman N.R. Sahasrarama Aiyer

Cochin Constitutional Reforms Report (January 1938)

Cochin Fnquiry into Family Budgets of Industrial Labour (1948)

Cochin Industrial Development Committee (1944)

Cochin Enquiry into Condition of Industrial Labour (1946)

Cochin Agrarian Problem Enquiry Committee (1948)

Cochin Legislative Council Proceedings (1925-47)

PRIVATE PAPERS COLLECTION

Organisational

AICC Papers, NMML (1887-1947)
AISPC Papers, NMML (1934-1947)

INDIVIDUAL COLLECTIONS

Indian Leaders and Administrators

R.R. Diwakar Papers, KSA.
History of Freedom Movement Unit, Tarachand Papers, NAI
Jawaharlal Nehru Papers, NMML
M.R. Jayakar Papers, NAI
Mahatma Gandhi Papers, Gandhi Smarak Nidhi, New Delhi
Mirza Ismail Papers, NMML
Pattam Thanu Pillai Papers, NMML
Rajendra Prasad Papers, NAI
C.P. Ramaswami Aiyar Papers (mainly printed matters) available from C.P. Ramaswami Aiyar Foundation, Teynampet, Madras
B.R. Reddy Papers, NMML
T.B. Sapru Papers (on microfilm) NMML
V.D. Savarkar Papers (on microfilm) NMML
Shanmugham Chetty Papers (on microfilm) NMML
T.R. Sharma Collection—Karnataka State Archives
Siddalingiah, *A Short History of His Life* (available in the private collection of Professor Dr. Kamath, Bangalore)
Sivaswami Iyer Papers, NAI
V.S. Srinivasa Sastri Papers, NAI

British Administrators—(Available in microfilm at NAI and NMML)

Attlee Papers, NAI
Birkenhead Collection, NMML
Chelmsford Collection, NMML
Halifax Collection, NMML
Harcourt Butler Collection, NMML

Linlithgow Collection, NAI
Montagu Collection, NMML
Templewood Collection, NMML
Willingdon Collection, NAI
Zetland Collection, NMML
For period after 1942 see Mansergh and Lumby—*Transfer of Power*, published by His Majesty's Stationery

Transcripts from Oral History Section, NMML

A. Achyuthan—ACC No. 85
Shri Kelappan—ACC No. 73
Neelakantan Nambudiripad—ACC No. 147
G. Ramachandran—ACC No. 54
Kunju Raman—ACC No. 100
R. Sankar—ACC No. 72

NON-GOVERNMENT RECORDS

Indian National Congress Publications

Report of the All Parties Conference (Nehru Report) (1928)
Indian National Congress, Annual Reports 1928 to 1940
Resolutions passed by the INC, particularly for the years 1920-23, 1927, 1928, 1930-34, 1934-36 and 1941 to 1946

ISPC and AISPC Publications—General

Hosakappa Krishna Rao—*Swaraj Constitution* (1928) (This constitution was endorsed by the South Indian States People's Conference meeting in 1928)

Visvesvarayya—*Swaraj Constitution* (Sponsored by the SISPC—1929)

G.R. Abhyankar—*Work in England of the Deputation of Indian States People's Conference* (1929)

Memorandum Presented to the Indian States Committee by the Indian States People's Conference (1928)

Address of the President, Indian States People's Conference (1929)

Presidential Address to the ISPC—by C.Y. Chintamani (undated)

Presidential Address to the ISPC—by R. Chatterjee (1931)

Presidential Address to the ISPC—by N.C. Kelkar (1933)

Memorandum of the Indian States People, presented to the Indian National Congress (1931)

Presidential Address at AISPC—by Jawaharlal Nehru (1937 and 1945)

Resolutions passed by the AISPC—1939-1946

Mysore-Karnataka Pradesh Congress Committee and other Publications

United Karnataka—Case for Karnataka unification (1928) issued by the Karnataka Union Sub-Committee of KPCC

The Mysore Struggle (*1940*) by K.T. Bhashyam—published by Karnataka PCC, available in typescripts in AICC Papers, NMML

Linguistic Provinces and the Karnataka Problem—a detailed statement by KPCC on Karnataka Ekakiran Mahasamiti (1948)

Travancore-Cochin—AISPC and other Publications

Malayali Memorial—Submitted to the Government of Travancore, 1891

Ezhava Memorial—Submitted to the Government of Travancore, 1895

Travancore Today, Her Struggle for Freedom—Published by Travancore State Congress (1938)

Travancore Before and After—Parliamentary Delegation and Travancore, Ernakulam, 29 January 1946

Native Newspaper Reports, Madras States

Bangalore Post, 14 January-May 1891

Bangalore Spectator, 14 January-May 1891

Bharati, 7 August 1908

Chakravarthi, 15 December 1915, 2 October 1915

Daily Post, 6 September 1911

Deshabhimani, 22 January 1916

Dhanawandari, 30 October 1913

Jagadguru, 9 August 1908

Justice, 14 January 1918, 19 December 1920

Karnataka, 29 May 1915

Karnataka Prokasika, 30 August 1886, 25 September 1886 and 19 January 1891

Keralabhimani, 18 July 1918, 5 November 1918

Kerala Bharati, 28 March 1919

Kerala Mitram, January 1884 to March 1884

Kerala Nandini, 23 January 1891

Kerala Patrika, 30 June 1906, 13 June 1908, 15 October 1910

Keralodayom, 18 April 1916, May 1916

Kerala Sanchari, 17 October 1900

Kesari, 12 August 1908

Loka Prakasam, 21 January 1918

Madras Standard, 29 August 1911, 30 August 1911, 20 March 1914

Malabar Herald, 8 October 1910, 7 March 1914

Malayala Manorama, 10 February 1900, 2 March 1901, 21 September 1903

Malayali, 9 March 1901, 21 March 1903, 12 January 1907, 9 February 1907, 28 September 1907, 28 September 1910, 3 December 1910, 21 May 1919

Mysore Herald, 24 January 1891

Mysore Standard, 8 May 1905

Mysore Star, 1 November 1910, 15 December 1912

Mysore State, 16 October 1905, 16 December 1912

Nadegannadi, 19 March 1901, 22 December 1905

Nazrani Dipika, 7 February 1901, 14 June 1905, 25 April 1909

New India 1911

Patriot, 12 December 1911, 1 March 1912

Sadhvi, 15 July 1912, 17 January 1913, 19 November 1912

Samadarshi, 13 July 1918, 31 May 1919

Sampadabhyudaya, 29 March 1915, 19 July 1917

Sarvodaya, February 1907

Suryodaya Prakasika, 14 November 1900, 12 December 1900, 11 September 1901, 12 July 1905, 6 September 1905, 25 October 1905, 27 June 1906, 17 June 1907

Sathianadam, 3 April 1914

Satyavadi, 22 May 1905
Srivazhumcode, 23 May 1919
Sujana Nandini, 25 July 1905
Suprabhatam, 2 October 1915
Swadeshamitram, 17 October 1905, 16 November 1907, 11 October 1908, 11 August 1908, 9 August 1918
Swadeshi, 5 January 1907
United India and the Native States, 5 November 1910, 17 December 1910, 13 May 1911, 27 July 1916
Vokhaligara Patrika, 7 January 1920
Vrithanta Chintamani, 17 January 1894, 17 January 1904, 19 June 1907, 1[illegible] August 1904, 26 August 1908
Vrittanta Patrika, 21 March 1901
Wednesday Review, 27 November 1907, 12 August 1908
West Coast Reformer, 27 October 1910
West Coast Spectator, 15 October 1908
Western Star, 19 January 1891

Newspapers and Periodicals—Indian and Foreign

Asia
Asian Affairs
Asiatic Review
Bengal Past and Present
Commonwealth
Contemporary Review
Economic and Political Weekly
Economist
Foreign Affairs
Foreign Policy Reports
Harijan
Hindu
Hindustan Times
Historical Journal
Indo British Review
Indian Annual Register, (Earlier quarterly and Half yearly)
Indian Economic and Social History Review
Indian Express
Indian Journal of Political Science
Indian Review

International Conciliation
Journal of Asian Studies
Journal of Kerala Studies
Journal of Royal Institute of International Studies
Labour Monthly
Liberal Magazine
Kerala Society Papers
Madras Review
Malabar Herald
Malabar Quarterly Review
Modern Asian Studies
Modern Review
Mysore Orientalist
Mysore Review
National Herald
New India (Political Forum)
New India—an occasional bulletin from 1937-1939 in two volumes
New India (Daily Political Journal)
New India—(a Fortnightly Journal)
New India Weekly
Political Scientist
Rama Varma Research Institute Bulletin
Round Table
Servant of India
South Asia
South Asian Review
Statesman
Times of India
United India
Young India

RELEVANT ARTICLES PUBLISHED IN PERIODICALS

Adams, John, 'Economic, Political and Social Dimensions of an Indian State: A Factor Analysis for District Data for Rajasthan', *Journal of Asian Studies*, November 1973, pp. 5-23.

Arnold, David, 'Caste Associations in South India, A Comparative Analysis', *Indian Economic and Social History Review*,

July-September 1976, pp. 353-373.

Balakrishnan, P.K., 'Caste System in Kerala', *Quest*, March-April 1976, pp. 9-15.

Banerjee, Albion, 'Indian States and the Constitution Bill', *Contemporary Review*, March 1935, pp. 313-320.

Barton, William, 'The Deadlock in India and the Indian States', *Quarterly Review*, July 1943, pp. 16-27.

———, 'Princes and Politics in India', *The Asiatic Review*, October 1944, pp. 357-366.

———, 'Postwar Development Scheme in the States of South India', *Asiatic Review*, October 1945.

———, 'The Indian Princes and the Cabinet Mission', *Quarterly Review*, January 1947, pp. 126-138.

Benn, Wedgwood, Address by—at the Round Table Conference, *Journal of the Royal Institute of International Affairs*, March 1931, pp. 147-149.

———, 'Accusation of Conservatives—in India Again,' *The Economist*, 25 November 1933, p. 1009.

Bhargava, Kusum, 'Rajasthan Politics and Princely Rulers', *Indian Journal of Political Science*, October-December 1972, pp. 413-430.

Bikaner Maharaja of, 'The Indian Constitution and States', *The Asiatic Review*, 12 February 1946.

Bisson, T.A., 'A New Constitution for India', *Foreign Policy Reports*, 17 July 1935, pp. 119-120.

Blunt, W.S., 'Ideas About India—The Native States', *Fortnightly Review*, February 1885, pp 234-248.

Boulger, Demetrius, 'Constitutional Government in Mysore—An Account of the Government in the States', *Contemporary Review*, March 1905, pp. 402-12.

Brailsford, H.H., 'The Indian Settlement'—*The New Statesman and Nation*, 25 May 1946.

Brock, R.W., 'Industrial Development in Indian States', *Asiatic Review*, July 1945.

Brock, R.W., 'India, Pakistan and Indian States', *Asiatic Review*, 1946, pp. 225-227.

Chatterjee, Ramanand, 'The Indian States', *Modern Review*, July 1931, pp. 29-43.

Chaturvedi, J.P., 'States Peoples Movement', See articles in *Mainstream* dated 14 February 1976, pp. 25-26, 28 February

1976, pp. 18-22, 6 March 1976, pp. 19-23, 3 April 1976, pp. 26-29, 8 May 1976, pp. 24-26, 19 June 1976, pp. 23-25 and 7 August 1976, pp. 24-27 and 34.

Coatman, John, 'India Today and Tomorrow, 1939, *Foreign Affairs*, pp. 316-318.

Copland, Ian, 'Maharaja of Kolhapur and the Non-Brahmin Movement 1902-1910', *Modern Asian Studies*, April 1973. pp. 209-225.

Das Taraknath, 'The Status of Hyderabad during and after British Rule in India', *Modern Review*, January 1949, pp. 21-30.

Darda, R.S., 'Political Movement in the Princely States of Rajasthan', *Quarterly Review of Historical Studies*, 1973-74, pp. 23-28.

Davis Sir Godfrey, 'Kashmir a Sovereign State', *The Asiatic Review*, pp. 30 and 133.

Dharmpal, 'British Policy Towards the Native States of India', *Journal of Indian History*, August 1947, pp. 217-239.

Dhringadhara, 'Indian Princes in the Ebb of British Retraction', *Indo-British Review*, 1973/74, pp. 58-65 (Review of Conrad Corfields book—*Princely India I Knew*)

Dolobrant, Rt. Hon, Lord Lloyd of, 'Problem of Constitutional Reform in India', *Journal of the Royal Institute of International Affairs*, September 1933, pp. 598-601.

Edwin, P.G., 'Travancore and Paramount Power—A Study of War Time Relationship', *Journal of Indian History*, August 1973, pp. 407-423.

Finlay, Mark, 'The Changing Role of the Indian Princes', *Contemporary Review*, October 1949, pp. 230-235.

Fisher, William, 'The Maharajas of India', *United Nation's World*, 1948.

Fuller, C.J., 'Kerala Christians and the Caste System'—*Man*, March 1976, pp. 53-70.

Furber, Holden, 'The Unification of India 1947-51', *Asian Affairs*, December 1951, pp. 352-371.

Gandhi, M.K., 'The Future of India', Address to the Institute on 20 October 1931, *Journal of the Royal Institute of International Affairs*, November 1931, p. 725.

Garratt, G.T., 'Indian India', *Asia*, November 1930.

Greer, James Frederick, 'India's Struggle for Independence',

Foreign Policy Reports, 1 June 1940, pp. 83-84.

Gupta, D.C., 'A Survey of the Present Constitutional Position of Indian States', *Modern Review*, September 1936.

Halifax, Viscount of, 'Indian Constitutional Reforms', *Journal of the Royal Institute of International Affairs*, March 1935, pp. 203-204.

———, 'The Political Future of India', *Foreign Affairs*, 1934, p. 424, and pp. 426-428.

———, 'India Two Hundred Years', *Foreign Affairs*, October 1947, pp. 108-09.

Harrison, 'Rulers and the Ruled', *South Asian Review*, October 1969, pp. 59-71.

Hayne, Edward G., 'British Policy Towards the Indian States', 1803-1870, Intervention, Adoption, Minority, *Journal of Rajasthan Institute of Historical Research*, October-December 1975, pp. 14-28.

Hurd, John, 'Economic Consequences of Indirect Rule in India', *Indian Economic and Social History Review*, April-June 1975, pp. 169-182.

———, 'Influence of British Policy on Industrial Development in the Princely States of India 1880-1933', *Indian Economic and Social History Review*, October-December 1975, pp. 409-424.

Hydari, Sir Akbar, 'The Indian Bill Moves on', *The Economist*, 4 May 1935, p. 1004.

Iqbal, Ali Shah Sirdar, 'The Future of Indian States', *The Fortnightly*, August, 1947.

James, Sir Frederick, 'The Indian Political Scene', *International Affairs*, April 1947.

Jeffrey, Robin, 'Sources for Modern Kerala History', *Indian Archives*, July-December 1972, pp. 6-9.

Kane, 'The Indian Problem—A Review', *Austrian Quarterly*, March 1945.

Kapadia, Rangildas, 'Rise and Growth of All India States Peoples Conference', *National Herald*, 24 December 1945.

Kibe, M.V., 'Principles of Taxation in Native States', *Hindustan Review*, April 1915, pp. 377-381.

Klatt, 'Caste, Class and Communism in Kerala', *Asian Affairs*, October 1972, pp. 275-287.

Knight, Lionel, 'British Paramountcy and the Education of the

Mysore Prince', *Bengal Past and Present*, January-June 1973, pp. 37-57.

Koshy, M.J., 'Genesis of Political Consciousness in Travancore', *Journal of Indian History*, April 1972, pp. 173-183.

Koshy, M.J., 'Political Awakening and Struggle for Freedom in Travancore', *Journal of Indian History*, August 1972, pp. 471-490.

Kurup, T. Narayana, 'Price of Rural Credit—An Empirical Analysis in Kerala', *Economic and Political Weekly*, 3 July 1976, pp. 998-1006.

Kusuman, K.K., 'Punnapra-Vayalar Uprising 1946', *Journal of Kerala Studies*, March, 1976, pp. 137-159.

La Foy, Margaret, 'India's Role in World Conflict—The Princes', *Foreign Policy Report*, 1 May 1942, p. 41.

Lothian, Arthur, 'A Neglected Aspect of Indian History', *Quarterly Review*, October 1962.

Mahmood, Sir Maqbool, 'The Indian States and British Commonwealth of Nations', *Asiatic Review*, April 1945.

Manor, James, 'Kengal Hanumanthaiya in Mysore', *South Asia*, October 1974, pp. 21-30.

———, 'Princely Mysore Before the Storm, the State Level Political System of India's Model State, 1920-1936', *Modern Asian Studies*, February 1975, pp. 30-58.

Mountbatten, Sir Louis, 'Speech as Guest of East India Association', *Asiatic Review*, 29 June 1948, pp. 351-353.

Nair, N. Gopinathan, 'Birth and Growth of Communists in Kerala', *Indian Left Review*, March 1976, April 1976, pp. 12-25, and pp. 19-34.

Nair, Karunakaran, 'Genesis of the Travancore State Congress', *Journal of Kerala Studies*, January 1974, pp. 327-344.

Nair, Ramakrishna R., 'Ruling Class and Its Governing Elite of Kerala', *Journal of Kerala Studies*, July 1975, pp. 33-47.

Nair, T.P. Sankaran Kutty, 'Rama Varma Saktan Tampuran, Forgotten Heroes of Kerala', *Indian Review*, February 1976, pp. 33-34, 36-37.

Nehru, Jawaharlal, 'Presidential Address—AISPC Conference, Ludhiana,' 15 February 1939, *The Selected Works of Jawaharlal Nehru*, p. 41.

———, 'What of the Indian States', 27 April 1940, JN Papers, ML.

———, 'Presidential Address, AISPC Conference, Udaipur Session,' 31 December 1945, JN Papers, NMML.

Oomen, T.K., 'Agrarian Legislation and Movement as Sources of Change—the Case of Kerala', *Economic and Political Weekly*, 4 October 1975, pp. 775-784.

Oren, Stephen, 'Killing a Myth'—A Note on the Lingayat Matters of Mysore State and their Political Influence, *Journal of Indian History*, Golden Jubilee Volume (1975), pp. 775-784.

Panikkar, K.M., 'The Position of Indian States—a Discussion', *Asiatic Review*, 1926, pp. 251-268.

———, 'The Princes and India's Future—Their Rights to Self-Determination', *Foreign Affairs*, April 1943, pp. 511-573.

Patil, N.S., 'English Education—National Awakening in Karnataka', *Modern Review*, January 1975, pp. 17-21.

———, 'Allur Venkat Rao: His Dreams of a United Karnataka', *Modern Review*, January 1976, pp. 16-18.

Pullapilly, Cyriac K., 'Ezhavas of Kerala and Their Historic Struggle for Acceptance in the Hindu Society', *Journal of Asian and African Studies*, January-April 1976, pp. 24-26.

Rajagopalachari, C., 'Reconciliation in India', *Foreign Affairs*, pp. 431-434.

Rajkumar, N.V., 'Evolution and Working of the Government in Travancore', *Indian Journal of Political Science*, October 1940, pp. 217-240.

Ramachandran, P., 'Suchindram Satyagraha', *Journal of Kerala Studies*, June 1976, pp. 229-237.

Rao, Lakshmana, and Leonard, Cane, 'Religious Parties in Kerala—a Multiple Repression Analysis', *Political Scientist*, 1972-74, pp. 75-96.

Ravindran, T.K., 'Kurichya Rebellion of 1812,' *Journal of Kerala Studies*, September-December 1976, pp. 533-544.

Reading (Lord), 'Constitutional Reform in India', *Foreign Affairs*, July 1933, pp. 618-19.

Reed, Sir Stanley, 'The Governance of India', *Journal of Royal Institute of International Affairs*, 26 April 1927, pp. 324-325.

Richter, William L. and Rumusack Barbara, 'The Chamber and the Consultation: Changing Forms of Princely Association in India', *Journal of Asian Studies*, 3 May 1975, pp. 755-776.

Rosenthal, Donald, B., 'From Reformist Princes to Cooperative Kings', *Economic and Political Weekly*, 2 June 1973, pp. 995-1000.

Roy, Choudhary, 'Vaikkom Satyagaraha', *Indian Review*, January 1972, pp. 17-21.

Saklatwala Shapurji, 'The Indian Round Table Conference', *The Labour Monthly*, February 1931, pp. 85-88, and p. 92.

Sapru, Tej Bahadur and Khan, Zafrulla, 'Indian Public Opinion on the White Paper', *Journal of the Royal Institute of International Affairs*, September 1933, p. 617.

Saradamoni, 'How Aggrestic Slavery was Abolished in Kerala', *Indian Economic and Social History Review*, June-September 1974.

Sheikh, Abdulla, 'Not Guilty', *The Labour Monthly*, October 1946, pp. 311-314.

Shah, M.H., 'Fundamental Rights in Baroda', *The Asiatic Review*, 1947, pp. 246-247.

Shiva Rao, B., 'The Vicious Circle in India', *Foreign Affairs*, 1941, pp. 847-850.

Singh, A., 'Twilight of the Princes', *Asia*, May 1937, pp. 366-370.

Singh, Bhupinder (Maharaja of Patiala), 'The Problem of the Indian States', paper read by—*Journal of the Royal Institute of International Affairs*, November 1928, pp. 389-406.

Singh, Gurumukh Nihal, 'United States of India or Princely States', *Asia*, pp. 414-21.

———, 'The Evolution of Modern Institutions in Mysore', *Modern Review*, November-December, 1936, pp. 537-541.

Spodek, Howard, 'Urban Politics in the Local Kingdoms of India', *Modern Asian Studies*, April 1973, pp. 253-275.

———, 'Rulers, Merchants and other Groups in the City States of Saurashtra', *Comparative Studies in Society and History*, September 1974, pp. 448-470.

Talbot, Philips, 'The Independence of India, the Indian States', *Foreign Policy Reports*, 15 June 1947, p. 94.

———, 'India and Pakistan—Progress Report of Princely States', *Foreign Policy Reports*, 15 June 1949, pp. 82-83.

Venkatachar, C.S., 'Last Year of British Rule in India', *Indo-British Review*, April-September 1970, pp. 7-12.

———, 'The Unmaking of Indian Princes', *Indo-British Review*,

April-September 1971, pp. 7-11.

Wadia, Ramesh, 'Praja Mandal Movement in the East Punjab State', *Punjab Past and Present*, April 1972, pp. 203-211.

Watson, Sir Alfred, 'If British Quit India', *Asiatic Review*, July 1944, p. 251.

———, 'India Raising up the Curtain, the Indian States', *Asiatic Review*, 1947, p. 310.

Yesudas, R.N.T., 'Travancore Rebellion of 1809—Its Anti-Christian Origin', *Journal of Kerala Studies*, June 1935, pp. 91-103.

Zetland, Marquis of, 'After the Indian Conference', *Foreign Affairs*, April 1932, p. 372.

Ph.D Thesis and other Unpublished Papers Available on Micro-film and in Indian Universities

Abhyankar Udayan, 'State Policy and Economic Development in Mysore State', 1887-1930, University of London, 1930.

Deshpande Narayan Raghunath, 'Constitution Making in India', University of Columbia, 1951.

Fritz Daniel Allen, 'Roles and Relationship of Local Politicians and Administrators in Mysore State, India', 1973.

Gustafson Donald Randolph, 'Mysore 1881-1902. The Making of a Model State', University of Wisconsin, 1969.

Hurd John, 'Some Economic Characteristics of the Princely States of India 1901-1931', University of Pennsylvania, 1969.

Jeffrey Robin, 'Decline of Nayar Dominance in Society and of Politics in Travancore', University of Sussex, 1973.

Koshy, M.J., 'The History of the Legislature of Travancore-Cochin up to 1956', University of Kerala, 1956.

Oren Stephen, A., 'Religious Groups at Political Organizations : A Comparative Analysis of three Indian States', University of Columbia, 1969.

Ramusack Barbara, 'Indian Princes as Imperial Politicians 1914-1939', University of Michigan, 1969.

Retzlaff Ralph Herbert, 'Constituent Assembly of India and the Problem of Indian Unity', University of Cornell-1960.

Smith Ray Thomas Jr., 'Liberals' in the Indian Nationalist Movement (1918-1947)', University of California, 1964.

Subbaramiah, S., 'The Economics of Public Enterprise in India with Special Reference to Mysore', University of Madras.

Wood John Ray, 'Political Integration of British and Princely Gujarat—Historical Political Dimension of Indian State Politics', University of Columbia, 1972.

Zachariah Mathew, 'Whither Kerala? A Social Change in Twentieth Century Kerala', University of Minnesota, 1968.

II—SECONDARY SOURCES

(a) General

Abhyankar, G.R. *Problem of Indian States*, Arya Bhushan Press, Poona, 1928.

Aitchison, C.U. *A Collection of Treaties, Engagement and Sanads*, Vols. IX, and X, Superintendent of Government Printing, Calcutta, 1909.

Aitchison, C.U. *The Native States of India, The Principles which Underlie their Relation with the British Government.*

Bagchi, Amiya Kumar *Private Investment in India 1900-1939*, Cambridge University Press, London, 1972.

Barton, William *The Princes of India* (with an Introduction by Viscount Halifax), Nisbet and Company, London, 1934

Beotra, B.R. *The Two Indias*, W. Newman and Company, Calcutta, 1927.

Bowring, L.B. *Eastern Experiences*, King and Company, London, 1871.

Butler, Harcourt *India Insistent*, William Heinemann, London, 1931.

Campbell-Johnson Alan *Mission with Mountbatten*, Robert Hale Limited, London, 1951.

Chopra, K.N. *Law Relating to the Protection of the Administration of States in India*, The University Book Agency, Lahore, 1940.

Chudgar, P.L. *Indian Princes Under British Protection*, Williams and Norgate, London, 1929.

Coen, Terence Creagh *Indian Political Service or Study in*

	Indirect Rule, Allied Publishers, Bombay, 1971.
Concord for India (a) (brought out by the Princes on the Privy purse issue.)	*The Privy Purse Issue and Other Consultation Papers*, Union Printers Co-operative Industrial Society, New Delhi, 1967.
(b)	*Cullings Regarding the Princes Position*, India Lodge, New Delhi, 1969.
Corfield Conrad	*Princely India I Knew—From Reading to Mountbatten*, Indo-British Historical Society, Madras, 1975.
Coupland, R.	*The Cripps Mission*, Oxford University Press, London, 1942.
Coupland, R.	*The Indian Problem*, Part I (1933-1935) and Part II (1935-42). Oxford University Press, London, 1943.
Coupland, R.	*Future of India*, Oxford University Press, London, 1943.
Coupland, R.	*Indian Politics Since 1926-1942*, Oxford University Press, London, 1944.
Das Taraknath	*Sovereign Rights of the Indian Princes*, Ganesh and Company, Madras, 1924.
Davies Collin, C.—Memorial Volumes	A Festschrift—refer article by Williams Donavan, 'The Adoption Despatch of 1867 and its Origin and Significance', Asia Publishing House, Bombay, 1973.
Deo, N.G.	*The Princes of India*, The Times Press, Bombay, 1921.
Desai, A.K.R.L.	*Indian Feudal States and National Liberation Struggle*, Bombay, 1938.
Desai, Bhulabhai	*Speeches (1934-38)*, Natesan and Company, Madras, 1938.
Dhavan, Shanti	*What are the Indian States* (Foreword by Jawaharlal Nehru), Allahabad Law Journal Press, Allahabad, 1939.
Diver, Maud	*Royal India*, Hodder and Stoughton Limited, London, 1942.
Durgadas— edited by	*Patel Correspondence, 1945-1950,*

10 volumes, Navajivan Press, Ahmedabad, 1974-75.

Edwardes, Michael — *The Last Years of British in India*, Allied Publishers, Bombay, 1963.

Fitze, Sir Kenneth — *Twilight of the Maharajas*, John Murray Limited, London, 1956.

Forbes Rosita — *India of the Princes*, The Right Book Club, London, 1939.

Gandhi, M.K. — *To the Princes and Their People*, Navajivan Press, Ahmedabad, 1942.

Gandhi, M.K. — *The Indian States Problem*, Navajivan Press, Ahmedabad, 1941.

Gandhi, M.K. — *Collected Works of Mahatma Gandhi*, Vol. XII to XXXXIX—XII to XXVI of special significance, Publication Division, Ministry of Information and Broadcasting, New Delhi.

Gauba, K.L. — *His Highness or the Pathology of the Princes*, The Times Publishing Company Lahore, 1930.

Gundappa, D.V. — *The States and Their People in the Indian Constitution*, Karnataka Publishing House, Mysore, 1931.

Gurmukh, Nihal Singh — *Indian States and British India—Their Future Relations* (Foreword by T.B. Sapru), Nand Kishore Bros, Benares, 1930.

Gwyer, Maurice and Appadorai — *Speeches and Documents on the Indian Constitution* (1921-47), 2 volumes, Oxford University Press, London, 1957.

Haksar Sir Kailas — *Indian States and the Federation*, D.B. Taraporewala and Sons, Bombay, 1939.

Haksar, K.N. and Panikkar K.M. — *Federal India*, Martin Hopkinson Limited, London, 1930.

Handa, R.L. — *History of Freedom Struggle in Princely States* (Foreword by S. Nijalingappa), Central News Agency, N. Delhi, 1968.

Ismail, Mirza — *My Public Life—Recollections and Reflections*, George Allen and Unwin Limited, London, 1924.

Ismail, Mirza — *Views and Opinions on His Retirement from Service*, Bangalore Press Bangalore, 1942.

Iyengar, S. Srinivasa — *Swaraj Constitution*, 192[illegible].

Iyer Sivaswami — *Indian Constitutional Problems*.

Jadhava Khasherao, B. — *Wake Up Princes*, Karnataka Printing Press, Bombay, 1920.

Jadhava Khasherao and Mehta V.B. — *Indian States*, Published by V.B. Mehta, Bombay, 1920.

Jarmani Das Diwan — *Maharajas: Lives and Loves and Intrigues of Indian Princes*, Allied Publishers, N. Delhi, 1969.

Kayco, J.W. — *Life of Metcalfe*

Kipling Rudyard — *Departmental Ditties and other Works*

Kipling Rudyard — *Plain Tales from the Hills*

Karni Singh — *Break up of Privy Purse*, 1970.

Karni Singh — *The Relations of the House of Bikaner with the Central Powers*—1865-1949, Munshiram Manoharlal, New Delhi, 1974.

Krishnamurthi, Y.G. — *Indian States and the Federal Plan* (With a Foreword by Bhulabhai Desai), Ratansey Parker and Company, Bombay, 1939.

Kulkarni, V.B. — *The Future of Indian States*, Thacker and Company, Bombay, 1944.

Latthe, A.B. — *Problems of Indian States*, Arya Bhushan Press, Poona, 1930.

Lee-Warner William — *Native States of India*, Macmillan and Company, London, 1910.

Lord John — *The Maharajahs*, Hutchinson and Company, London, 1972.

Lothian, A.C. — *Kingdom of Yesterday*, John Murray, London, 1951.

Low Sir Sidney — *The Indian States and Ruling Princes*, Ernest Benn, London, 1929.

Lumby, E.W.R. — *Transfer of Power in India*, George Allen and Unwin Limited, London, 1954.

Lumby, E.W.R. and — *Transfer of Power*, Vol. 1-8, His

Mansergh — Majesty's Stationery Office, London, 1970-80.

Macmunn George — *The Indian States and Princes,* Jarrolds, London, 1936.

Mankekar, D.R. — *Accession to Extinction—The Story of the Indian Princes,* Vikas Publishing House, Private Limited, Delhi, 1974.

Mehta, Mohan Sinha — *Lord Hastings and the Indian States,* Taraporewala and Sons, Bombay, 1930.

Mehtab Harekrushna — *Beginning of the End* (Foreword by Sardar Vallabhbhai Patel), Cuttack Students Store, Cuttack, 1949.

Menon, V.P. — *The Story of the Integration of the Indian States,* Orient Longmans Limited, Calcutta, 1956.

Menon, V.P. — *Transfer of Power in India,* Orient Longmans, New Delhi, 1968.

Moghe, K.P. — *The Indian States in their Relations with the British Paramount Power and the Government of British India,* published by K.B. Moghe, Bombay, 1928.

Montmorency Geoffrey De — *The Indian States and Indian Federation,* University Press, Cambridge, 1942.

Moon, Penderal — *Divide and Quit,* Chatto and Windus, London, 1961.

Moon, Penderal—edited by — *The Viceroy's Journal,* Oxford University Press, London, 1973.

Moore R.J. — *Crisis in Indian Unity 1917-1940,* Oxford University Press, New Delhi, 1974.

Mosley, Leonard — *The Last Days of the British Raj,* Hillman and Sons, Frome, 1962.

Naravane D.N. — *The Indian States in the Federation of India,* Karnataka Publishing House, Bombay, 1939.

Natwarsinghji (Maharaja of Porbandar) — *India's Problems, Reflections of an Ex-Ruler,* Orient Longmans, Madras, 1979.

Nehru, Jawaharlal — *Selected Works of Jawaharlal Nehru,* Vol. 1-9, Edited by S. Gopal, Orient Longmans, Delhi, 1972-80.

Nehru, Jawaharlal — *Unity of India,* Lindsay Drummond, London, 194'.

Nicholson, A.P. — *Scraps of Paper—India's Broken Treaties, Her Princes and the Problem,* Ernest Benn Limited, London, 1930.

O'Malley, L.S.S. — *Modern India and the West—A Study in the Interaction of their Civilization,* Oxford University Press, London, 1968.

Oza, Kewalram C. — *Indian States in Free India,* Vora and Company, Bombay, 1947.

Palmer Julian — *Sovereignty and Paramountcy in India,* Stevens and Sons Limited, London 1930.

Pandit, R.S. — *Dominion Status and Indian States—* Criticism of the Butler Committee, Allahabad Law Journal Press, Allahabad, 1930.

Panikkar, K.M. — *The Evolution of British Policy Towards Indian States* (1774-1868), Lahiri and Company, Calcutta, 1929.

Panikkar, K M. — *H.H. the Maharaja of Bikaner,* Oxford University Press, London, 1937.

Panikkar, K.M. — *The History of Kerala* (1498-1801), Annamalai University, Annamalai Nagar, 1960.

Panikkar, K.M. — *The Indian Princes in Council,* Oxford University Press, London, 1936.

Panikkar, K.M. — *The Indian States and the Government of India,* Martin Hopkinson, London, 1932.

Panikkar, K.M. — *The States and the Constitutional Settlement,* Institute of Pacific Relation International Secretariat, New York, 1942.

Panikkar, K.M. — *Relations of Indian States with Government of India,* M. Hopkinson, London, 1927.

Pathik, Bijai Singh — *What Are Indian States*—With illustrative Documents (date of publication not given).

Pattabhi Sitaramayya, B. — *History of Indian National Congress*—2 Vols., Padma Publication, Bombay, 1969.

Phadnis, Urmila — *Towards the Integration of Indian States* (1919-1947) Asia Publishing House, Delhi, 1968.

Philips, C.H. — *Partition cf India*, George Allen and Unwin, London, 1970.

Philips, C.H. (Edited by) — *Select Documents on the History of India and Pakistan*, Vols. I to IV, Oxford University Press, London, 1970.

Puttaswamy, B.S. — *Should the Indian States Enter Federation*, The World Press and Publishing House, Mysore, 1935.

Raghavan, S.R.S. — *Indian States and Indian Polity* (with an introduction by G.R. Abhyankar), Indian Press, Bangalore, 1931.

Raghubir Singh — *Indian States and theNew Regime*, (with a foreword by C.P. Ramaswami Aiyar) D.B. Taraporewala and Sons, Bombay, 1938.

Ramusack Barbara, N. — *The Princes of India in the Twilight of the Empire*, Ohio State University Press, Columbus, 1978.

Ranadive, R.K. — *The Legal Rights of the Indian States and of Their Subjects—or the Truth About the Indian States*, The Good Companion, Baroda, 1950.

Rao, Hosakappa Krishna — *Swaraj Constitution*, Published by the Indian States Peoples Conference, Bangalore, 1928.

A. Recluse — *Letters to an Indian Raja*, 1919.

Ruthnaswami, M. — *Relation of Indian States with Government of India*, Pearl Press, Cochin, 1931.

Ruthnaswami, M. — *Essays in Constitution Making*, The Good Pastor Press, Madras, 1946.

Sastri, K.R.R. — *Indian States*, Kitabistan, Allahabad, 1941.

Sastri, V.S. Srinivasa — *The Future of the Indian States*

Sen D.K. — *The Indian States—their Status, Rights*

and Obligations, Sweet and Maxwell 1930.

Shankar, V. — *My Reminiscences of Sardar Patel*, 2 vols., Macmillan and Co., Delhi, 1974.

Shiva Rao — *Framing of India's Constitution*—5 volumes, Indian Institute of Public Administration, New Delhi, 1966-68.

Srinivasachari, Chidambaram, S. — *The Inwardness of British Annexations in India*, University of Madras, Madras 1951.

Syama Sankar — *Nature and Evolution of the Political Relations between the Indian States and British Imperial Government*, 1931.

Tendulkar — *Mahatma, Life of Mohandas Karamchand Gandhi*, Publications Division, Delhi, 1960-63.

Thompson Edward — *Making of the Indian Princes*, Oxford University Press, London, 1943.

Thompson and Garrat — *Rise and Fulfilment of British Rule in India*, Central Book Depot, Allahabad, 1958.

Vaijnath — *Riyasthon Ka Saval* (The Problems of the Indian States, with a foreword by Pattabhi Sitaramayya), 1946

Varadarajan, M.K. — *The Indian States and the Federation*, Oxford University Press, London, 1939.

Westlake — *Collected Papers*

(b) Books with Particular Reference to MYSORE

Addressee unknown — *The Rajah and Principality of Mysore* (1865)—A letter to Rt. Hon. Lord Stanley MP.

Balakrishnan, R. — *Industrial Development of Mysore*, Doctoral Thesis, University of London, 1940.

Diwakar, R.R. (Commemorative Volume) — *Karnataka Darshana* (An Anthology of Articles), Published by R.S. Hukkerikar, Bombay, 1965.

Gundappa, D.V — *All About Mysore*, Karnataka Publishing

House, Bangalore, 1931.

Gopal, M.H. — *Tipu Sulṭan's Mysore—An Economic Study*, 1971.

Halappa, G.S. — *History of Freedom Movement in Karnataka*, in two volumes, Government of Mysore Publication, Bangalore, 1964.

Halappa, G.S.—edited by — *Studies in State Administration* 1970—An Anthology, Chapters on Revenue Administration by K. Balasubramaniam and Local Self-Government of some relevance, Karnataka University, Dharwar, 1970.

Rao, Hayavadana — *Mysore Gazetteer*, Part IV and V relevant, Mysore Government Press, Mysore, 1940.

Josyer, G.R. — *History of Mysore*, Published by G.R. Josyer, Mysore, 1935.

Ramachandriah, N.S. — *Mysore*, National Book Trust, New Delhi, 1972.

Rao, M. Shama — *Modern Mysore*, Higginbothams, Bangalore, 1936.

Row, N.S. — *Ten Years of Native Rule in Mysore—Account of Administration for 1881-1891.*

Sitaramaiah, V. — *M. Visvesvaraya* (1971).

(c) Books with Particular Reference to TRAVANCORE & COCHIN

Fic Victor, M. — *Kerala Yenan of India—Rise of Communist Power 1937-1969*, Nachiketa Publications, Bombay, 1970.

Fic Victor, M. — *Peaceful Transition to Communism in India*, Nachiketa Publications, Bombay, 1969.

George, K.C. — *Immortal Punnapra-Vayalar*, Communist Party Publication, Delhi, 1975.

Gopalan, A.K. — *Kerala, Past and Present*, Lawrence and Wishart, London, 1959.

Jeffrey, Robin — *Decline of Nayar Dominance—Society and Politics in Travancore 1847-1908—*

Vikas Publishing House, New Delhi, 1975.

Koshy, M.J. *Genesis of Political Consciousness in Kerala*, Kerala Political Society, Trivandrum, 1972.

Koshy, M.J. *Last Days of Monarchy in Kerala*, Kerala Historical Society, Trivandrum, 1973.

Koshy, M.J. *K.C. Mammen Mappilai, The Man and his Vision*, Kerala Historical Society, Trivandrum, 1976.

Krishna Aiyar, K.V. *A Short History of Kerala*, Pai and Company, Ernakulam, 1966.

Krishnamurthy, K.G. and Lakshmana Rao *Political Preferences in Kerala*, Radhakrishna Prakashan, Delhi, 1968.

Kusuman, K.K. *Slavery in Travancore*, Kerala Historical Society, Trivandrum, 1973.

Kusuman, K.K. *Extremist Movement in Kerala*, Charitram Publication, Trivandrum, 1977.

Mankekar, D.R. *The Red Riddle of Kerala*, Manektalab, Bombay 1965.

Mateer, Samuel *Native Life in Travancore*, W.H. Allen, London, 1883.

Menon, Achyutha *Cochin State Manual*, Cochin State Press, Ernakulam, 1911.

Menon, P.K.K. *The History of Freedom Movement in Kerala*, in 2 volumes compiled by the Regional Records Survey Committee, Trivandrum, 1970.

Menon, Sreedhara *Survey of Kerala History*, in 4 volumes, Sahitya Pravarthaka Cooperative Society Limited, Kottayam, 1967.

Menon, Sreedhara *A Social and Cultural History of Kerala*, Sterling Publishers, Delhi, 1979.

Nagam, Aiya *Travancore State Manual*, in 4 vols, Government Press, Trivandrum, 1906.

Namboodripad, E.M.S. *Autobiography* in Malayalam, Desabhiman Book House, 1970.

Namboodripad, E.M S. *How I Became a Communist*, Chinta Press, Trivandrum, 1976.

Namboodripad, *Kerala Yesterday, Today and Tomor-*

E.M.S.	*row*, National Book Agency, Private Limited, Calcutta, 1967,
Nair, K. Ramabhadran	*Industrial Relations in Kerala*, 1973.
Nair, R. Ramakrishna	*Constitutional Experiments in Kerala*, The Kerala Academy of Political Science, Trivendrum, 1964.
Pillai, Elamkulam Kunjan	*Studies in Kerala History*, Valsa Printers Trivandrum, 1970.
Ramanath Aiyar, S.	*A Brief Sketch of Travancore the Model State of India*, Western Star Press, Trivandrum, 1903.
Ramaswami Aiyar, C.P.	A Festschrift, C.P. Ramaswami Aiyar Foundation, Madras, 1959.
Ramaswami Aiyar, C.P.	*Convocation Address*, C.P. Ramaswami Aiyar Foundation, Madras, 1950.
Ramaswami Aiyar, C.P.	*Corporation and Panchayats with other Necessary Reforms—Presidential Address*, C.P. Ramaswami Aiyar Foundation Madras, 1970.
Ramaswami Aiyar, C.P.	*Selections from His Writings and Speeches*, 2 Volumes, C.P. Ramaswami Aiyar Foundation, Madras.
Ravindran, T.K.	*Asan and Social Revolution in Kerala*, Historical Society, Trivandrum, 1972.
Ravindran, T.K.	*Vaikkam Satyagraha and Gandhi*, Sri Narayana Institute of Social Affairs and Cultural Development, Trivandrum, 1975.
Velayudhan, R.	*Kerala the Red Rain Land*, Indian Institute of Social Affairs, Delhi, 1958.
Velu Pillai, T.K.	*Travancore State Manual*, in 4 volumes, Government Press, Trivandrum, 1940.
Visalakshi, N.R.	*Administration of Village Panchayat in Kerala*, The Education Supplies Department, Trivandrum, 1967.

Index